Microsoft Foundation Class Hierarchy

CObject

Classes Not Derived from C

Graphical Drawing

- CDC
  - CClientDC
  - CMetaFileDC
  - CPaintDC
  - CWindowDC

Control Support

- CDockState
- CImageList

Graphical Drawing Objects

- CGdiObject
  - CBitmap
  - CBrush
  - CFont
  - CPalette
  - CPen
  - CRgn

Menus

- CMenu

Command Line

- CCommandLineInfo

ODBC Database Support

- CDatabase
- CRecordset

    user recordsets

- CLongBinary

DAO Database Support

- CDaoDatabase
- CDaoQueryDef
- CDaoRecordset
- CDaoTableDef
- CDaoWorkspace

Synchronization

- CSyncObject
  - CCriticalSection
  - CEvent
  - CMutex
  - CSemaphore

Arrays

- CArray(Template)
- CByteArray
- CDWordArray
- CObArray
- CPtrArray
- CStringArray
- CUintArray
- CWordArray

— arrays of user types

Lists

- CList (Template)
- CPtrList
- CObList
- CStringList

— lists of user types

Maps

- CMap (Template)
- CMapWordToPtr
- CMapPtrToWord
- CMapPtrToPtr
- CMapWordToOb
- CMapStringToPtr
- CMapStringToOb
- CMapStringToString

— maps of user types

Internet Services

- CInternetSession
- CInternetConnection
  - CFtpConnection
  - CGopherConnection
  - CHttpConnection
- CFileFind
  - CFtpFileFind
  - CGopherFileFind
- CGopherLocator

Windows Sockets

- CAsyncSocket
  - CSocket

Internet Server API

- CHtmlStream
- CHttpFilter
- CHttpFilterContext
- CHttpServer
- CHttpServerContext

Runtime Object Model Support

- CArchive
- CDumpContext
- CRuntimeClass

Simple Value Types

- CPoint
- CRect
- CSize
- CString
- CTime
- CTimeSpan

Structures

- CCreateContext
- CMemoryState
- COleSafeArray
- CPrintInfo

- CCmdUI
  - COleCmdUI
- CDaoFieldExchange
- CDataExchange
- CDBVariant
- CFieldExchange
- COleDataObject
- COleDispatchDriver
- CPropExchange
- CRectTracker
- CWaitCursor

Typed Template Collections

- CTypedPtrArray
- CTypedPtrList
- CTypedPtrMap

OLE Type Wrappers

- CFontHolder
- CPictureHolder

OLE Automation Types

- COleCurrency
- COleDateTime
- COleDateTimeSpan
- COleVariant

Synchronization

- CMultiLock
- CSingleLock

SAMS Teach Yourself in 24 Hours MFC

Microsoft Foundation Class Hierarchy - Version 6.0

(Shaded boxes are new to version 6.0)

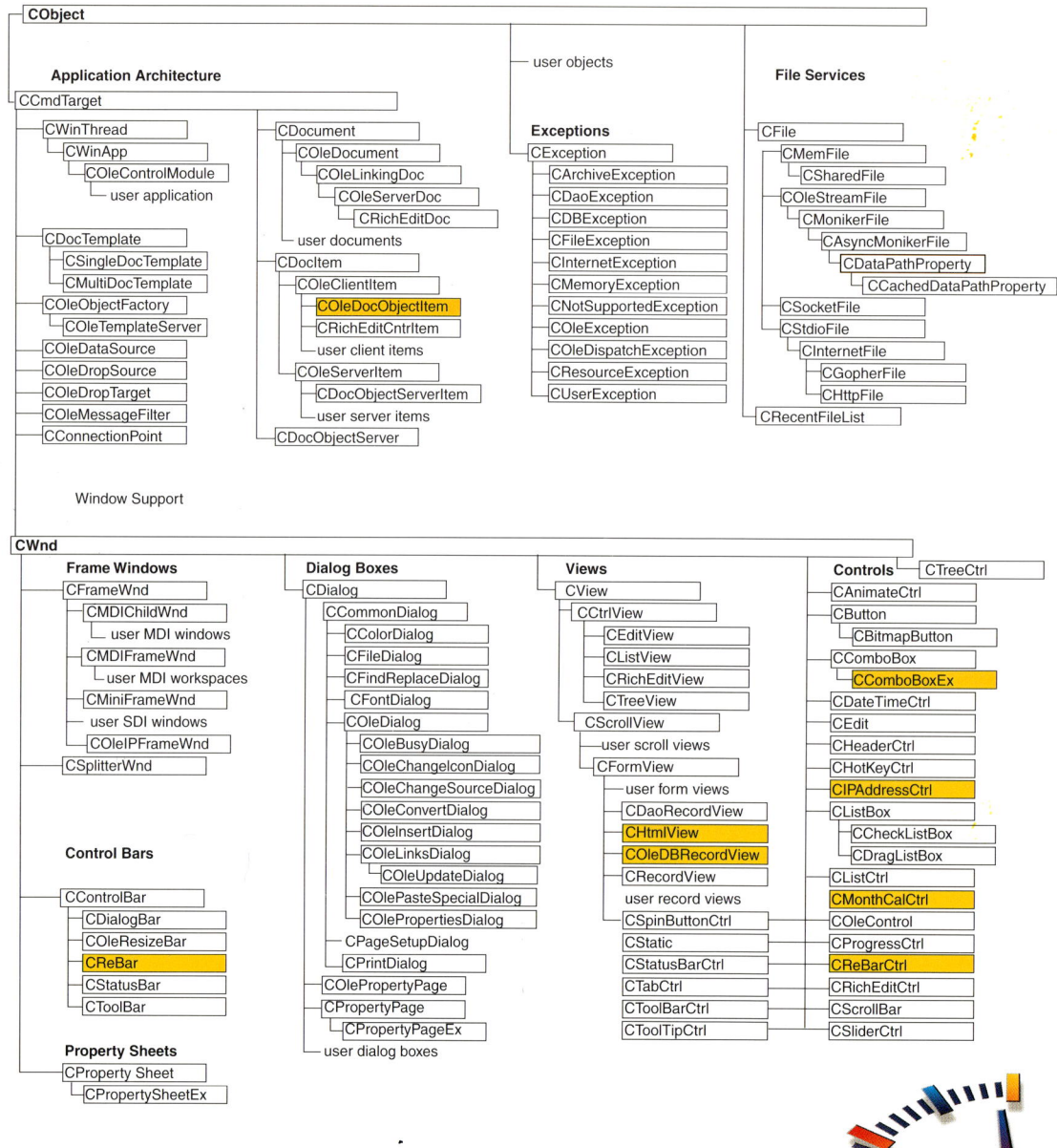

- CObject
  - **Application Architecture**
    - CCmdTarget
      - CWinThread
        - CWinApp
          - COleControlModule
          - user application
      - CDocTemplate
        - CSingleDocTemplate
        - CMultiDocTemplate
      - COleObjectFactory
        - COleTemplateServer
      - COleDataSource
      - COleDropSource
      - COleDropTarget
      - COleMessageFilter
      - CConnectionPoint
    - CDocument
      - COleDocument
        - COleLinkingDoc
          - COleServerDoc
            - CRichEditDoc
      - user documents
    - CDocItem
      - COleClientItem
        - COleDocObjectItem
        - CRichEditCntrItem
      - user client items
      - COleServerItem
        - CDocObjectServerItem
      - user server items
    - CDocObjectServer
  - user objects
  - **Exceptions**
    - CException
      - CArchiveException
      - CDaoException
      - CDBException
      - CFileException
      - CInternetException
      - CMemoryException
      - CNotSupportedException
      - COleException
      - COleDispatchException
      - CResourceException
      - CUserException
  - **File Services**
    - CFile
      - CMemFile
        - CSharedFile
      - COleStreamFile
      - CMonikerFile
        - CAsyncMonikerFile
          - CDataPathProperty
            - CCachedDataPathProperty
      - CSocketFile
      - CStdioFile
        - CInternetFile
          - CGopherFile
          - CHttpFile
    - CRecentFileList

Window Support

- CWnd
  - **Frame Windows**
    - CFrameWnd
      - CMDIChildWnd
        - user MDI windows
      - CMDIFrameWnd
        - user MDI workspaces
      - CMiniFrameWnd
      - user SDI windows
      - COleIPFrameWnd
    - CSplitterWnd
  - **Control Bars**
    - CControlBar
      - CDialogBar
      - COleResizeBar
      - CReBar
      - CStatusBar
      - CToolBar
  - **Property Sheets**
    - CPropertySheet
      - CPropertySheetEx
  - **Dialog Boxes**
    - CDialog
      - CCommonDialog
        - CColorDialog
        - CFileDialog
        - CFindReplaceDialog
        - CFontDialog
        - COleDialog
          - COleBusyDialog
          - COleChangeIconDialog
          - COleChangeSourceDialog
          - COleConvertDialog
          - COleInsertDialog
          - COleLinksDialog
            - COleUpdateDialog
          - COlePasteSpecialDialog
          - COlePropertiesDialog
        - CPageSetupDialog
        - CPrintDialog
      - COlePropertyPage
      - CPropertyPage
        - CPropertyPageEx
      - user dialog boxes
  - **Views**
    - CView
      - CCtrlView
        - CEditView
        - CListView
        - CRichEditView
        - CTreeView
      - CScrollView
        - user scroll views
        - CFormView
          - user form views
          - CDaoRecordView
          - CHtmlView
          - COleDBRecordView
          - CRecordView
          - user record views
      - CSpinButtonCtrl
      - CStatic
      - CStatusBarCtrl
      - CTabCtrl
      - CToolBarCtrl
      - CToolTipCtrl
  - **Controls**
    - CTreeCtrl
    - CAnimateCtrl
    - CButton
      - CBitmapButton
    - CComboBox
      - CComboBoxEx
    - CDateTimeCtrl
    - CEdit
    - CHeaderCtrl
    - CHotKeyCtrl
    - CIPAddressCtrl
    - CListBox
      - CCheckListBox
      - CDragListBox
    - CListCtrl
    - CMonthCalCtrl
    - COleControl
    - CProgressCtrl
    - CReBarCtrl
    - CRichEditCtrl
    - CScrollBar
    - CSliderCtrl

Sams Teach Yourself MFC in 24 Hours
0-672-31553-x

SAMS

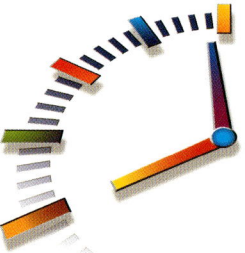

Michael Morrison

SAMS Teach Yourself
MFC in 24 Hours

SAMS
201 West 103rd St., Indianapolis, Indiana, 46290 USA

Sams Teach Yourself MFC in 24 Hours

Copyright © 1999 by Sams Publishing

All rights reserved. No part of this book shall be reproduced, stored in a retrieval system, or transmitted by any means, electronic, mechanical, photocopying, recording, or otherwise, without written permission from the publisher. No patent liability is assumed with respect to the use of the information contained herein. Although every precaution has been taken in the preparation of this book, the publisher and author assume no responsibility for errors or omissions. Neither is any liability assumed for damages resulting from the use of the information contained herein.

International Standard Book Number: 0-672-31553-X

Library of Congress Catalog Card Number: 98-88866

Printed in the United States of America

First Printing: March 1999

01   00   99   4   3   2   1

Trademarks

All terms mentioned in this book that are known to be trademarks or service marks have been appropriately capitalized. Sams Publishing cannot attest to the accuracy of this information. Use of a term in this book should not be regarded as affecting the validity of any trademark or service mark.

Warning and Disclaimer

Every effort has been made to make this book as complete and as accurate as possible, but no warranty or fitness is implied. The information provided is on an "as is" basis. The authors and the publisher shall have neither liability nor responsibility to any person or entity with respect to any loss or damages arising from the information contained in this book.

EXECUTIVE EDITOR
Bradley L. Jones

AQUISITIONS EDITOR
Chris Webb

DEVELOPMENT EDITOR
Matt Purcell

MANAGING EDITOR
Jodi Jensen

SENIOR EDITOR
Susan Ross Moore

COPY EDITOR
Linda Morris

INDEXER
Kevin Kent

PROOFREADER
Mona Brown

TECHNICAL EDITOR
Paul Schmidt

TEAM COORDINATOR
Carol Ackerman

INTERIOR DESIGN
Gary Adair

COVER DESIGN
Aren Howell

LAYOUT TECHNICIANS
Brian Borders
Susan Geiselman
Mark Walchle

Contents at a Glance

	Introduction	1
Hour 1	Welcome to MFC	3
2	Building MFC Applications	21
3	Creating and Using Application Resources	41
Hour 4	Interacting with the User	59
5	Making Use of Controls	75
6	Using Common Dialog Boxes	97
7	Retrieving Information with Custom Dialog Boxes	113
8	Manipulating Menus	131
9	Drawing Graphics	149
Hour 10	Managing Data with MFC	173
11	Organizing Data with MFC's Collection Classes	187
12	Managing Application Data with Documents	207
13	Viewing Application Data	227
Hour 14	Enhanced User Interfaces	241
15	Utilizing Control Bars	261
16	Managing Multiple Documents	275
Hour 17	Inside Printing	293
18	Accessing Databases with DAO	317
19	ADO and the Future of Databases	351
20	Connecting to the Web	361
21	Multimedia and DirectX	377
22	Creating DLLs	399
Hour 23	Creating Custom Controls	415
24	Creating Wizards	431
Appendix A	Quiz Answers	455
B	MFC Information Resources	477
C	MFC and Visual Development Tools	481
	Index	483

Contents

INTRODUCTION 1

HOUR 1 WELCOME TO MFC 3
    Win32 Basics 3
        Windows 4
        Window Procedures, Events, and Messages 5
        Strange Data Types 6
        The `WinMain()` Function 7
    The MFC Alternative 7
    A Skeletal MFC Application 8
        The Application Object 11
        The Main Frame Window 13
        Application Resources 16
    Summary 17
    Q&A 18
    Workshop 18
        Quiz 18
        Exercises 19

HOUR 2 BUILDING MFC APPLICATIONS 21
    Document-Centric Applications 22
    The Structure of an MFC Application 23
        Inside the `Application` Object 24
        Modeling Data with Documents 25
        Looking at Data with Views 26
    MFC Naming Conventions 26
    The Skeleton Application Revisited 28
        The `Document` Object 28
        The `View` Object 32
        Other Document/View Changes 35
    Summary 38
    Q&A 39
    Workshop 39
        Quiz 39
        Exercises 40

HOUR 3 CREATING AND USING APPLICATION RESOURCES 41
    Understanding the Role of Resources 42
    Types of Resources 44
    Defining Resources in a Resource Script 45
        Accelerators 45
        Bitmaps 46

Cursors	46
Icons	47
Menus	47
Dialog Boxes	49
String Tables	50
Version Resources	51
Using Resources in an Application	51
Summary	56
Q&A	56
Workshop	57
Quiz	57
Exercises	57

Hour 4 Interacting with the User   59

The Importance of User Input	59
Working with Message Maps	60
Using Message Map Macros	61
Writing Message Handlers	62
Handling User Input Messages	63
Keyboard Messaging Basics	64
Handling Keyboard Messages	66
Mouse Messaging Basics	67
Handling Mouse Messages	69
Summary	71
Q&A	72
Workshop	72
Quiz	72
Exercises	73

Hour 5 Making Use of Controls   75

Understanding Controls	75
Traditional Windows Controls	76
Common Controls	78
Controls and MFC	80
Creating Controls with MFC	81
Handling Control Notifications	82
ActiveX Controls	85
Putting Controls to Work	86
Summary	93
Q&A	94
Workshop	94
Quiz	94
Exercises	95

Hour 6 Using Common Dialog Boxes — 97

- Origins of Common Dialog Boxes — 98
- Exploring the Common Dialog Boxes — 98
- MFC Common Dialog Box Classes — 99
  - File Open and File Save As — 100
  - Color Selection — 101
  - Font Selection — 102
  - Find Text and Replace Text — 103
  - Page Setup — 104
  - Print — 105
- Using Common Dialog Boxes — 105
  - Opening Files — 107
  - Selecting Color — 109
- Summary — 111
- Q&A — 111
- Workshop — 111
  - Quiz — 111
  - Exercises — 112

Hour 7 Retrieving Information with Custom Dialog Boxes — 113

- Using Message Boxes — 114
- Modal and Modeless Dialog Boxes — 115
- MFC Dialog Box Support — 117
  - Dialog Box Data — 117
  - Dialog Box Messaging — 118
  - Creating a CDialog Object — 118
- Dialog Box Resources — 118
- Building Simple Dialog Boxes — 120
  - Creating the Dialog Box Resource — 121
  - Creating the Dialog Box Class — 123
  - Invoking the Dialog Box — 126
- Summary — 128
- Q&A — 128
- Workshop — 129
  - Quiz — 129
  - Exercises — 129

Hour 8 Manipulating Menus — 131

- Responding to Menu Events — 132
- Analyzing the System Menu — 132
  - Obtaining a System Menu Object — 133
  - Adding a System Menu Item — 133
- Dynamically Modifying Menus — 134
  - Getting Menus and Pop-up Menus — 135
  - Adding Menu Items — 135
  - Dynamic Menus and Animator3 — 136

Contents

Using Floating Pop-up Menus	140
Updating Menus	142
MFC's Command Update Message Handlers	142
Updating the Animator3 Menu	143
Summary	145
Q&A	146
Workshop	146
Quiz	146
Exercises	147

HOUR 9 DRAWING GRAPHICS — 149

Graphics Fundamentals	149
The Importance of Device Contexts	150
Basic Graphics Components	151
The Windows Graphics Coordinate System	152
Understanding Color	153
GDI and MFC	155
Painting Windows	156
Drawing Graphics Primitives	157
Lines	157
Rectangles	158
Ellipses	159
Drawing Text	160
Drawing Bitmaps	161
Loading a Bitmap	162
Painting a Bitmap	162
Putting It All Together	163
Summary	171
Q&A	171
Workshop	172
Quiz	172
Exercises	172

HOUR 10 MANAGING DATA WITH MFC — 173

Getting a Handle on Data Structures	174
MFC's Data Classes	175
Basic Data Structures	175
Data Collections	176
Support Classes	177
A Serialization Primer	178
Working with Strings	179
Creating Strings	179
Accessing String Characters	180
Concatenating Strings	181
Comparing Strings	181
Strings and `char` Pointers	182

	Working with Time	182
	Summary	184
	Q&A	184
	Workshop	184
	Quiz	185
	Exercises	185
HOUR 11	**ORGANIZING DATA WITH MFC'S COLLECTION CLASSES**	**187**
	Revisiting the MFC Collection Classes	188
	Array	188
	List	189
	Map	189
	Choosing Collections	190
	Using the Collection Classes	191
	Putting Arrays to Work	192
	`CArray`	192
	`CTypedPtrArray`	194
	Organizing Data into Lists	194
	`CList`	195
	`CTypedPtrList`	196
	Mapping Data	197
	`CMap`	197
	`CTypedPtrMap`	199
	Enhancing the Doodle Application	199
	Summary	205
	Q&A	205
	Workshop	206
	Quiz	206
	Exercises	206
HOUR 12	**MANAGING APPLICATION DATA WITH DOCUMENTS**	**207**
	Document Basics	208
	MFC's Document Support	209
	Documents and Serialization	210
	Creating Documents	212
	Applying Documents to Doodle	212
	The Main Frame Window and `Application Object`	212
	Application Resources	215
	The `Document` Class	217
	Serializing the `CGraphic` Class	221
	What's Missing?	225
	Summary	225
	Q&A	225
	Workshop	226
	Quiz	226
	Exercises	226

Hour 13 Viewing Application Data — 227

- Understanding Views — 227
  - Printing and Views — 228
  - View Windows — 229
- MFC's View Support — 229
- Creating Views — 232
- Adding a View to Doodle — 232
- Summary — 238
- Q&A — 238
- Workshop — 239
  - Quiz — 239
  - Exercises — 239

Hour 14 Enhanced User Interfaces — 241

- Optimizing Views — 241
  - Updating the View — 242
  - Drawing the View — 244
- Scrolling Views — 245
  - Sizing Up the Document — 245
  - Scrolling the View — 247
- Using Multiple Views — 251
  - Splitting the Views — 251
  - An Alternative View for Doodle — 253
- Summary — 259
- Q&A — 259
- Workshop — 260
  - Quiz — 260
  - Exercises — 260

Hour 15 Utilizing Control Bars — 261

- Understanding Control Bars — 261
- Using Toolbars — 264
- Using Status Bars — 266
- Showing and Hiding Control Bars — 269
- Working with ToolTips — 270
- Summary — 273
- Q&A — 273
- Workshop — 273
  - Quiz — 273
  - Exercises — 274

Hour 16 Managing Multiple Documents — 275

- MDI Fundamentals — 276
- Inside MDI Applications — 278
  - A Template for Multiple Documents — 279
  - Framing an MDI Application — 279

The MDI Client Window	279
Child Document Windows	280
Menus and MDI Applications	280
Building an MDI Application	280
Resources	281
The Application	284
The Main Frame Window	287
Summary	291
Q&A	291
Workshop	292
Quiz	292
Exercises	292

Hour 17 Inside Printing 293

Printing Basics	293
MFC's Support for Printing	294
Printing in the View	295
The `PrintInfo` Object	297
Standard Print Commands	298
Printing and GDI Mapping Modes	299
Printing Doodle Documents	301
Resources	301
The Application	304
The View	304
The Document	310
The Document's Final Stages	311
Summary	314
Q&A	314
Workshop	314
Quiz	315
Exercises	315

Hour 18 Accessing Databases with DAO 317

Databases and MFC	318
The DAO Object Model	319
The `DBEngine` Object	319
The `Workspace` Object	320
The `Database` Object	320
Internal Database Objects	320
The MFC DAO Classes	320
MFC, DAO, and Form-Based Applications	321
Creating a Custom Record Set Class	322
The Document and View	323
Building a Database Application	324
Resources	325
Database Support	329

	The Document	337
	The View	340
	Summary	347
	Q&A	347
	Workshop	348
	Quiz	348
	Exercises	349
HOUR 19	**ADO AND THE FUTURE OF DATABASES**	**351**
	Getting a Handle on the Big Picture	352
	VBSQL	352
	ODBC	353
	DAO	353
	RDO	353
	OLE DB	354
	ADO	354
	The Benefits of ADO	354
	Digging into ADO Objects	355
	The ADO Data Control	357
	ADO and MFC	358
	Summary	359
	Q&A	359
	Workshop	359
	Quiz	360
	Exercises	360
HOUR 20	**CONNECTING TO THE WEB**	**361**
	Understanding Web-Enabled Applications	361
	The WebBrowser Control	363
	An HTML View	364
	Using the CHtmlView Class	364
	For Internet Explorer Only	366
	Building a Simple Web Browser	366
	Resources	367
	The View	369
	Summary	374
	Q&A	374
	Workshop	375
	Quiz	375
	Exercises	376
HOUR 21	**MULTIMEDIA AND DIRECTX**	**377**
	Multimedia Basics	378
	What Is DirectX?	378
	DirectX Foundation	379
	DirectX Media	380

The DirectX Media Player Control	381
MFC and the Media Player Control	383
Using the Media Player Control	384
Resources	385
The Application	389
The Main Window	391
Summary	397
Q&A	397
Workshop	398
Quiz	398
Exercises	398

HOUR 22 CREATING DLLS 399

DLL Fundamentals	399
To Dynamically Link or Not	402
DLL Mechanics	403
Managing DLLs with DLLMain()	404
Creating an MFC Extension DLL	405
Using an MFC Extension DLL	411
Summary	413
Q&A	413
Workshop	414
Quiz	414
Exercises	414

HOUR 23 CREATING CUSTOM CONTROLS 415

When Standard Controls Aren't Enough	416
Deriving from an Existing Control	417
Creating a Control from Scratch	420
Testing Controls	423
Summary	428
Q&A	428
Workshop	428
Quiz	428
Exercises	429

HOUR 24 CREATING WIZARDS 431

Simplifying Tasks with Wizards	431
Property Sheets, Property Pages, and Wizards	433
MFC's Support for Property Sheets and Wizards	435
The CPropertySheet Class	435
The CPropertyPage Class	437
Creating a Simple Wizard	438
The Resources	439
The Wizard Data	444
The Wizard Pages	445

The Wizard	450
Testing the Investment Wizard	452
Summary	452
Q&A	453
Workshop	453
Quiz	453
Exercises	454

APPENDIX A QUIZ ANSWERS

Hour 1, "Welcome to MFC"	455
Quiz Answers	455
Hour 2, "Building MFC Applications"	456
Quiz Answers	456
Exercise Answers	456
Hour 3, "Creating and Using Applications Resources"	456
Quiz Answers	456
Hour 4, "Interacting with the User"	457
Quiz Answers	457
Exercise Answers	457
Hour 5, "Making Use of Controls"	459
Quiz Answers	459
Exercise Answers	459
Hour 6, "Using Common Dialog Boxes"	459
Quiz Answers	459
Exercise Answers	460
Hour 7, "Retrieving Information with Custom Dialog Boxes"	460
Quiz Answers	460
Exercise Answers	461
Hour 8, "Manipulating Menus"	461
Quiz Answers	461
Exercise Answers	462
Hour 9, "Drawing Graphics"	462
Quiz Answers	462
Hour 10, "Managing Data with MFC"	463
Quiz Answers	463
Exercise Answers	463
Hour 11, "Organizing Data with MFC's Collection Classes"	464
Quiz Answers	464
Exercise Answers	464
Hour 12, "Managing Application Data with Documents"	465
Quiz Answers	465
Exercise Answers	465
Hour 13, "Viewing Application Data"	466
Quiz Answers	466
Exercise Answers	466

Hour 14, "Enhanced User Interfaces" 467
    Quiz Answers..467
    Exercise Answers..467
Hour 15, "Utilizing Control Bars" 468
    Quiz Answers..468
    Exercise Answers..468
Hour 16, "Managing Multiple Documents" 469
    Quiz Answers..469
Hour 17, "Inside Printing" 469
    Quiz Answers..469
Hour 18, "Accessing Databases with DAO"..470
    Quiz Answers..470
    Exercise Answers..470
Hour 19, "ADO and the Future of Databases" 471
    Quiz Answers..471
Hour 20, "Connecting to the Web" 472
    Quiz Answers..472
    Exercise Answers..472
Hour 21, "Multimedia and DirectX" 473
    Quiz Answers..473
    Exercise Answers..474
Hour 22, "Creating DLLs" 474
    Quiz Answers..474
    Exercise Answers..475
Hour 23, "Creating Custom Controls" 475
    Quiz Answers..475
    Exercise Answers..475
Hour 24, "Creating Wizards" 475
    Quiz Answers..475
    Exercise Answers..476

APPENDIX B MFC INFORMATION RESOURCES   **477**

    Online Resources 478
    Periodicals..478

APPENDIX C MFC AND VISUAL DEVELOPMENT TOOLS   **481**

About the Author

MICHAEL MORRISON is a skateboarder, cyclist, toy inventor, and the author of a variety of programming books including *Windows 95 Game Developer's Guide Using the Game SDK* (Sams), *Java 1.1 Unleashed* (Sams), and *The Complete Idiot's Guide to Java* (Que). Michael is also a professional MFC programmer with experience developing games, multimedia applications, and software development tools. Michael is the instructor of DigitalThink's Win32 Programming Series, a Web-based training series for learning Win32 API programming. When not tinkering with his computer, Michael enjoys lazy weekends with his wife, Mahsheed.

Dedication

For my grandfather, Bob Hart, who gave more than my family could ever hope to repay him. We miss you!—Michael Morrison

Acknowledgments

Thanks to all of the folks at Sams Publishing, especially Chris Webb, who kept me on track and patiently listened to my excuses as the unfinished deadlines rolled by. I'd also like to thank Matt Purcell and Brad Jones, both of whom had lots of insight toward improving the content and organization of the book.

I'd like to thank my literary agent, Chris Van Buren, for his wisdom and guidance in improving my writing career.

Thanks also to my good friends Keith and Josh, who were kind enough to get me addicted to yet another sport (roller hockey). I look forward to many brutal crosschecks in the name of friendship!

I'd like to thank my parents for their unwavering love and support.

Finally, thanks to my wife, Mahsheed, the most beautiful and loving person I've ever met.

Tell Us What You Think!

As the reader of this book, *you* are our most important critic and commentator. We value your opinion and want to know what we're doing right, what we could do better, what areas you'd like to see us publish in, and any other words of wisdom you're willing to pass our way.

As the Executive Editor for the Advanced Programming team at Macmillan Computer Publishing, I welcome your comments. You can fax, email, or write me directly to let me know what you did or didn't like about this book—as well as what we can do to make our books stronger.

Please note that I cannot help you with technical problems related to the topic of this book, and that due to the high volume of mail I receive, I might not be able to reply to every message.

When you write, please be sure to include this book's title and author as well as your name and phone or fax number. I will carefully review your comments and share them with the author and editors who worked on the book.

Fax: 317-817-7070

Email: adv_prog@mcp.com

Mail: Bradley L. Jones
         Executive Editor
         Advanced Programming
         Macmillan Computer Publishing
         201 West 103rd Street
         Indianapolis, IN 46290 USA

Introduction

This book is written for programmers who have experience with C++ and would like to learn how to build Windows applications using Microsoft Foundation Classes (MFC). This book cuts to the chase by jumping straight into MFC programming and presenting lots of hands-on examples. You aren't burdened with any theory beyond what is absolutely required to explain a given topic. You'll find lots of examples that you can use as a basis for MFC development efforts of your own in each hour. Although you are free to type in the example code covered throughout the book, you may want to download it from the companion Web site.

How This Book Is Structured

This book is divided into 24 hour-long chapters, each of which delves into a different aspect of Windows programming with MFC:

Hours 1-3 introduce MFC and the coding conventions used by Windows programmers, as well as the basic construction techniques required to build simple MFC applications.

Hours 4-9 tackle user interface issues such as responding to the mouse and keyboard, using controls and dialog boxes, working with menus, and drawing graphics.

Hours 10-13 take a look at how MFC applications manage data. Topics include MFC's data structure classes, creating document classes, and designing views for displaying application data.

Hours 14-16 dig deeper into user interfaces by examining enhanced views, demonstrating how to use control bars, and exploring Multiple Document Interface (MDI) applications.

Hours 17-22 address some applied areas of MFC such as printing, database access, interacting with the Web, providing help, and creating DLLs.

Hours 23 and 24 explore user interfaces with an eye toward providing a more customized feel for an application. Topics include how to create custom controls and how to design and build wizards.

The lessons in the book are designed to take you roughly an hour each to complete. I encourage you to try to read the book sequentially because most of the material builds on earlier material. Each hour begins with a list of learning objectives, and then jumps into the first topic. The focus of the book is to learn by doing, so you'll notice that discussions are intertwined with hands-on examples that demonstrate a particular facet of MFC.

The end of each hour contains a Q&A section, a quiz, and exercises designed to test your knowledge and understanding of the hour's material. The answers to the quizzes are located in Appendix A, "Quiz Answers." Appendix B, "MFC Information Resources," includes a list of MFC resources that you'll find useful for learning more about MFC. Appendix C, "MFC and Visual Development Tools," provides information about third-party visual development tools that support MFC.

What You'll Need

This book assumes you have a solid working knowledge of the C++ programming language. It also assumes that you are familiar with the Windows 95/98 or Windows NT operating system at least from a user's perspective. You aren't expected to know anything about the Win32 API or Windows programming; the premise of the book is to teach you Windows programming using MFC.

You will need a computer running Windows 95/98 or Windows NT, along with a suitable C++ compiler that supports the Win32 API and MFC. It also wouldn't hurt to use a development tool with an integrated Windows debugger. Currently there are three commercial visual development environments available that include C++ compilers/debuggers and support for the Win32 API and MFC. Please refer to Appendix C for more information about these tools.

That's all you need to get started learning MFC. Go ahead and turn to Hour 1 for your first taste of MFC.

Hour 1

Welcome to MFC

Welcome to the first hour of an exciting journey through Windows programming using Microsoft Foundation Classes (MFC)! As you will soon learn, MFC has lots to offer the Windows developer. In this hour, you are introduced to MFC and will gain some perspective on why it is such a useful technology. You will also take a peek at a skeletal MFC application.

Following are some of the main things you learn about in this hour:

- The basics of Win32 programming
- The benefits of using MFC
- How to build a skeletal MFC application

Win32 Basics

Before I get into MFC and what it is, it's important to establish some ground rules regarding the operating environment that MFC targets. MFC is designed for building applications that run on the Win32 computing platform, which encompasses Windows 95, Windows 98, and Windows NT. Although these operating systems differ in some ways with respect to each other, they all share the common bond of being based on the Win32 platform.

The significance of Win32 is that it establishes the features and capabilities available to Windows applications. Win32 is responsible for all the neat graphical features you've come to expect as a Windows user, not to mention some behind-the-scenes features that you might not even know about. Why should you care about Win32? Because MFC is based entirely on the Win32 API, which is the standard programming interface for developing Win32 applications.

In the not so distant past, before MFC came into being, all Windows applications were developed in C using the Windows API. The Windows API defines a massive set of C functions and data structures that are used to interact with Win32 platform features. Unfortunately, Win32 API programming was very difficult, requiring even the simplest tasks to be carried out using hundreds of lines of code. The complexity of Win32 API programming is ultimately what led to the development of MFC. The Win32 API, however, still lurks below the surface of all Windows applications, including those developed using MFC. In fact, you will still find yourself interacting with the Win32 API when building MFC applications.

Windows

Because you must still work with the Win32 API when using MFC, it's important to understand some of the basic principles associated with Win32 API programming. In Win32, as well as MFC, everything begins with the concept of a window. A window is defined simply as a rectangular region on the screen that can receive input and display graphical information. Many types of windows are defined in Win32 ranging from application windows, to buttons, to scroll bars. Figure 1.1 shows a basic application window, with which you are no doubt familiar.

The application window shown in the figure is divided into two primary parts: the client area and the nonclient area. The client area is the rectangular part of the window over which an application has complete control. The rest of the window is considered the nonclient area, and is managed for the most part by Win32. I say "for the most part" because you can tweak the nonclient area to some extent, but generally speaking Win32 is in control of it.

The Win32 API includes a wide range of functions for manipulating windows. It also defines a number of window classes that define different types of windows. A window class is a template of window characteristics used as a basis for creating windows. As an example, a button has an associated window class that defines window characteristics specific to buttons. The window class for a window also contains a pointer to a window procedure, which determines the functionality of a window.

FIGURE 1.1
A basic Win32 application window.

Nonclient Area

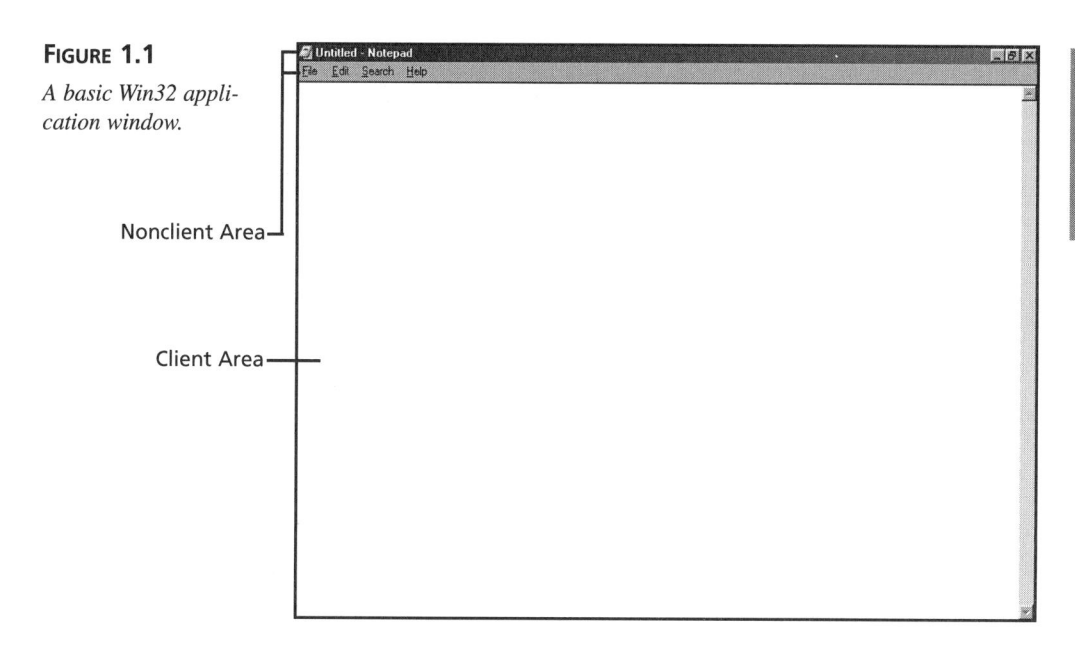

Client Area

> **NEW TERM**   A *window class* is a template of window characteristics in Win32 that is used as a basis for creating windows.

Window Procedures, Events, and Messages

The functional core of a Win32 window lies in the window procedure, which is a special function that contains all the code that drives a window's behavior. More specifically, the window procedure for a window contains a huge `switch` statement which responds to the various messages that a window handles. What's a message? Good question. Win32 uses messages to notify windows of events that have taken place such as the user dragging the mouse or pressing a key. There are also lower-level messages corresponding to a window's creation and destruction, for example. A window's behavior is ultimately determined by the messages it receives and how it handles them.

> **NEW TERM**   A *window procedure* is a special function which contains all the code that drives a window's behavior.

When I say that a message is sent to a window, I really mean that the window procedure for the window is called. The specific message is identified in the arguments to the window procedure. The big `switch` statement in the window procedure is necessary to distinguish between the different messages the window receives; Win32 defines hundreds of different messages. A window can respond to as few or as many messages as is necessary to carry out its function. Following are some messages commonly handled by Win32 applications:

- `WM_CREATE`—sent when a window is created
- `WM_PAINT`—sent when a window needs to repaint itself
- `WM_MOUSEMOVE`—sent when the mouse is moved over a window
- `WM_LBUTTONDOWN`—sent when the left mouse button is pressed over a window
- `WM_CLOSE`—sent when a window is about to close

If you've never programmed in Windows, the whole notion of messages might seem a little strange. Windows programming is known as *event-driven programming*, which means that applications are driven by external events. These events are delivered to an application as messages. As you get more comfortable with events, you will see that almost any change in an application's environment can trigger an event. As an application developer, you have the ability and often the responsibility of handling these events.

Because of the inherently graphical nature of Windows, it will become more apparent why Win32's event-driven programming model is not only convenient, but also downright necessary. With multiple applications running at once and on-the-fly system configuration changes, as well as a multitude of other things happening, events and messages are practically the only way an application could keep up with everything going on in a Windows session.

Strange Data Types

Although MFC shields you from many of the details of the Win32 API, you will still run across some of the strange data types that are a standard part of Win32 programming. One of the most commonly used Win32 data types is the handle, which is a unique integer *identifier* used to identify an object or piece of memory. A handle is sort of like an indirect pointer in that it references memory but not directly. Handles are necessary in Win32 because Windows often moves memory around without your knowledge. Because handles don't directly point to memory, you don't have to worry about whether a piece of memory has been moved.

New Term An *identifier* is a value, usually numeric, that is used to uniquely identify a piece of information.

New Term A *handle* is a unique integer identifier used in Win32 to identify an object or piece of memory.

You will primarily deal with handles when working with resources such as icons, menus, and bitmaps. Handles are typically defined with respect to a specific data type. For example, a handle to an icon is named `HICON`. Similarly, a handle to a menu is called `HMENU`. A generic `HANDLE` data type is also used to reference chunks of memory.

Another data type commonly used in Win32 is `BOOL`, which represents a Boolean value of `TRUE` or `FALSE`. Internally the `BOOL` data type is really an `int`, but you should get in the habit of thinking of it as a 1-bit data type with the only legal values of `TRUE` or `FALSE`.

Win32 also defines some very useful mathematical data types such as `POINT` and `RECT`. The `POINT` data type contains integer x and y members, and is used to represent a physical point such as the corner of a window. The `RECT` data type contains integer `left`, `top`, `right`, and `bottom` members, and is used to represent a physical rectangle such as the size and location of a window. Although it's possible that you'll encounter these data types while using MFC, you'll more than likely use the MFC class counterparts `CPoint` and `CRect`.

The `WinMain()` Function

If you've done any traditional C/C++ programming, you are no doubt familiar with the `main()` function. The operating system calls `main()` when a program is run, and the program code starts executing from within `main()`. Win32 has a similar function called `WinMain()` that serves as the starting point for Windows applications. However, `WinMain()`, unlike `main()`, merely creates and initializes some things and then eases out of the picture. After `WinMain()` creates a main window, the rest of the application executes through the window procedure by responding to messages (events). This is the fundamental difference between procedural and event-driven programming; procedural programs make calls to the operating system to receive input, whereas event-driven programs receive input by processing messages from the operating system.

> **FORGET ABOUT `WinMain()`**
> As you learn in just a moment, MFC hides the implementation of the `WinMain()` function, which means that you don't have to worry about it in MFC applications. This is a nice convenience because most of the code in `WinMain()` is standard overhead code required by all Win32 (and MFC) applications.

The MFC Alternative

I've already made mention of MFC numerous times, and I've yet to really tell you what it is. MFC is a library of C++ classes used to build Win32 applications. Without MFC, there really is no easy way to develop Win32 applications in C++ because the Win32 API is based solely on C. MFC serves as a wrapper around the Win32 API that packages Win32 functions and data types within C++ constructs. Additionally, MFC includes much of the standard overhead code required in functions such as `WinMain()`, which alleviates you from having to provide it yourself. This is a real benefit because a surprising amount of overhead code exists in even a minimal Win32 application.

Although MFC certainly adds some functionality and a great deal of organization not found in the Win32 API, the overriding goal of MFC was to create an object-oriented C++ library for building Win32 applications. Knowing this, it's not surprising that in some respects MFC serves only as a thin layer over the Win32 API. In other words, some MFC objects such as `CRect` are just class wrappers around existing Win32 API data structures. The `CRect` class wraps the `RECT` data structure and provides member functions that call the standard `RECT` Win32 API functions.

The most significant of the MFC wrapper classes is `CWnd`, which encapsulates the vast majority of the windowing functionality in the Win32 API. The huge benefit of using the `CWnd` class is the simplicity it offers when creating and manipulating windows. Creating a window in C with the Win32 API requires using multiple data structures along with several function calls. MFC simplifies things by allowing you to instantiate a `CWnd` object and call a couple of member functions. This simplicity of using objects over C data structures and global functions applies to the entire MFC library.

MFC also simplifies and improves the way an application responds to messages. Instead of developing a window procedure with a huge `Switch` statement, you map messages to member functions and write a member function to handle each specific message. This results in much cleaner code that is easier to understand and maintain. This benefit will become apparent in Hour 4, "Interacting with the User," when you learn to write message handler member functions.

In addition to wrapping the Win32 API and improving its use and organization with an object library, MFC also adds some powerful features of its own. One of these features is a document/view architecture that allows you to logically separate an application's data from the user interface that displays and manipulates the data. You learn more about MFC's document/view architecture in the next hour, "Building MFC Applications," and throughout the rest of the book.

A Skeletal MFC Application

Just in case you're afraid that I'm going to spend half the book rambling about the philosophical implications of Win32 and MFC, let me set the record straight with an example. The remainder of this hour focuses on a skeletal MFC application called Skeleton. The Skeleton application represents the minimum amount of code possible to create an MFC application. Skeleton basically does nothing but create and manage a main window, which is still more than you or I could do if we were just skeletons.

As a minimal application, Skeleton still manages to

- Respond to window resizing
- Display a custom icon
- Be minimized and maximized
- Share system resources with other applications

To help set the tone for the book, let's jump right into the details of how the Skeleton application works. The complete source code for the application is available from the book's companion Web site. Figure 1.2 shows what the Skeleton application looks like in action.

FIGURE 1.2

The Skeleton minimal MFC application.

As simple as Skeleton may be, it still requires eight source code files, one of which is a special resource file:

- StdAfx.h
- StdAfx.cpp
- Skeleton.h
- Skeleton.cpp
- MainFrame.h
- MainFrame.cpp

- Resource.h
- Skeleton.rc

The StdAfx files don't actually contain any source code. They are used to help generate precompiled headers, which greatly improve compilation speed. StdAfx.h contains `#include` directives for the standard MFC header files. StdAfx.cpp serves as the source code placeholder for StdAfx.h, which is necessary for creating precompiled headers. You will include these two files in all MFC applications that you build throughout the book.

> **THE BENEFIT OF PRECOMPILED HEADERS**
>
> Since the MFC library defines lots of classes, compiling the standard MFC AfxWin.h and AfxExt.h header files can get to be a pain, especially since their contents never change. Most modern compilers support the use of precompiled headers to deal with situations such as this. A file such as StdAfx.h includes the MFC header files and is then included in a source file such as StdAfx.cpp. This source code file triggers the compilation of the MFC class definitions as a separate entity that eliminates the dependency on other application code. The bottom line is that you don't have to wait for the MFC headers to recompile whenever you make a change to application-specific code and do a partial rebuild. Hence the benefit of precompiled headers!

Listings 1.1 and 1.2 contain the source code for the StdAfx.h and StdAfx.cpp files.

LISTING 1.1 THE STDAFX.H HEADER FILE FOR SKELETON

```
 1: #ifndef __STDAFX_H__
 2: #define __STDAFX_H__
 3:
 4: //----------------------------------------------------------------
 5: // Inclusions
 6: //----------------------------------------------------------------
 7: #include <AfxWin.h>
 8: #include <AfxExt.h>
 9:
10: #endif
```

LISTING 1.2 THE STDAFX.CPP SOURCE CODE FILE FOR SKELETON

```
1: //----------------------------------------------------------------
2: // Inclusions
3: //----------------------------------------------------------------
4: #include "StdAfx.h"
```

The rest of the source files in the Skeleton application define the structure and function of the application. More specifically, they define two fundamental elements that comprise an MFC application: an application object and a main frame window. Every MFC application has an associated application object that manages the overall operation of the application. Part of the responsibility of the application object is to create a main frame window, which is itself an object. The main frame window is what you actually see when you run an application; the application object works behind the scenes.

The Application Object

The files Skeleton.h and Skeleton.cpp provide the code for the Skeleton application object. Listings 1.3 and 1.4 contain these files.

LISTING 1.3 THE SKELETON.H HEADER FILE FOR SKELETON

```
 1: #ifndef __SKELETON_H__
 2: #define __SKELETON_H__
 3:
 4: //----------------------------------------------------------------
 5: // CSkeletonApp Class - Skeleton Application Object
 6: //----------------------------------------------------------------
 7: class CSkeletonApp : public CWinApp {
 8:   // Public Constructor(s)/Destructor
 9: public:
10:               CSkeletonApp();
11:   virtual     ~CSkeletonApp();
12:
13:   // Public Member Functions
14: public:
15:   virtual BOOL   InitInstance();
16:
17:   // Message Map & Runtime Support
18: protected:
19:   DECLARE_MESSAGE_MAP()
20: };
21:
22: #endif
```

LISTING 1.4 THE SKELETON.CPP SOURCE CODE FILE FOR SKELETON

```
 1: //----------------------------------------------------------------
 2: // Inclusions
 3: //----------------------------------------------------------------
 4: #include "StdAfx.h"
```

continues

LISTING 1.4 CONTINUED

```
 5: //----------------------------------------------------------------
 6: #include "Skeleton.h"
 7: #include "MainFrame.h"
 8:
 9: //----------------------------------------------------------------
10: // MFC Debugging Support
11: //----------------------------------------------------------------
12: #ifdef _DEBUG
13: #undef THIS_FILE
14: static char BASED_CODE THIS_FILE[] = __FILE__;
15: #endif
16:
17: //----------------------------------------------------------------
18: // Global Variables
19: //----------------------------------------------------------------
20: CSkeletonApp theApp;
21:
22:
23: //----------------------------------------------------------------
24: // Message Map & Runtime Support
25: //----------------------------------------------------------------
26: BEGIN_MESSAGE_MAP(CSkeletonApp, CWinApp)
27: END_MESSAGE_MAP()
28:
29: //----------------------------------------------------------------
30: // Public Constructor(s)/Destructor
31: //----------------------------------------------------------------
32: CSkeletonApp::CSkeletonApp() {
33: }
34:
35: CSkeletonApp::~CSkeletonApp() {
36: }
37:
38: //----------------------------------------------------------------
39: // Public Member Functions
40: //----------------------------------------------------------------
41: BOOL CSkeletonApp::InitInstance() {
42:   // Create main window
43:   m_pMainWnd = new CMainFrame;
44:   ASSERT(m_pMainWnd);
45:   if (((CMainFrame*)m_pMainWnd)->Create(m_pszAppName))
46:   {
47:     m_pMainWnd->ShowWindow(m_nCmdShow);
48:     m_pMainWnd->UpdateWindow();
49:     return TRUE;
50:   }
51:
52:   return FALSE;
53: }
```

The Skeleton.h header file defines a class named `CSkeletonApp` that derives from `CWinApp`. `CWinApp` serves as the base class for all MFC application objects. An application object provides the overhead for initializing and running an MFC application. Only one application object is associated with an application, and you must always create a global instance of it.

Although there is only one application object, Windows enables several copies of an application to run at the same time. To support this, application initialization is divided conceptually into two parts:

- One-time initialization—performed the very first time an application runs
- Instance initialization—performed each time an instance of an application runs, including the first time an application is run

Application initialization code is placed in the `InitInstance()` member function, which is defined in `CWinApp`. MFC's internal implementation of `WinMain()` automatically calls `InitInstance()` to initialize an application. The Skeleton application uses `InitInstance()` to create the main window object, `CMainFrame`, which corresponds to the application's main frame window.

The newly created `CMainFrame` window object is assigned to the inherited member `m_pMainWnd`. After constructing the `CMainFrame` object, `CMainFrame::Create()` is called to handle the actual creation of the window. I'll get into the specifics of the `Create()` member function a little later when I discuss the `CMainFrame` class. For now, note that `Create()` must return `TRUE` in order for the application to initialize successfully. The `InitInstance()` member function finishes up by displaying the newly created window and forcing it to be painted with calls to `ShowWindow()` and `Update()`. That wraps up the application object.

The Main Frame Window

Let's now take a look at the `CMainFrame` class to find out how the main frame window works. Listings 1.5 and 1.6 contain the source code for MainFrame.h and MainFrame.cpp.

LISTING 1.5 THE MAINFRAME.H HEADER FILE FOR SKELETON

```
1: #ifndef __MAINFRAME_H__
2: #define __MAINFRAME_H__
3:
4: //-------------------------------------------------------------
5: // CMainFrame Class - Main Frame Window Object
```

continues

LISTING 1.5 CONTINUED

```
 6: //----------------------------------------------------------------
 7: class CMainFrame : public CFrameWnd {
 8:    // Public Constructor(s)/Destructor
 9: public:
10:         CMainFrame();
11:    virtual ~CMainFrame();
12:
13:    // Public Member Functions
14: public:
15:    BOOL    Create(const CString& sTitle);
16:
17:    // Message Map & Runtime Support
18: protected:
19:    DECLARE_MESSAGE_MAP()
20:    DECLARE_DYNCREATE(CMainFrame)
21: };
22:
23: #endif
```

LISTING 1.6 THE MAINFRAME.CPP SOURCE CODE FILE FOR SKELETON

```
 1: //----------------------------------------------------------------
 2: // Inclusions
 3: //----------------------------------------------------------------
 4: #include "StdAfx.h"
 5: //----------------------------------------------------------------
 6: #include "MainFrame.h"
 7: #include "Resource.h"
 8:
 9: //----------------------------------------------------------------
10: // MFC Debugging Support
11: //----------------------------------------------------------------
12: #ifdef _DEBUG
13: #undef THIS_FILE
14: static char BASED_CODE THIS_FILE[] = __FILE__;
15: #endif
16:
17:
18: //----------------------------------------------------------------
19: // Message Map & Runtime Support
20: //----------------------------------------------------------------
21: BEGIN_MESSAGE_MAP(CMainFrame, CFrameWnd)
22: END_MESSAGE_MAP()
23:
24: IMPLEMENT_DYNCREATE(CMainFrame, CFrameWnd)
25:
```

```
26: //----------------------------------------------------------------
27: // Public Constructor(s)/Destructor
28: //----------------------------------------------------------------
29: CMainFrame::CMainFrame() {
30: }
31:
32: CMainFrame::~CMainFrame() {
33: }
34:
35: //----------------------------------------------------------------
36: // Public Member Functions
37: //----------------------------------------------------------------
38: BOOL CMainFrame::Create(const CString& sTitle) {
39:   CString sClassName;
40:
41:   sClassName = AfxRegisterWndClass(CS_HREDRAW | CS_VREDRAW,
42:     ::LoadCursor(NULL, IDC_ARROW),
43:     (HBRUSH)(COLOR_WINDOW + 1),
44:     ::LoadIcon(AfxGetInstanceHandle(),
45:     MAKEINTRESOURCE(IDR_SKELETON)));
46:
47:   return CFrameWnd::Create(sClassName, sTitle);
48: }
```

The declaration of the CMainFrame class in MainFrame.h is pretty simple; it contains only a constructor, destructor, and the Create() member function. The DECLARE_MESSAGE_MAP macro near the bottom of the listing defines a message map for the class, which is how the class processes messages. A message map essentially defines which member functions respond to which messages. The CMainFrame class doesn't process any messages in this case, but I include the message map code anyway because you will be using it in most of the examples throughout the book. You place actual message map entries in the CMainFrame.cpp file between the BEGIN_MESSAGE_MAP and END_MESSAGE_MAP macros.

NEW TERM A *message map* is an MFC coding structure that associates member functions with messages.

The DECLARE_DYNCREATE macro in the header file is used to enable MFC objects to be dynamically created at runtime. This is a powerful feature of MFC and is required for frame window classes. The IMPLEMENT_DYNCREATE macro is the partner of DECLARE_DYNCREATE and must be included with the class definition in order for dynamic object creation to function properly. These two macros always work in pairs—one in the header file and one in the source file.

Moving right along, `CMainFrame` performs its initialization in the `Create()` member function. `Create()` first calls `AfxRegisterWndClass()`, which is an MFC function that is used to modify window class attributes and register new classes. By registering a new window class, you can define new window characteristics of your own such as custom icons and cursors. In Skeleton, arguments are passed to `AfxRegisterWndClass()` that specify horizontal and vertical window updating, a standard arrow cursor, a standard background window color, and a custom Skeleton icon.

Application Resources

The custom Skeleton icon is defined in the application's resource file, which is discussed in a moment. To load the Skeleton icon, the `AfxGetInstanceHandle()` function is called. The `AfxGetInstanceHandle()` function gets a module handle for the application, which specifies that the Skeleton icon is physically located in the Skeleton application's .exe file (module). Contrasting this approach, notice that to load the arrow cursor you pass NULL as the module handle; this is done because the arrow cursor is a standard system resource.

Application resources include icons, cursors, menus, and bitmaps, among other things. All resources in an application must have a unique identifier associated with them so that they can be identified and used. Resource identifiers are used in the resource file to actually define resources as part of the application. Resource.h is the file that contains identifiers for all the resources in an application. Listing 1.7 contains the code for the Skeleton application's Resource.h file.

LISTING 1.7 THE RESOURCE.H HEADER FILE FOR SKELETON

```
1: //------------------------------------------------------------------
2: // Icons                    Range : 1000 - 1999
3: //------------------------------------------------------------------
4: #define IDR_SKELETON         1000
```

There isn't much going on in Skeleton's Resource.h file. Because Skeleton only uses one custom resource, only one corresponding identifier is listed in Resource.h. The resource identifier for the Skeleton icon is defined as `1000`. It is a good organizational practice to use ranges of numbers for different types of resources. This convention will become more apparent throughout the course as you work through examples that use more resources.

The last file in the Skeleton application is the resource file, Skeleton.rc, which is shown in Listing 1.8.

LISTING 1.8 THE SKELETON.RC RESOURCE FILE FOR SKELETON

```
 1: //----------------------------------------------------------------
 2: // Inclusions
 3: //----------------------------------------------------------------
 4: #include "AfxRes.h"
 5: #include "Resource.h"
 6:
 7: //----------------------------------------------------------------
 8: // Icons
 9: //----------------------------------------------------------------
10: IDR_SKELETON   ICON "Skeleton.ico"
11:
12: //----------------------------------------------------------------
13: // Strings
14: //----------------------------------------------------------------
15: STRINGTABLE
16: BEGIN
17:     AFX_IDS_APP_TITLE "Skeleton v1.0"
18: END
```

The Skeleton icon is defined in Skeleton.rc by using the Icon statement. The Icon statement specifies that the icon stored in the file Skeleton.ico will be compiled into the application and referenced by IDR_SKELETON. Figure 1.3 shows what the icon in the file Skeleton.ico looks like.

FIGURE 1.3

The Skeleton application's custom icon, which is stored in Skeleton.ico.

In addition to defining the icon resource, Skeleton.rc also defines a string resource containing the application title Skeleton. The application title is identified with the built-in MFC identifier AFX_IDS_APP_TITLE, which is used internally by MFC to establish the application's title upon initialization. This title string is displayed in the caption of the application's main frame window.

Summary

In this hour, you were introduced to MFC. You began by learning some fundamentals about Win32 API programming, which is the precursor to MFC programming. You then learned how MFC provides a layer above the Win32 API that makes Windows application development a much simpler task. You finished up the hour by building a minimal MFC application called Skeleton.

Q&A

Q Can I use MFC with any compiler I choose?

A Yes. Although MFC is integrated tightly with the Visual C++ development environment, you can use it with any 32-bit compiler provided you have all of the headers and libraries. Refer to Appendix C, "MFC and Visual Development Tools," for a list of some of the more popular development environments that include compilers supporting MFC.

Q You mention that MFC supports a document/view architecture, but there is no mention of documents or views in the Skeleton application. What gives?

A Although the document/view architecture is an important feature in MFC, it isn't necessarily something you will want to use in every MFC application. Being a minimal example of MFC, it makes sense that the Skeleton application should be as bare bones as possible, no pun intended. Besides, in the next hour you improve the Skeleton application to support MFC's document/view architecture.

Workshop

The Workshop is designed to help you anticipate possible questions, review what you've learned, and begin thinking ahead to put your knowledge into practice. The answers to the quiz are in Appendix A, "Quiz Answers."

Quiz

1. What operating systems does the Win32 platform encompass?
2. What is the rectangular part of a window over which an application has complete control?
3. What is a template of window characteristics in Win32 that is used as a basis for creating windows?
4. What does Win32 use to notify windows of events that have taken place such as the user dragging the mouse or pressing a key?
5. What is the special function that contains all the code that drives a window's behavior?

6. What is the relationship between MFC and the Win32 API?
7. What is the name of the MFC class that encapsulates the vast majority of the windowing functionality in the Win32 API?
8. What is the purpose of precompiled headers?
9. What is an MFC coding structure that associates member functions with messages?
10. Why is it necessary to define resource identifiers in the Resource.h file?

Exercises

1. Modify the icon (Skeleton.ico) for the Skeleton application in a resource editor and rebuild the application.
2. Change the name of the application in the resource file (Skeleton.rc) to `"My Skeleton Application"` and rebuild the application.

HOUR 2

Building MFC Applications

This hour opens a thorough discussion of application development with MFC by exploring MFC's document/view architecture. You not only learn about the basis of document-centric applications in general, but also about MFC's specific support for building applications with documents and views. By the end of the hour you will have created a new SkeletonDV application that makes use of MFC's document/view architecture.

In this hour, you will learn about

- The importance of document-centric applications
- The overall structure of an MFC application
- The naming conventions commonly used in MFC programming
- How to build a skeletal application based on MFC's document/view architecture

Document-Centric Applications

One of the most important features provided by MFC is its document/view architecture, which makes a clear distinction between an application's data and user interface. The significance of the document/view architecture is that it allows application developers to delineate between an application's data and the presentation of that data. It also benefits a user running an application because she is free to focus on the information the application manipulates, as opposed to the application itself. Applications that make use of a document/view architecture are known as document-centric applications.

New Term: *Document-centric* is an application description implying that an application makes use of a document/view architecture, which enables the user to focus on the manipulation of documents.

To better understand document-centric applications, consider a word processor such as WordPad, which ships with Windows 95/98. The WordPad application operates solely on word processing documents, typically in the Word document format. If you double-click a .doc file in Windows Explorer, an instance of WordPad will be launched with the file opened as a document. Files of type .DOC are associated with the WordPad application because it is designed specifically to work with Word documents.

It's easy to see how WordPad could be a document-centric application because you already tend to think of word processing files as documents. But what about other types of applications? There are a variety of different applications that could fit into a document/view architecture if you just expand your notion of a document. For example, Paint and Solitaire can both be implemented as document-centric applications. It is not surprising that Paint can be implemented this way because thinking of an image as a document isn't too much of a stretch. Solitaire is a little different, however, because there is no data being directly modified by the user. The game state information itself can be considered a document, though. In other words, the arrangement of the cards on the screen can be represented as a document.

In both of these examples, making distinctions between the documents and views improves the organization of the applications. Consider the Paint application for a moment. Assuming the document is simply the image being painted, the view is the client area that allows the user to view and modify the image. The view would communicate with the document to properly display and manipulate the image. The loading and saving of images are tasks solely performed by the document. Likewise, the view is completely responsible for interacting with the user and communicating changes to the document.

In addition to documents and views, MFC document-centric applications employ a document template that makes the association between the document, view, and application frame window. In MFC, you create the document, view, and frame window classes, and then allow the standard MFC document template to connect them all together appropriately. You will learn a great deal more about the relationship between documents and views later in the book. Nonetheless, I wanted to give you a quick introduction here because you'll be modifying the Skeleton application to be document-centric a little later in the hour.

New Term A *document template* is a special object that associates a document, view, frame window, and application resources with each other.

The Structure of an MFC Application

Although I showed you the source code for the Skeleton application in the previous hour, I didn't spend much time explaining the overall structure of MFC applications. Let's take a moment to build a more solid foundation on how MFC applications are structured. Regardless of whether an application uses MFC's document/view architecture, all MFC applications have a few things in common:

- An application object
- A main frame window
- User interface elements
- Application data
- Resources

The application object is the foundation for all MFC applications. It works behind the scenes to orchestrate the startup, execution, and termination of an application. The application object is responsible for creating a main frame window, which serves as the basis for an application's user interface. The main frame window houses the user interface elements such as buttons and toolbars that are used to carry out application tasks.

Practically all MFC applications operate on some type of data, whether it is text, graphics, database records, or custom application–specific data. This data is typically viewed and manipulated within the client area of the main frame window. In addition to the application–specific data involved in the primary function of an application, there is also special data associated with all applications. This data comes in the form of application resources such as icons and menus. Application resources are created and associated with an application during development, then compiled directly into an application's executable .EXE file. You explore resources more thoroughly in Hour 3, "Creating and Using Application Resources."

Inside the `Application` Object

You learned about the `Application` object in the last hour, but didn't dig into the details of what it does for an application. The purpose of the application object is to control the initialization, running, and termination of an application. Aside from encapsulating the Win32 `WinMain()` function for an application, the `Application` object provides some important member functions that can be used to control the execution of an application:

- `InitInstance()`
- `Run()`
- `OnIdle()`
- `ExitInstance()`

Figure 2.1 shows the relationship between these member functions and the `WinMain()` function.

FIGURE 2.1

The relationship between application object member functions and the `WinMain()` *function.*

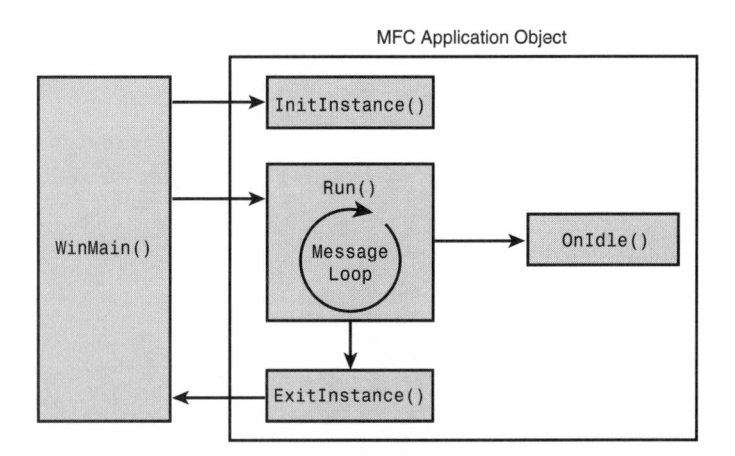

From Figure 2.1, it is apparent that `WinMain()` still runs the show behind the scenes in an MFC application. However, the application object neatly provides access to important sections of the `WinMain()` function through its member functions. The next few sections examine each of these member functions.

The `InitInstance()` Member Function

The `InitInstance()` member function is called near the start of `WinMain()` to perform instance initialization, which occurs for each instance of an application that is executed. `InitInstance()` is without a doubt the most important member function in application objects because practically all applications are concerned with instance initialization.

In fact, you are required to override the `InitInstance()` member function in your own application classes. Typically, you override `InitInstance()` to construct your main window object and set the inherited m_pMainWnd data member to point to that window.

The `Run()` Member Function

In an application built solely with the Win32 API, the `WinMain()` function spends the vast majority of its time in a message loop that waits for and processes incoming messages. This message loop is ultimately responsible for receiving messages and dispatching them to the main frame window of an application. In an MFC application, `WinMain()` delegates the message loop to the `Run()` member function. `Run()` loops continually wait for a message. If no messages are available, which is often the case, `Run()` calls the `OnIdle()` member function to perform idle processing. When the application is terminated, `Run()` calls the `ExitInstance()` member function.

The `OnIdle()` Member Function

The `OnIdle()` member function is used to perform idle processing that isn't immediately critical to the operation of an application. You typically override `OnIdle()` to perform background tasks such as a lengthy calculation. The default version of `OnIdle()` updates the state of user interface elements such as menu items and toolbar buttons.

The `ExitInstance()` Member Function

The `ExitInstance()` member function is called when an instance of an application is terminated. `ExitInstance()` is called by the `Run()` member function, usually in response to the user closing an application. You typically override `ExitInstance()` to perform the cleanup of objects created throughout the execution of an application. However, keep in mind that MFC automatically cleans up standard objects such as documents, views, and frame windows.

Modeling Data with Documents

The description of application structure thus far follows the Skeleton application example from the previous hour. How does it change when an application is moved to the document/view architecture? Surprisingly enough, things don't change too much. The primary change is organizational; the application object and main frame window aren't very different in a document/view application. The first noticeable change is the packaging of application-specific data into a document class. This document class derives from the MFC `CDocument` class, which provides features common to all documents.

The `CDocument` class supports standard operations such as creating a document, loading it, and saving it. You learn more about how to use the `CDocument` class to model application data with documents in Hour 12, "Managing Application Data with Documents."

Looking at Data with Views

In MFC's document view/architecture, views take on the role of providing a user interface for viewing and editing document data. A view typically takes up the client area of an application's main frame window, and can contain any number of user interface elements. However, standard application user interface elements such as the menu at the top of the frame window don't belong to a view. Neither do toolbars and status bars. Views are allowed to use pop-up menus and floating tool palettes. A particular view on document data is implemented in a view class, which must be derived from the MFC CView class.

The CView class provides the basic windowing functionality necessary for creating views. View classes derived from CView are always attached to a document class, and can be thought of as an intermediary between the user and the document. It's worth noting that views are child windows of an application's main frame window. You learn how to use the CView class to create interesting views of documents in Hour 13, "Viewing Application Data."

Figure 2.2 sums up what you've learned by providing a look at the relationship between the different parts of a document/view application.

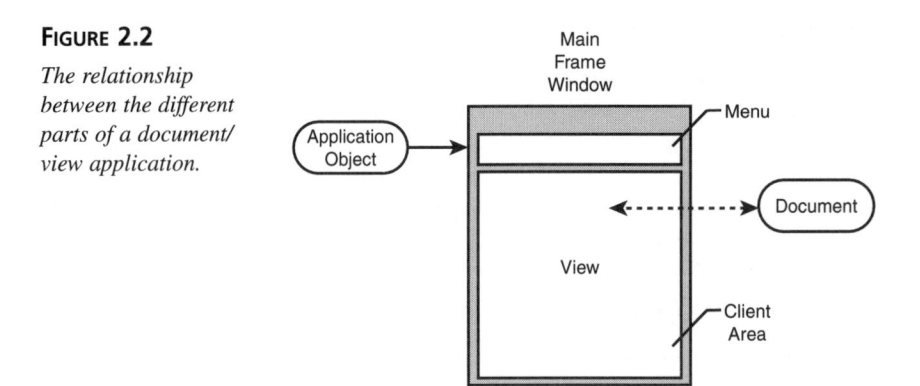

FIGURE 2.2

The relationship between the different parts of a document/view application.

MFC Naming Conventions

Before I move on to tackle a new version of the Skeleton application that supports documents and views, I'd like to clear up some of the naming conventions used in MFC programming. You've probably already caught on to some of these, such as MFC class names always beginning with the letter C. However, to keep you from stumbling later in the book, let's go over the most important of the naming conventions right now:

Building MFC Applications

- Functions are named as phrases with each word capitalized. Examples include `WinMain()`, `MessageBox()`, and `GetWindowRect()`.
- Classes are named like functions with the addition of a beginning letter `C`. Examples include `CWnd`, `CDocument`, and `CMenu`.
- Variables are named like functions, but they have a lowercase prefix that identifies the data type. Additionally, instance members of classes use the prefix `m_` to signify that they are members; static members don't use any special prefix. Examples include `szText`, `m_hWnd`, and `bEnabled`. Table 2.1 lists some of the more commonly used data prefixes.
- Data types specific to Win32 are defined in all uppercase. Examples include `HANDLE`, `HWND`, and `POINT`.
- Constants such as messages and resource identifiers are defined in all uppercase. Examples include `WM_CREATE`, `IDR_MAINFRAME`, and `IDI_MYICON`.
- Win32 API functions are always called by explicitly using the scope resolution operator, `::`. This is done to distinguish between calling Win32 API functions and MFC member functions of the same name. An example of this is `::GetMessage()`.

TABLE 2.1 COMMONLY USED DATA TYPE PREFIXES FOR NAMING VARIABLES

Prefix	Data Type
h	A handle (`HWND`, `HICON`, and so on)
w	A `WORD` (16-bit unsigned integer)
l	A `LONG` (32-bit signed integer)
p	A pointer
lp	A long (far) pointer
sz	A null-terminated string (terminated by a zero byte)
lpsz	A long pointer to a null-terminated string
b	A Boolean (`BOOL`)
rc	A rectangle structure (`RECT`)
pt	A point structure (`POINT`)

Programmers have long struggled with the problem of writing code that is easy to understand. Windows exacerbates this problem by introducing lots of different data types, which makes it difficult to keep up with which variables are of which type. Using the prefixes listed in Table 2.1 to name variables makes it easier to determine the data type of a variable without having to reference the variable declaration. This naming convention is known as Hungarian notation, and is named after the Hungarian Microsoft programmer Charles Simonyi, who initially came up with the scheme.

> **NEW TERM** *Hungarian notation* is the variable-naming convention of beginning a variable name with a lowercase letter or letters that indicate the data type of the variable.

The Skeleton Application Revisited

You now have sufficient knowledge of the structure of MFC applications to revisit the Skeleton application and apply MFC's document/view architecture to it. The new Skeleton application is called SkeletonDV. It will remain very minimal but will fully support the MFC document/view architecture. This is beneficial because you will then have starter code for the remainder of the sample applications covered throughout the book, whether or not they require documents and views.

The task of structuring the Skeleton application as a document/view application can be broken down into four main parts:

- Create a document class
- Create a view class
- Modify existing application code
- Modify existing application resources

The next few sections tackle each of these tasks.

The Document Object

As you learned earlier in this hour, all document classes must derive from the CDocument class. Because the goal in the Skeleton application is to keep things minimal, you'll notice that there isn't a whole lot to do beyond deriving from CDocument. Listings 2.1 and 2.2 contain the source code for the SkeletonDoc.h and SkeletonDoc.cpp files.

LISTING 2.1 THE SKELETONDOC.H HEADER FILE FOR SKELETONDV

```
 1: #ifndef __SKELETONDOC_H__
 2: #define __SKELETONDOC_H__
 3:
 4: //-----------------------------------------------------------------
 5: // CSkeletonDoc Class - Skeleton Document Object
 6: //-----------------------------------------------------------------
 7: class CSkeletonDoc : public CDocument {
 8:    // Public Constructor(s)/Destructor
 9: public:
10:              CSkeletonDoc();
```

```
11:     virtual      ~CSkeletonDoc();
12:
13:     // Public Member Functions
14: public:
15:     virtual BOOL   OnNewDocument();
16:     virtual void   Serialize(CArchive& ar);
17:
18:     // Diagnostic Functions
19: public:
20: #ifdef _DEBUG
21:     virtual void   AssertValid() const;
22:     virtual void   Dump(CDumpContext& dc) const;
23: #endif //_DEBUG
24:
25:     // Message Map & Runtime Support
26: protected:
27:     DECLARE_MESSAGE_MAP()
28:     DECLARE_DYNCREATE(CSkeletonDoc)
29: };
30:
31: #endif
```

LISTING 2.2 THE SKELETONDOC.CPP SOURCE CODE FILE FOR SKELETONDV

```
 1: //----------------------------------------------------------------
 2: // Inclusions
 3: //----------------------------------------------------------------
 4: #include "StdAfx.h"
 5: //----------------------------------------------------------------
 6: #include "SkeletonDoc.h"
 7:
 8: //----------------------------------------------------------------
 9: // MFC Debugging Support
10: //----------------------------------------------------------------
11: #ifdef _DEBUG
12: #undef THIS_FILE
13: static char BASED_CODE THIS_FILE[] = __FILE__;
14: #endif
15:
16:
17: //----------------------------------------------------------------
18: // Message Map & Runtime Support
19: //----------------------------------------------------------------
20: BEGIN_MESSAGE_MAP(CSkeletonDoc, CDocument)
21: END_MESSAGE_MAP()
22:
23: IMPLEMENT_DYNCREATE(CSkeletonDoc, CDocument)
```

continues

LISTING 2.1 CONTINUED

```
24:
25: //-----------------------------------------------------------
26: // Public Constructor(s)/Destructor
27: //-----------------------------------------------------------
28: CSkeletonDoc::CSkeletonDoc() {
29: }
30:
31: CSkeletonDoc::~CSkeletonDoc() {
32: }
33:
34: //-----------------------------------------------------------
35: // Public Member Functions
36: //-----------------------------------------------------------
37: BOOL CSkeletonDoc::OnNewDocument() {
38:   if (!CDocument::OnNewDocument())
39:     return FALSE;
40:
41:   // Initialize new document
42:   // TODO
43:
44:   return TRUE;
45: }
46:
47: void CSkeletonDoc::Serialize(CArchive& ar) {
48:   if (ar.IsStoring()) {
49:     // Store document data
50:     // TODO
51:   }
52:   else {
53:     // Load document data
54:     // TODO
55:   }
56: }
57:
58: //-----------------------------------------------------------
59: // Diagnostic Functions
60: //-----------------------------------------------------------
61: #ifdef _DEBUG
62: void CSkeletonDoc::AssertValid() const {
63:   CDocument::AssertValid();
64: }
65:
66: void CSkeletonDoc::Dump(CDumpContext& dc) const {
67:   CDocument::Dump(dc);
68: }
69: #endif //_DEBUG
```

Beyond providing an empty constructor and destructor, the `CSkeletonDoc` class defines member functions named `OnNewDocument()` and `Serialize()`.

The `OnNewDocument()` function is called in response to the user selecting New from an application's File menu. In other words, it is responsible for properly initializing an empty document. Because the `CSkeletonDoc` class doesn't actually define any document data, it isn't necessary for the `OnNewDocument()` function to do anything. Notice that there is a commented placeholder for inserting code to perform the initialization of document data.

> You'll find comments in the code throughout the book that serve as placeholders for inserting code. These comments are clearly marked with the word TODO, which means this is something "to do" later. In the Skeleton application, the TODO comment is used to show where you would normally place application code. The Skeleton application is so minimal that it doesn't require code in places where other applications would require it.

The `Serialize()` function is called to load or save the document data. The `If` statement checks to see whether the function is to load or save the document data. Again, I used comments to show where you would normally place functioning code.

In addition to the `OnNewDocument()` and `Serialize()` member functions, the `CSkeletonDoc` class also provides two diagnostic functions, `AssertValid()` and `Dump()`. I refer to these functions as diagnostic functions because they are only used for testing purposes during the development of the SkeletonDV application, which is why they are placed within the `_DEBUG` macro. Code placed within the `_DEBUG` macro is compiled into only the debug version of an application. You might have to set this up with your specific compiler to work properly. Visual C++ defines the `_DEBUG` macro by default when the compile target is set to debug.

The `AssertValid()` member function performs a validity check on an object by checking its internal state. In addition to calling its base class `AssertValid()` function, a class should check the integrity of its own data members. The `CSkeletonDoc` class doesn't define any data members of its own, which is why there isn't any additional code in its `AssertValid()` function.

The `Dump()` member function dumps the contents of an object so that its internal state can be examined. A `CDumpContext` object is provided as the only argument to the function. This dump context is what you use to actually dump the contents of an object. Because the `CSkeletonDoc` class doesn't define any data members of its own, it isn't necessary to dump anything in the `Dump()` function.

That wraps up the `CSkeletonDoc` document class. Let's move on to the view class.

The `View` Object

Similar to document classes, view classes must derive from a special MFC class; all view classes must derive from the `CView` class. Much like the `CSkeletonDoc` class, you'll notice that there isn't a whole lot of code in the view class beyond deriving from `CView`. Listings 2.3 and 2.4 contain the source code for the SkeletonView.h and SkeletonView.cpp files.

LISTING 2.3 THE SKELETONVIEW.H HEADER FILE FOR SKELETONDV

```
 1: #ifndef __SKELETONVIEW_H__
 2: #define __SKELETONVIEW_H__
 3:
 4: //----------------------------------------------------------------
 5: // CSkeletonView Class - Skeleton Document Object
 6: //----------------------------------------------------------------
 7: class CSkeletonView : public CView {
 8:     // Public Constructor(s)/Destructor
 9: public:
10:                 CSkeletonView();
11:     virtual     ~CSkeletonView();
12:
13:     // Public Member Functions
14: public:
15:     CSkeletonDoc* GetDocument();
16:     virtual BOOL  PreCreateWindow(CREATESTRUCT& cs);
17:     virtual void  OnDraw(CDC* pDC);
18:
19:     // Diagnostic Functions
20: public:
21: #ifdef _DEBUG
22:     virtual void  AssertValid() const;
23:     virtual void  Dump(CDumpContext& dc) const;
24: #endif //_DEBUG
25:
26:     // Message Map & Runtime Support
27: protected:
28:     DECLARE_MESSAGE_MAP()
29:     DECLARE_DYNCREATE(CSkeletonView)
30: };
31:
32: #ifndef _DEBUG
33: inline CSkeletonDoc* CSkeletonView::GetDocument() {
34:     return (CSkeletonDoc*)m_pDocument;
35: }
36: #endif //_DEBUG
37:
38: #endif
```

LISTING 2.4 THE SKELETONVIEW.CPP SOURCE CODE FILE FOR SKELETONDV

```
 1: //---------------------------------------------------------------
 2: // Inclusions
 3: //---------------------------------------------------------------
 4: #include "StdAfx.h"
 5: //---------------------------------------------------------------
 6: #include "SkeletonDoc.h"
 7: #include "SkeletonView.h"
 8:
 9: //---------------------------------------------------------------
10: // MFC Debugging Support
11: //---------------------------------------------------------------
12: #ifdef _DEBUG
13: #undef THIS_FILE
14: static char BASED_CODE THIS_FILE[] = __FILE__;
15: #endif
16:
17:
18: //---------------------------------------------------------------
19: // Message Map & Runtime Support
20: //---------------------------------------------------------------
21: BEGIN_MESSAGE_MAP(CSkeletonView, CView)
22: END_MESSAGE_MAP()
23:
24: IMPLEMENT_DYNCREATE(CSkeletonView, CView)
25:
26: //---------------------------------------------------------------
27: // Public Constructor(s)/Destructor
28: //---------------------------------------------------------------
29: CSkeletonView::CSkeletonView() {
30: }
31:
32: CSkeletonView::~CSkeletonView() {
33: }
34:
35: //---------------------------------------------------------------
36: // Public Member Functions
37: //---------------------------------------------------------------
38: BOOL CSkeletonView::PreCreateWindow(CREATESTRUCT& cs) {
39:    // Initialize the view window properties
40:    // TODO
41:
42:    return CView::PreCreateWindow(cs);
43: }
44:
45: void CSkeletonView::OnDraw(CDC* pDC) {
46:    // Get a pointer to the document
47:    CSkeletonDoc* pDoc = GetDocument();
```

continues

LISTING 2.4 CONTINUED

```
48:     ASSERT_VALID(pDoc);
49:
50:     // Draw the view
51:     // TODO
52: }
53:
54: //----------------------------------------------------------------
55: // Diagnostic Functions
56: //----------------------------------------------------------------
57: #ifdef _DEBUG
58: void CSkeletonView::AssertValid() const {
59:     CView::AssertValid();
60: }
61:
62: void CSkeletonView::Dump(CDumpContext& dc) const {
63:     CView::Dump(dc);
64: }
65:
66: CSkeletonDoc* CSkeletonView::GetDocument() {
67:     ASSERT(m_pDocument->IsKindOf(RUNTIME_CLASS(CSkeletonDoc)));
68:     return (CSkeletonDoc*)m_pDocument;
69: }
70: #endif //_DEBUG
```

In addition to providing an empty constructor and destructor, the `CSkeletonView` class defines member functions named `GetDocument()`, `PreCreateWindow()`, and `OnDraw()`.

The `GetDocument()` member function is called to get the document associated with the view. The `GetDocument()` function performs an extremely important role because it is the only way a view can gain access to the document to which it is associated. The source code for the `GetDocument()` function is interesting in that there are two different versions. The version in the SkeletonView.cpp file is a diagnostic debug version because it takes on the responsibility of making sure the document class is of the correct type. The version of `GetDocument()` in the SkeletonView.h file is the release version, and is more streamlined.

The `PreCreateWindow()` member function is called before the underlying Win32 window object is created for an MFC `CWnd` object. The significance of the function is that you can use it to tweak the styles for a window before the window is created. Classes derived from `CWnd` typically add functionality to the overridden version of `PreCreateWindow()`. Because the `CSkeletonView` window is minimal, it isn't necessary to modify any of its styles.

Building MFC Applications

The `OnDraw()` member function is called whenever the document data is to be rendered on the view. This is a very important function because it is solely responsible for rendering a graphical representation of document data. Because the SkeletonDV application has no document data, it isn't necessary to do anything special in the `OnDraw()` member function. Notice, however, that there is code to get a pointer to the document object and verify its validity.

> You might have noticed the use of the ASSERT and ASSERT_VALID macros throughout the Skeleton and SkeletonDV application sample code. These macros are used to perform validity tests during the development of an application. The ASSERT macro expects a Boolean result that is TRUE if the program operates normally and FALSE if there is an error. If the Boolean result is FALSE, the ASSERT macro halts the application with an error. It's important to note that all code used in the ASSERT macro is only compiled under debug mode. For the code to execute in both debug and release modes, use the VERIFY macro instead. It works just like ASSERT except that it still allows the test code to compile in release mode.
>
> The ASSERT_VALID macro is similar to ASSERT except it is used to check the integrity of objects. The ASSERT_VALID macro first checks to make sure an object pointer is non-NULL, and it then calls the object's `AssertValid()` member function. Any failure results in the application halting with an error.

Other Document/View Changes

In addition to creating document and view classes for the SkeletonDV application, you must also modify some of the original Skeleton application code to support the document/view architecture. First off is the application class, which requires a new and improved `InitInstance()` member function, as shown in Listing 2.5.

LISTING 2.5 THE `CSkeletonApp::InitInstance()` MEMBER FUNCTION FOR SKELETONDV

```
1: BOOL CSkeletonApp::InitInstance() {
2:   // Register the application's document templates
3:   CSingleDocTemplate* pDocTemplate;
4:   pDocTemplate = new CSingleDocTemplate(IDR_SKELETON,
5:     RUNTIME_CLASS(CSkeletonDoc),
6:     RUNTIME_CLASS(CMainFrame),
7:     RUNTIME_CLASS(CSkeletonView));
8:   AddDocTemplate(pDocTemplate);
9:
```

continues

LISTING 2.5   CONTINUED

```
10:      // Parse command line for standard shell commands
11:      CCommandLineInfo cmdInfo;
12:      ParseCommandLine(cmdInfo);
13:
14:      // Dispatch commands specified on the command line
15:      if (!ProcessShellCommand(cmdInfo))
16:        return FALSE;
17:
18:      // Show and update the main window
19:      m_pMainWnd->ShowWindow(SW_SHOW);
20:      m_pMainWnd->UpdateWindow();
21:
22:      return TRUE;
23: }
```

This version of `InitInstance()` is a little busier than the one you saw last hour in the Skeleton application. The main difference between the two is the addition of code for establishing the document/view connection. A document template is created that associates the document class, view class, and main frame window class together. It also uses a resource string identified by the `IDR_SKELETON` constant to specify additional application attributes. You learn about this resource string in a moment.

The command related code in the `InitInstance()` function makes the application a little more extensible by allowing it to process command-line arguments. Command-line arguments enable you to specify what document to open when you launch an application, which is sometimes convenient. You can also define application-specific options that are passed as command-line arguments.

Next on the agenda of SkeletonDV application changes is the removal of the `Create()` member function and the addition of the `PreCreateWindow()` member function. The `Create()` member function isn't necessary in document/view applications because MFC handles the details of creating the main frame window for you. However, you still might want to modify the frame window properties, which is where the `PreCreateWindow()` function comes into play. Listing 2.6 contains the source code for `PreCreateWindow()`.

LISTING 2.6   THE `CMainFrame::PreCreateWindow()` MEMBER FUNCTION FOR SKELETONDV

```
1: BOOL CMainFrame::PreCreateWindow(CREATESTRUCT& cs) {
2:     // Initialize the frame window properties
3:     // TODO
4:
5:     return CFrameWnd::PreCreateWindow(cs);
6: }
```

Building MFC Applications

As you can see, this function is really just a placeholder for functionality that you would add in a more interesting application. Nonetheless, it gives you a head start toward tweaking the properties of frame windows.

In addition to the code changes you've already made, there are a few resources that must be added to the SkeletonDV application for it to fully support MFC's document/view architecture. The first of these resources is a string that defines document information for the application. Listing 2.7 contains both of the string resources used in the SkeletonDV application, including the new `IDR_SKELETON` document string.

LISTING 2.7 THE STRING RESOURCES FOR SKELETONDV

```
1: //-----------------------------------------------------------
2: // Strings
3: //-----------------------------------------------------------
4: STRINGTABLE
5: BEGIN
6:     AFX_IDS_APP_TITLE   "Skeleton"
7:     IDR_SKELETON        "Skeleton\n\n\n\n\n\n"
8: END
```

The `IDR_SKELETON` document string contains a collection of substrings that define document properties. The substrings are separated from each other with newline characters (\n). Following is the format of the document string:

`"App\nDocName\nDocType\nFileType\n.Ext\nRegType\nRegName"`

Table 2.2 lists the meanings of each of the parts of the document string format.

TABLE 2.2 COMPONENTS OF THE DOCUMENT STRING FORMAT

String Component	Meaning
App	The application name
DocName	The default document name for new documents
DocType	A descriptive name for the document type
FileType	A descriptive name for the document file type
.Ext	The file extension for document files
RegType	The document file type used by Windows for file association
RegName	The readable name of the document file type

A quick examination of the `IDR_SKELETON` document string shows that it only specifies the App substring, which identifies the application name. It's OK to leave the other substrings blank because the SkeletonDV application doesn't really define its own document type; the `CSkeletonDoc` class is too minimal to be classified as a functioning document type.

If you recall, the whole point of creating the `IDR_SKELETON` document string was to create the document template, which ties the document and view together with the frame window. This was performed back in the `InitInstance()` method of the `CSkeletonApp` class. Along with using the `IDR_SKELETON` document string to identify document properties, the document template also looks for standard application resources such as an icon, menu, and accelerator table. If resources of these types are provided in the resource file with the `IDR_SKELETON` identifier, the document template will automatically find them and associate them with the application. Listing 2.8 contains the code for the SkeletonDV menu, which uses the `IDR_SKELETON` identifier.

LISTING 2.8   THE MENU RESOURCES FOR SKELETONDV

```
 1: //-----------------------------------------------
 2: // Menus
 3: //-----------------------------------------------
 4: IDR_SKELETON MENU
 5: BEGIN
 6:     POPUP "&File"
 7:     BEGIN
 8:         MENUITEM "E&xit",              ID_APP_EXIT
 9:     END
10: END
```

You don't really learn about the ins and outs of menus until Hour 8, "Manipulating Menus," but it's worth taking a quick look at the SkeletonDV menu. Even though the SkeletonDV application is designed to be minimal, I decided to give it a menu because document/view applications are expected to have one. The menu resource for the application defines a File pop-up menu much like you are accustomed to seeing in Windows applications. There is one menu item within the pop-up menu named Exit that is used to exit the application. The standard MFC identifier `ID_APP_EXIT` is used to tie the menu item to code that exits the application.

Summary

This hour built on the previous hour by digging deeper into application development with MFC. More specifically, you learned about document-centric applications and MFC's document/view architecture. You studied the application object a little closer, and then learned about the MFC classes that enable you to create documents and views. From there you learned about the naming conventions commonly used in MFC programming. Finally, you wrapped up the hour by creating a new SkeletonDV application that utilizes MFC's document/view architecture.

Q&A

Q When is it necessary to add code to the `PreCreateWindow()` member function?

A Any time you want to modify frame window styles. More specifically, if you wanted to set the initial size or position of a frame window, you could do so in the `PreCreateWindow()` function (see the Exercises). You can also set styles that alter window properties such as whether the window is sizeable.

Q What is the significance of building both the Skeleton and SkeletonDV applications?

A To have the option of selectively using MFC's document/view architecture. Although the document/view architecture is often beneficial, it isn't necessary in all applications. By having two types of skeletal applications, you can keep from using the document/view architecture unnecessarily. You will use both Skeleton and SkeletonDV throughout the rest of the book as the basis for other sample applications.

Workshop

The Workshop is designed to help you anticipate possible questions, review what you've learned, and begin thinking ahead to put your knowledge into practice. The answers to the quiz are in Appendix A, "Quiz Answers."

Quiz

1. What is the significance of MFC's document/view architecture?
2. What is the special object that associates documents, views, frame windows, and application resources with each other?
3. What works behind the scenes to orchestrate the startup, execution, and termination of an application?
4. What member function is called near the start of `WinMain()` to perform instance initialization for an application?
5. What member function is used to perform idle processing that isn't immediately critical to the operation of an application?

6. From what MFC class must all document classes derive?
7. What is Hungarian notation?
8. Why is the scope resolution operator (::) used to call Win32 API functions in MFC applications?
9. What is the purpose of the `AssertValid()` member function?
10. What is the difference between the `ASSERT` and `VERIFY` diagnostic macros?

Exercises

1. Insert the following code in the `CMainFrame::PreCreateWindow()` member function to size the frame window to half the screen size and center it.

   ```
   cs.cx = ::GetSystemMetrics(SM_CXSCREEN) / 2;
   cs.cy = ::GetSystemMetrics(SM_CYSCREEN) / 2;
   cs.x = ((cs.cx * 2) - cs.cx) / 2;
   cs.y = ((cs.cy * 2) - cs.cy) / 2;
   ```

2. Fill in the missing substrings of the `IDR_SKELETON` document string so that the Skeleton document properties are fully defined.

Hour 3

Creating and Using Application Resources

This hour introduces you to application resources, which are special data objects used to construct an application's graphical user interface. Actually, not all resources are used specifically for GUI purposes, but in general you can think of them as GUI elements. You learn in this hour how resources fit into the structure of applications, along with the different types of resources used in MFC applications. You then learn how to create and use resources within MFC applications.

In this hour, you will learn

- About the different types of resources used in MFC applications
- How to create a resource script
- How to use resources within MFC applications

Understanding the Role of Resources

All applications deal with data in one way or another. When you think of application data, you typically think of information specific to the operation of a particular application. However, there is data of a more general form that all Windows applications require. I'm referring to application resources, which are special data objects that are used primarily to construct an application's graphical user interface. Examples of resources include menus, icons, bitmaps, and strings.

New Term A *resource* is a special data object associated with an application that typically defines portions of the application's graphical user interface.

Resources are notably different from other types of application data because they are defined during the development of an application and are actually compiled into the executable file of the application. In other words, resources are compiled into binary form and linked into an executable file just like application source code. Of course, a special resource compiler is used to compile resources, but the compilation process is similar to that used for source code. Figure 3.1 shows how resources fit into the application development process.

> Resources can also be compiled into dynamic link libraries (DLLs), which are special libraries of compiled code that can be called by an application. You learn about DLLs in Hour 22, "Creating DLLs."

New Term A *resource compiler* is an application that creates a binary resource file based on a resource script containing definitions of application resources.

As you can see in Figure 3.1, the resource compiler compiles resources into a binary resource file with an .RES extension. This file is then handed off to the linker, which combines it with the .OBJ files containing compiled source code. The result is the finished application, which is stored in an .EXE file. There really is nothing magical about resources when you understand how they are integrated with an application during development.

Creating and Using Application Resources 43

FIGURE 3.1

The role resources play in the application development process.

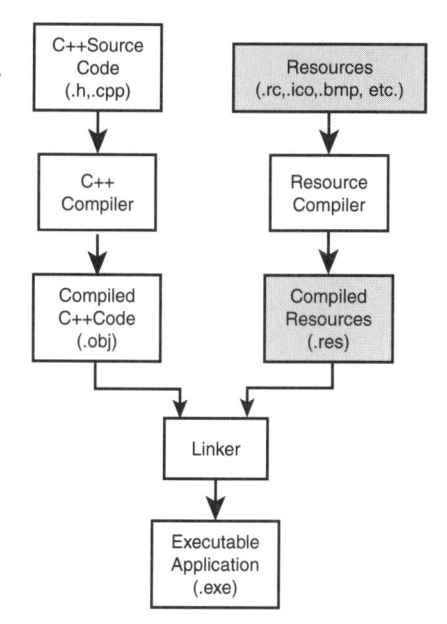

```
C++Source Code          Resources
  (.h,.cpp)           (.rc,.ico,.bmp, etc.)
      |                      |
      v                      v
   C++                   Resource
  Compiler               Compiler
      |                      |
      v                      v
  Compiled              Compiled
  C++Code               Resources
   (.obj)                 (.res)
       \                   /
        \                 /
         v               v
            Linker
              |
              v
          Executable
          Application
             (.exe)
```

Even though you now understand how resources fit into an application, you still might be curious as to why it's necessary to compile them into an application's executable file. The primary reason for compiling resources is organizational; things are simpler if an application's icon is physically attached to the application's executable code. Without this arrangement, an application would have to ship with an executable file and a bunch of other resource files on which the executable is dependent. If a user opens one of the resource files and makes an inadvertent change, it could cripple the application.

Another reason for compiling resources is that it's much more efficient for an application to load and reference resources directly from its executable file than from an external file. Also, resources such as menus can be compiled into an efficient binary format that is quickly accessible.

> Sometimes it is beneficial to compile resources into a separate DLL module if you want to keep the .EXE file size small or if you plan to support multiple languages. As an example, you could have English, Spanish, and French versions of a resource DLL that stores strings in each language. The application could easily switch languages by referencing a different DLL.

Types of Resources

Although the discussion of resources thus far has centered on MFC applications, resources are actually defined by Win32. In other words, applications written in C using the Win32 API rely on the same resources as an MFC application written in C++. In fact, Win32 defines a set of standard resource types that are available for use in applications. You can also define custom resources, although typically the standard Win32 resources are sufficient. Table 3.1 contains the standard resources supported by Win32.

TABLE 3.1 THE STANDARD WIN32 RESOURCES

Resource	Description
Accelerator	Provide keyboard shortcuts for commonly used commands
Bitmap	Graphical images that can be used in a variety of ways
Cursor	Alternate mouse cursors that you can create and use instead of the standard arrow cursor
Icon	Small bitmaps of a set size (32×32 or 16×16) that are used to identify an application when it is minimized
Menu	Describe the structure of an application's menu, which is displayed just below the caption at the top of the main frame window
Dialog box	Special windows used to retrieve information from the user
String table	Allow you to store a string of text as a resource, which can then be referenced from application code
Version	Define version information for an application

> I mentioned that it's possible to create user-defined resources. User-defined resources are custom resources that require special code to be added to an application in order to use them. Even though they require some programming overhead, they come in handy in certain situations. As an example, I once wrote a Windows game that stored the sound effects as user-defined resources.

Just in case you aren't familiar with all the standard resources, they each will be quickly gone over in the rest of this chapter.

Defining Resources in a Resource Script

All resources are defined in a resource script, which is a special text file with an .RC extension. An application's resource script lists all the resources used by the application. You use a resource compiler to compile a resource script into a binary resource file with a .RES extension. This binary resource file is then linked with an application's object code to create a complete executable application.

The compilation process for resources is quite different than the process for C code, and requires a special resource compiler. The resource compiler's main job is to assemble all the resources defined in a resource script into a single binary file. Even though a resource compiler is different than a C compiler, it does share an important similarity: A resource compiler supports preprocessor directives such as `#define` and `#include`. This allows you to include C/C++ header files containing identifiers that can be used to identify resources in a resource script.

It is common practice in MFC programming to define resource constants in a special header file named Resource.h. This header file is included in the application's resource file and in any source code files that reference resources. Listing 3.1 contains the code for the Resource.h file used in the Skeleton application you studied in Hour 1.

LISTING 3.1   THE RESOURCE.H HEADER FILE FOR THE SKELETON APPLICATION

```
1: //-------------------------------
2: // Strings              Range : 1000 - 1999
3: //-------------------------------
4: #define IDR_SKELETON       1000
```

This file defines one resource identifier, `IDR_SKELETON`, which is used to identify the icon for the Skeleton application. A single identifier is often used to identify multiple resources as long as the resources are of differing types. For example, the SkeletonDV application in the previous hour used the `IDR_SKELETON` identifier to define icon, menu, and string resources.

Now that you have an understanding of how resources are identified, I'll look at the specifics of how to create some different resources.

Accelerators

Accelerators are used to provide keyboard shortcuts for commonly used commands. For example, the popular Ctrl+C, Ctrl+X, and Ctrl+V shortcuts for performing copy, cut, and paste are actually just accelerators. You create an accelerator by defining a key combination and a menu command with which the combination is associated. Listing 3.2 shows an accelerator definition as it would appear in a resource script.

LISTING 3.2 AN ACCELERATOR RESOURCE DEFINITION

```
1: IDR_MYAPP ACCELERATORS
2: BEGIN
3:     "X",          ID_EDIT_CUT,        VIRTKEY,CONTROL
4:     "C",          ID_EDIT_COPY,       VIRTKEY,CONTROL
5:     "V",          ID_EDIT_PASTE,      VIRTKEY,CONTROL
6: END
```

As you can see, an accelerator definition can actually consist of multiple key assignments. This example shows how to wire the cut, copy, and paste key combinations to the standard menu commands identified by ID_EDIT_CUT, ID_EDIT_COPY, and ID_EDIT_PASTE. The letter in quotes indicates the base key, whereas the word CONTROL indicates that the Ctrl key is used in combination with the base key. VIRTKEY indicates that this is a virtual key assignment, as opposed to an ASCII assignment.

The accelerator resource is itself identified by the IDR_MYAPP identifier; this identifier is defined in the Resource.h file included in the resource script. The ACCELERATORS keyword identifies this resource as a list of accelerators.

Bitmaps

Bitmaps are graphical images that can be used in a variety of ways in an application. The most common use of bitmaps in MFC applications is to store the button graphics for toolbar buttons. Bitmaps are always referenced from a separate file (.BMP) that is created in an image editor such as Windows Paint. Unlike accelerators, bitmap resources are referenced from external files. Following is an example of defining a bitmap resource:

```
IDR_MYIMAGE BITMAP "MyImage.bmp"
```

The resource is identified by the IDR_MYIMAGE identifier, which would be defined in the Resource.h file included in the resource script. The BITMAP keyword identifies this resource as a bitmap, whereas the filename MyImage.bmp specifies the external bitmap file.

Cursors

Cursors are simply alternative mouse cursors that you can create and use instead of the standard arrow cursor. Applications use cursor resources to give the mouse cursor a custom appearance. Cursors are really a lot like small, black-and-white bitmaps, except that cursors have a hotspot associated with them. The hotspot identifies the specific location in the cursor image that represents the point of the cursor. As an example, the tip of the standard arrow cursor is the cursor's hotspot. Like bitmaps, cursors are stored in separate files (.CUR) that are created in a cursor editor. Most Windows development environments come standard with a cursor editor.

Cursor resources are defined similarly as bitmaps, except that they use the CURSOR keyword, like this:

```
IDR_MYAPP CURSOR  "MyApp.cur"
```

The resource is identified by the IDR_MYAPP identifier. The CURSOR keyword specifies that this resource is a cursor, whereas the MyApp.cur filename references the external cursor file for the resource.

Icons

Icons are small bitmaps of a set size (32×32 or 16×16) that are used to identify an application when it is minimized. Icons serve a very important role in graphically identifying applications, so it is common for every application to have at least an icon resource. Icons are also stored in separate files (.ICO) that are created in an icon editor. Most Windows development environments come standard with an icon editor.

Icons are defined very much like cursors and bitmaps but they use the ICON keyword, like this:

```
IDR_MYAPP ICON "MyApp.ico"
```

The identifier IDR_MYAPP identifies the resource, whereas the filename MyApp.ico references the external icon file. The size of the icon in this file can be either 32×32 or 16×16, depending on how you are going to use it; the default icon size for an application is 32×32.

> Windows also supports small 16×16 icons, which are displayed in places such as the Windows Taskbar. By default, Windows will automatically shrink a 32×32 icon to the smaller size if you don't provide a smaller icon.

Menus

Menu resources describe the structure of an application's menu, which is displayed just below the caption at the top of the main frame window. Menu resources describe the hierarchical structure of an application's menu along with the different commands available on the menu. Each menu command is assigned an identifier that is used in the application code to route the menu command to code that responds to it. This identifier is the same one used to associate accelerators with menu commands. You will learn how to do interesting things with menus in Hour 8, "Manipulating Menus."

Menu definitions in resource scripts are sometimes referred to as menu templates. A menu template defines the structure of a menu, including pop-up submenus and menu items, along with their associated identifiers and options. Listing 3.3 contains an example of a menu template that defines the ever-popular File and Help menus for an application that deals with files.

LISTING 3.3 A MENU RESOURCE DEFINITION

```
 1: IDR_MYAPP MENU
 2: BEGIN
 3:    POPUP "&File"
 4:       BEGIN
 5:          MENUITEM "&New\tCtrl+N",          ID_FILE_NEW
 6:          MENUITEM "&Open...\tCtrl+O",      ID_FILE_OPEN
 7:          MENUITEM "&Save\tCtrl+S",         ID_FILE_SAVE, GRAYED
 8:          MENUITEM "Save &As...",           ID_FILE_SAVE_AS, GRAYED
 9:          MENUITEM SEPARATOR
10:          MENUITEM "E&xit",                 ID_APP_EXIT
11:       END
12:    POPUP "&Help"
13:       BEGIN
14:          MENUITEM "&About MyApp...",       ID_APP_ABOUT
15:       END
16: END
```

The Menu resource statement is used to identify the start of the menu resource template. Also, the Popup statement is used to identify pop-up submenus, whereas the Menuitem statement is used to identify menu items. The formatting of the menu item names specifies the Alt key and menu accelerator associated with each item. The ID_XXX identifiers are constants that uniquely identify each menu item. These identifiers are sent back to the application as command messages when the user selects a menu item. The Separator statement specifies that a menu item is to provide division between the menu items above and below it. Finally, the GRAYED menu option used on the Save and Save As menu items initially disables the menu items.

> Although most resource identifiers are defined in Resource.h, MFC provides standard identifiers to represent common resources. The menu item identifiers used in Listing 3.3 are all standard MFC identifiers, and therefore don't have to be provided in Resource.h. These standard identifiers are defined in the file AfxRes.h, which is included in the resource script along with Resource.h.

Formatting Menu Item Names

The text for menu item names indicates information about the item beyond the name alone. The ampersand character (&) is used to specify which letter in the item name is underlined; this also determines the letter used in combination with the Alt key to access the menu item. The tab character (\t) is used to insert a tab between the item name and any accelerator text. Accelerator text such as Ctrl+N is used to identify the keyboard accelerator (shortcut) for the menu item.

Menu Options

Menu options are used to specify the initial state of menu items and pop-up submenu headings. Table 3.2 contains the menu options supported by Windows.

TABLE 3.2 WINDOWS MENU OPTIONS

Option	Usage
CHECKED	Places a checkmark by the menu item; only applicable to menu items
GRAYED	Grays the menu text and makes the menu item or pop-up submenu heading inactive
INACTIVE	Makes the menu item or pop-up submenu heading inactive without altering the menu text
MENUBREAK	The menu item or pop-up submenu heading appears in a new menu column
MENUBARBREAK	The menu item appears in a new menu column with a vertical line separating the columns; only applicable to menu items
HELP	The menu item or pop-up submenu heading is right-justified

Menu options can be combined using the bitwise OR symbol, except for the pairs GRAYED/INACTIVE and MENUBREAK/MENUBARBREAK, which cannot be used together.

Dialog Boxes

Dialog boxes are special windows used to retrieve information from the user. Unlike frame windows, which typically have a client area that displays application data, dialog boxes typically contain a group of GUI elements that are used to query the user for information. A dialog box resource defines the appearance of a dialog box, including the size of the dialog box window and the GUI elements it contains. You must still write code to control the inner workings of a dialog box, but you rely on a resource to describe the overall structure of the dialog box. You will learn a great deal about creating dialog box resources in Hour 7, "Retrieving Information with Custom Dialog Boxes."

Dialog box resources are by far the most complex of all the standard resources because they can define an entire GUI. For this reason, a thorough examination of dialog boxes is a little beyond the scope of this chapter. You learn how to create and work with dialog box resources in Hour 7. Even so, I think giving you a peek at a dialog box resource definition, or dialog box template, is worthwhile. Listing 3.4 contains the code for a dialog box resource definition.

LISTING 3.4 A DIALOG BOX RESOURCE DEFINITION

```
 1: IDD_ABOUTBOX DIALOG 0, 0, 217, 55
 2: CAPTION "About MyApp"
 3: STYLE DS_MODALFRAME | WS_POPUP | WS_CAPTION | WS_SYSMENU
 4: FONT 8, "MS Sans Serif"
 5: BEGIN
 6:    ICON          IDR_MYAPP, IDC_STATIC, 11, 17, 20, 20
 7:    LTEXT         "MyApp Version 1.0", IDC_STATIC, 40, 10,
 8:                  119, 8, SS_NOPREFIX
 9:    LTEXT         "Copyright (c) 1998 Michael Morrison", IDC_STATIC,
10:                  40, 25, 119, 8
11.    DEFPUSHBUTTON "OK", IDOK, 178, 7, 32, 14, WS_GROUP
12: END
```

The first few lines of code describe the resource type along with the size, caption, styles, and font of the dialog box. The remainder of the resource definition lists the individual graphical elements that form the dialog box's graphical user interface. These elements include an icon, two static text controls, and an OK pushbutton.

String Tables

String table resources are a little different than the other resources you've learned about because they aren't graphical. String table resources enable you to store a string of text as a resource, which can then be referenced from application code. String resources are useful at times when you want to isolate a string from application code. As an example, the name of an application is typically stored as a string resource.

You've already seen string tables at work a few times in the Skeleton and SkeletonDV applications. Even so, let's take another look at them to understand exactly what's going on. Listing 3.5 contains the code for a string table resource definition.

LISTING 3.5 A STRING TABLE RESOURCE DEFINITION

```
1: STRINGTABLE
2: BEGIN
3:   AFX_IDS_APP_TITLE   "MyApp"
4: END
```

The first line of code in this resource definition establishes that this is a string table resource. The strings that comprise the string table are then listed inside the BEGIN and END keywords. In this case, only one string is listed. The identifier used to reference the string is AFX_IDS_APP_TITLE, which is a standard MFC identifier used to identify the name of an application.

Version Resources

Last on the resource list is version resources, which are used to define version information for an application. Version information is important because of its role in installation routines that must analyze the versions of applications and support modules for compatibility. Compatibility problems can arise if a newer version of an application is installed and used with an older version of a support module, or vice-versa. Providing a version resource in an application gives installation routines the capability to ascertain the version of an application or support module and try to avoid such problems.

Using Resources in an Application

It's fine to understand how to build a resource script containing resources, but how does that translate to using resources in an application? The remainder of the hour answers this question by showing you how to build a simple application that makes use of a few different resources. More specifically, the Resourceful application builds on the SkeletonDV application from the last hour by supporting five different kinds of resources. Let's learn how it works.

Like most applications, the Resourceful application's support for resources begins with the Resource.h header file, which defines the application's resource identifiers. Listing 3.6 contains the code for the Resource.h header file.

LISTING 3.6 THE RESOURCE.H HEADER FILE FOR RESOURCEFUL

```
1: //-------------------------------
2: // Strings                Range : 1000 - 1999
3: //-------------------------------
4: #define IDR_RESOURCEFUL   1000
5:
6: //-------------------------------
7: // Dialog Boxes           Range : 2000 - 2999
8: //-------------------------------
9: #define IDD_ABOUTBOX      2000
```

As you can see, there are only two resource identifiers defined for the Resourceful application. The IDR_RESOURCEFUL identifier is used to identify the majority of the resources used by the application, whereas `IDD_ABOUTBOX` identifies a dialog box resource. This dialog box and the other resources for the application are defined in the resource script Resourceful.rc, which is shown in Listing 3.7.

LISTING 3.7 THE RESOURCEFUL.RC RESOURCE SCRIPT FOR RESOURCEFUL

```
 1: //-------------------------------
 2: // Icons
 3: //-------------------------------
 4: IDR_RESOURCEFUL ICON "Resourceful.ico"
 5:
 6: //-------------------------------
 7: // Menus
 8: //-------------------------------
 9: IDR_RESOURCEFUL MENU
10: BEGIN
11:   POPUP "&File"
12:     BEGIN
13:       MENUITEM "&New\tCtrl+N",           ID_FILE_NEW
14:       MENUITEM "&Open...\tCtrl+O",       ID_FILE_OPEN
15:       MENUITEM "&Save\tCtrl+S",          ID_FILE_SAVE
16:       MENUITEM "Save &As...",            ID_FILE_SAVE_AS
17:       MENUITEM SEPARATOR
18:       MENUITEM "E&xit",                  ID_APP_EXIT
19:     END
20:   POPUP "&Edit"
21:     BEGIN
22:       MENUITEM "&Undo\tCtrl+Z",          ID_EDIT_UNDO
23:       MENUITEM SEPARATOR
24:       MENUITEM "Cu&t\tCtrl+X",           ID_EDIT_CUT
25:       MENUITEM "&Copy\tCtrl+C",          ID_EDIT_COPY
26:       MENUITEM "&Paste\tCtrl+V",         ID_EDIT_PASTE
27:     END
28:   POPUP "&Help"
29:     BEGIN
30:       MENUITEM "&About Resourceful...",  ID_APP_ABOUT
31:     END
32: END
33:
34:
35: //-------------------------------
36: // ACCELERATORS
37: //-------------------------------
38: IDR_RESOURCEFUL ACCELERATORS
39: BEGIN
40:     "N",         ID_FILE_NEW,           VIRTKEY,CONTROL
41:     "O",         ID_FILE_OPEN,          VIRTKEY,CONTROL
42:     "S",         ID_FILE_SAVE,          VIRTKEY,CONTROL
43:     "Z",         ID_EDIT_UNDO,          VIRTKEY,CONTROL
```

```
44:      "X",            ID_EDIT_CUT,        VIRTKEY,CONTROL
45:      "C",            ID_EDIT_COPY,       VIRTKEY,CONTROL
46:      "V",            ID_EDIT_PASTE,      VIRTKEY,CONTROL
47:      VK_BACK,        ID_EDIT_UNDO,       VIRTKEY,ALT
48:      VK_DELETE,      ID_EDIT_CUT,        VIRTKEY,SHIFT
49:      VK_INSERT,      ID_EDIT_COPY,       VIRTKEY,CONTROL
50:      VK_INSERT,      ID_EDIT_PASTE,      VIRTKEY,SHIFT
51:      VK_F6,          ID_NEXT_PANE,       VIRTKEY
52:      VK_F6,          ID_PREV_PANE,       VIRTKEY,SHIFT
53: END
54:
55: //--------------------------------
56: // Dialog Boxes
57: //--------------------------------
58: IDD_ABOUTBOX DIALOG 0, 0, 217, 55
59: CAPTION "About Resourceful"
60: STYLE DS_MODALFRAME ¦ WS_POPUP ¦ WS_CAPTION ¦ WS_SYSMENU
61: FONT 8, "MS Sans Serif"
62: BEGIN
63:     ICON            IDR_RESOURCEFUL, IDC_STATIC, 11, 17, 20, 20
64:     LTEXT           "Resourceful Version 1.0", IDC_STATIC, 40, 10,
65:                     119, 8, SS_NOPREFIX
66:     LTEXT           "Copyright (c) 1998 Michael Morrison", IDC_STATIC,
67:                     40, 25, 119, 8
68:     DEFPUSHBUTTON "OK", IDOK, 178, 7, 32, 14, WS_GROUP
69: END
70:
71:
72: //--------------------------------
73: // Strings
74: //--------------------------------
75: STRINGTABLE
76: BEGIN
77:     AFX_IDS_APP_TITLE   "Resourceful"
78:     IDR_RESOURCEFUL     "Resourceful\n\n\n\n\n\n"
79: END
```

This resource script defines an icon, a menu, a set of accelerators, a dialog box, and a couple of strings in a string table. You've already learned the basics of what these resource definitions mean, so I won't go into details about them. Instead, let's see how these resources are used in the Resourceful application.

You'll be glad to learn that most of the work of associating resources with an application is handled automatically by MFC. If you make use of MFC's document/view architecture, then the icon, menu, accelerators, and strings for an application are automatically utilized when possible. For the Resourceful application there is little to do beyond writing the code to make the dialog box work. The dialog box defined in the resource script is an About dialog box, which should be displayed when the user selects About from the Help menu. This menu command is handled in the Resourceful application class source code where the dialog box is then displayed. The necessary line of code in the header file that defines the message handler is

```
afx_msg void OnAppAbout();
```

This message handler member function is called whenever the user selects About from the Help menu. Listing 3.8 contains the source code for the message map in the application class's source code file:

LISTING 3.8 THE APPLICATION CLASS'S MESSAGE MAP FOR RESOURCEFUL

```
1: BEGIN_MESSAGE_MAP(CResourcefulApp, CWinApp)
2:   ON_COMMAND(ID_FILE_NEW, CWinApp::OnFileNew)
3:   ON_COMMAND(ID_FILE_OPEN, CWinApp::OnFileOpen)
4:   ON_COMMAND(ID_APP_ABOUT, OnAppAbout)
5: END_MESSAGE_MAP()
```

This code maps the File, New; File, Open; and Help, About menu commands to appropriate message handlers. Listing 3.9 contains the code for the `OnAppAbout()` message handler, which creates the About dialog box.

LISTING 3.9 THE CResourcefulApp::OnAppAbout() MESSAGE HANDLER

```
1: void CResourcefulApp::OnAppAbout() {
2:   CAboutDlg aboutDlg;
3:   aboutDlg.DoModal();
4: }
```

This code relies on the `CAboutDlg` class, which is a special class used to drive the dialog box resource. Listings 3.10 and 3.11 contain the header and source code for this class.

LISTING 3.10 THE ABOUTDLG.H HEADER FILE FOR RESOURCEFUL

```
1: #ifndef __ABOUTDLG_H__
2: #define __ABOUTDLG_H__
3:
4: //-------------------------------
5: // Inclusions
6: //-------------------------------
7: #include "Resource.h"
8:
9: //-------------------------------
```

```
10: // CAboutDlg Class - About Dialog Object
11: //---------------------------------
12: class CAboutDlg : public CDialog {
13:   // Member Constants
14:   enum { IDD = IDD_ABOUTBOX };
15:
16:   // Public Constructor(s)/Destructor
17: public:
18:                CAboutDlg();
19:   virtual      ~CAboutDlg();
20:
21:   // Message Map & Runtime Support
22: protected:
23:   DECLARE_MESSAGE_MAP()
24: };
25:
26: #endif
```

LISTING 3.11 THE ABOUTDLG.CPP SOURCE CODE FILE FOR RESOURCEFUL

```
 1: //---------------------------------
 2: // Inclusions
 3: //---------------------------------
 4: #include "StdAfx.h"
 5: //---------------------------------
 6: #include "AboutDlg.h"
 7:
 8: //---------------------------------
 9: // MFC Debugging Support
10: //---------------------------------
11: #ifdef _DEBUG
12: #undef THIS_FILE
13: static char BASED_CODE THIS_FILE[] = __FILE__;
14: #endif
15:
16:
17: //---------------------------------
18: // Message Map & Runtime Support
19: //---------------------------------
20: BEGIN_MESSAGE_MAP(CAboutDlg, CDialog)
21: END_MESSAGE_MAP()
22:
23: //---------------------------------
24: // Public Constructor(s)/Destructor
25: //---------------------------------
26: CAboutDlg::CAboutDlg() : CDialog(CAboutDlg::IDD) {
27: }
28:
29: CAboutDlg::~CAboutDlg() {
30: }
```

It isn't incredibly important that you understand the ins and outs of this code at this point. I mainly just wanted you to understand that it does take real source code behind the scenes to make a dialog box resource function properly. You return to this code later in the book when you dig deeper into dialog boxes. Figure 3.1 shows the completed Resourceful application, along with the About dialog box.

FIGURE 3.2

The completed Resourceful application displaying the About dialog box.

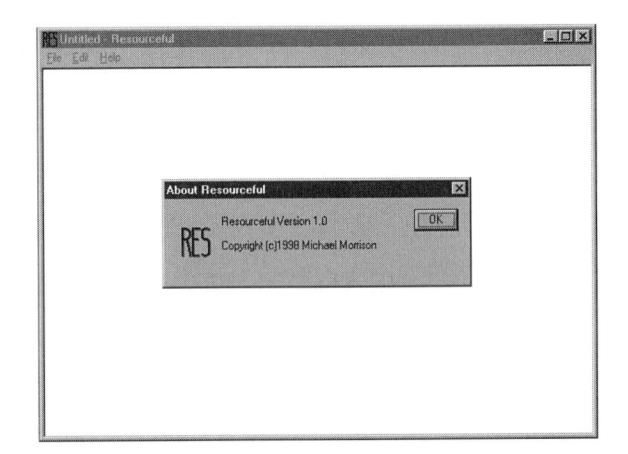

Summary

This hour cleared up some of the mysteries from the first two hours by clarifying exactly what resources are, and how they are used in MFC applications. You learned about the different types of standard Win32 resources and how to create them in resource scripts. At the end of the hour you took a look at an application that made use of a variety of different resources.

Q&A

Q Why are dialog boxes defined as resources and not just created from source code like frame windows?

A Because dialog boxes typically make use of multiple GUI elements such as buttons, text labels, and check boxes, it is much easier to define them as resources. Without resources, you would have to manually create every GUI control in source code, which is very tedious and time-consuming. Creating dialog boxes as resources is also beneficial because you can use resource editors to further simplify and speed up the process.

Q How does a resource editor work?

A A resource editor is a graphical tool used to create and edit resources in a visual manner. Resource editors typically let you create icons, cursors, and bitmaps as images much as you draw images in Paint. They also let you create menus graphically, which makes it easy to see the hierarchy of menu items. Most importantly, however, is that resource editors enable you to graphically layout dialog boxes. Regardless of how graphical they might be, however, resource editors ultimately generate an .RC file similar to what you studied in this chapter.

Workshop

The Workshop is designed to help you anticipate possible questions, review what you've learned, and begin thinking ahead to put your knowledge into practice. The answers to the quiz are located in Appendix A, "Quiz Answers."

Quiz

1. What is a text file with an .RC extension that defines resources known as?
2. What is the default size for an application icon?
3. How are resources notably different from other types of application data?
4. What are accelerators used for?
5. What is the name of the MFC header file used to define resource constants?
6. What is a resource compiler?
7. What is the most common use of bitmaps in MFC applications?
8. What does the hotspot of a cursor identify?
9. When defining menu resources, how do you combine menu options?
10. What is the standard MFC identifier used to identify the name of an application?

Exercises

1. Try out the accelerators for the Resourceful application and make sure they correspond to the appropriate menu item selection. Also, open the About dialog box by selecting About Resourceful... from the Help menu.
2. Swap some of the identifiers for the accelerators in Resourceful, rebuild the application, and run it. Notice how the accelerators have changed.

Hour 4

Interacting with the User

This hour tackles a very important part of MFC application development: user input. It's practically impossible to develop an application without dealing with some degree of user input. Fortunately, responding to keyboard and mouse input is a very straightforward task. By the end of this hour, you will have created a pretty interesting application that can be manipulated with the keyboard and mouse.

In this hour, you will learn

- Why user input is such an important part of MFC applications
- The ins and outs of message maps
- How to handle keyboard and mouse messages

The Importance of User Input

Regardless of how powerful or useful a purpose an application serves, it won't be of any use if it doesn't effectively handle user input. User input encompasses the entire communications between a user and an application, so it deserves close attention from a developer's perspective.

For the most part, user input consists of keeping track of the keyboard and mouse. Unfortunately, some Windows developers have a tendency to favor the mouse because it is such a commonly used input device. Granted, the mouse plays a pivotal role in most Windows applications, which is only to be expected in a graphical environment. However, just because mice are standard fare on computers these days doesn't mean that you should ignore the keyboard when designing the user interface for an application. As useful as it might be, the mouse is still an input device designed to work in addition to the keyboard, not in place of it.

Consider the situation of someone who has a physical disability and can't maneuver the mouse. They might find it easier to use the keyboard. Also, some laptop users find it much easier to use a keyboard than a portable mouse or some other portable pointing device. The point I'm trying to make is that you need to make a serious effort to fully support both the mouse and keyboard in your applications because there are people out there who might find it easier to use one or the other.

Working with Message Maps

Message maps are MFC constructs that are used to map messages to member functions. Message maps represent a dramatic improvement in the way an application responds to messages. In traditional Win32 applications written in C, messages were handled by a huge `Switch` statement. Each `case` within the `Switch` statement corresponded to a different message. With most applications responding to tens of messages, this approach proved cumbersome. There had to be a better way!

In designing a C++ wrapper around the Win32 API, Microsoft knew they had to improve the way messages are handled. This is where message maps come into play. Message maps move message handling into the OOP world by associating messages with member functions. When a message is delivered to an application, the message map is used to determine which member function should be called to handle the message. For this reason, these member functions are often referred to as message handlers.

New Term A *message map* is an MFC construct used to improve the manner in which an application responds to messages. A message map associates messages with message handler member functions.

New Term A *message handler* is a member function called in response to a message being delivered.

If you're the curious type, you might be wondering why the folks at Microsoft didn't just use virtual member functions to handle messages as opposed to the more layered approach of message maps. This is a very reasonable question to raise because message maps require extra work that wouldn't be necessary if virtual functions were automatically associated with messages. However, using virtual functions would introduce some serious efficiency issues. Let's examine why.

If you wanted to handle messages via virtual functions, you would first create a master base class that defines a virtual member function (message handler) for every possible message to which an object might respond. There are hundreds of messages defined in the Win32 API, so the class would define literally hundreds of message handlers. The problem here is that virtual functions are stored in a special part of a class known as the v-table, which is a list of virtual function pointers. This list must accompany every class derived from the base message handling class. So, every derived class will automatically have a v-table with hundreds of entries.

When you consider that a class hierarchy such as MFC consists of hundreds of different classes, it's simply too inefficient to have huge v-tables in classes that don't really need them. The message map approach allows a class to define only the message handlers it needs to use, which is very efficient and a lot faster than the virtual function approach.

Using Message Map Macros

Although message maps ultimately provide a much cleaner method for handling messages than traditional Win32 API programming, they do require a little extra coding overhead. For classes that choose to respond to messages, you must use a set of message map macros to indicate that the class is to handle messages. At the end of the declaration for the class in the header file, you must include the following macro statement:

`DECLARE_MESSAGE_MAP()`

This statement simply states that the class supports a message map for responding to messages. The specifics of the message map are listed in the source code implementation of the class. Listing 4.1 contains the two message map macros that must be placed in the implementation file for a class.

LISTING 4.1 THE MESSAGE MAP MACROS REQUIRED IN THE IMPLEMENTATION FILE FOR A CLASS

```
1: BEGIN_MESSAGE_MAP(CMainFrame, CFrameWnd)
2:   // Message map entries go here!
3: END_MESSAGE_MAP()
```

Specific message mappings are placed between these two macros. As an example, Listing 4.2 shows the message map for the Resourceful application you built in the previous hour.

LISTING 4.2 THE MESSAGE MAP FOR THE RESOURCEFUL APPLICATION

```
1: BEGIN_MESSAGE_MAP(CResourcefulApp, CWinApp)
2:     ON_COMMAND(ID_FILE_NEW, CWinApp::OnFileNew)
3:     ON_COMMAND(ID_FILE_OPEN, CWinApp::OnFileOpen)
4:     ON_COMMAND(ID_APP_ABOUT, OnAppAbout)
5: END_MESSAGE_MAP()
```

This message map defines three message mappings for menu commands. The `ON_COMMAND` macro is used to map commands to message handlers. This macro takes two parameters: the identifier of the command, and the name of the message handler to call when the command message is sent. As you can see in the entries for the `ID_FILE_NEW` and `ID_FILE_OPEN` commands, it is possible to map messages to message handlers in a parent class.

The `ON_COMMAND` macro is designed for use with command messages that would typically be sent via the `WM_COMMAND` message. There are also other macros for use when handling different types of messages. The `ON_WM_XXXX` macro is used to respond to predefined Windows messages. As an example, the `WM_PAINT` message handler macro would be named `ON_WM_PAINT`. The `ON_UPDATE_COMMAND_UI` macro is used to respond to user interface updates such as modifying the state of a toolbar button. The `ON_MESSAGE` macro is used to handle user-defined messages. There are a few other message-mapping macros but I'll spare you the details of them for the time being. The majority of your message mapping work will involve using the `ON_COMMAND` and `ON_WM_XXXX` macros.

Writing Message Handlers

Writing message handlers is a little different than writing any other member functions, with the exception that the name and parameter list for message handlers is predetermined by MFC. Following is an example of a message handler declaration for the Resourceful application:

```
afx_msg void   OnAppAbout();
```

The main thing that distinguishes this member function is the presence of the `afx_msg` keyword at the beginning of the function declaration. This keyword simply identifies the member function as a message handler. It is important to include it in all message handler declarations, however. Listing 4.3 contains the implementation of the `OnAppAbout()` message handler.

LISTING 4.3 THE `CResourceful::OnAppAbout()` MESSAGE HANDLER

```
1: void CResourcefulApp::OnAppAbout() {
2:   CAboutDlg aboutDlg;
3:   aboutDlg.DoModal();
4: }
```

Notice that the `afx_msg` keyword isn't required in the method implementation. There really is nothing special about the method's definition other than the fact that it doesn't accept any parameters; all command message handlers take no parameters. Parameters are actually an important part of message handlers. Following is a message handler that takes some parameters:

`afx_msg void OnSize(UINT nType, int cx, int cy);`

The `OnSize()` message handler is associated with the `WM_SIZE` message, which is sent after a window has been resized. The parameters to the `OnSize()` message handler indicate the type of sizing that took place (`nType`), along with the new width (`cx`) and height (`cy`) of the window's client area. Clearly, the information contained in these parameters is very useful to the message handler. Incidentally, the message map entry for the `OnSize()` message handler follows:

`ON_WM_SIZE()`

> If you happen to be using Microsoft Visual C++ (Visual Studio) as your development environment, you can use Class Wizard to map messages to message handlers. It will prompt you to select a message and then it will automatically generate the message handler ready for you to add code. Of course, I don't assume that you're using Visual C++ so I'll continue to show you how to do things manually.

Handling User Input Messages

Handling user input messages is as simple as determining the specific messages you want to handle and then creating the appropriate message handlers for them. There are a variety of different keyboard and mouse messages supported by Win32, so it's important to make sure you are handling the proper messages to achieve your desired functionality. To recap, following are the steps required to handle any message:

1. Declare a message handler member function in the appropriate header file.
2. Create a message map entry binding the message to the message handler.
3. Write the code for the message handler in the appropriate source code file.

Keyboard Messaging Basics

Before jumping into the specifics of how to handle keyboard messages, let's take a moment to learn about how Windows manages keyboard messages. When you press a key in a Windows application, Windows generates a keyboard message. This message is sent to the application whose main frame window has keyboard focus. The application then handles the message and does whatever it needs to do with the keystroke information. In the case of a word processor, the application might store away a character based on the key press and draw the character on the screen.

It's important to note that keyboard messages aren't directly associated with specific characters because this would cause problems with multilingual applications. Instead, the Win32 API defines virtual key codes that are mapped to each key on the keyboard. Virtual key codes serve as device-independent identifiers for keys on the keyboard. Applications always interpret keystrokes as virtual key codes instead of raw characters. Following are some examples of virtual key codes defined in the Win32 API:

- VK_A
- VK_B
- VK_C
- VK_F1
- VK_F2
- VK_RETURN
- VK_DELETE

NEW TERM A *virtual key code* is a device-independent identifier for keys on the keyboard.

Keyboard messages are sent to the window with input focus. Input focus is a temporary property that only one window at a time is capable of having. Input focus is associated with the currently active window, which is often identifiable by a highlighted caption bar, dialog frame, or caption text, depending on the type of window. Although input focus plays an important role in determining where keyboard messages are sent, it doesn't tell the whole story. Allow me to explain.

Keyboard focus determines when a window actually receives keyboard messages. Keyboard focus is a more specific type of input focus that requires that a window not be minimized. As an example, a minimized word processor shouldn't accept keyboard input because you can't see what you're typing. Thanks to keyboard focus, applications don't receive keyboard messages when they're minimized.

Each time you press and release a key in Windows, a keyboard message is generated. In fact, an individual message is generated both for the key press and the key release. Table 4.1 lists the Win32 messages associated with keystrokes, along with the MFC message handlers for each.

TABLE 4.1 WIN32 KEYSTROKE MESSAGES AND THEIR MFC MESSAGE HANDLERS

Message	Message Handler
WM_KEYDOWN	OnKeyDown()
WM_KEYUP	OnKeyUp()
WM_CHAR	OnChar()
WM_SYSKEYDOWN	OnSysKeyDown()
WM_SYSKEYUP	OnSysKeyUp()

The WM_KEYDOWN and WM_KEYUP messages are used to process the vast majority of keystrokes. The WM_CHAR message is similar to the WM_KEYDOWN message, except it contains a translated character associated with the key press. The WM_CHAR message is sent after a WM_KEYDOWN and WM_KEYUP message combination. The WM_SYSKEYDOWN and WM_SYSKEYUP messages are sent in response to system keystrokes such as key combinations involving the Alt key.

> Windows automatically handles system keystrokes such as using the Alt key to access menus. It is rare that you would want to handle system keystrokes in an application. Windows also handles keyboard accelerators, which are used as shortcuts to invoke some menu commands.

Following is the declaration for the OnKeyDown() message handler, which indicates the parameters accepted by all the keyboard message handlers:

```
afx_msg void OnKeyDown(UINT nChar, UINT nRepCnt, UINT nFlags);
```

The nChar parameter specifies the virtual-key code of the key being pressed. The nRepCnt parameter specifies the repeat count, which applies if a key is being held down and the typematic repeat function of the keyboard is invoked. Finally, the nFlags parameter specifies additional information such as whether the Alt key was down when the key was pressed.

> Typically, keyboard messages come in "key down"/"key up" pairs. However, when a key is held down and the typematic repeat for the keyboard kicks in, Windows sends a series of "key down" messages followed by a single "key up" message when the key is released.

Handling Keyboard Messages

Now that you've learned all about keyboard messages and how to respond to them with message handlers, let's try putting some of this information to work in a real application. In keeping with the spirit of the Skeleton application from the first hour, you're going to add keyboard support to an application named Ghost that allows you to control a ghost with the keyboard. The Ghost application is based on the Skeleton application so it doesn't rely on MFC's document/view architecture.

Typically, moving an image around would require special animation code. Because animation is relatively complex to implement, you're going to cheat in the Ghost application by controlling the mouse cursor instead of a separate image. However, you can get the same effect by simply changing the mouse cursor to look like a ghost.

The real importance of the Ghost application is its support for keyboard interaction. The following line of code shows the `OnKeyDown()` message handler declaration, which appears in the Ghost application's main frame window class:

```
afx_msg void   OnKeyDown(UINT nChar, UINT nRepCnt, UINT nFlags);
```

For this message handler to work, it must have an entry in the message map for the main frame class. Following is the line added to the message map:

```
ON_WM_KEYDOWN()
```

Now all that's missing is a message handler implementation to actually move the mouse cursor in response to the user pressing a key. Listing 4.4 contains the source code for the `OnKeyDown()` message handler.

LISTING 4.4 THE `CMainFrame::OnKeyDown()` MESSAGE HANDLER IN GHOST

```
 1: void CMainFrame::OnKeyDown(UINT nChar, UINT nRepCnt, UINT nFlags) {
 2:   CPoint  ptCurPos;
 3:
 4:   // Calculate new cursor position based on key press
 5:   if (::GetCursorPos(&ptCurPos))
 6:   {
 7:     // Get the client area rect and convert to screen coordinates
```

```
 8:        CRect rcClient;
 9:        GetClientRect(&rcClient);
10:        ClientToScreen(&rcClient);
11:
12:        switch (nChar) {
13:          case VK_LEFT:
14:            ptCurPos.x -= 5;
15:            if (rcClient.PtInRect(ptCurPos))
16:              ::SetCursorPos(ptCurPos.x, ptCurPos.y);
17:            break;
18:
19:          case VK_RIGHT:
20:            ptCurPos.x += 5;
21:            if (rcClient.PtInRect(ptCurPos))
22:              ::SetCursorPos(ptCurPos.x, ptCurPos.y);
23:            break;
24:
25:          case VK_UP:
26:            ptCurPos.y -= 5;
27:            if (rcClient.PtInRect(ptCurPos))
28:              ::SetCursorPos(ptCurPos.x, ptCurPos.y);
29:            break;
30:
31:          case VK_DOWN:
32:            ptCurPos.y += 5;
33:            if (rcClient.PtInRect(ptCurPos))
34:              ::SetCursorPos(ptCurPos.x, ptCurPos.y);
35:            break;
36:        }
37:      }
38: }
```

The OnKeyDown() message handler gets the current mouse cursor position and modifies it based on the key pressed. The four arrow keys are used to control the cursor, which explains the virtual key codes VK_LEFT, VK_RIGHT, VK_UP, and VK_DOWN. The cursor is actually moved by calling the Win32 API function SetCursorPos() and providing the new cursor position.

Mouse Messaging Basics

When you move the mouse or press a mouse button, Windows generates a mouse message. Unlike keyboard messages, mouse messages are sent to any window that the mouse cursor passes over or that the mouse is clicked over, regardless of input focus. Every window is responsible for responding to mouse messages according to its own particular needs.

> Windows automatically handles many mouse functions, such as displaying menus that are clicked and altering the state of pushbuttons and check boxes that are clicked.

The mouse is represented on the screen by a mouse cursor, which is typically in the shape of an arrow. The mouse cursor has a single-pixel hotspot that pinpoints an exact location on the screen. The hotspot of the mouse cursor is significant because the position of all mouse operations is based on the hotspot. Figure 4.1 shows the hotspot location on the standard arrow mouse cursor.

FIGURE 4.1
The hotspot location on the standard arrow mouse cursor.

Although I'm sure that you're well-versed in the different ways a mouse can be used in Windows, it's best to leave no stone unturned. So, let me briefly clarify the different operations that can be performed with a mouse in Windows:

- Clicking—pressing and releasing a mouse button
- Double-clicking—pressing and releasing a mouse button twice in quick succession
- Moving—moving the mouse around without pressing any buttons
- Dragging—moving the mouse around while holding down a button

These operations are important because they help determine the kinds of mouse messages generated by Windows. Mouse messages are divided into two types: client area messages and non-client area messages. Client area messages are by far the more commonly used of the two types, and are therefore the ones I'm going to focus on. Table 4.2 lists the Win32 messages associated with the mouse, along with the MFC message handlers for each.

TABLE 4.2 WIN32 MOUSE MESSAGES AND THEIR MFC MESSAGE HANDLERS

Message	Message Handler
WM_MOUSEMOVE	OnMouseMove()
WM_LBUTTONDOWN	OnLButtonDown()
WM_MBUTTONDOWN	OnMButtonDown()
WM_RBUTTONDOWN	OnRButtonDown()
WM_LBUTTONUP	OnLButtonUp()

WM_MBUTTONUP	OnMButtonUp()
WM_RBUTTONUP	OnRButtonUp()
WM_LBUTTONDBLCLK	OnLButtonDblClk()
WM_MBUTTONDBLCLK	OnMButtonDblClk()
WM_RBUTTONDBLCLK	OnRButtonDblClk()

The WM_MOUSEMOVE message is sent when the mouse moves over the client area of a window. The WM_XBUTTONDOWN messages are sent when a mouse button is pressed within the client area of a window, whereas the WM_XBUTTONUP messages are sent when a mouse button is released. The WM_XBUTTONDBLCLK messages are sent when a mouse button is double-clicked in the client area of a window. All the button messages come in three versions that correspond to the left, right, and middle mouse buttons. Some mice don't have a middle button, in which case they aren't capable of generating middle mouse button messages.

Following is the declaration for the OnMouseMove() message handler, which indicates the parameters accepted by all the mouse message handlers:

```
afx_msg void OnMouseMove(UINT nFlags, CPoint point);
```

The nFlags parameter indicates whether various virtual keys are down. This parameter can be any combination of the following values:

- MK_LBUTTON—set if the left mouse button is down
- MK_MBUTTON—set if the middle mouse button is down
- MK_RBUTTON—set if the right mouse button is down
- MK_CONTROL—set if the Ctrl key is down
- MK_SHIFT—set if the Shift key is down

The other parameter, point, specifies the X and Y coordinates of the mouse cursor. These coordinates indicate the specific position of the mouse cursor's hotspot, and are relative to the upper-left corner of the window the mouse is over.

Handling Mouse Messages

To try out handling mouse messages, let's return to the Ghost application. A neat enhancement would be to display an image of the word "Boo!" at the mouse cursor position any time that you click the left mouse button. As you will soon find out, adding this functionality is easier than you might think. Let's get started by writing a mouse message handler to respond to the WM_LBUTTONDOWN message. The following line of code shows the OnLButton() message handler declaration, which appears in the Ghost application's main frame window class:

```
afx_msg void  OnLButtonDown(UINT nFlags, CPoint point);
```

This message handler must have an entry in the message map for the main frame class. Following is the line added to the message map:

```
ON_WM_LBUTTONDOWN()
```

The next step is to develop the source code for the `OnLButtonDown()` message handler, which displays an image at the current mouse cursor position. Listing 4.5 contains the source code for the `OnLButtonDown()` message handler.

LISTING 4.5 THE `CMainFrame::OnLButtonDown()` MESSAGE HANDLER IN GHOST

```
1: void CMainFrame::OnLButtonDown(UINT nFlags, CPoint point) {
2:     // Draw the "Boo!" image
3:     CClientDC dc(this);
4:     DrawBoo(&dc, point);
5: }
```

This message handler is probably much simpler than you expected. That's primarily due to the fact that it delegates much of its work to the `DrawBoo()` support function, which is shown in Listing 4.6.

LISTING 4.6 THE `CMainFrame::DrawBoo()` SUPPORT MEMBER FUNCTION IN GHOST

```
 1: void CMainFrame::DrawBoo(CDC* pdc, CPoint ptPos) {
 2:     CDC        dcMem;
 3:     CBitmap    bmBoo;
 4:     CBitmap*   pbmOld;
 5:     BITMAP     bmInfo;
 6:     CSize      sizBoo;
 7:
 8:     // Load boo bitmap
 9:     VERIFY(bmBoo.LoadBitmap(IDB_BOO));
10:
11:     // Get size of boo bitmap
12:     bmBoo.GetObject(sizeof(BITMAP), &bmInfo);
13:     sizBoo.cx = bmInfo.bmWidth;
14:     sizBoo.cy = bmInfo.bmHeight;
15:
16:     // Setup memory DC
17:     ASSERT(pdc);
18:     dcMem.CreateCompatibleDC(pdc);
19:     VERIFY(pbmOld = dcMem.SelectObject(&bmBoo));
20:
21:     // Draw boo image
22:     pdc->BitBlt(ptPos.x, ptPos.y - bmInfo.bmHeight, sizBoo.cx,
23:       sizBoo.cy, &dcMem, 0, 0, SRCAND);
```

```
24:
25:    // Cleanup memory DC
26:    VERIFY(dcMem.SelectObject(pbmOld));
27: }
```

The `DrawBoo()` member function heads into some territory that is no doubt unfamiliar to you. It's not terribly important for you to understand the details of it at this point, but I will give you some idea as to how it works. The `DrawBoo()` function first loads the "Boo!" bitmap using the resource identifier `IDB_BOO`, and then determines the size of the bitmap. The bitmap is then drawn to a device context, which is a Win32 drawing surface. The function finishes up by cleaning up the device context.

Figure 4.2 shows the Ghost application complete with "Boo!" images.

FIGURE 4.2
The Ghost application.

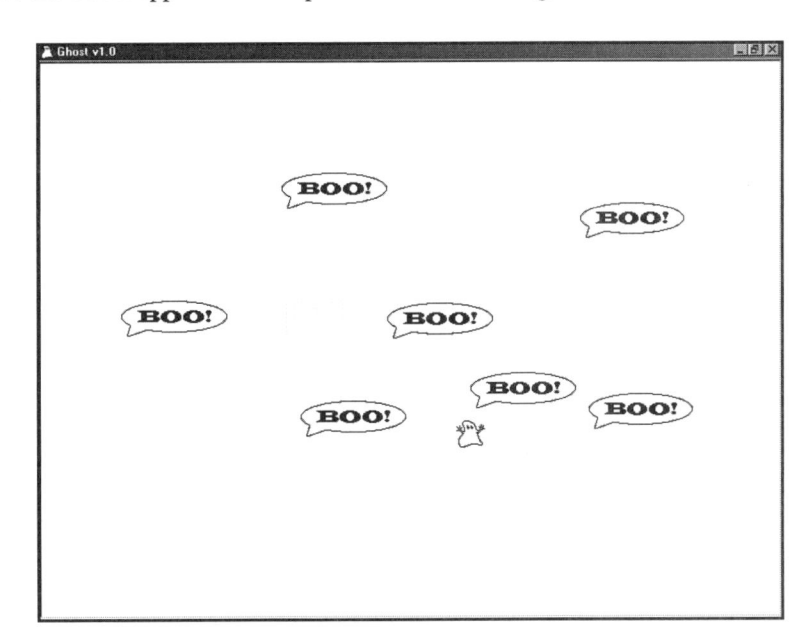

Summary

This hour introduces you to user input and how it is handled in MFC applications. You learned about the significance of user input and how it is important in practically all applications. You then learned about message maps and how they are used to make message handling cleaner and more efficient in MFC applications. Finally, you wrapped up the hour by learning how to create message handlers that respond to keyboard and mouse messages.

Q&A

Q **What happens to messages that aren't handled?**

A MFC defines a message processing hierarchy based on the inheritance tree of a class. If a class doesn't provide a message handler for a particular message, the message is passed up the tree to the parent class. This process continues on until the message maps of all base classes have been searched. If none of the classes handle the message, the message undergoes default processing.

Q **How do you know when to handle mouse and keyboard messages?**

A In general, you will only handle mouse and keyboard messages in user-defined windows that you create, such as application frame windows. Other types of windows, such as standard Windows buttons, already handle mouse and keyboard messages for themselves. If you add a button to your application, you don't have to write any message handlers for the button itself to visually respond to a mouse click. However, you will have to write a message handler if your application should respond to the button being clicked.

Workshop

The Workshop is designed to help you anticipate possible questions, review what you've learned, and begin thinking ahead to put your knowledge into practice. The answers to the quiz are in Appendix A, "Quiz Answers."

Quiz

1. What is a message map?
2. What is a member function called in response to a message being delivered?
3. Why doesn't MFC use virtual functions instead of message maps to respond to messages?
4. What is a device-independent identifier for keys on the keyboard?
5. How many windows can have input focus at any given time?
6. Which message should be handled to process characters typed on the keyboard?
7. What is required for a window to have keyboard focus?
8. What keystrokes does Windows automatically handle?
9. When does Windows sends a series of "key down" messages followed by a single "key up" message?
10. When would the `OnMButtonDblClk()` message handler be called in an application?

Exercises

1. Add a new `case` section for the Spacebar (`VK_SPACE`) in the `OnKeyDown()` message handler for the Ghost application. Add code to make the mouse cursor move to a random location when the user presses the Spacebar. You can use the standard C `rand()` function to generate the random numbers.

2. Add an `OnRButtonDown()` message handler that is called in response to the user pressing the right mouse button in the Ghost application. In this message handler add code to display a message box:

```
MessageBox("I'm a ghost!");
```

HOUR 5

Making Use of Controls

This hour delves into the world of controls, which is full of mystery and intrigue. (Not really, but controls are very interesting as building blocks when it comes to assembling the user interface for applications.) This hour introduces you to the two main types of controls used in MFC programming, and culminates in a neat application that uses a variety of controls together.

In this hour, you will learn

- The difference between traditional Windows controls and common controls
- The relationship between MFC and the underlying Windows controls
- How to create controls and respond to control notifications

Understanding Controls

It is often useful to nest windows within other windows, in which case a relationship is formed between the two windows known as a parent-child relationship. A parent window owns any child windows created within it. Child windows, such as a button, that perform a common, reusable function are often referred to as controls. The purpose of controls is to delegate functionality so that the parent window has less responsibility. For example, it doesn't make sense for an application window to worry about the details of push button logic when that logic can be encapsulated within a button control. The button control is self-contained in that it knows how to draw itself and respond to user input. It only reports back to the parent when an event occurs, such as the user clicking the button.

New Term A child window that performs a common, reusable function is called a *control*.

There are two primary types of controls used to develop Windows applications: traditional Windows controls and common controls. Both types of controls are standard in Win32, but each are handled a little differently. The reason for the two different control types goes back to the origins of Windows. Early versions of Windows shipped with a standard suite of basic controls, such as buttons and scroll bars. If you wanted to do anything fancy, you had to develop a custom control, which back then wasn't a very fun proposition.

As of Windows 95, a newer set of controls was introduced that offered a more modern user interface, including tree views, sliders, and progress gauges. These controls are referred to as common controls and are largely responsible for the revamped look and feel of the Windows 95/98 user interface.

As a Win32 developer, you have at your disposal both traditional Windows controls and the more advanced common controls. Fortunately, there isn't much difference between using the two different types of controls. The primary difference has to do with how you respond to messages sent by the controls. MFC provides wrapper classes for all the controls, which also helps smooth out the differences between the underlying Win32 implementations. Let's move on and learn some specifics about the different controls.

Traditional Windows Controls

The traditional Windows controls date back to early versions of Windows and should be very familiar to you. Even though they've been around a while, the traditional controls are still very useful. Table 5.1 lists these controls.

TABLE 5.1 TRADITIONAL WINDOWS CONTROLS

Control	Description
Button	A small window that can be clicked on and off
Static	An output-only window that can be used to display a text string, box, rectangle, icon, cursor, or image

Scroll bar	A window containing arrows and a thumb selector used as a means of identifying and modifying the current position in a document
Edit	A window in which the user can enter text
List box	A window that displays a list of items that the user can view and select

Figure 5.1 shows a File Open dialog box, which contains many of the traditional Windows controls.

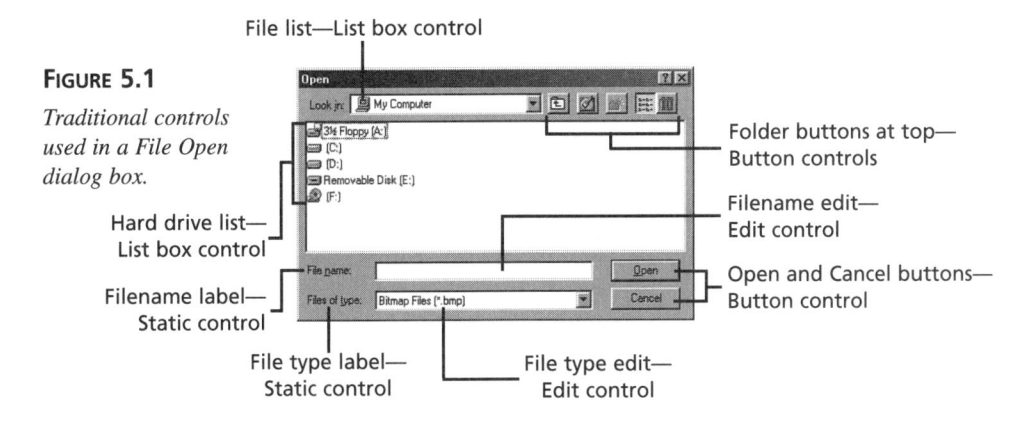

FIGURE 5.1

Traditional controls used in a File Open dialog box.

Unlike other types of predefined child window controls, button controls come in a few different varieties. The same button window class can be used to create button controls in the following forms:

- Push button—a button that can be pushed to trigger some event
- Check box—a two-state button that is either checked or unchecked
- Radio button—a two-state button used in groups to provide a means of performing a mutually exclusive selection (only one button in the group can be selected at a time)

Each different traditional control has an associated set of styles that determine the look and feel of the control. Additionally, each control has a set of notification codes that are used to convey information about control events. Notification codes are sent to a control's parent as part of the WM_COMMAND message. However, they are handled a little differently than other commands sent via the WM_COMMAND message. More on this a little later in the hour.

New Term: A special code used to convey information about control events to a control's parent is known as a *control notification*.

In addition to predefined child window controls, which are also sometimes referred to as dialog box controls, Windows supports common controls. Common controls are more modern user interface controls that were added to Windows as of Windows 95. Let's move on and take a look at the common controls and see what they have to offer.

Common Controls

Unlike the traditional Windows controls that have been a part of Windows since its early days, common controls are relatively new. Common controls form the cornerstone of the modern user interface introduced in Windows 95. Common controls are derived from controls such as toolbars and status bars that application developers traditionally had to create themselves. There are seventeen common controls, so there are plenty of options when it comes to building an application's user interface.

One of the biggest sources of confusion surrounding common controls is the difference between common controls and the standard Windows dialog box controls. In terms of function, there isn't much difference. The main difference lies in the motivation for each. The standard dialog box controls were present in the earliest versions of Windows back when the Windows user interface was in its infancy. Common controls are more of an afterthought and are aimed at refreshing the Windows user interface with a more modern look and feel. Additionally, common controls are meant to standardize the Windows user interface by providing standard implementations of common user interface elements such as toolbars, status bars, and tree views.

At a technical level, the primary difference between standard dialog box controls and common controls is how they communicate with applications. The standard dialog box controls communicate with applications by sending `WM_COMMAND` messages, whereas common controls typically send `WM_NOTIFY` messages. I use the word "typically" because there is an exception to this rule that you will find out about later in the hour. Regardless of the messaging differences, standard dialog box controls and common controls are used in essentially the same way.

All the common controls but one (image list) are implemented as window classes. After a common control is created, you interact with it just like you would any other window. Common controls can be moved, resized, hidden, and can send and receive messages.

When building an application that uses common controls, you must include the CommCtrl.h header file in any source code file that references common controls. This is due to the fact that common controls aren't referenced in the standard Windows.h header file. Additionally, you need to make sure the static common control library (COMCTL32.LIB) is linked into your application. Otherwise you will get linker errors.

There are a variety of different common controls available for jazzing up the user interface of your Win32 applications. Table 5.2 lists the Windows common controls, along with their function.

TABLE 5.2 WINDOWS COMMON CONTROLS

Control	Description
Toolbar	A container for command shortcut buttons
Tooltip	A window that displays brief floating help text
Status bar	A context-sensitive information window placed at the bottom of an application's frame window
Property sheet	A container for multiple Property Pages
Property page	A modeless dialog box acting as a single page in a property sheet
List	A list of items identified by a bitmap and text
Tree	A hierarchically organized list of items
Animate	A window that displays an animated sequence of images
Image list	A non-window control that stores a set of images
Progress bar	A window that displays a progress gauge for long operations
Rich edit	An advanced edit control that supports rich text
Slider	An input control for selecting a value in a specific range
Spin button	An input control for incrementing or decrementing a value

Figure 5.2 shows how some of the common controls are used within the Windows Explorer application.

FIGURE 5.2

Common controls used in the Windows Explorer application.

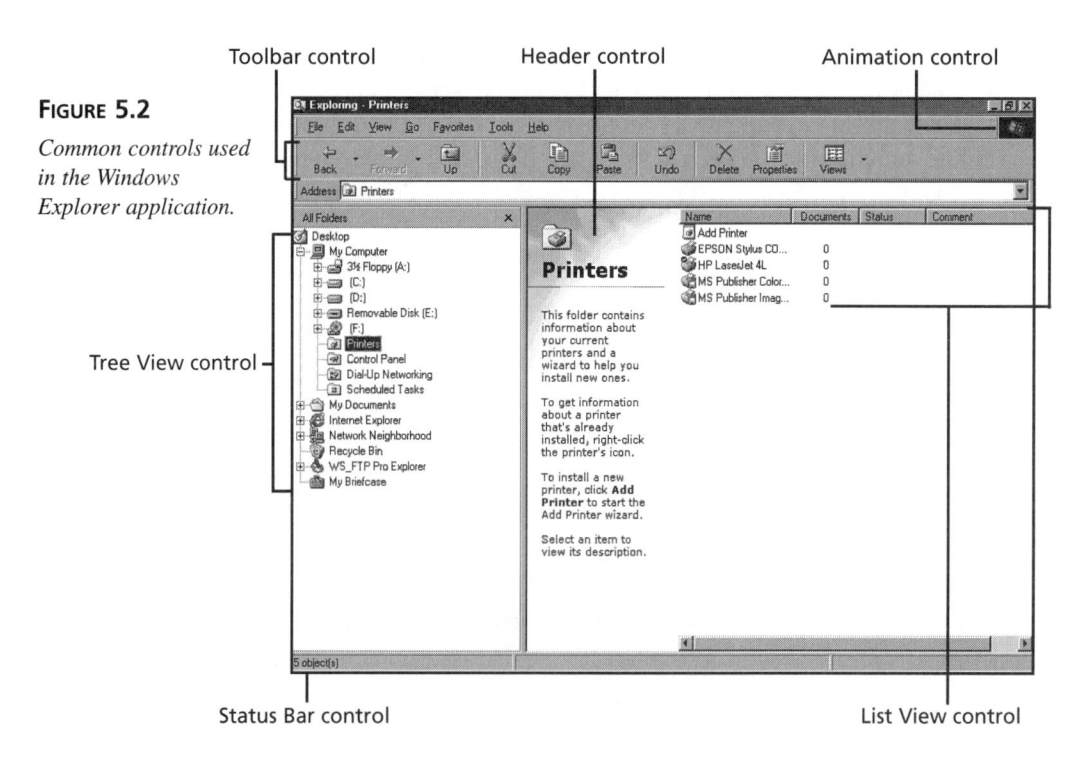

[Figure showing Windows Explorer with labels: Toolbar control, Header control, Animation control, Tree View control, Status Bar control, List View control]

Controls and MFC

To help make it easier to use controls from within an MFC application, MFC provides wrapper classes for both the traditional and common controls you've learned about thus far in the hour. You can use these wrapper classes to create and manipulate controls in an application. Table 5.3 lists the MFC control classes along with the underlying controls with which they are associated.

TABLE 5.3 MFC CONTROL CLASSES AND THE CONTROLS WITH WHICH THEY ARE ASSOCIATED

MFC Class	Control
CButton	Button
CStatic	Static
CScrollBar	Scroll bar
CEdit	Edit
CListBox	List box
CToolBarCtrl	Toolbar
CToolTipCtrl	Tooltip

`CStatusBarCtrl`	Status bar
`CPropertySheet`	Property sheet
`CPropertyPage`	Property page
`CListCtrl`	List
`CTreeCtrl`	Tree
`CAnimateCtrl`	Animate
`CImageList`	Image list
`CProgressCtrl`	Progress bar
`CRichEditCtrl`	Rich edit
`CSliderCtrl`	Slider
`CSpinButtonCtrl`	Spin button

Creating Controls with MFC

Creating controls in MFC typically involves three steps:

1. Create a unique integer identifier for the control in the Resource.h header file.
2. Create an object using an MFC wrapper class, which results in the object's constructor being called.
3. Call the `Create()` member function on the object and pass in the unique identifier.

The first step has to do with the fact that controls are always created using unique integer identifiers. These identifiers are used by Windows to distinguish between the different controls in an application. This might seem like a hassle, but specifying a unique identifier for each control you create actually requires very little work. You basically just pass the identifier as one of the parameters to the `Create()` member function of the MFC object. Control identifiers are typically defined in Resource.h along with resource identifiers.

The second step creates the MFC wrapper object for a control, which is then capable of creating the underlying Windows object. The third step is what actually results in the creation of the underlying Windows object. Remember that MFC is just a wrapper around the Win32 API; without calling `Create()` you would simply have an empty wrapper. You can think of the second step as creating the wrapper around a Big Mac hamburger, whereas the third step actually provides the sandwich itself. The `Create()` member therefore provides the beef in this scenario. I apologize, but that pun was irresistible!

Most of the time you will be creating and using controls within dialog boxes, which you learn how to do in Hour 7, "Retrieving Information with Custom Dialog Boxes."

However, there are times when you might want to create a control directly in an application's frame window. The issue of creating a control in a frame window raises the question of where to perform the creation. You might think that the constructor for the frame window is a good place, or maybe the overridden Create() member function instead.

It turns out that the best place to create a control in a frame window is in the OnCreate() message handler, which is called in response to the window receiving a WM_CREATE message. The WM_CREATE message is sent to a window just after the window is created, but before it becomes visible. This makes the OnCreate() message handler an ideal spot to create any child window controls used by a frame window. You work through an example that uses the OnCreate() message handler to create controls a little later in the hour.

Handling Control Notifications

As any parent will tell you, communicating with a child can often be difficult. Not so in MFC! Controls communicate with parent windows by sending notification messages, which are relatively easy to handle. You wire message handlers to control notification messages in much the same way as you connect message handlers to other Windows messages. The only caveat to handling control notification messages is that they aren't all sent in exactly the same way.

Controls communicate with parent windows using one of two messaging mechanisms, WM_COMMAND or WM_NOTIFY. The WM_COMMAND message is used by traditional Windows controls such as buttons and list boxes, whereas the WM_NOTIFY message is used by most of the common controls. The message handlers themselves aren't really any different in each case, but the message map macros used to associate them with messages do differ a little. Let's first consider the case of traditional Windows controls that make use of the WM_COMMAND message.

WM_COMMAND Notifications

As you learned in the previous hour, WM_COMMAND messages are typically handled using the ON_COMMAND macro. Although this approach applies to menu commands, it doesn't hold up for control notifications. I know it might seem confusing, but control notifications require different message map macros even though they are sent through the WM_COMMAND message. This is due to the fact that control notifications ultimately involve more information because they must indicate a specific event that has occurred within a control. For example, an Edit control generates different notifications when it is scrolled horizontally and vertically, as well as when it gains and loses focus. Listing 5.1 shows a message map that maps these four notifications to an Edit control.

LISTING 5.1   A MESSAGE MAP THAT HANDLES FOUR EDIT CONTROL NOTIFICATIONS

```
1: BEGIN_MESSAGE_MAP(CMainFrame, CFrameWnd)
2:    ON_EN_HSCROLL(ID_ET_EDIT, OnETEditHScroll)
3:    ON_EN_VSCROLL(ID_ET_EDIT, OnETEditVScroll)
4:    ON_EN_SETFOCUS(ID_ET_EDIT, OnETEditSetFocus)
5:    ON_EN_KILLFOCUS(ID_ET_EDIT, OnETEditKillFocus)
6: END_MESSAGE_MAP()
```

In this example, message handlers are mapped to the Edit control identified by the ID_ET_EDIT identifier. The Edit control notifications handled are EN_HSCROLL, EN_VSCROLL, EN_SETFOCUS, and EN_KILLFOCUS. All controls define control-specific notifications to which you can respond. Table 5.4 lists the notification codes defined for the Edit control (CEdit).

TABLE 5.4   EDIT CONTROL NOTIFICATION CODES

Notification Code	Description
EN_CHANGE	Text has been altered in the control
EN_UPDATE	The control is about to display altered text
EN_HSCROLL	The user clicked the control's horizontal scroll bar
EN_VSCROLL	The user clicked the control's vertical scroll bar
EN_KILLFOCUS	The control has lost input focus
EN_SETFOCUS	The control has received input focus
EN_MAXTEXT	The control has reached its maximum limit of characters
EN_ERRSPACE	The control has run out of memory

Notice in the example that the message map macro for the control notifications are named based on the notification code. For example, the macro for EN_SETFOCUS is named ON_EN_SETFOCUS. You are free to name the corresponding message handlers anything you choose. However, the message handlers must conform to the following function prototype:

`afx_msg void OnXXXX();`

Control notification message handlers don't accept parameters or return any arguments, which makes using them quite simple. Now that you understand how control notifications for traditional Windows controls work, let's take a quick look at how the common controls are handled.

`WM_NOTIFY` Notifications

I mentioned earlier that most of the common controls use the `WM_NOTIFY` message to deliver control notifications instead of `WM_COMMAND`. This isn't just something the Win32 architects did to make Windows programming more difficult. They had already done a good enough job of that! No, using the `WM_NOTIFY` message allows controls to send additional information along with the message, which is very important in many of the common controls. This is apparent by the fact that `WM_NOTIFY` message handlers accept parameters, unlike their `WM_COMMAND` counterparts. Following is the function prototype that these message handlers must use:

```
afx_msg void OnXXXX(NMHDR* pNotifyStruct, LRESULT* result)
```

The first parameter is a control-specific structure containing information relating to the notification. You typically cast this pointer to a data structure specific to a given control. The second parameter is a result code that you use to return information from the message handler.

The message map macro used to wire message handlers with the `WM_NOTIFY` message is called `ON_NOTIFY`, and works similar to the macros for `WM_COMMAND` messages. The main difference is that the `ON_NOTIFY` macro requires an additional parameter indicating notification code of the event. Listing 5.2 contains an example of a message map that uses the `ON_NOTIFY` macro.

LISTING 5.2 A MESSAGE MAP THAT HANDLES TWO SLIDER CONTROL NOTIFICATIONS

```
1: BEGIN_MESSAGE_MAP(CMainFrame, CFrameWnd)
2:   ON_NOTIFY(TB_LINEUP, ID_TB_SLIDER, OnTBSliderLineUp)
3:   ON_NOTIFY(TB_LINEDOWN, ID_TB_SLIDER, OnTBSliderLineDown)
4: END_MESSAGE_MAP()
```

This example maps the `TB_LINEUP` and `TB_LINEDOWN` notifications for the Slider control identified by `ID_TB_SLIDER`. As you can see, the `WM_NOTIFY` approach is a little more complicated than the `WM_COMMAND` approach, but then again most of the common controls are significantly more powerful then the traditional Windows controls.

Rogue Notifications

There is one more class of notifications that I want to address before I move on. I'm referring to custom control notifications that use the `WM_COMMAND` message. These notifications work just like the ones you've already seen in this hour, except for the fact that they don't have macros predefined for each type of notification code. Instead, they rely on the `ON_CONTROL` macro to map their message handlers. Why is this relevant to the discussion? Because one of the most interesting common controls, Animate, relies on this control notification technique. Listing 5.3 contains an example of a message map involving an Animate control.

LISTING 5.3 A MESSAGE MAP THAT HANDLES TWO ANIMATE CONTROL NOTIFICATIONS

```
1: BEGIN_MESSAGE_MAP(CMainFrame, CFrameWnd)
2:   ON_CONTROL(ACN_START, ID_AN_ANIMATION, OnANStart)
3:   ON_CONTROL(ACN_STOP, ID_AN_ANIMATION, OnANStop)
4: END_MESSAGE_MAP()
```

The `ACN_START` and `ACN_STOP` notifications are sent when an animation starts and stops playing, respectively. As you can see, the `ON_CONTROL` macro requires a notification code, a control identifier, and a message handler function. Like all message handlers called in response to the `WM_COMMAND` message, `OnANStart()` and `OnANStop()` neither accept parameters nor return arguments.

ActiveX Controls

Before moving on to an example involving controls, allow me to address a topic that you might be curious about. I'm referring to ActiveX controls, which have received lots of media attention as of late. ActiveX controls are a special breed of controls that are much more powerful than the controls you've learned about in this hour. ActiveX controls are designed to be extremely extensible and provide a high degree of interoperability with applications and other controls. Unlike the controls you've learned about thus far, ActiveX controls don't use the Windows messaging architecture but instead communicate through COM, which stands for Component Object Model. ActiveX controls are also designed with networking in mind, which makes them ideal for applications that involve processing information over the Internet.

The main distinction between ActiveX controls and the other controls you've learned about in this hour is that ActiveX controls are software components that provide true reusability on a broad scale. Just as Henry Ford and his assembly line approach to manufacturing sparked a whole new level of efficiency, software developers are now attempting to dramatically improve their efficiency using software components. A software component is a piece of software isolated into a discrete, easily reusable structure. Software components are ideally supposed to act as software building blocks that can be easily used and reused together to create applications without perpetually reinventing the proverbial wheel.

NEW TERM A *software component* is a piece of software isolated into a discrete, easily reusable structure.

What does all this mean in the context of MFC? Well, MFC supports ActiveX and provides a framework of classes for creating and working with ActiveX controls. However, ActiveX is a complex enough topic that could easily take up an entire book. For this reason, I want to spend the rest of the hour building an application that uses controls you've already learned about.

Putting Controls to Work

The remainder of the hour focuses on the development of an application called Animator that displays animations. The Animator application makes use of three different kinds of controls that all interact with each other. Figure 5.3 shows the Animator application in action, which should give you an idea as to how it works.

FIGURE 5.3

The Animator application in action.

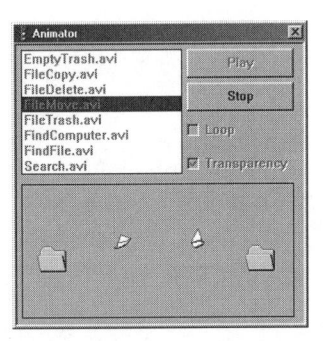

The items in the Animator application's list box are animation filenames. You play an animation by selecting a filename and clicking the Play button. The Stop button stops playing an animation. The Loop check box causes an animation to play over and over until you click the Stop button. Finally, the Transparency check box displays an animation with the background showing up behind it, which makes it look more natural.

> The animations used in the Animator application are in the AVI (Audio Video Interleaved) format, which is a file format that Microsoft created for animations and movies. Although many AVI files include sound tracks, the Animate control doesn't support sound. Consequently, the Animate control is typically used to view simple animations.

Making Use of Controls

The Animator application makes use of six controls. Four of the controls are Button controls and the other two are a ListBox control and an Animate control. Identifiers for these controls are defined in the Resource.h header file, which is shown in Listing 5.4.

> If you recall from earlier in the hour, buttons come in a variety of different forms. More specifically, you can use the Button control to create a push button, a check box, or a radio button. The Animator application uses the Button control to create push buttons and check boxes.

LISTING 5.4 THE RESOURCE.H HEADER FILE FOR THE ANIMATOR APPLICATION

```
 1: //---------------------------------
 2: // Strings              Range : 1000 - 1999
 3: //---------------------------------
 4: #define IDR_ANIMATOR      1000
 5:
 6: //---------------------------------
 7: // Controls             Range : 2000 - 2999
 8: //---------------------------------
 9: #define ID_LB_ANIMLISTBOX    2000
10: #define ID_PB_PLAY           2001
11: #define ID_PB_STOP           2002
12: #define ID_CK_LOOP           2003
13: #define ID_CK_TRANSPARENCY   2004
14: #define ID_AN_ANIMATION      2005
```

I've attempted to create identifiers that reflect the type of control they identify. For instance, the ListBox identifier begins with ID_LB, whereas the two Button (push button) identifiers begin with ID_PB. The identifier names can really be anything you choose, but it is good to stick with some type of consistent naming convention.

Everything in the Animator application pretty much takes place in the CMainFrame class. Listing 5.5 contains the code for the MainFrame.h header file.

LISTING 5.5 THE MAINFRAME.H HEADER FILE FOR THE ANIMATOR APPLICATION

```
 1: //---------------------------------
 2: // Inclusions
 3: //---------------------------------
 4: #include "AfxCmn.h"
 5:
 6: //---------------------------------
 7: // CMainFrame Class - Main Frame Window Object
```

continues

LISTING 5.5 CONTINUED

```
 8: //--------------------------------
 9: class CMainFrame : public CFrameWnd {
10:     // Member Variables
11: protected:
12:     CListBox        m_AnimListBox;
13:     CButton         m_PlayButton;
14:     CButton         m_StopButton;
15:     CButton         m_LoopCheckbox;
16:     CButton         m_TransCheckbox;
17:     CAnimateCtrl    m_Animation;
18:
19:     // Public Constructor(s)/Destructor
20: public:
21:             CMainFrame();
22:     virtual ~CMainFrame();
23:
24:     // Public Member Functions
25: public:
26:     BOOL            Create(const CString& sTitle);
27:     virtual BOOL    PreCreateWindow(CREATESTRUCT& cs);
28:
29:     // Message Handlers
30: protected:
31:     afx_msg int     OnCreate(LPCREATESTRUCT lpCreateStruct);
32:     afx_msg void    OnPBPlayClicked();
33:     afx_msg void    OnPBStopClicked();
34:     afx_msg void    OnCKTransparencyClicked();
35:     afx_msg void    OnANStart();
36:     afx_msg void    OnANStop();
37:
38:     // Message Map & Runtime Support
39: protected:
40:     DECLARE_MESSAGE_MAP()
41:     DECLARE_DYNCREATE(CMainFrame)
42: };
43:
44: #endif
```

The most important thing to notice in the header file is the declaration of the control member variables; the `CMainFrame` class contains a member variable corresponding to each of the controls it uses. You will examine the creation of these controls in a moment. For now, try to keep your attention focused on the member functions defined in the `CMainFrame` class.

The `Create()` member function is borrowed directly from the Skeleton application and is required to register and create the Windows frame window. The `PreCreateWindow()` member function is used to alter the style of the frame window as well as its size.

Making Use of Controls

The message handlers in `CMainFrame` all relate to controls. `OnCreate()` is used to create and initialize the controls. The remaining message handlers respond to control notifications. To understand how these work, you need to turn your attention to the MainFrame.cpp source code file (Listing 5.6), which contains the implementation of the `CMainFrame` class.

LISTING 5.6 THE MAINFRAME.CPP SOURCE CODE FILE FOR THE ANIMATOR APPLICATION

```
 1: //---------------------------------
 2: // Inclusions
 3: //---------------------------------
 4: #include "StdAfx.h"
 5: //---------------------------------
 6: #include "MainFrame.h"
 7: #include "Resource.h"
 8:
 9: //---------------------------------
10: // MFC Debugging Support
11: //---------------------------------
12: #ifdef _DEBUG
13: #undef THIS_FILE
14: static char BASED_CODE THIS_FILE[] = __FILE__;
15: #endif
16:
17:
18: //---------------------------------
19: // Message Map & Runtime Support
20: //---------------------------------
21: BEGIN_MESSAGE_MAP(CMainFrame, CFrameWnd)
22:     ON_WM_CREATE()
23:     ON_BN_CLICKED(ID_PB_PLAY, OnPBPlayClicked)
24:     ON_BN_CLICKED(ID_PB_STOP, OnPBStopClicked)
25:     ON_BN_CLICKED(ID_CK_TRANSPARENCY, OnCKTransparencyClicked)
26:     ON_CONTROL(ACN_START, ID_AN_ANIMATION, OnANStart)
27:     ON_CONTROL(ACN_STOP, ID_AN_ANIMATION, OnANStop)
28: END_MESSAGE_MAP()
29:
30: IMPLEMENT_DYNCREATE(CMainFrame, CFrameWnd)
31:
32: //---------------------------------
33: // Public Constructor(s)/Destructor
34: //---------------------------------
35: CMainFrame::CMainFrame() {
36: }
37:
38: CMainFrame::~CMainFrame() {
39: }
40:
```

continues

LISTING 5.6 CONTINUED

```
41: //-------------------------------
42: // Public Member Functions
43: //-------------------------------
44: BOOL CMainFrame::Create(const CString& sTitle) {
45:   CString sClassName;
46:
47:   sClassName = AfxRegisterWndClass(CS_HREDRAW | CS_VREDRAW,
48:     ::LoadCursor(NULL, IDC_ARROW),
49:     (HBRUSH)::GetStockObject(LTGRAY_BRUSH),
50:     ::LoadIcon(AfxGetInstanceHandle(),
51:     MAKEINTRESOURCE(IDR_ANIMATOR)));
52:
53:   return CFrameWnd::Create(sClassName, sTitle);
54: }
55:
56: BOOL CMainFrame::PreCreateWindow(CREATESTRUCT& cs) {
57:   // Create a window without min/max buttons or sizable border
58:   cs.style = WS_OVERLAPPED | WS_SYSMENU | WS_BORDER;
59:
60:   // Set the window size
61:   cs.x = 5; cs.y = 5;
62:   cs.cx = 320; cs.cy = 320;
63:
64:   return CFrameWnd::PreCreateWindow(cs);
65: }
66:
67: //-------------------------------
68: // Message Handlers
69: //-------------------------------
70: int CMainFrame::OnCreate(LPCREATESTRUCT lpCreateStruct) {
71:   // Create and initialize the list box control
72:   RECT rc = { 5, 5, 180, 140 };
73:   m_AnimListBox.Create(WS_CHILD | WS_VISIBLE | LBS_STANDARD,
74:     rc, this, ID_LB_ANIMLISTBOX);
75:   m_AnimListBox.AddString("FileCopy.avi");
76:   m_AnimListBox.AddString("FileMove.avi");
77:   m_AnimListBox.AddString("FileDelete.avi");
78:   m_AnimListBox.AddString("FileTrash.avi");
79:   m_AnimListBox.AddString("EmptyTrash.avi");
80:   m_AnimListBox.AddString("FindFile.avi");
81:   m_AnimListBox.AddString("FindComputer.avi");
82:   m_AnimListBox.AddString("Search.avi");
83:
84:   // Create the button controls
85:   rc.left = 185; rc.top = 5; rc.right = 300; rc.bottom = 35;
86:   m_PlayButton.Create("Play", WS_CHILD | WS_VISIBLE | BS_PUSHBUTTON,
87:     rc, this, ID_PB_PLAY);
88:   rc.left = 185; rc.top = 40; rc.right = 300; rc.bottom = 70;
```

```
 89:    m_StopButton.Create("Stop", WS_CHILD | WS_VISIBLE | BS_PUSHBUTTON |
 90:      WS_DISABLED, rc, this, ID_PB_STOP);
 91:    rc.left = 185; rc.top = 75; rc.right = 300; rc.bottom = 105;
 92:    m_LoopCheckbox.Create("Loop", WS_CHILD | WS_VISIBLE |
 93:      BS_AUTOCHECKBOX, rc, this, ID_CK_LOOP);
 94:    rc.left = 185; rc.top = 110; rc.right = 300; rc.bottom = 140;
 95:    m_TransCheckbox.Create("Transparency", WS_CHILD | WS_VISIBLE |
 96:      BS_AUTOCHECKBOX, rc, this, ID_CK_TRANSPARENCY);
 97:
 98:    // Create the animation control
 99:    rc.left = 5; rc.top = 145; rc.right = 300; rc.bottom = 285;
100:    m_Animation.Create(WS_CHILD | WS_VISIBLE | WS_BORDER | ACS_CENTER,
101:      rc, this, ID_AN_ANIMATION);
102:
103:    // Set the focus to the list box
104:    m_AnimListBox.SetCurSel(0);
105:
106:    return 0;
107: }
108:
109: void CMainFrame::OnPBPlayClicked() {
110:    // Make sure an animation is selected
111:    if (m_AnimListBox.GetCurSel() != LB_ERR) {
112:      // Get the currently selected animation filename
113:      CString sAnimFile;
114:      m_AnimListBox.GetText(m_AnimListBox.GetCurSel(), sAnimFile);
115:
116:      // Determine if the animation is to be looped
117:      BOOL bLoop = (m_LoopCheckbox.GetCheck() == 1);
118:
119:      // Open and play the animation
120:      m_Animation.Open(sAnimFile);
121:      m_Animation.Play(0, -1, bLoop ? -1 : 1);
122:    }
123: }
124:
125: void CMainFrame::OnPBStopClicked() {
126:    // Stop playing the animation
127:    m_Animation.Stop();
128: }
129:
130: void CMainFrame::OnCKTransparencyClicked() {
131:    // Toggle the transparent style
132:    DWORD dwStyle = m_Animation.GetStyle();
133:    if (m_TransCheckbox.GetCheck() == 1)
134:      dwStyle |= ACS_TRANSPARENT;
135:    else
136:      dwStyle &= ~ACS_TRANSPARENT;
137:
138:    // Set the new style in the animation control
```

continues

LISTING 5.6   CONTINUED

```
139:     ::SetWindowLong(m_Animation.GetSafeHwnd(), GWL_STYLE, dwStyle);
140: }
141:
142: void CMainFrame::OnANStart() {
143:     // Enable/disable the controls when the animation starts
144:     m_AnimListBox.EnableWindow(FALSE);
145:     m_PlayButton.EnableWindow(FALSE);
146:     m_StopButton.EnableWindow(TRUE);
147:     m_LoopCheckbox.EnableWindow(FALSE);
148:     m_TransCheckbox.EnableWindow(FALSE);
149: }
150:
151: void CMainFrame::OnANStop() {
152:     // Enable/disable the controls when the animation stops
153:     m_AnimListBox.EnableWindow(TRUE);
154:     m_PlayButton.EnableWindow(TRUE);
155:     m_StopButton.EnableWindow(FALSE);
156:     m_LoopCheckbox.EnableWindow(TRUE);
157:     m_TransCheckbox.EnableWindow(TRUE);
158: }
```

First on the agenda is the message map, which associates all the message handlers with messages. The `ON_WM_CREATE` macro connects the `OnCreate()` message handler with the `WM_CREATE` message. The three `ON_BN_CLICKED` macros connect the Play, Stop, and Transparency Button controls to the `WM_COMMAND` message and the `BN_CLICKED` Button control notification. The last two `ON_CONTROL` macros connect the Animate control to the `ACN_START` and `ACN_STOP` notifications, which are also sent through the `WM_COMMAND` message.

The `Create()` member is clearly borrowed from the Skeleton application but with one important change: the background color is changed to light gray. This is accomplished by calling the `GetStockObject()` Win32 API function and retrieving a light gray brush. A brush is a graphical Windows resource that functions much like a paintbrush in the real world. The brush specified in the `Create()` member function is used to paint the background of the frame window.

NEW TERM   A *brush* is a graphical Windows resource that functions much like a paintbrush in the real world.

The `PreCreateWindow()` member function is overridden in order to alter the styles and size of the frame window. The styles are set so that the window doesn't have minimize or maximize buttons, or a sizable border. This is helpful because there is no reason for the window to be sizeable; allowing the user to resize the window would only cause problems accessing the controls.

Making Use of Controls

The `OnCreate()` member function tackles the creation and initialization of the controls. Every control requires a `RECT` structure as part of its creation parameters to indicate its rectangular position within the client area of the frame window. The ListBox control is the first control created in `OnCreate()`. The control is also initialized by adding a series of animation filename strings to it.

The buttons are then created; the push buttons are created using the `BS_PUSHBUTTON` style, whereas the check boxes are created with the `BS_CHECKBOX` style. The Stop button also uses the `WS_DISABLED` style so that it is initially created in the disabled state. The last control created is the Animate control. After creating this control, the first string in the ListBox control is selected.

The remainder of the member functions in the `CMainFrame` class are control notification message handlers. The `OnPBPlayClicked()` message handler gets the currently selected animation filename from the ListBox control and then plays it using the Animate control. In doing so, it examines the Loop check box to see if the animation is to be looped. The `OnPBStopClicked()` message handler simply stops the currently playing animation by calling the `Stop()` member function on the Animate control.

The `OnCKTransparencyClicked()` message handler is definitely the trickiest of the handlers. It toggles the transparency of the Animate control by tweaking the styles of the underlying Windows object. The Transparency check box is first examined to see whether the `ACS_TRANSPARENT` style is to be added or removed from the control. The newly altered style is then set using the `SetWindowLong()` Win32 API function.

The last two message handlers in `CMainFrame` are `OnANStart()` and `OnANStop()`, which are called when an animation starts and stops, respectively. The Animator application uses these message handlers to make the user interface a little more intuitive. More specifically, these handlers enable and disable all the controls except the Animate control to reflect the status of the animation. This results in the Stop button being disabled when an animation is not being played, which makes sense. Likewise, the ListBox control, Play Button control, and check boxes are disabled while an animation is playing.

That wraps up the Animator application! I realize it introduced a few tricks here and there, but overall it's pretty straightforward. Please spend some time going back over the code if it didn't click the first time through.

Summary

This hour introduced you to controls and the role they play as user interface building blocks. You learned about the different types of controls available for use in MFC, as well as how to use them. More specifically, you learned how to create controls and then respond to events that occur within them. You wrapped up the hour by building an application that relied on a variety of controls to play animations.

Q&A

Q Is there an easier way to position controls than the approach used in the Animator application?

A Yes. When you use controls in a dialog box you can specify their positions in a resource script. Furthermore, you can use a dialog editor to graphically position controls within a dialog box window, which makes the task very easy. Unfortunately, when you use controls directly in an application's main frame window, you have to position them by hand when they are created.

Q Why is `this` passed into the `Create()` member function when creating each control in the Animator application?

A Because controls are child windows, it is necessary to specify their parent window. In the Animator application the `CMainFrame` window is the parent of all the child controls. So, passing `this` from within a `CMainFrame` member function sets the parent window of each control to `CMainFrame`.

Workshop

The Workshop is designed to help you anticipate possible questions, review what you've learned, and begin thinking ahead to put your knowledge into practice. The answers to the quiz are in Appendix A, "Quiz Answers."

Quiz

1. What is a child window that performs a common, reusable function?
2. What are the two primary types of controls used to develop Windows applications?
3. What are the three types of buttons that can be created using the Button control?
4. What is a control notification?
5. What is the difference between traditional Windows controls and common controls?
6. What is the purpose of control identifiers?
7. Where is the best place to create a control in a frame window?
8. What two Windows messages are used to communicate control notifications?

9. What is a software component?
10. For what purpose is a brush used in the Animator application?

Exercises

1. Add a message map entry that responds to the `LBN_DBLCLK` ListBox notification, and have it call the `OnPBPlayClicked()` message handler. This change will enable you to double click an animation in the list box to play it.

   `ON_LBN_DBLCLK(ID_LB_ANIMLISTBOX, OnPBPlayClicked)`

2. Add a string to the ListBox control in the Animator application that allows you to play the animation named Drill.avi.

Hour 6

Using Common Dialog Boxes

This hour presents the Windows common dialog boxes, which offer a suite of standard user interfaces for performing common user interface tasks, such as selecting files for opening and saving. You learn about each of the different common dialog boxes available for use, along with how MFC provides classes for working with the dialogs in C++. You finish up the hour by adding common dialog support to the Animator application from the previous hour.

In this hour, you will learn

- About the different common dialog boxes available for use in Windows applications
- How MFC classes are used to create and manipulate common dialog boxes
- How to put common dialog boxes to use in an application

Origins of Common Dialog Boxes

There was a time in the early days of Windows when a graphical user interface was still a novelty. It was fun to use and even more fun to make jokes about an interesting new device called the mouse. Options for building a Windows application's user interface at that time were limited, consisting primarily of the traditional controls you learned about in the previous hour. Anything outside the boundaries of those controls had to be developed by hand. Oh, the good old days!

The Windows user interface has matured a great deal since the early versions. More importantly, the user interface has been standardized so that applications function similarly. This standardization is a result of Windows providing additional functionality that applications can leverage. By sharing a standard suite of user interface elements, Windows applications become more intuitive and are ultimately easier to learn and use.

To illustrate the point of user interface standardization, consider the File Open dialog box that is used so prominently in Windows applications. As recently as Windows 3.0, every Windows application had to provide its own implementation of the File Open dialog box. Not only did this require extra work for developers, but it also resulted in every application having a different user interface for opening files. In Windows 3.1, Microsoft remedied this problem by integrating a standard set of dialog boxes into the Windows API. These standard dialog boxes helped perform common user interface tasks such as opening files and selecting fonts. The dialog boxes were eventually carried over into the Win32 API and are now known as the common dialog boxes.

NEW TERM *Common dialog boxes* are a standard set of dialog boxes that help perform common user interface tasks such as opening files and selecting fonts.

Exploring the Common Dialog Boxes

The whole idea behind common dialog boxes is to encapsulate the functionality required to perform common user interface tasks such as opening files and selecting fonts. The Windows architects studied the most common user interface tasks and decided on a set of common dialog boxes that encompass a relatively wide range of functionality. Even though the common dialogs are designed to address specific needs, they are designed to be very customizable. As an example, you can specify the type of file and default file extension for the *File Open* dialog box, among other things.

Table 6.1 lists the different common dialog boxes supported in the Win32 API.

TABLE 6.1 WINDOWS COMMON DIALOG BOXES

Dialog Box	Description
File Open	Navigate to a directory and select a file to open
File Save As	Navigate to a directory and select a file to save
Color selection	Select a color from a palette of colors
Font selection	Select a font by setting font attributes
Find text	Enter text for a find operation
Replace text	Enter text for a replace operation
Page Setup	Setup the properties of a page
Print	Display the status of a print job

Most of the dialog boxes listed in the table are probably familiar to you already because they are widely used throughout Windows applications. Nonetheless, it's worth taking a look at each one to make sure you understand the role it plays in the standard Windows user interface.

> There are two main types of dialog boxes used in Windows: modal and modeless. Modal dialogs query the user for information and don't return control to an application until the user exits the dialog. They are called modal because they enforce somewhat of a dialog-input mode, which means that an application is inactive while the dialog box is in use. An example of a modal dialog box is the File Open dialog. Modeless dialog boxes don't enforce any kind of mode, which means that the user can still work in an application while a modeless dialog is in use. An example of a modeless dialog box is the Find dialog. Actually, the Find and Replace dialog boxes are the only two common dialogs that are modeless.

MFC Common Dialog Box Classes

Like all Win32 windows, MFC provides an object-oriented interface for working with common dialog boxes. More specifically, MFC provides a set of classes that serve as wrappers around the common dialog boxes. All the common dialog classes derive from a common base class, `CCommonDialog`. You rarely need to interact directly with the `CCommonDialog` class. Table 6.2 lists the MFC common dialog classes that derive from `CCommonDialog`, along with the Win32 dialog boxes for which they serve as wrappers.

TABLE 6.2 MFC COMMON DIALOG BOX CLASSES AND THE DIALOG BOXES WITH WHICH THEY ARE ASSOCIATED

MFC Class	Dialog Box
`CFileDialog`	File Open, File Save As
`CColorDialog`	Color selection
`CFontDialog`	Font selection
`CFindReplaceDialog`	Find text, Replace text
`CPageSetupDialog`	Page Setup
`CPrintDialog`	Print

Although the MFC common dialog boxes are wrappers around Win32, they give you full control over customizing each dialog box within a given application. Each MFC common dialog box class defines a constructor and a set of member functions for altering the attributes of the dialog box. Additionally, you can alter the resource for a common dialog box and manipulate the controls contained within.

Keep in mind that from the user's perspective the main benefit of common dialog boxes is their consistent appearance and functionality from application to application. Therefore, it is important that you customize a common dialog box only when it is absolutely necessary. Otherwise, the consistent appearance and benefits of a standardized user interface will cease to exist. In general, if you stick with customizing the custom dialogs by using only their member functions you will stay well within the bounds of retaining their standardized look and feel. Changing the window size and adding or removing controls is where you enter territory that could potentially harm the benefits of their standard appearance.

It's worth mentioning at this point that each common dialog box has an associated Win32 data structure that is used behind the scenes to coordinate the properties of the dialog box. In traditional Win32 programming you must create one of these data structures each time you use a common dialog box. MFC hides the details of the dialog data structures and provides an interface to many of the dialog box properties in the parameters to each dialog class's constructor. In other words, instead of creating a structure and filling out all its members, you can simply pass pertinent information about a dialog box to the constructor of the dialog box's MFC class.

File Open and File Save As

The `CFileDialog` class is used to invoke File Open and File Save As dialog boxes, which look almost identical; Figures 6.1 and 6.2 show each of them in action.

FIGURE 6.1

The File Open common dialog box.

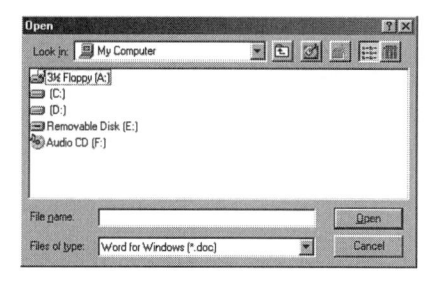

FIGURE 6.2

The File Save As common dialog box.

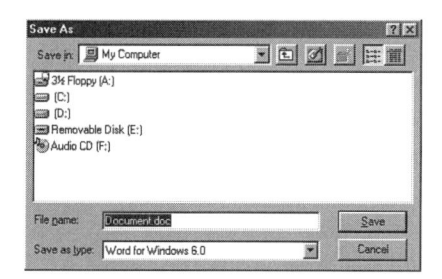

The File Open dialog box displays lists of drives, directories, and filename extensions from which the user can select to display a list of filenames. The user then has the option of typing a filename or selecting one from a list to identify the file to be opened. The File Save As dialog box works similarly but its purpose is to specify a file in which to save something. In terms of how the dialogs operate, the File Open dialog box checks to ensure that a file exists before allowing you to continue. If the file doesn't exist, the dialog box will inform you with an error message and wait for you to specify another file. The File Save As dialog box, on the other hand, expects no file to exist with the filename and path specified. If a file exists with the same name, you will receive a message asking if you want to overwrite the file.

The difference between the two dialog boxes might seem subtle, but it does dramatically impact how the dialog boxes are used. Even so, it's clear that the user interface for each dialog is really the same. For this reason, the Win32 API uses the same dialog box resource for each of these dialog boxes. In terms of MFC, you use the same MFC class to create both types of dialog boxes. You learn how to do this in a moment.

Color Selection

The `CColorDialog` class is used to invoke the Color selection dialog box, which allows the user to select a color from a palette of colors. Figure 6.3 shows the Color dialog box at work selecting a standard color.

FIGURE 6.3

Using the Edit Color selection common dialog box to select a standard color.

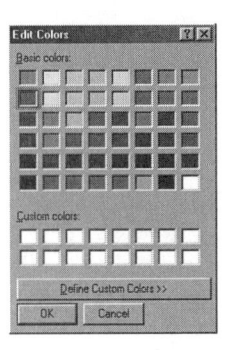

As you can see, the Color dialog box provides an intuitive user interface for selecting colors. This dialog box is useful in just about any application that allows the user to set the color of some graphical element. If the standard colors shown in the dialog box aren't enough, you can also define custom colors of your own. This is accomplished by clicking the Define Custom Colors button, which results in the dialog box expanding to reveal a custom color selector (see Figure 6.4).

FIGURE 6.4

Using the Edit Color selection common dialog box to select a custom color.

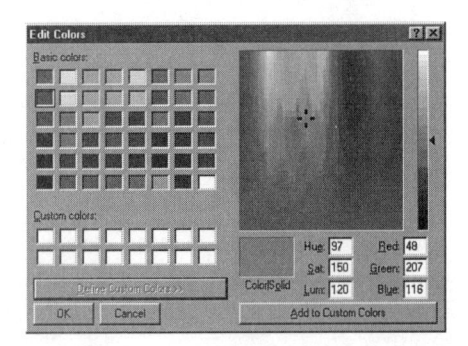

Custom colors are selected by moving a cross-hair over the range of colors in the right side of the dialog box. A custom color can immediately be selected by clicking the OK button, or you can add it to the custom color palette by clicking the Add to Custom Colors button. The custom color palette is preserved throughout an application session.

Font Selection

Similar to colors, fonts are also commonly selected and customized in Windows applications. The `CFontDialog` class is used to invoke the Font selection dialog box, which allows the user to modify many font attributes (see Figure 6.5).

FIGURE 6.5

The Font selection common dialog box.

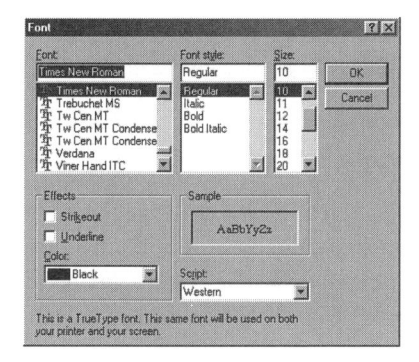

The Font dialog box allows you to modify the font family (name), font style, font size, font effects, and font color for a particular font. It also displays a sample of the font so you can see what you've selected before accepting the selection. This is a nice touch that makes the dialog box much handier to use.

Find Text and Replace Text

If you're like me and you find yourself sitting in front of a word processor for hours on end, you've no doubt come to appreciate find and replace text functions. The `CFindReplaceDialog` class is used to invoke the Find text and Replace text common dialog boxes, which provide simple and effective user interfaces for entering text to be found or replaced. Figures 6.6 and 6.7 show the Find and Replace dialog boxes.

FIGURE 6.6

The Find text common dialog box.

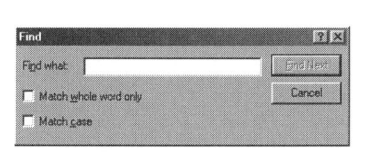

FIGURE 6.7

The Replace text common dialog box.

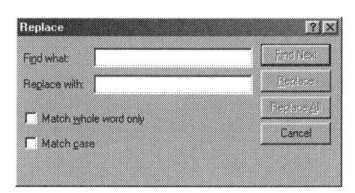

The Find dialog box allows the user to type in a string to find. The user can also specify search options such as the search direction and whether the search is case-sensitive. The Replace dialog box is similar to the Find dialog but has an additional edit control for entering text to replace the found text. The Replace dialog box allows the user to type in a string to find and a replacement string. Like the Find dialog, the user can specify search options, but they can also specify replacement options such as the scope of replacement.

Page Setup

The `CPageSetupDialog` class is used to invoke the Page Setup dialog box, which is used to setup page properties that an application uses for printing a paginated document. The page setup for an application impacts how a page is printed because it involves information such as page orientation and paper size. Figure 6.8 shows the Page Setup common dialog box.

FIGURE 6.8
The Page Setup common dialog box.

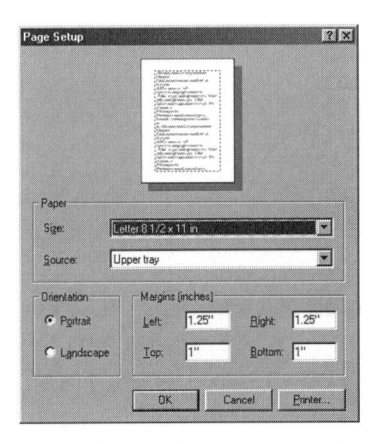

The Page Setup dialog box allows the user to modify page setup information such as page orientation, paper size, paper source, and margins. The Page Setup dialog also includes a Printer button that allows the user to modify printer properties. This actually invokes a Printer Properties dialog box that is managed by the Windows system. This is the same Printer Properties dialog box that is invoked from the Printers folder in Windows Explorer.

> The Win32 API also defines a Print Setup common dialog box that performs a very similar function as the Page Setup dialog box. The Print Setup dialog is provided for backward compatibility with earlier versions of Windows and shouldn't be used. Instead, just stick with the Page Setup dialog box.

Print

The last common dialog box is the Print dialog box, which is invoked using the `CPrintDialog` class. The Print dialog box is used to control parameters related to the printing of a document. Figure 6.9 shows the Print common dialog box.

FIGURE 6.9

The Print common dialog box.

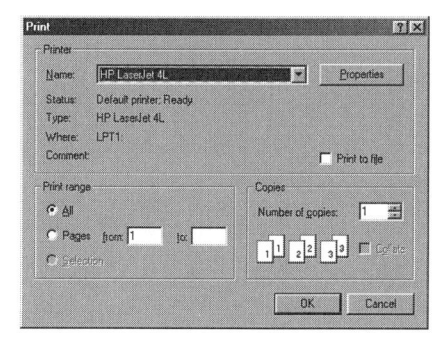

The Print common dialog box displays information about the installed printer and its configuration, and allows the user to select print job options such as the range of pages to print and the number of copies. The Print dialog also serves as the starting point for initiating the printing process.

Using Common Dialog Boxes

For the functionality that they provide, you might be surprised at how easy it is to create and manipulate common dialog boxes in MFC. Using common dialog boxes in MFC typically involves three steps:

1. Create a dialog box object using an MFC wrapper class, making sure to initialize the dialog by passing parameters to the object's constructor.
2. Call the `DoModal()` member function on the object; the return value from `DoModal()` indicates how the dialog box was exited (`IDOK` or `IDCANCEL`).
3. If the `DoModal()` function returns `IDOK`, retrieve the user's selections using `GetXXXX()` member functions.

> This discussion on creating and using common dialog boxes focuses solely on modal dialogs, which include all the common dialog boxes except the Find and Replace dialogs. Modeless dialog boxes are trickier to work with and are ultimately beyond the scope of this hour.

The first step to creating a common dialog box simply involves creating an object for the dialog box from one of the MFC dialog box classes. Following is an example of creating a File Open dialog box object using the `CFileDialog` class:

```
CFileDialog dlg(TRUE);
```

The only parameter passed into the constructor is a Boolean that indicates whether the dialog box is File Open or File Save As. This is necessary because the `CFileDialog` class is used for both dialog boxes. Passing `TRUE` for this parameter results in a File Open dialog box, whereas `FALSE` results in File Save As. There are other parameters for the `CFileDialogBox` constructor that you can use to customize the dialog box, but they have default values that are often suitable.

The second step is what actually invokes a dialog box. When you call the `DoModal()` member function on a common dialog, the dialog box is displayed and the application goes inactive. The dialog box has complete control until the user exits the dialog by clicking the OK or Cancel button. Following is an example of invoking the File Open dialog box you created a moment ago:

```
dlg.DoModal();
```

The third step involves processing the results of the dialog box to determine what information the user provided. The key is to first look at the return value of the `DoModal()` function because this value identifies which button the user clicked to close the dialog. A return value of `IDOK` indicates that the OK button was clicked, whereas `IDCANCEL` means that the user clicked the Cancel button. If `DoModal()` returns `IDCANCEL`, you know you can go on about your business because the user changed their mind about providing information to the dialog box. However, if it returns `IDOK`, you must query the dialog class for information provided by the user. Listing 6.1 shows how to get the filename of a file selected using the File Open dialog box.

LISTING 6.1 RETRIEVING THE FILENAME OF A FILE SELECTED USING THE FILE OPEN DIALOG BOX

```
1: CFileDialog dlg(TRUE);
2: if (dlg.DoModal() == IDOK)
3:    CString s = dlg.GetFileName();
```

In this example, the `GetFileName()` member function is called to get the filename selected. Notice that this information is retrieved after the dialog exits from the `DoModal()` function. Each MFC dialog class provides member functions for getting information specific to the context of the dialog boxes.

Opening Files

Now that you have an understanding of how to use the common dialog boxes with MFC, let's look at a practical example of how to use them. In the previous hour you developed an application called Animator that allowed you to select an animation file from a list box and play it using the Animate control. The remainder of this hour focuses on the development of the Animator2 application, which adds a couple of neat features to Animator. The first change has to do with the fact that in Animator the user has to select from a predetermined group of animation files in a list box. It would be better if the application also allowed you to open animation files from anywhere you want using the File Open common dialog box.

You need some intuitive way of invoking the File Open dialog box. Instead of adding an *Open* button to the application, it would be neat to add a special list box entry that indicates you want to browse and select a file. It is standard Windows practice to use an ellipsis (...) to indicate that a command invokes a dialog box. So, why not use an ellipsis entry in the list box as an indication that an animation file is to be selected via the File Open dialog box? Adding the following line of code to the `CMainFrame::OnCreate()` member function does the trick:

```
m_AnimListBox.AddString("...");
```

Just in case you aren't sure how this line of code fits into the `OnCreate()` member function, Listing 6.2 shows the new version of the function in its entirety.

LISTING 6.2 THE `CMainFrame::OnCreate()` MEMBER FUNCTION FOR THE ANIMATOR2 APPLICATION

```
 1: int CMainFrame::OnCreate(LPCREATESTRUCT lpCreateStruct) {
 2:   // Create and initialize the list box control
 3:   RECT rc = { 5, 5, 180, 140 };
 4:   m_AnimListBox.Create(WS_CHILD | WS_VISIBLE | LBS_STANDARD,
 5:     rc, this, ID_LB_ANIMLISTBOX);
 6:   m_AnimListBox.AddString("...");
 7:   m_AnimListBox.AddString("FileCopy.avi");
 8:   m_AnimListBox.AddString("FileMove.avi");
 9:   m_AnimListBox.AddString("FileDelete.avi");
10:   m_AnimListBox.AddString("FileTrash.avi");
11:   m_AnimListBox.AddString("EmptyTrash.avi");
12:   m_AnimListBox.AddString("FindFile.avi");
13:   m_AnimListBox.AddString("FindComputer.avi");
14:   m_AnimListBox.AddString("Search.avi");
15:   m_AnimListBox.AddString("Drill.avi");
16:
17:   // Create the button controls
```

continues

LISTING 6.2   CONTINUED

```
18:      rc.left = 185; rc.top = 5; rc.right = 300; rc.bottom = 35;
19:      m_PlayButton.Create("Play", WS_CHILD | WS_VISIBLE | BS_PUSHBUTTON,
20:        rc, this, ID_PB_PLAY);
21:      rc.left = 185; rc.top = 40; rc.right - 300; rc.bottom = 70;
22:      m_StopButton.Create("Stop", WS_CHILD | WS_VISIBLE | BS_PUSHBUTTON |
23:        WS_DISABLED, rc, this, ID_PB_STOP);
24:      rc.left = 185; rc.top = 75; rc.right = 300; rc.bottom = 105;
25:      m_LoopCheckbox.Create("Loop", WS_CHILD | WS_VISIBLE |
26:        BS_AUTOCHECKBOX, rc, this, ID_CK_LOOP);
27:      rc.left = 185; rc.top = 110; rc.right = 300; rc.bottom = 140;
28:      m_TransCheckbox.Create("Transparency", WS_CHILD | WS_VISIBLE |
29:        BS_AUTOCHECKBOX, rc, this, ID_CK_TRANSPARENCY);
30:
31:      // Create the animation control
32:      rc.left = 5; rc.top = 145; rc.right = 300; rc.bottom = 285;
33:      m_Animation.Create(WS_CHILD | WS_VISIBLE | WS_BORDER | ACS_CENTER,
34:        rc, this, ID_AN_ANIMATION);
35:
36:      // Set the focus to the list box
37:      m_AnimListBox.SetCurSel(0);
38:
39:      return 0;
40:  }
```

Of course, adding the ellipsis list box entry doesn't actually invoke the dialog box; you still have to add some code to the `CMainFrame::OnPBPlayClicked()` member function. Checking to see if the user selected the ellipsis item in the list box is as simple as adding an `If` statement to the `OnPBPlayClicked()` member function. The body of the `If` statement is where you invoke the File Open common dialog box. Listing 6.3 contains the code for the new and improved `OnPBPlayClicked()` member function.

LISTING 6.3   THE `CMainFrame::OnPBPlayClicked()` MEMBER FUNCTION FOR THE ANIMATOR2 APPLICATION

```
 1:  void CMainFrame::OnPBPlayClicked() {
 2:      // Make sure an animation is selected
 3:      if (m_AnimListBox.GetCurSel() != LB_ERR) {
 4:          // Get the currently selected animation filename
 5:          CString sAnimFile;
 6:          m_AnimListBox.GetText(m_AnimListBox.GetCurSel(), sAnimFile);
 7:
 8:          // Check to see if "..." was selected
 9:          if (sAnimFile == "...") {
10:              // Select an animation filename using the File Open dialog box
11:              CFileDialog dlg(TRUE, "avi");
```

```
12:            if (dlg.DoModal() == IDOK)
13:                sAnimFile = dlg.GetFileName();
14:            else
15:                return;
16:        }
17:
18:        // Determine if the animation is to be looped
19:        BOOL bLoop = (m_LoopCheckbox.GetCheck() == 1);
20:
21:        // Open and play the animation
22:        m_Animation.Open(sAnimFile);
23:        m_Animation.Play(0, -1, bLoop ? -1 : 1);
24:    }
25: }
```

The == operator is used to see if the selected list box item file matches the ellipsis. This operator is an overloaded operator defined in the `CString` MFC class, which represents text strings. If the ellipsis has been selected, then a `CFileDialog` object is created. The first parameter to the dialog's constructor, `TRUE`, indicates that the dialog box is a File Open dialog as opposed to a File Save As dialog. The second parameter, `"avi"`, indicates the default file extension to be used if the user doesn't specify one when selecting a file.

If the user clicks the OK button in the File Open dialog box, the filename of the selected file is retrieved and stored in the `sAnimFile` variable, and the animation is opened and played. If not, the `OnPBPlayClicked()` member function returns without doing anything more; the user clicking the Cancel button is an indication that no animation is to be played.

Selecting Color

The addition of the File Open dialog box to the Animator application is a very practical improvement. Although I'm all for practicality, I'm now making a change that has more to do with fun than being practical. I thought it might be interesting to use the Color common dialog box to enable the user to select a new background color for the application's frame window. An easy way to invoke the dialog box is by detecting a right mouse click anywhere on the frame window.

The first step in making this application enhancement is to add a right mouse button message map entry to the `CMainFrame` class, like this:

`ON_WM_RBUTTONUP()`

This message map entry requires an associated message handler function declaration in the header file. Following is the declaration for the `OnRButtonUp()` message handler:

```
afx_msg void  OnRButtonUp(UINT nFlags, CPoint point);
```

The real work takes place in the implementation of the `OnRButtonUp()` message handler, which is shown in Listing 6.4.

LISTING 6.4 THE `CMainFrame::OnRButtonUp()` MEMBER FUNCTION FOR THE ANIMATOR2 APPLICATION

```
 1: void CMainFrame::OnRButtonUp(UINT nFlags, CPoint point) {
 2:   // Select a background color using the Color dialog box
 3:   CColorDialog dlg(RGB(192, 192, 192));
 4:   if (dlg.DoModal() == IDOK) {
 5:     // Set the new background color for the frame window
 6:     CBrush brBackground(dlg.GetColor());
 7:     ::SetClassLong(GetSafeHwnd(), GCL_HBRBACKGROUND,
 8:       (LONG)(HBRUSH)brBackground);
 9:     Invalidate();
10:   }
11: }
```

The `OnRButtonUp()` message handler first creates a `CColorDialog` object, which is necessary for invoking a Color selection dialog box. The parameter to the constructor identifies the default color that is initially selected when the dialog is invoked. The RGB value (`192, 192, 192`) is the light gray color that serves as the default for most windows. You can tinker with RGB values in the Color dialog box when creating custom colors.

> In Windows, colors are formed by combining varying intensities of the colors red, green, and blue. This color system is known as RGB (Red Green Blue) and is standard across most graphical computer systems. Each component (red, green, and blue) of a color is represented by a number in the range 0–255. The Win32 API defines a macro called RGB that packs these three numeric color components into a single 32-bit number that is suitable for most color operations. This 32-bit color representation is known as a COLORREF value.

The Color dialog box is invoked with a call to the `DoModal()` member function. If the user clicks OK, the selected color is retrieved from the dialog object with a call to `GetColor()`. This color is used as the basis for creating a brush, which is then set as the frame window's background brush. The frame window is then invalidated with a call to `Invalidate()`, which results in it repainting itself in the new background color. Incidentally, you learn more about window invalidation and painting in Hour 9, "Drawing Graphics."

Summary

In this hour you learned about common dialog boxes and how they improve the Windows user interface. You found out that common dialog boxes help to make Windows applications more consistent and predictable by providing standard user interfaces for commonly performed tasks. You also learned about the MFC classes that provide a C++ interface for working with the common dialog boxes. Finally, you finished up the hour by modifying the Animator application to support a couple of common dialog boxes.

Q&A

Q Do I have to add anything special to my resource file to accommodate common dialog boxes?

A No. Although the common dialog boxes certainly utilize dialog box resources behind the scenes, these resources are already defined within the Windows API. All an application must do in order to use the dialog box is create the appropriate MFC wrapper object for a common dialog. It is worth mentioning that an application can replace the resource for a common dialog box to alter its functionality, but this should be avoided because it defeats the whole purpose of a standardized user interface.

Q How do I detect an error if one occurs within a common dialog box?

A The return values from the `DoModal()` member function don't indicate errors, so you must use a special Win32 function to check for common dialog box errors. More specifically, a return value of `IDCANCEL` isn't distinguishable from an error, so you must call the Win32 `CommDlgExtendedError()` function to see if an error occurred. This function defines a set of error codes that indicate a wide range of errors.

Workshop

The Workshop is designed to help you anticipate possible questions, review what you've learned, and begin thinking ahead to put your knowledge into practice. The answers to the quiz are in Appendix A, "Quiz Answers."

Quiz

1. What is a common dialog box?
2. What version of Windows introduced common dialog boxes?
3. What are the two main types of dialog boxes used in Windows?

4. From what common base class do all common dialog box classes derive?
5. What common dialog boxes are wrapped by the `CFileDialog` class?
6. What is used behind the scenes to coordinate the properties of a common dialog box?
7. How do you initially set the properties of a common dialog box?
8. What member function do you call to invoke a modal common dialog box?
9. How do you know if the user clicked the OK button to exit a common dialog box?
10. What does the first parameter of the `CFileDialog` constructor specify?

Exercises

1. Modify the `CMainFrame::OnRButtonUp()` member function in Animator2 so that the background color is stored in a static variable. Use this variable to set the initial color in the Color dialog box so that it reflects the current color of the frame window.

2. Pass an additional parameter to the constructor for the `CFileDialog` object in the `CMainFrame::OnPBPlayClicked()` member function of Animator2 so that the initial filename selected is `*.avi`.

HOUR 7

Retrieving Information with Custom Dialog Boxes

Dialog boxes are typically used to obtain information from the user that can't be retrieved through a simple menu selection. Dialog boxes are different than other types of windows because Windows takes on much of the management of the child controls in a dialog box. Although you learned about common dialog boxes in the previous hour, you haven't explored custom dialog boxes. This hour focuses on how to create and use custom dialog boxes.

In this hour, you will learn

- How to use message boxes as a primitive form of custom dialog box
- About MFC's support for custom dialog boxes
- How to assemble a dialog box resource
- How to create and invoke a dialog box

Using Message Boxes

Although the focus of this hour is on retrieving information with custom dialog boxes, it's worth starting the hour by learning about message boxes. Message boxes without a doubt provide the easiest way to create a primitive type of custom dialog box. The catch is that message boxes are limited in the degree to which they can be customized. You are no doubt familiar with message boxes due to their common usage in Windows. Figure 7.1 shows a message box that you might have seen before.

FIGURE 7.1

The Save confirmation message box in WordPad.

The message box in the figure is used in many applications in response to the user closing a document without saving. This message box is a standard part of Windows and can be easily created and manipulated to get simple input from the user. The `MessageBox()` member function, which is defined in the `CWnd` class, is the key to using message boxes:

```
int MessageBox(LPCTSTR lpszText, LPCTSTR lpszCaption = NULL,
➥UINT nType = MB_OK);
```

The first parameter to `MessageBox()` is the text message displayed in the message box. The second parameter is the text caption displayed in the message box's caption bar. Accepting the default value of `NULL` results in the message box displaying the application name. The last parameter to `MessageBox()` is the style of the message box, which is a combination of standard message box styles. There are four different types of message box styles, the first of which determines the type of the message box:

- `MB_ABORTRETRYIGNORE`—the message box contains Abort, Retry, and Ignore buttons
- `MB_OK`—the message box contains a single OK button
- `MB_OKCANCEL`—the message box contains OK and Cancel buttons
- `MB_RETRYCANCEL`—the message box contains Retry and Cancel buttons
- `MB_YESNO`—the message box contains Yes and No buttons
- `MB_YESNOCANCEL`—the message box contains Yes, No, and Cancel buttons

The second type of message box style determines the modality of a message box:

- `MB_APPLMODAL`—the user must respond to the message box before continuing work in the current window, but they are free to move to other applications (this is the default modality style)

- `MB_SYSTEMMODAL`—all applications are suspended until the user responds to the message box

The third type of message box style determines the icon displayed in a message box:

- `MB_ICONEXCLAMATION`—an exclamation-point icon
- `MB_ICONQUESTION`—a question-mark icon
- `MB_ICONINFORMATION`—an icon displaying the letter "i" in a circle
- `MB_ICONSTOP`—an icon displaying the letter "x" in a circle

The last type of message box style determines which button is the default button for the dialog box:

- `MB_DEFBUTTON1`—the first button is the default (this is the default button style)
- `MB_DEFBUTTON2`—the second button is the default
- `MB_DEFBUTTON3`—the third button is the default

> You are capable of declaring any button within a dialog box as the default button. The significance of a default dialog box button is that it can be pushed by using the Enter key on the keyboard. Typically the OK button is declared as the default button for most dialog boxes, in which case pressing the Enter key yields the same effect as clicking the OK button.

The style for a message box can consist of one of each of the previous style types. However, in most cases you will only need to specify the type of message box and the icon displayed within it. Following is an example of how to create a message box with OK and Cancel buttons and a stop-sign icon:

```
MessageBox("Would you like to continue?", "My Application",
  MB_OKCANCEL | MB_ICONSTOP);
```

The return value of this function is either `IDOK` or `IDCANCEL` depending on which button the user pushes to exit the message box. The `MessageBox()` member function is also capable of returning `IDYES`, `IDNO`, `IDABORT`, `IDRETRY`, or `IDIGNORE` if you specify that those buttons are to be used in a message box.

Modal and Modeless Dialog Boxes

In the previous hour I briefly mentioned the distinction between modal and modeless dialog boxes. Let's revisit this topic to make sure you understand the difference between these two primary types of dialog boxes. Modal dialogs are by far the most commonly used type of dialog box. Modal dialog boxes query the user for information and do not return control to an application until the user exits the dialog. An About dialog box such as the one in Figure 7.2 is a good example of a modal dialog box because you can't interact with the application window until you click the OK button and exit the dialog box.

FIGURE 7.2

The About dialog box in Notepad.

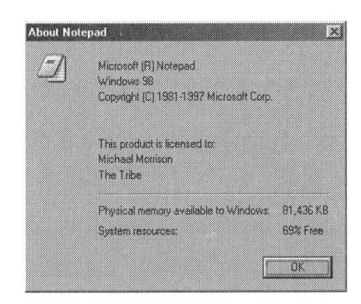

Modal dialog boxes are called "modal" because they enforce somewhat of a dialog-input mode, which means that an application is inactive while the dialog box is in use. You can think of a modal dialog box as a window to which you must provide information before continuing on with an application task. Another good example of a modal dialog box is the File Open dialog, which requires you to select a file before exiting the dialog box.

Unlike their modal counterparts, modeless dialog boxes don't enforce any kind of input mode. This means that the user can still work in an application while a modeless dialog is in use. Information that is provided to a modeless dialog box typically isn't critical to performing a given task. Examples of modeless dialog boxes include the Find dialog box and the Replace dialog box used in word processors and text editing applications such as the standard Windows WordPad and Notepad. Figure 7.3 shows the Find dialog box as used in the Notepad application.

FIGURE 7.3

The Find dialog box in Notepad.

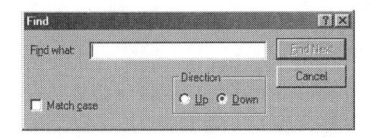

NEW TERM A *modal dialog box* is a dialog box that requires the user to close the dialog box before accessing any other windows in an application.

NEW TERM A *modeless dialog box* is a dialog box that allows the user to access other windows in an application.

From a programming perspective, modeless dialog boxes are considerably more difficult to work with than modal dialog boxes. This is because a modeless dialog must run concurrently with the application in which it appears. In other words, you have to address the complications that arise when a user interacts with an application while the dialog box is displayed. Modal dialog boxes don't have this complication because they don't enable users to interact with any other part of an application while they are being used.

MFC Dialog Box Support

Like most Win32 user interface elements, MFC provides rich support for creating and using custom dialog boxes. MFC's dialog box support starts with the `CDialog` class, which serves as the basis for all custom dialog box classes. The `CDialog` class provides a base level of support necessary to carry out general functions of a dialog box.

Unlike other MFC window objects, an instantiated `CDialog` objects consists of a combination of a dialog box resource and a dialog box class derived from `CDialog`. In other words, a `CDialog` object requires a dialog box resource to define the structure of the dialog box, along with a customized class derived from `CDialog`. A dialog box resource is defined in an application's resource file, and specifies the layout of and controls used within a dialog box. The composition of dialog boxes is interesting because it is defined using resources (dialog resources). Contrast this with an application's frame window, for example, which requires you to manually create all controls used in the window.

> Dialog box resources are also sometimes referred to as dialog box templates. So, if you ever run across a "dialog box template," you can rest easy in knowing that it is the same thing as a dialog box resource.

Dialog Box Data

Dialog boxes are perfectly capable of storing data using member variables. It is often beneficial to associate a dialog box's member variables with controls used in the dialog box. MFC provides a special mechanism called dialog data exchange (DDX) that automatically converts and transfers the state of controls to dialog box member variables. MFC also allows you to perform validations (DDV) on member variables that are connected to dialog controls. You learn how to use dialog data exchange a little later in the hour.

New Term: A *dialog data exchange* is a special mechanism that automatically converts and transfers the state of controls to dialog box member variables.

Dialog Box Messaging

The `CDialog` class is derived from `CWnd`, which means that dialog boxes are capable of performing the same types of operations as traditional windows. Like any other window, dialog boxes receive messages from Windows. The messages most commonly handled by a dialog box are notification messages sent from the dialog's controls. These notification messages are associated with message handler member functions using message maps, with which you already have some experience.

Creating a `CDialog` Object

Creating a `CDialog` object is as simple as using one of the constructors provided by the `CDialog` class:

```
CDialog(LPCTSTR lpszTemplateName, CWnd* pParentWnd = NULL);
CDialog(UINT nIDTemplate, CWnd* pParentWnd = NULL);
CDialog();
```

The first constructor creates a `CDialog` object based on the dialog resource name provided as the first parameter, `lpszTemplateName`. The second parameter is an optional parent window for the dialog box. The default value of `NULL` results in the main application window being used as the dialog's parent. The second constructor is similar to the first constructor except the dialog box resource is identified with an integer ID as opposed to a string name. Finally, the last constructor is simply a default constructor and doesn't handle associating a resource with the dialog object.

Although you will derive your own specific dialog classes from `CDialog`, it is very important that you call one of the first two `CDialog` constructors and identify the dialog box resource. You will carry out this task in the constructor for your dialog box class, in which case you simply call the `CDialog` constructor and pass in a string resource name or integer resource identifier.

Dialog Box Resources

Dialog box resources define the structure and layout of dialog boxes. These resources appear within an application's resource file along with other application resource definitions. Dialog box resources must be defined using the `DIALOG` resource statement, which enforces a standard format for specifying dialog attributes such as the caption, size, and controls appearing in a dialog box. Listing 7.1 shows the format of the `DIALOG` resource statement.

Listing 7.1 The Format of the DIALOG Resource Statement

```
1: DialogName DIALOG X, Y, Width, Height
2: CAPTION Caption
3: STYLE Styles
4: FONT FontSize, FontName
5: BEGIN
6:     ControlList
7: END
```

The `DIALOG` resource statement defines all the structural attributes of a dialog box. The statement begins with the name of the dialog box, which is specified in `DialogName`. The location if the upper-left corner of the dialog box is specified in *X* and *Y*. Additionally, the width and height of the dialog box are specified in Width and Height.

The caption that appears in a dialog box's caption bar is specified in `Caption`. Now things get slightly trickier. Dialog boxes, like other windows, have styles that determine what they look like and how they operate. Styles identifies the styles for the dialog box. There are lots of different dialog box styles, so I won't try to cover them all. Instead, check out the following list of styles commonly used in dialog boxes:

- `DS_MODALFRAME`—creates a dialog box with a non-sizeable border
- `WS_POPUP`—creates a pop-up window
- `WS_CAPTION`—creates a window with a caption bar
- `WS_SYSMENU`—creates a window with a system menu

The first style is what gives dialog boxes their familiar border that doesn't enable you to resize them. The last three styles aren't specific to dialog boxes only, but because dialog boxes are really just windows, they work fine.

> In addition to the `DIALOG` resource statement, there is also a `DIALOGEX` resource statement that allows you to specify extended dialog box information such as context sensitive help identifiers for dialog box controls. The `DIALOGEX` statement also allows you to use extended control styles, which are often useful.

Getting back to the `DIALOG` resource statement, the font of a dialog box is specified in `FontSize` and `FontName`. Finally, the remainder of a dialog resource definition consists of the individual controls contained within a dialog box (`ControlList`). `ControlList` consists of a list of controls, along with their respective locations, sizes, and styles.

Following is an example of defining OK and Cancel buttons within a dialog box resource:

```
DEFPUSHBUTTON  "OK",      IDOK,     162,  7, 50, 14
PUSHBUTTON     "Cancel",  IDCANCEL, 162, 24, 50, 14
```

As you can see, the OK button is identified as the default button and is given an identifier of IDOK. Its upper left corner is located at the relative position (162, 7) in the dialog box. Also, the OK button is 50 pixels wide and 14 pixels in height. The Cancel button has the identifier IDCANCEL, the position (162, 24), and is 50 pixels wide and 14 pixels in height.

All dialog box controls are defined using this approach. There are a variety of control types you can use to define different controls. These control types are used in the same capacity as DEFPUSHBUTTON and PUSHBUTTON in the previous example. You see some of these control types in action later in the hour when you create a dialog box resource for a financial application.

> Although it is certainly valuable to understand the intricate details of a how a dialog box resource is laid out, it isn't really practical to code them by hand. The physical positioning of controls is simply too difficult to accurately carry out with straight coding. For this reason, I encourage you to use a visual dialog box editor to create dialog box resources. I used the dialog box editor in Visual C++ to create the dialog box resources for this book. The only problem with dialog box editors is that they typically will overwrite the resource file and also attempt to make changes to your Resource.h header file. For this reason, I create dialog box resources in a temporary resource file and then copy the code over to my own application resource file. That way the dialog editor doesn't get the opportunity to monkey around with my resource code.

Building Simple Dialog Boxes

Building and integrating a custom dialog box into an application involves a few simple steps. The first step is creating the dialog box resource and adding it to the application's resource file. You also have to define identifiers used to uniquely identify the different child controls used in the dialog box; these identifiers are declared in the Resource.h header file. In addition to creating a dialog resource, you must also create a custom dialog box class that derives from the CDialog class. After the dialog box class is created, you are free to create a dialog box object from application code. Following is a summary of the steps required to create a custom dialog box for an application:

1. Create a dialog box resource in the application's resource script.
2. Declare identifiers in the Resource.h header file.
3. Create a custom dialog box class that derives from `CDialog`.
4. Invoke the dialog box from application code.

You've already learned how to complete the first three steps, so let's focus on invoking dialog boxes. In the previous hour, you learned how to invoke common dialog boxes using the `DoModal()` member function; this same function is used to invoke custom dialog boxes. When you call the `DoModal()` member function on a custom dialog, the dialog box is displayed and the application goes inactive. The dialog box has complete control until the user exits the dialog by clicking a suitable button. When a dialog box exits, it returns a code indicating which button was pushed to exit.

Applications must look at the return value of the `DoModal()` function to determine which button the user clicked to close the dialog. A return value of `IDOK` indicates that the OK button was clicked, whereas `IDCANCEL` means that the user clicked the Cancel button. A custom dialog box can also return a custom value if you want to use buttons other than OK and Cancel. After a custom dialog box returns from the `DoModal()` function, you are free to interact with dialog data using the dialog box object just as you did with common dialog boxes in the previous hour.

The remainder of the hour uses the steps you just learned in this section to create a custom dialog box and integrate it with a financial application named Finance.

Creating the Dialog Box Resource

The Finance application contains two dialog boxes: Personal Information and About. The Personal Information dialog box is a custom dialog box that retrieves information including a person's name and investment strategy. The About dialog box is roughly the same dialog box you created back in Hour 3, and is shown in Figure 7.4. I thought it was worth reusing in the Finance application because you now understand much more about how it works. The Personal Information dialog box is shown in Figure 7.5. Listing 7.2 contains the resource identifiers defined in the Resource.h header file, which includes identifiers used by the two custom dialog boxes.

FIGURE 7.4

The About dialog box in Finance.

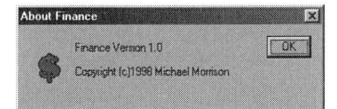

FIGURE 7.5

The Personal Information dialog box in Finance.

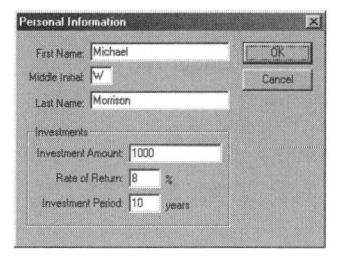

LISTING 7.2 THE RESOURCE IDENTIFIERS DEFINED IN THE RESOURCE.H HEADER FILE

```
 1: //--------------------------------
 2: // Strings                 Range : 1000 - 1999
 3: //--------------------------------
 4: #define IDR_FINANCE         1000
 5:
 6: //--------------------------------
 7: // Commands                Range : 2000 - 2999
 8: //--------------------------------
 9: #define ID_FILE_PERSONALINFO 2000
10:
11: //--------------------------------
12: // Dialog Boxes            Range : 3000 - 3999
13: //--------------------------------
14: #define IDD_PERSONALINFOBOX  3000
15: #define IDD_ABOUTBOX         3001
16:
17: //--------------------------------
18: // Controls                Range : 4000 - 4999
19: //--------------------------------
20: #define IDC_FNAME            4000
21: #define IDC_MINITIAL         4001
22: #define IDC_LNAME            4002
23: #define IDC_AMOUNT           4003
24: #define IDC_RETURNRATE       4004
25: #define IDC_PERIOD           4005
```

The `IDD_PERSONALINFOBOX` and `IDD_ABOUTBOX` identifiers are used to identify the two custom dialog box resources. The various `IDC_XXXX` identifiers are used to identify controls within the Personal Information dialog box. All these identifiers are used in the dialog box resources located in the application's resource file. Listing 7.3 contains the resource definition for the Personal Information dialog box.

LISTING 7.3 THE PERSONAL INFORMATION DIALOG BOX RESOURCE DEFINITION

```
 1: IDD_PERSONALINFOBOX DIALOGEX 0, 0, 219, 137
 2: CAPTION "Personal Information"
 3: STYLE DS_MODALFRAME | WS_POPUP | WS_CAPTION | WS_SYSMENU
 4: FONT 8, "MS Sans Serif"
 5: BEGIN
 6:    RTEXT          "First Name:", IDC_STATIC, 7, 10, 42, 8, 0
 7:    EDITTEXT       IDC_FNAME, 53, 7, 99, 12
 8:    RTEXT          "Middle Initial:", IDC_STATIC, 7, 25, 42, 8, 0
 9:    EDITTEXT       IDC_MINITIAL, 53, 22, 16, 12
10:    RTEXT          "Last Name:", IDC_STATIC, 7, 42, 42, 8, 0
11:    EDITTEXT       IDC_LNAME, 53, 38, 99, 12
12:    GROUPBOX       "Investments", IDC_STATIC, 7, 60, 146, 65
13:    RTEXT          "Investment Amount:", IDC_STATIC, 13, 74, 64, 8, 0
14:    RTEXT          "Rate of Return:", IDC_STATIC, 13, 90, 64, 8, 0
15:    EDITTEXT       IDC_AMOUNT, 81, 72, 66, 12, ES_NUMBER
16:    EDITTEXT       IDC_RETURNRATE, 81, 88, 23, 12, ES_NUMBER
17:    LTEXT          "%", IDC_STATIC, 107, 91, 8, 8
18:    RTEXT          "Investment Period:", IDC_STATIC, 13, 106, 64, 8, 0
19:    EDITTEXT       IDC_PERIOD, 81, 104, 23, 12, ES_NUMBER
20:    LTEXT          "years", IDC_STATIC, 108, 107, 17, 8
21:    DEFPUSHBUTTON  "OK", IDOK, 162, 7, 50, 14
22:    PUSHBUTTON     "Cancel", IDCANCEL, 162, 24, 50, 14
23: END
```

The Personal Information dialog box resource uses the `DIALOGEX` resource statement to define a dialog box with a variety of different controls. Following are the different types of controls used in the Personal Information dialog box resource definition:

- `RTEXT`—displays right-justified static text
- `LTEXT`—displays left-justified static text
- `EDITTEXT`—displays text for editing
- `GROUPBOX`—displays a title and border for grouping other controls
- `PUSHBUTTON`—a basic button
- `DEFPUSHBUTTON`—a basic button set as the dialog's default button

You might notice that three of the `EDITTEXT` controls include an additional parameter specifying the style `ES_NUMBER`. This extended style indicates that the text in the edit control is actually a number, and prevents the user from entering anything that isn't numeric.

Creating the Dialog Box Class

With the dialog box resource in place, you're ready to move on and create a custom dialog box class derived from `CDialog`. Listing 7.4 contains the header code for the `CPersonalInfoDlg` dialog box class.

LISTING 7.4 THE PERSONALINFODLG.H HEADER FILE FOR FINANCE

```
 1: #ifndef __PERSONALINFODLG_H__
 2: #define __PERSONALINFODLG_H__
 3:
 4: //-------------------------------
 5: // Inclusions
 6: //-------------------------------
 7: #include "Resource.h"
 8:
 9: //-------------------------------
10: // CPersonalInfoDlg Class - PersonalInfo Dialog Object
11: //-------------------------------
12: class CPersonalInfoDlg : public CDialog {
13:     // Member Constants
14:     enum { IDD = IDD_PERSONALINFOBOX };
15:
16:     // Member Variables
17: public:
18:     CString m_sFName;
19:     CString m_sMInitial;
20:     CString m_sLName;
21:     float   m_fAmount;
22:     float   m_fReturnRate;
23:     int     m_nPeriod;
24:
25:     // Public Constructor(s)/Destructor
26: public:
27:             CPersonalInfoDlg();
28:     virtual ~CPersonalInfoDlg();
29:
30:     // Public Member Functions
31: public:
32:     void    DoDataExchange(CDataExchange* pDX);
33:
34:     // Message Map & Runtime Support
35: protected:
36:     DECLARE_MESSAGE_MAP()
37: };
38:
39: #endif
```

The most important thing to note about the CPersonalInfoDlg class declaration is the IDD member constant, which is set to the dialog box resource identifier, IDD_PERSONALINFOBOX. The IDD member constant will be used in the constructor to associate the dialog box resource with the class. Also important in the CPersonalInfoDlg class are the member variables, which are declared public so that the Finance application can easily access them. These member variables directly correspond to dialog box controls.

Retrieving Information with Custom Dialog Boxes

You might be curious about the `DoDataExchange()` member function declared in `CPersonalInfoDlg`. This function is responsible for carrying out dialog data exchange for the dialog box, which involves tying member variables to dialog box controls. The usage of this function is a little easier to grasp when you see its implementation. Speaking of implementations, the source code for the `CPersonalInfoDlg` class is shown in Listing 7.5.

LISTING 7.5 THE PERSONALINFODLG.CPP SOURCE CODE FILE FOR FINANCE

```
 1: //-----------------------------------
 2: // Inclusions
 3: //-----------------------------------
 4: #include "StdAfx.h"
 5: //-----------------------------------
 6: #include "PersonalInfoDlg.h"
 7:
 8: //-----------------------------------
 9: // MFC Debugging Support
10: //-----------------------------------
11: #ifdef _DEBUG
12: #undef THIS_FILE
13: static char BASED_CODE THIS_FILE[] = __FILE__;
14: #endif
15:
16:
17: //-----------------------------------
18: // Message Map & Runtime Support
19: //-----------------------------------
20: BEGIN_MESSAGE_MAP(CPersonalInfoDlg, CDialog)
21: END_MESSAGE_MAP()
22:
23: //-----------------------------------
24: // Public Constructor(s)/Destructor
25: //-----------------------------------
26: CPersonalInfoDlg::CPersonalInfoDlg() : CDialog(CPersonalInfoDlg::IDD) {
27:   m_fAmount = 1000.0;
28:   m_fReturnRate = 8.0;
29:   m_nPeriod = 10;
30: }
31:
32: CPersonalInfoDlg::~CPersonalInfoDlg() {
33: }
34:
35: //-----------------------------------
36: // Public Member Functions
37: //-----------------------------------
38: void CPersonalInfoDlg::DoDataExchange(CDataExchange* pDX) {
```

continues

LISTING 7.5 CONTINUED

```
39:     CDialog::DoDataExchange(pDX);
40:
41:     DDX_Text(pDX, IDC_FNAME, m_sFName);
42:     DDX_Text(pDX, IDC_MINITIAL, m_sMInitial);
43:     DDX_Text(pDX, IDC_LNAME, m_sLName);
44:     DDX_Text(pDX, IDC_AMOUNT, m_fAmount);
45:     DDX_Text(pDX, IDC_RETURNRATE, m_fReturnRate);
46:     DDX_Text(pDX, IDC_PERIOD, m_nPeriod);
47: }
```

The constructor for `CPersonalInfoDlg` initializes the numeric member variables for the class. It also performs a very important chore by calling the parent `CDialog` constructor and passing the `IDD` constant. Without this call, the `CPersonalInfoDlg` class wouldn't know about the dialog box resource and would be pretty useless. The destructor for `CPersonalInfoDlg` doesn't do anything; by the time the dialog's destructor is called, all of its child window controls have been destroyed. I provided the destructor as a placeholder if you should ever want to go back and add new features that require cleanup.

The `DoDataExchange()` member function is by far the most interesting part of the `CPersonalInfoDlg` class. It first calls the `DoDataExchange()` function in the parent `CDialog` class. It then calls the `DDX_Text()` function to connect member variables with text edit controls. In each call to `DDX_Text()` a text edit control identifier and member variable are provided. MFC's built-in dialog data exchange functionality ensures that the state of the control is reflected in the member variable. This makes it very easy to query the state of a dialog box after it has been exited.

> The `DDX_Text()` function isn't the only function available for connecting controls and member variables together using dialog data exchange. There are also `DDX_Check()`, `DDX_Radio()`, and `DDX_Scroll()` functions for wiring member variables to check boxes, radio buttons, and scroll bars, respectively. There is also a set of dialog data validation functions that can be used to validate information such as minimum and maximum limits on a numeric value.

Invoking the Dialog Box

The final step in assembling the Finance application is creating a menu command for the Personal Information dialog box and adding code to its message handler. Listing 7.6 contains the menu resource definition for the Finance application menu.

LISTING 7.6 THE FINANCE MENU RESOURCE DEFINITION

```
 1: IDR_FINANCE MENU
 2: BEGIN
 3:     POPUP "&File"
 4:     BEGIN
 5:         MENUITEM "&Personal Info...",      ID_FILE_PERSONALINFO
 6:         MENUITEM SEPARATOR
 7:         MENUITEM "E&xit",                  ID_APP_EXIT
 8:     END
 9:     POPUP "&Help"
10:     BEGIN
11:         MENUITEM "&About Finance...",      ID_APP_ABOUT
12:     END
13: END
```

The ID_FILE_PERSONALINFO command is wired to the OnFilePersonalInfo() message handler with the following message map entry:

ON_COMMAND(ID_FILE_PERSONALINFO, OnFilePersonalInfo)

Likewise, you must provide a member function declaration in the application's header file. Following is this function declaration:

afx_msg void OnFilePersonalInfo();

Finally, the implementation of the OnFilePersonalInfo() member function shows exactly how the Personal Information dialog box is used. Listing 7.7 contains the source code for the function.

LISTING 7.7 THE CMainFrame::OnFilePersonalInfo() MEMBER FUNCTION FOR THE FINANCE APPLICATION

```
 1: void CMainFrame::OnFilePersonalInfo() {
 2:     // Retrieve personal information
 3:     CPersonalInfoDlg personalInfoDlg;
 4:     if (personalInfoDlg.DoModal() == IDOK) {
 5:         // Calculate the investment
 6:         float fTotal = personalInfoDlg.m_fAmount;
 7:         for (int i = 0; i < personalInfoDlg.m_nPeriod; i++)
 8:             fTotal += (fTotal * (personalInfoDlg.m_fReturnRate / 100));
 9:
10:         // Display the result
11:         CString sResult;
12:         sResult.Format("%s %s. %s's total investment after %d years is
            ➥$%.2f.",
13:             personalInfoDlg.m_sFName, personalInfoDlg.m_sMInitial,
14:             personalInfoDlg.m_sLName, personalInfoDlg.m_nPeriod, fTotal);
```

continues

LISTING 7.7 CONTINUED

```
15:     MessageBox(sResult);
16:   }
17: }
```

As you can see in the listing, the dialog box is created by simply instantiating a `CPersonalInfoDlg` object and calling its `DoModal()` member function. If this function returns `IDOK`, the investment is calculated and the results displayed in a message box. The `CString::Format()` function is used to format the result string. You learn more about how to format strings in Hour 11, "Organizing Data with MFC's Collections Classes." Figure 7.6 shows the message box containing the investment results.

FIGURE 7.6

The message box investment results in Finance.

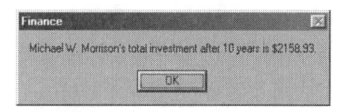

Summary

This hour introduces you to the user interface possibilities made available by custom dialog boxes. You learned about the simplest type of custom dialog box, the message box. You also learned about MFC's support for custom dialog boxes. From there, you moved on to finding out how to define the structure of a custom dialog box using dialog box resources. You finished up the hour by creating and integrating a custom dialog box into a financial application.

Q&A

Q Where is the best place to perform dialog box initialization?

A The `OnInitDialog()` member function, which is defined in the `CDialog` class. This function is called in response to a dialog box being invoked, just before the dialog is displayed.

Q How can I close a dialog box programmatically?

A By calling the `EndDialog()` function, which is defined in the `CDialog` class. Both the `OnOK()` and `OnCancel()` standard message handlers call `EndDialog()` to close a dialog box.

Workshop

The Workshop is designed to help you anticipate possible questions, review what you've learned, and begin thinking ahead to put your knowledge into practice. The answers to the quiz are in Appendix A, "Quiz Answers."

Quiz

1. What is the easiest way to create a primitive type of custom dialog box?
2. What is the significance of a default dialog box button?
3. What does the `MessageBox()` function return if the user clicks the OK button?
4. What class serves as the basis for all custom dialog box classes?
5. What is a dialog box template?
6. What is used to define dialog box resources?
7. What is the difference between the `DEFPUSHBUTTON` and `PUSHBUTTON` dialog box controls?
8. Why is it beneficial to use a visual dialog box editor to create dialog box resources?
9. What function do you use to invoke custom dialog boxes?
10. How do you use dialog data exchange to connect member variables with text edit controls?

Exercises

1. Try changing the values of the position and size for the controls in the Personal Information dialog box resource to get a feel for the difficulty involved in hand-coding dialog boxes.
2. Add a confirmation message box to the Personal Information dialog box that asks the user for confirmation on exiting the dialog using the Cancel button.

HOUR 8

Manipulating Menus

Although you've worked with menus a little throughout the book thus far, you haven't gone much beyond the absolute basics of them. This hour digs a little deeper into menus and shows you how to do some pretty interesting things. More specifically, you learn how to respond to menu events, how to dynamically manipulate menus, how to use floating pop-up menus, and how to update the state of menu items. You should definitely gain a different perspective on menus by the time you finish this hour.

In this hour, you will learn

- How to respond to menu events
- The significance of the system menu
- How to dynamically modify menus
- How to use floating pop-up menus
- How to update the state of menu items

Responding to Menu Events

As you learned back in Hour 3, menus form an integral part of the user interface in most applications. Although you learned in Hour 3 how to create a menu resource script, you didn't get too far into the details of how to respond to menu commands using menu message handlers. The good news is that menu commands are delivered via the WM_COMMAND message, with which you already have some experience.

As you might recall, the ON_COMMAND macro is designed for use with command messages such as menu commands that are sent via the WM_COMMAND message. You supply two parameters to the macro to map menu commands to message handlers. These parameters include the identifier of the menu command and the name of the message handler to call when the command message is sent. You used this macro in the previous hour to map menu commands in the Finance application, as the following code shows:

```
BEGIN_MESSAGE_MAP(CMainFrame, CFrameWnd)
  ON_COMMAND(ID_FILE_PERSONALINFO, OnFilePersonalInfo)
  ON_COMMAND(ID_APP_ABOUT, OnAppAbout)
END_MESSAGE_MAP()
```

This message map connects the message handlers OnFilePersonalInfo() and OnAppAbout() to the menu commands identified by ID_FILE_PERSONALINFO and ID_APP_ABOUT, respectively. This is the same approach you will use to map menu commands in all MFC applications.

Analyzing the System Menu

Throughout the book thus far you've focused on application menus, which are custom menus containing commands specific to an application. Although this type of menu is what you are probably the most familiar with, it isn't the only type of menu used in Windows applications. Most Windows applications also have a system menu, which contains standard system commands supported by Windows. Following is a list of these standard system commands:

- *Restore*—restores a minimized application frame window
- *Move*—moves the application frame window
- *Size*—resizes the application frame window
- *Minimize*—minimizes the application frame window
- *Maximize*—maximizes the application frame window
- *Close*—closes the application

You can invoke the system menu for an application by either clicking the small icon in the upper left corner of an application's frame window or by pressing Alt+Space on the keyboard.

Obtaining a System Menu Object

The reason I'm making an issue out of the system menu is because you can alter the system menu to include application-specific menu commands. This might be useful in an application that doesn't have a traditional application menu. To modify the system menu you must first call the `GetSystemMenu()` member function, which is defined in the `CWnd` class. Following is an example of obtaining a `CMenu` object that represents the system menu:

```
CMenu* pSysMenu = GetSystemMenu(FALSE);
```

The Boolean parameter to the `GetSystemMenu()` function is used to either retrieve or restore the system menu. A value of `FALSE` retrieves the system menu, whereas a value of `TRUE` restores the default system menu.

Adding a System Menu Item

When you have a `CMenu` object, you can easily add a menu item using the `AppendMenu()` member function, like this:

```
pSysMenu->AppendMenu(MF_STRING | MF_ENABLED, ID_APP_ABOUT,
    ""&About Animator...""");
```

This adds a menu item named `About Animator...` with the command identifier `ID_APP_ABOUT` to an application's system menu. This particular example might be useful in the Animator application you developed earlier in the book because it didn't have an application menu. You can also add a menu separator to a menu by passing `MF_SEPARATOR` to the `AppendMenu()` function, like this:

```
pSysMenu->AppendMenu(MF_SEPARATOR);
```

There is one catch to adding menu items to the system menu for an application; unlike normal menu commands, system menu commands are delivered to an application via the `WM_SYSCOMMAND` message instead of `WM_COMMAND`. So, to handle menu command events you must create an `OnSysCommand()` message handler that responds to the `WM_SYSCOMMAND` message. Following is the macro for the `WM_SYSCOMMAND` message that must be placed in an application's message map:

```
ON_WM_SYSCOMMAND()
```

The corresponding declaration for the `OnSysCommand()` message handler follows:

`afx_msg void  OnSysCommand(UINT nID, LPARAM lParam);`

Because the `OnSysCommand()` message handler is used to handle all system command messages, it is necessary to check the value of the `nID` parameter to see which system menu command was actually selected. Listing 8.1 shows an implementation of `OnSysCommand()` that displays an About dialog box in response to the `ID_APP_ABOUT` command that was added to the system menu.

LISTING 8.1 THE `CMainFrame::OnSysCommand()` MESSAGE HANDLER FOR ANIMATOR3

```
 1: void CMainFrame::OnSysCommand(UINT nID, LPARAM lParam) {
 2:   // Check for the About menu item
 3:   switch (nID) {
 4:   case ID_APP_ABOUT:
 5:     CAboutDlg aboutDlg;
 6:     aboutDlg.DoModal();
 7:     return;
 8:   }
 9:
10:   CFrameWnd::OnSysCommand(nID, lParam);
11: }
```

The code in Listing 8.1, along with the other system menu modifying code you just learned about, is included in the Animator3 application. You will continue to make modifications to the Animator3 application throughout this hour.

Dynamically Modifying Menus

Although the previous discussion focused on altering the system menu, you are actually free to modify any menu, including the main application menu. Typically you create an application menu as a resource and use it in an application without modification. However, there are times when it is useful to alter this menu or even swap it out with an entirely different menu. MFC's `CMenu` class gives you complete control over dynamically modifying menus. Following are the member functions that make this possible:

- `GetSubMenu()`—gets a pop-up menu (sub-menu) within a menu
- `GetMenuItemCount()`—gets the number of items in a menu
- `AppendMenu()`—adds an item to the end of a menu
- `InsertMenu()`—inserts an item at some point within a menu
- `DeleteMenu()`—deletes a menu item
- `ModifyMenu()`—modifies a menu item

These member functions enable you to dynamically alter a menu in just about any way you want. You'll be using these member functions throughout the rest of this hour to modify the menu for the Animator3 application. Before I move on to modifying a menu, however, let me take a quick look at how menus and pop-up menus are retrieved.

Getting Menus and Pop-up Menus

In order to modify a menu or pop-up menu, you must first create a CMenu object based on the application menu. Because an application will typically already have a menu, you can obtain a CMenu object pointer from the application frame window instead of actually creating a CMenu object yourself. You obtain a CMenu object pointer from an application frame window by calling the GetMenu() member function on the window object, like this:

```
CMenu* pMenu = GetMenu();
```

You can make this call within any member function of your frame window class. However, if you are modifying a menu upon application initialization, a good place to put this call is in the OnCreate() member function. This is the approach you used earlier in the hour to retrieve a pointer to the system menu object.

It's important to note that the menu pointer obtained with GetMenu() is for the top level menu bar, and doesn't enable direct access to pop-up menu items. Generally speaking, the majority of menu modification takes place in pop-up menus. So, it is necessary to use a member function of CMenu to obtain a pop-up menu pointer. To get a menu pointer for a pop-up menu, you must call the GetSubMenu() function on the top level menu object, like this:

```
CMenu* pFileMenu = GetMenu()->GetSubMenu(0);
```

This code gets a menu pointer to the first pop-up menu in the application menu, which is typically the File pop-up menu.

Adding Menu Items

When you have a CMenu object pointer, you are ready to use the menu modification functions to dynamically alter the application menu. One of the most useful functions is InsertMenu(), which inserts a new menu item at a specific location within a menu. If you use the InsertMenu() function on a top level menu it will insert a new pop-up menu. To insert a menu item to the top of a pop-up menu, you use the InsertMenu() member function:

```
pFileMenu->InsertMenu(0, MF_BYPOSITION | MF_STRING | MF_ENABLED,
  ID_FILE_PLAY, ""&Play"");
```

The first parameter is an integer that has different meanings based on the flags specified in the second parameter (see Table 8.1).

TABLE 8.1 FLAGS USED BY THE CMenu::InsertMenu() MEMBER FUNCTION

Flag	Description
MF_BYCOMMAND	Indicates that the first parameter to InsertMenu() is the menu command identifier of an existing menu item; the new menu item is inserted at this position
MF_BYPOSITION	Indicates that the first parameter to InsertMenu() is a zero-based integer index for the menu position; the new menu item is inserted at this position
MF_CHECKED	The menu item is initially checked
MF_UNCHECKED	The menu item is initially unchecked
MF_HILITE	The menu item is initially highlighted
MF_UNHILITE	The menu item is initially unhighlighted
MF_ENABLED	The menu item is initially enabled
MF_DISABLED	The menu item is initially disabled
MF_GRAYED	The menu item is initially grayed
MF_STRING	The menu item is a normal menu item
MF_POPUP	The menu item is a new pop-up menu

Based on the InsertMenu() flags shown in the table you might be able to guess that the previous example code adds a menu item named Play as the first item under the File pop-up menu. Also, the integer identifier ID_FILE_PLAY identifies the menu item.

If you just want to add a menu item to the end of a pop-up menu, you can use the AppendMenu() member function, like this:

```
pSysMenu->AppendMenu(MF_STRING | MF_ENABLED, ID_APP_ABOUT,
  "&About Animator...");
```

This is code you saw earlier in the hour when you modified the system menu of the Animator3 application. Now you have a better understanding of what is taking place with the parameters to the function.

Dynamic Menus and Animator3

I've mentioned the Animator3 application a few times throughout the discussion of dynamic menus in this hour. In this section you put some of your dynamic menu knowledge to use in the Animator3 application. Before getting into the details of the dynamic menu code, however, you need to add a basic File menu to the application. Listing 8.2 contains the code for a menu resource with a File pop-up menu and an Exit menu item.

LISTING 8.2 THE MENU RESOURCE FOR ANIMATOR3

```
1: IDR_ANIMATOR MENU
2: BEGIN
3:   POPUP "&File"
4:     BEGIN
5:       MENUITEM "E&xit",    ID_APP_EXIT
6:     END
7: END
```

This menu is associated with the Animator3 application in the `Create()` member function. Listing 8.3 contains the code for the new version of the `Create()` member function.

LISTING 8.3 THE NEW CMainFrame::Create() MEMBER FUNCTION FOR ANIMATOR3

```
 1: BOOL CMainFrame::Create(const CString& sTitle) {
 2:     CString sClassName;
 3:
 4:     sClassName = AfxRegisterWndClass(CS_HREDRAW | CS_VREDRAW,
 5:         ::LoadCursor(NULL, IDC_ARROW),
 6:         (HBRUSH)::GetStockObject(LTGRAY_BRUSH),
 7:         ::LoadIcon(AfxGetInstanceHandle(),
 8:         MAKEINTRESOURCE(IDR_ANIMATOR)));
 9:
10:     RECT rc = { 5, 5, 320, 345 };
11:     return CFrameWnd::Create(sClassName, sTitle, WS_OVERLAPPED |
12:         WS_SYSMENU | WS_BORDER, rc, NULL, MAKEINTRESOURCE(IDR_ANIMATOR));
13: }
```

The menu for Animator3 is set in the call to the parent `CFrameWnd::Create()` member function; the last parameter to this function specifies the application menu. You might also notice that the window styles and window size of the frame window are provided in this function call. In Animator2 this code appeared in the `PreCreateWindow()` member function; Animator2 doesn't need the `PreCreateWindow()` member function. This is a good example of how there is sometimes more than one way to achieve a desired effect in MFC.

Now that Animator3 has a basic menu, you're ready to start modifying it dynamically. Most of the menu modification code for Animator3 is located in the `OnCreate()` message handler. Listing 8.4 contains partial source code for the `OnCreate()` message handler of Animator3.

LISTING 8.4 DYNAMIC MENU CODE ADDED TO THE `CMainFrame::OnCreate()` MESSAGE HANDLER FOR ANIMATOR3

```
 1: // Add an About menu item to the system menu
 2: CMenu* pSysMenu = GetSystemMenu(FALSE);
 3: pSysMenu->AppendMenu(MF_SEPARATOR);
 4: pSysMenu->AppendMenu(MF_STRING | MF_ENABLED, ID_APP_ABOUT,
 5:   "&About Animator...");
 6:
 7: // Add menu items to the application menu
 8: CMenu* pFileMenu = GetMenu()->GetSubMenu(0);
 9: pFileMenu->InsertMenu(0, MF_BYPOSITION | MF_STRING | MF_ENABLED,
10:   ID_FILE_PLAY, "&Play");
11: pFileMenu->InsertMenu(1, MF_BYPOSITION | MF_STRING | MF_ENABLED,
12:   ID_FILE_STOP, "&Stop");
13: pFileMenu->InsertMenu(2, MF_BYPOSITION | MF_SEPARATOR);
14: pFileMenu->InsertMenu(3, MF_BYPOSITION | MF_STRING | MF_ENABLED,
15:   ID_FILE_LOOP, "&Loop");
16: pFileMenu->InsertMenu(4, MF_BYPOSITION | MF_STRING | MF_ENABLED,
17:   ID_FILE_TRANSPARENCY, "&Transparency");
18: pFileMenu->InsertMenu(5, MF_BYPOSITION | MF_SEPARATOR);
19: pFileMenu->InsertMenu(6, MF_BYPOSITION | MF_STRING | MF_ENABLED,
20:   ID_FILE_CHANGECOLOR, "Change &Color...");
21: pFileMenu->InsertMenu(7, MF_BYPOSITION | MF_SEPARATOR);
```

The code shown in the listing is dynamic menu creation code that should be added to the existing `OnCreate()` message handler in Animator3. This code adds an About Animator menu item to the system menu and the following menu items to the File menu: Play, Stop, Loop, Transparency, and Change Color. These new File menu items provide a menu interface to supplement the existing control interface.

> Although adding menu support to the Animator3 application might seem unnecessary, you have to consider that some users prefer using a menu. A supplemental menu interface is often valuable for users with disabilities who have trouble maneuvering the mouse. Also, some laptop users find menus easier to work with than the small trackball mice commonly found in laptops.

Following are the message map additions for the new menu items added to the Animator3 menu:

```
ON_COMMAND(ID_FILE_PLAY, OnPBPlayClicked)
ON_COMMAND(ID_FILE_STOP, OnPBStopClicked)
ON_COMMAND(ID_FILE_LOOP, OnFileLoop)
```

```
ON_COMMAND(ID_FILE_TRANSPARENCY, OnFileTransparency)
ON_COMMAND(ID_FILE_CHANGECOLOR, OnFileChangeColor)
```

Notice that the first two message map entries call the existing functions `OnPBPlayClicked()` and `OnPBStopClicked()`. This demonstrates how selecting Play or Stop from the menu is functionally no different than clicking the Play or Stop buttons. The remaining message map entries require their own message handlers. Following are the corresponding menu command message handler declarations for Animator3:

```
afx_msg void   OnFileLoop();
afx_msg void   OnFileTransparency();
afx_msg void   OnFileChangeColor();
```

The implementation of these message handlers is pretty straightforward, as Listing 8.5 shows.

LISTING 8.5 THE NEW MENU COMMAND MESSAGE HANDLERS FOR ANIMATOR3

```
 1: void CMainFrame::OnFileLoop() {
 2:   // Toggle the Loop check box
 3:   m_LoopCheckbox.SetCheck(1 - m_LoopCheckbox.GetCheck());
 4: }
 5:
 6: void CMainFrame::OnFileTransparency() {
 7:   // Toggle the Transparency check box
 8:   m_TransCheckbox.SetCheck(1 - m_TransCheckbox.GetCheck());
 9:
10:   // Respond to the transparency change
11:   OnCKTransparencyClicked();
12: }
13:
14: void CMainFrame::OnFileChangeColor() {
15:   // Select a background color using the Color dialog box
16:   CColorDialog dlg(RGB(192, 192, 192));
17:   if (dlg.DoModal() == IDOK) {
18:     // Set the new background color for the frame window
19:     CBrush brBackground(dlg.GetColor());
20:     ::SetClassLong(GetSafeHwnd(), GCL_HBRBACKGROUND,
21:       (LONG)(HBRUSH)brBackground);
22:     Invalidate();
23:   }
24: }
```

The `OnFileLoop()` message handler simply checks or unchecks the Loop check box to reflect the menu selection. The `OnFileTransparency()` message handler does the same thing for the Transparency check box. However, `OnFileTransparency()` must also call the `OnCKTransparencyClicked()` handler so that the transparency change is reflected in the Animation control. The `OnFileChangeColor()` message handler is called to change the background color of the Animator3 application frame window. The code in this handler should look familiar because it originally appeared in the `OnRButtonUp()` message handler of Animator2. As you soon find out, the Animator3 application uses the `OnRButtonUp()` message handler to display a floating pop-up menu, which is why the color change code is moved into `OnFileChangeColor()`.

Using Floating Pop-up Menus

Originally seeing their start as fancy user interface enhancements in a few applications, floating pop-up menus eventually made their way into the Windows user interface as a standard fixture. You've no doubt used floating pop-up menus in Windows applications such as Windows Explorer. These pop-up menus are typically context-sensitive, and are invoked with the right mouse button. For this reason, floating pop-up menus are sometimes referred to as context menus. You might be surprised at how easy it is to support floating pop-up menus in MFC applications.

The key to using floating pop-up menus is the `TrackPopupMenu()` member function of `CMenu`. The `TrackPopupMenu()` function displays a floating pop-up menu representing the `CMenu` object on which it is called. Following is an example of displaying a floating pop-up menu using the `TrackPopupMenu()` function:

```
pFileMenu->TrackPopupMenu(TPM_CENTERALIGN | TPM_LEFTBUTTON,
  x, y, this);
```

The first parameter to `TrackPopupMenu()` is a flag indicating the alignment and mouse button used to select menu items from the pop-up menu. Table 8.2 shows the flags used by `TrackPopupMenu()`.

TABLE 8.2 FLAGS USED BY THE `CMenu::TrackPopupMenu()` MEMBER FUNCTION

Flag	Description
TPM_CENTERALIGN	The menu is centered horizontally on the X position of the menu
TPM_LEFTALIGN	The left edge of the menu is aligned with the X position of the menu
TPM_RIGHTALIGN	The right edge of the menu is aligned with the X position of the menu
TPM_LEFTBUTTON	The left mouse button is used to make menu selections
TPM_RIGHTBUTTON	The right mouse button is used to make menu selections

The X position referenced in the table is the second parameter to `TrackPopupMenu()`, which indicates the horizontal position of the menu relative to the screen. The third parameter is the Y position of the menu. The last parameter is a pointer to the parent window of the menu; it is sufficient to pass this if TrackPopupMenu() is called from a CMainFrame member function.

Now that you know how the TrackPopupMenu() function works, try it out in the Animator3 application. Listing 8.6 contains the new version of the OnRButtonUp() message handler, which supports a floating pop-up menu containing the menu commands in the File menu.

LISTING 8.6 THE NEW VERSION OF THE CMainFrame::OnRButtonUp() MESSAGE HANDLER FOR ANIMATOR3

```
void CMainFrame::OnRButtonUp(UINT nFlags, CPoint point) {
  // Display the File menu as a floating pop-up menu
  CMenu* pFileMenu = GetMenu()->GetSubMenu(0);
  ClientToScreen(&point);
  pFileMenu->TrackPopupMenu(TPM_CENTERALIGN | TPM_LEFTBUTTON,
    point.x, point.y, this);
}
```

As you can see, the OnRButtonUp() message handler first obtains a menu pointer for the File pop-up menu using the GetSubMenu() member function of CMenu. Before displaying the floating pop-up menu, OnRButtonUp() calls the ClientToScreen() member function of CWnd to convert the client window position in the point parameter to screen coordinates. This call is necessary because the TrackPopupMenu() function expects the pop-up menu position in screen coordinates, not client window coordinates. The OnRButtonUp() message handler finishes up by calling TrackPopupMenu() to display a pop-up menu containing the File menu commands. Figure 8.1 shows this floating pop-up menu in action.

FIGURE 8.1

The floating pop-up menu in Animator3.

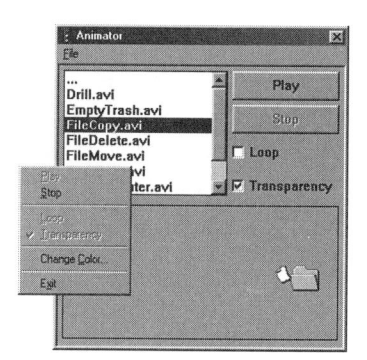

> The Animator3 application showed how to display a floating pop-up menu based on one in the main application menu. You can also create custom pop-up menus as resources that aren't necessarily used elsewhere in the application. To do this you must first create a menu resource in the application's resource file. You then create a CMenu object and call the LoadMenu() member function to load a menu from a resource. This menu object can then be used with the TrackPopupMenu() member function to display the menu as a floating pop-up menu.

Updating Menus

The last topic on this hour's agenda has to do with the way in which menu items are presented. More specifically, you've probably noticed that most commercial Windows applications seem to intelligently enable and disable menu items based on the state of the application. For example, the WordPad application that ships with Windows intelligently enables and disables the Copy and Cut menu items in its Edit menu based on whether you have any text selected. Take a second to try it out and see what I mean.

Prior to MFC, injecting this type of menu state intelligence into an application could get very tricky. Even if you managed to get your menu states worked out correctly, there was no good technique for reflecting these states in an application's toolbar buttons, which typically correspond to menu items. MFC solved this problem with a very elegant and easy-to-use solution for dealing with the state of user interface elements including menu items, toolbar buttons, and status bar text. For now you're going to focus on how to manage the state of menu items.

MFC's Command Update Message Handlers

MFC's answer to user interface state management comes in the form of command update message handlers. A command update message handler is associated with an individual user interface element such as a menu item or a toolbar button. This handler is called to refresh the state of the user interface element in question. In the case of pop-up menu items, the command update message handler is called just before a pop-up menu is displayed.

As you might be guessing, each command update message handler requires a message map entry that ties the handler to a given user interface element. The ON_UPDATE_COMMAND_UI macro is used to carry out this connection. Following is an example of wiring a command update message handler to a menu item:

```
ON_UPDATE_COMMAND_UI(ID_FILE_PLAY, OnUpdateFilePlay)
```

This code wires the `OnUpdateFilePlay()` command update message handler to the menu item identified by `ID_FILE_PLAY`. This handler is called just before the Play menu item is displayed to the user. Following is the prototype of the `OnUpdateFilePlay()` command update message handler:

```
afx_msg void  OnUpdateFilePlay(CCmdUI* pCmdUI);
```

The parameter to `OnUpdateFilePlay()`, `pCmdUI`, is sent to all update command message handlers, and provides a means of modifying the state of the user interface element. Following are the primary member functions used in conjunction with the `CCmdUI` class:

- `Enable()`—enables or disables the user interface element
- `SetCheck()`—checks or unchecks the user interface element
- `SetRadio()`—checks or unchecks the radio state of the user interface element
- `SetText()`—sets the text of the user interface element

Following is an example of enabling a user interface element using the `Enable()` member function:

```
pCmdUI->Enable(TRUE);
```

Disabling a user interface element is as simple as calling the same member function and passing `FALSE`, like this:

```
pCmdUI->Enable(FALSE);
```

The other member functions of the `CCmdUI` class work in roughly the same way. You see some of them in action later in the book.

> By default, the MFC command update mechanism automatically disables any menu items that don't have a command message handler. This makes it apparent to you (and the user) that a menu item isn't currently operational.

Updating the Animator3 Menu

Perhaps the best way to understand how a command update message handler works is to take a look at an example. The Animator3 menu items are in real need of command update message handlers so that the user can tell when different commands are available for use. Before looking into the handlers themselves, it is necessary to add some support code that keeps track of the state of the animation. Following is the declaration of the `m_bPlaying` member variable, which keeps track of whether the Animation control is currently playing an animation:

```
BOOL  m_bPlaying;
```

This member variable is set in the `OnANStart()` and `OnANStop()` member functions, which are called when the Animation control stops and starts an animation. Listing 8.7 contains the modified code for these member functions.

LISTING 8.7 THE NEW VERSIONS OF THE ANIMATION CONTROL MESSAGE HANDLERS FOR ANIMATOR3

```
 1: void CMainFrame::OnANStart() {
 2:    // Enable/disable the controls when the animation starts
 3:    m_AnimListBox.EnableWindow(FALSE);
 4:    m_PlayButton.EnableWindow(FALSE);
 5:    m_StopButton.EnableWindow(TRUE);
 6:    m_LoopCheckbox.EnableWindow(FALSE);
 7:    m_TransCheckbox.EnableWindow(FALSE);
 8:
 9:    // Set the Playing flag
10:    m_bPlaying = TRUE;
11: }
12:
13: void CMainFrame::OnANStop() {
14:    // Enable/disable the controls when the animation stops
15:    m_AnimListBox.EnableWindow(TRUE);
16:    m_PlayButton.EnableWindow(TRUE);
17:    m_StopButton.EnableWindow(FALSE);
18:    m_LoopCheckbox.EnableWindow(TRUE);
19:    m_TransCheckbox.EnableWindow(TRUE);
20:
21:    // Clear the Playing flag
22:    m_bPlaying = FALSE;
23: }
```

Now that you have a member variable indicating the state of the Animation control, you can move on to implementing the command update message handlers. Following are the message map entries for the command update message handlers in Animator3:

```
ON_UPDATE_COMMAND_UI(ID_FILE_PLAY, OnUpdateFilePlay)
ON_UPDATE_COMMAND_UI(ID_FILE_STOP, OnUpdateFileStop)
ON_UPDATE_COMMAND_UI(ID_FILE_LOOP, OnUpdateFileLoop)
ON_UPDATE_COMMAND_UI(ID_FILE_TRANSPARENCY, OnUpdateFileTransparency)
```

Following are the corresponding command update message handler declarations for Animator3:

```
afx_msg void   OnUpdateFilePlay(CCmdUI* pCmdUI);
afx_msg void   OnUpdateFileStop(CCmdUI* pCmdUI);
afx_msg void   OnUpdateFileLoop(CCmdUI* pCmdUI);
afx_msg void   OnUpdateFileTransparency(CCmdUI* pCmdUI);
```

The implementation of these message handlers is shown in Listing 8.8.

LISTING 8.8 THE COMMAND UPDATE MESSAGE HANDLERS FOR ANIMATOR3

```
 1: void CMainFrame::OnUpdateFilePlay(CCmdUI* pCmdUI) {
 2:   // Update the File¦Play menu item
 3:   pCmdUI->Enable(!m_bPlaying);
 4: }
 5:
 6: void CMainFrame::OnUpdateFileStop(CCmdUI* pCmdUI) {
 7:   // Update the File¦Stop menu item
 8:   pCmdUI->Enable(m_bPlaying);
 9: }
10:
11: void CMainFrame::OnUpdateFileLoop(CCmdUI* pCmdUI) {
12:   // Update the File¦Loop menu item
13:   pCmdUI->Enable(!m_bPlaying);
14:   if (m_LoopCheckbox.GetCheck() == 1)
15:     pCmdUI->SetCheck(1);
16:   else
17:     pCmdUI->SetCheck(0);
18: }
19:
20: void CMainFrame::OnUpdateFileTransparency(CCmdUI* pCmdUI) {
21:   // Update the File¦Transparency menu item
22:   pCmdUI->Enable(!m_bPlaying);
23:   if (m_TransCheckbox.GetCheck() == 1)
24:     pCmdUI->SetCheck(1);
25:   else
26:     pCmdUI->SetCheck(0);
27: }
```

The `OnUpdateFilePlay()` and `OnUpdateFileStop()` message handlers simply enable or disable the respective menu items based on whether the animation is playing. The `OnUpdateFileLoop()` and `OnUpdateFileTransparency()` handlers work similarly, but they must also deal with checking and unchecking the menu items based on the state of the corresponding check box controls.

Summary

This hour explored menus and many of the things you can do to make them a more useful part of an application's user interface. You began the hour by learning the details of how to respond to menu events. You then learned about the role of the system menu along with how to add menu items to it. From there you learned about how to dynamically modify menus. You finished up the hour by exploring floating pop-up menus and the importance of updating menu item states.

Q&A

Q Is it possible to disable the default disabling of menu items that don't have message handlers?

A Yes. As you learned in this hour, any menu item that doesn't have a corresponding command message handler is automatically disabled by MFC's command update mechanism. You can disable this feature by setting the inherited m_bAutoMenuEnable member variable to FALSE in your application frame window class.

Q How does the MFC command update mechanism work with respect to floating pop-up menus?

A Floating pop-up menu items have identifiers just like any other menu items, which means they can have command update message handlers to manage their states. If a floating pop-up menu is based on part of the main application menu, such as in the Animator3 application, the main menu command update message handlers will automatically work for the pop-up menu as well.

Workshop

The Workshop is designed to help you anticipate possible questions, review what you've learned, and begin thinking ahead to put your knowledge into practice. The answers to the quiz are in Appendix A, "Quiz Answers."

Quiz

1. How do you invoke the system menu for an application using the keyboard?
2. What CWnd member function do you use to obtain a system menu pointer?
3. What is the purpose of the OnSysCommand() message handler?
4. How do you obtain a menu pointer for a pop-up menu?
5. What menu flag is used to add a menu separator to a menu using the AppendMenu() or InsertMenu() member functions of CMenu?
6. What is the purpose of the MF_BYPOSITION flag that is used in the InsertMenu() member function of CMenu?
7. What CMenu member function is used to display a floating pop-up menu?
8. What macro is used to wire command update message handlers to menu items?
9. What is the purpose of the CCmdUI class?
10. What CCmdUI member function do you use to enable and disable the state of menu items?

Exercises

1. Try commenting out the message map entry for the Change Color menu command message handler in the Animator3 application. Notice that the menu item is disabled due to MFC's default menu item disabling feature.

2. Add a custom floating pop-up menu to the Animator3 application that contains Play and Stop buttons, and that is invoked with the right mouse button.

HOUR 9

Drawing Graphics

To me, graphics represents one of the most fun and entertaining areas of Windows programming. This hour jumps into Windows graphics and gives you a solid foundation upon which to create MFC applications that utilize graphics. You start off by learning some fundamentals about graphics in Windows, and then quickly progress on to finding out how to use MFC classes to put graphics in action. The hour culminates in the development of a simple drawing application named Doodle.

In this hour, you will learn

- The importance of graphics device contexts
- About the Windows graphics coordinate system
- MFC and the Windows Graphics Device Interface
- How windows are painted
- How to draw lines, rectangles, ellipses, text, and bitmaps

Graphics Fundamentals

As you already know, Windows supports all kinds of different graphical output devices such as monitors, printers, and plotters. Although I often take for granted the fact that I can easily plug in a new output device and render graphics to it, a lot goes on under the hood to make this happen. For example, every graphics output device must have a Windows driver for the device to be useable in Windows. More importantly, however, is the underlying application code that paints graphics to a given device.

To seamlessly support a wide range of graphical output devices, Windows abstracts the process of painting graphics. This abstraction comes in the form of the Graphics Device Interface, or GDI, which is a programmatic interface for painting graphics in a generic manner. GDI operations work in concert with Windows graphics drivers to communicate with physical graphics devices such as monitors, printers, and plotters. Figure 9.1 shows the architecture of the GDI.

FIGURE 9.1

The architecture of the Windows GDI.

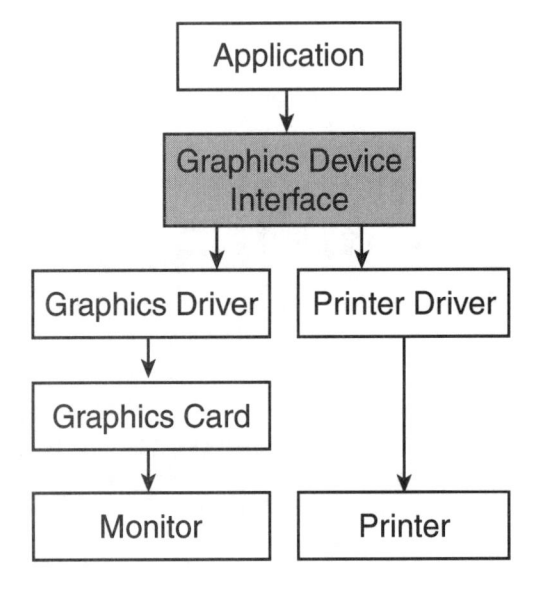

> Although I use the term "generic" to describe GDI graphics, please understand that the Win32 API provides a broad range of GDI graphics operations. You learn about many of the basic GDI operations throughout this hour.

The Importance of Device Contexts

The key component in GDI graphics is the graphics device context, which acts as a gateway to a physical graphics device. You can think of a device context as an abstract surface to which graphics are painted. Device contexts provide the abstraction necessary to facilitate device-independent graphics.

NEW TERM A *graphics device context* is an abstract surface to which graphics are painted.

Device-independent graphics are the main motivation for having device contexts. You might not immediately see the importance of device independence, so please allow me to try to paint the picture. Without device independence, every application would be responsible for supporting specific graphics hardware. For example, an image editing application would have to take direct responsibility for painting graphics differently, depending on the make and model of the graphics card in use. This is clearly an unreasonable amount of responsibility at the application level, especially considering the wide range of hardware available for PCs these days. Yet this is exactly the problem DOS programmers had to deal with for years.

The Graphics Device Interface remedies this problem by severing the direct link between applications and graphics hardware. The GDI acts as an intermediary between the two and provides a well-defined interface for graphical communication. An application now must only concern itself with painting to a "generic" device context, which is then translated to a specific graphics device via Windows graphics drivers. The responsibility of providing a compatible Windows graphics driver is placed in the hands of hardware manufacturers, which is where it rightly belongs.

Basic Graphics Components

In addition to device contexts, the GDI also supports the following common graphics components:

- Pens
- Brushes
- Palettes
- Bitmaps
- Fonts

Pens in GDI are analogous to ink pens in the real world; they are used to draw lines and curves. Pens can be created with varying widths and of different colors. Brushes in GDI are analogous to paint brushes in the real world; they are used to paint the interior of polygons, ellipses, and paths. Brushes can also be defined based on a bitmap pattern, which means they paint in a pattern instead of as a solid.

NEW TERM A *pen* is a GDI object used to draw lines and curves.

New Term A *brush* is a GDI object used to paint the interior of regions such as rectangles and ellipses.

A palette is a set of colors used by GDI when rendering an image. As an example, many images are stored as 256-color images, which means they use colors from a palette of 256 colors. A bitmap is a graphical image stored as an array of pixels. Bitmaps are rectangular, so the number of pixels in a bitmap is the width of the bitmap multiplied by its height. Bitmaps can contain multiple colors and are often based on a specific palette of colors. As you probably already know, fonts are objects that determine the size and style of text.

New Term A *palette* is a set of colors used by GDI when rendering an image.

New Term A graphical image stored as an array of pixels is known as a *bitmap*.

New Term A *font* is an object that determines the style of text displayed graphically.

Pens, brushes, palettes, and bitmaps are all properties of a device context, which means they are used to perform graphics operations within a device context. You can select one of each of these graphics components into a device context.

The Windows Graphics Coordinate System

When you draw a picture on a piece of paper, you make some assumptions about the orientation of the paper and the manner in which it is being viewed. Additionally, if you want to center the picture, you might measure in from the edges of the paper to determine the paper's center, and then draw from there. When you make considerations such as these, you are effectively utilizing your own primitive graphics coordinate system.

Graphical computing systems also rely on graphics coordinate systems, and Windows is no exception. Coordinate systems typically specify the axes (X and Y) and directions of increasing value for each of the axes. It is also important for a coordinate system to indicate the location of the origin, which is the reference point (0, 0). Coordinate values increase and decrease from this point along the coordinate axes. Check out Figure 9.2 to see what I'm talking about.

Notice in the figure that there are X and Y axes, and that they increase in value from the origin to the right and up. Coordinate values to the left or below the origin have negative values. Windows supports a variety of different coordinate systems, which are also referred to as graphics mapping modes. The default Windows mapping mode is called MM_TEXT, and is shown in Figure 9.3.

FIGURE 9.2

The traditional mathematical coordinate system.

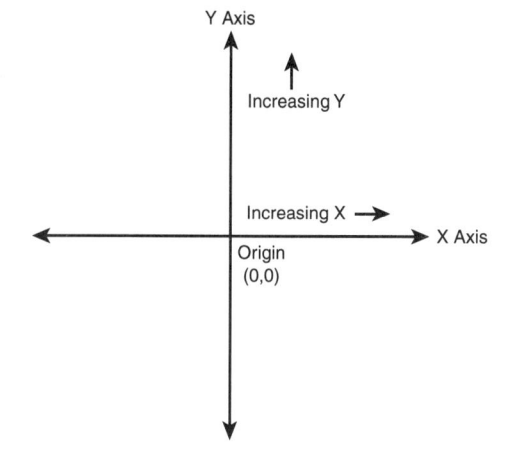

FIGURE 9.3

The default Windows graphics mapping mode.

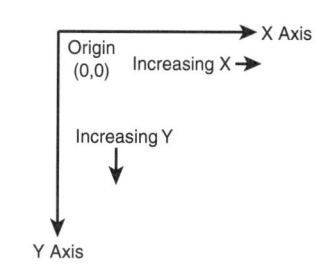

As the figure shows, the default Windows graphics coordinate system doesn't support negative coordinate values. Its X-axis increases to the right, whereas its Y-axis increases down. When you map this coordinate system to an application window, the origin ends up being located in the upper left corner of the window's client area. This means that all graphics coordinates in the default Windows mapping mode are specified relative to the upper left corner of a window's client area. You will primarily use this mapping mode as the basis for GDI operations such as drawing lines, rectangles, and bitmaps.

Understanding Color

You can't get very far in discussing graphics without taking a moment to explore color and how it impacts graphics in Windows. To fully understand the role color plays in Windows graphics, you have to take a step back and examine color in computer systems in general. The main function of color in a computer system is to accurately reflect the physical nature of color within the confines of a graphical system.

Your color monitor provides a very useful insight into how computer systems handle color. A color monitor has three electron guns: red, green, and blue. The output from these three guns converges on each pixel of the screen to produce a color. The color itself is determined by the intensities of each of the guns. Figure 9.4 illustrates how electron guns combine colors in a monitor.

FIGURE 9.4

Electron guns are used to combine colors in a color computer monitor.

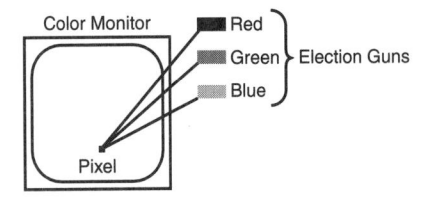

The software color system used by Windows is very similar to the hardware color system used by color monitors; unique colors are formed by combining varying intensities of the colors red, green, and blue. Windows programs use numeric color intensities to determine the mix of a color, which in turn tell the monitor how hard to fire each electron gun. Combinations of the numeric intensities of the primary colors red, green, and blue therefore represent Windows colors. This color system is known as RGB (Red Green Blue) and is standard across most graphical computer systems.

Each component (red, green, and blue) of a Windows color is represented by a number in the range 0–255. Table 9.1 shows the numeric values for the color components of some basic colors. If you pay attention to the primary colors red, green, and blue, you'll see that they consist solely of one color component at the maximum value of 255.

TABLE 9.1 NUMERIC RGB VALUES FOR SOME BASIC COLORS

Color	Red	Green	Blue
Red	255	0	0
Green	0	255	0
Blue	0	0	255
Black	0	0	0
White	255	255	255
Light Gray	192	192	192
Dark Gray	128	128	128
Yellow	255	255	0
Purple	255	0	255

Colors are represented in Windows programs by the `COLORREF` data type, which packs the RGB components of a color into a single numeric value. You can create a `COLORREF` value from individual RGB components using the `RGB` macro, like this:

```
COLORREF color = RGB(255, 0, 0);
```

This example creates a `COLORREF` value representing the color red. Most of the GDI operations that make use of color expect you to provide the color as a `COLORREF` value. After you have a `COLORREF` color value, you can extract individual RGB color components using the `GetRValue`, `GetGValue`, and `GetBValue` macros. Following is an example of extracting the red color component from a `COLORREF` value:

```
BYTE redComp = GetRValue(color);
```

GDI and MFC

Thus far the discussion of Windows graphics has mentioned nothing of MFC. It's now time to see how MFC fits into the scheme of painting graphics in an application. A large part of the functionality of the GDI is encapsulated in a single MFC class, `CDC`, which is a device context class. The `CDC` class represents an abstract graphics drawing surface (device context), and provides lots of member functions for performing a wide range of graphics operations. The `CDC` class supports the basic graphics components you learned about earlier, including palettes, bitmaps, pens, and brushes. You can also use the `CDC` class to draw graphics primitives such as lines, rectangles, and ellipses, as well as text.

There are three sub-classes of CDC worth knowing about: `CPaintDC`, `CClientDC`, and `CWindowDC`. The `CPaintDC` class is associated with the `WM_PAINT` message, which is sent to a window that needs to be painted. You learn more about this message a little later in the hour. The `CClientDC` class manages a device context associated with a window's client area, whereas the `CWindowDC` class manages a device context associated with an entire window, including its frame and controls. You will typically use either `CPaintDC` or `CClientDC` in most applications to perform painting operations.

Because graphics device contexts (DCs) are generic in nature, it's sometimes helpful to be able to find out information about the underlying hardware that they represent. For example, you might want to find out the width and height of the screen in order to resize a window appropriately. You determine the capabilities of a device context using the `GetDeviceCaps()` member function of the CDC class:

```
int GetDeviceCaps(int nIndex);
```

You obtain a specific device context attribute by providing a constant in the `nIndex` parameter. Following are some of the more commonly used constants accepted by the `GetDeviceCaps()` function:

- `HORZSIZE`—width of the physical screen in millimeters
- `VERTSIZE`—height of the physical screen in millimeters
- `HORZRES`—width of the physical screen in pixels
- `VERTRES`—height of the physical screen in pixels
- `BITSPIXEL`—number of adjacent color bits for each pixel
- `NUMCOLORS`—number of entries in the device's color table

As an example, you can determine the width and height of a graphical output device, in pixels, like this:

```
int width = dc.GetDeviceCaps(HORZRES);
int height = dc.GetDeviceCaps(VERTRES);
```

Painting Windows

You understand that device contexts are used to paint a window using the `CDC` class or one of its subclasses. However, you haven't learned when to paint a window. Unfortunately, you don't really have any say over when a window is painted; it is handled automatically by Windows. When a window needs to be painted, Windows sends it a `WM_PAINT` message. This can occur when a window is first created, when a window is uncovered from behind other windows, or a variety of other reasons. The bottom line is that you must handle the `WM_PAINT` message in order to paint the client area of a window.

> When I refer to painting or drawing to a window, I'm really referring to a client window, which is positioned in the client area of a window. In case you forgot, this is the rectangular part of a window inside the window's border that doesn't include the window frame, caption, menu, system menu, or scroll bars. The coordinates of a client window follow the Windows coordinate system, which means that they begin in the upper left corner of the window and increase down and to the right. This coordinate system is very important because most GDI graphics operations are based on them.

Handling the `WM_PAINT` message involves mapping and creating an `OnPaint()` message handler. You must use the `ON_WM_PAINT` message map macro to map the message handler to the message, like this:

```
BEGIN_MESSAGE_MAP(CMainFrame, CFrameWnd)
    ON_WM_PAINT()
```

```
END_MESSAGE_MAP()
```

Following is the declaration of the `OnPaint()` message handler:

```
afx_msg void OnPaint();
```

To actually paint graphics within the `OnPaint()` message handler, you must create a `CPaintDC` object. This is necessary because painting operations are always performed on a device context. Following is a skeletal `OnPaint()` message handler:

```
afx_msg void CMainFrame::OnPaint() {
  CPaintDC dc(this);
  // add painting code here
}
```

With the `CPaintDC` object created, you are free to paint to the device context at will. Let's learn about some of the different things you can paint using a device context.

Drawing Graphics Primitives

Graphics primitives form a fundamental part of any graphical system. The Windows GDI supports a wide range of graphics primitives, which you can paint to a device context using a `CDC` object. Each graphics primitive is drawn using the current pen, which is a property of the `CDC` object. The current pen defines the color and width of lines used in painting graphics primitives. Following are the major graphics primitives you can paint using a `CDC` object:

- Lines
- Rectangles
- Ellipses
- Polygons
- Pies
- Arcs

You learn how to draw a few of these graphics primitives in the next few sections.

Lines

Lines are painted using the `MoveTo()` and `LineTo()` member functions, which operate under the premise of a current graphics position. The current graphics position is an invisible point used as the starting point for lines. You set this point using the `MoveTo()` member function. There are two versions of the `MoveTo()` member function, which accept the current position as either a pair of integers or as a `POINT` structure:

```
CPoint MoveTo(int x, int y);
```

```
CPoint MoveTo(POINT point);
```

The `MoveTo()` member functions both return the previous current position as a `CPoint` object. The `LineTo()` member function draws a line connecting the current position to a specified end point. Following are the two versions of the `LineTo()` member function:

```
BOOL LineTo(int x, int y);
BOOL LineTo(POINT point);
```

The `LineTo()` member functions both return `TRUE` if the line was successfully drawn, and `FALSE` otherwise. You can get the current graphics position using the `GetCurrentPosition()` member function:

```
CPoint GetCurrentPosition();
```

Listing 9.1 contains an `OnPaint()` message handler that uses the `MoveTo()` and `LineTo()` member functions to draw a line.

LISTING 9.1 AN `OnPaint()` MESSAGE HANDLER THAT DRAWS A LINE

```
1: afx_msg void CMainFrame::OnPaint() {
2:     CPaintDC dc(this);
3:
4:     // Draw a line
5:     dc.MoveTo(0, 0);
6:     dc.LineTo(50, 75);
7: }
```

> An XY coordinate in Windows is referred to as a point, and is often represented by the Win32 `POINT` structure. The `POINT` structure is used throughout the Win32 API to represent coordinates for a variety of different operations. The `POINT` structure consists solely of two long integer fields, X and Y. MFC wraps the `POINT` structure with the `CPoint` class, which is used to specify XY coordinates in many of the `CDC` painting member functions.

Rectangles

Rectangles are painted using the `Rectangle()` function, which comes in two forms:

```
BOOL Rectangle(int x1, int y1, int x2, int y2);
BOOL Rectangle(LPCRECT lpRect);
```

The only difference between the two versions of `Rectangle()` is that one accepts a rectangle as two pairs of integer coordinates specifying the upper left and lower right corners of the rectangle, whereas the other takes a pointer to a `RECT` structure. The `CDC` class also provides a `FillRect()` member function that enables you to draw a rectangle filled with a given color.

> One really nice feature of many of the MFC wrapper classes is that they have overloaded operators for converting them to standard Win32 data types. For example, the `CRect` class has an overloaded `operator LPCRECT()` member function that converts a `CRect` object to a pointer to `RECT` structure. This enables you to pass a `CRect` object to a member function expecting a pointer to `RECT` structure (LPCRECT or LPRECT), such as the `CDC::Rectangle()` member function. Since `CRect` inherits directly from `RECT`, there is no overhead involved in the conversion.

Listing 9.2 contains an `OnPaint()` message handler that uses the `Rectangle()` member function to draw a rectangle.

LISTING 9.2 AN `OnPaint()` MESSAGE HANDLER THAT DRAWS A RECTANGLE

```
1: afx_msg void CMainFrame::OnPaint() {
2:    CPaintDC dc(this);
3:
4:    // Draw a rectangle
5:    RECT rc = { 0, 0, 100, 150 };
6:    dc.Rectangle(&rc);
7: }
```

> You can paint perfect squares using the `Rectangle()` function by specifying the same value for the width and height of the bounding rectangle.

Ellipses

Ellipses are painted using the `Ellipse()` member function, which functions very much like the `Rectangle()` member function. The `Ellipse()` member function comes in two forms:

`BOOL Ellipse(int x1, int y1, int x2, int y2);`

`BOOL Ellipse(LPCRECT lpRect);`

The rectangle specified in each `Ellipse()` function represents the bounding rectangle for the ellipse to be painted. Listing 9.3 contains an `OnPaint()` message handler that uses the `Ellipse()` member function to draw an ellipse.

Hour 9

LISTING 9.3 AN `OnPaint()` MESSAGE HANDLER THAT DRAWS AN ELLIPSE

```
1: afx_msg void CMainFrame::OnPaint() {
2:     CPaintDC dc(this);
3:
4:     // Draw an ellipse (circle in this case)
5:     RECT rc = { 0, 0, 100, 100 };
6:     dc.Ellipse(&rc);
7: }
```

> You can paint perfect circles using the `Ellipse()` function by specifying the same value for the width and height of the bounding rectangle.

Drawing Text

In Windows, text is treated no differently than graphics, which means that text is painted using GDI functions. Of course, this means that an MFC application paints text using a member function of the `CDC` class. The primary member function used to paint text is `TextOut()`:

`BOOL TextOut(int x, int y, const CString& str);`

The first two parameters to the `TextOut()` function, x and y, identify the coordinates of the upper left corner of the first text character. Figure 9.5 shows how these coordinates relate to the painted text. The last parameter, str, contains the string of text to be drawn.

FIGURE 9.5

Text coordinates identify the upper left corner of the first text character.

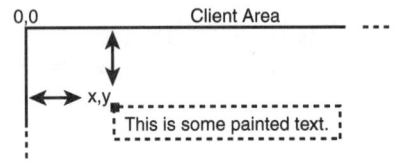

Listing 9.4 contains an `OnPaint()` message handler that uses the `TextOut()` member function to draw a string of text.

LISTING 9.4 AN `OnPaint()` MESSAGE HANDLER THAT DRAWS A STRING OF TEXT

```
1: afx_msg void CMainFrame::OnPaint() {
2:     CPaintDC dc(this);
3:
4:     // Draw a string of text
```

```
5:    CString str = "This is some text!";
6:    dc.TextOut(10, 30, str);
7: }
```

Drawing Bitmaps

You learned earlier in this hour that the primary colors red, green, and blue converge inside your monitor to produce different colored pixels on the screen. A bitmap is a rectangular grouping of pixels. To better understand this, consider the bitmap in Figure 9.6.

FIGURE 9.6

A rectangular bitmap.

At this size it's hard to visualize the fact that an image is just a grouping of pixels. But when you zoom in, things take on a whole new perspective. Figure 9.7 shows a magnified portion of the same image.

FIGURE 9.7

Zooming in on a bitmap reveals that it is just a rectangular grouping of pixels.

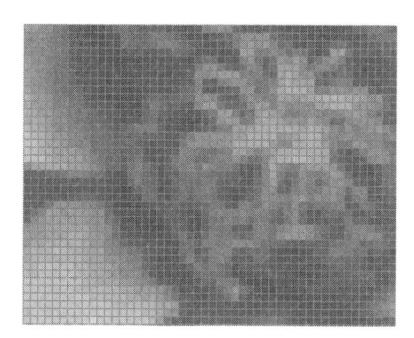

As you can see, a bitmap is just a bunch of different colored pixels arranged in a rectangular shape.

Loading a Bitmap

Now that you have an idea about what bitmaps are, let's focus on how to load and display them. Before you can display a bitmap, you must first load it into the computer's memory. If you don't see the significance of loading a bitmap before displaying it, imagine trying to view a slideshow without loading slides into the slide projector.

Before you can even get into the details of loading and painting a bitmap, you must specify the bitmap as a resource in your application's resource script. Following is the resource definition for a bitmap stored in the file Mine.bmp with an identifier named IDB_MYBITMAP.

```
IDB_MYBITMAP BITMAP   "Mine.bmp"
```

In MFC, bitmaps are represented by the `CBitmap` class. The `CBitmap` class provides a member function named `LoadBitmap()` that is used to load a bitmap after you've created a `CBitmap` object. You load a bitmap by providing a bitmap resource identifier to the `LoadBitmap()` function, like this:

```
CBitmap bm;
bm.LoadBitmap(IDB_MYBITMAP);
```

Painting a Bitmap

After you've loaded a bitmap into a `CBitmap` object, you're ready to paint the bitmap using the `BitBlt()` member function provided by the `CDC` class. Unfortunately, painting a bitmap isn't as easy as just calling one member function. You must first create a memory device context and select the bitmap into it. You then copy the bitmap from the memory device context to the output device context. To summarize, following are the steps required to paint a bitmap:

1. Create a memory device context.
2. Select the bitmap into the memory device context.
3. Copy the bitmap from the memory device context to the output device context using the `BitBlt()` member function.

Listing 9.5 contains an `OnPaint()` message handler that uses the `BitBlt()` member function to draw a bitmap.

LISTING 9.5 AN OnPaint() MESSAGE HANDLER THAT DRAWS A BITMAP

```
1: afx_msg void CMainFrame::OnPaint() {
2:   CPaintDC dc(this);
3:
```

```
 4:    // Load the bitmap
 5:    CBitmap bm;
 6:    bm.LoadBitmap(IDB_MYBITMAP);
 7:
 8:    // Create the memory DC
 9:    CDC memDC;
10:    memDC.CreateCompatibleDC(&dc);
11:
12:    // Select the bitmap into the memory DC
13:    memDC.SelectObject(&bm);
14:
15:    // Paint the bitmap
16:    dc.BitBlt(10, 20, 32, 32, &memDC, 0, 0, SRCCOPY);
17: }
```

The first two parameters of the `BitBlt()` function are the X and Y coordinates of where the bitmap is to be painted. The third and fourth parameters specify the width and height of the bitmap, which should match the physical dimensions of the bitmap. The fifth parameter is the source device context containing the bitmap. The sixth and seventh parameters are the coordinates within the bitmap from which to copy pixels. These coordinates will always be `0, 0` unless you want to draw only a portion of a bitmap. The last parameter to `BitBlt()` is the raster operation to be performed, which determines the manner in which the bitmap pixels are painted. You will typically use the `SRCCOPY` or `SRCAND` raster operations to paint bitmaps. The `SRCCOPY` operation copies each bitmap pixel over the background pixels, whereas the `SRCAND` operation performs a bitwise `AND` between each bitmap pixel and the background pixels.

Putting It All Together

You've seen some small examples of how to paint graphics using the `CDC` class throughout the hour. The remainder of the hour focuses on the development of an application called Doodle that demonstrates some of the graphics functions you've learned about. Figure 9.8 shows the Doodle application, which enables you to use the mouse to draw some graphics primitives including lines, rectangles, ellipses, and bitmaps.

The Doodle application begins with a Resource.h header file, which is shown in Listing 9.6.

FIGURE 9.8.

The Doodle application.

LISTING 9.6 THE RESOURCE.H HEADER FILE FOR DOODLE

```
 1: //-------------------------------------------------------------
 2: // Strings                    Range : 1000 - 1999
 3: //-------------------------------------------------------------
 4: #define IDR_DOODLE            1000
 5:
 6: //-------------------------------------------------------------
 7: // Bitmaps                    Range : 2000 - 2999
 8: //-------------------------------------------------------------
 9: #define IDB_CRITTER           2000
10:
11: //-------------------------------------------------------------
12: // Commands                   Range : 3000 - 3999
13: //-------------------------------------------------------------
14: #define ID_DRAW_LINE          3000
15: #define ID_DRAW_RECTANGLE     3001
16: #define ID_DRAW_ELLIPSE       3002
17: #define ID_DRAW_CRITTER       3003
18: #define ID_DRAW_CHANGECOLOR   3004
19:
20: //-------------------------------------------------------------
21: // Dialog Boxes               Range : 4000 - 4999
22: //-------------------------------------------------------------
23: #define IDD_ABOUTBOX          4000
```

This header file defines identifiers for a bitmap resource and a host of commands used with the application's menu. Listing 9.7 shows the Doodle application's resource file, which actually defines the resources.

LISTING 9.7 THE DOODLE.RC RESOURCE FILE FOR DOODLE

```
 1: //-----------------------------------------------------------
 2: // Inclusions
 3: //-----------------------------------------------------------
 4: #include "AfxRes.h"
 5: #include "Resource.h"
 6:
 7: //-----------------------------------------------------------
 8: // Icons
 9: //-----------------------------------------------------------
10: IDR_DOODLE  ICON   "Doodle.ico"
11:
12: //-----------------------------------------------------------
13: // Bitmaps
14: //-----------------------------------------------------------
15: IDB_CRITTER BITMAP  "Critter.bmp"
16:
17: //-----------------------------------------------------------
18: // Menus
19: //-----------------------------------------------------------
20: IDR_DOODLE MENU
21: BEGIN
22:    POPUP "&File"
23:      BEGIN
24:        MENUITEM "E&xit",              ID_APP_EXIT
25:      END
26:    POPUP "&Draw"
27:      BEGIN
28:        MENUITEM "&Line",              ID_DRAW_LINE
29:        MENUITEM "&Rectangle",         ID_DRAW_RECTANGLE
30:        MENUITEM "&Ellipse",           ID_DRAW_ELLIPSE
31:        MENUITEM "&Critter",           ID_DRAW_CRITTER
32:        MENUITEM SEPARATOR
33:        MENUITEM "Change C&olor...",   ID_DRAW_CHANGECOLOR
34:      END
35:    POPUP "&Help"
36:      BEGIN
37:        MENUITEM "&About Doodle...",   ID_APP_ABOUT
38:      END
```

continues

LISTING 9.7 CONTINUED

```
39: END
40:
41: //-----------------------------------------------------------
42: // Dialog Boxes
43: //-----------------------------------------------------------
44: IDD_ABOUTBOX DIALOG 0, 0, 217, 55
45: CAPTION "About Doodle"
46: STYLE DS_MODALFRAME ¦ WS_POPUP ¦ WS_CAPTION ¦ WS_SYSMENU
47: FONT 8, "MS Sans Serif"
48: BEGIN
49:     ICON            IDR_DOODLE, IDC_STATIC, 11, 17, 20, 20
50:     LTEXT           "Doodle Version 1.0", IDC_STATIC, 40, 10,
51:                     119, 8, SS_NOPREFIX
52:     LTEXT           "Copyright (c)1998 Michael Morrison", IDC_STATIC,
53:                     40, 25, 119, 8
54:     DEFPUSHBUTTON "OK", IDOK, 178, 7, 32, 14, WS_GROUP
55: END
56:
57: //-----------------------------------------------------------
58: // Strings
59: //-----------------------------------------------------------
60: STRINGTABLE
61: BEGIN
62:     AFX_IDS_APP_TITLE   "Doodle"
63: END
```

This resource script defines an icon resource, a bitmap resource, a menu resource, and the familiar About dialog box resource. The critter bitmap used in Doodle is stored in the file Critter.bmp and identified by IDB_CRITTER. Also, notice that the menu resource defines a Draw pop-up menu containing drawing modes (Line, Rectangle, Ellipse, Critter) and a menu item (Change Color) for changing the drawing color.

Rather than list the entire source code for the Doodle application, let's focus on the most important parts. Listing 9.8 contains the message map for the CMainFrame class.

LISTING 9.8 THE CMainFrame MESSAGE MAP FOR DOODLE

```
1: BEGIN_MESSAGE_MAP(CMainFrame, CFrameWnd)
2:     ON_WM_LBUTTONDOWN()
3:     ON_COMMAND(ID_DRAW_LINE, OnDrawLine)
4:     ON_COMMAND(ID_DRAW_RECTANGLE, OnDrawRectangle)
5:     ON_COMMAND(ID_DRAW_ELLIPSE, OnDrawEllipse)
6:     ON_COMMAND(ID_DRAW_CRITTER, OnDrawCritter)
```

```
 7:    ON_COMMAND(ID_DRAW_CHANGECOLOR, OnDrawChangeColor)
 8:    ON_COMMAND(ID_APP_ABOUT, OnAppAbout)
 9:    ON_UPDATE_COMMAND_UI(ID_DRAW_LINE, OnUpdateDrawLine)
10:    ON_UPDATE_COMMAND_UI(ID_DRAW_RECTANGLE, OnUpdateDrawRectangle)
11:    ON_UPDATE_COMMAND_UI(ID_DRAW_ELLIPSE, OnUpdateDrawEllipse)
12:    ON_UPDATE_COMMAND_UI(ID_DRAW_CRITTER, OnUpdateDrawCritter)
13: END_MESSAGE_MAP()
```

This message map wires message handlers for the WM_LBUTTONDOWN message, along with the different menu commands. It also establishes menu command update message handlers for the drawing mode menu items. Before I get into the details of these message handlers, let's take a quick look at the member variables for the CMainFrame class:

```
enum     { DM_LINE, DM_RECTANGLE, DM_ELLIPSE, DM_CRITTER };
int      m_nDrawMode;
CPen     m_pen;
```

The m_nDrawMode member variable keeps track of the current drawing mode. The m_pen member variable is the current pen used to draw graphics primitives. Any time you change the drawing color, the old pen is deleted and a new one is created and stored in the m_pen member. Following is the CMainFrame constructor, which initializes these two member variables:

```
CMainFrame::CMainFrame() : m_nDrawMode(DM_LINE),
  m_pen(PS_SOLID, 2, RGB(0, 0, 0)) {
}
```

The initial drawing mode is set to DM_LINE, whereas the initial pen is a solid black pen that is two pixels wide. The constructor for CPen enables you to create solid and dashed pens of varying widths and colors.

Listing 9.9 contains the Doodle menu command message handlers, which set the drawing mode and enable you to change the drawing color.

LISTING 9.9 THE CMainFrame MENU COMMAND MESSAGE HANDLERS FOR DOODLE

```
1: void CMainFrame::OnDrawLine() {
2:   // Set the drawing mode to Line
3:   m_nDrawMode = DM_LINE;
4: }
5:
6: void CMainFrame::OnDrawRectangle() {
```

continues

LISTING 9.9 CONTINUED

```
 7:     // Set the drawing mode to Rectangle
 8:     m_nDrawMode = DM_RECTANGLE;
 9: }
10:
11: void CMainFrame::OnDrawEllipse() {
12:     // Set the drawing mode to Ellipse
13:     m_nDrawMode = DM_ELLIPSE;
14: }
15:
16: void CMainFrame::OnDrawCritter() {
17:     // Set the drawing mode to Critter
18:     m_nDrawMode = DM_CRITTER;
19: }
20:
21: void CMainFrame::OnDrawChangeColor() {
22:     // Select a pen color using the Color dialog box
23:     CColorDialog dlg;
24:     if (dlg.DoModal() == IDOK) {
25:         // Create a new pen with the selected color
26:         m_pen.DeleteObject();
27:         m_pen.CreatePen(PS_SOLID, 2, dlg.GetColor());
28:     }
29: }
30:
31: void CMainFrame::OnAppAbout() {
32:     CAboutDlg aboutDlg;
33:     aboutDlg.DoModal();
34: }
```

The first four message handlers respond to each drawing mode menu command by setting the drawing mode appropriately. The OnDrawChangeColor() message handler uses a Color common dialog box to enable the user to select a new drawing color. This color is used to create a new pen that is used to draw the graphics primitives in the application.

Listing 9.10 contains the Doodle menu command update message handlers, which enforce a mutually exclusive radio button style for the drawing mode menu items.

LISTING 9.10 THE CMainFrame MENU COMMAND UPDATE MESSAGE HANDLERS FOR DOODLE

```
1: void CMainFrame::OnUpdateDrawLine(CCmdUI* pCmdUI) {
2:     // Update the Draw¦Line menu item
3:     pCmdUI->SetRadio(m_nDrawMode == DM_LINE);
4: }
5:
6: void CMainFrame::OnUpdateDrawRectangle(CCmdUI* pCmdUI) {
7:     // Update the Draw¦Rectangle menu item
```

Drawing Graphics

```
 8:     pCmdUI->SetRadio(m_nDrawMode == DM_RECTANGLE);
 9:   }
10:
11:   void CMainFrame::OnUpdateDrawEllipse(CCmdUI* pCmdUI) {
12:     // Update the Draw|Ellipse menu item
13:     pCmdUI->SetRadio(m_nDrawMode == DM_ELLIPSE);
14:   }
15:
16:   void CMainFrame::OnUpdateDrawCritter(CCmdUI* pCmdUI) {
17:     // Update the Draw|Critter menu item
18:     pCmdUI->SetRadio(m_nDrawMode == DM_CRITTER);
19:   }
```

The `SetRadio()` member function of `CCmdUI` is used to set a radio style check mark next to a menu item; passing `TRUE` sets the mark, whereas `FALSE` clears it.

The last code of interest in Doodle is the `OnLButtonDown()` message handler, which is shown in Listing 9.11.

LISTING 9.11 THE `CMainFrame::OnLButtonDown` MESSAGE HANDLER FOR DOODLE

```
 1: void CMainFrame::OnLButtonDown(UINT nFlags, CPoint point) {
 2:   // Start the "rubber band" rectangle tracker
 3:   CRectTracker tracker;
 4:   tracker.TrackRubberBand(this, point);
 5:
 6:   // Create a DC and select the pen
 7:   CClientDC dc(this);
 8:   dc.SelectObject(m_pen);
 9:   dc.SelectObject(CBrush::FromHandle((HBRUSH)::GetStockObject
      ➥(NULL_BRUSH)));
10:
11:   // Draw graphics based on the drawing mode
12:   switch (m_nDrawMode) {
13:   case DM_LINE:
14:     // Draw a line
15:     dc.MoveTo(tracker.m_rect.TopLeft());
16:     dc.LineTo(tracker.m_rect.BottomRight());
17:     break;
18:
19:   case DM_RECTANGLE:
20:     // Draw a rectangle
21:     dc.Rectangle(tracker.m_rect);
22:     break;
23:
```

continues

LISTING 9.11   CONTINUED

```
24:     case DM_ELLIPSE:
25:       // Draw an ellipse
26:       dc.Ellipse(tracker.m_rect);
27:       break;
28:
29:     case DM_CRITTER:
30:       // Load the critter bitmap
31:       CBitmap   bmCritter;
32:       BITMAP    bmInfo;
33:       VERIFY(bmCritter.LoadBitmap(IDB_CRITTER));
34:       bmCritter.GetObject(sizeof(BITMAP), &bmInfo);
35:
36:       // Setup the memory DC
37:       CDC       dcMem;
38:       dcMem.CreateCompatibleDC(&dc);
39:       VERIFY(pbmOld = dcMem.SelectObject(&bmCritter));
40:
41:       // Draw the critter image
42:       dc.StretchBlt(tracker.m_rect.left, tracker.m_rect.top,
43:         tracker.m_rect.Width(), tracker.m_rect.Height(), &dcMem, 0, 0,
44:         bmInfo.bmWidth, bmInfo.bmHeight, SRCAND);
45:       break;
46:   }
47: }
```

The `OnLButtonDown()` member function uses a `CRectTracker` object to draw a "rubber band" style rectangle that stretches as you hold down the left mouse button and drag the mouse. This tracker provides a visual indicator of the bounding rectangle for the graphics operation being performed.

> One interesting thing about the Doodle application is that it doesn't rely on the `OnPaint()` message handler to perform its painting. This is because the goal of Doodle is to paint graphics in direct response to the user dragging the mouse around. The downside of Doodle is that all the painting is lost when the window is repainted due to the fact that the `OnPaint()` message handler knows nothing about the graphics operations that have taken place. In reality, the Doodle application should store each of the graphics operation and then render them in the `OnPaint()` method. However, this requires some advanced usage of data structures that you aren't quite prepared for just yet.

Because the `OnLButtonDown()` message handler doesn't provide a device context like `OnPaint()`, you must create one yourself. A `CClientDC` object is easy enough to create and use, as the code for the function shows. The `m_pen` member is selected into the newly created device context, along with a null brush. The null brush ensures that all graphics operations will have transparent backgrounds. The remainder of the `OnLButtonDown()` handler paints each of the graphics primitives using code that should be very familiar to you.

There are a couple of new tricks in the way the bitmap is painted, however. First of all, the `StretchBlt()` member function is used to copy the bitmap to the output device context instead of `BitBlt()`. This was done to allow the user to stretch and shrink the bitmap to different sizes. Also, the size of the bitmap was obtained by calling the `GetObject()` member function on the bitmap. This function fills out a `BITMAP` structure with information about a bitmap.

Summary

This hour covered a lot of territory by teaching you the ins and outs of Windows graphics. You began the hour by learning about device contexts, graphics components, the Windows graphics coordinate system, and color. You then moved on to learn about MFC's role in graphics and how windows are painted. From there you focused on how to draw graphics primitives, text, and bitmaps. You wrapped up the hour by developing a pretty neat application that showed off much of your newfound graphics knowledge.

Q&A

Q Do GDI graphics operations always use pixels to specify units?

A No. In fact, all GDI graphics operations use logical units, and not actual pixel units. The GDI makes use of a mapping mode to map logical units to physical graphics device units (pixels). The default mapping mode happens to map one logical unit to one pixel unit, which is why it appears that you are dealing directly with pixels. Other mapping modes are used in special circumstances where you want to scale graphics to a particular device.

Q Can you force a window to repaint itself?

A Yes. Even though you can never call the `OnPaint()` message handler directly, you can cause it to be called by invalidating the window. This is accomplished by calling the `Invalidate()` member function of `CWnd`.

Workshop

The Workshop is designed to help you anticipate possible questions, review what you've learned, and begin thinking ahead to put your knowledge into practice. The answers to the quiz are in Appendix A, "Quiz Answers."

Quiz

1. What is the Windows Graphics Device Interface (GDI)?
2. What is a graphics device context?
3. What is the significance of device-independent graphics?
4. What is a set of colors used by GDI when rendering an image?
5. What is a bitmap?
6. In which directions do the X-axis and Y-axis of the Windows coordinate system increase in value?
7. What macro is used to pack color components into a COLORREF value?
8. When does Windows send a window a WM_PAINT message?
9. What is the role of the CClientDC class?
10. How do you draw a perfect circle using the CDC class?

Exercises

1. Experiment with the m_pen member variable in the Doodle application by trying different parameters in the call to the CreatePen() member function. Some valid pen styles include PS_SOLID, PS_DASH, and PS_DOT. You can also change the width of the pen by changing the second parameter to CreatePen().
2. Create a bitmap of your own and use it in place of the Critter.bmp bitmap in Doodle. Make sure to change the bitmap name referenced in the resource file for the application.

HOUR 10

Managing Data with MFC

Although you might think of data structures as a general programming topic outside of the realm of Windows programming in MFC, data structures actually play an important role in both Windows and MFC. This hour explores the basics of data structures and how they fit into MFC. You will spend some time getting acquainted with strings, which are a basic yet powerful data structure supported by MFC.

In this hour, you will learn

- The basics of data structures
- MFC's support for data structures
- How to use the `CString` class to work with strings
- How to manipulate time using the `CTime` and `CTimeSpan` classes

Getting a Handle on Data Structures

You might be a little curious about the purpose of this hour because Windows applications don't necessarily require any unique usage of data structures. Even though this is the case, an argument could be made that all applications typically utilize data structures even if they are basic arrays and strings. For this reason, Microsoft felt it necessary to build some pretty powerful data structure support into MFC. More specifically, MFC provides a variety of data structure classes for representing simple data structures such as rectangles and strings, as well as more complex collections of data.

Before I get into the specific MFC data classes, let's take a moment to clarify the importance of data structures. Practically every Windows application works with information to some degree, and therefore has its own set of data requirements that greatly affect the applicability of different data structures. If you don't understand the full range of programming options in terms of data structures, you'll find yourself trying to solve every problem with an array. This tendency to rely on one solution for all your programming problems will end up getting you into trouble. In other words, by understanding how to use a wide variety of data structures, you broaden your perspective on how to solve the inevitable problems arising from new programming challenges. End of sermon.

Now that I've bored you with my treatise on why data structures are important, allow me to get a little more specific about how they are used. Beyond the primitive data types such as `int` and `float`, the array is probably the most simple data structure used in C++. To refresh your memory, an array is simply an aggregate series of data elements of the same type. Arrays are referred to as "aggregate" because they are treated as a single entity, just like any other variable. However, they actually contain multiple elements that can be accessed independently. Based on this description, it's logical to assume that arrays are useful any time you need to store and access a group of information that is all the same type. However, the glaring limitation with arrays is that they can't change in size to accommodate more (or fewer) elements. Additionally, you must always access array elements using an integer index. These two limitations often make it impossible for some applications to use arrays.

As you might have already surmised, MFC offers support for data structures that go well beyond the confines of standard C++ arrays. And not all the MFC data structures are designed to store collections of data; some of them simply encapsulate a commonly used data type such as a string. Let's examine the different data structure classes that MFC has to offer.

MFC's Data Classes

Data structures in MFC are implemented as classes, which allows them to provide an interface (member functions) for interacting with the data they contain. MFC's data structure classes can be broken down into three major types:

- Basic data structures
- Data collections
- Support classes

The next couple of sections examine the MFC classes for each of these types of data structures.

Basic Data Structures

Basic MFC data structures are used to represent a single element of data that is somehow more complex than a primitive data type. Most of the basic MFC data structure classes are wrappers around existing Win32 structures implemented in C. You'll typically find the MFC classes much easier to work with than traditional C structures. Following are the basic MFC data structures:

- `CPoint`—the XY coordinate of a point (wraps `POINT`)
- `CSize`—the width and height of a rectangle (wraps `SIZE`)
- `CRect`—a rectangle (wraps `RECT`)
- `CString`—a string of text
- `CTime`—an absolute date and time
- `CTimeSpan`—a relative time span

The `CPoint`, `CSize`, and `CRect` classes all wrap existing Win32 data structures. You already have some experience using `CPoint` and `CRect`. The `CSize` class is very similar to `CPoint`, except that `CSize` internally uses the `int` type to represent a rectangular width and height, whereas `CPoint` uses the `LONG` type. It's worth noting that in some cases you might want to use the Win32 data structures instead of these classes to minimize overhead. For example, you used a `RECT` structure directly in the Animator3 application to set the initial window size:

```
RECT rc = { 5, 5, 320, 345 };
```

Because Animator3 didn't need to use any of the member functions of `CRect`, it was a little more efficient to use a `RECT` structure. If you wanted to stick with the MFC `CRect` class, you could have also used the following code:

```
CRect rc = new CRect(5, 5, 320, 345);
```

Getting back to the basic MFC data structures, the `CString`, `CTime`, and `CTimeSpan` classes aren't based on any existing Win32 data structures. You spend some time later in the hour learning more details about these classes, so let's move on and learn about the MFC collection classes.

Data Collections

Data collections are special data structures that contain multiple items of a given type. Arrays are considered a primitive form of a data collection even though they aren't implemented as classes. MFC's data collection classes provide lots of flexibility when it comes to storing collections of data. The MFC classes are based on C++ templates, which are mechanisms for generating classes based on type parameters. Templates enable you to design a single class that operates on data of many types, as opposed to creating a separate class for each type.

NEW TERM A *template (C++)* is a mechanism for generating classes based on type parameters.

To understand how templates fit into MFC collections, consider an array implemented as a class. The member functions for an array class would have to accept and return data of a specific type such as `int` or `char`, or maybe even a class type. You would have to create a different array class for each different date type you want to store in the array. So, you might have different array classes named `IntArray`, `CharArray`, and maybe `ObjectArray`. This approach to building an array class is clearly a hassle because the class performs the exact same function regardless of the data it contains. Using templates, you could create one generic array class that operates on any data type.

MFC provides template-based classes for the following collections:

- Array—a list of elements that can dynamically shrink and grow
- List—an ordered list of elements that can dynamically shrink and grow; also allows the insertion of elements
- Map—a "dictionary" that maps unique keys to values; each element in a map is a key/value pair, where a key is a special piece of data that uniquely identifies a value, such as a social security number

> MFC actually provides a set of collection classes that aren't based on templates. However, these classes are remnants of prior versions of MFC and shouldn't be used anymore. The template-based collections are more convenient and provide better type safety than the old collection classes.

Although these collections all store a set of elements, they are each geared toward a specific purpose. For example, arrays are optimized for access via an integer index, but suffer when it comes to inserting and deleting elements because other elements have to be shifted around. Likewise, lists are optimized for insertion and deletion, but aren't very effective when it comes to accessing an element via an index. Finally, maps are useful when you want to use a key to lookup a piece of information. Maps are sometimes referred to as dictionaries because of the way they are used to lookup data.

MFC supports two different approaches to template-based collections. There is a simple set of collection classes that are used to contain objects derived from the `CObject` class. There is also a set of collection classes that are used to contain pointers to objects of a specific type. Both of these approaches enforce type-safety, so it's OK to use either one of them. The next hour focuses on collections and gets into more detail regarding the different types of MFC collections and how they are used.

Support Classes

In addition to the basic data structures and collections, MFC also provides a few support classes that are used throughout the MFC framework. Following is a list of these classes:

- `CObject`—the base class for most MFC classes; provides basic object services
- `CDumpContext`—a diagnostic class for outputting diagnostic information about objects
- `CArchive`—a binary stream that supports the serialization of objects
- `CFile`—the base class for MFC file classes; provides file I/O services

The `CObject` class forms the basis of the MFC class hierarchy, and works in concert with the other support classes to provide basic services such as serialization, runtime class information, and diagnostic output.

The `CDumpContext` class is a diagnostic class used to output diagnostic information about an object. This class is useful in that it outputs diagnostic information from a stream as readable text. There is a standard `CDumpContext` object named `afxDump` that can be used to dump most objects. The `CDumpContext` class and `afxDump` object are only used in debug versions of an application.

> **NEW TERM** A medium through which diagnostic data is displayed for an object is called a *dump context*.

The `CArchive` class is used to implement object serialization, which is the capability of reading and writing objects as streams of binary data. The `CArchive` class itself acts as a binary stream and supports the reading and writing of objects. `CArchive` objects are typically associated with files, in which case objects are actually written to and retrieved from persistent files. Unlike standard C++ I/O streams, the `CArchive` class deals solely in binary data and is therefore more efficient at reading and writing binary objects.

The `CFile` class serves as the base class for MFC file classes, and provides support for file binary I/O. There are also classes derived from `CFile` that support text files and memory mapped files. It's important to understand that the `CFile` class works in conjunction with the `CArchive` class to support the serialization of MFC objects.

A Serialization Primer

The previous discussion of the MFC data structure support classes touched on object serialization. I want to take a moment to explain serialization because it is tightly linked to MFC's data structure classes. Serialization is the process of reading or writing an object as a stream of bytes. Serialization is extremely useful for storing and retrieving MFC objects to and from non-volatile locations, such as disk files. The key to serialization is the representation of an object's state in a serialized form that is capable of being restored. When serialized, an object is basically converted to a series of bytes that sufficiently represents the state of the object. The `CObject` and `CArchive` classes are largely responsible for supporting serialization in MFC. Figure 10.1 provides a visual look at how serialization works.

NEW TERM The process of reading or writing an object as a stream of bytes is known as *serialization*.

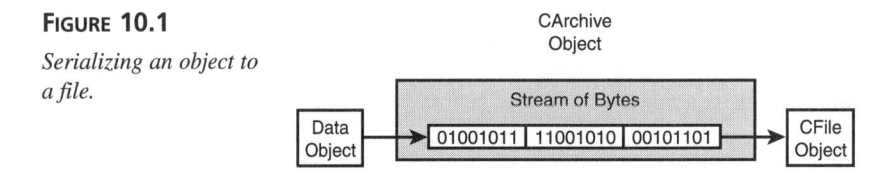

FIGURE 10.1

Serializing an object to a file.

As the figure shows, a data object is serialized into a stream of bytes using the `CArchive` class. The `CArchive` class then uses the `CFile` class to write the stream of bytes to a file. The `CArchive` and `CFile` classes are used heavily in MFC's document/view architecture to save and retrieve document data. You will use this approach to serialization in Hour 12, "Managing Application Data with Documents," when you learn how to create a serialized document.

Working with Strings

Now that you've spent some time learning about the different data structures supported by MFC, it's time to dig into the details of one of them. The `CString` class represents a string of text, and provides lots of different member functions for manipulating the text. The `CString` class is intended to be used in lieu of the standard C runtime string functions. I think you'll find the `CString` class so convenient to use that you won't miss any of the old C runtime functions. It's worth noting that `CString` is one of the few MFC classes that isn't derived from `CObject`.

The `CString` class provides member functions and overloaded operators that greatly simplify the handling of strings. You can think of a `CString` object as representing an actual string of text. Granted, deep down the `CString` class manages a string as a sequence of characters, but you can think of `CString` as a string type.

> As of MFC version 3.0, the `CString` class supports Unicode and Multibyte Character Sets (MBCS). These character sets make it much easier to create international applications that support multiple languages. To make use of this support, you should always format string literals using the _T macro. For example, my name as a Unicode string literal would be coded as _T("Michael"). I don't use the _T macro in the example code in this book because I want to keep things simple.

Creating Strings

Creating strings using the `CString` class is very simple. Following is an example of creating a `CString` object from a string literal:

```
CString string = "This is a string of text."
```

Notice that it isn't necessary to use a constructor because the `CString` class provides an overloaded operator for creating a `CString` object from a string literal. Just as you can assign a literal string to create a `CString` object, you can also assign `CString` objects, as the following code shows:

```
CString string = "This is a string of text."
CString stringCopy = string;
```

It's important to note that the first string is not copied when it is assigned to the second string. In other words, the two string objects share a reference to the same string data. If one of the strings is later modified, then a copy will be made so that the strings contain different string data. The reason that copied strings initially share a reference to the same data is because it is much more efficient than always performing a copy of the string data.

The `CString` class does provide constructors that can be used to create string objects. Following are a few examples of creating string objects using `CString` constructors:

```
CString s1();
CString s2("This is a string of text.");
CString s3(s2);
CString s4('z');
```

The first example creates an empty string object using the default `CString` constructor. The second example creates a string object from a string literal, and is functionally equivalent to the earlier assignment creation example. The third example creates a string object as a copy of another string object. Finally, the fourth example creates a string from a single character.

Accessing String Characters

Speaking of characters, you can access the individual characters within a `CString` object by using the `GetAt()` and `SetAt()` member functions. `CString` also supports the array subscript operator (`[ ]`), which performs exactly the same operation as the `GetAt()` member function.

> The `GetAt()` member function and subscript operator (`[ ]`) do not perform bounds checking on the character indices passed into them. This means that if you attempt to access a character beyond the end of a string, an application will either assert or perform a general protection fault, depending on whether it is a debug build or a release build.

Following is an example of using these different approaches to access string characters:

```
CString string = "ABCDEFG";
char f = string.GetAt(5);
string.SetAt(3, 'X');
char x = string[3];
```

Because the position parameter to `GetAt()` is zero-based, the call to `GetAt()` gets the sixth character in the string. The call to `SetAt()` results in the D character being replaced by X. Finally, the last line of code gets the fourth character in the string, which is the newly set X character.

Concatenating Strings

Concatenation is perhaps the most interesting aspect of working with `CString` objects, simply because it's so easy. To support concatenation, the `CString` class provides overloaded operators for = and +=. This allows you to concatenate strings as if they were numbers being added together. Following is an example to illustrate:

```
CString s1 = "Don't ";
CString s2 = "Shirley";
s1 += "call ";
CString message = s1 + "me " + s2 "!";
```

This example uses both of the overloaded `CString` concatenation operators. The resulting message string is `"Don't call me Shirley!"`.

Comparing Strings

It is often necessary to compare strings to see if they are the same. The `CString` class provides overloaded == and != operators, and a set of member functions for comparing strings. The `Compare()` member function is roughly equivalent to the == operator except that it returns 0 if the strings are equivalent. The `CompareNoCase()` member function is similar to `Compare()` but it compares strings without regard to case. Both of the functions and the overloaded operator compare string objects to see if they contain the same text. Following is an example:

```
CString name1 = "Jeffrey";
CString name2 = "Geoffrey";
if (name1 == "Jeffrey")
  MessageBox("Hello Jeffrey!");
else if (name1.Compare("Geoffrey") == 0)
  MessageBox("Oh, it's you Geoffrey!");
else
  MessageBox("Who are you?");
```

This example code uses the == operator and the `Compare()` member function to compare strings. As you can see, comparing strings in MFC is very simple and straightforward, thanks to the `CString` class.

> The `CString` class also provides overloaded relational operators for <, <=, >, and >=. These operators perform a lexicographical comparison between two string objects that is similar in function to the `strcmp()` C runtime function.

Strings and `Char` Pointers

Although you will likely use the `CString` class for most of your string handling needs, there will inevitably be times when you call a function and it expects a `char` pointer. This isn't a problem because the `CString` class provides an overloaded operator that converts a `CString` object to a `char` pointer. More specifically, the overloaded operator converts a `CString` object to the Win32 `LPCTSTR` data type, which is essentially a `const char` pointer. Following is an example of passing a `CString` object to a member function that expects a `char` pointer:

```
CString message = "Busy...";
PCmdUI->SetText(message);
```

This example sets the command update text of a graphical user interface element using a `CString` object. The `CCmdUI:SetText()` member function actually takes a `LPCTSTR` parameter, but the overloaded `CString` operator smoothes everything out. It's important to note that you shouldn't modify a `CString` object while referencing a `char` pointer obtained with the `LPCTSTR` operator. This is due to the fact that it's possible for the internal memory of the string object to be moved in memory, thus invalidating the pointer. The `CString` class does provide two member functions, `GetBuffer()` and `ReleaseBuffer()`, that temporary lock the string's memory in place so that you can directly modify it through a character pointer.

Working with Time

The `CTime` class represents an absolute date and time based on Greenwich Mean Time (GMT). The `CTime` class includes a host of member functions for retrieving information about the date and time. Following is an example of creating a `CTime` object set to the current date and time:

```
CTime time = CTime::GetCurrentTime();
```

Although the `CTime` object defines a variety of different constructors, the easiest way to get the current time is to use the static `GetCurrentTime()` member function, as the code shows. After you've created a `CTime` object, you can get specific date/time information using the following member functions:

- `GetYear()`—get the year as an integer
- `GetMonth()`—get the month as an integer in the range 1 through 12
- `GetDay()`—get the day of the month as an integer in the range 1 through 31
- `GetDayOfWeek()`—get the day of the week in the range 1 through 7 (1 = Sunday, 2 = Monday, and so on)

- `GetHour()`—get the hour of the local time in the range 0 through 23
- `GetMinute()`—get the minute of the local time in the range 0 through 59
- `GetSecond()`—get the second of the local time in the range 0 through 59
- `Format()`—format the date and time as a string

The `GetXXX()` member functions are used to get components of the date and time as integers. More useful perhaps is the `Format()` member function, which formats a date and time as a string. The `Format()` function takes a single string parameter that specifies the manner in which the date and time are formatted. Following are some of the most useful format codes supported by the `Format()` function:

- `%A`—full weekday name
- `%B`—full month name
- `%d`—day of month as an integer in the range 1 through 31
- `%H`—hour as an integer in the range 0 through 23 (24-hour format)
- `%I`—hour as an integer in the range 1 through 12 (12-hour format)
- `%M`—minute as an integer in the range 0 through 59
- `%p`—A.M./P.M. indicator for 12-hour clock
- `%S`—second as an integer in the range 0 through 59
- `%y`—year as integer in the range 00 through 99 (without century)
- `%Y`—year as integer (with century)
- `%Z`—time-zone name
- `%%`—percent sign

Following is an example of formatting a `CString` object using the `Format()` function:

```
CString s = t.Format( "%A, %B %d, %Y" );
```

This code results in the variable s containing the string `"Monday, August 24, 1970"`.

Another class useful when dealing with time is `CTimeSpan`, which represents a relative time span. A `CTimeSpan` object represents the difference between two `CTime` objects. Following is an example of using the `CTimeSpan` class to measure an elapsed period of time:

```
CTime startTime = CTime::GetCurrentTime();
// perform time-consuming operation here
CTime endTime = CTime::GetCurrentTime();
CTimeSpan alapsedTime = endTime - startTime;
LONG lElapsedSeconds = elapsedTime.GetTotalSeconds();
```

This code could be used to measure how long it takes to carry out a lengthy operation. The `CTimeSpan` object supports many of the same `GetXXX()` member functions as the `CTime` object, which makes it easy to find out information about the time span.

Summary

This hour introduced you to data structures as they apply to MFC. You began the hour by learning about the different data structure classes MFC has to offer. You then got a quick introduction to serialization, which forms an integral part of data management in MFC. From there you dove into the `CString` class, and learned how to use it to store and manipulate strings. You finished up the hour by exploring the MFC classes used to represent date and time.

Q&A

Q Is it possible to directly modify the character sequence stored within a `CString` object?

A Yes. The `CString` class provides a member function named `GetBuffer()` that returns a `char` pointer that you can use to directly alter the string's internally stored character buffer. You must always call the `ReleaseBuffer()` member function to let the `CString` object know that you are finished altering the character buffer. The `char` pointer shouldn't be used after calling `ReleaseBuffer()`.

Q What is Greenwich Mean Time (GMT)?

A Greenwich Mean Time (GMT) is a timekeeping system that was originally created to aid naval navigation in the fifteenth century. It is named for Britain's national center for time, Greenwich, and was adopted by British Parliament in 1880. The United States adopted Greenwich Mean Time in 1883 when telegraph lines transmitted time signals to all major cities. Greenwich Mean Time (GMT) was adopted universally in 1884 at the International Meridian Conference in Washington, DC.

Workshop

The Workshop is designed to help you anticipate possible questions, review what you've learned, and begin thinking ahead to put your knowledge into practice. The answers to the quiz are in Appendix A, "Quiz Answers."

Quiz

1. What are the two limitations of arrays?
2. What type of data does the CSize class represent?
3. Why would you sometimes want to use a Win32 struct instead of an equivalent MFC wrapper class?
4. What is a C++ template?
5. If you wanted to use a key to lookup a piece of information in a data collection, what type of collection would work best?
6. What MFC class would you use to output diagnostic information about an object?
7. What is the purpose of the CArchive class?
8. Why should you not modify a CString object while referencing a char pointer obtained with the LPCTSTR operator?
9. What does the CTime class represent?
10. What is the relationship between the CTime class and the CTimeSpan class?

Exercises

1. Write code to take two CString objects containing your first and last name, concatenate them together into one name string, and then use them to display a sentence in a message box that reads "Good afternoon, YOUR NAME!".
2. Modify the previous code to include the date and time so that the message reads "Good afternoon, YOUR NAME, it is CURRENT DATE AND TIME!".

HOUR 11

Organizing Data with MFC's Collection Classes

In the previous hour I touched on MFC's data collection classes and explained how they are used to provide flexibility in building data structures containing multiple items of a given type. This hour digs deeper into these collection classes by showing you exactly how they are used. You not only learn about the different collection classes provided by MFC, but you also learn how to use them within the context of a real application.

In this hour, you will learn

- About the different collection classes in MFC
- How to create collections of data using arrays, lists, and maps
- How to enhance an existing application to utilize collections

Revisiting the MFC Collection Classes

As you already know, collection classes are used as a storage medium for data. Unlike arrays, MFC's collection classes store data in different ways according to their purpose, and provide member functions that are used to manipulate the data. Additionally, most of the MFC collection classes are based on templates, which make them very robust in dealing with different types of data.

> MFC also provides an older set of collection classes that aren't based on templates. The template-based collections are more modern, more convenient, and provide better type safety than the old collection classes. So, I discourage you from directly using the older MFC collection classes. However, you will still encounter them indirectly when using some of the template-based collection classes.

MFC provides template-based classes for the following collections:

- Array—a list of elements that can dynamically shrink and grow
- List—an ordered list of elements that can dynamically shrink and grow; also allows the insertion and removal of elements
- Map—a "dictionary" that maps unique keys to values; each element in a map is a key/value pair

Array

The array collection offers a dynamically sized, ordered, and integer-indexed array of elements. Traditional C++ arrays cannot be sized, which is often a significant limitation. MFC's array collection gives you much more flexibility because it can shrink and grow to accommodate changes in the data it contains. Elements in an array collection are accessed via an integer index. Figure 11.1 shows a visual representation of the array collection.

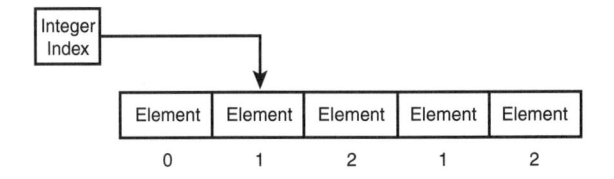

FIGURE 11.1

A visual representation of the array collection.

Arrays are useful in situations where you need to access elements based on their absolute position within the array. Arrays are very efficient if all you intend to do is append to and remove from the end of the array. However, it is very inefficient to insert or remove elements at a particular point within an array. You should use a list collection if you require this type of functionality.

List

The list collection provides an ordered, non-indexed list of elements that is implemented as a doubly linked list. A linked list is a data structure containing linked elements that can be navigated in a single direction; a doubly linked list can be navigated in either direction. A list collection has a "head" and a "tail," which serve as the beginning and end of the list. You can visualize a list collection as a train where the engine is the head, the caboose is the tail, and each of the cars is an element in between. You can add or remove elements from the head or tail of a list, or insert or delete elements in the middle. Figure 11.2 shows a visual representation of the list collection.

NEW TERM A *linked list* is a non-indexed data structure containing linked elements that can be navigated in either direction.

FIGURE 11.2

A visual representation of the list collection.

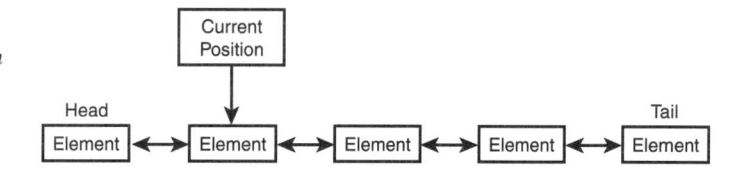

Lists are very useful in situations where you need to navigate through the list an element at a time. Unlike arrays, lists facilitate inserting or removing elements from any point within a list in a very efficient manner. The weakness of lists is revealed when you need to access a list element at an absolute position. Unlike arrays, which use integer indices to access any element at an absolute position, an element in a list is accessed relative to other elements. In other words, you have to navigate through the list to find a particular element.

Map

The map collection is very different from the array and list collections in that it uses two pieces of information for each element that it contains. One of the pieces of information is the element itself, which is often referred to as the value, whereas the other is a key used to access the value. Keys in a map are unique and serve as look-up values for finding elements. You can think of a map as being akin to a dictionary, where the words correspond to keys and the definitions correspond to elements. In other words, you use a word to look up its definition in a dictionary the same way you use a key to look up an element in a map. Not surprisingly, maps are often referred to as dictionaries. Figure 11.3 shows a visual representation of the map collection.

FIGURE 11.3

A visual representation of the map collection.

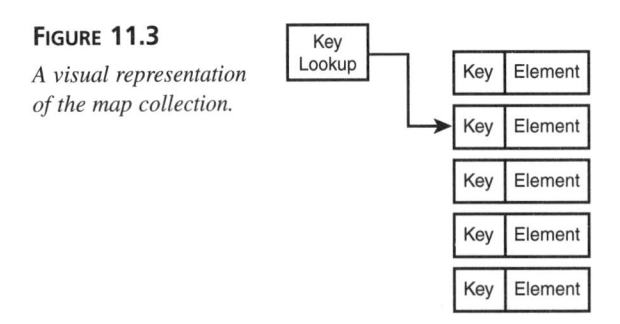

Maps are extremely useful in situations when you need to access elements based on some value. For example, you might want to store a list of employees and access them based on their Social Security numbers. A map is ideal in this situation because it allows you to use the Social Security number as a key look-up for employee elements. Maps are certainly more specialized than arrays and lists, but they can come in handy in some situations.

Choosing Collections

The MFC collection classes each are geared toward storing data of a particular type. As such, each type of collection has strengths and weaknesses that must be assessed before deciding which one is the most appropriate in a given situation. Table 11.1 contrasts the different collection types and highlights their strengths and weaknesses. Depending on how you intend to use a collection, you can use this table as a basis for determining which collection type is most appropriate.

TABLE 11.1 CONTRASTING THE MFC COLLECTION TYPES

Collection	Ordered?	Indexed?	Insert	Search
Array	Yes	By int	Slow	Slow
List	Yes	No	Fast	Slow
Map	No	By key	Fast	Fast

It's worth pointing out that both lists and maps involve more overhead than arrays, especially when dealing with primitive data types. For example, an element in a list requires storage for the data itself, as well as numeric pointers for the previous and next element. If you were storing `floats` in a list as opposed to an array, each element would incur triple the memory overhead due to the pointers. This overhead is less of an issue when you store objects in a list, because the size of an object is typically significantly greater than the pointers.

After you've decided on a collection type, you must then decide how you want to use the collection. MFC provides two different approaches to using its template-based collections. Both approaches are type-safe, so you don't have to worry about casting object types regardless of which you choose. The approaches differ with respect to how they store data in a given collection; one approach stores actual objects, whereas the other approach stores pointers to objects. The classes associated with the first collection approach are referred to as simple collection classes, whereas the classes associated with the second approach are referred to as typed pointer collection classes. The real distinction between the two approaches is whether you want to store objects or pointers to objects. The manner in which you're using a collection might dictate one approach or the other.

As an example, it typically makes sense to store primitive (intrinsic) data types such as `int` and `float` in a simple collection class. On the other hand, many object types need to be stored in a typed pointer collection class because you might want to store derived classes that contain additional data. Additionally, a typed pointer collection is usually much more efficient in handling complex objects because it only manipulates pointers; a simple collection class usually manipulates entire objects in memory. The general rule of thumb is to use simple collection classes for primitive data types and very simple objects, and then use the typed pointer collection classes for complex objects.

Using the Collection Classes

Let's break away from the theory and learn how to use the collection classes. To use the collection classes, you must typically perform two basic steps:

1. Declare a variable of the collection class type
2. Manipulate the collection object by calling its member functions

The first step is obviously the most important. Following is an example of creating a variable using the `CList` simple collection class:

```
CList<float, float>  floatList;
```

This code creates a simple list collection variable that contains elements of type `float`. To manipulate the collection as mentioned in the second step, you call member functions defined in the `CList` class, like this:

```
floatList.AddHead(3.14);
floatList.AddTail(5280.0);
floatList.RemoveAll();
```

This code adds an element to the head and tail of the list, and then removes all the elements contained in the list. You learn more about the `CList` member functions a little later in the hour.

> The MFC collection classes are declared in a special header file named AfxTempl.h, which must be included in any source code files that reference collection classes.

Putting Arrays to Work

MFC supports type-safe array collections through two classes:

- CArray
- CTypedPtrArray

The `CArray` class is a simple array collection class that is used to store objects in an array, whereas `CTypedPtrArray` expects you to store object pointers. The next couple of sections show you how to use each of these classes to create array collections.

CArray

The `CArray` class implements a zero-based array that can dynamically shrink and grow. Creating an array collection based on `CArray` requires two parameters, `TYPE` and `ARG_TYPE`, which are shown in the following template prototype for `CArray`:

```
template<class TYPE, class ARG_TYPE> class CArray : public CObject
```

The `TYPE` parameter specifies the data type of the objects stored in the array. The `ARG_TYPE` parameter specifies the data type used to access objects stored in the array; the `ARG_TYPE` data type is used in most of the member functions for `CArray`. The significance of `ARG_TYPE` is that sometimes you might want to pass an object by reference instead of by value. For example, you would typically pass a `CObject`-derived object by reference, but you would pass primitive data types by value. To better understand how these parameters are used, check out the following example:

Organizing Data with MFC's Collection Classes

```
CArray<int, int> intArray;
CArray<CRect, CRect&> rectArray;
```

The first line of example code declares an array collection named `intArray` that contains elements of type `int`. The second line declares an array collection named `rectArray` that contains `CRect` objects. However, these objects are accessed using a reference to a `CRect` object (`CRect&`) as opposed to an actual `CRect` object. This is typically more efficient when dealing with objects.

You manipulate elements in an array collection by calling member functions defined in `CArray`. Table 11.2 lists some of the most useful member functions found in the `CArray` class.

TABLE 11.2 THE `CArray` COLLECTION CLASS MEMBER FUNCTIONS

Member Function	Description
`GetSize()`	Gets the number of elements in the array
`SetSize()`	Sets the number of elements to be contained in the array
`Add()`	Adds an element to the end of the array, growing the array if necessary
`GetAt()`	Gets the element at a specific index
`SetAt()`	Sets the element at a specific index, not allowing the array to grow
`SetAtGrow()`	Sets the element at a specific index, growing the array if necessary
`InsertAt()`	Inserts an element at a specific index
`RemoveAt()`	Removes an element at a specific index
`RemoveAll()`	Removes all elements from the array
`ElementAt()`	Gets a temporary reference to an element at a specific index
`operator []`	Gets or sets the element at a specific index

Following is an example of creating an array collection, setting its size, adding a few elements to it, accessing an element with `operator []`, and removing all the elements:

```
CArray<CRect, CRect&> rectArray;
rectArray.SetSize(5);
CRect rc1(10, 10, 60, 60);
CRect rc2(70, 10, 130, 60);
rectArray.Add(rc1);
rectArray.Add(rc2);
CRect rc3 = rectArray[1];
rectArray.removeAll();
```

> You will probably want to call the `SetSize()` member function of an array collection before using the collection. This establishes the size of the array and allocates memory for it. If you do not call `SetSize()`, adding elements

CTypedPtrArray

The `CTypedPtrArray` class serves as a wrapper around a zero-based array of typed object pointers. Unlike the `CArray` class, `CTypedPtrArray` doesn't store objects themselves, but pointers to objects. Creating an array collection based on `CTypedPtrArray` requires two parameters, `BASE_CLASS` and `TYPE`, which are shown in the following template prototype for `CTypedPtrArray`:

```
template<class BASE_CLASS, class TYPE> class CTypedPtrArray : public BASE_CLASS
```

The `BASE_CLASS` parameter identifies the base collection class of the array collection, which must be one of MFC's non-template array collection classes (`CPtrArray` or `CObArray`). This is evidence of the fact that `CTypedPtrArray` is a type-safe wrapper around an underlying array implementation. The `TYPE` parameter specifies the data type of the objects stored in the array. To better understand how these parameters are used, check out the following example:

```
CTypedPtrArray<CObArray, CRect*> rectArray;
```

This example code declares an array collection named `rectArray` that contains `CRect` object pointers. Objects in this array are accessed using a pointer to a `CRect` object (`CRect*`) as opposed to a `CRect` object or reference. The same member functions are used to manipulate a `CTypedPtrArray` object as those used with `CArray` (refer to Table 11.2).

> You should use `CObArray` as the base class for `CTypedPtrArray` if the elements you are going to store in the array are derived from `CObject`. Otherwise, you should use `CPtrArray` as the base class.

Organizing Data into Lists

MFC supports type-safe list collections through two classes:

- `CList`
- `CTypedPtrList`

The `CList` class is a simple list collection class that can be used to store objects in a list, whereas `CTypedPtrList` expects you to store object pointers. The next couple of sections show you how to use each of these classes to create list collections.

CList

The `CList` class implements an ordered list of elements that are accessed either sequentially or by value. Creating a list collection based on `CList` requires two parameters, `TYPE` and `ARG_TYPE`, which are the same parameters you learned about for `CArray`. Following is the template prototype for `CList`:

```
template<class TYPE, class ARG_TYPE> class CList : public CObject
```

The `TYPE` parameter specifies the data type of the objects stored in the list, whereas `ARG_TYPE` specifies the data type used to access objects stored in the list. Take a look at the following example of creating list collections:

```
CList<int, int> intList;
CList<CRect, CRect&> rectList;
```

The example declares a list collection named `intList` that contains elements of type `int`. The second example declares a list collection named `rectList` that contains `CRect` objects.

You manipulate elements in a list collection by calling member functions defined in `CList`. Many of these member functions operate on a variable of type `POSITION`, which serves as a marker that indicates a position within a list. You can use the `POSITION` data type as an iterator for moving through a list sequentially. It's important to note, however, that a position within a list is not the same as an array index. Table 11.3 lists some of the most useful member functions found in the `CList` class.

TABLE 11.3 THE `CList` COLLECTION CLASS MEMBER FUNCTIONS

Member Function	Description
`GetCount()`	Gets the number of elements in the list
`GetHead()`	Gets the head element of the list
`GetTail()`	Gets the tail element of the list
`GetHeadPosition()`	Gets the position of the head element of the list
`GetTailPosition()`	Gets the position of the tail element of the list
`GetNext()`	Gets the next element in the list
`GetPrev()`	Gets the previous element in the list
`GetAt()`	Gets the element at a specific position

continues

TABLE 11.3 CONTINUED

SetAt()	Sets the element at a specific position
AddHead()	Adds an element to the head of the list
AddTail()	Adds an element to the tail of the list
InsertBefore()	Inserts an element before a specific position
InsertAfter()	Inserts an element after a specific position
RemoveHead()	Removes the element at the head of the list
RemoveTail()	Removes the element at the tail of the list
RemoveAt()	Removes an element at a specific position
RemoveAll()	Removes all elements from the list
Find()	Gets the position of an element matching a pointer value
FindIndex()	Gets the position of an element at a specific index
IsEmpty()	Checks to see if the list is empty

Following is an example of creating a list collection and adding a few elements to it:

```
CList<CRect, CRect&> rectList;
CRect rc1(10, 10, 60, 60);
CRect rc2(70, 10, 130, 60);
rectList.AddHead(rc1);
rectList.AddHead(rc2);
```

Following is another example that iterates through the list collection:

```
POSITION pos = rectList.GetHeadPosition();
while (pos != NULL) {
  CRect& rc = rectList.GetNext(pos);
}
```

CTypedPtrList

The CTypedPtrList class serves as a wrapper around an ordered list of elements that are accessed either sequentially or by value. Unlike the CList class, CTypedPtrList doesn't store objects themselves, but pointers to objects. Creating a list collection based on CTypedPtrList requires two parameters, BASE_CLASS and TYPE, which are shown in the following template prototype for CTypedPtrList:

```
template<class BASE_CLASS, class TYPE> class CTypedPtrArray : public
BASE_CLASS
```

These parameters should be familiar to you from learning about the CTypedPtrArray class a little earlier. The BASE_CLASS parameter identifies the base collection class of the array collection, whereas the `TYPE` parameter specifies the data type of the objects stored in the array. To better understand how these parameters are used, check out the following example:

```
CTypedPtrList<CObList, CRect*> rectList;
```

This example code declares a list collection named `rectList` that contains `CRect` object pointers. Objects in this list are accessed using a pointer to a `CRect` object (`CRect*`). The same member functions are used to manipulate a `CTypedPtrList` object as those used with `CList` (refer to Table 11.3).

Mapping Data

MFC supports type-safe map collections through two classes:

- `CMap`
- `CTypedPtrMap`

The `CMap` class is a simple map collection class that is used to store objects in a map, whereas `CTypedPtrMap` expects you to store object pointers. The next couple of sections show you how to use each of these classes to create map collections.

CMap

The `CMap` class implements a dictionary collection that maps unique keys to values. Creating a map collection based on `CMap` requires four parameters: `KEY`, `ARG_KEY`, `VALUE`, and `ARG_VALUE`. Following is the template prototype for `CMap`:

```
template<class KEY, class ARG_KEY, class VALUE, class ARG_VALUE>
    ↪class CMap : public CObject
```

The `KEY` parameter specifies the data type of keys used to map values stored in the map, whereas `ARG_KEY` specifies the data type used to access these keys. Similarly, `VALUE` and `ARG_VALUE` serve the same purpose for determining the data type of values stored in the map. Take a look at the following example of creating a map collection:

```
CMap<int, int, CString, CString&> nameMap;
```

The example declares a map collection named `nameMap` that maps `int` keys to values of type `CString`. This means that you would use integer keys as the basis for looking up strings in the map. This would be useful if you wanted to store a person's name based on their employee ID or telephone number, for example. You would probably want to use a string key to identify employees based on their social security number, since social security numbers can have leading zeros.

You manipulate elements in a map collection by calling member functions defined in CMap. More specifically, you use keys to locate and access values stored in a map. You can also use the POSITION data type as an iterator for moving through a map from a given position. However, unlike list collections, this iteration isn't sequential with respect to key values. Table 11.4 lists some of the most useful member functions found in the CMap class.

TABLE 11.4 THE CMap COLLECTION CLASS MEMBER FUNCTIONS

Member Function	Description
GetCount()	Gets the number of elements in the map
GetStartPosition()	Gets the position of the first element in the map
GetNextAssoc()	Gets the next element in the map
SetAt()	Inserts an element into the map, replacing an existing element if a matching key is found
Lookup()	Looks up the value mapped to a given key
RemoveKey()	Removes an element using a specific key
RemoveAll()	Removes all elements from the map
IsEmpty()	Checks to see if the map is empty
operator []	Inserts an element into the map (same as SetAt())

Following is an example of creating a map collection and adding a few elements to it:

```
CMap<int, int, CString, CString&> playerMap;
CString player1("Cliff Ronning");
CString player2("Scott Walker");
CString player3("Sergei Krivokrasov");
playerMap.SetAt(7, player1);
playerMap.SetAt(24, player2);
playerMap.SetAt(25, player3);
```

This example code shows how to create a map collection containing players for the Nashville Predators NHL hockey team. The neat thing about the map is that the players' names are stored based on their jersey number. In other words, the number on a player's jersey serves as the key for looking up the player's name. Someone wanting to know the name of a player based on a jersey number would simply look up the player like this:

```
CString name;
playerMap.Lookup(7, name);
```

CTypedPtrMap

The `CTypedPtrMap` class serves as a wrapper around a dictionary collection of key/value pairs. Unlike the `CMap` class, `CTypedPtrMap` doesn't store objects themselves, but pointers to objects. Creating a map collection based on `CTypedPtrMap` requires three parameters: `BASE_CLASS`, `KEY`, and `VALUE`. Following is the template prototype for `CTypedPtrMap`:

```
template<class BASE_CLASS, class KEY, class VALUE> class CTypedPtrMap :
    public BASE_CLASS
```

These parameters should be familiar to you from learning about the other typed pointer collection classes earlier. The `BASE_CLASS` parameter identifies the base collection class of the map collection, whereas the `KEY` and `VALUE` parameters specify the data type of the map's keys and values, respectively. The base class must be one of MFC's non-template map collection classes (`CMapPtrToPtr`, `CMapPtrToWord`, `CMapWordToPtr`, and `CMapStringToPtr`). To better understand how the `CTypedPtrMap` parameters are used, check out the following example:

```
CTypedPtrMap<CMapWordToPtr, int, CString*> nameMap;
```

This example code declares a map collection named `nameMap` that uses keys of type `int` to look up `CString` object pointers. The same member functions are used to manipulate a `CTypedPtrMap` object as those used with `CMap` (refer to Table 11.4).

Enhancing the Doodle Application

Now that you understand the ins and outs of MFC's collection classes, let's work through an example that puts them to good use. If you recall from Hour 9, "Drawing Graphics," you developed an application called Doodle that allowed you to draw lines, rectangles, ellipses, and bitmapped images. The drawback to Doodle was that it didn't keep up with the graphics as you drew them, so there was no way to refresh the client area if the application was minimized and restored, for example.

If you created a class to store each graphic and then stored objects of this class in a collection, it would be possible to keep up with everything drawn in Doodle. This is the approach you use in developing Doodle2 throughout the remainder of this hour. Listing 11.1 contains the header code for the `CGraphic` class.

LISTING 11.1   THE GRAPHIC.H HEADER FILE FOR DOODLE2

```
1: #ifndef __GRAPHIC_H__
2: #define __GRAPHIC_H__
3:
4: //----------------------------------
```

continues

LISTING 11.1   CONTINUED

```
 5: // Inclusions
 6: //-----------------------------------
 7:
 8: //-----------------------------------
 9: // CGraphic Class - Graphic Object
10: //-----------------------------------
11: class CGraphic : public CObject {
12:   // Public Member Constants
13: public:
14:   enum  { LINE, RECTANGLE, ELLIPSE, CRITTER };
15:
16:   // Member Variables
17: private:
18:   int       m_nType;
19:   CRect     m_rcPosition;
20:   COLORREF  m_crColor;
21:
22:   // Public Constructor(s)/Destructor
23: public:
24:   CGraphic(int nType, CRect& rcPosition, COLORREF crColor);
25:
26:   // Public Member Functions
27: public:
28:   void Draw(CDC* pDC);
29: };
30:
31: #endif
```

The CGraphic class encapsulates information common to all the graphics types drawn in Doodle. It uses an enumeration to distinguish between the different graphic types. It also includes member variables for keeping track of the rectangular position and color of a graphic. The CGraphic class also declares a single constructor and a Draw() method that draws the graphic to a device context. Listing 11.2 contains the source code for CGraphic, which shows exactly how the class works.

LISTING 11.2   THE GRAPHIC.CPP SOURCE CODE FILE FOR DOODLE2

```
1: //-----------------------------------
2: // Inclusions
3: //-----------------------------------
4: #include "StdAfx.h"
5: //-----------------------------------
6: #include "Graphic.h"
7: #include "Resource.h"
8:
```

```
 9: //--------------------------------
10: // MFC Debugging Support
11: //--------------------------------
12: #ifdef _DEBUG
13: #undef THIS_FILE
14: static char BASED_CODE THIS_FILE[] = __FILE__;
15: #endif
16:
17:
18: //--------------------------------
19: // Public Constructor(s)/Destructor
20: //--------------------------------
21: CGraphic::CGraphic(int nType, CRect& rcPosition, COLORREF crColor) {
22:   m_nType = nType;
23:   m_rcPosition = rcPosition;
24:   m_crColor = crColor;
25: }
26:
27: //--------------------------------
28: // Member Functions
29: //--------------------------------
30: void CGraphic::Draw(CDC* pDC) {
31:   ASSERT_VALID(pDC);
32:
33:   // Select the pen and brush
34:   CPen pen(PS_SOLID, 2, m_crColor);
35:   CPen* ppenOld;
36:   CBrush* pbrOld;
37:   VERIFY(ppenOld = pDC->SelectObject(&pen));
38:   VERIFY(pbrOld = pDC->SelectObject(
39:     CBrush::FromHandle((HBRUSH)::GetStockObject(NULL_BRUSH))));
40:
41:   // Draw graphic based on the type
42:   switch (m_nType) {
43:   case LINE:
44:     // Draw a line
45:     pDC->MoveTo(m_rcPosition.TopLeft());
46:     pDC->LineTo(m_rcPosition.BottomRight());
47:     break;
48:
49:   case RECTANGLE:
50:     // Draw a rectangle
51:     pDC->Rectangle(m_rcPosition);
52:     break;
53:
54:   case ELLIPSE:
55:     // Draw an ellipse
56:     pDC->Ellipse(m_rcPosition);
57:     break;
58:
```

continues

LISTING 11.2 CONTINUED

```
59:    case CRITTER:
60:      // Load the critter bitmap
61:      CBitmap    bmCritter;
62:      BITMAP     bmInfo;
63:      VERIFY(bmCritter.LoadBitmap(IDB_CRITTER));
64:      bmCritter.GetObject(sizeof(BITMAP), &bmInfo);
65:
66:      // Setup the memory DC
67:      CDC        dcMem;
68:      dcMem.CreateCompatibleDC(pDC);
69:      VERIFY(pbmOld = dcMem.SelectObject(&bmCritter));
70:
71:      // Draw the critter image
72:      pDC->StretchBlt(m_rcPosition.left, m_rcPosition.top,
73:        m_rcPosition.Width(), m_rcPosition.Height(), &dcMem, 0, 0,
74:        bmInfo.bmWidth, bmInfo.bmHeight, SRCAND);
75:      break;
76:    }
77:
78:    // Cleanup the DC
79:    VERIFY(pDC->SelectObject(ppenOld));
80:    VERIFY(pDC->SelectObject(pbrOld));
81: }
```

The constructor for `CGraphic` simply sets its member variables based on passed parameters. The `Draw()` member function draws the graphic to a provided device context. This drawing code was pulled from the original `CMainFrame` class in Doodle; delegating the drawing of a graphic to the `CGraphic` class makes perfect sense from an OOP perspective.

At this point you're probably wondering where collections fit into all this code. Collections enter the picture when you turn your attention to the `CMainFrame` class. Following are the member variables for `CMainFrame`:

```
CTypedPtrList <CObList, CGraphic*>  m_graphicList;
int                                 m_nDrawMode;
COLORREF                            m_crColor;
```

The `CMainFrame` class uses a typed pointer list collection named `m_graphicList` to store `CGraphic` object pointers. It also makes use of a `COLORREF` member variable to keep track of the current drawing color instead of a `CPen` object, which was used in the original Doodle application.

Another change required in Doodle2 is the inclusion of the AfxTempl.h collection class header file. Because this is a standard header that doesn't change, it makes sense to add

Organizing Data with MFC's Collection Classes 203

it to StdAfx.h and benefit from it going into the application's precompiled headers. Listing 11.3 contains the source code for the StdAfx.h header file for Doodle2.

LISTING 11.3 THE STDAFX.H HEADER FILE FOR DOODLE2

```
 1: #ifndef __STDAFX_H__
 2: #define __STDAFX_H__
 3:
 4: //---------------------------------
 5: // Inclusions
 6: //---------------------------------
 7: #include <AfxWin.h>
 8: #include <AfxExt.h>
 9: #include <AfxTempl.h>
10:
11: #endif
```

The constructor for `CMainFrame` is responsible for setting the initial drawing mode and color:

```
CMainFrame::CMainFrame() : m_nDrawMode(CGraphic::LINE),
  m_crColor(RGB(0, 0, 0)) {
}
```

Notice that the drawing mode is now based on the enumerations defined in `CGraphic`. This impacts the `OnDrawXXX()` message handlers, as well as the `OnUpdateDrawXXX()` command update message handlers. I'll skip showing the code for those because it simply involves changing the enumerations. Also note in the `CMainFrame` constructor that the drawing color is now a `COLORREF` value instead of a `CPen` object.

Getting back to a collection topic, typed pointer collections don't automatically free the memory of the objects they contain. So, it is necessary for you to free the `CGraphic` objects manually in the `CMainFrame` destructor:

```
CMainFrame::~CMainFrame() {
  // Cleanup the graphics list
  while (!m_graphicList.IsEmpty())
    delete m_graphicList.RemoveHead();
}
```

As you can see, the destructor for `CMainFrame` iterates through the list of graphic objects and deletes each one as it is removed.

Not surprisingly, the `OnLButtonDown()` message handler in `CMainFrame` requires some significant changes. The new version of `OnLButtonDown()` is shown in Listing 11.4.

LISTING 11.4 THE CMainFrame::OnLButtonDown() MESSAGE HANDLER FOR DOODLE2

```
 1: void CMainFrame::OnLButtonDown(UINT nFlags, CPoint point) {
 2:   // Start the "rubber band" rectangle tracker
 3:   CRectTracker tracker;
 4:   tracker.TrackRubberBand(this, point);
 5:
 6:   // Add new graphic based on the drawing mode
 7:   CGraphic* pGraphic;
 8:   switch (m_nDrawMode) {
 9:   case CGraphic::LINE:
10:     // Add a line to the graphics list
11:     pGraphic = new CGraphic(CGraphic::LINE, tracker.m_rect,
12:       m_crColor);
13:     m_graphicList.AddTail(pGraphic);
14:     break;
15:
16:   case CGraphic::RECTANGLE:
17:     // Add a rectangle to the graphics list
18:     pGraphic = new CGraphic(CGraphic::RECTANGLE, tracker.m_rect,
19:       m_crColor);
20:     m_graphicList.AddTail(pGraphic);
21:     break;
22:
23:   case CGraphic::ELLIPSE:
24:     // Add an ellipse to the graphics list
25:     pGraphic = new CGraphic(CGraphic::ELLIPSE, tracker.m_rect,
26:       m_crColor);
27:     m_graphicList.AddTail(pGraphic);
28:     break;
29:
30:   case CGraphic::CRITTER:
31:     // Add a critter to the graphics list
32:     pGraphic = new CGraphic(CGraphic::CRITTER, tracker.m_rect,
33:       m_crColor);
34:     m_graphicList.AddTail(pGraphic);
35:     break;
36:   }
37:
38:   // Repaint the window
39:   Invalidate();
40: }
```

The big change in OnLButtonDown() is that it now creates a CGraphic object and adds it to the list collection instead of drawing each graphic directly to the screen. The client area is then forced to repaint itself with the call to Invalidate(). Speaking of painting, the last code change in Doodle2 is the OnPaint() message handler, which is entirely new. Listing 11.5 contains the code for OnPaint().

LISTING 11.5 THE `CMainFrame::OnPaint()` MESSAGE HANDLER FOR DOODLE2

```
 1: void CMainFrame::OnPaint() {
 2:   CPaintDC dc(this);
 3:
 4:   // Paint the graphics
 5:   POSITION pos = m_graphicList.GetHeadPosition();
 6:   while (pos != NULL) {
 7:     CGraphic* pGraphic = m_graphicList.GetNext(pos);
 8:     pGraphic->Draw(&dc);
 9:   }
10: }
```

The `OnPaint()` message handler simply iterates through the graphic list and calls the `Draw()` member function on each `CGraphic` object, resulting in each graphic being drawn.

Summary

This hour introduced you to MFC collections and the role they play in storing application data. You began the hour by learning about the different MFC collection classes and the considerations to be made in determining when to use them. You then explored each class in detail and learned exactly how they are used to store application data. The hour concluded by leading you through the modification of the Doodle application to add support for collections.

Q&A

Q Is it possible to derive from the MFC collection classes to add custom collection behavior?

A Yes. The MFC collection classes can be used as base classes for custom collections of your own. For example, you might need a collection that contains a list of strings sorted into alphabetical order. You could derive a class from `CArray` and implement this sorting functionality.

Q Can you store object pointers in the simple collection classes (CArray, CList, or CMap)?

A Yes. Although the simple collection classes are designed to contain objects, they can certainly be used to contain object pointers. However, it is generally more efficient to use the typed pointer collection classes instead.

Workshop

The Workshop is designed to help you anticipate possible questions, review what you've learned, and begin thinking ahead to put your knowledge into practice. The answers to the quiz are in Appendix A, "Quiz Answers."

Quiz

1. Why should you not use MFC's old collection classes that aren't based on templates?
2. Which type of collection should you use in situations where you need to access elements based on their absolute position within the collection?
3. Which type of collection should you use in situations where you need to navigate through the collection an element at a time?
4. What type of collection is very inefficient at inserting or removing elements at a particular point?
5. What is a linked list?
6. Which type of collection is the fastest for performing searches?
7. Which type of collection is not ordered?
8. Which file must be included in any source code files that work with MFC collection classes?
9. What is the difference between `CArray` and `CTypedPtrArray`?
10. Why should you call the `SetSize()` member function of an array collection before using the collection?

Exercises

1. Write code to create an array collection variable named `messageArray` that stores elements of type `CString`.
2. Write code to create a map collection variable named `propertyMap` that maps keys of type `CString` to values of type `BOOL`.

Hour 12

Managing Application Data with Documents

This hour tackles documents, which are special classes used to store data in document-centric MFC applications. Together with views, documents form the basis of MFC's document/view architecture. You initially learned about the document/view architecture back in Hour 2, "Building MFC Applications," when you built a skeletal document/view application. In this hour you begin modifying the Doodle application to fit into MFC's document/view architecture. This will give the application much more power with little additional effort.

In this hour, you will learn

- The basics of documents and how they work
- About MFC's support for documents
- How to create and use documents

Document Basics

A document is a special class that stores and provides access to application data. More specifically, a document represents the unit of data that you associate with the File, Open and File, Save menu commands in an application. Documents represent half of the document/view equation; views form the other half. Even in the absence of views, documents are quite powerful. Although most applications only operate on one document type, there is nothing limiting an application from supporting multiple document types. Likewise, each document type can have multiple views. Figure 12.1 shows how a single document can have multiple views.

FIGURE 12.1

A document with multiple views.

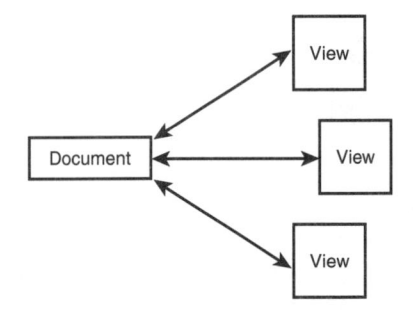

Documents provide a highly structured approach to managing application data, including the storage and retrieval of application data. In other words, documents make it very easy to read and write application data on a persistent storage medium such as a file on a hard disk. To summarize, documents really serve two main purposes in an application:

- Provide a structured interface for accessing and manipulating application data
- Save and restore application data

Within a document/view application, a document object sits alongside one or more view objects, as well as a document template object, a main frame window object, and an application object. The application object creates a document template object, which in turn creates the document, view, and main frame window objects. The document template object is ultimately responsible for associating a document with its views.

The good news for you is that most of the details of the document/view object relationships are hidden within MFC. This means that you are free to focus on the details of developing the document and view classes while MFC worries about how they interact within the context of an application. Incidentally, I realize that you already learned some of this back in Hour 2, but I wanted to recap just to make sure you understand the role documents play in document/view applications.

MFC's Document Support

You might think that a massive hierarchy of classes is necessary to support documents in MFC. You might be surprised to learn that MFC provides only one class to support the creation of documents, CDocument. This is due to the fact that documents are highly application-specific, which means that there really is no way to provide a generic document framework consisting of multiple classes. So, MFC provides a single document class from which you must derive your own document classes that model data specific to a given application.

The CDocument class provides the basic functionality required of application-specific document classes including creating documents, loading documents, saving documents, and keeping track of the state of documents. The member functions defined by CDocument are used by other classes in MFC's document/view architecture. As an example, the CView class serves as the base class for document views, and interacts with the CDocument class via a document template. Table 12.1 lists the most commonly used member functions in the CDocument class.

TABLE 12.1 THE MOST COMMONLY USED CDocument MEMBER FUNCTIONS

Member Function	Description
OnNewDocument()	Called to create a new document
OnOpenDocument()	Called to open an existing document
OnSaveDocument()	Called to save the document
OnCloseDocument()	Called to close the document
Serialize()	Called to store or retrieve the contents of the document
DeleteContents()	Delete the contents of the document
SetModifiedFlag()	Sets the document's "modified" flag
UpdateAllViews()	Updates all the document's views

You might notice that the member functions listed in the table are used in different ways; some are called automatically whereas others you must call yourself. This reflects that automatic nature of the document/view architecture. The standard menu commands File, New; File, Save; File, Open; and File, Close are automatically wired to the appropriate member functions in CDocument. This makes it particularly easy to support the standard Windows File menu in document/view applications.

The other member function automatically called by the framework is Serialize(), which is called to store or retrieve the document data. The Serialize() member function is interesting because it performs both the task of storing and retrieving document data. You learn more about the `Serialize()` function a little later in the hour.

The remaining `CDocument` member functions are used to carry out common tasks related to the management of a document. `DeleteContents()` is called to clear the document of all data and restore it to the state of a newly created document. The `SetModifiedFlag()` function is used to set the "modified" flag for the document. This flag determines if document data has been modified since the last save, and is used as the basis for presenting a prompt allowing the user to save the document before closing it. In other words, this flag is responsible for the familiar "Do you want to save changes?" message that is used in most Windows applications.

The last of the `CDocument` member functions is `UpdateAllViews()`, which is used to update the views of a document in response to changes in document data. Any time a view should change as a result of a document change, you need to call `UpdateAllViews()` to carry out the change. All views associated with the document will be updated and redraw themselves in response to calling `UpdateAllViews()`.

Documents and Serialization

Before I move on to the details of how documents are created and used, it's worth examining serialization and its relationship to documents. Serialization is one of the major benefits of using MFC's document/view architecture because it makes the storage and retrieval of document data incredibly easy to carry out. The serialization support in the `CDocument` class operates through the `Serialize()` member function, which is itself tightly linked to the `CArchive` class.

In Hour 10, "Managing Data with MFC," you learned about the `CArchive` class and how it acts as a binary stream that supports the reading and writing of objects. The `Serialize()` member function accepts a `CArchive` object as its only parameter:

```
virtual void Serialize(CArchive& ar);
```

This member function is actually defined in `CObject`, so every MFC class has the capability of overriding it to support serialization. You must override the `Serialize()` member function in your document class for it to support serialization. Following is the general structure of the `Serialize()` function:

```
void CSkeletonDoc::Serialize(CArchive& ar) {
  if (ar.IsStoring()) {
    // Store document data
    // TODO
  }
  else {
```

```
    // Load document data
    // TODO
  }
}
```

This code is pulled straight from the SkeletonDV application you saw in Hour 2. Notice how the `IsStoring()` member function of the `CArchive` object is called to see if the document data is being stored or retrieved. The code in the `if` branch stores the document data, whereas the code in the `else` branch retrieves the document data. When I refer to the storage and retrieval of document data, I'm really referring to the exchange of information between the document class's member variables and a disk file.

> Serialization isn't limited to disk files, although files are the most common medium for serializing application data. Technically, you could also serialize data to/from memory or across a network connection.

The real power of document serialization is in the `CArchive` class, which supports overridden << and >> operators for reading and writing basic data types. As an example, consider a document consisting of employee information. Let's assume the document contains the following member variables that keep track of an employee:

```
String m_sFName;
String m_sLName;
CTime  m_tHireDate;
float  m_fSalary;
```

Assuming that these member variables represent the entire state of the document, the following `Serialize()` member function would sufficiently support the serialization of the document data:

```
void CEmployeeDoc::Serialize(CArchive& ar) {
  if (ar.IsStoring()) {
    // Store document data
    ar << m_sFName;
    ar << m_sLName;
    ar << m_tHireDate;
    ar << m_fSalary;
  }
  else {
    // Load document data
    ar >> m_sFName;
    ar >> m_sLName;
    ar >> m_tHireDate;
    ar >> m_fSalary;
  }
}
```

The << operator is used to write a piece of data to the archive, whereas the >> operator reads a piece of data from the archive. Notice that this `Serialize()` function is not only reading and writing simple data types, but also a couple of object types (`CString` and `CTime`). These objects must support the << and >> operators for being stored to and retrieved from an archive. Optionally, some objects support the `Serialize()` member function. You must support one of these serialization approaches in any user-defined classes that you use as part of an application's document data. You learn exactly how to do this later in this hour when you build the Doodle3 application.

Creating Documents

You're probably itching to create a functioning document. Fortunately, you'll be glad to know that creating documents isn't too difficult; the main work involved is creating a `CDocument`-derived class that represents application-specific data. Following are the main steps involved in creating a document:

1. Derive a class from `CDocument`
2. Add member variables to model the document's data
3. Create member functions for accessing and manipulating the document's data
4. Override the `CObject::Serialize()` member function to support serialization

As you can tell, the steps to creating a document are very straightforward. Even so, I think an example is in order to help clarify exactly how a real document is created. The remainder of the hour focuses on building a document class for the Doodle3 application.

Applying Documents to Doodle

As I mentioned earlier, the Doodle application you've worked on in the past few hours is an ideal application for MFC's document/view architecture. The Doodle2 application you developed in Hour 11, "Organizing Data with MFC's Collection Classes," is still lacking in that it doesn't support the storage and retrieval of Doodle drawings. Modifying the application to support documents and views makes it particularly easy to add support for reading and writing Doodle drawing files.

The Main Frame Window and `Application` Object

Perhaps the best place to start with Doodle3 is the `CMainFrame` class, which is now surprisingly lean. Listings 12.1 and 12.2 show the code for the MainFrame.h header file and MainFrame.cpp source code file.

Managing Appliction Data with Documents 213

LISTING 12.1 THE MAINFRAME.H HEADER FILE FOR DOODLE3

```
 1: #ifndef __MAINFRAME_H__
 2: #define __MAINFRAME_H__
 3:
 4: //-------------------------------------------------------------
 5: // CMainFrame Class - Main Frame Window Object
 6: //-------------------------------------------------------------
 7: class CMainFrame : public CFrameWnd {
 8:    // Public Constructor(s)/Destructor
 9: public:
10:                CMainFrame();
11:    virtual    ~CMainFrame();
12:
13:    // Public Member Functions
14: public:
15:    virtual BOOL   PreCreateWindow(CREATESTRUCT& cs);
16:
17:    // Message Map & Runtime Support
18: protected:
19:    DECLARE_MESSAGE_MAP()
20:    DECLARE_DYNCREATE(CMainFrame)
21: };
22:
23: #endif
```

LISTING 12.2 THE MAINFRAME.CPP SOURCE CODE FILE FOR DOODLE3

```
 1: //-------------------------------------------------------------
 2: // Message Map & Runtime Support
 3: //-------------------------------------------------------------
 4: BEGIN_MESSAGE_MAP(CMainFrame, CFrameWnd)
 5: END_MESSAGE_MAP()
 6:
 7: IMPLEMENT_DYNCREATE(CMainFrame, CFrameWnd)
 8:
 9: //-------------------------------------------------------------
10: // Public Constructor(s)/Destructor
11: //-------------------------------------------------------------
12: CMainFrame::CMainFrame() {
13: }
14:
15: CMainFrame::~CMainFrame() {
16: }
17:
18: //-------------------------------------------------------------
19: // Public Member Functions
```

continues

LISTING 12.2 THE MAINFRAME.CPP SOURCE CODE FILE FOR DOODLE3

```
20: //------------------------------------------------------------
21: BOOL CMainFrame::PreCreateWindow(CREATESTRUCT& cs) {
22:   // Initialize the frame window properties
23:   // TODO
24:
25:   return CFrameWnd::PreCreateWindow(cs);
26: }
```

If you recall, this class contained a decent amount of code in Doodle2. However, this code must now be relocated into the document and view classes for the application. The `CMainFrame` class now acts only as a simple window class, which makes sense within the document/view architecture.

Before I get into the document class for Doodle3, it's worth noting some other changes necessary to support documents and views. The `InitInstance()` member function in the `CDoodleApp` class is responsible for creating a document template that associates the document, view, and main frame window objects. Listing 12.3 contains the source code for this function.

LISTING 12.3 THE CDoodleApp::InitInstance MEMBER FUNCTION FOR DOODLE3

```
 1: BOOL CDoodleApp::InitInstance() {
 2:   // Register the application's document templates
 3:   CSingleDocTemplate* pDocTemplate;
 4:   pDocTemplate = new CSingleDocTemplate(IDR_DOODLE,
 5:     RUNTIME_CLASS(CDoodleDoc),
 6:     RUNTIME_CLASS(CMainFrame),
 7:     RUNTIME_CLASS(CDoodleView));
 8:   AddDocTemplate(pDocTemplate);
 9:
10:   // Parse command line for standard shell commands
11:   CCommandLineInfo cmdInfo;
12:   ParseCommandLine(cmdInfo);
13:
14:   // Dispatch commands specified on the command line
15:   if (!ProcessShellCommand(cmdInfo))
16:     return FALSE;
17:
18:   // Show and update the main window
19:   m_pMainWnd->ShowWindow(SW_SHOW);
20:   m_pMainWnd->UpdateWindow();
21:
22:   return TRUE;
23: }
```

Most of the code in this function should look familiar from other applications you've built. The main difference is the creation of the document template, which is necessary for all document/view applications. Notice that the document, view, and main frame window classes are identified in the creation of the document template. You'll also notice that a resource identifier (IDR_DOODLE) is used in the creation of the document template; this resource identifier specifies the menu, accelerators, icon, and string resource for the application.

> You might be curious about the name of the document template class, CSingleDocTemplate, which appears to imply that only one document type is permitted. The CSingleDocumentTemplate class is in fact used to support the document/view architecture in single document applications, which are applications that can only have one document open at a time. There is also a CMultiDocumentTemplate class that is used to manage documents and views in a multiple document application. These applications are referred to as Multiple Document Interface (MDI) applications, and are covered in Hour 16, "Managing Multiple Documents."

Application Resources

Speaking of application resources, Listing 12.4 contains the menu resource definition for Doodle3, which includes a few new commands and a new popup menu.

LISTING 12.4 THE MENU RESOURCE DEFINITION FOR DOODLE3

```
 1: IDR_DOODLE MENU
 2: BEGIN
 3:     POPUP "&File"
 4:     BEGIN
 5:         MENUITEM "&New\tCtrl+N",            ID_FILE_NEW
 6:         MENUITEM "&Open...\tCtrl+O",        ID_FILE_OPEN
 7:         MENUITEM "&Save\tCtrl+S",           ID_FILE_SAVE
 8:         MENUITEM "Save &As...",             ID_FILE_SAVE_AS
 9:         MENUITEM SEPARATOR
10:         MENUITEM "E&xit",                   ID_APP_EXIT
11:     END
12:     POPUP "&Edit"
13:     BEGIN
14:         MENUITEM "Clear &All",              ID_EDIT_CLEAR_ALL
15:     END
16:     POPUP "&Draw"
```

continues

LISTING 12.4 CONTINUED

```
17:       BEGIN
18:         MENUITEM "&Line",               ID_DRAW_LINE
19:         MENUITEM "&Rectangle",          ID_DRAW_RECTANGLE
20:         MENUITEM "&Ellipse",            ID_DRAW_ELLIPSE
21:         MENUITEM "&Critter",            ID_DRAW_CRITTER
22:         MENUITEM SEPARATOR
23:         MENUITEM "Change C&olor..."     ID_DRAW_CHANGECOLOR
24:       END
25:     POPUP "&Help"
26:       BEGIN
27:         MENUITEM "&About Doodle...", ID_APP_ABOUT
28:       END
29: END
```

The Doodle3 menu now includes the standard File, New; File, Save; File, Open; and File, Close menu items, as well as an Edit popup menu with a Clear All menu item. You learn about this new menu command a little later in the hour.

I mentioned earlier that the IDR_DOODLE resource identifier specified the menu, accelerators, icon, and string resource for the application, but I didn't clarify how the string resource is used. You actually learned about this string resource in Hour 2, but I'll refresh your memory because that was almost half a day ago!

The string resource in question is actually a document string that contains a collection of substrings defining document properties. The substrings are separated from each other with newline characters (\n). Following is the format of the document string:

`"App\nDocName\nDocType\nFileType\n.Ext\nRegType\nRegName"`

Table 12.2 lists the meanings of each of the parts of the document string format.

TABLE 12.2 COMPONENTS OF THE DOCUMENT STRING FORMAT

String Component	Meaning
App	The application name
DocName	The default document name for new documents
DocType	A descriptive name for the document type
FileType	A descriptive name for the document file type
.Ext	The file extension for document files
RegType	The document file type used by Windows for file association
RegName	The readable name of the document file type

Managing Appliction Data with Documents

Following is the document string for the Doodle3 application, which adheres to the document string format:

`"Doodle\n\n\nDoodle Files (*.doo)\n.doo\nDoodle.Document\nDoodle Document"`

All the document substrings are filled out except for `DocName` and `DocType`. It isn't necessary to provide a `DocName` substring because MFC will use the name `Untitled` for unnamed documents automatically. Also, the `DocType` substring is really only necessary in applications that support multiple document types.

The Document Class

Now that you have a handle on the Doodle3 application resources, you're ready to move on to the actual document class, `CDoodleDoc`. The best way to learn about this class is to just jump into the code. Listing 12.5 contains the code for the DoodleDoc.h header file.

LISTING 12.5 THE DOODLEDOC.H HEADER FILE FOR DOODLE3

```
 1: #ifndef __DOODLEDOC_H__
 2: #define __DOODLEDOC_H__
 3:
 4: //-----------------------------------------------------------------
 5: // Inclusions
 6: //-----------------------------------------------------------------
 7: #include "Graphic.h"
 8:
 9: //-----------------------------------------------------------------
10: // CDoodleDoc Class - Doodle Document Object
11: //-----------------------------------------------------------------
12: class CDoodleDoc : public CDocument {
13:   // Member Variables
14: public:
15:   CTypedPtrList <CObList, CGraphic*>  m_graphicList;
16:
17:   // Public Constructor(s)/Destructor
18: public:
19:             CDoodleDoc();
20:   virtual   ~CDoodleDoc();
21:
22:   // Public Member Functions
23: public:
24:   virtual BOOL   OnNewDocument();
25:   virtual BOOL   OnOpenDocument(LPCTSTR lpszPathName);
26:   virtual void   DeleteContents();
27:   virtual void   Serialize(CArchive& ar);
28:   void           AddGraphic(CGraphic* pGraphic);
29:
```

continues

LISTING 12.5 CONTINUED

```
30:    // Message Handlers
31: public:
32:    afx_msg void   OnEditClearAll();
33:    afx_msg void   OnUpdateEditClearAll(CCmdUI* pCmdUI);
34:
35:    // Diagnostic Functions
36: public:
37: #ifdef _DEBUG
38:    virtual void   AssertValid() const;
39:    virtual void   Dump(CDumpContext& dc) const;
40: #endif //_DEBUG
41:
42:    // Message Map & Runtime Support
43: protected:
44:    DECLARE_MESSAGE_MAP()
45:    DECLARE_DYNCREATE(CDoodleDoc)
46: };
47:
48: #endif
```

The document data for `CDoodleDoc` consists of a single member variable, `m_graphicList`, which is a list collection of `CGraphic` object pointers. In Doodle2 this member variable belonged to `CMainFrame`. The `m_graphicList` member variable is sufficient for modeling the document data for the Doodle3 application.

The `CDoodleDoc` class overrides the familiar `CDocument` member functions you learned about earlier in the hour. It also adds an additional member function named `AddGraphic()` that is called by the view object to add a new graphic to the graphic list. The `CDoodleDoc` class also includes a command message handler, `OnEditClearAll()`, and a command update handler, `OnUpdateEditClearAll()`, that correspond to the Edit, Clear All menu command. To understand how all these member functions work, please turn your attention to Listing 12.6, which contains the implementation of `CDoodleDoc`.

LISTING 12.6 THE DOODLEDOC.CPP SOURCE CODE FILE FOR DOODLE3

```
1: //----------------------------------------------------------------
2: // Inclusions
3: //----------------------------------------------------------------
4: #include "StdAfx.h"
5: //----------------------------------------------------------------
6: #include "DoodleDoc.h"
7: #include "Resource.h"
8:
9: //----------------------------------------------------------------
```

Managing Appliction Data with Documents

```
10: // MFC Debugging Support
11: //-------------------------------------------------------------
12: #ifdef _DEBUG
13: #undef THIS_FILE
14: static char BASED_CODE THIS_FILE[] = __FILE__;
15: #endif
16:
17:
18: //-------------------------------------------------------------
19: // Message Map & Runtime Support
20: //-------------------------------------------------------------
21: BEGIN_MESSAGE_MAP(CDoodleDoc, CDocument)
22:   ON_COMMAND(ID_EDIT_CLEAR_ALL, OnEditClearAll)
23:   ON_UPDATE_COMMAND_UI(ID_EDIT_CLEAR_ALL, OnUpdateEditClearAll)
24: END_MESSAGE_MAP()
25:
26: IMPLEMENT_DYNCREATE(CDoodleDoc, CDocument)
27:
28: //-------------------------------------------------------------
29: // Public Constructor(s)/Destructor
30: //-------------------------------------------------------------
31: CDoodleDoc::CDoodleDoc() {
32: }
33:
34: CDoodleDoc::~CDoodleDoc() {
35: }
36:
37: //-------------------------------------------------------------
38: // Public Member Functions
39: //-------------------------------------------------------------
40: BOOL CDoodleDoc::OnNewDocument() {
41:   return CDocument::OnNewDocument();
42: }
43:
44: BOOL CDoodleDoc::OnOpenDocument(LPCTSTR lpszPathName) {
45:   return CDocument::OnOpenDocument(lpszPathName);
46: }
47:
48: void CDoodleDoc::DeleteContents() {
49:   // Cleanup graphic list
50:   while (!m_graphicList.IsEmpty())
51:     delete m_graphicList.RemoveHead();
52: }
53:
54: void CDoodleDoc::Serialize(CArchive& ar) {
55:   // Store/retrieve graphic list
56:   m_graphicList.Serialize(ar);
57: }
58:
```

continues

LISTING 12.6 CONTINUED

```
59: void CDoodleDoc::AddGraphic(CGraphic* pGraphic) {
60:    // Add a new graphic to end of graphic list
61:    ASSERT_VALID(pGraphic);
62:    m_graphicList.AddTail(pGraphic);
63:
64:    // Flag document as modified and update view
65:    SetModifiedFlag();
66:    UpdateAllViews(NULL);
67: }
68:
69: //-----------------------------------------------------------
70: // Message Handlers
71: //-----------------------------------------------------------
72: void CDoodleDoc::OnEditClearAll() {
73:    // Clear the document
74:    DeleteContents();
75:    SetModifiedFlag();
76:    UpdateAllViews(NULL);
77: }
78:
79: void CDoodleDoc::OnUpdateEditClearAll(CCmdUI* pCmdUI) {
80:    // Update the Edit¦Clear All menu item
81:    pCmdUI->Enable(!m_graphicList.IsEmpty());
82: }
83:
84: //-----------------------------------------------------------
85: // Diagnostic Functions
86: //-----------------------------------------------------------
87: #ifdef _DEBUG
88: void CDoodleDoc::AssertValid() const {
89:    CDocument::AssertValid();
90: }
91:
92: void CDoodleDoc::Dump(CDumpContext& dc) const {
93:    CDocument::Dump(dc);
94: }
95: #endif //_DEBUG
```

This looks like a lot of code but you'll find that it's pretty easy to understand. Let's start with the member functions that are overridden from CDocument. The OnNewDocument() function is called to create a new document, and corresponds to the user selecting the File, New menu command. In some applications you would perform special processing associated with the creation of a new document. However, CDoodleDoc is simple enough that it simply calls the base class version of the function. The OnOpenDocument() function performs a similar role, except that it responds to the user selecting the File, Open menu command.

Managing Appliction Data with Documents 221

The `DeleteContents()` member function is where things really start to get interesting. This function is responsible for clearing out the document data and freeing up any memory allocated for the data. In this case, the document data is the list collection of `CGraphic` object pointers. This code should look familiar to you because it appeared in the `CMainFrame` destructor in Doodle2. This is the first of many changes where functionality is shifted from the main frame window to the document and view classes.

The `Serialize()` member function is called to store and retrieve the document data to and from a `CArchive` object. The list collection provides its own `Serialize()` member function that handles the details of serializing a list of object pointers, so all you have to do is call this function on the `m_graphicList` member variable.

The `AddGraphic()` member function isn't an overridden function from `CDocument`. Instead, it provides an interface for adding new `CGraphic` objects to the graphic list. It first takes the `CGraphic` object pointer parameter and adds it to the list collection. It then calls the `SetModifiedFlag()` function to flag the document as being modified. Finally, the `UpdateAllViews()` function is called to update all document views so that they reflect the newly added graphic. `NULL` is passed to `UpdateAllViews()` because there is no specific view being targeted for updating.

> The `CDocument::SetModifiedFlag()` member function accepts a Boolean parameter that determines whether the document has been modified. The function assumes a default parameter of `TRUE`, which means that the document has indeed been modified. This is why it's OK to call the function without passing in a parameter.

The `CDoodleDoc` class also includes a couple of message handlers, `OnEditClearAll()` and `OnUpdateEditClearAll()`. The `OnEditClearAll()` handler carries out the Edit, Clear All menu command by deleting the contents of the document. It also makes sure to set the "modified" flag for the document and update the document's views. The `OnUpdateEditClearAll()` command update handler simply checks to see if the graphic list is empty. If so, it disables the menu item.

Serializing the `CGraphic` Class

The last code modification necessary for the Doodle3 application's document support is in the `CGraphic` class, which requires changes to support serialization. Listings 12.7 and 12.8 contain the code for the Graphic.h header file and Graphic.cpp source code file.

LISTING 12.7 THE GRAPHIC.H HEADER FILE FOR DOODLE3

```
 1: #ifndef __GRAPHIC_H__
 2: #define __GRAPHIC_H__
 3:
 4: //----------------------------------------------------------------
 5: // CGraphic Class - Graphic Object
 6: //----------------------------------------------------------------
 7: class CGraphic : public CObject {
 8:     // Public Member Constants
 9: public:
10:     enum   { LINE, RECTANGLE, ELLIPSE, CRITTER };
11:
12:     // Member Variables
13: private:
14:     int       m_nType;
15:     CRect     m_rcPosition;
16:     COLORREF  m_crColor;
17:
18:     // Constructor(s)/Destructor
19: protected:
20:     CGraphic(); // for serialization only
21: public:
22:     CGraphic(int nType, CRect& rcPosition, COLORREF crColor);
23:
24:     // Public Member Functions
25: public:
26:     void          Draw(CDC* pDC);
27:     virtual void  Serialize(CArchive& ar);
28:
29:     // Serialization Support
30: protected:
31:     DECLARE_SERIAL(CGraphic)
32: };
33:
34: #endif
```

LISTING 12.8 THE GRAPHIC.CPP SOURCE CODE FILE FOR DOODLE3

```
 1: //----------------------------------------------------------------
 2: // Inclusions
 3: //----------------------------------------------------------------
 4: #include "StdAfx.h"
 5: //----------------------------------------------------------------
 6: #include "Graphic.h"
 7: #include "Resource.h"
 8:
 9: //----------------------------------------------------------------
10: // MFC Debugging Support
```

```
11: //---------------------------------------------------------------
12: #ifdef _DEBUG
13: #undef THIS_FILE
14: static char BASED_CODE THIS_FILE[] = __FILE__;
15: #endif
16:
17:
18: //---------------------------------------------------------------
19: // Serialization Support
20: //---------------------------------------------------------------
21: IMPLEMENT_SERIAL(CGraphic, CObject, 1)
22:
23: //---------------------------------------------------------------
24: // Public Constructor(s)/Destructor
25: //---------------------------------------------------------------
26: CGraphic::CGraphic() {
27: }
28:
29: CGraphic::CGraphic(int nType, CRect& rcPosition, COLORREF crColor) {
30:   m_nType = nType;
31:   m_rcPosition = rcPosition;
32:   m_crColor = crColor;
33: }
34:
35: //---------------------------------------------------------------
36: // Member Functions
37: //---------------------------------------------------------------
38: void CGraphic::Draw(CDC* pDC) {
39:   ASSERT_VALID(pDC);
40:
41:   // Select the pen and brush
42:   CPen  pen(PS_SOLID, 2, m_crColor);
43:   CPen* ppenOld;
44:   CBrush* pbrOld;
45:   VERIFY(ppenOld = pDC->SelectObject(&pen));
46:   VERIFY(pbrOld = pDC->SelectObject(
47:     CBrush::FromHandle((HBRUSH)::GetStockObject(NULL_BRUSH))));
48:
49:   // Draw graphic based on the type
50:   switch (m_nType) {
51:   case LINE:
52:     // Draw a line
53:     pDC->MoveTo(m_rcPosition.TopLeft());
54:     pDC->LineTo(m_rcPosition.BottomRight());
55:     break;
56:
57:   case RECTANGLE:
58:     // Draw a rectangle
59:     pDC->Rectangle(m_rcPosition);
60:     break;
61:
```

continues

LISTING 12.8 CONTINUED

```
 62:   case ELLIPSE:
 63:     // Draw an ellipse
 64:     pDC->Ellipse(m_rcPosition);
 65:     break;
 66:
 67:   case CRITTER:
 68:     // Load the critter bitmap
 69:     CBitmap    bmCritter;
 70:     BITMAP     bmInfo;
 71:     VERIFY(bmCritter.LoadBitmap(IDB_CRITTER));
 72:     bmCritter.GetObject(sizeof(BITMAP), &bmInfo);
 73:
 74:     // Setup the memory DC
 75:     CDC        dcMem;
 76:     dcMem.CreateCompatibleDC(pDC);
 77:     VERIFY(dcMem.SelectObject(&bmCritter));
 78:
 79:     // Draw the critter image
 80:     pDC->StretchBlt(m_rcPosition.left, m_rcPosition.top,
 81:       m_rcPosition.Width(), m_rcPosition.Height(), &dcMem, 0, 0,
 82:       bmInfo.bmWidth, bmInfo.bmHeight, SRCAND);
 83:     break;
 84:   }
 85:
 86:   // Cleanup the DC
 87:   VERIFY(pDC->SelectObject(ppenOld));
 88:   VERIFY(pDC->SelectObject(pbrOld));
 89: }
 90:
 91: void CGraphic::Serialize(CArchive& ar) {
 92:   if (ar.IsStoring()) {
 93:     ar << (WORD)m_nType;
 94:     ar << m_rcPosition;
 95:     ar << m_crColor;
 96:   }
 97:   else {
 98:     WORD w;
 99:     ar >> w;
100:     m_nType = w;
101:     ar >> m_rcPosition;
102:     ar >> m_crColor;
103:   }
104: }
```

The first change to note in CGraphic is the IMPLEMENT_SERIAL macro, which is used to help give the class serialization support. This macro requires the class name, base class name, and schema for the serialized class. A schema is a special number used to distinguish between different versions of a serialized class. This enables future versions of a class to successfully serialize themselves from older versions. Passing a value of 1 as the schema is like identifying the class as version 1.0.

New Term A *schema* is a special number used to distinguish between different versions of a serialized class.

You'll also notice in the new version of `CGraphic` that there is now a default constructor. Even though the default constructor doesn't contain any actual code in `CGraphic`, it is necessary to have the constructor for serialization purposes.

The only other change in `CGraphic` is the `Serialize()` member function, which reads and writes the member variables of the class. This code is pretty straightforward except for the handling of the `m_nType` member variable. Because this member variable is of type `int`, which isn't guaranteed to be the same size on all platforms, it must be converted to a portable size (`WORD`) before being stored. Likewise, the data read from the archive must be first stored in a `WORD` variable and then cast to an `int` for the serialization to work properly. It's very important that the member variables are stored to and retrieved from the archive in the same order in each part of the `if` branch.

What's Missing?

Although you've done a lot of work toward making the Doodle3 application document-centric, you aren't quite finished. However, I want to save the last step for the next hour, which shows you how to create views. In the next hour you finish up the Doodle3 application by creating a view for the `CDoodleDoc` class.

Summary

This hour revisited MFC's document/view architecture and showed you the inner workings of documents. You learned about the `CDocument` class and what it has to offer, along with how important serialization is to documents. You also learned how to create documents, and wrapped up the hour by adding document support to the Doodle application. In the next hour you complete the new and improved Doodle3 application by adding a view to go along with the document.

Q&A

Q In this hour it was mentioned that some data types such as **int** aren't safe for serialization because their size can change across different systems. What data types are safe to use with the << and >> operators for serialization purposes?

A Portable data types that support the << and >> operators include `float`, `double`, `BYTE`, `WORD`, `LONG`, `DWORD`, `SIZE`, `POINT`, `RECT`, `CString`, `CTime`, and `CTimeSpan`. Also keep in mind that you can implement serialization support in your own classes, as was done in the `CGraphic` class for Doodle3.

Q Is the `DeleteContents()` member function ever called by the MFC document/view framework?

A Yes. `DeleteContents()` is called by the framework to delete a document's data before destroying the `CDocument` object. In other words, it is called just before a document is destroyed. The Doodle3 application also used `DeleteContents()` as the basis for an Edit, Clear All menu command.

Workshop

The Workshop is designed to help you anticipate possible questions, review what you've learned, and begin thinking ahead to put your knowledge into practice. The answers to the quiz are in Appendix A, "Quiz Answers."

Quiz

1. What is a document?
2. How many document types can an application use?
3. Can a document have more than one view?
4. What is the role of a document template object?
5. What class provides the basic functionality required of documents?
6. What is the purpose of a document's `Serialize()` member function?
7. What is the purpose of a document's "modified" flag?
8. How does a document notify its views of a change in document data?
9. Within the `Serialize()` member function, how do know if a document is being stored or retrieved?
10. What is the purpose of the schema used by the `IMPLEMENT_SERIAL` macro?

Exercises

1. Pretend that for some reason the `CGraphic` class requires an additional member variable of type `CString` that is named `m_sName`. Modify the `Serialize()` member function to properly serialize this member variable along with the other member variables already being serialized.
2. Compare the code you learned about in this hour with the code in the `CMainFrame` class in the Doodle2 application (Hour 11). Think about what functionality is likely to be included in the view class for the Doodle3 application. You develop this class in the next hour.

HOUR 13

Viewing Application Data

In the previous hour, you learned about documents and how they are used within the context of a document/view application. This hour continues the discussion by examining the view part of the document/view equation. You learn the basics of views and how to create views based on the CView class. You also finish up the Doodle3 application by creating a view for the Doodle document data.

In this hour, you will learn

- How views fit into document/view applications
- About the different MFC classes that support views
- How to create and use views

Understanding Views

MFC's document/view architecture is logically divided into two parts, documents and views. You learned in the previous hour that documents are used to encapsulate an application's data. Views work hand-in-hand with documents and provide a visual glimpse at a document's data. Views also provide a graphical user interface for interacting with the data contained in a document. If you think of your computer in terms of a document/view architecture, the information contained within logically represents the document, whereas the monitor, keyboard, and mouse together constitute the view.

A view is responsible for providing a visualization of a document's data. However, it isn't necessarily possible for a view to display all a document's data at a given time because views are constrained to fit within a certain physical space. Figure 13.1 shows how a view might display a portion of a document's data.

FIGURE 13.1

A view that displays a portion of a document's data.

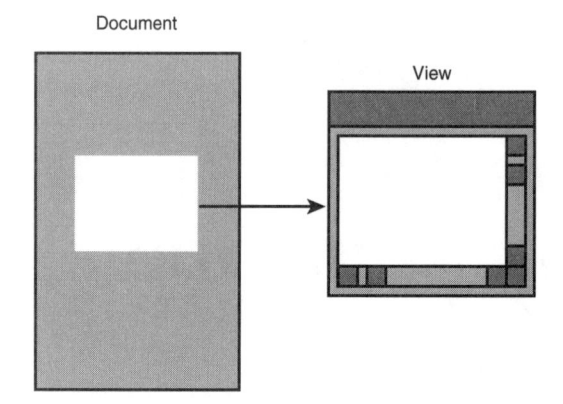

Because it is possible to represent some kinds of data in more than one way, it is possible to have multiple views associated with a given document. As an example, you could think of different types of graphs in a spreadsheet as multiple views on the same set of numeric data. It's not imperative to provide multiple views for every document, but it is always a nice option to have.

The beauty of views is that they can be created and modified without ever having to make changes to the document with which they are associated. The whole premise of MFC's document/view architecture is to make a clear distinction between application data and the visualization and manipulation of the data. Views are responsible for providing both the visualization and manipulation of document data.

Printing and Views

You might be surprised to learn that printing is very closely related to views. In fact, supporting the printing of documents is one of the responsibilities of views. Every view is required to have a special member function that renders document data to a device context. This member function is used to draw a document to the screen and to print a document to a printer because a device context is an abstraction of a drawing surface. In this way, views are responsible for rendering a visualization of document data to a variety of different output destinations.

View Windows

Unlike documents, views are actually windows and derive from the `CWnd` class. This is a testament to the visual nature of views. In many cases, views take up the client area of an application's frame window, which might lead you to think that they aren't windows to themselves. It's important to understand that views are always created as separate windows regardless of where they appear. This is evident in applications that utilize splitter windows to display multiple views. In this case, multiple view windows can coexist in the client area of a frame window. Figure 13.2 shows multiple view windows separated by a splitter window in Microsoft Word.

NEW TERM A *splitter window* is a special window that hosts two or more other windows, called panes, separated by one or more dividers.

FIGURE 13.2

Multiple view windows separated by a splitter window in Microsoft Word.

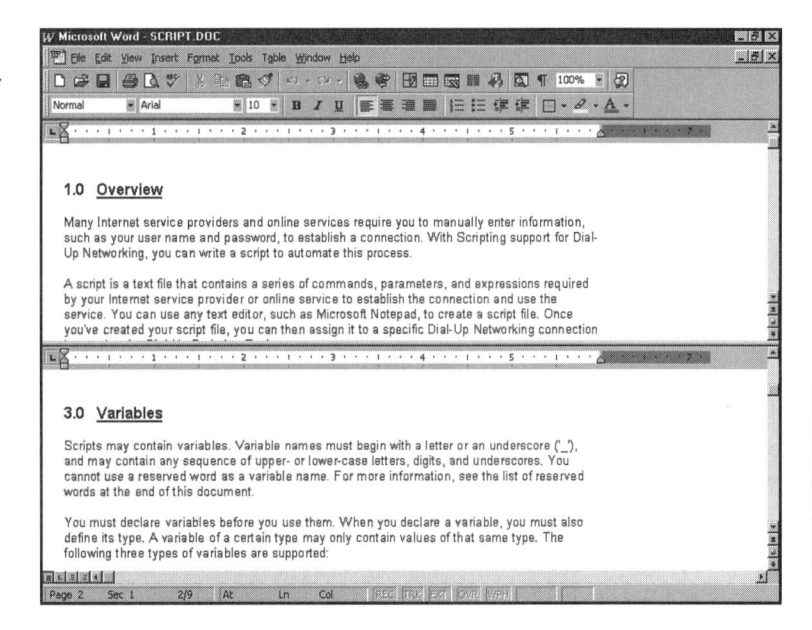

MFC's View Support

MFC provides plenty of support for views, including a set of classes that are tailored to specific types of views. Like the `CDocument` class, however, the general functionality of a view is encapsulated in a single view class, `CView`. The `CView` class provides member functions for accessing the document associated with the view, as well as a special draw member function for drawing the document data. You have the option of deriving your own view classes from `CView` or from a more specific view class that provides a view tailored to a certain type of visual presentation. Following are the different `CView`-derived view classes provided by MFC:

- `CScrollView`—A scrollable view
- `CEditView`—A text edit view
- `CListView`—A view that contains a list box control
- `CTreeView`—A view that contains a tree control
- `CCtrlView`—A view that serves as the base for other control views
- `CFormView`—A scrollable view that is based on a dialog box resource
- `CRichEditView`—A view that contains a rich edit control
- `CRecordView`—A view that displays database records
- `CDaoRecordView`—A view that displays database records using Database Access Objects
- `CHtmlView`—A view that displays HTML Web content and serves as a mini Web browser

You can use any of these view classes or derive from them to create views for your applications. Although most of these classes are very specific in how they display document data, they simplify things a great deal if you need a similar functionality. For the purposes of this hour, I'm going to stick with the `CView` class. You learn how to use some of the specialized view classes in the next hour, "Enhanced User Interfaces."

Getting back to the `CView` class, it provides some important member functions that you will commonly use when developing your own view classes. Table 13.1 lists the most commonly used member functions in the `CView` class.

TABLE 13.1 THE MOST COMMONLY USED CView MEMBER FUNCTIONS

Member Function	Description
OnDraw()	Called to render the view's document
OnUpdate()	Called when the view's document is modified (usually calls OnDraw())
OnPrint()	Called to print the view's document
GetDocument()	Gets the view's document

The brevity of this list of member functions might surprise you, but in fact a view class serves a relatively simple purpose that doesn't require much overhead. The only real requirement of a view class is that it provide an implementation of the OnDraw() member function. This requirement is evident in the fact that OnDraw() is declared as pure virtual in the CView class:

```
virtual void OnDraw(CDC* pDC) = 0;
```

> It isn't necessary to override the OnDraw() member function in CFormView because all of the child controls in the view draw themselves.

It is certainly possible to create a view whose only member function is OnDraw() because the other member functions in Table 13.1 have default implementations often suitable for simple views. However, it is typically useful to override GetDocument() and provide a type-safe version that safely casts the returned CDocument object to the appropriate application-specific document type.

The OnUpdate() member function is called when the document is modified and the view must be updated to reflect the change. It is only necessary to override OnUpdate() if you want to update only those view regions that correspond to the modified portions of the document. In this case the document must pass special information to the view when calling the UpdateAllViews() member function to update the view. The view receives this information in OnUpdate() and uses it as the basis for updating only a region of a view window. In this way the OnUpdate() member function serves as an optimization for drawing views quicker.

I mentioned earlier in the hour that a single draw function is responsible for drawing a view to both the screen and to a printer. I was referring to the OnDraw() member function. If the OnDraw() function handles printing a document, then what is the purpose of the OnPrint() member function? The OnPrint() member function is called by the framework to print or preview a page of document data, and is responsible for preparing the printer device context for printing. The default implementation of OnPrint() calls OnDraw() and passes it the printer device context. You only need to override OnPrint() if you are printing a multipage document, or if you want the printed document to somehow look different than it does on the screen.

> CFormView represents another exception to the rule in that it doesn't support default printing through the OnPrint() member function.

Creating Views

Creating a view is quite simple, and can often involve implementing only a couple of member functions. Following are the main steps involved in creating a view:

1. Derive a class from `CView` or one of the specialized view classes
2. Add member variables keep track of the view's user interface
3. Create message handlers to manage the view's user interface
4. Implement the `OnDraw()` member function to render the view

The steps to creating a view aren't too complicated, but it certainly helps to see a real example. The remainder of the hour focuses on finishing up the Doodle3 application by developing a view class for it.

Adding a View to Doodle

When you last left the Doodle3 application in the previous hour, it was in dire need of a view class. You developed a document class and modified other parts of the application to support MFC's document/view architecture. All it needs at this point is a view class that renders a visual representation of the `CDoodleDoc` class and provides a user interface for drawing Doodle graphics. Listing 13.1 contains the code for the DoodleView.h header file, which declares the `CDoodleView` class.

LISTING 13.1 THE DOODLEVIEW.H HEADER FILE FOR DOODLE3

```
 1: #ifndef __DOODLEVIEW_H__
 2: #define __DOODLEVIEW_H__
 3:
 4: //-----------------------------------------------------------------
 5: // CDoodleView Class - Doodle View Object
 6: //-----------------------------------------------------------------
 7: class CDoodleView : public CView {
 8:     // Member Variables
 9: protected:
10:     int        m_nDrawMode;
11:     COLORREF   m_crColor;
12:
13:     // Public Constructor(s)/Destructor
14: public:
15:                CDoodleView();
16:     virtual    ~CDoodleView();
17:
18:     // Public Member Functions
19: public:
```

```
20:    virtual void   OnDraw(CDC* pDC);
21:    CDoodleDoc*    GetDocument();
22:
23:    // Message Handlers
24: public:
25:    afx_msg void   OnLButtonDown(UINT nFlags, CPoint point);
26:    afx_msg void   OnDrawLine();
27:    afx_msg void   OnDrawRectangle();
28:    afx_msg void   OnDrawEllipse();
29:    afx_msg void   OnDrawCritter();
30:    afx_msg void   OnDrawChangeColor();
31:    afx_msg void   OnAppAbout();
32:    afx_msg void   OnUpdateDrawLine(CCmdUI* pCmdUI);
33:    afx_msg void   OnUpdateDrawRectangle(CCmdUI* pCmdUI);
34:    afx_msg void   OnUpdateDrawEllipse(CCmdUI* pCmdUI);
35:    afx_msg void   OnUpdateDrawCritter(CCmdUI* pCmdUI);
36:
37:    // Diagnostic Functions
38: public:
39: #ifdef _DEBUG
40:    virtual void   AssertValid() const;
41:    virtual void   Dump(CDumpContext& dc) const;
42: #endif //_DEBUG
43:
44:    // Message Map & Runtime Support
45: protected:
46:    DECLARE_MESSAGE_MAP()
47:    DECLARE_DYNCREATE(CDoodleView)
48: };
49:
50: #ifndef _DEBUG
51: inline CDoodleDoc* CDoodleView::GetDocument() {
52:    return (CDoodleDoc*)m_pDocument;
53: }
54: #endif //_DEBUG
55:
56: #endif
```

You might immediately notice that much of the functionality present in the CMainFrame class in Doodle2 now appears in CDoodleView. This is due to the fact that a view is responsible not only for providing a visual representation of a document, but also for establishing a graphical user interface for manipulating the document. In Doodle2, the main frame window assumed this responsibility, but now it lies squarely on the shoulders of CDoodleView. Fortunately, the change consisted simply of moving the code to the CDoodleView class from CMainFrame.

The only member functions in CDoodleView that didn't come from CMainFrame are GetDocument() and OnDraw(). As you learned earlier in the hour, these are two member functions that are commonly implemented in view classes. In fact, you are required to provide an `OnDraw()` function because the base class version is pure virtual.

You might be curious about the code at the bottom of DoodleView.h that defines an inline `GetDocument()` member function. This code is an optimization that only appears in release (non-debug) builds of the Doodle3 application. The debug version appears in the DoodleView.cpp source code file, and performs type checking on the document class to make sure it is of the correct type. Because type checking is primarily used for tracking tricky bugs, it is more efficient to only perform it in the debug version of the application.

To understand how the debug version of `GetDocument()` works, along with the `OnDraw()` member function, you need to turn your attention to the class implementation for `CDoodleView`. Listing 13.2 contains the complete source code for the `CDoodleView` class implementation, which is located in the file DoodleView.cpp.

LISTING 13.2 THE DOODLEVIEW.CPP SOURCE CODE FILE FOR DOODLE3

```
 1: //-----------------------------------------------------------------
 2: // Inclusions
 3: //-----------------------------------------------------------------
 4: #include "StdAfx.h"
 5: //-----------------------------------------------------------------
 6: #include "DoodleDoc.h"
 7: #include "DoodleView.h"
 8: #include "AboutDlg.h"
 9:
10: //-----------------------------------------------------------------
11: // MFC Debugging Support
12: //-----------------------------------------------------------------
13: #ifdef _DEBUG
14: #undef THIS_FILE
15: static char BASED_CODE THIS_FILE[] = __FILE__;
16: #endif
17:
18:
19: //-----------------------------------------------------------------
20: // Message Map & Runtime Support
21: //-----------------------------------------------------------------
22: BEGIN_MESSAGE_MAP(CDoodleView, CView)
23:    ON_WM_LBUTTONDOWN()
24:    ON_COMMAND(ID_DRAW_LINE, OnDrawLine)
25:    ON_COMMAND(ID_DRAW_RECTANGLE, OnDrawRectangle)
26:    ON_COMMAND(ID_DRAW_ELLIPSE, OnDrawEllipse)
27:    ON_COMMAND(ID_DRAW_CRITTER, OnDrawCritter)
28:    ON_COMMAND(ID_DRAW_CHANGECOLOR, OnDrawChangeColor)
29:    ON_COMMAND(ID_APP_ABOUT, OnAppAbout)
```

```
30:    ON_UPDATE_COMMAND_UI(ID_DRAW_LINE, OnUpdateDrawLine)
31:    ON_UPDATE_COMMAND_UI(ID_DRAW_RECTANGLE, OnUpdateDrawRectangle)
32:    ON_UPDATE_COMMAND_UI(ID_DRAW_ELLIPSE, OnUpdateDrawEllipse)
33:    ON_UPDATE_COMMAND_UI(ID_DRAW_CRITTER, OnUpdateDrawCritter)
34: END_MESSAGE_MAP()
35:
36: IMPLEMENT_DYNCREATE(CDoodleView, CView)
37:
38: //----------------------------------------------------------------
39: // Public Constructor(s)/Destructor
40: //----------------------------------------------------------------
41: CDoodleView::CDoodleView() : m_nDrawMode(CGraphic::LINE),
42:   m_crColor(RGB(0, 0, 0)) {
43: }
44:
45: CDoodleView::~CDoodleView() {
46: }
47:
48: //----------------------------------------------------------------
49: // Public Member Functions
50: //----------------------------------------------------------------
51: #ifdef _DEBUG
52: CDoodleDoc* CDoodleView::GetDocument() {
53:   ASSERT(m_pDocument->IsKindOf(RUNTIME_CLASS(CDoodleDoc)));
54:   return (CDoodleDoc*)m_pDocument;
55: }
56: #endif //_DEBUG
57:
58: void CDoodleView::OnDraw(CDC* pDC) {
59:   // Get a pointer to the document
60:   CDoodleDoc* pDoc = GetDocument();
61:   ASSERT_VALID(pDoc);
62:
63:   // Draw the view (paint the graphics)
64:   POSITION pos = pDoc->m_graphicList.GetHeadPosition();
65:   while (pos != NULL) {
66:     CGraphic* pGraphic = pDoc->m_graphicList.GetNext(pos);
67:     pGraphic->Draw(pDC);
68:   }
69: }
70:
71: //----------------------------------------------------------------
72: // Message Handlers
73: //----------------------------------------------------------------
74: void CDoodleView::OnLButtonDown(UINT nFlags, CPoint point) {
75:   // Get a pointer to the document
76:   CDoodleDoc* pDoc = GetDocument();
77:   ASSERT_VALID(pDoc);
78:
```

continues

LISTING 13.2 CONTINUED

```
79:       // Start the "rubber band" rectangle tracker
80:       CRectTracker tracker;
81:       tracker.TrackRubberBand(this, point);
82:
83:       // Add new graphic based on the drawing mode
84:       switch (m_nDrawMode) {
85:       case CGraphic::LINE:
86:          // Add a line to the graphics list
87:          pDoc->AddGraphic(new CGraphic(CGraphic::LINE, tracker.m_rect,
88:             m_crColor));
89:          break;
90:
91:       case CGraphic::RECTANGLE:
92:          // Add a rectangle to the graphics list
93:          pDoc->AddGraphic(new CGraphic(CGraphic::RECTANGLE,
              ↪tracker.m_rect,
94:             m_crColor));
95:          break;
96:
97:       case CGraphic::ELLIPSE:
98:          // Add an ellipse to the graphics list
99:          pDoc->AddGraphic(new CGraphic(CGraphic::ELLIPSE, tracker.m_rect,
100:            m_crColor));
101:         break;
102:
103:      case CGraphic::CRITTER:
104:         // Add a critter to the graphics list
105:         pDoc->AddGraphic(new CGraphic(CGraphic::CRITTER, tracker.m_rect,
106:            m_crColor));
107:         break;
108:      }
109: }
110:
111: void CDoodleView::OnDrawLine() {
112:    // Set the drawing mode to Line
113:    m_nDrawMode = CGraphic::LINE;
114: }
115:
116: void CDoodleView::OnDrawRectangle() {
117:    // Set the drawing mode to Rectangle
118:    m_nDrawMode = CGraphic::RECTANGLE;
119: }
120:
121: void CDoodleView::OnDrawEllipse() {
122:    // Set the drawing mode to Ellipse
123:    m_nDrawMode = CGraphic::ELLIPSE;
124: }
125:
126: void CDoodleView::OnDrawCritter() {
```

```
127:    // Set the drawing mode to Critter
128:    m_nDrawMode = CGraphic::CRITTER;
129: }
130:
131: void CDoodleView::OnDrawChangeColor() {
132:    // Select a pen color using the Color dialog box
133:    CColorDialog dlg(m_crColor);
134:    if (dlg.DoModal() == IDOK) {
135:      // Change the current color
136:      m_crColor = dlg.GetColor();
137:    }
138: }
139:
140: void CDoodleView::OnAppAbout() {
141:    CAboutDlg aboutDlg;
142:    aboutDlg.DoModal();
143: }
144:
145: void CDoodleView::OnUpdateDrawLine(CCmdUI* pCmdUI) {
146:    // Update the Draw¦Line menu item
147:    pCmdUI->SetRadio(m_nDrawMode == CGraphic::LINE);
148: }
149:
150: void CDoodleView::OnUpdateDrawRectangle(CCmdUI* pCmdUI) {
151:    // Update the Draw¦Rectangle menu item
152:    pCmdUI->SetRadio(m_nDrawMode == CGraphic::RECTANGLE);
153: }
154:
155: void CDoodleView::OnUpdateDrawEllipse(CCmdUI* pCmdUI) {
156:    // Update the Draw¦Ellipse menu item
157:    pCmdUI->SetRadio(m_nDrawMode == CGraphic::ELLIPSE);
158: }
159:
160: void CDoodleView::OnUpdateDrawCritter(CCmdUI* pCmdUI) {
161:    // Update the Draw¦Critter menu item
162:    pCmdUI->SetRadio(m_nDrawMode == CGraphic::CRITTER);
163: }
164:
165: //-----------------------------------------------------------------
166: // Diagnostic Functions
167: //-----------------------------------------------------------------
168: #ifdef _DEBUG
169: void CDoodleView::AssertValid() const {
170:    CView::AssertValid();
171: }
172:
173: void CDoodleView::Dump(CDumpContext& dc) const {
174:    CView::Dump(dc);
175: }
176: #endif //_DEBUG
```

The debug version of the `GetDocument()` member function is responsible for performing a runtime type check on the document class, and then returning a pointer to the document object. This is accomplished using the `CObject::IsKindOf()` member function and the `RUNTIME_CLASS` macro. The `ASSERT` macro in `GetDocument()` will fail if the document isn't of type `CDoodleDoc`.

The other member function of interest in `CDoodleView` is `OnDraw()`, which is responsible for drawing the document to the view window. The `OnDraw()` function in a view class is actually very similar to the `OnPaint()` function in a window class, except that `OnDraw()` is provided with a device context pointer with which it must perform all drawing operations. The first task in `OnDraw()` is to obtain a document pointer by calling the `GetDocument()` member function. From there, the `OnDraw()` member function simply iterates through the graphic list in the document and draws each graphic.

The remainder of the `CDoodleView` class implementation is transplanted code from the `CMainFrame` class, with which you are already familiar. That pretty well wraps up the view class for the Doodle3 application.

Summary

This hour in many ways served as a continuation of the previous hour by exploring the details of how views fit into the document/view architecture of document-centric applications. You learned about the different view classes supported by MFC, as well as how to create custom views of your own. The hour concluded by leading you through the creation of a view for the Doodle3 application, which completed the transformation of Doodle to a document/view application.

Q&A

Q How does the `OnDraw()` member function know if it is drawing to the screen or to a printer?

A It doesn't. The neat thing about the `OnDraw()` member function is that it doesn't need to know anything about the device on which it is drawing, except of course for the device context of the device. This abstraction is precisely what gives the `OnDraw()` function such flexibility. If you need to tweak the output of a printed document, you can always do so in the `OnPrint()` member function.

Q Is it really necessary to move so much of the functionality of the Doodle application's user interface from `CMainFrame` to `CDoodleView`?

A Technically, no. The Doodle3 application places most of the user interface functionality in `CDoodleView`, but that isn't a strict requirement of the document/view architecture. However, it's a good idea to think of a view as being solely responsible for the user interface of a document, in which case it usually makes sense to push the user interface functionality onto the view.

Workshop

The Workshop is designed to help you anticipate possible questions, review what you've learned, and get you thinking about how to put your knowledge into practice. The answers to the quiz are in Appendix A, "Quiz Answers."

Quiz

1. In addition to providing a visual glimpse at a document's data, what else is an application's view responsible for doing?
2. In terms of inheritance, what is the main distinguishing factor between documents and views?
3. What class encapsulates the general functionality of a view?
4. Which specialized view class supports a view containing a list box control?
5. What is the purpose of the `OnDraw()` member function?
6. When is the `OnUpdate()` member function called?
7. In what situations would you need to override the `OnPrint()` member function of a view?
8. Why is the `OnDraw()` member function declared as pure virtual in the `CView` class?
9. What role does a view play when it comes to printing a document?
10. What is a splitter window, and what does it have to do with views?

Exercises

1. Run the Doodle3 application and experiment with drawing some graphics and then saving the document to disk. Next, try opening the document to make sure that everything was properly saved. You might also want to try out the Edit, Clear All menu command because it is new to this version of Doodle.

2. You might have noticed that the Doodle3 application doesn't include the current graphic color as part of the document. This means that the color isn't saved as part of the document and is always set back to black when you open a document. To correct this, move the m_crColor member variable to the CDoodleDoc class. You might also want to move the OnDrawChangeColor() message handler to the document class because it is directly related to this member variable. Also, don't forget to serialize the m_crColor member in the document's Serialize() member function.

Hour 14

Enhanced User Interfaces

In the previous hour you learned about views, and how they fit into the overall scheme of an application. You also created a view for the Doodle application. This hour examines some techniques for altering views to enhance the user interface of applications. More specifically, this hour touches on the optimization of views, scrolling views, and using multiple views within an application. You revisit the familiar Doodle application in this hour to develop a significantly improved Doodle4 application.

In this hour, you will learn

- How to optimize the drawing of views
- How to support the scrolling of data within views
- How to use a splitter window to display two views
- How to use two different types of views in a single application

Optimizing Views

If you've spent any time trying out the Doodle application up to this point, you might have noticed that the speed in which it repaints the graphic list becomes noticeable as you add lots of graphic elements. There is a distinct flicker each time you add a new graphic element because the view is redrawing the entire list with the addition of each new graphic. Although this flicker isn't really a functional problem with the application, it is something that should be fixed if at all possible. Fortunately, MFC provides a mechanism for dealing with this exact situation.

> If you happen to have a graphics card with an obscene amount of memory or a supercharged accelerator, you might not experience the flicker to which I'm referring. However, keep in mind that you are typically developing applications for others to use, and you can't count on everyone having a hotrod computer. It's sometimes worth making optimizations for the sake of those who have run-of-the-mill computers with average speed performance.

Updating the View

The flicker is ultimately caused by the `CDoodleView::OnUpdate()` member function, which is responsible for determining how to update the view in response to a change in document data. The default implementation of `OnUpdate()` simply calls the `Invalidate()` member function to redraw the entire view in response to any change in document data. To reduce the flicker, you would invalidate only the region surrounding the newly added graphic. This requires the document to somehow communicate information about the graphic to the view's `OnUpdate()` function.

Support for this communication is built into the `OnUpdate()` member function, as the following prototype shows:

```
virtual void OnUpdate(CView* pSender, LPARAM lHint, CObject* pHint);
```

The first parameter, `pSender`, is a pointer to the view that caused the change in the document; this parameter is passed as `NULL` if all views are to be updated, which is the case with Doodle4. The second and third parameters enable you to pass custom information known as hints regarding the impact of the document change on the view. You can pass an object pointer as a hint in the third parameter, `pHint`, as long as the object is derived from `CObject`.

NEW TERM A *hint* is a piece of information used to inform a view of how it should be updated in response to a document change.

Before you get into the code for the Doodle4 application's `CDoodleView::OnUpdate()` member function, let's clarify the two situations when the function is called by the framework:

Enhanced User Interfaces

1. When a new graphic element is added to the document
2. Any time the view needs to be repainted

The difference between these two situations is that the first one benefits from using hints, whereas the second one doesn't. It is necessary for the `OnUpdate()` function to respond differently based on whether a hint is provided. Because a hint is required only when the `OnUpdate()` function is called in response to a new graphic element, it makes sense to use the `CGraphic` object as the hint. Passing a hint to the `OnUpdate()` function from the document is as simple as providing the hint to the `UpdateAllViews()` function in `CDoodleDoc::AddGraphic()`, which is shown in Listing 14.1.

LISTING 14.1 THE `CDoodleDoc::AddGraphic()` MEMBER FUNCTION FOR DOODLE4

```
1: void CDoodleDoc::AddGraphic(CGraphic* pGraphic) {
2:    // Add a new graphic to end of graphic list
3:    ASSERT_VALID(pGraphic);
4:    m_graphicList.AddTail(pGraphic);
5:
6:    // Flag document as modified and update view
7:    SetModifiedFlag();
8:    UpdateAllViews(NULL, 0L, pGraphic);
9: }
```

If you recall, the call to `UpdateAllViews()` in Doodle3 passed `NULL` as the hint pointer. The hint is processed in the `CDoodleView::OnUpdate()` member function, which is shown in Listing 14.2.

LISTING 14.2 THE `CDoodleView::OnUpdate()` MEMBER FUNCTION FOR DOODLE4

```
1: void CDoodleView::OnUpdate(CView* pSender, LPARAM lHint, CObject*
   ➥pHint) {
2:    // Make sure the hint is valid
3:    if (pHint != NULL) {
4:       if (pHint->IsKindOf(RUNTIME_CLASS(CGraphic))) {
5:          // Invalidate only the rectangular position of the new graphic
6:          CGraphic* pGraphic = DYNAMIC_DOWNCAST(CGraphic, pHint);
7:          CRect rc = pGraphic->GetPosition();
8:          InvalidateRect(&rc);
9:          return;
10:      }
11:   }
12:
13:   // Invalidate the entire view
14:   Invalidate();
15: }
```

Because it's possible that you might use hints of different types, the `OnUpdate()` function first checks to see if the hint is of type `CGraphic`. If so, the position rectangle of the graphic is retrieved and used as the basis for invalidating the view. The `InvalidateRect()` member function is used to specify a rectangular area of the view to invalidate. Because the position rectangle of a graphic element is usually much smaller than a view's rectangular extents, this is a significant improvement in the updating of a view. Notice that the entire view is invalidated if the hint type is anything other than `CGraphic`.

> The `CDoodleView::OnUpdate()` member function uses the `DYNAMIC_DOWNCAST` macro to safely cast the hint pointer to a `CGraphic` object pointer. The `DYNAMIC_DOWNCAST` macro is safer than performing a normal C++ cast because it checks to make sure the cast is legal.

Incidentally, the graphic position rectangle of the `CGraphic` hint was retrieved using the `GetPosition()` member function of `CGraphic`, which follows:

```
CRect& GetPosition() { return m_rcPosition; }
```

Drawing the View

In addition to the modifications made to the Doodle4 application's view code, you must also change the way the view is drawn. In other words, the `OnDraw()` function must factor in the update rectangle when drawing the view. Listing 14.3 contains the code for the view's `OnDraw()` member function.

LISTING 14.3 THE `CDoodleView::OnDraw()` MEMBER FUNCTION FOR DOODLE4

```
 1: void CDoodleView::OnDraw(CDC* pDC) {
 2:    // Get a pointer to the document
 3:    CDoodleDoc* pDoc = GetDocument();
 4:    ASSERT_VALID(pDoc);
 5:
 6:    // Get the clipping rect for the DC
 7:    CRect rcClip, rcGraphic;
 8:    pDC->GetClipBox(&rcClip);
 9:
10:    // Draw the view (paint the graphics)
11:    POSITION pos = pDoc->m_graphicList.GetHeadPosition();
12:    while (pos != NULL) {
13:       // Get the next graphic
14:       CGraphic* pGraphic = pDoc->m_graphicList.GetNext(pos);
```

```
15:
16:        // Only draw if the graphic rect intersects the clipping rect
17:        rcGraphic = pGraphic->GetPosition();
18:        if (rcGraphic.IntersectRect(&rcGraphic, &rcClip))
19:          pGraphic->Draw(pDC);
20:      }
21: }
```

This version of `OnDraw()` takes into consideration the clipping rectangle of the device context, which is the same update rectangle specified in `OnUpdate()`. The clipping rectangle of a device context specifies the area of the device context to which graphics can be drawn; nothing is drawn outside of the clipping rectangle. When drawing the graphic elements, `OnDraw()` checks to make sure that each element's position rectangle intersects the clipping rectangle before being drawn. Any graphic elements that don't intersect the clipping rectangle are not drawn. This results in much more efficient drawing of the view.

NEW TERM A *clipping rectangle* is a rectangle associated with a device context that specifies the area of the device context to which graphics can be drawn; nothing is drawn outside of the clipping rectangle.

Scrolling Views

You might have noticed that the Doodle application allows you to draw outside of the view window, even though there is no way to view the portion of a graphic element that extends beyond the view window. A common expectation of views is to support the display of document data that doesn't fit within the confines of a view window. In this case, views are expected to provide scrollbars that enable the user to scroll around and view different parts of the document data. The Doodle application is no different in this regard, and could certainly benefit from a scrollable view. Let's take a look at how to add this functionality.

Sizing Up the Document

The implementation of scrolling views begins with the concept of every document having a size. This means that you must declare a physical size (width and height) for a document before you can add scrolling support. In Doodle4, this requires you to add a member variable in the `CDoodleDoc` class:

```
CSize m_sizDoc;
```

You also need to add a member function that retrieves the document size:

`CSize& GetDocSize() { return m_sizDoc; }`

Finally, the document size needs to be initialized to some default in the class constructor:

```
CDoodleDoc::CDoodleDoc() : m_sizDoc(800, 600) {
}
```

This document size is specified in pixels, and is arbitrary for the most part. I chose the same width to height ratio that monitors use because it's likely that the Doodle4 application will be run maximized. Because the document size is something you want to store and keep up with, you need to persistently store and retrieve it in the `Serialize()` member function. Listing 14.4 contains the new `Serialize()` function for Doodle4.

LISTING 14.4 THE CDoodleDoc::Serialize() MEMBER FUNCTION FOR DOODLE4

```
 1: void CDoodleDoc::Serialize(CArchive& ar) {
 2:    // Store/retrieve the document size
 3:    if (ar.IsStoring()) {
 4:      ar << m_sizDoc;
 5:    }
 6:    else {
 7:      ar >> m_sizDoc;
 8:    }
 9:
10:    // Store/retrieve graphic list
11:    m_graphicList.Serialize(ar);
12: }
```

The `Serialize()` member function simply uses the `<<` and `>>` operators to read and write the `m_sizDoc` member variable to and from the archive.

Things get more interesting in the `AddGraphic()` member function for the document, which must enlarge the document when a new graphic is added that is outside of the document's bounds. Listing 14.5 contains the code for the newly revised `CDoodleDoc::AddGraphic()` member function.

LISTING 14.5 THE NEW CDoodleDoc::AddGraphic() MEMBER FUNCTION FOR DOODLE4

```
 1: void CDoodleDoc::AddGraphic(CGraphic* pGraphic) {
 2:    // Add a new graphic to end of graphic list
 3:    ASSERT_VALID(pGraphic);
 4:    m_graphicList.AddTail(pGraphic);
 5:
```

```
 6:     // Enlarge the document size if necessary
 7:     CSize sizGraphic = pGraphic->GetPosition().BottomRight();
 8:     if ((sizGraphic.cx > m_sizDoc.cx) || (sizGraphic.cy > m_sizDoc.cy)) {
 9:        m_sizDoc.cx = max(m_sizDoc.cx, sizGraphic.cx);
10:        m_sizDoc.cy = max(m_sizDoc.cy, sizGraphic.cy);
11:     }
12:
13:     // Flag document as modified and update view
14:     SetModifiedFlag();
15:     UpdateAllViews(NULL, 0L, pGraphic);
16: }
```

The new code added to the `AddGraphic()` member function checks to see if the right or bottom edge of the new graphic element is located outside of the current document size. If so, the document size is adjusted to include the graphic. That finishes up the changes to the document required to support scrolling. Let's move on to the view.

Scrolling the View

To help make supporting scrolling views a little easier, MFC provides a `CScrollView` class that handles a lot of the dirty work associated with scrolling views. The first step to supporting scrolling views in Doodle4 is to derive the `CDoodleView` class from `CScrollView` instead of `CView`. Following is the new class declaration for `CDoodleView` that accomplishes this task:

```
class CDoodleView : public CScrollView {
   ...
}
```

When you change the parent class for `CDoodleView` to `CScrollView`, you have to make some other changes for things to work properly. One of these changes is in the message map and dynamic creation macros:

```
BEGIN_MESSAGE_MAP(CDoodleView, CScrollView)
   ...
END_MESSAGE_MAP()

IMPLEMENT_DYNCREATE(CDoodleView, CScrollView)
```

You also have to change the code for the diagnostic `AssertValid()` and `Dump()` member functions, both of which reference the parent of the `CDoodleView` class. Listing 14.6 contains the new code for these functions.

LISTING 14.6 THE `CDoodleView::AssertValid()` AND `CDoodleView::Dump()` MEMBER FUNCTIONS FOR DOODLE4

```
1: #ifdef _DEBUG
2: void CDoodleView::AssertValid() const {
3:    CScrollView::AssertValid();
4: }
5:
6: void CDoodleView::Dump(CDumpContext& dc) const {
7:    CScrollView::Dump(dc);
8: }
9: #endif //_DEBUG
```

Okay, so `CDoodleView` is now technically a scrolling view, but it doesn't really know any specifics about how it should scroll. The first step to solving this problem lies in the `OnInitialUpdate()` member function, which is called to initially update a view upon creation:

```
virtual void OnInitialUpdate();
```

Listing 14.7 contains the source code for the `OnInitialUpdate()` member function, which sets the initial scroll size for the view.

LISTING 14.7 THE `CDoodleView::OnInitialUpdate()` MEMBER FUNCTION FOR DOODLE4

```
1: void CDoodleView::OnInitialUpdate() {
2:    // Set the document size for scrolling purposes
3:    SetScrollSizes(MM_TEXT, GetDocument()->GetDocSize());
4: }
```

The scroll size for a view is the same as the document size you added to the `CDoodleDoc` class. You set the scroll size for a view by calling the `SetScrollSizes()` member function, as the `OnInitialUpdate()` function demonstrates.

Because the document size can change any time a new graphic is added, it's necessary to also set the scroll size in the `OnUpdate()` member function, as shown in Listing 14.8.

LISTING 14.8 THE NEW `CDoodleView::OnUpdate()` MEMBER FUNCTION FOR DOODLE4

```
1: void CDoodleView::OnUpdate(CView* pSender, LPARAM lHint, CObject*
     ➥pHint) {
2:    // Make sure the hint is valid
3:    if (pHint != NULL) {
4:       if (pHint->IsKindOf(RUNTIME_CLASS(CGraphic))) {
5:          // Update the scroll sizes
```

```
 6:        CDoodleDoc* pDoc = GetDocument();
 7:        ASSERT_VALID(pDoc);
 8:        SetScrollSizes(MM_TEXT, pDoc->GetDocSize());
 9:
10:        // Invalidate only the rectangular position of the new graphic
11:        CGraphic* pGraphic = DYNAMIC_DOWNCAST(CGraphic, pHint);
12:        CClientDC dc(this);
13:        OnPrepareDC(&dc);
14:        CRect rc = pGraphic->GetPosition();
15:        dc.LPtoDP(&rc);
16:        rc.InflateRect(1, 1);
17:        InvalidateRect(&rc);
18:        return;
19:     }
20:  }
21:
22:  // Invalidate the entire view
23:  Invalidate();
24: }
```

If `OnUpdate()` determines that a new graphic element has been added to the document, it first sets the scroll size to the document size. You might also notice some new code to the portion of `OnUpdate()` that invalidates the rectangle of the new graphic element. This code converts logical coordinates to device coordinates, and is necessary because a scrolling view uses a different coordinate system than the document data. In prior versions of Doodle it was safe to assume that the origin of the document matched that of the view window. However, the view window can now be scrolled around to display different portions of a document. It is necessary to convert logical document coordinates to the device coordinates used by the view window. The `LPtoDP()` member function of the `CDC` class handles this chore.

NEW TERM *Logical coordinates* are a coordinate system that is based on a logical entity such as a document.

NEW TERM *Device coordinates* are a coordinate system that is based on a physical entity such as a window; device coordinates are also sometimes referred to as physical coordinates.

The coordinate disparity also reveals itself in the `OnLButtonDown()` member function, because it must take a mouse position in device coordinates and convert it to logical coordinates for the position of a graphic element. Listing 14.9 contains the revised code for the `OnLButtonDown()` member function.

LISTING 14.9 THE `CDoodleView::OnLButtonDown()` MEMBER FUNCTION FOR DOODLE4

```
 1: void CDoodleView::OnLButtonDown(UINT nFlags, CPoint point) {
 2:   // Get a pointer to the document
 3:   CDoodleDoc* pDoc = GetDocument();
 4:   ASSERT_VALID(pDoc);
 5:
 6:   // Start the "rubber band" rectangle tracker
 7:   CRectTracker tracker;
 8:   tracker.TrackRubberBand(this, point);
 9:
10:   // Convert the tracker rect from device to logical coordinates
11:   CClientDC dc(this);
12:   OnPrepareDC(&dc);
13:   dc.DPtoLP(&tracker.m_rect);
14:
15:   // If the width or height of the rect is negative, fix it
16:   if (tracker.m_rect.left > tracker.m_rect.right) {
17:     LONG l = tracker.m_rect.left;
18:     tracker.m_rect.left = tracker.m_rect.right;
19:     tracker.m_rect.right = l;
20:   }
21:   if (tracker.m_rect.top > tracker.m_rect.bottom) {
22:     LONG l = tracker.m_rect.top;
23:     tracker.m_rect.top = tracker.m_rect.bottom;
24:     tracker.m_rect.bottom = l;
25:   }
26:
27:   // Add new graphic based on the drawing mode
28:   switch (m_nDrawMode) {
29:   case CGraphic::LINE:
30:     // Add a line to the graphics list
31:     pDoc->AddGraphic(new CGraphic(CGraphic::LINE, tracker.m_rect,
32:       m_crColor));
33:     break;
34:
35:   case CGraphic::RECTANGLE:
36:     // Add a rectangle to the graphics list
37:     pDoc->AddGraphic(new CGraphic(CGraphic::RECTANGLE, tracker.m_rect,
38:       m_crColor));
39:     break;
40:
41:   case CGraphic::ELLIPSE:
42:     // Add an ellipse to the graphics list
43:     pDoc->AddGraphic(new CGraphic(CGraphic::ELLIPSE, tracker.m_rect,
44:       m_crColor));
45:     break;
46:
47:   case CGraphic::CRITTER:
48:     // Add a critter to the graphics list
49:     pDoc->AddGraphic(new CGraphic(CGraphic::CRITTER, tracker.m_rect,
```

Enhanced User Interfaces

```
50:            m_crColor));
51:        break;
52:    }
53: }
```

In addition to performing the coordinate conversion, the `OnLButtonDown()` member function also includes a fix for a subtle problem that was introduced earlier in the hour when you improved the drawing optimization of the view. If the mouse was dragged left or up to create a new graphic, as opposed to right or down, the graphic would have a negative width or height. A negative width or height causes problems with the code in `OnDraw()` that checks for the intersection of rectangles. `OnLButtonDown()` solves the problem by swapping the sides of a rectangle if they would result in a negative width or height.

That concludes the scrolling modifications required for the Doodle4 application. Figure 14.1 shows Doodle4 with support for scrolling.

FIGURE 14.1

The Doodle4 application with support for scrolling.

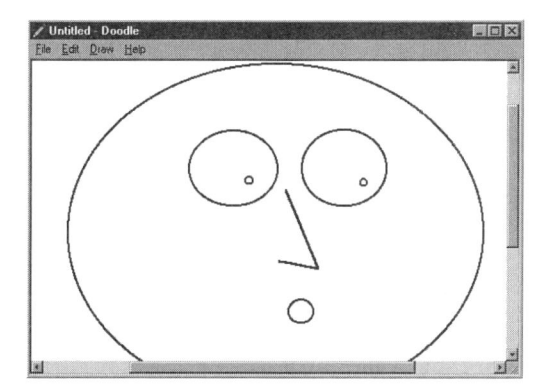

Using Multiple Views

Up until this point you've designed and built the Doodle application with regard to a single view for the `CDoodleDoc` class. It is sometimes useful to support multiple views in order to provide an alternative means of viewing or modifying document data. The last user interface enhancement you're going to make to the Doodle4 application involves creating another type of view and integrating it into the application's user interface.

Splitting the Views

A good way to manage multiple views is to use a splitter window, which divides the client area of an application into separate panes. Each pane of a splitter window contains a view. You can use the splitter window to adjust the sizes of the views. Figure 14.2 should give you an idea of how a splitter window supports multiple views.

FIGURE 14.2

A splitter window used to support multiple views.

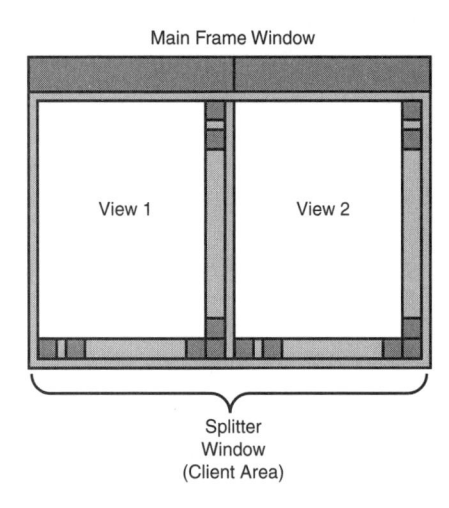

```
                    Main Frame Window
          ┌─────────────────────────────────┐
          │                                 │
          │    ┌─────────┐ ┌─────────┐     │
          │    │         │ │         │     │
          │    │ View 1  │ │ View 2  │     │
          │    │         │ │         │     │
          │    └─────────┘ └─────────┘     │
          └─────────────────────────────────┘
                     └────────┬────────┘
                           Splitter
                           Window
                         (Client Area)
```

> **NEW TERM** A *pane* is one of a set of windows that is displayed on either side of a splitter window; moving the splitter window adjusts the sizes of the panes.

Fortunately, it's pretty easy to add a splitter window to the Doodle4 application. The first step is to declare a member variable of type `CSplitterWnd`:

`CSplitterWnd  m_wndSplitter;`

The `CSplitterWnd` class is defined in the AfxCView.h header file, which should be added to the Doodle4 application's StdAfx.h header file. Listing 14.10 contains the new code for this header file.

LISTING 14.10   THE STDAFX.H HEADER FILE FOR DOODLE4

```
 1: #ifndef __STDAFX_H__
 2: #define __STDAFX_H__
 3:
 4: //----------------------------------------------------------------
 5: // Inclusions
 6: //----------------------------------------------------------------
 7: #include <AfxWin.h>
 8: #include <AfxExt.h>
 9: #include <AfxTempl.h>
10: #include <AfxCView.h>
11:
12: #endif
```

The splitter window should be created in the `OnCreateClient()` member function of `CMainFrame` because the splitter window resides in the client area of `CMainFrame`.

Following is the prototype for the `OnCreateClient()` member function:

```
virtual BOOL OnCreateClient(LPCREATESTRUCT lpcs, CCreateContext*
➥pContext);
```

Listing 14.11 contains the source code for the `OnCreateClient()` member function, which creates the splitter window as well as the two views residing in each splitter pane.

LISTING 14.11 THE `CMainFrame::OnCreateClient()` MEMBER FUNCTION FOR DOODLE4

```
 1: BOOL CMainFrame::OnCreateClient(LPCREATESTRUCT lpcs, CCreateContext*
 2:    pContext) {
 3:    // Create the splitter window and views
 4:    m_wndSplitter.CreateStatic(this, 1, 2);
 5:    m_wndSplitter.CreateView(0, 0, RUNTIME_CLASS(CDoodleView),
 6:       CSize(400, 400), pContext);
 7:    m_wndSplitter.CreateView(0, 1, RUNTIME_CLASS(CDoodleListView),
 8:       CSize(400, 400), pContext);
 9:    return TRUE;
10: }
```

The `CreateStatic()` member function is used to create the splitter window. The second and third parameters to this function indicate the number of rows and columns of panes in the splitter window. A 1∞2 splitter window consists of two panes separated by a vertical splitter bar. The two calls to `CreateView()` create the views associated with each pane. The left pane (0, 0) is of type `CDoodleView`, with which you are already familiar. The right pane (0, 1) is of type `CDoodleListView`, which is an entirely new view type. Both views are given a size of 400∞400 upon creation, which is arbitrary.

> The `CSplitterWnd` class also supports a `Create()` member function that is used to create dynamic splitter windows. Dynamic splitter windows are limited to supporting views of the same class, unlike Doodle4. The `CreateStatic()` member function must be used to create a static splitter window if you want to use views of differing types.

An Alternative View for Doodle

It's now time to turn your attention to the new view, `CDoodleListView`. As you might guess from the name, this view displays the Doodle document's graphic elements as a list. More specifically, the list view displays a list of text items that indicate the type and size of each graphic element. `CDoodleListView` is derived from the `CListView` class, which is a specialized view that contains a list control. You manipulate text entries in the list view by interacting with the underlying list control.

Because the `CDoodleListView` class implements an output-only view, its code is relatively simple. Listing 14.12 contains the code for the DoodleListView.h header file.

LISTING 14.12 THE DOODLELISTVIEW.H HEADER FILE FOR DOODLE4

```
 1: #ifndef __DOODLELISTVIEW_H__
 2: #define __DOODLELISTVIEW_H__
 3:
 4: //-----------------------------------------------------------------
 5: // CDoodleListView Class - Doodle View Object
 6: //-----------------------------------------------------------------
 7: class CDoodleListView : public CListView {
 8:    // Public Constructor(s)/Destructor
 9: public:
10:                 CDoodleListView();
11:    virtual      ~CDoodleListView();
12:
13:    // Public Member Functions
14: public:
15:    virtual void  OnUpdate(CView* pSender, LPARAM lHint, CObject*
          ➥pHint);
16:    virtual void  OnInitialUpdate();
17:    CDoodleDoc*   GetDocument();
18:
19:    // Diagnostic Functions
20: public:
21: #ifdef _DEBUG
22:    virtual void  AssertValid() const;
23:    virtual void  Dump(CDumpContext& dc) const;
24: #endif //_DEBUG
25:
26:    // Runtime Support
27: protected:
28:    DECLARE_DYNCREATE(CDoodleListView)
29: };
30:
31: #ifndef _DEBUG
32: inline CDoodleDoc* CDoodleListView::GetDocument() {
33:    return (CDoodleDoc*)m_pDocument;
34: }
35: #endif //_DEBUG
36:
37: #endif
```

As you can see, the `CDoodleListView` class relies on the familiar view functions `OnUpdate()` and `OnInitialUpdate()`, as well as a few other support and diagnostic functions. Listing 14.13 contains the implementation of the `CDoodleListView` class.

LISTING 14.13 THE DOODLELISTVIEW.CPP SOURCE CODE FILE FOR DOODLE4

```
 1: //------------------------------------------------------------------
 2: // Inclusions
 3: //------------------------------------------------------------------
 4: #include "StdAfx.h"
 5: //------------------------------------------------------------------
 6: #include "DoodleDoc.h"
 7: #include "DoodleListView.h"
 8:
 9: //------------------------------------------------------------------
10: // MFC Debugging Support
11: //------------------------------------------------------------------
12: #ifdef _DEBUG
13: #undef THIS_FILE
14: static char BASED_CODE THIS_FILE[] = __FILE__;
15: #endif
16:
17:
18: //------------------------------------------------------------------
19: // Runtime Support
20: //------------------------------------------------------------------
21: IMPLEMENT_DYNCREATE(CDoodleListView, CListView)
22:
23: //------------------------------------------------------------------
24: // Public Constructor(s)/Destructor
25: //------------------------------------------------------------------
26: CDoodleListView::CDoodleListView() {
27: }
28:
29: CDoodleListView::~CDoodleListView() {
30: }
31:
32: //------------------------------------------------------------------
33: // Public Member Functions
34: //------------------------------------------------------------------
35: #ifdef _DEBUG
36: CDoodleDoc* CDoodleListView::GetDocument() {
37:    ASSERT(m_pDocument->IsKindOf(RUNTIME_CLASS(CDoodleDoc)));
38:    return (CDoodleDoc*)m_pDocument;
39: }
40: #endif //_DEBUG
41:
```

continues

LISTING 14.13 CONTINUED

```
42: void CDoodleListView::OnUpdate(CView* pSender, LPARAM lHint, CObject*
       ➥pHint) {
43:     // Get a pointer to the document
44:     CDoodleDoc* pDoc = GetDocument();
45:     ASSERT_VALID(pDoc);
46:
47:     // Make sure the hint is valid
48:     if (pHint != NULL) {
49:         // A new graphic has been added by the user
50:         if (pHint->IsKindOf(RUNTIME_CLASS(CGraphic))) {
51:             // Add the new graphic to the list control
52:             CGraphic* pGraphic = (CGraphic*)pHint;
53:             CRect    rc = pGraphic->GetPosition();
54:             CString  sItem;
55:             sItem.Format("%s : %dx%d", pGraphic->GetTypeAsString(),
56:                 rc.Width(), rc.Height());
57:             GetListCtrl().InsertItem(GetListCtrl().GetItemCount(), sItem);
58:         }
59:         // A new graphic list has been opened
60:         else if (pHint->IsKindOf(RUNTIME_CLASS(CObList))) {
61:             // First delete all items from the list control
62:             GetListCtrl().DeleteAllItems();
63:
64:             // Then add each graphic to the list control
65:             POSITION pos = pDoc->m_graphicList.GetHeadPosition();
66:             while (pos != NULL) {
67:                 CGraphic* pGraphic = pDoc->m_graphicList.GetNext(pos);
68:                 CRect    rc = pGraphic->GetPosition();
69:                 CString  sItem;
70:                 sItem.Format("%s : %dx%d", pGraphic->GetTypeAsString(),
71:                     rc.Width(), rc.Height());
72:                 GetListCtrl().InsertItem(GetListCtrl().GetItemCount(),
                        ➥sItem);
73:             }
74:         }
75:     }
76:     // The graphic list has been cleared
77:     else if (pDoc->m_graphicList.IsEmpty()) {
78:         // Delete all items from the list control
79:         GetListCtrl().DeleteAllItems();
80:     }
81: }
82:
83: void CDoodleListView::OnInitialUpdate() {
84:     // Set the style of the list control
85:     DWORD dwStyle = GetListCtrl().GetStyle() | LVS_LIST;
86:     ::SetWindowLong(GetListCtrl().GetSafeHwnd(), GWL_STYLE, dwStyle);
87: }
```

```
 88:
 89:
 90: //--------------------------------------------------------------
 91: // Diagnostic Functions
 92: //--------------------------------------------------------------
 93: #ifdef _DEBUG
 94: void CDoodleListView::AssertValid() const {
 95:   CListView::AssertValid();
 96: }
 97:
 98: void CDoodleListView::Dump(CDumpContext& dc) const {
 99:   CListView::Dump(dc);
100: }
101: #endif //_DEBUG
```

The `OnUpdate()` member function is the real workhorse in the `CDoodleListView` class because it is responsible for adding new text entries to the list control as new graphic elements are added to the document. The function looks for two different kinds of hints: `CGraphic` objects and `CObList` objects. You are already familiar with the `CGraphic` hint. The `CObList` hint is used to inform the list view that a document has been opened. This is a tricky way of filling the list control with entries when the user opens an existing document; the `CObList` hint is the document's graphic list.

The `OnInitialUpdate()` member function is used to alter the style of the list control. The list control's style is set to `LVS_LIST`, which indicates that the list is to be a simple text list. There are other styles that you can apply to create more interesting lists such as multicolumn lists with graphics.

You might have noticed that the `GetTypeAsString()` member function of `CGraphic` was used in `OnUpdate()` to get the text name of the graphic type. This is a new function to the `CGraphic` class, and is declared as follows:

`CString GetTypeAsString();`

Listing 14.14 contains the source code for the `CGraphic::GetTypeAsString()` member function.

LISTING 14.14 THE `CGraphic::GetTypeAsString()` MEMBER FUNCTION FOR DOODLE4

```
1: CString CGraphic::GetTypeAsString() {
2:   switch (m_nType) {
3:     case LINE:
4:       return CString("Line");
5:
```

continues

LISTING 14.14 CONTINUED

```
 6:    case RECTANGLE:
 7:      return CString("Rectangle");
 8:
 9:    case ELLIPSE:
10:      return CString("Ellipse");
11:
12:    case CRITTER:
13:      return CString("Critter");
14:
15:    default:
16:      return CString("Unknown");
17:    }
18: }
```

The CGraphic::GetTypeAsString() member function returns a string representation of the graphic type. There's not really anything tricky going on here!

The last code changes required to make the multiview version of Doodle4 work properly are in the OnNewDocument() and OnOpenDocument() member functions. Listing 14.15 contains the source code for these functions.

LISTING 14.15 THE CDoodleDoc::OnNewDocument() AND CDoodleDoc::OnOpenDocument() MEMBER FUNCTIONS FOR DOODLE4

```
 1: BOOL CDoodleDoc::OnNewDocument() {
 2:   if (!CDocument::OnNewDocument())
 3:     return FALSE;
 4:   UpdateAllViews(NULL);
 5:   return TRUE;
 6: }
 7:
 8: BOOL CDoodleDoc::OnOpenDocument(LPCTSTR lpszPathName) {
 9:   if (!CDocument::OnOpenDocument(lpszPathName))
10:     return FALSE;
11:   UpdateAllViews(NULL, 0L, &m_graphicList);
12:   return TRUE;
13: }
```

An interesting caveat to using different view types within a single application is that the views aren't automatically updated when you use the File, New and File, Open menu commands. The OnNewDocument() and OnOpenDocument() member functions both call UpdateAllViews() to make sure the views are updated. The OnOpenDocument() function is a little different because it passes the graphic list in as a hint to UpdateAllViews().

This is how the `OnUpdate()` member function knows how to fill the list control for the list view when a document is opened. I know this is a sneaky approach to updating the list view, but it just so happens to work!

By the way, the completed Doodle4 application is shown in Figure 14.3.

FIGURE 14.3

The Doodle4 application with two different types of views separated by a splitter window.

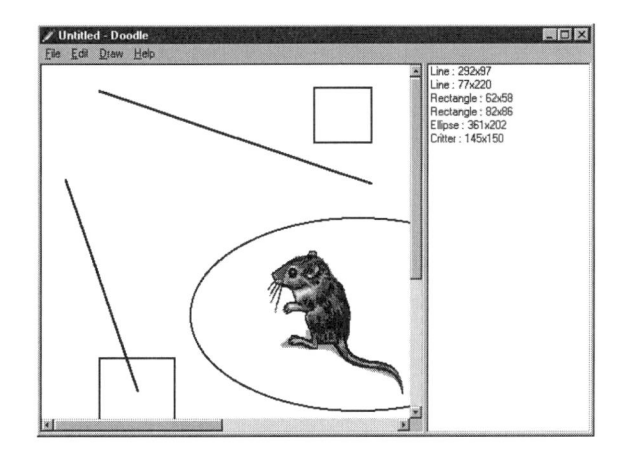

Summary

This hour jumped headfirst into some interesting code for modifying the graphical user interface of the Doodle application. If you had any complaints about not seeing enough source code thus far in the book, then this hour certainly delivered! You learned how views can be optimized to draw themselves more efficiently. You also learned how to support scrolling in views, as well as how to use multiple view types in a single application.

Q&A

Q Is it necessary to keep track of the document size in order to support a scrolling view?

A Yes. However, it isn't necessary to support a document that changes in size. In other words, you are free to set a fixed document size that doesn't ever change.

Q What is the significance of static and dynamic splitter windows?

A The physical structure of static splitter windows cannot be modified after a splitter window has been created, whereas dynamic splitter windows can be dynamically altered. On the other hand, static splitter windows are more flexible in that they can contain panes with different types of views and can have more panes than dynamic splitter windows. An example of a static splitter window is the one dividing the two main views in Windows Explorer, whereas Microsoft Word is an example of an application that uses dynamic splitter windows.

Workshop

The Workshop is designed to help you anticipate possible questions, review what you've learned, and begin thinking ahead to put your knowledge into practice. The answers to the quiz are in Appendix A, "Quiz Answers."

Quiz

1. How does the default implementation of the `CView::OnUpdate()` member function update a view?
2. In regard to documents and views, what is a hint?
3. What is the difference between the `Invalidate()` and `InvalidateRect()` member functions?
4. What is a clipping rectangle?
5. What member function of `CScrollView` do you use to set the scroll size for a view?
6. What is the difference between logical coordinates and device coordinates?
7. What is a pane?
8. What standard MFC header file must you include to use the `CSplitterWnd` class?
9. What is the significance of the rows and columns in a splitter window?
10. What MFC view class supports a specialized view that contains a list control?

Exercises

1. Add a member function to `CGraphic` called `GetColor()` that returns the color of the graphic.
2. Modify the `CDoodleListView` class so that it displays the color of the graphic in addition to the type and size. You should use the new `GetColor()` member function of `CGraphic` to obtain the color, and then specify the color in terms of its RGB components.

HOUR 15

Utilizing Control Bars

This hour takes a look at a graphical user interface feature that has become extremely popular in modern Windows applications. I'm referring to control bars, which typically take the form of toolbars and status bars. Toolbars are commonly used as a quick alternative to selecting commands within an application. Status bars are used to provide a primitive form of Help for commands, as well as other information about the status of an application.

In this hour, you will learn

- The basics of control bars and how they are used
- How to create and use toolbars
- How to create and use status bars
- How to use ToolTips to enhance a toolbar

Understanding Control Bars

You don't have to look very far to find a Windows application that uses control bars in one way or another as part of its graphical user interface. Control bars consist of toolbars, status bars, and dialog bars. The primary purpose of control bars is to enhance the user interface of applications and provide an alternative means of issuing commands and altering application settings. The WordPad application that ships with Windows 95/98 contains one of each type of control bar, as shown in Figure 15.1.

FIGURE 15.1

The WordPad application with a toolbar, status bar, and dialog bar.

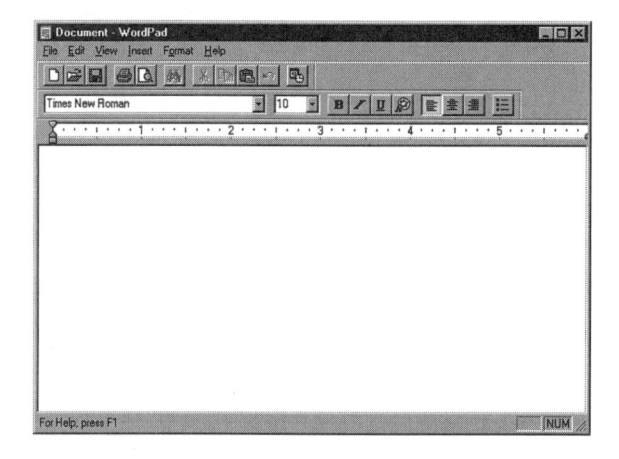

Toolbars and dialog bars are similar in that they both can contain buttons. However, dialog bars are more flexible in that they can contain any control. On the other hand, toolbars are easier to use and more efficient if you only need buttons.

Not surprisingly, MFC provides a set of classes that model each type of control bar, as well as a general base class from which each control bar class is derived. Following are the MFC classes that support control bars:

- CControlBar
- CToolBar
- CStatusBar
- CDialogBar

The CControlBar class provides the basic support required of all control bars, and serves as the base class for the other control bar classes. The CControlBar class supports a control bar window that can be aligned to the left or right edge of a frame window. One neat feature of control bars is docking, which allows a floating control bar to be attached to the edge of a frame window. Most control bars are docked by default; you initially make a control bar float by dragging it away from the edge of a frame window. Generally speaking, control bar windows are children of an application's frame window, and siblings of the client window.

New Term — *Docking* is the capability of a floating control bar to be attached to the edge of a frame window.

The `CToolBar` class implements a control bar with a row of bitmap buttons and optional separators. Each button in a toolbar contains a bitmap image, and can act like a pushbutton, a check box, or a radio button. In the latter two cases, a button remains depressed to indicate that it is checked. Toolbars are typically placed at the top of an application's frame window in between the menu and the client area.

The `CStatusBar` class implements a control bar with a row of text panes that display information about the state of an application. These panes are commonly used to show help messages and keyboard status indicators such as the state of the Caps Lock, Num Lock, and Scroll Lock keys. Perhaps the most important usage of status bars is the display of help messages for menu commands. When the user highlights a command on a menu, a help message is displayed in the status bar containing information about the command. Status bars are typically placed at the bottom of an application's frame window just below the client area.

The `CDialogBar` class implements a control bar that is much like a dialog box in that it can contain different types of controls. In fact, you can create a dialog bar from a dialog box resource. Dialog bars are often placed at the top of an application's frame window like a toolbar, but depending on the needs of a particular application, they might appear on the left or right side of the frame window, or even at the bottom. Figure 15.2 shows the Paint application that ships with Windows 95/98, which contains a dialog bar on the left side of the frame window, and another one at the bottom of the frame window just above the status bar.

Figure 15.2

The Paint application with two dialog bars at different locations.

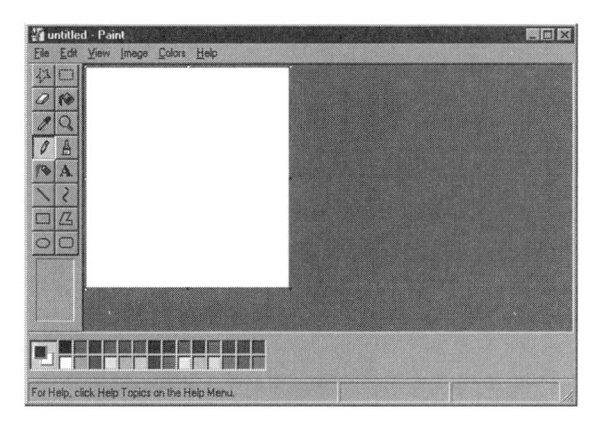

Using Toolbars

As you just learned, toolbars consist of a row of bitmap buttons that are typically used as an alternative means of issuing menu commands. You'll be glad to know that toolbars are very easy to create and use, especially considering how much they can improve the graphical user interface of an application. The vast majority of toolbar functionality is encapsulated in the CToolBar class, and is automatically enabled after you create and initialize a CToolBar object. Following are the steps required to create a toolbar:

1. Create a toolbar bitmap and include it in the application as a bitmap resource
2. Create a toolbar resource
3. Create a CToolBar object
4. Call the Create() member function to create the toolbar
5. Call the LoadToolBar() member function to load the toolbar resource and bitmap

Each button in a toolbar has a bitmap image associated with it that is displayed on the button. To make the development of toolbars a little simpler, toolbar button images are specified in a single toolbar bitmap. You can think of this bitmap as an array of button images. Figure 15.3 shows a zoomed view of the toolbar bitmap image for the Doodle5 application.

FIGURE 15.3

A zoomed view of the toolbar bitmap image for Doodle5.

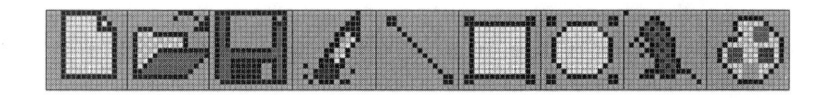

As you can see, the individual button images are tiled from left to right across the toolbar bitmap. Each button image is 16∞15 pixels, which is the standard size for most Windows applications. This image is stored in the file ToolBar.bmp, and must be included as a bitmap resource in the resource script for Doodle5:

IDR_DOODLE BITMAP   "ToolBar.bmp"

After you've created a toolbar bitmap and included it as a bitmap resource, you're ready to create a toolbar resource. Listing 15.1 contains the toolbar resource for the Doodle5 application.

LISTING 15.1 THE TOOLBAR RESOURCE DEFINITION FOR DOODLE5

```
1: IDR_DOODLE TOOLBAR  16, 15
2: BEGIN
3:    BUTTON      ID_FILE_NEW
```

```
 4:    BUTTON      ID_FILE_OPEN
 5:    BUTTON      ID_FILE_SAVE
 6:    SEPARATOR
 7:    BUTTON      ID_EDIT_CLEAR_ALL
 8:    SEPARATOR
 9:    BUTTON      ID_DRAW_LINE
10:    BUTTON      ID_DRAW_RECTANGLE
11:    BUTTON      ID_DRAW_ELLIPSE
12:    BUTTON      ID_DRAW_CRITTER
13:    BUTTON      ID_DRAW_CHANGECOLOR
14: END
```

A toolbar resource is similar in some ways to a menu resource, except that a toolbar resource is much simpler. Each button in the toolbar is defined by assigning it a menu command identifier. Keep in mind that the number of buttons in the toolbar resource must match the number of tiled button bitmaps in the toolbar bitmap. Also notice that the size of the button images (16∞15) is specified at the start of the toolbar resource. Spaces between buttons are created using the SEPARATOR identifier.

With the toolbar resource in place, you're now ready to create a CToolBar object. The first step in doing this is to declare a CToolBar member variable in the CMainFrame class:

```
CToolBar m_wndToolBar;
```

The best place to create and initialize a toolbar is in the OnCreate() message handler for an application's main frame window, which is associated with the WM_CREATE message. Of course, you must first add a message map entry for this message in order for the handler to get called:

```
BEGIN_MESSAGE_MAP(CMainFrame, CFrameWnd)
  ON_WM_CREATE()
END_MESSAGE_MAP()
```

Following is the prototype for the OnCreate() message handler, which must be added to the CMainFrame class declaration:

```
afx_msg int OnCreate(LPCREATESTRUCT lpCreateStruct);
```

Last, but certainly not least, is the code for the OnCreate() message handler, which is responsible for creating and initializing the toolbar (see Listing 15.2).

LISTING 15.2 THE CMainFrame::OnCreate() MESSAGE HANDLER FOR DOODLE5

```
1: int CMainFrame::OnCreate(LPCREATESTRUCT lpCreateStruct) {
2:    if (CFrameWnd::OnCreate(lpCreateStruct) == -1)
3:       return -1;
```

continues

LISTING 15.2 CONTINUED

```
 4:
 5:    // Create toolbar
 6:    if (!m_wndToolBar.Create(this) ||
 7:      !m_wndToolBar.LoadToolBar(IDR_DOODLE))
 8:      return -1;
 9:
10:    return 0;
11: }
```

The Create() member function is first called on the CToolBar object to create the toolbar. However, at this stage the toolbar resource hasn't been associated with the toolbar, so the toolbar really isn't of much use. The toolbar is properly initialized by calling the LoadToolBar() member function, which loads the toolbar resource and bitmap. Figure 15.4 shows the Doodle5 application with its new toolbar.

FIGURE 15.4

The Doodle5 application with a toolbar.

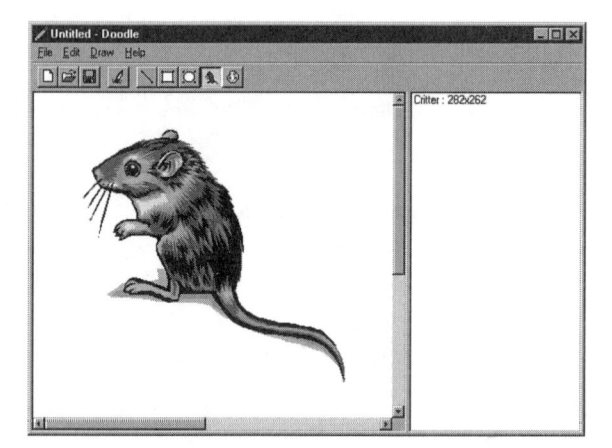

Using Status Bars

Status bars are used to convey information to the user such as help messages and keyboard status indicators. Help messages are displayed in the main section of a status bar, whereas all other information is displayed in panes that appear inset with respect to the status bar. In addition to keyboard status indicators, status bar panes can be used to display application-specific information.

Similar to a toolbar, the functionality of a status bar is largely automatic after you create and initialize the status bar object. Following are the steps required to create a status bar:

1. Create string resources for the status bar help messages and keyboard status indicators.

2. Create a `CStatusBar` object.
3. Create a static `UINT` array specifying the panes for the status bar.
4. Call the `Create()` member function to create the status bar.
5. Call the `SetIndicators()` member function to set the panes for the status bar.

A status bar requires two different sets of string resources: a set identifying the help messages for menu commands and a set identifying the panes. Listing 15.3 contains the string resources for the Doodle5 application's status bar help messages.

LISTING 15.3 THE HELP MESSAGE STRING RESOURCE DEFINITIONS FOR DOODLE5'S STATUS BAR

```
 1: STRINGTABLE
 2: BEGIN
 3:    ID_FILE_NEW            "Create a new drawing"
 4:    ID_FILE_OPEN           "Open an existing drawing"
 5:    ID_FILE_SAVE           "Save the drawing"
 6:    ID_FILE_SAVE_AS        "Save the drawing with a new name"
 7:    ID_APP_EXIT            "Quit the application; prompts to save drawing"
 8:
 9:    ID_EDIT_CLEAR_ALL      "Clear the entire drawing"
10:
11:    ID_DRAW_LINE           "Draw a line"
12:    ID_DRAW_RECTANGLE      "Draw a rectangle"
13:    ID_DRAW_ELLIPSE        "Draw an ellipse"
14:    ID_DRAW_CRITTER        "Draw an image of a critter"
15:    ID_DRAW_CHANGECOLOR    "Change the current drawing color"
16: END
```

As you can see, there is nothing magical about associating status bar help messages with menu commands. It's as simple as identifying the menu command identifier and the text message associated with it. Listing 15.4 is a little more interesting in that it specifies the keyboard status indicators used in Doodle5's status bar panes.

LISTING 15.4 THE KEYBOARD STATUS INDICATOR STRING RESOURCE DEFINITIONS FOR DOODLE5'S STATUS BAR

```
1: STRINGTABLE
2: BEGIN
3:    ID_INDICATOR_CAPS      "CAP"
4:    ID_INDICATOR_NUM       "NUM"
5:    ID_INDICATOR_SCRL      "SCRL"
6: END
```

The identifiers used in the keyboard status indicators are standard identifiers defined in MFC. They represent the Caps Lock, Num Lock, and Scroll Lock keys, respectively. The purpose of these string resources is simply to determine the size of each keyboard status indicator pane within the status bar. More specifically, each pane is automatically sized so that it will fit the string resource. The creation of the panes is handled in a moment after you create the status bar object.

The creation of the `CStatusBar` object is handled by simply declaring a `CMainFrame` member variable of type `CStatusBar`:

```
CStatusBar m_wndStatusBar;
```

The panes for this status bar are specified using a static array of `UINT` pane identifiers:

```
static UINT indicators[] = { ID_SEPARATOR, ID_INDICATOR_CAPS,
  ID_INDICATOR_NUM, ID_INDICATOR_SCRL };
```

The `ID_SEPARATOR` identifier is used to place the panes on the right side of the status bar, which leaves room for help messages to be displayed on the left side. This array of identifiers is used to establish the status bar panes in the `CMainFrame::OnCreate()` message handler, which is shown in Listing 15.5.

LISTING 15.5 THE REVISED `CMainFrame::OnCreate()` MESSAGE HANDLER FOR DOODLE5

```
 1: int CMainFrame::OnCreate(LPCREATESTRUCT lpCreateStruct) {
 2:   if (CFrameWnd::OnCreate(lpCreateStruct) == -1)
 3:     return -1;
 4:
 5:   // Create toolbar
 6:   if (!m_wndToolBar.Create(this) ||
 7:     !m_wndToolBar.LoadToolBar(IDR_DOODLE))
 8:     return -1;
 9:
10:   // Create status bar
11:   if (!m_wndStatusBar.Create(this) ||
12:     !m_wndStatusBar.SetIndicators(indicators,
             ➥sizeof(indicators)/sizeof(UINT)))
13:     return -1;
14:
15:   return 0;
16: }
```

As you can see, the status bar is created with a call to `Create()`, whereas the panes are set with a call to `SetIndicators()`. The resulting status bar is shown in action in Figure 15.5.

FIGURE 15.5
The Doodle5 application with a status bar.

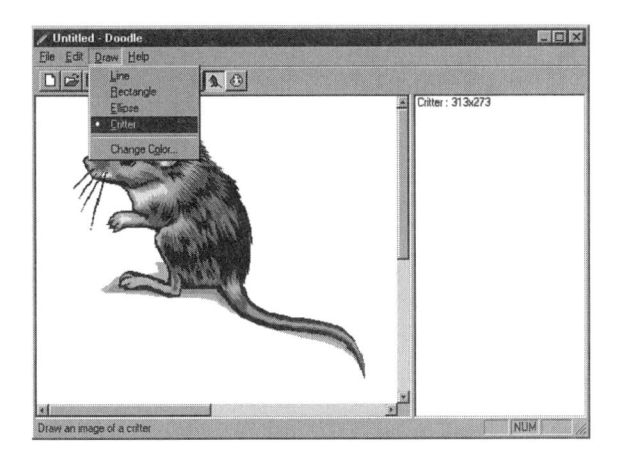

Showing and Hiding Control Bars

Although control bars are typically viewed as an enhancement to the graphical user interface of an application, there might be situations where a user would prefer not having them around. Therefore, it is nice to enable the user to easily hide control bars if desired. This makes your applications a little more customizable to each user's tastes, which is very important. The good news is that it is painfully easy to add this functionality to MFC applications.

The first step is to add menu commands that can be used to show and hide the toolbar and status bar of an application. Listing 15.6 shows the menu resource definition for Doodle5, which defines a View popup menu containing the commands `Toolbar` and `Status Bar`.

LISTING 15.6 THE MENU RESOURCE DEFINITION FOR DOODLE5

```
 1: IDR_DOODLE MENU
 2: BEGIN
 3:     POPUP "&File"
 4:     BEGIN
 5:         MENUITEM "&New\tCtrl+N",            ID_FILE_NEW
 6:         MENUITEM "&Open...\tCtrl+O",        ID_FILE_OPEN
 7:         MENUITEM "&Save\tCtrl+S",           ID_FILE_SAVE
 8:         MENUITEM "Save &As...",             ID_FILE_SAVE_AS
 9:         MENUITEM SEPARATOR
10:         MENUITEM "E&xit",                   ID_APP_EXIT
11:     END
12:     POPUP "&Edit"
13:     BEGIN
```

continues

LISTING 15.6 CONTINUED

```
14:        MENUITEM "Clear &All",         ID_EDIT_CLEAR_ALL
15:      END
16:   POPUP "&Draw"
17:      BEGIN
18:        MENUITEM "&Line",              ID_DRAW_LINE
19:        MENUITEM "&Rectangle",         ID_DRAW_RECTANGLE
20:        MENUITEM "&Ellipse",           ID_DRAW_ELLIPSE
21:        MENUITEM "&Critter",           ID_DRAW_CRITTER
22:        MENUITEM SEPARATOR
23:        MENUITEM "Change C&olor..."    ID_DRAW_CHANGECOLOR
24:      END
25:   POPUP "&View"
26:      BEGIN
27:        MENUITEM "&Toolbar",           ID_VIEW_TOOLBAR
28:        MENUITEM "&Status Bar",        ID_VIEW_STATUS_BAR
29:      END
30:   POPUP "&Help"
31:      BEGIN
32:        MENUITEM "&About Doodle...",   ID_APP_ABOUT
33:      END
34: END
```

The beauty of the View menu commands is that they use standard menu command identifiers (ID_VIEW_TOOLBAR and ID_VIEW_STATUS_BAR) that automatically invoke the show/hide functionality for control bars. In other words, the Doodle5 application gains the capability to show and hide its toolbar and status bar by simply supporting two menu commands. It's times like this that you really have to appreciate MFC!

Working with ToolTips

One final touch that is worth adding to any applications that use a toolbar is ToolTips. ToolTips are shorthand help messages that are displayed when you pause the mouse cursor over a toolbar button. ToolTips aren't necessarily critical to the user interface of an application, but they certainly provide a nice touch. And when you see how little work is required to support them, you'll probably want to use them in all your applications.

NEW TERM A *ToolTip* is a shorthand help message that is displayed when you pause the mouse cursor over a toolbar button.

Support for ToolTips is actually a toolbar style, which means that you can alter the style of a toolbar to enable ToolTips. You alter the style of a toolbar using the SetBarStyle() member function. The toolbar style for supporting ToolTips is CBRS_TOOLTIPS, which should be added to the toolbar styles when calling `SetBarStyle()`. Listing 15.7 contains the final version of the `CMainFrame::OnCreate()` message handler for Doodle5.

LISTING 15.7 THE FINAL `CMainFrame::OnCreate()` MESSAGE HANDLER FOR DOODLE5

```
 1: int CMainFrame::OnCreate(LPCREATESTRUCT lpCreateStruct) {
 2:   if (CFrameWnd::OnCreate(lpCreateStruct) == -1)
 3:     return -1;
 4:
 5:   // Create toolbar
 6:   if (!m_wndToolBar.Create(this) ||
 7:     !m_wndToolBar.LoadToolBar(IDR_DOODLE))
 8:     return -1;
 9:
10:   // Create status bar
11:   if (!m_wndStatusBar.Create(this) ||
12:     !m_wndStatusBar.SetIndicators(indicators,
           sizeof(indicators)/sizeof(UINT)))
13:     return -1;
14:
15:   // Enable tooltips
16:   m_wndToolBar.SetBarStyle(m_wndToolBar.GetBarStyle() |
17:     CBRS_TOOLTIPS | CBRS_FLYBY | CBRS_SIZE_DYNAMIC);
18:
19:   // Set toolbar as dockable
20:   m_wndToolBar.EnableDocking(CBRS_ALIGN_ANY);
21:   EnableDocking(CBRS_ALIGN_ANY);
22:   DockControlBar(&m_wndToolBar);
23:   return 0;
24: }
```

The `SetBarStyle()` member function is used to set the `CBRS_TOOLTIPS` style for the toolbar. Two other styles, `CBRS_FLYBY` and `CBRS_SIZE_DYNAMIC`, are also specified. These styles are used to jazz up the toolbar a little. The `CBRS_FLYBY` style results in the display of status bar help messages for toolbar buttons any time a ToolTip is activated. Without this style, a help message is only displayed when the user clicks a button. The `CBRS_SIZE_DYNAMIC` style allows the user to resize the toolbar window when it is detached from the application's frame window and used as a floating toolbar.

You might also notice some new code at the end of the `OnCreate()` message handler. This code adds support for toolbar docking, which allows the user to detach the toolbar from the application's frame window and use it as a floating toolbar, or dock it to any side of the frame window.

At this point the Doodle5 toolbar is ready to use ToolTips, but you've yet to actually provide any of them. The actual text for ToolTips is provided as part of the status bar help messages for each menu command. You accomplish this by inserting a newline (\n) character at the end of each help message, followed by the ToolTip text. Listing 15.8 shows the new help message string resources with ToolTip text added.

LISTING 15.8 THE REVISED HELP MESSAGE STRING RESOURCE DEFINITIONS FOR DOODLE5'S STATUS BAR

```
 1: STRINGTABLE
 2: BEGIN
 3:     ID_FILE_NEW            "Create a new drawing\nNew"
 4:     ID_FILE_OPEN           "Open an existing drawing\nOpen"
 5:     ID_FILE_SAVE           "Save the drawing\nSave"
 6:     ID_FILE_SAVE_AS        "Save the drawing with a new name\nSave As"
 7:     ID_APP_EXIT            "Quit application; prompts to save drawing\nExit"
 8:
 9:     ID_EDIT_CLEAR_ALL      "Clear the entire drawing\nClear All"
10:
11:     ID_DRAW_LINE           "Draw a line\nDraw Line"
12:     ID_DRAW_RECTANGLE      "Draw a rectangle\nDraw Rectangle"
13:     ID_DRAW_ELLIPSE        "Draw an ellipse\nDraw Ellipse"
14:     ID_DRAW_CRITTER        "Draw an image of a critter\nDraw Critter"
15:     ID_DRAW_CHANGECOLOR    "Change the current drawing color\nChange Color"
16: END
```

Hopefully you're pleasantly surprised by how simple it is to create and use ToolTips. Figure 15.6 shows the Doodle5 application with a ToolTip being displayed over one of the toolbar buttons.

FIGURE 15.6

The Doodle5 application with support for ToolTips.

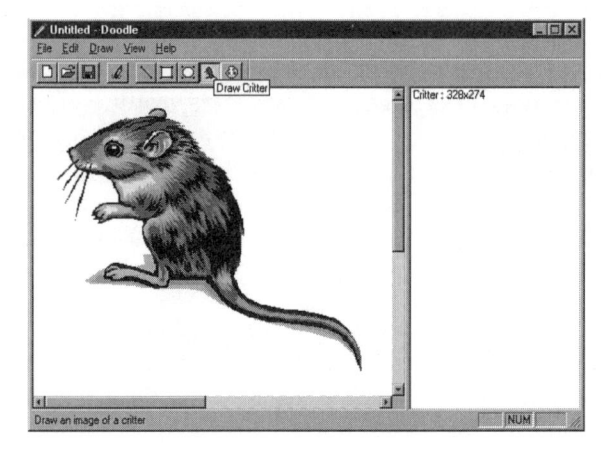

Summary

This hour explored some very interesting graphical user interface components that are used in most modern Windows applications. The general classification of these components is control bars, but they typically appear in the form of toolbars and status bars. MFC also supports dialog bars, which look a lot like toolbars but aren't limited to buttons. In this hour, you learned how to create and use toolbars and status bars, as well as how to spice up toolbars with ToolTips.

Q&A

Q Can I create a toolbar with larger button images?

A Absolutely. Although 16∞15 is the standard size used for toolbar button images, you are free to create larger images if you so choose. Just keep in mind that all the button images in a given toolbar must be the same size. Additionally, you must specify the button image size in the toolbar resource definition.

Q How do I display application-specific information in a status bar?

A Understand that any information beyond menu command help messages must be displayed in a status bar pane. To add a custom information pane, you must first create an identifier for the pane and add it to the `indicators` array that is used to set the panes for the status bar. You must also create a string resource with the identifier that establishes the size of the pane. Finally, you must create a command update message handler for the pane and map it to the pane's identifier using the `ON_UPDATE_COMMAND_UI` macro, like you do for menus. Inside this message handler is where you set the text that is displayed in the pane.

Workshop

The Workshop is designed to help you anticipate possible questions, review what you've learned, and begin thinking ahead to put your knowledge into practice. The answers to the quiz are in Appendix A, "Quiz Answers."

Quiz

1. What is the difference between toolbars and dialog bars?
2. What MFC class provides the basic support required of all control bars?
3. What is docking?
4. What is the relationship between dialog bars and dialog boxes?

5. How do you specify the individual button images for toolbar buttons?
6. How do you create space between buttons on a toolbar?
7. What is the purpose of the array of identifiers that is used when initializing a status bar?
8. What are the two standard MFC identifiers used to support the showing and hiding of toolbars and status bars?
9. What is a ToolTip?
10. How do you specify the text for a ToolTip?

Exercises

1. Add a button to the Doodle5 application's toolbar that displays the About dialog box when clicked. Hint: the menu command ID for the Help, About Doodle menu item is `ID_APP_ABOUT`.
2. Add a status bar message and ToolTip for the new About button on the Doodle5 application's toolbar.

Hour 16

Managing Multiple Documents

The document/view applications you've developed throughout the book thus far enable you to have one document open at any given time. This type of application is known as a single document application. Windows also supports multiple document applications, also known as MDI (Multiple Document Interface) applications, which enable you to have multiple documents open at a time. This hour explores MDI applications and how they impact MFC.

In this hour, you will learn

- The basics of MDI applications
- About the different components of MFC applications
- How to create an MDI application

MDI Fundamentals

MDI stands for Multiple Document Interface, and is a Windows standard for building applications that enable you to have more than one document open at a time. Applications that utilize the Multiple Document Interface are known as MDI applications. MDI applications are similar to single document applications in that they both utilize documents and views to manipulate document data. Single document applications are sometimes referred to as SDI (Single Document Interface) applications. The main difference between MDI and SDI applications is the fact that MDI applications enable you to have multiple documents open at once.

> MDI is implemented in the Win32 API but MFC provides a set of classes that encapsulate its functionality.

Even though MDI applications perform roughly the same function as single document applications, there are some differences between the two types of applications that you need to understand. Following are some attributes of MDI applications that are different from single document applications:

- Document content is displayed and manipulated via document windows, which are child windows within the frame window's client area.
- The client area of the application frame window is used only for managing document windows.
- Only one child document window is active at a time.
- The application menu changes to reflect the currently active child document window.
- Child document windows can be traversed via a Window popup menu that supports actions such as cascading and tiling the windows.
- A list of the open child document windows is displayed in the Window popup menu.

The main application frame window in an MDI application is responsible for creating the client window that supports MDI document windows. This frame window serves as the anchor around which the MDI user interface is built. However, the frame's MDI client window really performs the bulk of the work in terms of MDI window management. All child document windows are created and managed for the most part by the MDI client window. Figure 16.1 shows the relationship between these windows.

Managing Multiple Documents

FIGURE 16.1

The relationship between windows in an MDI application.

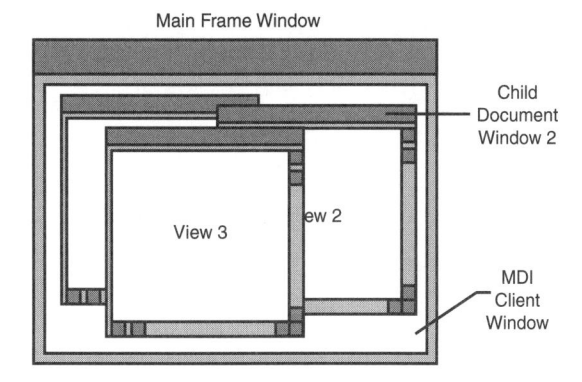

An MDI application may support more than one document type, in which case it must have document windows that are capable of displaying each type of document. The application menu typically changes based on the type of document window that is active.

Microsoft Word is a good example of an MDI application. Figure 16.2 shows how Word supports multiple documents by using child document windows.

FIGURE 16.2

Microsoft Word is a good example of an MDI application.

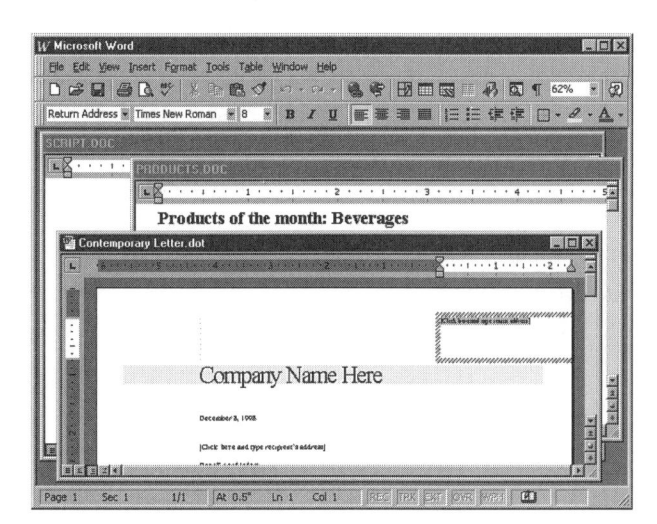

In contrast to Word is the WordPad application that ships with Windows 95/98, which is a single document application. Figure 16.3 shows the WordPad application with a single document open.

FIGURE 16.3

Windows WordPad is a good example of a single document application.

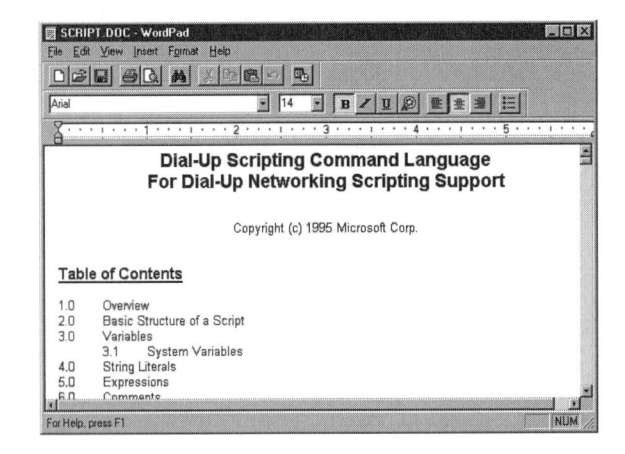

> The Doodle application you've developed throughout the book is also a single document application. You remedy this situation toward the end of this hour by converting Doodle into an MDI application.

Before you move on to learning the details of how MDI applications work, it's worth mentioning that there is still some debate in the development community regarding the virtues of MDI. As an operating system, Windows is evolving to become much more document-centric, which means that emphasis is being placed more on documents and data types rather than on applications. SDI applications actually make more sense in a document-centric operating environment.

However, there are certainly situations where it is beneficial to access and manipulate multiple documents within a single application. Therefore, I think it's safe to assume that MDI will be around a long time. You don't have to look any further than Microsoft's office suite, Microsoft Office, to see a host of MDI applications. Until Microsoft abandons MDI, I don't think anyone has to worry about its future.

Inside MDI Applications

Like SDI applications, MDI applications consist of a group of windows and related user interface components. However, there is more work involved for the user interface in an MDI application simply because MDI applications are more complex than SDI applications. In other words, it takes additional effort to maintain multiple document windows. This effort translates into more responsibility on the part of the windows and user interface components in an MDI application. To get a better understanding of what I'm talking about, let's take a look at the major parts of an MDI application:

- Document template
- Main frame window
- MDI client window
- Child document windows
- Menus

The next few sections examine these parts of an MDI application and their responsibilities in more detail.

A Template for Multiple Documents

As you may recall, the document template for an SDI application is responsible for making the connection between the document, view, and main frame window of the application. You've already built SDI applications that make use of the `CSingleDocTemplate` class to create a document template object. For MDI applications, MFC offers the `CMultiDocTemplate` class, which is used to associate the document, view, and child document window of the application. The child document window in an MDI application plays a similar role as the main frame window in an SDI application, which is why the `CMultiDocTemplate` class associates the document and view of an application with a type of child document window.

Framing an MDI Application

The main frame window of an MDI application serves as the anchor around which the application's user interface is built. You might be surprised to learn that an MDI frame window really isn't too much different than a normal application window in an SDI application. An MDI frame window is responsible for creating and maintaining an application's menu, toolbar, and status bar. More importantly, it serves as the parent for the MDI client window, which does most of the actual work of managing the child document windows.

MFC provides a class named `CMDIFrameWnd` that supports the additional functionality required of an MDI frame window. If you recall, the SDI frame window class is `CFrameWnd`. The nice thing about `CMDIFrameWnd` is that it hides most of the details of how an MDI frame window creates and manages an MDI client window.

The MDI Client Window

The real workhorse of an MDI application is the MDI client window, which is a child of the main frame window. The Win32 API provides a window class called `MDICLIENT` that provides the standard functionality required of an MDI client window. When using MFC, you don't ever really do anything with the MDI client window because it is buried within the implementation of `CMDIFrameWnd`. Trust me, this is a good thing! Developing MDI applications the old fashioned way without MFC was no fun at all.

Child Document Windows

The big idea behind MDI is to enable you to view and edit multiple documents within an application at once. This capability is highly dependent on child document windows, which act much like frame windows in SDI applications. A child document window typically contains a view that is used to display document data and to provide a user interface for manipulating document data. MFC supports MDI child windows with the `CMDIChildWnd` class, which provides the functionality of an MDI child window.

Menus and MDI Applications

Now that you have a clue about the different windows that comprise an MDI application, let's turn our attention to menus. In SDI applications you usually have a menu for accessing commands that somehow alter document data or application settings. MDI applications put a twist on this scenario by supporting multiple menus that are displayed depending on the type of content in the currently active child document window. There is still only one menu displayed at any given time, but that menu can change depending on the active child document window. Additionally, an abbreviated menu is displayed if no child document windows are open; this abbreviated menu is also displayed when an MDI application initially starts.

You define multiple menus for an MDI application by creating multiple menu resources in the resource file for the application. The menus are automatically swapped out by MFC in response to the user opening, closing, or otherwise selecting child document windows.

> In addition to supporting multiple menus, MDI applications also make use of multiple icons. Each type of document supported by an MDI application has its own icon, not to mention the icon for the application itself. So, every MDI application uses at least two icons.

Building an MDI Application

I've alluded to the fact that MFC hides much of the support required to implement an MDI application. In fact, it really requires very little effort to build an MDI application due to MFC's MDI support. The remainder of the hour focuses on converting an SDI application to an MDI application, which will give you a good idea as to how an MDI application is constructed. You will revisit the familiar Doodle application and convert it to MDI. More specifically, you will build the Doodle6 application based on the Doodle5 application you developed in the previous hour.

The conversion of the Doodle application from SDI to MDI involves a few steps. These steps impact different parts of the application. Following are the major changes that are necessary to modify the Doodle application to support MDI:

- Create a document resource identifier
- Create a document icon
- Create an "empty" menu resource
- Create an application name string
- Change the document template code in the `CDoodleApp` class to use the `CMultiDocTemplate` class
- Explicitly create a `CMainFrame` window object
- Change the `CMainFrame` class to derive from `CMDIFrameWnd` instead of `CFrameWnd`
- Move the About message handler to the `CDoodleApp` class

This may seem like a big list of changes but most of them are pretty straightforward. It's interesting to note that no changes are required in the document or view classes when moving an application from SDI to MDI. This is an indication that the two types of applications are very similar in their support for MFC's document/view architecture.

Resources

Because MDI applications must be able to distinguish between different document types, it is necessary to create an identifier that uniquely identifies each document type. Because the Doodle application only supports one document type, `CDoodleDoc`, only one identifier is required. Following is the new Doodle document resource identifier for the Doodle6 application:

```
#define IDR_DOODLETYPE      1001
```

In addition to a unique identifier, each document type in an MDI application requires an icon that is displayed in the upper-left corner of the child document window. Following is the new document icon resource used by the Doodle6 application:

```
IDR_DOODLETYPE   ICON   "DoodleType.ico"
```

One of the interesting things about MDI applications is how they use multiple menus. Unlike SDI applications, which always display a single document, MDI applications are capable of displaying multiple documents of different types or no documents at all. A single menu couldn't possibly apply to all these different scenarios, so MDI applications change menus based on the currently active child document window. MDI applications also provide an "empty" menu that is used when no child document windows are open.

In the SDI Doodle5 application from the previous hour, the application menu is geared toward supporting the Doodle document. In Doodle6, this menu is displayed when a child document window is active. Its menu resource name must be changed to IDR_DOODLETYPE to reflect its affiliation with the Doodle document type. You must create a new "empty" menu for the Doodle6 application that has the original IDR_DOODLE resource name. Listing 16.1 contains the Doodle6 menu resources for these two menus.

LISTING 16.1 THE MENU RESOURCE DEFINITIONS FOR DOODLE6

```
 1: IDR_DOODLE MENU
 2: BEGIN
 3:   POPUP "&File"
 4:     BEGIN
 5:       MENUITEM "&New\tCtrl+N",        ID_FILE_NEW
 6:       MENUITEM "&Open...\tCtrl+O",    ID_FILE_OPEN
 7:       MENUITEM SEPARATOR
 8:       MENUITEM "Recent File",         ID_FILE_MRU_FILE1, GRAYED
 9:       MENUITEM SEPARATOR
10:       MENUITEM "E&xit",               ID_APP_EXIT
11:     END
12:   POPUP "&View"
13:     BEGIN
14:       MENUITEM "&Toolbar",            ID_VIEW_TOOLBAR
15:       MENUITEM "&Status Bar",         ID_VIEW_STATUS_BAR
16:     END
17:   POPUP "&Help"
18:     BEGIN
19:       MENUITEM "&About Doodle...",    ID_APP_ABOUT
20:     END
21: END
22:
23: IDR_DOODLETYPE MENU
24: BEGIN
25:   POPUP "&File"
26:     BEGIN
27:       MENUITEM "&New\tCtrl+N",        ID_FILE_NEW
28:       MENUITEM "&Open...\tCtrl+O",    ID_FILE_OPEN
29:       MENUITEM "&Save\tCtrl+S",       ID_FILE_SAVE
30:       MENUITEM "Save &As...",         ID_FILE_SAVE_AS
31:       MENUITEM SEPARATOR
32:       MENUITEM "Recent File",         ID_FILE_MRU_FILE1,GRAYED
33:       MENUITEM SEPARATOR
34:       MENUITEM "E&xit",               ID_APP_EXIT
35:     END
36:   POPUP "&Edit"
```

```
37:         BEGIN
38:             MENUITEM "Clear &All",              ID_EDIT_CLEAR_ALL
39:         END
40:         POPUP "&Draw"
41:         BEGIN
42:             MENUITEM "&Line",                   ID_DRAW_LINE
43:             MENUITEM "&Rectangle",              ID_DRAW_RECTANGLE
44:             MENUITEM "&Ellipse",                ID_DRAW_ELLIPSE
45:             MENUITEM "&Critter",                ID_DRAW_CRITTER
46:             MENUITEM SEPARATOR
47:             MENUITEM "Change C&olor..."         ID_DRAW_CHANGECOLOR
48:         END
49:         POPUP "&View"
50:         BEGIN
51:             MENUITEM "&Toolbar",                ID_VIEW_TOOLBAR
52:             MENUITEM "&Status Bar",             ID_VIEW_STATUS_BAR
53:         END
54:         POPUP "&Window"
55:         BEGIN
56:             MENUITEM "&New Window",             ID_WINDOW_NEW
57:             MENUITEM "&Cascade",                ID_WINDOW_CASCADE
58:             MENUITEM "&Tile",                   ID_WINDOW_TILE_HORZ
59:             MENUITEM "&Arrange Icons",          ID_WINDOW_ARRANGE
60:         END
61:         POPUP "&Help"
62:         BEGIN
63:             MENUITEM "&About Doodle...",        ID_APP_ABOUT
64:         END
65: END
```

You may notice a new menu item in each of these menu resources. I'm referring to the Recent File menu item, which uses the identifier ID_FILE_MRU_FILE1. This menu item supports a "most recently used" (MRU) file list, which you may be familiar with in other Windows applications. The Recent File menu item serves as a placeholder for recently used files. These files are displayed in the File menu in place of the Recent File menu item for quick selection. MFC automatically provides the functionality of the MRU list based on the ID_FILE_MRU_FILE1 identifier. There is nothing about the Recent File menu item that is specifically associated with MDI, I just thought it might be a good time to introduce it.

The last resource change required for Doodle6 involves a string resource containing the application name. MFC requires MDI applications to provide an application name in the string resource identified by the main application resource identifier. In the case of Doodle6, this identifier is IDR_DOODLE. Listing 16.2 contains the main application string resources for the Doodle6 application.

LISTING 16.2   THE MAIN APPLICATION STRING RESOURCES FOR DOODLE6

```
 1: STRINGTABLE
 2: BEGIN
 3:     IDR_DOODLE          "Doodle"
 4:     AFX_IDS_APP_TITLE "Doodle"
 5:     IDR_DOODLETYPE      "\nDoodle\nDoodle\nDoodle Files" \
 6:         "(*.doo)\n.doo\nDoodle.Document\nDoodleDocument"
 7:     AFX_IDS_IDLEMESSAGE "Ready"
 8: END
```

The last two resources in this list of string resources appeared in previous versions of Doodle. However, the document string has been renamed to `IDR_DOODLETYPE` instead of `IDR_DOODLE`. This is a subtle change that reflects the fact that MDI applications are sometimes responsible for managing multiple document types.

The Application

Not surprisingly, moving an SDI application to MDI requires some changes in the application class. Fortunately, these changes are very straightforward. One change you might not have suspected is moving the Help, About Doodle menu message handler to the application class. In Doodle5, this code appeared in the `CDoodleView` class, and there wasn't any problem because there was always a view window.

In Doodle6 it is possible to close all the view windows in the application because views are contained within child document windows. This would result in the About Doodle menu item becoming inaccessible when no child document windows are open. Granted, this isn't a huge bug, but it is one of those inconsistencies that should be avoided. Simply moving the message handler code to the `CDoodleApp` class solves the problem. Listing 16.3 contains the code for the new Doodle.h header file.

LISTING 16.3   THE DOODLE.H HEADER FILE FOR DOODLE6

```
 1: #ifndef __DOODLE_H__
 2: #define __DOODLE_H__
 3:
 4: //-----------------------------------------------------------------
 5: // Inclusions
 6: //-----------------------------------------------------------------
 7: #include "Resource.h"
 8:
 9: //-----------------------------------------------------------------
10: // CDoodleApp Class - Doodle Application Object
11: //-----------------------------------------------------------------
12: class CDoodleApp : public CWinApp {
```

Managing Multiple Documents

```
13:    // Public Constructor(s)/Destructor
14: public:
15:                CDoodleApp();
16:    virtual    ~CDoodleApp();
17:
18:    // Public Member Functions
19: public:
20:    virtual BOOL   InitInstance();
21:
22:    // Message Handlers
23: public:
24:    afx_msg void   OnAppAbout();
25:
26:    // Message Map & Runtime Support
27: protected:
28:    DECLARE_MESSAGE_MAP()
29: };
30:
31: #endif
```

Moving the About Doodle menu message handler to the CDoodleApp class isn't the only change required to the class. If you recall from earlier in the hour, MDI applications use a different document template object than SDI applications. The InitInstance() member function of CDoodleApp is where this document template object is created. Doodle6 creates a document template object of type CMultiDocTemplate, and uses the CMDIChildWnd class as the frame window type. Listing 16.4 contains the new source code for the CDoodleApp class.

LISTING 16.4 THE DOODLE.CPP SOURCE CODE FILE FOR DOODLE6

```
 1: //-----------------------------------------------------------------
 2: // Inclusions
 3: //-----------------------------------------------------------------
 4: #include "StdAfx.h"
 5: //-----------------------------------------------------------------
 6: #include "Doodle.h"
 7: #include "MainFrame.h"
 8: #include "DoodleDoc.h"
 9: #include "DoodleView.h"
10: #include "AboutDlg.h"
11:
12: //-----------------------------------------------------------------
13: // MFC Debugging Support
14: //-----------------------------------------------------------------
15: #ifdef _DEBUG
16: #undef THIS_FILE
17: static char BASED_CODE THIS_FILE[] = __FILE__;
```

continues

LISTING 16.4 CONTINUED

```
18: #endif
19:
20: //--------------------------------------------------------------
21: // Global Variables
22: //--------------------------------------------------------------
23: CDoodleApp theApp;
24:
25:
26: //--------------------------------------------------------------
27: // Message Map & Runtime Support
28: //--------------------------------------------------------------
29: BEGIN_MESSAGE_MAP(CDoodleApp, CWinApp)
30:   ON_COMMAND(ID_FILE_NEW, CWinApp::OnFileNew)
31:   ON_COMMAND(ID_FILE_OPEN, CWinApp::OnFileOpen)
32:   ON_COMMAND(ID_APP_ABOUT, OnAppAbout)
33: END_MESSAGE_MAP()
34:
35: //--------------------------------------------------------------
36: // Public Constructor(s)/Destructor
37: //--------------------------------------------------------------
38: CDoodleApp::CDoodleApp() {
39: }
40:
41: CDoodleApp::~CDoodleApp() {
42: }
43:
44: //--------------------------------------------------------------
45: // Public Member Functions
46: //--------------------------------------------------------------
47: BOOL CDoodleApp::InitInstance() {
48:   // Load the MRU list
49:   LoadStdProfileSettings();
50:
51:   // Register the application's document templates
52:   CMultiDocTemplate* pDocTemplate;
53:   pDocTemplate = new CMultiDocTemplate(IDR_DOODLETYPE,
54:     RUNTIME_CLASS(CDoodleDoc),
55:     RUNTIME_CLASS(CMDIChildWnd),
56:     RUNTIME_CLASS(CDoodleView));
57:   AddDocTemplate(pDocTemplate);
58:
59:   // Create main MDI frame window
60:   CMainFrame* pMainFrame = new CMainFrame;
61:   if (!pMainFrame->LoadFrame(IDR_DOODLE))
62:     return FALSE;
63:   m_pMainWnd = pMainFrame;
64:
```

```
65:    // Parse command line for standard shell commands
66:    CCommandLineInfo cmdInfo;
67:    ParseCommandLine(cmdInfo);
68:
69:    // Dispatch commands specified on the command line
70:    if (!ProcessShellCommand(cmdInfo))
71:      return FALSE;
72:
73:    // Show and update the main window
74:    pMainFrame->ShowWindow(SW_SHOW);
75:    pMainFrame->UpdateWindow();
76:
77:    return TRUE;
78: }
79:
80: //-----------------------------------------------------------------
81: // Message Handlers
82: //-----------------------------------------------------------------
83: void CDoodleApp::OnAppAbout() {
84:    CAboutDlg aboutDlg;
85:    aboutDlg.DoModal();
86: }
```

You may recall that in prior versions of Doodle the document frame window was set to `CMainFrame` in the creation of the document template object. This resulted in the automatic creation of a `CMainFrame` object. Because the document frame window in Doodle6 is set to `CMDIChildWnd`, it is necessary to manually create the application frame window, `CMainFrame`. The application resources for the main frame window are then loaded with a call to the `LoadFrame()` member function.

One other interesting piece of code in the `InitInstance()` member function is at the very beginning of the function. The `LoadStdProfileSettings()` member function is called to enable the MRU file list and load any previously stored files in the list. Files in the MRU file list are stored in the Windows Registry. After you call this function, the MRU file list is maintained entirely by MFC.

The Main Frame Window

The last coding change for the Doodle6 MDI application involves the `CMainFrame` class. As you now know, MFC provides a `CMDIFrameWnd` class that supports the functionality required of an MDI application frame window. The `CMainFrame` class in Doodle6 should derive from `CMDIFrameWnd` instead of `CFrameWnd`. Listing 16.5 contains the code for the new MainFrame.h header file.

LISTING 16.5 THE MAINFRAME.H HEADER FILE FOR DOODLE6

```
 1: #ifndef __MAINFRAME_H__
 2: #define __MAINFRAME_H__
 3:
 4: //----------------------------------------------------------------
 5: // CMainFrame Class - Main Frame Window Object
 6: //----------------------------------------------------------------
 7: class CMainFrame : public CMDIFrameWnd {
 8:    // Member Variables
 9: protected:
10:    CToolBar      m_wndToolBar;
11:    CStatusBar    m_wndStatusBar;
12:    CSplitterWnd  m_wndSplitter;
13:
14:    // Public Constructor(s)/Destructor
15: public:
16:                  CMainFrame();
17:    virtual       ~CMainFrame();
18:
19:    // Public Member Functions
20: public:
21:    virtual BOOL  PreCreateWindow(CREATESTRUCT& cs);
22:
23:    // Message Handlers
24: public:
25:    afx_msg int OnCreate(LPCREATESTRUCT lpCreateStruct);
26:
27:    // Message Map & Runtime Support
28: protected:
29:    DECLARE_MESSAGE_MAP()
30:    DECLARE_DYNCREATE(CMainFrame)
31: };
32:
33: #endif
```

The implementation of the `CMainFrame` class shows some different areas where the parent frame window class is revealed. Listing 16.6 contains the new source code for the `CMainFrame` class.

LISTING 16.6 THE MAINFRAME.CPP SOURCE CODE FILE FOR DOODLE6

```
 1: //----------------------------------------------------------------
 2: // Inclusions
 3: //----------------------------------------------------------------
 4: #include "StdAfx.h"
```

```
 5: //----------------------------------------------------------------
 6: #include "MainFrame.h"
 7: #include "Resource.h"
 8: #include "DoodleDoc.h"
 9: #include "DoodleView.h"
10:
11: //----------------------------------------------------------------
12: // MFC Debugging Support
13: //----------------------------------------------------------------
14: #ifdef _DEBUG
15: #undef THIS_FILE
16: static char BASED_CODE THIS_FILE[] = __FILE__;
17: #endif
18:
19:
20: //----------------------------------------------------------------
21: // Message Map & Runtime Support
22: //----------------------------------------------------------------
23: BEGIN_MESSAGE_MAP(CMainFrame, CMDIFrameWnd)
24:    ON_WM_CREATE()
25: END_MESSAGE_MAP()
26:
27: IMPLEMENT_DYNCREATE(CMainFrame, CMDIFrameWnd)
28:
29: //----------------------------------------------------------------
30: // Static Members
31: //----------------------------------------------------------------
32: static UINT indicators[] = { ID_SEPARATOR, ID_INDICATOR_CAPS,
33:    ID_INDICATOR_NUM, ID_INDICATOR_SCRL };
34:
35: //----------------------------------------------------------------
36: // Public Constructor(s)/Destructor
37: //----------------------------------------------------------------
38: CMainFrame::CMainFrame() {
39: }
40:
41: CMainFrame::~CMainFrame() {
42: }
43:
44: //----------------------------------------------------------------
45: // Public Member Functions
46: //----------------------------------------------------------------
47: BOOL CMainFrame::PreCreateWindow(CREATESTRUCT& cs) {
48:    return CMDIFrameWnd::PreCreateWindow(cs);
49: }
50:
51: //----------------------------------------------------------------
52: // Message Handlers
```

continues

LISTING 16.6 CONTINUED

```
53: //-----------------------------------------------------------------
54: int CMainFrame::OnCreate(LPCREATESTRUCT lpCreateStruct) {
55:   if (CMDIFrameWnd::OnCreate(lpCreateStruct) == -1)
56:     return -1;
57:
58:   // Create toolbar
59:   if (!m_wndToolBar.Create(this) ||
60:     !m_wndToolBar.LoadToolBar(IDR_DOODLE))
61:     return -1;
62:
63:   // Create status bar
64:   if (!m_wndStatusBar.Create(this) ||
65:     !m_wndStatusBar.SetIndicators(indicators,
66:     sizeof(indicators)/sizeof(UINT)))
67:     return -1;
68:
69:   // Enable tooltips
70:   m_wndToolBar.SetBarStyle(m_wndToolBar.GetBarStyle() |
71:     CBRS_TOOLTIPS | CBRS_FLYBY | CBRS_SIZE_DYNAMIC);
72:
73:   // Set tool bar as dockable
74:   m_wndToolBar.EnableDocking(CBRS_ALIGN_ANY);
75:   EnableDocking(CBRS_ALIGN_ANY);
76:   DockControlBar(&m_wndToolBar);
77:   return 0;
78: }
```

As you can see in the `CMainFrame` implementation, the message map and `IMPLEMENT_DYNCREATE` macro both are modified to reference the new `CMDIFrameWnd` parent class. Additionally, the `PreCreateWindow()` and `OnCreate()` member functions now call the respective versions in the `CMDIFrameWnd` parent class.

One other change worth mentioning in the `CMainFrame` class is the removal of the `OnCreateClient()` member function, which was used to create a splitter window and view panes in the Doodle5 application. I wanted to keep the document/view code simple in Doodle6, so I decided to remove the splitter window and list view from the application's user interface. That pretty well wraps up the changes to the Doodle6 application required to support MDI. Figure 16.4 shows the finished application with multiple documents open.

FIGURE 16.4

The Doodle6 MDI application.

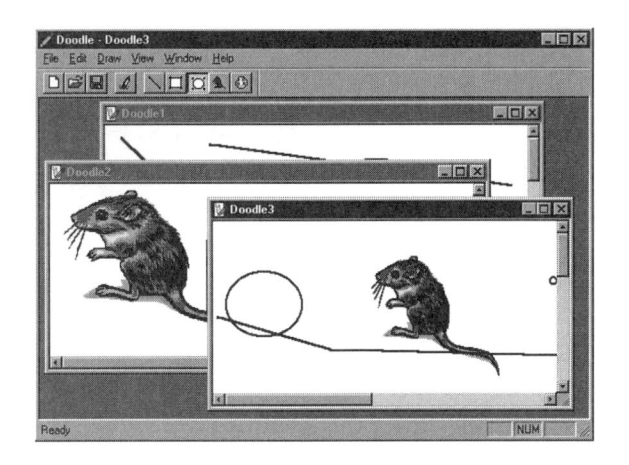

Summary

This hour introduced you to the Multiple Document Interface (MDI), which is used to create document/view applications that enable you to open multiple documents. You learned the basics of MDI and took a look at the different parts of an MDI application. You also learned how to create MDI applications by converting an existing single document application to support multiple documents.

Q&A

Q How are menu command messages routed from an MDI application's menu down to a specific view window?

A An application's MDI frame window delegates menu command messages down through the MDI client window and on to MDI child windows before it tries to handle them itself. In other words, messages are passed through a bottom-up hierarchy of windows where each window has the opportunity of responding before allowing its parent to handle the message. If a message arrives at the main frame window and still isn't handled, it gets passed along to the application class. This is the approach that was taken with the About Doodle menu command message in Doodle6.

Q What object owns the document and view in an MDI application?

A Each child document window in an MDI application owns its respective document and view. In other words, each MDI child document window object contains a document object and a view window object that is used to display document data and provide a graphical user interface to the document. In this way, MDI child document windows act similarly to main frame windows in SDI applications.

Workshop

The Workshop is designed to help you anticipate possible questions, review what you've learned, and begin thinking ahead to put your knowledge into practice. The answers to the quiz are in Appendix A, "Quiz Answers."

Quiz

1. Which window in an MDI application serves as the anchor around which an MDI user interface is built?
2. Which window in an MDI application manages and orchestrates the child document windows?
3. How many child document windows can be active at a given time?
4. What MFC class is used to associate the document, view, and child document window of an MDI application?
5. What MFC class supports the functionality required of an MDI application frame window?
6. What MFC class supports the functionality of an MDI child frame window?
7. When is the menu of an MDI application changed?
8. If an application supports two different document types, how many menus must it support?
9. What is a "most recently used" (MRU) file list?
10. Why was the Help, About Doodle menu message handler moved from the view class to the application class in the Doodle6 application?

Exercises

1. Try out the MDI functionality of the Doodle6 application by creating multiple documents and drawing different graphic elements in each. Make sure to save each document so that the files get added to the MRU file list, and then close all the windows. Notice that the menu changes when you close all the child document windows.
2. Test out the Window menu commands to arrange the different child document windows. Also try out the MRU file list under File menu to open the files you saved earlier.

HOUR 17

Inside Printing

This hour digs into printing, which is a very important topic that affects many applications. You may be a little worried that printing is going to be extremely complicated and require lots of tricky coding. If this book were about traditional Windows programming using the Win32 API, you would be on the right track. However, you're learning how to program Windows with MFC, which makes tasks like printing infinitely easier than the old school approach. I think you'll be pleased with how MFC supports printing. Let's get started!

In this hour, you will learn

- The basics of printing in Windows
- How MFC supports printing
- How to print documents

Printing Basics

You learned earlier in the book that Windows utilizes a device-independent graphics architecture that allows you to draw graphics without worrying about the physical device to which the graphics are being drawn. Printers fit into this device-independent architecture as an output device much like a monitor. This means that printing to a printer is logically no different than drawing to the screen—in both cases you obtain a device context and draw to it. Recall that a device context is an abstract drawing surface that is associated with an underlying hardware device such as a printer or monitor.

The fact that drawing graphics to a printer is just like drawing to the screen can be very beneficial in some applications. For example, an application such as the Doodle application that you've built throughout the book could print the exact same graphics that it displays in its view. On the other hand, some applications such as database applications often must provide specialized printing facilities to generate reports based on a particular subset of data. How its printing support is implemented is really up to each individual application.

Regardless of what specific information an application intends to print, it is beneficial to support Print Preview, which has become a standard feature in most Windows applications. Print Preview is a visualization of a document on the screen as it will appear on the printed page. You can think of Print Preview as a simulated print to a special preview window. Fortunately, it is common to use the same printing code to implement Print Preview.

NEW TERM *Print Preview* is a visualization of a document on the screen as it will appear on the printed page.

MFC's Support for Printing

In traditional Win32 programming, printing was a real chore and could often become a coding nightmare. The problem wasn't that drawing graphics to the printer is difficult but because it required myriad Win32 function calls to move the process along. There were also complex data structures that you had to initialize and use properly. And last but not least, you were responsible for implementing a special modeless dialog box that allowed the user to cancel out of printing a lengthy document.

I'm happy to report that MFC has simplified the process of printing significantly. As a matter of fact, MFC's document/view architecture provides you with default support for printing without you have to do any additional work. By default, MFC will use the OnDraw() member function in your view class to print a document. If you recall, OnDraw() accepts a pointer to a CDC object as its only parameter. When printing, this CDC object represents a printer device context instead of a screen device context.

Printing in the View

The majority of MFC's printing support is encapsulated in the CView class, which means that all document/view applications have some form of default printing. There is also a set of special printing member functions in CView that you can use to alter the way in which documents are printed. As an example, you must alter the default CView printing functionality if you want to print multiple pages or if you want to print a header or footer on a page.

Table 17.1 lists the most important CView member functions used for printing.

TABLE 17.1 THE MOST IMPORTANT CView MEMBER FUNCTIONS USED FOR PRINTING

Member Function	Description
OnPreparePrinting()	Called before a document is printed or previewed
DoPreparePrinting()	Displays the Print dialog box and creates a printer DC; called from OnPreparePrinting()
OnBeginPrinting()	Called when a print job begins; allocates print-related GDI resources
OnPrepareDC()	Called before OnDraw() to prepare a DC for drawing
OnPrint()	Called to print or preview a document page
OnEndPrintPreview()	Called when the user exits preview mode
OnEndPrinting()	Called when a print job ends; free print-related GDI resources

NEW TERM The *print job* is the document in the process of being printed.

The member functions listed in the table represent a printing sequence that is common across all document/view applications. To get a handle on how this process works, check out Figure 17.1.

When the user first requests to print a document, the OnPreparePrinting() member function is called by the framework to display the Print dialog box and get things started. OnPreparePrinting() carries out this request by delegating the work to the DoPreparePrinting() function, which actually handles displaying the Print dialog box and creating a printer DC. You can alter the default values displayed in the Print dialog box by overriding the OnPreparePrinting() function and altering the CPrintInfo object that is passed into DoPreparePrinting(). You learn more about the CPrintInfo object in a moment.

FIGURE 17.1

The `CView` member functions called in the standard MFC printing sequence.

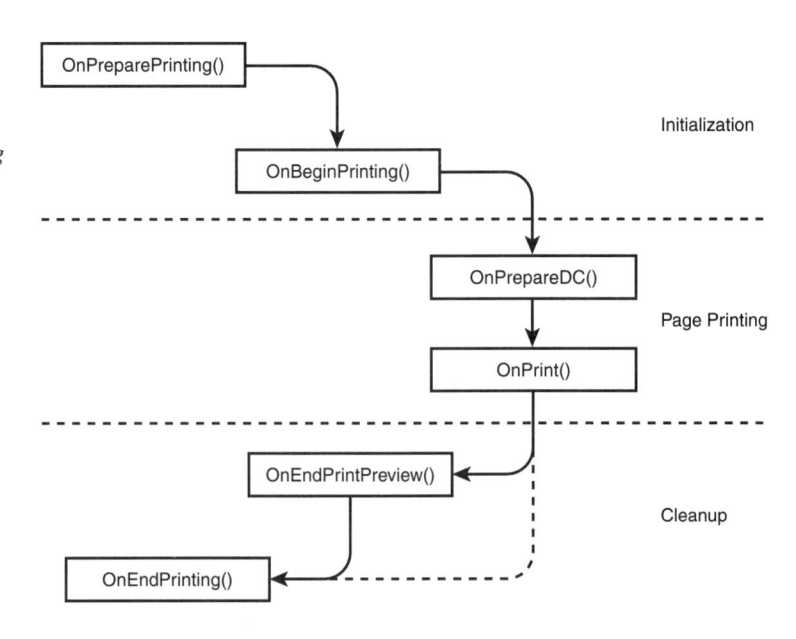

```
                    OnPreparePrinting()
                              |
                              |                    Initialization
                              v
                    OnBeginPrinting()
    - - - - - - - - - - - - - | - - - - - - - - - - - - - - - -
                              v
                         OnPrepareDC()
                              |                    Page Printing
                              v
                           OnPrint()
    - - - - - - - - - - - - - | - - - - - - - - - - - - - - - -
                    OnEndPrintPreview()  <---+
                              |              |    Cleanup
                              v              |
                    OnEndPrinting()  <- - - -+
```

Getting back to the print sequence, the `OnBeginPrinting()` member function is called by the framework at the beginning of a print or Print Preview job, after `OnPreparePrinting()` has been called. The main purpose of `OnBeginPrinting()` is to provide a convenient place to allocate any GDI resources specifically required for printing, such as fonts. Once the `OnBeginPrinting()` function returns, printing commences one page at a time.

The `OnPrepareDC()` and `OnPrint()` member functions are called for each page that is printed. `OnPrepareDC()` is responsible for making any modifications to the device context required to print the current page. It is also used to analyze attributes of the `CPrintInfo` object, such as the number of pages in the document. If a document length isn't specified, `OnPrepareDC()` assumes the document is one page long and stops the printing sequence after one page.

The `OnPrint()` member function is called just after `OnPrepareDC()`, and is used to perform any graphical output specific to printing. Many applications call the `OnDraw()` function from `OnPrint()` to print the document as it appears in the view. These applications typically use `OnPrint()` to print page elements such as headers and footers. Other applications might use `OnPrint()` to print a document completely independent of the `OnDraw()` function. These applications typically have a view whose `OnDraw()` function isn't helpful for printing. An example of such an application would be one that uses `CFormView`, which is a view containing controls based on a dialog resource.

When a document is finished printing, the `OnEndPrinting()` member function is called to free any GDI resources allocated for printing. These resources are typically allocated in the `OnBeginPrinting()` function. If the print sequence was issued for a Print Preview instead of an actual print job, the `OnEndPrintPreview()` function is called just before `OnEndPrinting()`. The default `OnEndPrintPreview()` function actually calls `OnEndPrinting()` after destroying the view window and restoring the application window to its original state.

Now that you have an idea how a view fits into the print sequence, let's clarify exactly what an application's view is responsible for in terms of printing. An application's view class must take on the following responsibilities to support printing:

- Inform the framework how many pages are in the document (or accept the default of one page).
- Allocate and free any GDI resources required for printing.
- When asked to print a specific page, draw that portion of the document.

That seems simple enough. To understand why you are required to do so little, let's examine the framework's printing responsibilities. The MFC framework must take on the following responsibilities to support printing:

- Display the Print dialog box
- Create a suitable `CDC` object for the printer
- Inform the view class which page should be printed
- Call `CView` member functions that can be overridden at the appropriate times

The `PrintInfo` Object

I've mentioned the `CPrintInfo` object a few times when discussing the `CView` member functions associated with printing. The `CPrintInfo` object maintains information about a print or Print Preview job. You don't ever need to create a `CPrintInfo` object yourself; the framework automatically creates it when the print sequence begins.

The `CPrintInfo` object contains information such as the range of pages to be printed and the current page being printed. This information is accessible through public data members of the `CPrintInfo` class. Following are the most commonly used public data members in the `CPrintInfo` class:

- `m_nCurPage`—identifies the page currently being printed
- `m_nNumPreviewPages`—identifies the number of pages displayed in the Print Preview (1 or 2)

- `m_bPreview`—indicates whether the document is being previewed
- `m_rectDraw`—specifies the usable page area for printing

The first two members, `m_nCurPage` and `m_nNumPreviewPages`, are useful for controlling the printing of a multiple page document. The `m_bPreview` member is used to determine if the document is being printed to the printer or displayed in a Print Preview window. Finally, the `m_rectDraw` member contains a rectangle that represents the usable page area for printing. You can shrink this rectangle to reduce the page area available for printing. This is a useful technique when drawing headers and footers on a page.

The `CPrintInfo` object plays a very important role in MFC printing because it serves as a means of exchanging information between an application's view and MFC's built-in printing functionality. A `CPrintInfo` object is passed between the framework and your view class during the printing process. As an example, your view class knows which page to print because the framework sets the `m_nCurPage` member of `CPrintInfo`.

Standard Print Commands

To help make supporting printing a little easier, MFC defines standard identifiers for commonly used menu commands. Following are the standard print command identifiers defined by MFC:

- `ID_FILE_PRINT_SETUP`
- `ID_FILE_PRINT`
- `ID_FILE_PRINT_DIRECT`
- `ID_FILE_PRINT_PREVIEW`

The really neat thing about these standard identifiers is that MFC provides default implementations for their message handlers. The `CWinApp::OnFilePrintSetup()` message handler for the `ID_FILE_PRINT_SETUP` command invokes the standard print setup dialog that allows the user to alter the printer settings. All you must do to include this functionality in an application is provide the following message map entry in your application class:

`ON_COMMAND(ID_FILE_PRINT_SETUP, CWinApp::OnFilePrintSetup)`

The `CView::OnFilePrint()` message handler for the `ID_FILE_PRINT` command calls the `OnPreparePrinting()` function to display the standard Print dialog and create the printer DC. For each page, it calls `OnPrepareDC()` followed by a call to `OnPrint()` for that page. When complete, the `OnEndPrinting()` function is called, and the printing progress dialog is closed. The `ID_FILE_PRINT_DIRECT` command uses the `OnFilePrint()` message handler to print without displaying the Print dialog box; the default printer and related settings are used. The `ID_FILE_PRINT_DIRECT` command is typically used for toolbar Print buttons.

The `CView::OnFilePrintPreview()` message handler for the `ID_FILE_PRINT_PREVIEW` command initiates the Print Preview of a document. You don't have to do anything but provide a message map entry for this command to support Print Preview. Following are the view class message map entries required to include the functionality of the `ID_FILE_PRINT`, `ID_FILE_PRINT_DIRECT`, and `ID_FILE_PRINT_PREVIEW` commands in an application:

```
ON_COMMAND(ID_FILE_PRINT, CView::OnFilePrint)
ON_COMMAND(ID_FILE_PRINT_DIRECT, CView::OnFilePrint)
ON_COMMAND(ID_FILE_PRINT_PREVIEW, CView::OnFilePrintPreview)
```

Printing and GDI Mapping Modes

Before you move on and learn how to support printing in a real application, there is an important topic worth covering. I'm referring to GDI mapping modes and their impact on printing. Throughout the book thus far you've used the `MM_TEXT` mapping mode for all GDI operations. If you recall, this mapping mode performs a 1-to-1 mapping of physical device units to logical units. In other words, logical and physical units are equivalent in the `MM_TEXT` mapping mode. Furthermore, the coordinate system in this mapping mode increases down and to the right from the upper-left origin in a window.

Why does all this mapping mode stuff matter when it comes to printing? Well, think for a moment about the resolution of the screen. You probably are using a monitor with the resolution set at 800×600, 1024×768, or 1152×864 (my preference). As you are probably aware, these numbers reflect the number of individual pixels in the X and Y directions, respectively. Now consider the resolution of a laser printer. I've had my laser printer for a while so it has a resolution of only 300dpi. That means that there are 300 printer pixels for every inch of page. Wait a minute! Does that mean that an 8 1/2×11–inch page has a resolution of 2550×3300 pixels? Absolutely. If I were to print graphics on my printer using the `MM_TEXT` mapping mode, they would be displayed at around 45 percent of their screen size. Figure 17.2 illustrates the problem with the `MM_TEXT` mapping mode.

The source of the problem in this scenario is the `MM_TEXT` mapping mode, which doesn't take into account the variances in hardware device resolutions. As long as you're mapping logical units on a 1-to-1 basis with hardware pixels, you're guaranteed to get inconsistent results on different types of hardware. Is there a solution? Of course! The solution is to use a mapping mode that doesn't think in terms of pixels.

FIGURE 17.2

Graphics printed using the `MM_TEXT` *mapping mode will appear smaller on the printed page than they do on the screen.*

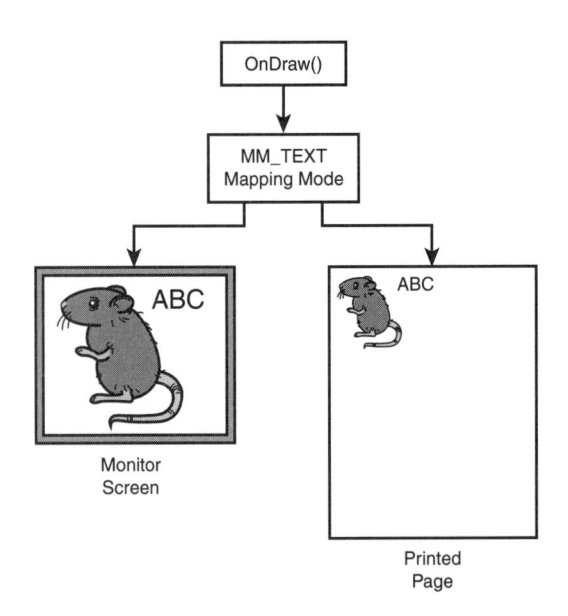

Win32 supports a few different mapping modes, but one that I like to use for printing is `MM_LOENGLISH`. The `MM_LOENGLISH` mapping mode maps a logical unit to a 0.01 inch physical unit. In other words, 100 logical units would appear as 1 inch regardless of the physical device. This functionality is expected in modern applications and is affectionately referred to as WYSIWIG (What You See Is What You Get). Figure 17.3 illustrates how the `MM_LOENGLISH` mapping mode solves the WYSIWIG problem.

FIGURE 17.3

The `MM_LOENGLISH` *mapping mode results in graphics appearing the same in print as they do on the screen.*

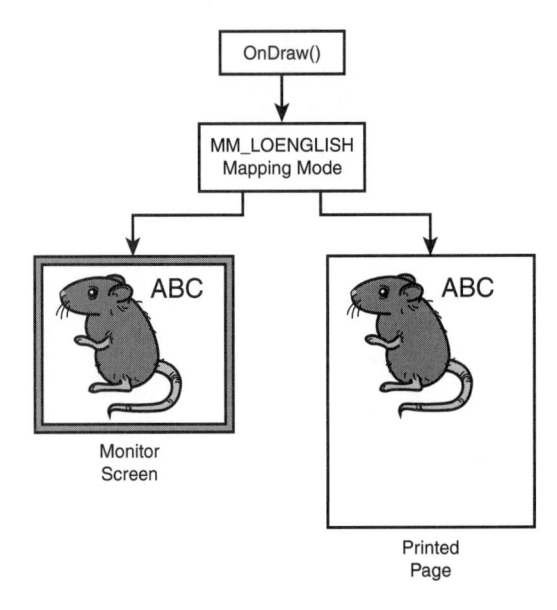

> The only caveat with the MM_LOENGLISH mapping mode is that the Y-axis increases in the opposite direction of MM_TEXT. This means that Y values decrease down from the origin in the upper-left corner of a window. This sometimes requires special handling since most applications aren't accustomed to dealing with negative graphics coordinates.

Printing Doodle Documents

Although I know you're probably just about doodled out, we're going to revisit the Doodle application yet again to demonstrate printing. You have to admit that the prospect of adding printing support to Doodle is kind of exciting because you can now save those precious works of art. All jokes aside, the Doodle application requires quite a few modifications to successfully support printing. Since MFC's printing functionality comes almost for free, most of the changes have to do with making Doodle's existing code more "printer friendly."

Resources

The printer-enabled Doodle7 application begins with some resource modifications, and perhaps the best place to start with those modifications is the menu resources. Listing 17.1 contains the revised menu resources for Doodle7.

LISTING 17.1 THE REVISED MENU RESOURCE DEFINITIONS FOR DOODLE7

```
 1: IDR_DOODLE MENU
 2: BEGIN
 3:    POPUP "&File"
 4:    BEGIN
 5:       MENUITEM "&New\tCtrl+N",         ID_FILE_NEW
 6:       MENUITEM "&Open...\tCtrl+O",     ID_FILE_OPEN
 7:       MENUITEM SEPARATOR
 8:       MENUITEM "P&rint Setup...",      ID_FILE_PRINT_SETUP
 9:       MENUITEM SEPARATOR
10:       MENUITEM "Recent File",          ID_FILE_MRU_FILE1, GRAYED
11:       MENUITEM SEPARATOR
12:       MENUITEM "E&xit",                ID_APP_EXIT
13:    END`
14:    POPUP "&View"
15:    BEGIN
16:       MENUITEM "&Toolbar",             ID_VIEW_TOOLBAR
17:       MENUITEM "&Status Bar",          ID_VIEW_STATUS_BAR
18:    END
```

continues

LISTING 17.1 CONTINUED

```
19:     POPUP "&Help"
20:       BEGIN
21:         MENUITEM "&About Doodle...",       ID_APP_ABOUT
22:       END
23: END
24:
25: IDR_DOODLETYPE MENU
26: BEGIN
27:     POPUP "&File"
28:       BEGIN
29:         MENUITEM "&New\tCtrl+N",           ID_FILE_NEW
30:         MENUITEM "&Open...\tCtrl+O",       ID_FILE_OPEN
31:         MENUITEM "&Save\tCtrl+S",          ID_FILE_SAVE
32:         MENUITEM "Save &As...",            ID_FILE_SAVE_AS
33:         MENUITEM SEPARATOR
34:         MENUITEM "&Print...\tCtrl+P",      ID_FILE_PRINT
35:         MENUITEM "Print Pre&view",         ID_FILE_PRINT_PREVIEW
36:         MENUITEM "P&rint Setup...",        ID_FILE_PRINT_SETUP
37:         MENUITEM SEPARATOR
38:         MENUITEM "Recent File",            ID_FILE_MRU_FILE1,GRAYED
39:         MENUITEM SEPARATOR
40:         MENUITEM "E&xit",                  ID_APP_EXIT
41:       END
42:     POPUP "&Edit"
43:       BEGIN
44:         MENUITEM "Clear &All",             ID_EDIT_CLEAR_ALL
45:       END
46:     POPUP "&Draw"
47:       BEGIN
48:         MENUITEM "&Line",                  ID_DRAW_LINE
49:         MENUITEM "&Rectangle",             ID_DRAW_RECTANGLE
50:         MENUITEM "&Ellipse",               ID_DRAW_ELLIPSE
51:         MENUITEM "&Critter",               ID_DRAW_CRITTER
52:         MENUITEM SEPARATOR
53:         MENUITEM "Change C&olor..."        ID_DRAW_CHANGECOLOR
54:       END
55:     POPUP "&View"
56:       BEGIN
57:         MENUITEM "&Toolbar",               ID_VIEW_TOOLBAR
58:         MENUITEM "&Status Bar",            ID_VIEW_STATUS_BAR
59:       END
60:     POPUP "&Window"
61:       BEGIN
62:         MENUITEM "&New Window",            ID_WINDOW_NEW
63:         MENUITEM "&Cascade",               ID_WINDOW_CASCADE
64:         MENUITEM "&Tile",                  ID_WINDOW_TILE_HORZ
65:         MENUITEM "&Arrange Icons",         ID_WINDOW_ARRANGE
```

```
66:        END
67:     POPUP "&Help"
68:     BEGIN
69:        MENUITEM "&About Doodle...",      ID_APP_ABOUT
70:     END
71: END
```

The `IDR_DOODLE` menu, which is displayed when no child document windows are open, simply picks up a new File, Print Setup command. The other print commands (File, Print and File, Print Preview) only apply to open documents so they are added to the `IDR_DOODLETYPE` menu.

What Print menu command would be complete without a toolbar button to match? Figure 17.4 shows a zoomed view of the toolbar bitmap image for the Doodle7 application, which includes the new Print button.

FIGURE 17.4

A zoomed view of the toolbar bitmap image for Doodle7.

This new button must be added to the Doodle7 toolbar resource. Listing 17.2 contains the new and improved toolbar resource for the Doodle7 application.

LISTING 17.2 THE REVISED TOOLBAR RESOURCE DEFINITION FOR DOODLE7

```
 1: IDR_DOODLE TOOLBAR  16, 15
 2: BEGIN
 3:     BUTTON      ID_FILE_NEW
 4:     BUTTON      ID_FILE_OPEN
 5:     BUTTON      ID_FILE_SAVE
 6:     BUTTON      ID_FILE_PRINT_DIRECT
 7:     SEPARATOR
 8:     BUTTON      ID_EDIT_CLEAR_ALL
 9:     SEPARATOR
10:     BUTTON      ID_DRAW_LINE
11:     BUTTON      ID_DRAW_RECTANGLE
12:     BUTTON      ID_DRAW_ELLIPSE
13:     BUTTON      ID_DRAW_CRITTER
14:     BUTTON      ID_DRAW_CHANGECOLOR
15: END
```

Notice that the command `ID_FILE_PRINT_DIRECT` is used for the Print button instead of `ID_FILE_PRINT`. This is done so that the button will print a document without displaying the Print dialog box, which is a little quicker for the user. This also happens to be the standard approach taken by most Windows applications.

Speaking of making things quicker for the user, the Doodle7 application includes a new accelerator that is used to print documents. Listing 17.3 contains the keyboard accelerator resources for the Doodle7 application.

LISTING 17.3 THE KEYBOARD ACCELERATOR RESOURCE DEFINITIONS FOR DOODLE7

```
1: IDR_DOODLE ACCELERATORS
2: BEGIN
3:     "N",        ID_FILE_NEW,        VIRTKEY,CONTROL
4:     "O",        ID_FILE_OPEN,       VIRTKEY,CONTROL
5:     "S",        ID_FILE_SAVE,       VIRTKEY,CONTROL
6:     "P",        ID_FILE_PRINT,      VIRTKEY,CONTROL
7: END
```

That wraps up the print-related resources required for the Doodle7 application. Let's move on the application code.

The Application

Since printing is mainly related to the documents and views of an application, it might seem strange that changes would be necessary in the `CDoodleApp` application class. However, the `ID_FILE_PRINT_SETUP` menu command appears on the "empty" menu for the application, which means the application class is a good place to locate the message handler. Fortunately, you don't have to implement a handler at all; you just need to provide a message map entry to the `CDoodleApp` class:

```
ON_COMMAND(ID_FILE_PRINT_SETUP, CWinApp::OnFilePrintSetup)
```

This is all that is required of the Doodle7 application to support the Print Preview command. Likewise, it's the only coding change you have to make in the application class.

The View

As you learned earlier in this hour, the view is responsible for supporting printing. It shouldn't come as a big surprise to learn that the `CDoodleView` class is where most of the work takes place in adding printing functionality to the Doodle7 application. Let's begin with the message map for the view, which is shown in Listing 17.4.

Inside Printing

LISTING 17.4 THE CDoodleView MESSAGE MAP FOR DOODLE7

```
 1: BEGIN_MESSAGE_MAP(CDoodleView, CScrollView)
 2:   ON_WM_LBUTTONDOWN()
 3:   ON_COMMAND(ID_FILE_PRINT, CView::OnFilePrint)
 4:   ON_COMMAND(ID_FILE_PRINT_DIRECT, CView::OnFilePrint)
 5:   ON_COMMAND(ID_FILE_PRINT_PREVIEW, CView::OnFilePrintPreview)
 6:   ON_COMMAND(ID_DRAW_LINE, OnDrawLine)
 7:   ON_COMMAND(ID_DRAW_RECTANGLE, OnDrawRectangle)
 8:   ON_COMMAND(ID_DRAW_ELLIPSE, OnDrawEllipse)
 9:   ON_COMMAND(ID_DRAW_CRITTER, OnDrawCritter)
10:   ON_COMMAND(ID_DRAW_CHANGECOLOR, OnDrawChangeColor)
11:   ON_UPDATE_COMMAND_UI(ID_DRAW_LINE, OnUpdateDrawLine)
12:   ON_UPDATE_COMMAND_UI(ID_DRAW_RECTANGLE, OnUpdateDrawRectangle)
13:   ON_UPDATE_COMMAND_UI(ID_DRAW_ELLIPSE, OnUpdateDrawEllipse)
14:   ON_UPDATE_COMMAND_UI(ID_DRAW_CRITTER, OnUpdateDrawCritter)
15: END_MESSAGE_MAP()
```

There are three new message map entries, all of which route messages to existing `CView` message handlers. MFC's printing architecture doesn't require you to provide application-specific message handlers for any of these printing commands. Instead, it allows you to override `CView` member functions that perform certain printing operations. You learned about these member functions earlier in the hour. Following is the declaration of one of them in the `CDoodleView` class:

`virtual BOOL  OnPreparePrinting(CPrintInfo* pInfo);`

If you recall, the `OnPreparePrinting()` member function is called by the `CView::OnFilePrint()` message handler to initiate the printing process. Following is the implementation of the `OnPreparePrinting()` member function for `CDoodleView`, which simply calls `DoPreparePrinting()` to delegate the work of starting the printing process:

```
BOOL CDoodleView::OnPreparePrinting(CPrintInfo* pInfo) {
  return DoPreparePrinting(pInfo);
}
```

Moving right along, you now know that the mapping mode for the Doodle7 application must be changed from `MM_TEXT` to `MM_LOENGLISH` so that graphics are drawn consistently on both the screen and printer. The mapping mode is set in the call to `SetScrollSizes()` in the `OnInitialUpdate()` member function, which follows:

```
void CDoodleView::OnInitialUpdate() {
  // Set the scroll sizes
  SetScrollSizes(MM_LOENGLISH, GetDocument()->GetDocSize());
}
```

The other place in the view where the SetScrollSizes() member function is called is in the OnUpdate() member function. Listing 17.5 contains the source code for the OnUpdate() member function.

LISTING 17.5 THE CDoodleView::OnUpdate() MEMBER FUNCTION FOR DOODLE7

```
 1: void CDoodleView::OnUpdate(CView* pSender, LPARAM lHint, CObject*
        ➥pHint) {
 2:     // Make sure the hint is valid
 3:     if (pHint != NULL) {
 4:         if (pHint->IsKindOf(RUNTIME_CLASS(CGraphic))) {
 5:             // Update the scroll sizes
 6:             CDoodleDoc* pDoc = GetDocument();
 7:             ASSERT_VALID(pDoc);
 8:             SetScrollSizes(MM_LOENGLISH, pDoc->GetDocSize());
 9:
10:             // Invalidate only the rectangular position of the new graphic
11:             CGraphic* pGraphic = (CGraphic*)pHint;
12:             CClientDC dc(this);
13:             OnPrepareDC(&dc);
14:             CRect rc = pGraphic->GetPosition();
15:             dc.LPtoDP(&rc);
16:             rc.InflateRect(1, 1);
17:             InvalidateRect(&rc);
18:             return;
19:         }
20:     }
21:
22:     // Invalidate the entire view
23:     Invalidate();
24: }
```

Things get a little more interesting in the OnDraw() member function, which has to deal with the issue of the MM_LOENGLISH mapping mode's Y-axis increasing in the negative direction. Listing 17.6 contains the source code for the OnDraw() member function.

LISTING 17.6 THE CDoodleView::OnDraw() MEMBER FUNCTION FOR DOODLE7

```
1: void CDoodleView::OnDraw(CDC* pDC) {
2:     // Get a pointer to the document
3:     CDoodleDoc* pDoc = GetDocument();
4:     ASSERT_VALID(pDoc);
5:
6:     // Get the clipping rect for the DC
```

```
 7:     CRect rcClip, rcGraphic;
 8:     pDC->GetClipBox(&rcClip);
 9:     rcClip.top = -rcClip.top;
10:     rcClip.bottom = -rcClip.bottom;
11:
12:     // Draw the view (paint the graphics)
13:     POSITION pos = pDoc->m_graphicList.GetHeadPosition();
14:     while (pos != NULL) {
15:       // Get the next graphic
16:       CGraphic* pGraphic = pDoc->m_graphicList.GetNext(pos);
17:
18:       // Only draw if the graphic rect intersects the clipping rect
19:       rcGraphic = pGraphic->GetPosition();
20:       rcGraphic.top = -rcGraphic.top;
21:       rcGraphic.bottom = -rcGraphic.bottom;
22:       if (rcGraphic.IntersectRect(&rcGraphic, &rcClip))
23:         pGraphic->Draw(pDC);
24:     }
25: }
```

The solution to the negative Y-axis problem in OnDraw() is to negate the Y components of each rectangle in the code. Notice that the top and bottom members of the rcClip and rcGraphic rectangles are both negated before the rectangles are used. This results in positive values for the Y components of the rectangles. Without making this change, the IntersectRect() function would have trouble interpreting the negative rectangle components, and would never detect a rectangle intersection.

That fixes the drawing code to work for both the screen and the printer but you haven't addressed the specifics of printing. The OnPrint() member function is responsible for performing any additional drawing when a document is being printed. Following is the declaration of OnPrint() in the CDoodleView class:

```
virtual void  OnPrint(CDC* pDC, CPrintInfo* pInfo);
```

Listing 17.7 contains the source code for the OnPrint() member function.

LISTING 17.7 THE CDoodleView::OnPrint() MEMBER FUNCTION FOR DOODLE7

```
1: void CDoodleView::OnPrint(CDC* pDC, CPrintInfo* pInfo) {
2:   // Get a pointer to the document
3:   CDoodleDoc* pDoc = GetDocument();
4:   ASSERT_VALID(pDoc);
5:
6:   // Print the page header and adjust the DC window origin
```

continues

LISTING 17.7 CONTINUED

```
 7:    CString sDocTitle = pDoc->GetTitle();
 8:    PrintPageHeader(pDC, pInfo, sDocTitle);
 9:    pDC->SetWindowOrg(pInfo->m_rectDraw.left, -pInfo->m_rectDraw.top);
10:
11:    // Print the document data
12:    OnDraw(pDC);
13: }
```

The `OnPrint()` member function takes on the task of printing the header on the page before allowing `OnDraw()` to draw the actual document data. Notice how the window origin of the device context is altered to reflect the drawing rectangle maintained by the `CPrintInfo` object. This is necessary so that the `OnDraw()` function can't draw up in the header; in fact, `OnDraw()` doesn't even know about the header.

Another member function that does know about the header is `PrintPageHeader()`, which is responsible for printing the document header. Following is the declaration of the `PrintPageHeader()` member function:

```
void PrintPageHeader(CDC* pDC, CPrintInfo* pInfo, CString& sHeader);
```

The `PrintPageHeader()` member function accepts a string as its third parameter and prints it, along with a horizontal line below the string that goes across the page. Listing 17.8 contains the source code for the `PrintPageHeader()` member function.

LISTING 17.8 THE `CDoodleView::PrintPageHeader()` MEMBER FUNCTION FOR DOODLE7

```
 1: void CDoodleView::PrintPageHeader(CDC* pDC, CPrintInfo* pInfo,
 2:    CString& sHeader) {
 3:    // Draw the header text aligned left
 4:    pDC->SetTextAlign(TA_LEFT);
 5:    pDC->TextOut(0, -25, sHeader);
 6:
 7:    // Draw a line across the page just below the header text
 8:    TEXTMETRIC tm;
 9:    pDC->GetTextMetrics(&tm);
10:    int y = -35 - tm.tmHeight;
11:    pDC->MoveTo(0, y);
12:    pDC->LineTo(pInfo->m_rectDraw.right, y);
13:
14:    // Adjust the drawing rect to not include the header
15:    y -= 25;
16:    pInfo->m_rectDraw.top += y;
17: }
```

Notice that the header text is drawn using a negative Y coordinate, which is necessary when working within the MM_LOENGLISH mapping mode. The value of -25 equates to 1/4 inch in this mapping mode since each logical unit is equivalent to 0.01 inch (25×0.01=0.25). A line is drawn across the page just below the text. After drawing the line, the PrintPageHeader() function adjusts the drawing rectangle to exclude the header.

The final change required in the CDoodleView class involves the OnLButtonDown() message handler, which is used to add new graphic elements to the document. Listing 17.9 contains the source code for the OnLButtonDown() message handler.

LISTING 17.9 THE CDoodleView::OnLButtonDown() MEMBER FUNCTION FOR DOODLE7

```
 1: void CDoodleView::OnLButtonDown(UINT nFlags, CPoint point) {
 2:     // Get a pointer to the document
 3:     CDoodleDoc* pDoc = GetDocument();
 4:     ASSERT_VALID(pDoc);
 5:
 6:     // Start the "rubber band" rectangle tracker
 7:     CRectTracker tracker;
 8:     tracker.TrackRubberBand(this, point);
 9:
10:     // Convert the tracker rect from device to logical coordinates
11:     CClientDC dc(this);
12:     OnPrepareDC(&dc);
13:     dc.DPtoLP(&tracker.m_rect);
14:
15:     // Add new graphic based on the drawing mode
16:     switch (m_nDrawMode) {
17:     case CGraphic::LINE:
18:         // Add a line to the graphics list
19:         pDoc->AddGraphic(new CGraphic(CGraphic::LINE, tracker.m_rect,
20:           m_crColor));
21:         break;
22:
23:     case CGraphic::RECTANGLE:
24:         // Add a rectangle to the graphics list
25:         pDoc->AddGraphic(new CGraphic(CGraphic::RECTANGLE, tracker.m_rect,
26:           m_crColor));
27:         break;
28:
29:     case CGraphic::ELLIPSE:
30:         // Add an ellipse to the graphics list
31:         pDoc->AddGraphic(new CGraphic(CGraphic::ELLIPSE, tracker.m_rect,
32:           m_crColor));
```

continues

LISTING 17.9 CONTINUED

```
33:       break;
34:
35:     case CGraphic::CRITTER:
36:       // Add a critter to the graphics list
37:       pDoc->AddGraphic(new CGraphic(CGraphic::CRITTER, tracker.m_rect,
38:         m_crColor));
39:       break;
40:     }
41: }
```

The change to the `OnLButtonDown()` message handler is the removal of the code that fixed rectangle components to eliminate the risk of a negative width or height. The changes you made to support the `MM_LOENGLISH` mapping mode now make this code unnecessary.

The Document

With the view behind us, we're almost home free. However, there are still a few changes necessary in the document to get the Doodle7 application ready to print. More specifically, you must make a slight change to the `AddGraphic()` member function due to the view's new mapping mode. Listing 17.10 contains the source code for the `AddGraphic()` member function.

LISTING 17.10 THE `CDoodleDoc::AddGraphic()` MEMBER FUNCTION FOR DOODLE7

```
 1: void CDoodleDoc::AddGraphic(CGraphic* pGraphic) {
 2:   // Add a new graphic to end of graphic list
 3:   ASSERT_VALID(pGraphic);
 4:   m_graphicList.AddTail(pGraphic);
 5:
 6:   // Enlarge the document size if necessary
 7:   CSize sizGraphic = pGraphic->GetPosition().BottomRight();
 8:   sizGraphic.cy = -sizGraphic.cy;
 9:   if ((sizGraphic.cx > m_sizDoc.cx) || (sizGraphic.cy > m_sizDoc.cy)) {
10:     m_sizDoc.cx = max(m_sizDoc.cx, sizGraphic.cx);
11:     m_sizDoc.cy = max(m_sizDoc.cy, sizGraphic.cy);
12:   }
13:
14:   // Flag document as modified and update view
15:   SetModifiedFlag();
16:   UpdateAllViews(NULL, 0L, pGraphic);
17: }
```

The only change to the `AddGraphic()` function is the negation of the Y component of the graphic element's size. This is necessary to account for the negative Y-axis in the `MM_LOENGLISH` mapping mode.

One tricky issue you might not have thought about is that the graphic elements now use negative coordinate values for the Y components of their position rectangle. Since the Doodle7 application fully expects negative graphic position values, there is a big problem if it tries to open Doodle documents saved with an earlier version of Doodle. To fix this problem, you must increment the schema for the document in the `IMPLEMENT_SERIAL` macro:

```
IMPLEMENT_SERIAL(CGraphic, CObject, 2)
```

If you try to open a document saved with an earlier version of Doodle, the Doodle7 application will complain about an unrecognized file format and not open the document. This is much more acceptable than opening the document and attempting to draw questionable document data. Of course, you could add extra serialization code to interpret old schemas and appropriately make the conversion, but that's a little beyond the focus of this hour.

The Document's Final Stages

The final change required in the Doodle7 application is in the `CGraphic` class. Unfortunately, the change required in this class doesn't have as much to do with printing as it does with GDI in general. Even though one of the big benefits of GDI graphics is that they are device-independent, there are some caveats. One of the big caveats in GDI programming has to do with printing device-dependent bitmaps.

A device-dependent bitmap is a bitmap that can only be displayed on an output device with certain specific characteristics. Although it is possible to use device-independent bitmaps in Win32, the `CBitmap` class only supports device-dependent bitmaps. So, short of developing our own bitmap class, we have to make the `CBitmap` class work for us.

NEW TERM   A *device-dependent bitmap* is a bitmap that can only be displayed on an output device with certain specific characteristics.

The device dependency of the `CBitmap` class hasn't mattered up to this point because you've only been dealing with a single output device, the screen. Not surprisingly, there is no problem drawing device-dependent bitmaps to the screen. However, they aren't compatible with printers, and therein lies the problem.

The solution to this problem is relatively simple. Before drawing a bitmap, you must first create a memory device context that is compatible with the screen, and select the bitmap into it. You must then create a memory device context compatible with the printer and copy the bitmap to it. Once you have the bitmap in a memory device context that is compatible with the printer, you're ready to roll. Following is a summary of these steps to help clarify:

1. Load the bitmap into a `CBitmap` object.
2. Create a memory DC compatible with the screen.
3. Select the bitmap into this screen memory DC.
4. Create a memory DC compatible with the printer.
5. Copy the bitmap from the screen memory DC to the printer memory DC.
6. Draw the bitmap from the printer memory DC to the printer DC.

Listing 17.11 contains the source code for the `CGraphic::Draw()` member function, which performs these steps.

LISTING 17.11 THE `CGraphic::Draw()` MEMBER FUNCTION FOR DOODLE7

```
 1: void CGraphic::Draw(CDC* pDC) {
 2:     ASSERT_VALID(pDC);
 3:
 4:     // Select the pen and brush
 5:     CPen    pen(PS_SOLID, 2, m_crColor);
 6:     CPen*   ppenOld;
 7:     CBrush* pbrOld;
 8:     VERIFY(ppenOld = pDC->SelectObject(&pen));
 9:     VERIFY(pbrOld = pDC->SelectObject(
10:         CBrush::FromHandle((HBRUSH)::GetStockObject(NULL_BRUSH))));
11:
12:     // Draw graphic based on the type
13:     switch (m_nType) {
14:     case LINE:
15:         // Draw a line
16:         pDC->MoveTo(m_rcPosition.TopLeft());
17:         pDC->LineTo(m_rcPosition.BottomRight());
18:         break;
19:
20:     case RECTANGLE:
21:         // Draw a rectangle
22:         pDC->Rectangle(m_rcPosition);
23:         break;
24:
```

```
25:    case ELLIPSE:
26:      // Draw an ellipse
27:      pDC->Ellipse(m_rcPosition);
28:      break;
29:
30:    case CRITTER:
31:      // Load the critter bitmap
32:      CBitmap   bmCritter1;
33:      BITMAP    bmInfo;
34:      VERIFY(bmCritter1.LoadBitmap(IDB_CRITTER));
35:      bmCritter1.GetObject(sizeof(BITMAP), &bmInfo);
36:
37:      // Create a DC and select the bitmap into it
38:      CDC dcMem1;
39:      dcMem1.CreateCompatibleDC(NULL);
40:      VERIFY(dcMem1.SelectObject(&bmCritter1));
41:
42:      // Create a compatible bitmap and DC
43:      CBitmap   bmCritter2;
44:      CDC       dcMem2;
45:      bmCritter2.CreateCompatibleBitmap(pDC, bmInfo.bmWidth,
              ↪bmInfo.bmHeight);
46:      dcMem2.CreateCompatibleDC(pDC);
47:      VERIFY(dcMem2.SelectObject(&bmCritter2));
48:
49:      // Copy the bitmap to the compatible DC
50:      dcMem2.BitBlt(0, 0, bmInfo.bmWidth, bmInfo.bmHeight, &dcMem1, 0,
              ↪0, SRCCOPY);
51:
52:      // Draw the critter image
53:      pDC->StretchBlt(m_rcPosition.left, m_rcPosition.top,
54:        m_rcPosition.Width(), m_rcPosition.Height(), &dcMem2, 0, 0,
55:        bmInfo.bmWidth, bmInfo.bmHeight, SRCAND);
56:      break;
57:  }
58:
59:  // Cleanup the DC
60:  VERIFY(pDC->SelectObject(ppenOld));
61:  VERIFY(pDC->SelectObject(pbrOld));
62: }
```

That finishes up the Doodle7 application. I encourage you to burn through a few reams of paper testing out the application.

Summary

This hour tackled a pretty big topic by introducing you to printing using MFC. You began the hour by learning some basics about printing and the role of Print Preview. You then moved on to learn about MFC's support for printing, and how it automates a great deal of the printing process. From there, you found out how GDI mapping modes impact printing. Finally, you wrapped up the hour by adding printing support to the Doodle application.

Q&A

Q Is it really necessary to override the `OnPreparePrinting()` member function in Doodle7?

A Yes. Even though Doodle7's `OnPreparePrinting()` member function consists of only a single call to the `CView::DoPreparePrinting()` member function, it is absolutely necessary. The default version of `OnPreparePrinting()` defined in the `CView` class does nothing at all. The Doodle7 application wouldn't print without overriding this member function.

Q Is it possible to ascertain the capabilities of a printer before attempting to print a document to it?

A Yes. You can use the `GetDeviceCaps()` member function on the printer DC to determine specific information about the types of graphics the printer supports. For example, you can call the `GetDeviceCaps()` member function to determine if a printer is capable of printing bitmaps. You should call `GetDeviceCaps()` in the `OnPreparePrinting()` member function and return `FALSE` if the printer isn't capable of printing the document; this results in the print job being cancelled.

Workshop

The Workshop is designed to help you anticipate possible questions, review what you've learned, and begin thinking ahead to put your knowledge into practice. The answers to the quiz are in Appendix A, "Quiz Answers."

Quiz

1. What is a Print Preview?
2. How does MFC support printing by default?
3. What class encapsulates the majority of MFC's printing support?
4. What is a print job?
5. What `CView` member function is called by the framework to display the Print dialog box and get the print sequence started?
6. How do you alter the default values displayed in the Print dialog box?
7. What pair of `CView` member functions is used to allocate and free GDI resources required for printing?
8. What MFC class is used to maintain information about a print or Print Preview job?
9. How do you reduce the page area available for printing to make room for headers and footers on a page?
10. Using the `MM_LOENGLISH` mapping mode, how many logical units would map to 3 inches in physical units?

Exercises

1. Try previewing a document using the File, Print Preview menu command, and then print the file to the printer. Compare the printed page with the preview window and notice how similar they are. This reveals how a Print Preview is rendered in the same way as a printed page.
2. Try opening a document in Doodle7 that was saved using an earlier version of Doodle. Notice how Doodle7 recognizes the different document schema number and notifies you of an unrecognized file type.

HOUR 18

Accessing Databases with DAO

This hour tackles the topic of databases, which are an important component of any MFC programmer's skill set. Even if you don't have lots of experience with databases, you should be able to follow along and understand how to use them with MFC. It's worth noting that there are a variety of different database technologies available for use in MFC applications. This hour focuses on DAO (Data Access Objects), which is currently the most straightforward approach to building MFC database applications. The next hour takes a deeper look at other database technologies that are gaining in popularity.

In this hour, you will learn

- How databases relate to MFC programming
- About the MFC DAO classes
- How to build an MFC application using DAO

Databases and MFC

When it comes to database programming, as an MFC programmer you have lots of options. MFC directly supports two different approaches to database development: ODBC and DAO. ODBC stands for Open Database Connectivity, and has been around for a while. DAO stands for Data Access Objects, and originated as a means of accessing Microsoft Jet databases using Visual Basic. ODBC and DAO both offer roughly the same functionality, but there are advantages and disadvantages to using each one.

Even though DAO now supports databases beyond Microsoft Jet databases, it does so through an ODBC layer. So, if you really want data source independence, you might want to stick with using ODBC directly. However, if you don't mind using a Jet database, DAO is more efficient and easier to use than ODBC. Under the hood, both ODBC and DAO are C-based APIs. MFC provides a suite of classes that wrap the APIs and make accessing databases much more intuitive.

> The Microsoft Jet databases directly supported by DAO are sometimes referred to as Microsoft Access databases because they are the native database format of the Microsoft Access application. The Jet name comes from Microsoft's Jet database engine, which is the database engine used by Microsoft Access. These databases have a file extension of .MDB, and should be familiar to you if you've ever done any database programming in Visual Basic or Access.

If you're building a new application and the format of the underlying database isn't critical, I encourage you to use DAO and an Access database. This mainly has to do with simplifying the MFC code and the upkeep of the database. More specifically, DAO offers the following advantages for building MFC database applications:

- Better performance in many cases when using Microsoft Jet (.MDB) databases
- Support for ODBC databases through an ODBC layer
- Direct access to data validation rules
- Capability of specifying relations between tables
- Support for Data Definition Language (DDL) and Data Manipulation Language (DML)

The DAO Object Model

Before I get into the details of how DAO is used with MFC, it's important to understand the structure of DAO. DAO defines an object model that specifies the objects used to manipulate a database. Following are the different objects that comprise the DAO object model:

- DBEngine
- Workspace
- Database
- TableDef
- QueryDef
- Recordset

Figure 18.1 shows the relationship between the objects in the DAO object model. The next few sections explain the relevance of each of these DAO objects.

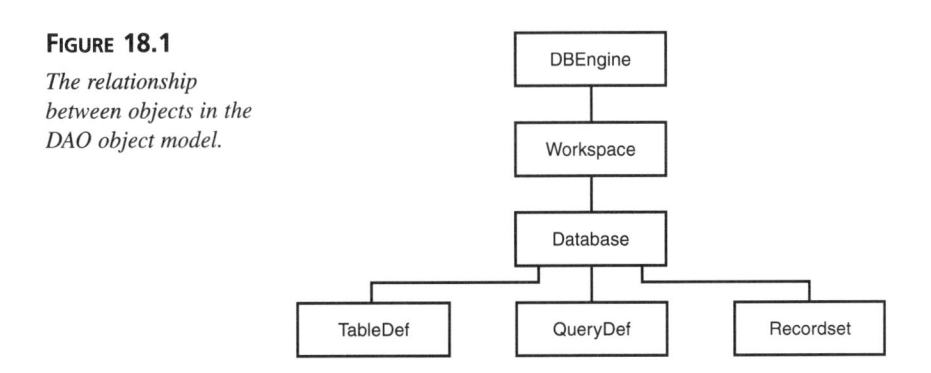

FIGURE 18.1

The relationship between objects in the DAO object model.

```
              DBEngine
                 |
              Workspace
                 |
              Database
          _____|_____
         |        |        |
      TableDef QueryDef Recordset
```

The DBEngine Object

The DBEngine object is the DAO database engine, and encapsulates the functionality of the Microsoft Jet database engine. Not surprisingly, the DBEngine object forms the root of the DAO object model. A major part of the database engine is support for SQL (Structured Query Language), which is the language used to query databases for information. Most database applications utilize SQL to some degree when extracting information from a database. The DBEngine object is responsible for supporting SQL in DAO.

The `Workspace` Object

A workspace in DAO consists of the memory used to perform a series of DAO operations. The `Workspace` object is used to represent a DAO workspace. Most applications use only one workspace but you are free to open more if you so choose. A default workspace is automatically created and assigned to an application when you open a database using DAO.

The `Database` Object

The `Database` object is where things start to get interesting with DAO because the `Database` object represents a Microsoft Jet database. A Jet database is a collection of tables, which themselves include data fields and indexes. Jet databases can also include database queries. The `Database` object effectively encapsulates an .MDB Jet database file.

Internal Database Objects

A database is ultimately a collection of tables containing fields of related information. The `TableDefs` object is a collection of all the tables in a database. Each `TableDef` object in the TableDefs collection corresponds to an individual table in the database. Similarly, the `QueryDefs` object is a collection of all the compiled SQL queries contained in a database. Each `QueryDef` object in the QueryDefs collection corresponds to an individual SQL command string.

The `Recordset` object is in many ways the most important of the DAO objects because it is the one you typically come in the most contact with when developing a database application. The `Recordset` object represents a set of records selected from a database. The records in a `Recordset` object can be obtained directly from a table or indirectly through a SQL query, and can come from multiple tables.

The MFC DAO Classes

Now that you have a basic understanding of how DAO is organized into objects, you're ready to take a look at how MFC wraps DAO with a set of MFC wrapper classes. In many respects, the relationship between MFC and DAO is like the relationship between MFC and the Win32 API; MFC encapsulates DAO through a set of MFC wrapper classes. Many of the MFC classes have a one-to-one relationship with DAO objects. Following are some of the MFC classes that wrap major DAO objects:

- `CDaoWorkspace`—wraps the DAO `Workspace` object
- `CDaoDatabase`—wraps the DAO `Database` object

- `CDaoTableDef`—wraps the DAO `TableDef` object
- `CDaoQueryDef`—wraps the DAO `QueryDef` object
- `CDaoRecordset`—wraps the DAO `Recordset` object

Although these MFC classes have a one-to-one relationship with respective DAO objects, MFC doesn't provide classes for all DAO objects. Some DAO objects are accessed via member functions defined in the `CDaoTableDef`, `CDaoQueryDef`, and `CDaoRecordset` MFC classes. These DAO objects relate to database fields, indexes, parameters, and relations.

Another difference between MFC's wrapper classes and DAO has to do with the DAO database engine, which is hidden in the MFC wrapper classes. The functionality supported by the DAO `DBEngine` object is still available in MFC but not in a discrete MFC class. Instead, MFC provides member functions in the `CDaoWorkspace` class that can be used to get and set properties of the Jet database engine.

In addition to MFC's direct support for DAO, MFC also provides a special view class that brings DAO into the realm of the familiar document/view architecture. The `CDaoRecordView` class represents a view on a DAO database record, and is extremely useful in building MFC database applications. You learn more about the `CDaoRecordView` class in the next section.

MFC, DAO, and Form-Based Applications

Although you are free to structure MFC database applications any way you choose, MFC makes it particularly straightforward to build form-based applications. A form-based application looks a lot like a dialog box because it uses a dialog box resource (form) as the basis for its user interface. The user interface in a form consists of controls that are used to view, enter, and manipulate data.

The key to building form-based applications in MFC is the `CDaoRecordView` class, which is designed specifically for form-based applications. When using the `CDaoRecordView` class, the document data for an application consists of a record set, or `CDaoRecordset` object. The view then consists of a group of dialog controls that provide a means of viewing and modifying the data in a given record within the record set. MFC provides all of the mechanisms required for shuttling information between the record set and the database, as well as between the record set and the dialog controls.

The `CDaoRecordView` class provides a default implementation for navigational operations such as moving from one record to the previous or next record. You can also navigate to the first or last record in a record set. The `CDaoRecordView` class includes message handlers for these navigational operations, which means that supporting them is as simple as adding navigation commands to your application's menu.

Creating a Custom Record Set Class

Creating a form-based MFC application using the `CDaoRecordView` class is very straightforward. Most of the work involves working with `CDaoRecordset` objects. More specifically, you will need to create a `CDaoRecordset`-derived class for each record set that you plan on using in the application. Within this class, there are a few important member functions that you must override:

- `GetDefaultDBName()`
- `GetDefaultSQL()`
- `DoFieldExchange()`

The `GetDefaultDBName()` member function returns the name of the default database. You should return a string containing the name of your database in the overridden version of `GetDefaultDBName()`. Following is an example of how this is accomplished:

```
CString CAnimalSet::GetDefaultDBName() {
  // Return the database name
  return "Zoo.mdb";
}
```

The `GetDefaultSQL()` member function returns the default SQL statement issued on the record set when it is first created. If you want to retrieve all the records in a given table, you can simply provide the table name in square brackets ([ ]), like this:

```
CString CAnimalSet::GetDefaultSQL() {
  // Return the default SQL statement
  return "[Animals]";
}
```

The last important member function you should override in your own record set classes is `DoFieldExchange()`, which is responsible for binding record set data fields with member variables in your record set class. MFC provides DAO record field exchange functions that you use to perform these bindings. Following is an example:

```
void CAnimalSet::DoFieldExchange(CDaoFieldExchange* pFX) {
  // Bind the record set columns to member variables
  pFX->SetFieldType(CDaoFieldExchange::outputColumn);
  DFX_Long(pFX, "[AnimalID]", m_AnimalID);
  DFX_Text(pFX, "[Type]", m_Type);
  DFX_Text(pFX, "[Name]", m_Name);
  DFX_Short(pFX, "[Age]", m_Age);
  DFX_Text(pFX, "[Location]", m_Location);
}
```

Of course, you must then define the appropriate member variables in your record set class, like this:

```
long     m_AnimalID;
CString  m_Type;
CString  m_Name;
short    m_Age;
CString  m_Location;
```

The only other requirement of a custom record set class is to initialize the member variables to default values in the constructor, like this:

```
CAnimalSet::CAnimalSet(CDaoDatabase* pdb) : CDaoRecordset(pdb) {
  // Initialize the record set data
  m_AnimalID = 0;
  m_Type = "";
  m_Name = "";
  m_Age = 0;
  m_Location = "";
  m_nFields = 5;
  m_nDefaultType = dbOpenDynaset;
}
```

The only potentially tricky thing in the constructor code is the inherited `m_nFields` member, which must be set to the number of fields of data in the record set. In this case there are five fields of data, which is evident by the member variables you added and the DAO record field exchange function calls.

The Document and View

You will typically want to embed a record set object in the document of a form-based MFC DAO database application. Of course, if the application uses multiple record sets, then you might want to define multiple member variable record sets. You can also create and use temporary record set objects if necessary. Other than containing record set objects, a document in a form-based MFC DAO application does very little. Following is an example of a record set object declaration as it would appear in a document:

```
CanimalSet m_animalSet;
```

Most of the work in a form-based MFC DAO application is taken on by the view. The view must derive from `CDaoRecordView` to inherit all the built-in form-based functionality. The view then communicates with the document to obtain information about record set data. There is one very important member function in `CDaoRecordView` that you must override. The `OnGetRecordset()` member function returns a pointer to the record set object associated with the view. This record set contains the records that the view displays in its controls. Following is an example of an `OnGetRecordset()` member function that returns a record set pointer:

```
CDaoRecordset* CZooView::OnGetRecordset() {
  CZooDoc* pDoc = GetDocument();
  return &pDoc->m_animalSet;
}
```

Building a Database Application

You now hopefully have a pretty good feel for how an MFC application is structured to provide a form-based interface to a DAO database. The remainder of the hour focuses on the construction of a database application named Hockey that keeps track of the teams in the National Hockey League (NHL). The Hockey application uses a Microsoft Jet database named Hockey.mdb that I created in Microsoft Access. Following are the tables defined in the Hockey.mdb database:

- Teams—The teams in the NHL
- Conferences—The conferences in the NHL
- Divisions—The divisions within NHL conferences

The main table in the Hockey.mdb database is Teams, which contains fields pertaining to different teams. Table 18.1 lists the fields in the Teams table.

TABLE 18.1 THE DATA FIELDS DEFINED IN THE TEAMS TABLE OF THE HOCKEY.MDB DATABASE

Field Name	Type	Description
TeamID	Long integer	Uniquely identifies each team
TeamName	String	Team name
Location	String	Location of the team
Coach	String	Coach of the team
Wins	Short integer	Number of wins
Losses	Short integer	Number of losses
Ties	Short integer	Number of ties
ConferenceID	Long integer	Key into the Conferences table
DivisionID	Long integer	Key into the Divisions table

The `ConferenceID` and `DivisionID` fields are keys into the Conferences and Divisions tables. This gives the database the flexibility to allow conferences and divisions to change without directly impacting the Teams table. The Conferences and Divisions tables are very similar in that they simply contain ID and name fields. Tables 18.2 and 18.3 list the fields in the Conferences and Divisions tables, respectively.

TABLE 18.2 THE DATA FIELDS DEFINED IN THE CONFERENCES TABLE OF THE HOCKEY.MDB DATABASE

Field Name	Type	Description
ConferenceID	Long integer	Uniquely identifies each conference
ConferenceName	String	Conference name

TABLE 18.3 THE DATA FIELDS DEFINED IN THE DIVISIONS TABLE OF THE HOCKEY.MDB DATABASE

Field Name	Type	Description
DivisionID	Long integer	Uniquely identifies each division
DivisionName	String	Division name

Getting back to the Hockey application, it uses the Teams table as the basis for its form-based view. In other words, you can navigate through the teams in the NHL and view and modify information about them. The Hockey application also supports the File, Best menu command, which checks to find the best team in the league. Incidentally, the Conferences and Divisions tables are still used indirectly as look-ups for the conference and division of each team. Let's get started putting the application together!

Resources

As in most applications you've learned about throughout the book, the Hockey application begins with resources. Listing 18.1 contains the Resource.h header file for Hockey, which contains identifiers for the application's resources.

LISTING 18.1 THE RESOURCE.H HEADER FILE FOR HOCKEY

```
 1: //----------------------------------------------------------------
 2: // Resource Identifiers
 3: // C++ Source - Resource.h
 4: //----------------------------------------------------------------
 5:
 6: //----------------------------------------------------------------
 7: // Strings                     Range : 1000 - 1999
 8: //----------------------------------------------------------------
 9: #define IDR_HOCKEY              1000
10:
```

continues

LISTING 18.1 CONTINUED

```
11: //----------------------------------------------------------------
12: // Commands                  Range : 2000 - 2999
13: //----------------------------------------------------------------
14: #define ID_FILE_BEST          2000
15:
16: //----------------------------------------------------------------
17: // Controls                   Range : 3000 - 3999
18: //----------------------------------------------------------------
19: #define IDC_TEAMNAME          3001
20: #define IDC_LOCATION          3002
21: #define IDC_COACH             3003
22: #define IDC_WINS              3004
23: #define IDC_LOSSES            3005
24: #define IDC_TIES              3006
25: #define IDC_CONFERENCE        3007
26: #define IDC_DIVISION          3008
27:
28: //----------------------------------------------------------------
29: // Dialog Boxes               Range : 4000 - 4999
30: //----------------------------------------------------------------
31: #define IDD_ABOUTBOX          4000
32: #define IDD_HOCKEYBOX         4001
```

The `ID_FILE_BEST` identifier is used to identify the menu command for finding the best team. The control identifiers are all associated with controls in the dialog box form for the record view. The `IDD_HOCKEYBOX` identifier uniquely identifies this dialog box form. To get an idea as to how this dialog box is structured, check out Listing 18.2, which contains the resource script for the Hockey application.

LISTING 18.2 THE HOCKEY.RC RESOURCE SCRIPT FOR HOCKEY

```
 1: //----------------------------------------------------------------
 2: // Hockey Resources
 3: // RC Source - Hockey.rc
 4: //----------------------------------------------------------------
 5:
 6: //----------------------------------------------------------------
 7: // Inclusions
 8: //----------------------------------------------------------------
 9: #include "AfxRes.h"
10: #include "Resource.h"
11:
12: //----------------------------------------------------------------
13: // Icons
14: //----------------------------------------------------------------
```

```
15: IDR_HOCKEY       ICON    "Hockey.ico"
16:
17: //-----------------------------------------------------------------
18: // Bitmaps
19: //-----------------------------------------------------------------
20: IDR_HOCKEY       BITMAP  "ToolBar.bmp"
21:
22: //-----------------------------------------------------------------
23: // Menus
24: //-----------------------------------------------------------------
25: IDR_HOCKEY MENU PRELOAD DISCARDABLE
26: BEGIN
27:   POPUP "&File"
28:     BEGIN
29:       MENUITEM "&Best...",                  ID_FILE_BEST
30:       MENUITEM SEPARATOR
31:       MENUITEM "E&xit",                     ID_APP_EXIT
32:     END
33:   POPUP "&Record"
34:     BEGIN
35:       MENUITEM "&First Record",             ID_RECORD_FIRST
36:       MENUITEM "&Previous Record",          ID_RECORD_PREV
37:       MENUITEM "&Next Record",              ID_RECORD_NEXT
38:       MENUITEM "&Last Record",              ID_RECORD_LAST
39:     END
40:   POPUP "&View"
41:     BEGIN
42:       MENUITEM "&Toolbar",                  ID_VIEW_TOOLBAR
43:       MENUITEM "&Status Bar",               ID_VIEW_STATUS_BAR
44:     END
45:   POPUP "&Help"
46:     BEGIN
47:       MENUITEM "&About Hockey...",          ID_APP_ABOUT
48:     END
49: END
50:
51: //-----------------------------------------------------------------
52: // Tool Bars
53: //-----------------------------------------------------------------
54: IDR_HOCKEY TOOLBAR DISCARDABLE   16, 15
55: BEGIN
56:   BUTTON      ID_RECORD_FIRST
57:   BUTTON      ID_RECORD_PREV
58:   BUTTON      ID_RECORD_NEXT
59:   BUTTON      ID_RECORD_LAST
60:   SEPARATOR
61:   BUTTON      ID_APP_ABOUT
62: END
63:
64: //-----------------------------------------------------------------
```

continues

LISTING 18.2 CONTINUED

```
65: // Dialog Boxes
66: //-----------------------------------------------------------------
67: IDD_ABOUTBOX DIALOG 0, 0, 217, 55
68: CAPTION "About Hockey"
69: STYLE DS_MODALFRAME | WS_POPUP | WS_CAPTION | WS_SYSMENU
70: FONT 8, "MS Sans Serif"
71: BEGIN
72:     ICON            IDR_HOCKEY, IDC_STATIC, 11, 17, 20, 20
73:     LTEXT           "Hockey Version 1.0", IDC_STATIC, 40, 10,
74:                     119, 8, SS_NOPREFIX
75:     LTEXT           "Copyright (c)1998 Michael Morrison", IDC_STATIC,
76:                     40, 25, 119, 8
77:     DEFPUSHBUTTON   "OK", IDOK, 178, 7, 32, 14, WS_GROUP
78: END
79:
80: IDD_HOCKEYBOX DIALOG 0, 0, 340, 77
81: CAPTION "Hockey"
82: STYLE WS_CHILD
83: FONT 8, "MS Sans Serif"
84: BEGIN
85:     RTEXT           "Team Name:", IDC_STATIC, 7, 8, 45, 8
86:     RTEXT           "Location:", IDC_STATIC, 7, 26, 45, 8
87:     RTEXT           "Conference:", IDC_STATIC, 177, 9, 45, 8
88:     RTEXT           "Division:", IDC_STATIC, 177, 26, 45, 8
89:     RTEXT           "Record:", IDC_STATIC, 7, 59, 45, 8
90:     EDITTEXT        IDC_TEAMNAME, 56, 7, 113, 12
91:     EDITTEXT        IDC_LOCATION, 55, 24, 113, 12
92:     EDITTEXT        IDC_WINS, 55, 58, 21, 12
93:     COMBOBOX        IDC_CONFERENCE, 226, 7, 107, 60,
94:                     CBS_DROPDOWNLIST | WS_VSCROLL | WS_TABSTOP
95:     COMBOBOX        IDC_DIVISION, 226, 24, 107, 60,
96:                     CBS_DROPDOWNLIST | WS_VSCROLL | WS_TABSTOP
97:     RTEXT           "Coach:", IDC_STATIC, 7, 43, 45, 8
98:     EDITTEXT        IDC_COACH, 55, 41, 102, 12
99:     EDITTEXT        IDC_LOSSES, 84, 58, 21, 12
100:    EDITTEXT        IDC_TIES, 115, 58, 21, 12
101:    CTEXT           "-", IDC_STATIC, 75, 59, 8, 8
102:    CTEXT           "-", IDC_STATIC, 106, 59, 8, 8
103:    LTEXT           "(Win - Lose - Tie)", IDC_STATIC, 140, 59, 55, 8
104: END
105:
106: //-----------------------------------------------------------------
107: // Strings
108: //-----------------------------------------------------------------
109: STRINGTABLE
110: BEGIN
111:     AFX_IDS_APP_TITLE     "Hockey"
112:     IDR_HOCKEY            "Hockey\n\nHockey\n\n\nHockey.Document\nHockey
            ➥Document"
```

```
113:    AFX_IDS_IDLEMESSAGE  "Ready"
114: END
115:
116: STRINGTABLE
117: BEGIN
118:    ID_INDICATOR_CAPS    "CAP"
119:    ID_INDICATOR_NUM     "NUM"
120:    ID_INDICATOR_SCRL    "SCRL"
121: END
122:
123: STRINGTABLE
124: BEGIN
125:    ID_FILE_BEST         "Find the best team in the NHL\nBest Team"
126:    ID_APP_EXIT          "Quit the application; prompts to save
          ➥drawing\nExit"
127:
128:    ID_RECORD_FIRST      "Move to first record\nFirst Record"
129:    ID_RECORD_LAST       "Move to final record\nLast Record"
130:    ID_RECORD_NEXT       "Move to next record\nNext Record"
131:    ID_RECORD_PREV       "Move to previous record\nPrevious Record"
132: END
```

There isn't really anything earth-shattering about the resources for the Hockey application. Undoubtedly, the most important resource is the IDD_HOCKEYBOX dialog box definition, which forms the basis of the application's user interface. Because it's difficult to get a feel for how the dialog box looks from the resource code, Figure 18.2 shows the dialog box in the Visual C++ dialog box editor.

FIGURE 18.2

The IDD_HOCKEYBOX *dialog box database form.*

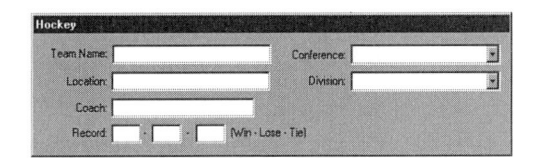

Database Support

A lot of the work involved in building a DAO database application in MFC is creating custom record set classes for each record set you intend to use. The Hockey application requires custom record set classes for all three of its database tables: Teams, Conferences, and Divisions. Because the Teams record set is the most important of the three, let's take a look at it first. Listings 18.3 and 18.4 contain the complete source code for the CTeamSet record set class.

LISTING 18.3 THE TEAMSET.H HEADER FILE FOR HOCKEY

```
 1: #ifndef __TEAMSET_H__
 2: #define __TEAMSET_H__
 3:
 4: //-------------------------------------------------------------------
 5: // CTeamSet Class - Team Set Recordset Object
 6: //-------------------------------------------------------------------
 7: class CTeamSet : public CDaoRecordset {
 8:    // Member Data
 9: public:
10:    long    m_TeamID;
11:    CString m_TeamName;
12:    CString m_Location;
13:    CString m_Coach;
14:    short   m_Wins;
15:    short   m_Losses;
16:    short   m_Ties;
17:    long    m_ConferenceID;
18:    long    m_DivisionID;
19:
20:    // Public Constructor
21: public:
22:                    CTeamSet(CDaoDatabase* pDatabase = NULL);
23:
24:    // Public Member Functions
25: public:
26:    virtual CString GetDefaultDBName();
27:    virtual CString GetDefaultSQL();
28:    virtual void    DoFieldExchange(CDaoFieldExchange* pFX);
29:
30:    // Diagnostic Functions
31: public:
32: #ifdef _DEBUG
33:    virtual void    AssertValid() const;
34:    virtual void    Dump(CDumpContext& dc) const;
35: #endif //_DEBUG
36:
37:    // Runtime Support
38: protected:
39:    DECLARE_DYNAMIC(CTeamSet)
40: };
41:
42: #endif
```

LISTING 18.4 THE TEAMSET.CPP SOURCE CODE FILE FOR HOCKEY

```
1: //-------------------------------------------------------------------
2: // Inclusions
```

```
 3: //------------------------------------------------------------
 4: #include "StdAfx.h"
 5: //------------------------------------------------------------
 6: #include "TeamSet.h"
 7:
 8: //------------------------------------------------------------
 9: // MFC Debugging Support
10: //------------------------------------------------------------
11: #ifdef _DEBUG
12: #undef THIS_FILE
13: static char BASED_CODE THIS_FILE[] = __FILE__;
14: #endif
15:
16:
17: //------------------------------------------------------------
18: // Runtime Support
19: //------------------------------------------------------------
20: IMPLEMENT_DYNAMIC(CTeamSet, CDaoRecordset)
21:
22: //------------------------------------------------------------
23: // Public Constructor(s)/Destructor
24: //------------------------------------------------------------
25: CTeamSet::CTeamSet(CDaoDatabase* pdb) : CDaoRecordset(pdb) {
26:     // Initialize the record set data
27:     m_TeamID = 0;
28:     m_TeamName = "";
29:     m_Location = "";
30:     m_Coach = "";
31:     m_Wins = 0;
32:     m_Losses = 0;
33:     m_Ties = 0;
34:     m_ConferenceID = 0;
35:     m_DivisionID = 0;
36:     m_nFields = 9;
37:     m_nDefaultType = dbOpenDynaset;
38: }
39:
40: //------------------------------------------------------------
41: // Public Member Functions
42: //------------------------------------------------------------
43: CString CTeamSet::GetDefaultDBName() {
44:     // Return the database name
45:     return "Hockey.mdb";
46: }
47:
48: CString CTeamSet::GetDefaultSQL() {
49:     // Return the default SQL statement
50:     return "[Teams]";
51: }
```

continues

LISTING 18.4 CONTINUED

```
52:
53: void CTeamSet::DoFieldExchange(CDaoFieldExchange* pFX) {
54:     // Bind the record set columns to member variables
55:     pFX->SetFieldType(CDaoFieldExchange::outputColumn);
56:     DFX_Long(pFX, "[TeamID]", m_TeamID);
57:     DFX_Text(pFX, "[TeamName]", m_TeamName);
58:     DFX_Text(pFX, "[Location]", m_Location);
59:     DFX_Text(pFX, "[Coach]", m_Coach);
60:     DFX_Short(pFX, "[Wins]", m_Wins);
61:     DFX_Short(pFX, "[Losses]", m_Losses);
62:     DFX_Short(pFX, "[Ties]", m_Ties);
63:     DFX_Long(pFX, "[ConferenceID]", m_ConferenceID);
64:     DFX_Long(pFX, "[DivisionID]", m_DivisionID);
65: }
66:
67: //-------------------------------------------------------------
68: // Diagnostic Functions
69: //-------------------------------------------------------------
70: #ifdef _DEBUG
71: void CTeamSet::AssertValid() const {
72:     CDaoRecordset::AssertValid();
73: }
74:
75: void CTeamSet::Dump(CDumpContext& dc) const {
76:     CDaoRecordset::Dump(dc);
77: }
78: #endif //_DEBUG
```

The CTeamSet record set class conforms very closely to the earlier description of how a CDaoRecordset-derived class must be structured. It defines member variables corresponding to each field in the Teams table, and then initializes these members in the constructor. The DoFieldExchange() member function binds the member variables to fields in the database. The database itself (Hockey.mdb) is named in the GetDefaultDBName() member function. Finally, all the records in the Teams table are included in the record set via the return value from the GetDefaultSQL() member function.

The Hockey application also requires a custom record set class for the Conferences table. Listings 18.5 and 18.6 contain the complete source code for the CConferenceSet record set class.

LISTING 18.5 THE CONFERENCESET.H HEADER FILE FOR HOCKEY

```
1: #ifndef __CONFERENCESET_H__
2: #define __CONFERENCESET_H__
3:
```

```
 4: //----------------------------------------------------------------
 5: // CConferenceSet Class - Conference Set Recordset Object
 6: //----------------------------------------------------------------
 7: class CConferenceSet : public CDaoRecordset {
 8:    // Member Data
 9: public:
10:    long    m_ConferenceID;
11:    CString m_ConferenceName;
12:
13:    // Public Constructor
14: public:
15:                    CConferenceSet(CDaoDatabase* pDatabase = NULL);
16:
17:    // Public Member Functions
18: public:
19:    virtual CString GetDefaultDBName();
20:    virtual CString GetDefaultSQL();
21:    virtual void    DoFieldExchange(CDaoFieldExchange* pFX);
22:
23:    // Diagnostic Functions
24: public:
25: #ifdef _DEBUG
26:    virtual void    AssertValid() const;
27:    virtual void    Dump(CDumpContext& dc) const;
28: #endif //_DEBUG
29:
30:    // Runtime Support
31: protected:
32:    DECLARE_DYNAMIC(CConferenceSet)
33: };
34:
35: #endif
```

LISTING 18.6 THE CONFERENCESET.CPP SOURCE CODE FILE FOR HOCKEY

```
 1: //----------------------------------------------------------------
 2: // Inclusions
 3: //----------------------------------------------------------------
 4: #include "StdAfx.h"
 5: //----------------------------------------------------------------
 6: #include "ConferenceSet.h"
 7:
 8: //----------------------------------------------------------------
 9: // MFC Debugging Support
10: //----------------------------------------------------------------
11: #ifdef _DEBUG
12: #undef THIS_FILE
13: static char BASED_CODE THIS_FILE[] = __FILE__;
```

continues

LISTING 18.6 CONTINUED

```
14: #endif
15:
16:
17: //-----------------------------------------------------------------
18: // Runtime Support
19: //-----------------------------------------------------------------
20: IMPLEMENT_DYNAMIC(CConferenceSet, CDaoRecordset)
21:
22: //-----------------------------------------------------------------
23: // Public Constructor(s)/Destructor
24: //-----------------------------------------------------------------
25: CConferenceSet::CConferenceSet(CDaoDatabase* pdb)
26:    : CDaoRecordset(pdb) {
27:    // Initialize the record set data
28:    m_ConferenceID = 0;
29:    m_ConferenceName = "";
30:    m_nFields = 2;
31:    m_nDefaultType = dbOpenDynaset;
32: }
33:
34: //-----------------------------------------------------------------
35: // Public Member Functions
36: //-----------------------------------------------------------------
37: CString CConferenceSet::GetDefaultDBName() {
38:    // Return the database name
39:    return "Hockey.mdb";
40: }
41:
42: CString CConferenceSet::GetDefaultSQL() {
43:    // Return the default SQL statement
44:    return "[Conferences]";
45: }
46:
47: void CConferenceSet::DoFieldExchange(CDaoFieldExchange* pFX) {
48:    // Bind the record set columns to member variables
49:    pFX->SetFieldType(CDaoFieldExchange::outputColumn);
50:    DFX_Long(pFX, "[ConferenceID]", m_ConferenceID);
51:    DFX_Text(pFX, "[ConferenceName]", m_ConferenceName);
52: }
53:
54: //-----------------------------------------------------------------
55: // Diagnostic Functions
56: //-----------------------------------------------------------------
57: #ifdef _DEBUG
58: void CConferenceSet::AssertValid() const {
59:    CDaoRecordset::AssertValid();
60: }
61:
62: void CConferenceSet::Dump(CDumpContext& dc) const {
```

Accessing Databases with DAO

```
63:     CDaoRecordset::Dump(dc);
64: }
65: #endif //_DEBUG
```

No surprises here! The `CConferenceSet` record set class is very similar to `CTeamSet`, with the obvious difference that it declares different member variables that bind to database fields in the Conferences table.

The last record set required for the Hockey application is `CDivisionSet`, which is associated with the Divisions table in the Hockey.mdb database. Listings 18.7 and 18.8 contain the complete source code for the `CDivisionSet` record set class.

LISTING 18.7   THE DIVISIONSET.H HEADER FILE FOR HOCKEY

```
 1: #ifndef __DIVISIONSET_H__
 2: #define __DIVISIONSET_H__
 3:
 4: //-----------------------------------------------------------------
 5: // CDivisionSet Class - Division Set Recordset Object
 6: //-----------------------------------------------------------------
 7: class CDivisionSet : public CDaoRecordset {
 8:     // Member Data
 9: public:
10:     long    m_DivisionID;
11:     CString m_DivisionName;
12:
13:     // Public Constructor
14: public:
15:     CDivisionSet(CDaoDatabase* pDatabase = NULL);
16:
17:     // Public Member Functions
18: public:
19:     virtual CString GetDefaultDBName();
20:     virtual CString GetDefaultSQL();
21:     virtual void    DoFieldExchange(CDaoFieldExchange* pFX);
22:
23:     // Diagnostic Functions
24: public:
25: #ifdef _DEBUG
26:     virtual void    AssertValid() const;
27:     virtual void    Dump(CDumpContext& dc) const;
28: #endif //_DEBUG
29:
30:     // Runtime Support
31: protected:
32:     DECLARE_DYNAMIC(CDivisionSet)
```

continues

LISTING 18.7 CONTINUED

```
33: };
34:
35: #endif
```

LISTING 18.8 THE DIVISIONSET.CPP SOURCE CODE FILE FOR HOCKEY

```
 1: //-----------------------------------------------------------------
 2: // Inclusions
 3: //-----------------------------------------------------------------
 4: #include "StdAfx.h"
 5: //-----------------------------------------------------------------
 6: #include "DivisionSet.h"
 7:
 8: //-----------------------------------------------------------------
 9: // MFC Debugging Support
10: //-----------------------------------------------------------------
11: #ifdef _DEBUG
12: #undef THIS_FILE
13: static char BASED_CODE THIS_FILE[] = __FILE__;
14: #endif
15:
16:
17: //-----------------------------------------------------------------
18: // Runtime Support
19: //-----------------------------------------------------------------
20: IMPLEMENT_DYNAMIC(CDivisionSet, CDaoRecordset)
21:
22: //-----------------------------------------------------------------
23: // Public Constructor(s)/Destructor
24: //-----------------------------------------------------------------
25: CDivisionSet::CDivisionSet(CDaoDatabase* pdb) : CDaoRecordset(pdb) {
26:     // Initialize the record set data
27:     m_DivisionID = 0;
28:     m_DivisionName = "";
29:     m_nFields = 2;
30:     m_nDefaultType = dbOpenDynaset;
31: }
32:
33: //-----------------------------------------------------------------
34: // Public Member Functions
35: //-----------------------------------------------------------------
36: CString CDivisionSet::GetDefaultDBName() {
37:     // Return the database name
38:     return "Hockey.mdb";
39: }
40:
```

LISTING 18.8 CONTINUED

```
41: CString CDivisionSet::GetDefaultSQL() {
42:   // Return the default SQL statement
43:   return "[Divisions]";
44: }
45:
46: void CDivisionSet::DoFieldExchange(CDaoFieldExchange* pFX) {
47:   // Bind the record set columns to member variables
48:   pFX->SetFieldType(CDaoFieldExchange::outputColumn);
49:   DFX_Long(pFX, "[DivisionID]", m_DivisionID);
50:   DFX_Text(pFX, "[DivisionName]", m_DivisionName);
51: }
52:
53: //-----------------------------------------------------------------
54: // Diagnostic Functions
55: //-----------------------------------------------------------------
56: #ifdef _DEBUG
57: void CDivisionSet::AssertValid() const {
58:   CDaoRecordset::AssertValid();
59: }
60:
61: void CDivisionSet::Dump(CDumpContext& dc) const {
62:   CDaoRecordset::Dump(dc);
63: }
64: #endif //_DEBUG
```

As you can see, the `CDivisionSet` class closely parallels the `CConferenceSet` class due to the similar structures of the database tables. Because you've already covered roughly the same code, I'll spare going through the details.

The Document

The document in the Hockey application is used as a container for the record set objects. An instance of each of the three custom record sets is stored in the document. This is evident in the `CHockeyDoc` class declaration, which is shown in Listing 18.9.

LISTING 18.9 THE HOCKEYDOC.H HEADER FILE FOR HOCKEY

```
1: #ifndef __HOCKEYDOC_H__
2: #define __HOCKEYDOC_H__
3:
4: //-----------------------------------------------------------------
5: // Inclusions
6: //-----------------------------------------------------------------
7: #include "TeamSet.h"
```

continues

LISTING 18.9 CONTINUED

```
 8: #include "ConferenceSet.h"
 9: #include "DivisionSet.h"
10:
11: //-----------------------------------------------------------------
12: // CHockeyDoc Class - Hockey Document Object
13: //-----------------------------------------------------------------
14: class CHockeyDoc : public CDocument {
15:    // Member Data
16: public:
17:    CTeamSet        m_teamSet;
18:    CConferenceSet  m_conferenceSet;
19:    CDivisionSet    m_divisionSet;
20:
21:    // Public Constructor(s)/Destructor
22: public:
23:                CHockeyDoc();
24:    virtual    ~CHockeyDoc();
25:
26:    // Public Member Functions
27: public:
28:    virtual BOOL  OnNewDocument();
29:
30:    // Diagnostic Functions
31: public:
32: #ifdef _DEBUG
33:    virtual void  AssertValid() const;
34:    virtual void  Dump(CDumpContext& dc) const;
35: #endif //_DEBUG
36:
37:    // Message Map & Runtime Support
38: protected:
39:    DECLARE_MESSAGE_MAP()
40:    DECLARE_DYNCREATE(CHockeyDoc)
41: };
42:
43: #endif
```

As the class declaration shows, the CHockeyDoc class is extremely streamlined and does little more than act as a container for record sets. Listing 18.10 contains the implementation of the CHockeyDoc class.

LISTING 18.10 THE HOCKEYDOC.CPP SOURCE CODE FILE FOR HOCKEY

```
1: //-----------------------------------------------------------------
2: // Inclusions
3: //-----------------------------------------------------------------
```

Accessing Databases with DAO

```
 4: #include "StdAfx.h"
 5: //---------------------------------------------------------------
 6: #include "HockeyDoc.h"
 7:
 8: //---------------------------------------------------------------
 9: // MFC Debugging Support
10: //---------------------------------------------------------------
11: #ifdef _DEBUG
12: #undef THIS_FILE
13: static char BASED_CODE THIS_FILE[] = __FILE__;
14: #endif
15:
16:
17: //---------------------------------------------------------------
18: // Message Map & Runtime Support
19: //---------------------------------------------------------------
20: BEGIN_MESSAGE_MAP(CHockeyDoc, CDocument)
21: END_MESSAGE_MAP()
22:
23: IMPLEMENT_DYNCREATE(CHockeyDoc, CDocument)
24:
25: //---------------------------------------------------------------
26: // Public Constructor(s)/Destructor
27: //---------------------------------------------------------------
28: CHockeyDoc::CHockeyDoc() {
29: }
30:
31: CHockeyDoc::~CHockeyDoc() {
32: }
33:
34: //---------------------------------------------------------------
35: // Public Member Functions
36: //---------------------------------------------------------------
37: BOOL CHockeyDoc::OnNewDocument() {
38:    if (!CDocument::OnNewDocument())
39:      return FALSE;
40:
41:    return TRUE;
42: }
43:
44: //---------------------------------------------------------------
45: // Diagnostic Functions
46: //---------------------------------------------------------------
47: #ifdef _DEBUG
48: void CHockeyDoc::AssertValid() const {
49:    CDocument::AssertValid();
50: }
51:
52: void CHockeyDoc::Dump(CDumpContext& dc) const {
```

continues

LISTING 18.10 CONTINUED

```
53:     CDocument::Dump(dc);
54: }
55: #endif //_DEBUG
```

The implementation of the `CHockeyDoc` class reveals that the class is in fact a skeletal container for record sets. I warned you that the view took on most of the responsibility in MFC DAO applications. The `CHockeyDoc` class is clear proof of this fact!

The View

The view of the Hockey application is the most interesting part of the application, at least from a programming perspective. Listing 18.11 contains the declaration of the `CHockeyView` class, which derives from `CDaoRecordView`.

LISTING 18.11 THE HOCKEYVIEW.H HEADER FILE FOR HOCKEY

```
 1: #ifndef __HOCKEYVIEW_H__
 2: #define __HOCKEYVIEW_H__
 3:
 4: //--------------------------------------------------------------
 5: // Inclusions
 6: //--------------------------------------------------------------
 7: #include "Resource.h"
 8:
 9: //--------------------------------------------------------------
10: // CHockeyView Class - Hockey View Object
11: //--------------------------------------------------------------
12: class CTeamSet;
13: class CHockeyView : public CDaoRecordView {
14: protected:
15:     // Member Data
16: public:
17:     enum { IDD = IDD_HOCKEYBOX };
18:     CTeamSet* m_pSet;
19:     CComboBox m_cbConferenceList;
20:     CComboBox m_cbDivisionList;
21:
22:     // Public Constructor(s)/Destructor
23: public:
24:                 CHockeyView();
25:     virtual     ~CHockeyView();
26:
27:     // Public Member Functions
```

```
28: public:
29:    CHockeyDoc*             GetDocument();
30:    virtual CDaoRecordset*  OnGetRecordset();
31:
32:    // Protected Member Functions
33: protected:
34:    virtual void            DoDataExchange(CDataExchange* pDX);
35:    virtual void            OnInitialUpdate();
36:
37:    // Message Handlers
38: public:
39:    afx_msg void            OnFileBest();
40:
41:    // Diagnostic Functions
42: public:
43: #ifdef _DEBUG
44:    virtual void  AssertValid() const;
45:    virtual void  Dump(CDumpContext& dc) const;
46: #endif //_DEBUG
47:
48:    // Message Map & Runtime Support
49: protected:
50:    DECLARE_MESSAGE_MAP()
51:    DECLARE_DYNCREATE(CHockeyView)
52: };
53:
54: #ifndef _DEBUG
55: inline CHockeyDoc* CHockeyView::GetDocument() {
56:    return (CHockeyDoc*)m_pDocument;
57: }
58: #endif //_DEBUG
59:
60: #endif
```

The CHockeyView class declares a few member variables. The m_pSet member maintains a pointer to the CTeamSet record set embedded in the document. This pointer member is mainly used as a convenience. The other two members, m_cbConferenceList and m_cbDivisionList, are CComboBox objects that are part of the dialog box form user interface. Using CComboBox objects makes it easier to fill the combo box controls with data from the Conferences and Divisions database tables.

The required OnGetRecordset() member function is overridden in CHockeyView. The DoDataExchange() and OnInitialUpdate() member functions are also declared, along with a message handler for the File, Best menu command. Listing 18.12 contains the implementation of the CHockeyView class.

LISTING 18.12 THE HOCKEYVIEW.CPP SOURCE CODE FILE FOR HOCKEY

```
 1: //-----------------------------------------------------------
 2: // Inclusions
 3: //-----------------------------------------------------------
 4: #include "StdAfx.h"
 5: //-----------------------------------------------------------
 6: #include "HockeyDoc.h"
 7: #include "HockeyView.h"
 8: #include "Resource.h"
 9:
10: //-----------------------------------------------------------
11: // MFC Debugging Support
12: //-----------------------------------------------------------
13: #ifdef _DEBUG
14: #undef THIS_FILE
15: static char BASED_CODE THIS_FILE[] = __FILE__;
16: #endif
17:
18:
19: //-----------------------------------------------------------
20: // Message Map & Runtime Support
21: //-----------------------------------------------------------
22: BEGIN_MESSAGE_MAP(CHockeyView, CDaoRecordView)
23:   ON_COMMAND(ID_FILE_BEST, OnFileBest)
24: END_MESSAGE_MAP()
25:
26: IMPLEMENT_DYNCREATE(CHockeyView, CDaoRecordView)
27:
28: //-----------------------------------------------------------
29: // Public Constructor(s)/Destructor
30: //-----------------------------------------------------------
31: CHockeyView::CHockeyView() : CDaoRecordView(CHockeyView::IDD) {
32:   m_pSet = NULL;
33: }
34:
35: CHockeyView::~CHockeyView() {
36: }
37:
38: //-----------------------------------------------------------
39: // Public Member Functions
40: //-----------------------------------------------------------
41: CDaoRecordset* CHockeyView::OnGetRecordset() {
42:   return m_pSet;
43: }
44:
45: //-----------------------------------------------------------
46: // Protected Member Functions
47: //-----------------------------------------------------------
48: void CHockeyView::DoDataExchange(CDataExchange* pDX) {
```

Accessing Databases with DAO

```
49:     CDaoRecordView::DoDataExchange(pDX);
50:
51:     // Bind the dialog controls with record set members
52:     DDX_FieldText(pDX, IDC_TEAMNAME, m_pSet->m_TeamName, m_pSet);
53:     DDV_MaxChars(pDX, m_pSet->m_TeamName, 64);
54:     DDX_FieldText(pDX, IDC_LOCATION, m_pSet->m_Location, m_pSet);
55:     DDV_MaxChars(pDX, m_pSet->m_Location, 64);
56:     DDX_FieldText(pDX, IDC_COACH, m_pSet->m_Coach, m_pSet);
57:     DDV_MaxChars(pDX, m_pSet->m_Coach, 64);
58:     DDX_FieldText(pDX, IDC_WINS, m_pSet->m_Wins, m_pSet);
59:     DDX_FieldText(pDX, IDC_LOSSES, m_pSet->m_Losses, m_pSet);
60:     DDX_FieldText(pDX, IDC_TIES, m_pSet->m_Ties, m_pSet);
61:     DDX_Control(pDX, IDC_CONFERENCE, m_cbConferenceList);
62:     DDX_FieldCBIndex(pDX, IDC_CONFERENCE, (int&)m_pSet->m_ConferenceID,
        ➥m_pSet);
63:     DDX_Control(pDX, IDC_DIVISION, m_cbDivisionList);
64:     DDX_FieldCBIndex(pDX, IDC_DIVISION, (int&)m_pSet->m_DivisionID,
        ➥m_pSet);
65: }
66:
67: void CHockeyView::OnInitialUpdate() {
68:     // Initialize the record set member variable
69:     CHockeyDoc* pDoc = GetDocument();
70:     m_pSet = &pDoc->m_teamSet;
71:     CDaoRecordView::OnInitialUpdate();
72:
73:     // Open the conference record set
74:     try {
75:         pDoc->m_conferenceSet.Open();
76:     }
77:     catch(CDaoException* e) {
78:         AfxMessageBox(e->m_pErrorInfo->m_strDescription);
79:         e->Delete();
80:         return;
81:     }
82:
83:     // Fill the conference combo box
84:     m_cbConferenceList.ResetContent();
85:     if (pDoc->m_conferenceSet.IsOpen()) {
86:         // Add an initial string to the combo box
87:         m_cbConferenceList.AddString("** CONFERENCES **");
88:
89:         while (!pDoc->m_conferenceSet.IsEOF()) {
90:             // Add the current conference name to the combo box
91:             m_cbConferenceList.AddString(pDoc-
                ➥>m_conferenceSet.m_ConferenceName);
92:
93:             // Move to the next record
94:             pDoc->m_conferenceSet.MoveNext();
```

continues

LISTING 18.12 CONTINUED

```
 95:        }
 96:     }
 97:     // Set the combo box selection to the current conference
 98:     m_cbConferenceList.SetCurSel((int)m_pSet->m_ConferenceID);
 99:
100:     // Open the division record set
101:     try {
102:        pDoc->m_divisionSet.Open();
103:     }
104:     catch(CDaoException* e) {
105:        AfxMessageBox(e->m_pErrorInfo->m_strDescription);
106:        e->Delete();
107:        return;
108:     }
109:
110:     // Fill the division combo box
111:     m_cbDivisionList.ResetContent();
112:     if (pDoc->m_divisionSet.IsOpen()) {
113:        // Add an initial string to the combo box
114:        m_cbDivisionList.AddString("** DIVISIONS **");
115:
116:        while (!pDoc->m_divisionSet.IsEOF()) {
117:           // Add the current division name to the combo box
118:           m_cbDivisionList.AddString(pDoc->m_divisionSet.m_DivisionName);
119:
120:           // Move to the next record
121:           pDoc->m_divisionSet.MoveNext();
122:        }
123:     }
124:     // Set the combo box selection to the current division
125:     m_cbDivisionList.SetCurSel((int)m_pSet->m_DivisionID);
126:
127:     // Size the view to fit the form
128:     GetParentFrame()->RecalcLayout();
129:     ResizeParentToFit();
130: }
131:
132: //----------------------------------------------------------------
133: // Message Handlers
134: //----------------------------------------------------------------
135: void CHockeyView::OnFileBest() {
136:     // Open the team record set
137:     CTeamSet teamSet;
138:     try {
139:        teamSet.Open();
140:     }
141:     catch(CDaoException* e) {
142:        AfxMessageBox(e->m_pErrorInfo->m_strDescription);
143:        e->Delete();
```

```
144:      return;
145:    }
146:
147:    // Look for the team with the most points
148:    int        curPoints, bestPoints = 0;
149:    COleVariant bookmark;
150:    if (teamSet.IsOpen())
151:      while (!teamSet.IsEOF()) {
152:        // Calculate the current team's points
153:        curPoints = teamSet.m_Wins * 2 + teamSet.m_Ties;
154:
155:        // Check to see if the current team has the most points
156:        if (curPoints > bestPoints) {
157:          // If so, then bookmark the team
158:          bestPoints = curPoints;
159:          bookmark = teamSet.GetBookmark();
160:        }
161:        teamSet.MoveNext();
162:      }
163:    // Set the current record to the last bookmarked team
164:    teamSet.SetBookmark(bookmark);
165:
166:    // Format and display the result
167:    CString sResult;
168:    sResult.Format("The %s are the best team in the NHL with %d wins, " \
169:      "%d losses, and %d ties for a total of %d points.",
170:      teamSet.m_TeamName, teamSet.m_Wins, teamSet.m_Losses,
        ➥teamSet.m_Ties,
171:      bestPoints);
172:    MessageBox(sResult);
173: }
174:
175: //-----------------------------------------------------------------
176: // Diagnostic Functions
177: //-----------------------------------------------------------------
178: #ifdef _DEBUG
179: void CHockeyView::AssertValid() const {
180:   CDaoRecordView::AssertValid();
181: }
182:
183: void CHockeyView::Dump(CDumpContext& dc) const {
184:   CDaoRecordView::Dump(dc);
185: }
186:
187: CHockeyDoc* CHockeyView::GetDocument() {
188:   ASSERT(m_pDocument->IsKindOf(RUNTIME_CLASS(CHockeyDoc)));
189:   return (CHockeyDoc*)m_pDocument;
190: }
191: #endif //_DEBUG
```

Perhaps the best place to start with the code is the constructor for `CHockeyView`, which initializes the `m_pSet` record set pointer to `NULL`. The `OnGetRecordset()` member function then returns the `m_pSet` member. Just in case you're worried about the `m_pSet` member being set to `NULL` at this point, let me assure you that it is set in the `OnInitialUpdate()` member function, which you learn about in a moment.

The `DoDataExchange()` member function is responsible for binding the view's dialog box controls with members in the `CTeamSet` record set class. Various dialog data exchange (DDX) functions are used to accomplish this task. Probably the most interesting DDX function is `DDXFieldCBIndex()`, which binds the index of a combo box to a record set ID. As long as the combo box has been properly filled from the same record set, this approach works very smoothly. The combo boxes in this case are filled in the `OnInitialUpdate()` member function.

The `OnInitialUpdate()` member function first sets the record set pointer for the view, `m_pSet`, to the `CTeamSet` object in the document. It then takes on the chore of filling the conferences and divisions combo boxes from their respective record sets in the document. The `Open()` member function is first called on the conference record set to open it. The `IsOpen()` member function is then called to make sure the record set was opened OK. `OnInitialUpdate()` then iterates through the record set using the `IsEOF()` and `MoveNext()` member functions. The conference combo box is filled during the record set iteration by adding the name of each conference to the combo box. The same process is carried out for the division record set and combo box.

The `OnFileBest()` message handler works similarly to the `OnInitialUpdate()` member function in that it iterates through a record set. However, the record set in this case is the team record set. Also, the purpose of the iteration is to determine the best team. In hockey, teams are awarded points based on their number of wins and ties. Each win is worth two points and each tie is worth one point, whereas a loss is worth nothing. The best team is the team with the most points.

The `OnFileBest()` message handler iterates through the team record set and looks for the team with the most points. It keeps track of the current best team by using a bookmark in the record set. The `GetBookmark()` member function of `CDaoRecordset` returns a bookmark for the current record. You can easily return to the record by passing the bookmark to the `SetBookmark()` member function. After determining the best team, the `OnFileBest()` message handler formats the information into a string and displays it in a message box.

Figure 18.3 shows the completed Hockey application with the current record set to my home team, the Nashville Predators.

FIGURE 18.3

Viewing a record in the Hockey application.

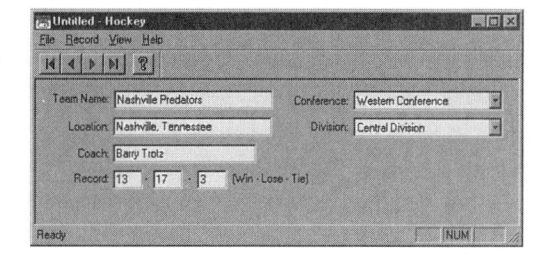

Figure 18.4 shows the Hockey application displaying information about the best team in the Hockey.mdb database.

FIGURE 18.4

Finding the best team in the Hockey application.

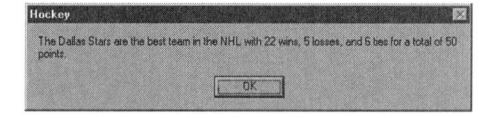

Summary

In this hour you learned about MFC database programming using Microsoft's Data Access Objects, or DAO. You began the hour by learning about two of the different approaches to database programming using MFC, including DAO. You then delved into DAO and learned about the different objects that comprise it. From there, you learned about the MFC wrapper classes that encapsulate DAO objects. You then explored the fundamentals of how a form-based DAO application is constructed using MFC's `CDaoRecordView` class. Finally, the hour concluded by leading you through the development of a complete MFC DAO application.

Q&A

Q Can I build an MFC database application that uses DAO but doesn't rely on MFC's document/view architecture?

A Absolutely. Although the `CDaoRecordView` class simplifies and helps automate the process of building database applications, you can certainly bypass it if you so desire. In fact, there might be situations where you want more flexibility in how the user interface connects to data in a database, in which case the `CDaoRecordView` class might not be the best approach. The important thing is that you can still use the MFC DAO classes and bind controls to database fields regardless of whether you use the `CDaoRecordView` class and MFC's document/view architecture.

Q Is it possible to filter a record set using the `CDaoRecordset` class?

A Yes. The `CDaoRecordset` class includes a public member variable named `m_strFilter` that can be used to filter a record set when it is initially created. Note that this member must be set prior to calling `Open()` on the record set. An example of a record set string filter is `"FirstName = 'Max'"`, which would filter a record set so that only records with the `FirstName` field set to `Max` are included in the set.

Workshop

The Workshop is designed to help you anticipate possible questions, review what you've learned, and begin thinking ahead to put your knowledge into practice. The answers to the quiz are in Appendix A, "Quiz Answers."

Quiz

1. What are the two different approaches to database development directly supported by MFC?
2. What's the difference between a Microsoft Jet database and a Microsoft Access database?
3. What type of database is best to use with DAO?
4. What is the role of the `DBEngine` object in DAO?
5. What is the role of the `Database` object in DAO?
6. What DAO object is used to represent a set of records selected from a database?
7. What MFC class is used as the basis for the user interface in form-based DAO applications?
8. What must you create in order to use record sets in a DAO application?
9. What is the purpose of the `GetDefaultDBName()` member function in `CDaoRecordSet`?
10. What is the purpose of the `OnGetRecordset()` member function of `CDaoRecordView`?

Exercises

1. After running the Hockey application, try opening the Hockey.mdb database in Microsoft Access to examine the table data. Now modify some of the data and run the application again to see the changes. Keep in mind that you can also modify the database using the Hockey application; record changes are written when you move to another record.

2. Add a File, Worst menu command that finds the worst team in the database. Be sure to add a menu command identifier, a message map entry for the message handler, and then write the code for the message handler itself.

HOUR 19

ADO and the Future of Databases

This hour takes a step back from the details and examines the different approaches to MFC database programming. More specifically, you learn about ActiveX Data Objects (ADO), which in many ways represent the future of database development for both MFC and Microsoft technologies in general. Although DAO is certainly a powerful and useful technology, as you learned in the previous hour, ADO represents the path that Microsoft is steering database developers toward.

In this hour, you will learn

- How ADO fits into the big picture of Microsoft's database interfaces
- What ADO has to offer
- About the ADO Data control
- How ADO can be used from MFC

Getting a Handle on the Big Picture

Before you learn about ActiveX Data Objects (ADO) in particular, it's important to get a perspective on Microsoft's database technologies as a whole. If you look at all the different database technologies offered by Microsoft, you might wonder why there are so many and why should you use one instead of another. It's not hard to get seriously confused when trying to sort out the different technologies.

Microsoft's entry into the database interface market began a few years back with the DB-Library interface for Visual Basic, which is also known as VBSQL. A steady stream of database interfaces has popped up since then, culminating in the latest interface, OLE DB. The good news is that each new database interface has added features not present in earlier ones. The bad news is that each interface presents a new learning curve and a new approach to accessing data.

The whole reason for having database interfaces is to make it easier for application developers to access information in a database. This keeps developers from having to deal with the specifics of different native database formats. Each subsequent database interface released by Microsoft helped to address a range of issues confronting application developers. At some point, however, Microsoft realized that they were spreading themselves thin with too many different interfaces. Consequently, they decided to work on a uniform database interface that would encompass the majority of the functionality found in all their previous database interfaces.

Following is a list of all Microsoft's database interfaces that have popped up over the past few years:

- VBSQL—Visual Basic SQL (Structured Query Language)
- ODBC—Open Database Connectivity
- DAO—Data Access Objects
- RDO—Remote Data Objects
- OLE DB—OLE Database (OLE stands for Object Linking and Embedding)
- ADO—ActiveX Data Objects

The next few sections discuss each of these database interfaces and give you some perspective regarding their relevance in Microsoft's grand database scheme.

VBSQL

VBSQL (Visual Basic SQL) is a C-based database interface designed for accessing Microsoft SQL Server databases. VBSQL exposed a set of C API (Application Programming Interface) functions to Visual Basic so that Visual Basic developers could access SQL Server databases. The obvious limitation of VBSQL is that it can only be used to access SQL Server databases. Microsoft is quickly abandoning VBSQL and doesn't plan to support it as of SQL Server version 7.0.

ODBC

ODBC (Open Database Connectivity) is a very popular database interface standard that can be used to access any relational database with an ODBC driver. ODBC defines a common C-based API that is used to access a database regardless of the underlying database format. The specific details of interacting with an underlying database are forced on the ODBC driver, which must fully support the ODBC API. ODBC works quite well at supporting a variety of different databases because of the abstraction between the generic ODBC API and the specific underlying database. Keep in mind, however, that ODBC is only for relational databases.

Aside from being limited to relational databases, ODBC is also fairly complex from a coding perspective. The ODBC API actually contains fewer functions than VBSQL, but the functions in the ODBC API require complex arguments. Consequently, developing a large database application using the ODBC API is relatively difficult. Even so, ODBC is still the most widely used means of accessing data in relational databases, simply because it is so flexible.

DAO

Unlike VBSQL and ODBC, DAO (Data Access Objects) presents an object-based interface for accessing databases. In other words, DAO relies on objects instead of functions to provide database access. DAO is designed specifically for use with Microsoft's Jet database engine, which is the engine used by Microsoft Access. You can also access ODBC databases through DAO but there is a performance hit because the databases are accessed through an ODBC layer.

The main benefit offered by DAO is ease of use. As you learned in the previous hour, MFC fully supports DAO and includes special classes for accessing databases using DAO. The capability of binding controls to database fields significantly improves the process of building database applications. Consequently, DAO has caught on and is now one of the most widely used object-based database interfaces. DAO is used even more in Visual Basic than in Visual C++, which accounts largely for its popularity.

RDO

RDO (Remote Data Objects) is similar to DAO in that it is an object-based interface for accessing databases. However, RDO is designed solely as an interface to ODBC and doesn't include direct support for Jet databases. Although RDO generally is as easy to use as DAO, it is somewhat limited because it can only be used to access relational databases through ODBC drivers. On the other hand, RDO offers support for more advanced database features such as stored procedures and complex result sets. As such, RDO has enjoyed popularity as a database interface for developers building complex database applications.

OLE DB

OLE DB (OLE Database) is one of Microsoft's latest object-based interfaces designed for universal data access. As a universal database interface, OLE DB is not limited to relational databases or any specific database format, for that matter. Unlike RDO and DAO, however, OLE DB is a low-level database interface, which means that it is difficult to use in application development. In fact, you can't even access OLE DB directly from Visual Basic. You could certainly use OLE DB directly in an MFC database application if you wanted, but there's a good reason not to. This reason is ADO (ActiveX Data Objects), which is a high-level database interface built on top of OLE DB.

ADO

ADO (ActiveX Data Objects) is an object-based interface built on top of OLE DB. The purpose of ADO is to provide a high-level interface to functionality offered by OLE DB. More specifically, ADO provides an interface similar to DAO that is based on the universal data access features of OLE DB. In many ways ADO represents the best of both worlds; a clean, relatively easy to use object-based interface that is capable of accessing any type of data.

The Benefits of ADO

As you learned in the previous section, ADO provides an object-based interface to accessing databases using OLE DB. OLE DB is a low-level interface that provides high-performance universal access to any data source. ADO consists of a set of objects that greatly simplify the development of database applications. Typical database operations such as connecting to a database and retrieving record sets are very straightforward to carry out using ADO.

> Examples of OLE DB data sources include both relational and non-relational databases, as well as email and file systems.

ADO grew out of a need for a broad approach to accessing data, which is due to the fact that the concept of an "application" has changed in the past couple of years. Applications now include both traditional standalone applications and Web-based applications that reside in Web pages. Web-based database applications require very extensible components that can be referenced from Web pages and manipulated with scripting languages. Of course, these same components must also be usable in traditional standalone database applications. ADO fits both of these requirements, and is designed to be somewhat of an all-encompassing database solution.

The primary benefits of ADO follow:

- High speed
- Relative ease of use
- Simplified object hierarchy
- Low overhead
- Small disk storage requirements

To get an idea about how important ADO is to Microsoft, consider the products that currently include ADO:

- Internet Information Server 4.0
- Internet Explorer 4.0
- Visual Studio
- Visual Basic
- Visual InterDev
- Visual C++

Additionally, Microsoft Office 2000 is expected to fully support ADO.

Digging into ADO Objects

ADO is very extensible because it is based on ActiveX, which is widely supported in both visual development tools and many end-user applications. The ADO object model consists of a set of ActiveX objects that represent different elements of a database. Table 19.1 contains a list of the objects that comprise ADO.

TABLE 19.1 THE OBJECTS THAT COMPRISE ADO

Object	Description
Connection	A connection to a data source
Recordset	A record set
Property	An ADO object attribute
Properties	All of the `Property` objects associated with an ADO object
Field	A column of data in a record set
Fields	All the `Field` objects associated with a `Recordset` object
Command	A SQL statement
Parameter	A parameter of a SQL statement
Parameters	All the `Parameter` objects associated with a `Command` object
Error	A database connection error
Errors	All of the `Error` objects associated with a single database connection failure

Figure 19.1 shows the relationship between the objects in the ADO object model.

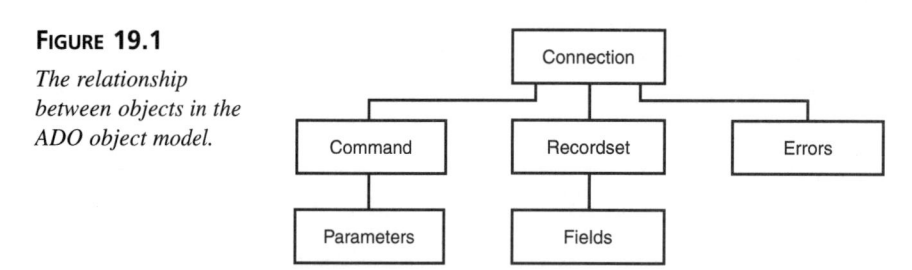

FIGURE 19.1

The relationship between objects in the ADO object model.

Although the ADO objects themselves are fairly self-explanatory, it doesn't hurt to consider the practical usage of each. Following is an example of a hypothetical database session that demonstrates the usage of some of the different ADO objects:

1. Make a connection to a data source using the `Connection` object.
2. Create a SQL command using the `Command` object.
3. Specify columns, tables, and field values in the SQL command using the `Parameter` object.
4. Execute the SQL command to obtain a `Recordset` object.

5. Sort, filter, and navigate through the data using the `Recordset` object.
6. Add, delete, or change rows and columns of data using the `Recordset` object.
7. Update the data source using the `Recordset` object.
8. Close the database connection using the `Connection` object.

Each ADO object defines member functions that you can use to carry out certain operations. For example, the `Connection` object provides an `Open()` member function that is used to open a connection to a database. There is also an `Execute()` member function that is used to execute SQL commands.

The `Recordset` object also contains some member functions that you'll find familiar. The `MoveNext()`, `MovePrevious()`, `MoveFirst()`, and `MoveLast()` member functions are used to navigate through records in a record set.

The ADO Data Control

To make ADO even easier to use, Microsoft offers an ADO Data control that encapsulates the functionality required to open a database and retrieve record sets using ADO. Using a visual development tool such as Visual C++, you can easily bind a data-aware control to the ADO Data control and build a database application with no coding. Granted, that's not really in the scope of this book, but it's still a powerful concept. Keep in mind that you can use ADO objects directly in an application to access a database, but the ADO Data control has the advantage of providing graphical navigational support.

> Data-aware ActiveX controls include Microsoft's `DataList`, `DataCombo`, and `DataGrid` controls, among others. These controls all include a `DataSource` property that must be set to the ID of the ADO Data control. Data-aware controls know how to retrieve data from a database and display it, which makes them quite powerful.

Even if you don't want to use a visual development tool, you can still utilize the ADO Data control to put ADO to work in your own MFC applications. In this case you would want to create an MFC wrapper class around the ADO Data control to make it easier to work with the control in MFC code. You manipulate the ADO Data control through its properties, some of which are listed in Table 19.2.

TABLE 19.2 SOME OF THE MOST IMPORTANT ADO DATA CONTROL PROPERTIES

Object	Description
ConnectionString	Connection settings
RecordSource	The SQL statement or query that is used to obtain a record set
UserName	The name of the user accessing the database
Password	The database password (if the database is password-protected)
Recordset	The record set returned by a SQL statement or query

The `ConnectionString` ADO Data control property is used to set connection settings such as the data provider and the database file name. The `RecordSource` property contains a SQL statement or query that is executed on the database to retrieve a record set, which is represented by the `Recordset` property. You can set the `ConnectionString` and `RecordSource` properties at design-time or dynamically at runtime.

ADO and MFC

So far this hour hasn't talked too much about how ADO relates to MFC. That's mainly because there is no direct relationship between ADO and MFC. Because ADO is implemented as a set of ActiveX objects, it is compatible with C++ by default. However, ADO objects are not implemented using MFC classes, and therefore aren't as straightforward to use in MFC code as the DAO MFC classes.

There are two main approaches to using ADO in an MFC application:

1. Use the ADO Data control in a form-based application.
2. Directly use the ADO objects through MFC wrapper classes.

The first approach involves embedding an ADO Data control in the dialog box for a form-based application. You will also want to connect the ADO control to a data-aware control such as the `DataList`, `DataCombo`, or `DataGrid` controls. This approach requires you to use a visual dialog editor because the ADO Data control has properties that must be set for the control to work properly. You also will more than likely need to use an MFC wrapper class around the ADO control to facilitate calling its member functions.

The second approach to using ADO involves MFC wrapper classes around each of the ADO objects. In this case, each ADO object would have a corresponding MFC class that you would use to access a database. The MFC wrapper classes for ADO objects would be similar in function to the MFC wrapper classes for DAO that you saw in the previous hour.

Both ADO approaches require you to use wrapper classes, which don't ship with ADO or MFC. However, you can use a visual development environment such as Visual C++ to generate MFC wrapper classes around ADO objects and the ADO Data control. This is somewhat beyond the scope of this book, however, so I'll let that be something for you to explore on your own.

Summary

This hour continued with the discussion of databases by introducing you to ADO, ActiveX Data Objects. You began the hour by learning how ADO fits into the grand scheme of Microsoft's database interface technologies. You then moved on to uncover the benefits of ADO, one of which is the ADO Data control. Finally, you wrapped up the hour by learning how to access ADO from within MFC applications.

Q&A

Q Why can't you use ADO objects directly in MFC code?

A Actually you can, but because ActiveX objects are structured differently than MFC classes, it isn't as straightforward as you might think. Keep in mind that ActiveX is programming language-independent, which means that there is nothing inherent in ActiveX that makes it usable in C++ or MFC. ActiveX is accessible from C++ and MFC using special interfaces that are in fact accessible from many different programming languages. The drawback is that the code is a little messier when working directly with ActiveX objects in MFC, which is why wrapper classes are helpful.

Q How do I generate wrapper classes around ADO objects?

A In Visual C++, you can do this using the Components and Controls Gallery, which is displayed when you add a component or control to a project.

Workshop

The Workshop is designed to help you anticipate possible questions, review what you've learned, and begin thinking ahead to put your knowledge into practice. The answers to the quiz are in Appendix A, "Quiz Answers."

Quiz

1. What is the name and purpose of Microsoft's first entry into the database interface market?
2. What kinds of databases can be accessed using ODBC?
3. How is DAO different from VBSQL and ODBC?
4. Why would you not want to use OLE DB directly in an MFC database application?
5. What are some examples of OLE DB data sources?
6. What ADO object is used to issue SQL commands?
7. What is the purpose of the `Field` ADO object?
8. What member functions are used to navigate through records in an ADO `Recordset` object?
9. What is the purpose of the `ConnectionString` ADO Data control property?
10. What is the advantage of using the ADO Data control over ADO objects?

Exercises

1. Open the documentation to ADO and take a look at the documentation for the different objects within ADO. Take note of the member functions provided by each object and the similarities they share with their DAO counterparts. This will give you an idea as to how similar the two technologies are from a usage perspective. Just keep in mind that ADO is much more extensible.
2. Use a visual dialog editor to insert an ADO Data control in a dialog box. Examine the properties of the control and then try wiring the control to a data-aware control.

HOUR 20

Connecting to the Web

As increasing numbers of individuals and businesses continue to connect to the Internet, it will become more important for applications to use the Web as an information source. Many applications such as Microsoft's Office Suite are already Web-enabled, which means that they understand how to connect to the Web and view Web content. This hour explores a feature of MFC that supports the viewing of Web content, and shows you how to build a simple Web browser application.

In this hour, you will learn

- The basics of Web-enabled applications
- About MFC's support for viewing Web content
- How to build a simple Web browser application

Understanding Web-Enabled Applications

A Web-enabled application is an application that somehow utilizes or generates Web content. Typically a Web-enabled application will support the viewing of Web pages that provide supplemental information related to the application. Microsoft Office applications are Web-enabled in that they enable you to open and view Web pages within them. As an example, you can embed hyperlinks in Word documents and use them to navigate and open Web pages.

A more extreme example of a Web-enabled application is Microsoft Money, which uses a Web page as its main application user interface. The Money toolbar provides familiar Web navigation commands such as forward and back. The neat thing about Money is that it displays financial news and information from the Web, and enables you to view Web pages directly in the Money application window. You can easily navigate between your Money financial data and news headlines from the Web. Figure 20.1 shows the Microsoft Money application and its Web-based user interface.

FIGURE 20.1

The Microsoft Money application and its Web-based user interface.

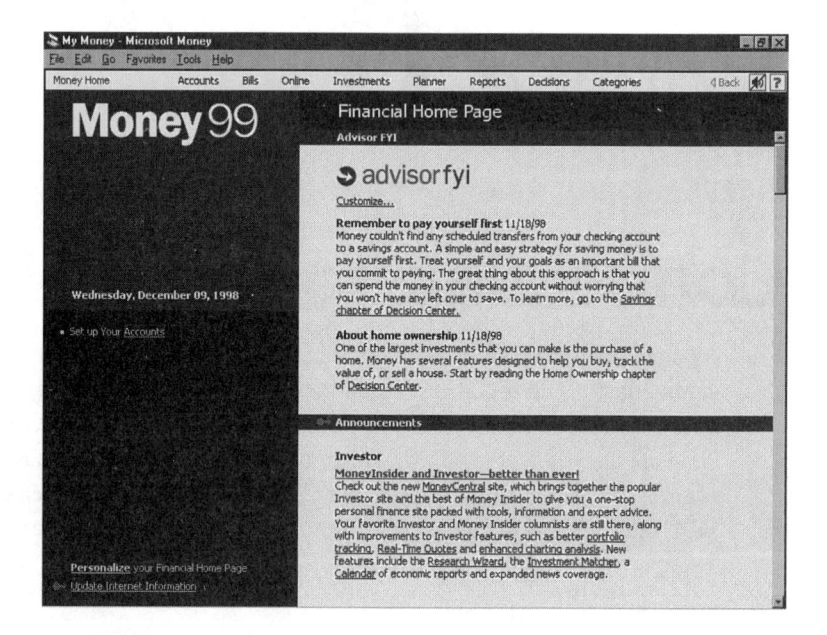

> Just so you'll know, Microsoft Office applications became Web-enabled as of the release of Office 97. Microsoft Money picked up its Web-based functionality in Money 98.

For the record, this isn't a product pitch for Microsoft Money; I just think that Money takes a particularly interesting approach to its support for Web content. You can expect to start seeing more applications take this approach as users come to expect up-to-the-minute news and information via the Web.

Your own applications will likely vary in their need to support Web content. In fact, many applications don't benefit at all from being Web-enabled. However, I encourage you to consider adding Web support if you think there is any way it might improve the usefulness of an application. It is surprisingly easy to integrate Web browsing capabilities into your own applications. Let's start learning how!

The WebBrowser Control

As of Internet Explorer 3.0, Microsoft moved the functionality of viewing Web content into an ActiveX control called WebBrowser. Internet Explorer itself uses this control as the basis for viewing Web pages. Because the Web functionality of Internet Explorer is encapsulated in the WebBrowser control, you can add full Web support to your own applications by simply using the WebBrowser control. The WebBrowser control supports viewing Web page content, browsing Web sites, and downloading raw data from the Internet.

Keep in mind that you always have the option of launching Internet Explorer, Netscape Communicator, or some other Web browser from within an application. However, it can be disruptive to the user to have to switch back and forth between a browser application and your application. The WebBrowser control brings Web browser functionality into your applications.

The WebBrowser control can display Web pages containing any of the following features:

- Standard HTML documents, as well as HTML enhancements such as floating frames and cascading style sheets
- Multimedia content, such as video and audio
- Java applets
- Scripts written in scripting languages such as VBScript or JavaScript
- Most Netscape Communicator plug-ins
- Other ActiveX controls
- 3D virtual worlds created in VRML (Virtual Reality Modeling Language)

> Although HTML documents are certainly the main focus of the WebBrowser control, they aren't the only game in town. The WebBrowser control can actually open any Active Document, which includes most Microsoft Office documents. For example, the WebBrowser control can be used to open and edit Microsoft Excel spreadsheets, Microsoft Word documents, and Microsoft PowerPoint presentations, provided Microsoft Office is installed on the user's system.

Like Internet Explorer, the `WebBrowser` control maintains a history list that keeps track of the Web pages a user has accessed. You can navigate through the history list using back and forward member functions of the `WebBrowser` control. You can also navigate to the default home page that is set in Internet Explorer.

An HTML View

The `WebBrowser` control sounds great, but how does it impact MFC? You'll be glad to know that MFC provides a really convenient class that encapsulates the `WebBrowser` control and integrates it with MFC's document/view architecture. I'm referring to the `CHtmlView` control, which implements a view class that contains a `WebBrowser` control. The `CHtmlView` class is derived from `CView`, and can be used like any other MFC view class to implement a Web-based application using the document/view architecture.

Applications that use the `CHtmlView` class will effectively have a Web browser window anywhere the view is used. You could use the view as a pane within a splitter window to include browser support in addition to some other view, or you could make it the main application view and effectively create your own Web browser application.

Using the `CHtmlView` Class

The `CHtmlView` class is extremely automated and therefore very easy to use. The class is declared in the standard MFC header file AfxHTML.h, which you must include in any source code files that utilize `CHtmlView`. Table 20.1 lists some of the most commonly used member functions in the `CHtmlView` class.

TABLE 20.1 THE MOST COMMONLY USED `CHtmlView` MEMBER FUNCTIONS

Member Function	Description
`Navigate()`	Navigates to a Web page identified by a URL
`Navigate2()`	Navigates to a Web page identified by a URL, or to a file identified by a file path
`GoHome()`	Navigates to Internet Explorer's default home Web page
`GoSearch()`	Navigates to Internet Explorer's default search Web page
`GoBack()`	Navigates to the previous Web page in the history list
`GoForward()`	Navigates to the next Web page in the history list
`Stop()`	Stops loading the current Web page
`Refresh()`	Reloads the current Web page
`GetBusy()`	Checks to see if a Web page is still being loaded

The first two member functions in the table are the only ones that require parameters. Following are the function prototypes for the `Navigate()` and `Navigate2()` member functions:

```
void Navigate(LPCTSTR lpszURL, DWORD dwFlags = 0,
  LPCTSTR lpszTargetFrameName = NULL, LPCTSTR lpszHeaders = NULL,
  LPVOID lpvPostData = NULL, DWORD dwPostDataLen = 0);
void Navigate2(LPCTSTR lpszURL, DWORD dwFlags = 0,
  LPCTSTR lpszTargetFrameName = NULL, LPCTSTR lpszHeaders = NULL,
  LPVOID lpvPostData = NULL, DWORD dwPostDataLen = 0);
```

As you can see, these functions take the exact same list of parameters. The first parameter to each function is a string identifying a URL, or in the case of `Navigate2()` it could also specify a file path. The second parameter is a navigation constant that determines how the Web page or file is opened. Table 20.2 lists the navigation constants supported by these functions.

TABLE 20.2 THE NAVIGATION CONSTANTS USED BY THE `Navigate()` AND `Navigate2()` MEMBER FUNCTIONS

Navigation Constant	Description
`navOpenInNewWindow`	Opens the URL/file in a new instance of Internet Explorer
`navNoHistory`	Opens the URL/file but doesn't add it to the navigation history list
`navAllowAutosearch`	Specifies that an automatic search should be performed if the URL/document isn't found; this search consists of appending common root domains to the URL or file path
`navBrowserBar`	Opens the URL/file using the current Internet Explorer browser bar

The remaining parameters to the `Navigate()` and `Navigate2()` member functions are used much less frequently than the first two. The vast majority of the time you will simply use their default values. Let's move on and take a look at an example of the `Navigate()` member function, which should help clarify its usage. Following is a line of code that navigates to my Web site using the `Navigate()` member function:

```
Navigate("http://www.thetribe.com/");
```

If for some reason you wanted to open the URL in a new instance of Internet Explorer, you would use the following code:

```
Navigate("http://www.thetribe.com/", navOpenInNewWindow);
```

Don't forget about the other member functions provided by the `CHtmlView` class. To stop loading a Web page you can call the `Stop()` member function, like this:

`Stop();`

Likewise, you can refresh a Web page with a simple call to the `Refresh()` member function:

`Refresh();`

You can also navigate backward or forward in the history list using the `GoBack()` and `GoForward()` member functions, as well as go to the default Internet Explorer home and search pages by calling `GoHome()` and `GoSearch()`, respectively.

For Internet Explorer Only

It's important to note that the `WebBrowser` control is a major part of the Internet Explorer application. Consequently, there are member functions defined in the control that only apply to Internet Explorer. This means that you shouldn't use these member functions in your own applications because they won't do anything. These member functions can also be found in the `CHtmlView` class. Following are the member functions in the `CHtmlView` class that are only for use in Internet Explorer:

- `GetFullName()`
- `GetAddressBar()`
- `SetAddressBar()`
- `GetStatusBar()`
- `SetStatusBar()`
- `SetFullScreen()`
- `SetMenuBar()`
- `SetToolBar()`

You are certainly free to call any of these functions in your own applications, but they will have no noticeable effect.

Building a Simple Web Browser

Because you now understand the ins and outs of the `CHtmlView` class, it only makes sense to put it through its paces in a real application. How about building a simple Web browser from scratch? I knew you'd be excited! The remainder of the hour focuses on the construction of the BrowseIt application, which relies heavily on the `CHtmlView` class and serves as a simple Web browser. The BrowseIt application is built upon the familiar SkeletonDV document/view application that you developed earlier in the book.

As you learned earlier in the hour, the `CHtmlView` class is declared in the AfxHTML.h header file, which must be added to the BrowseIt application's StdAfx.h header file. Listing 20.1 contains the new code for this header file.

LISTING 20.1 THE STDAFX.H HEADER FILE FOR BROWSEIT

```
 1: #ifndef __STDAFX_H__
 2: #define __STDAFX_H__
 3:
 4: //-----------------------------------------------------------------
 5: // Inclusions
 6: //-----------------------------------------------------------------
 7: #include <AfxWin.h>
 8: #include <AfxExt.h>
 9: #include <AfXHTML.h>
10:
11: #endif
```

Resources

Because the BrowseIt application is a Web browser, it makes sense to provide some of the familiar browser commands such as Stop, Refresh, Back, Forward, and Home. Listing 20.2 contains the menu resource definition for BrowseIt, which includes these menu commands.

LISTING 20.2 THE MENU RESOURCE DEFINITION FOR BROWSEIT

```
 1: IDR_BROWSEIT MENU
 2: BEGIN
 3:   POPUP "&File"
 4:   BEGIN
 5:     MENUITEM "E&xit",                ID_APP_EXIT
 6:   END
 7:   POPUP "&View"
 8:   BEGIN
 9:     MENUITEM "&Stop",                ID_VIEW_STOP
10:     MENUITEM "&Refresh",             ID_VIEW_REFRESH
11:     MENUITEM SEPARATOR
12:     MENUITEM "&Toolbar",             ID_VIEW_TOOLBAR
13:     MENUITEM "&Status Bar",          ID_VIEW_STATUS_BAR
14:   END
15:   POPUP "&Go"
16:   BEGIN
```

continues

LISTING 20.2 CONTINUED

```
17:        MENUITEM "&Back",              ID_GO_BACK
18:        MENUITEM "&Forward",           ID_GO_FORWARD
19:        MENUITEM SEPARATOR
20:        MENUITEM "&Home",              ID_GO_HOME
21:    END
22:    POPUP "&Help"
23:    BEGIN
24:        MENUITEM "&About Browse It...", ID_APP_ABOUT
25:    END
26: END
```

You might also notice that the BrowseIt menu includes a View popup menu for showing and hiding a toolbar and status bar. Speaking of toolbars, the BrowseIt toolbar needs to include the basic browser commands you just learned about. As you learned in Hour 15, "Utilizing Control Bars," a toolbar requires a special bitmap that contains the individual button images. Figure 20.2 shows a zoomed view of the toolbar bitmap image for the BrowseIt application.

FIGURE 20.2

A zoomed view of the toolbar bitmap image for BrowseIt.

Each individual button image in the toolbar image is 20∞20 pixels, which is larger than the standard 16∞15 size you used in the Doodle application. However, this is perfectly acceptable as long as you specify the larger size in the toolbar resource definition. Listing 20.3 contains the toolbar resource for the BrowseIt application.

LISTING 20.3 THE TOOLBAR RESOURCE DEFINITION FOR BROWSEIT

```
1: IDR_BROWSEIT TOOLBAR  20, 20
2: BEGIN
3:     BUTTON     ID_GO_BACK
4:     BUTTON     ID_GO_FORWARD
5:     BUTTON     ID_GO_HOME
6:     SEPARATOR
7:     BUTTON     ID_VIEW_STOP
8:     BUTTON     ID_VIEW_REFRESH
9: END
```

Don't forget that the toolbar image, ToolBar.bmp, must be included as a bitmap resource in the resource script for BrowseIt:

```
IDR_BROWSEIT BITMAP    "ToolBar.bmp"
```

That squares away the toolbar for BrowseIt, but you still need to do a little work for the status bar. Remember help messages? Help messages are those little text messages that are displayed in the status bar when the user selects a menu item. Listing 20.4 contains the string resources for the BrowseIt application's status bar help messages.

LISTING 20.4 THE HELP MESSAGE STRING RESOURCE DEFINITIONS FOR BROWSEIT'S STATUS BAR

```
 1: STRINGTABLE
 2: BEGIN
 3:     ID_APP_EXIT             "Quit the application\nExit"
 4:
 5:     ID_VIEW_STOP            "Stop loading the current Web page\nStop"
 6:     ID_VIEW_REFRESH         "Refresh the current Web page\nRefresh"
 7:
 8:     ID_GO_BACK              "Navigate back to a Web page\nGo Back"
 9:     ID_GO_FORWARD           "Navigate forward to a Web page\nGo Forward"
10:     ID_GO_HOME              "Go to the default home Web page\nGo Home"
11: END
```

Notice that the help messages for BrowseIt include support for ToolTips. This adds a nice touch to the graphical user interface of the application, and finishes up the resource requirements for BrowseIt.

The View

The real work of the BrowseIt application takes place in the view class. Fortunately for us, the CHtmlView class does most of this work. The CBrowseItView class derives from CHtmlView and primarily responds to menu commands only. Listing 20.5 contains the code for the BrowseItView.h header file.

LISTING 20.5 THE BROWSEITVIEW.H HEADER FILE FOR BROWSEIT

```
1: #ifndef __BROWSEITVIEW_H__
2: #define __BROWSEITVIEW_H__
3:
4: //----------------------------------------------------------------
5: // CBrowseItView Class - BrowseIt Document Object
6: //----------------------------------------------------------------
7: class CBrowseItView : public CHtmlView {
8:     // Public Constructor(s)/Destructor
```

continues

LISTING 20.5 CONTINUED

```
 9:  public:
10:                      CBrowseItView();
11:      virtual         ~CBrowseItView();
12:
13:      // Public Member Functions
14:  public:
15:      CBrowseItDoc*  GetDocument();
16:      virtual void   OnInitialUpdate();
17:
18:      // Diagnostic Functions
19:  public:
20:  #ifdef _DEBUG
21:      virtual void   AssertValid() const;
22:      virtual void   Dump(CDumpContext& dc) const;
23:  #endif //_DEBUG
24:
25:      // Message Handlers
26:  public:
27:      afx_msg void   OnViewStop();
28:      afx_msg void   OnViewRefresh();
29:      afx_msg void   OnGoBack();
30:      afx_msg void   OnGoForward();
31:      afx_msg void   OnGoHome();
32:      afx_msg void   OnUpdateViewStop(CCmdUI* pCmdUI);
33:
34:      // Message Map & Runtime Support
35:  protected:
36:      DECLARE_MESSAGE_MAP()
37:      DECLARE_DYNCREATE(CBrowseItView)
38:  };
39:
40:  #ifndef _DEBUG
41:  inline CBrowseItDoc* CBrowseItView::GetDocument() {
42:      return (CBrowseItDoc*)m_pDocument;
43:  }
44:  #endif //_DEBUG
45:
46:  #endif
```

As you can see, the `CBrowseItView` class overrides the `OnInitialUpdate()` member function and provides a group of message handlers for handling the browser menu command messages. Listing 20.6 contains the implementation of the `CBrowseItView` class.

LISTING 20.6 THE BROWSEITVIEW.CPP SOURCE CODE FILE FOR BROWSEIT

```
1:  //-----------------------------------------------------------------
2:  // Inclusions
3:  //-----------------------------------------------------------------
```

```
 4: #include "StdAfx.h"
 5: //----------------------------------------------------------------
 6: #include "BrowseItDoc.h"
 7: #include "BrowseItView.h"
 8: #include "Resource.h"
 9:
10: //----------------------------------------------------------------
11: // MFC Debugging Support
12: //----------------------------------------------------------------
13: #ifdef _DEBUG
14: #undef THIS_FILE
15: static char BASED_CODE THIS_FILE[] = __FILE__;
16: #endif
17:
18:
19: //----------------------------------------------------------------
20: // Message Map & Runtime Support
21: //----------------------------------------------------------------
22: BEGIN_MESSAGE_MAP(CBrowseItView, CHtmlView)
23:    ON_COMMAND(ID_VIEW_STOP, OnViewStop)
24:    ON_COMMAND(ID_VIEW_REFRESH, OnViewRefresh)
25:    ON_COMMAND(ID_GO_BACK, OnGoBack)
26:    ON_COMMAND(ID_GO_FORWARD, OnGoForward)
27:    ON_COMMAND(ID_GO_HOME, OnGoHome)
28:    ON_UPDATE_COMMAND_UI(ID_VIEW_STOP, OnUpdateViewStop)
29: END_MESSAGE_MAP()
30:
31: IMPLEMENT_DYNCREATE(CBrowseItView, CHtmlView)
32:
33: //----------------------------------------------------------------
34: // Public Constructor(s)/Destructor
35: //----------------------------------------------------------------
36: CBrowseItView::CBrowseItView() {
37: }
38:
39: CBrowseItView::~CBrowseItView() {
40: }
41:
42: //----------------------------------------------------------------
43: // Public Member Functions
44: //----------------------------------------------------------------
45: void CBrowseItView::OnInitialUpdate() {
46:    CHtmlView::OnInitialUpdate();
47:    Navigate("http://www.sincity.com/");
48: }
49:
50: //----------------------------------------------------------------
51: // Message Handlers
52: //----------------------------------------------------------------
53: void CBrowseItView::OnViewStop() {
54:    // Stop loading the current Web page
```

continues

LISTING 20.6   CONTINUED

```
55:    Stop();
56:  }
57:
58: void CBrowseItView::OnViewRefresh() {
59:    // Refresh the current Web page
60:    Refresh();
61:  }
62:
63: void CBrowseItView::OnGoBack() {
64:    // Navigate back to a Web page
65:    GoBack();
66:  }
67:
68: void CBrowseItView::OnGoForward() {
69:    // Navigate forward to a Web page
70:    GoForward();
71:  }
72:
73: void CBrowseItView::OnGoHome() {
74:    // Navigate to the default home Web page
75:    GoHome();
76:  }
77:
78: void CBrowseItView::OnUpdateViewStop(CCmdUI* pCmdUI) {
79:    // Update the View¦Stop menu item
80:    pCmdUI->Enable(GetBusy());
81:  }
82:
83: //-----------------------------------------------------------------
84: // Diagnostic Functions
85: //-----------------------------------------------------------------
86: #ifdef _DEBUG
87: void CBrowseItView::AssertValid() const {
88:    CHtmlView::AssertValid();
89:  }
90:
91: void CBrowseItView::Dump(CDumpContext& dc) const {
92:    CHtmlView::Dump(dc);
93:  }
94:
95: CBrowseItDoc* CBrowseItView::GetDocument() {
96:    ASSERT(m_pDocument->IsKindOf(RUNTIME_CLASS(CBrowseItDoc)));
97:    return (CBrowseItDoc*)m_pDocument;
98:  }
99: #endif //_DEBUG
```

If you recall, the `OnInitialUpdate()` member function is called by the framework when a view is first created. This gives you a great opportunity to perform any special view initialization tasks. In the case of `CBrowseItView`, the `Navigate()` member function is called to navigate to an initial Web site.

The `OnViewStop()`, `OnViewRefresh()`, `OnGoBack()`, `OnGoForward()`, and `OnGoHome()` member functions are very straightforward in that they each call one of the `CHtmlView` browser member functions you learned about earlier in the hour. The one interesting message handler is `OnUpdateViewStop()`, which enables the View, Stop menu command based on the status of the current Web page. The `GetBusy()` member function is called to see if the application is busy loading the page. If so, the View, Stop menu command is enabled; otherwise it is disabled.

I encourage you to spend some time tinkering with the BrowseIt application because it really does give you an incredible amount of functionality for a relatively small amount of development effort. Figure 20.3 shows the BrowseIt application upon startup after it navigates to the Sin City Web site.

FIGURE 20.3

The BrowseIt application with the Sin City Web site displayed.

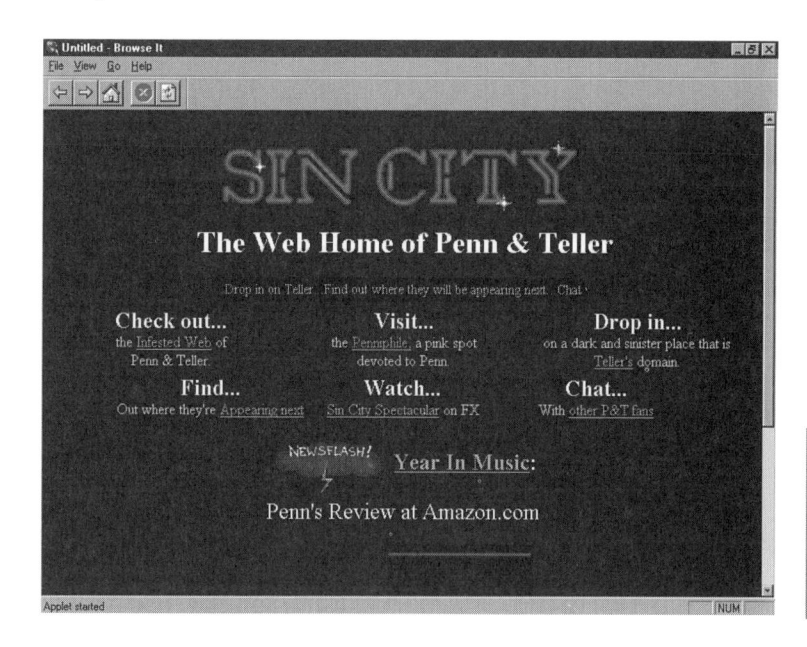

Before you get worried about the Sin City Web site, let me assure you that it's not quite what it sounds like. It's actually the Web home of the magic duo Penn and Teller, and is a really cool site. Getting back to BrowseIt, clicking the Go Home button results in the application navigating to the default Internet Explorer Web site, which on my computer happens to be the default Microsoft MSN site. Figure 20.4 shows the BrowseIt application with Microsoft's default home page displayed.

FIGURE 20.4

The BrowseIt application with Microsoft's default home page displayed.

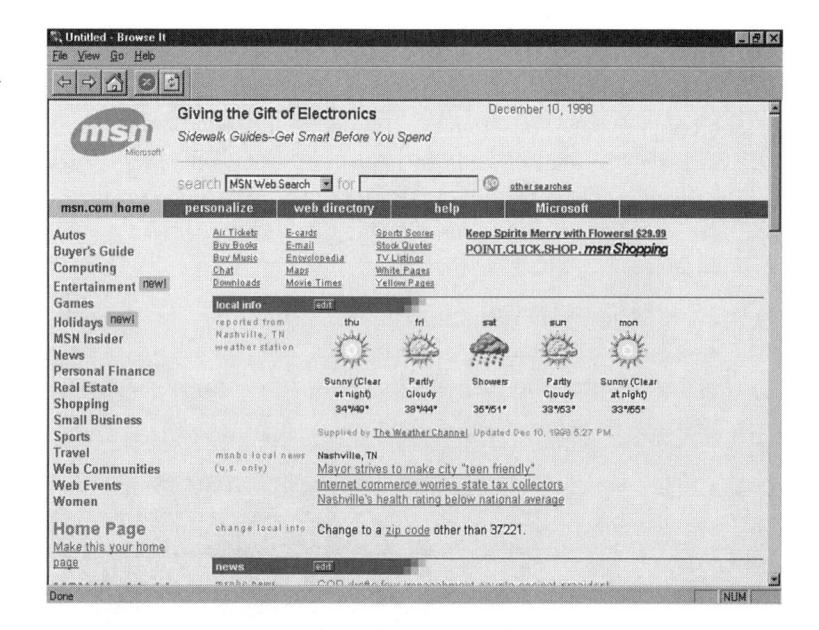

Summary

This hour expanded your MFC repertoire by introducing you to the `CHtmlView` class and showing you how to build a Web-enabled application. You began the hour by learning the basics of Web-enabled applications. You then moved on to learning about Internet Explorer's `WebBrowser` control and the `CHtmlView` MFC class. From there, you wrapped up the hour by building a simple Web browser called BrowseIt. I hope you are as surprised as I was about how easy it is to interact with the Web using MFC.

Q&A

Q What is the role of the document object in an application that uses the `CHtmlView` class as the basis for its view?

A Really nothing. Although you are required to provide a document for purposes of complying with the document/view architecture, the document object in an application that uses `CHtmlView` doesn't necessarily maintain any document data. On the other hand, you might want to build a specialized application that somehow is limited to navigating Web pages on an intranet, for example, in which case you might use the document object to store URLs for the pages.

Q Can I load a Web page from a resource using the `CHtmlView` class?

A Yes. There is an HTML resource type that is used to define Web page resources. You basically associate a URL string with an identifier and use HTML as the resource type. Instead of calling the `Navigate()` or `Navigate2()` member functions, you call the `LoadFromResource()` member function to load the Web page using its resource identifier.

Workshop

The Workshop is designed to help you anticipate possible questions, review what you've learned, and begin thinking ahead to put your knowledge into practice. The answers to the quiz are in Appendix A, "Quiz Answers."

Quiz

1. What version of Internet Explorer introduced the `WebBrowser` control?
2. How does the `WebBrowser` control keep track of the Web pages a user has accessed?
3. What is the relationship between the `CHtmlView` class and the `WebBrowser` control?
4. What standard MFC header file must you include in source code files that use `CHtmlView`?
5. What is the difference between the `Navigate()` and `Navigate2()` member functions of `CHtmlView`?
6. How do you use `CHtmlView` to open a Web page in a separate Internet Explorer browser window?
7. What `CHtmlView` member function do you call to navigate to the previous Web page in the history list?
8. How do you force a Web page to be reloaded using the `CHtmlView` class?
9. How can you tell when a Web page has finished loading using the `CHtmlView` class?
10. Why are there member functions defined in the `CHtmlView` class that have no noticeable effect if called from your own application?

Exercises

1. Add a Search menu item to the Go menu of BrowseIt, along with a new toolbar button. Don't forget to create a resource identifier named `ID_GO_SEARCH` and use it for the menu item and in the toolbar resource. You must also create a new button image within the toolbar bitmap.

2. Add a `CBrowseItView::OnGoSearch()` message handler to respond to the Go, Search menu command. Call the `GoSearch()` member function in this message handler to navigate to the default search Web page.

HOUR 21

Multimedia and DirectX

This hour explores a very powerful and exciting aspect of MFC programming: multimedia. Multimedia content has become an integral part of many Windows applications from productivity tools to games. Programming support for multimedia has evolved rapidly to meet the increasing demand for high-quality audio and video. Microsoft's DirectX technologies represent a major leap in multimedia support for Windows. This hour introduces you to DirectX and shows you how to create a simple multimedia player using DirectX.

In this hour, you will learn

- The basics of multimedia
- What the DirectX technologies have to offer
- How to use the DirectX Media Player control to build a multimedia application

Multimedia Basics

The term multimedia is used a lot when describing applications, but it isn't often clear what exactly qualifies an application as a multimedia application. Although you don't necessarily think of applications in terms of their content, the term multimedia really refers to the content displayed or manipulated by an application. In a general sense, any application content that contains audio or video elements could be considered multimedia content. However, I'd like to make a clearer distinction between multimedia content and other application content.

For the purposes of this hour, multimedia content is audio or video content that is time-based, which means that the content changes over time. This definition of multimedia eliminates static content such as still images. This isn't meant to lessen the importance of images in Windows applications. Rather, I'm trying to get the point across that multimedia content encompasses a specific type of data. Keep in mind that static images could still fit into a multimedia presentation as components of an animation that is time-based. However, our definition of multimedia is that the images are changed or altered over time.

NEW TERM *Multimedia content* is audio or video content that is time-based, which means that the content changes over time.

Practically all games are considered multimedia applications due to their heavy use of multimedia content. There are also multimedia applications that ship with Windows 95/98. The CD Player and Sound Recorder applications are multimedia applications used to play CDs and record audio clips. You could even think of Microsoft Word and some other productivity applications as multimedia applications because it's possible to embed audio and video clips within Word documents. Web browsers are also very good examples of multimedia applications.

What Is DirectX?

The support for multimedia in Windows has undergone a great deal of change over the years. The latest group of Windows multimedia technologies is collectively referred to as DirectX, and encompasses an incredibly wide range of multimedia features. DirectX is designed to allow applications to simultaneously display and manipulate 2D and 3D graphics, animation, video, and surround sound. DirectX also supports advanced user input devices and networked multiuser applications. DirectX has been integrated directly into the Windows operating system, not to mention the Internet Explorer Web browser. Many graphics-intensive games already use DirectX, and a wide range of applications are starting to warm up to it.

The main goal of DirectX is to promote Windows game development and eliminate the inconsistencies inherent in low-level multimedia programming. Because multimedia applications are typically very processor- and memory-intensive, programmers have a tendency to use lots of tricks to squeeze every ounce of performance out of the hardware. This has the unfortunate side effect of making some applications hardware-dependent. As you know, Windows doesn't take too kindly to hardware dependency. DirectX provides a single programming interface (API) that exposes many of the benefits of low-level hardware programming without the dependency problems.

DirectX also plays an important role in unifying many different multimedia content types. With DirectX you can combine 2D graphics animations, video clips, and CD-quality audio into a single presentation. Additionally, these different types of media can be synchronized together under a common timing mechanism. DirectX also supports surround sound, which is a particularly interesting media type.

DirectX frees multimedia developers from many of the mundane yet difficult tasks associated with low-level multimedia programming. More specifically, you can build applications using DirectX that automatically take advantage of advanced multimedia hardware without any additional work on your part. For example, if you use DirectX's 3D graphics features to create a game, the game will automatically detect and use 3D graphics hardware if any is installed. If there is no 3D graphics hardware installed on a user's system, DirectX will emulate the 3D functionality. DirectX is also designed to be extensible enough to support new multimedia features and media types.

The DirectX tools, APIs, controls, and other features are organized into two functional layers of DirectX:

- DirectX Foundation
- DirectX Media

The next couple of sections examine these DirectX layers in a little more detail. For more information on DirectX, you might want to check out Microsoft's DirectX Web site at http://www.microsoft.com/directx/. Figure 21.1 shows Microsoft's DirectX Web site, which contains late-breaking news on DirectX, not to mention lots of other useful information.

DirectX Foundation

DirectX Foundation is the low-level layer of DirectX, and supports core multimedia features such as 3D graphics, sound, music, advanced user input, and network support. The DirectX Foundation layer is implemented as a set of APIs that can be used to add media functionality to applications. These APIs provide a formal interface to the underlying low-level DirectX multimedia features. The DirectX Foundation APIs are used in conjunction with a set of components that are part of the Foundation layer:

FIGURE 21.1

Microsoft's DirectX Web site.

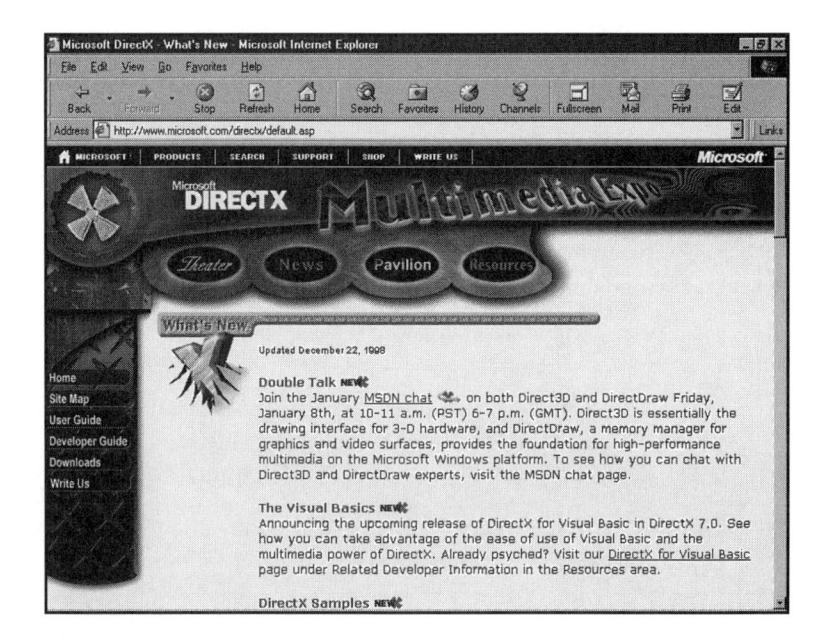

- DirectDraw—high-performance 2D graphics
- Direct3D—high-performance 3D graphics
- DirectSound—digital sound mixing and 3D audio
- DirectMusic—wavetable music synthesis
- DirectInput—advanced user input support for devices such as data gloves, flight yokes, and digital joysticks
- DirectPlay—multiuser networking

Each of these DirectX components is implemented as an ActiveX component or as a suite of ActiveX components. To utilize the DirectX Foundation layer, you simply plug in the appropriate ActiveX components, set their attributes, and let them go about their business. Admittedly, I'm simplifying things a great deal; the DirectX components still adhere to a set of low-level APIs and therefore require some work on the part of the developer. However, they offer huge benefits by hiding many of the complexities typically associated with multimedia development.

DirectX Media

DirectX Media is the higher-level layer of DirectX that sits on top of DirectX Foundation. The DirectX Media layer is responsible for high-level services such as animation and media streaming. Media streaming is the viewing of media content as it is transmitted over a network such as the Internet. The DirectX Media layer provides extensive support for viewing and manipulating many different types of media. Aside from being useful in applications, DirectX Media is also designed for use in Web pages, and is supported in the Internet Explorer Web browser. Similar to the DirectX Foundation layer, the DirectX Media layer is implemented as a suite of components:

- DirectShow—high-quality capture and playback of multimedia content streams
- DirectAnimation—animation and integration of diverse media types
- DirectX Transform—custom extensibility for DirectX

New Term *Media streaming* is the viewing of media content as it is transferred over a network.

The DirectX Media layer answers the need for a unified means of coordinating different media types into a single multimedia presentation. The DirectShow component is used to capture and play back streaming multimedia content in a variety of different formats. The DirectAnimation component then allows you to integrate and coordinate the playback of different media types within the context of a single animation. Using DirectAnimation, you can layer a 2D graphics object over a video clip and then synchronize it with sound and music. Finally, the DirectX Transform component allows third-party software vendors to extend DirectX and add their own features and components.

The DirectX Media Player Control

Based on the discussion of DirectX thus far, you may already have a clue that it's a very broad technology. In other words, you could fill an entire book covering the basics of the DirectX Foundation layer. For this reason, I want to focus on a particular aspect of DirectX and show you how it can be integrated with MFC. More specifically, you're going to focus on the DirectX `Media Player` control, which is an ActiveX control that is part of the DirectX Media layer.

The `Media Player` control is based on the DirectShow component of the DirectX Media layer and is used solely for the playback of multimedia content. The `Media Player` control acts as a universal player for most standard multimedia formats, including both streaming and nonstreaming media content. This makes the `Media Player` control extremely versatile; you can use the control in both applications and Web pages. The `Media Player` supports the following streaming media formats, which are typically used for playback over a network:

- Advanced Streaming Format (ASF)
- Video On Demand (VOD)

- Moving Picture Experts Group standard 1, 2, and 3 (MPEG-1, MPEG-2, and MPEG-3)
- RealAudio (RA) and RealVideo (RV)

> Advanced Streaming Format (ASF) is Microsoft's standard streaming media format recommended for use with the `Media Player` control. An ASF file is capable of storing both audio and video and is specially designed to be used over networks such as the Internet. ASF media content is delivered as a continuous flow of data with minimal wait time before playback begins. Of course, this is the benefit of all types of streaming media.

The `Media Player` control also supports the following nonstreaming media formats, which are typically used for local playback:

- Audio-Video Interleaved (AVI)
- QuickTime (MOV)
- Musical Instrument Digital Interface (MIDI)
- Indeo 5
- Waveform Audio (WAV)
- Sound File (SND)
- UNIX audio (AU)
- Audio Interchange File Format (AIFF)

You interact with the `Media Player` control by setting properties and calling member functions on the control. You can also respond to events that are generated by the control. Since the control is implemented as an ActiveX control, you can interact with it from applications written in a variety of different languages, or from a scripting language in a Web page. Using the properties and member functions exposed by the control, you can

- Control playback with operations such as start, stop, pause, rewind, and fast-forward
- Adjust the volume level or mute the audio entirely
- Monitor the performance of the media stream
- Retrieve media content information such as the author and title

The `Media Player` control is used as the basis for the Windows Media Player application that ships with Windows 98. The Windows Media Player application uses the standard user interface provided by the `Media Player` control, and allows you to open and play the different types of media supported by the control. This application is a good example of how the `Media Player` control can be used to play back media content. Figure 21.2 shows the Windows Media Player application in action.

> For more extensive information on the DirectX `Media Player` control, check out Microsoft's Windows Media Web site at http://www.microsoft.com/windows/windowsmedia/.

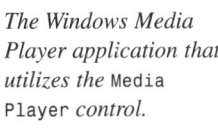

FIGURE 21.2

The Windows Media Player application that utilizes the `Media Player` *control.*

MFC and the `Media Player` Control

You've learned that the DirectX `Media Player` control is an ActiveX control, and can therefore be used in a wide range of programming languages. The `WebBrowser` control you learned about in the previous hour is also implemented as an ActiveX control. However, the `WebBrowser` control was encapsulated in the `CHtmlView` class that is a standard part of MFC. The `Media Player` control doesn't have a nice, clean view class to provide an MFC interface for the control.

Instead, the DirectX Media SDK (Software Development Kit) includes an MFC class named `CMediaPlayer` that serves as a C++ wrapper around the `Media Player` control. The `CMediaPlayer` class doesn't really provide any functionality of its own; it simply hides the details of making member function calls on the ActiveX control. Even so, the `CMediaPlayer` class is very convenient and keeps you from having to hassle with the calling conventions required when interacting with ActiveX controls.

> Because the `CMediaPlayer` class isn't part of a formal class library, you have to actually include the header (MediaPlayer.h) and source code (MediaPlayer.cpp) files in any projects that utilize the class.

Following are a few of the most commonly used member functions defined in the `CMediaPlayer` class:

- `GetVolume()`—gets the volume of the control
- `SetVolume()`—sets the volume of the control
- `SetFileName()`—sets the filename of the media clip to be played
- `Play()`—plays the current media clip
- `Pause()`—pauses the current media clip
- `Stop()`—stops the current media clip
- `GetCurrentPosition()`—gets the current playback position of the current media clip
- `SetCurrentPosition()`—sets the current playback position of the current media clip

This is only a very small subset of the member functions available for use in the `CMediaPlayer` class. In fact, the `CMediaPlayer` class defines over 150 member functions that are used to control a wide range of media playback parameters. To keep things simple, we'll stick to the basic media player functions.

Assuming that you already have a pointer to a `CMediaPlayer` object in the variable `pMediaPlayer`, following is an example of setting the player to an AVI video clip named Movie.avi:

`pMediaPlayer->SetFileName("Movie.avi");`

To start playing the video clip, you simply call the `Play()` member function, like this:

`pMediaPlayer->Play();`

You can then pause or stop the playback of the video clip by calling the `Pause()` or `Stop()` member functions.

Using the Media Player Control

Although the Windows Media Player application is very powerful and serves as a great all-purpose media player, you didn't get to join in the creation of it. You wouldn't be reading this book if you weren't interested in building your own applications. So, I want to lead you through the development of an MFC media player application named Projector that uses the `Media Player` control. You'll use the `CMediaPlayer` wrapper class to access the functionality of the `Media Player` control. Let's get started!

The Projector application is intended to function somewhat like a film projector. You load a "film" (media clip) and then you can play it, pause it, or stop it; stopping a media clip automatically results in it being rewound. Because the Projector application uses the `Media Player` control, it supports all kinds of different media types, including both streaming and nonstreaming media content.

The Projector application is structured a little differently than the other applications you've built throughout the book. Instead of creating a main frame window and adding the `Media Player` control to it, the main frame window is created from a dialog resource. In other words, the application's main frame window is really just a dialog box containing the `Media Player` control and a few buttons. This type of application is called a dialog-based application, or a form-based application. It's often very convenient because you can layout the application user interface using a visual dialog editor.

NEW TERM A *dialog-based application* is an application whose main frame window is based on a dialog box resource.

Resources

Because the main frame window for the Projector application is based on a dialog box resource, resources play an extremely important role in the application. Listing 21.1 shows the Resource.h header file for Projector, which contains the application's resource identifiers.

LISTING 21.1 THE RESOURCE.H HEADER FILE FOR PROJECTOR

```
 1: //-----------------------------------------------------------
 2: // Strings                        Range : 1000 - 1999
 3: //-----------------------------------------------------------
 4: #define IDR_PROJECTOR           1000
 5:
 6: //-----------------------------------------------------------
 7: // Commands                       Range : 2000 - 2999
 8: //-----------------------------------------------------------
 9: #define ID_ABOUT                2000
10:
11: //-----------------------------------------------------------
12: // Dialog Boxes                   Range : 3000 - 3999
13: //-----------------------------------------------------------
14: #define IDD_ABOUTBOX            3000
```

continues

LISTING 21.1 CONTINUED

```
15: #define IDD_PROJECTORBOX      3001
16:
17: //------------------------------------------------------------
18: // Controls               Range : 4000 - 4999
19: //------------------------------------------------------------
20: #define ID_PB_LOAD            4000
21: #define ID_PB_PLAY            4001
22: #define ID_PB_PAUSE           4002
23: #define ID_PB_STOP            4003
24: #define ID_MP_PLAYER          4004
```

The `ID_ABOUT` command identifier is used for the About Projector menu command, which displays an About dialog box. The `IDD_PROJECTORBOX` identifier is used to identify the dialog box resource that the main frame window is based on. This dialog box resource contains a `Media Player` control and a series of buttons used to manipulate the control, as you'll soon see. The buttons and the `Media Player` control are identified by the control constants near the end of the header file.

The actual resources for the Projector application are defined in the Projector.rc resource script, which is shown in Listing 21.2.

LISTING 21.2 THE PROJECTOR.RC RESOURCE SCRIPT FOR PROJECTOR

```
 1: //------------------------------------------------------------
 2: // Inclusions
 3: //------------------------------------------------------------
 4: #include "AfxRes.h"
 5: #include "Resource.h"
 6:
 7: //------------------------------------------------------------
 8: // Icons
 9: //------------------------------------------------------------
10: IDR_PROJECTOR ICON "Projector.ico"
11:
12: //------------------------------------------------------------
13: // Dialog Boxes
14: //------------------------------------------------------------
15: IDD_ABOUTBOX DIALOG 0, 0, 217, 55
16: CAPTION "About Projector"
17: STYLE DS_MODALFRAME | WS_POPUP | WS_CAPTION | WS_SYSMENU
18: FONT 8, "MS Sans Serif"
19: BEGIN
20:     ICON         IDR_PROJECTOR, IDC_STATIC, 11, 17, 20, 20
21:     LTEXT        "Projector Version 1.0", IDC_STATIC, 40, 10,
22:                  119, 8, SS_NOPREFIX
```

```
23:     LTEXT           "Copyright (c)1998 Michael Morrison", IDC_STATIC,
24:                     40, 25, 119, 8
25:     DEFPUSHBUTTON "OK", IDOK, 178, 7, 32, 14, WS_GROUP
26: END
27:
28: IDD_PROJECTORBOX DIALOGEX 0, 0, 311, 186
29: CAPTION "Projector"
30: STYLE DS_MODALFRAME | WS_MINIMIZEBOX | WS_POPUP | WS_VISIBLE |
31:     WS_CAPTION | WS_SYSMENU
32: EXSTYLE WS_EX_APPWINDOW
33: FONT 8, "MS Sans Serif"
34: BEGIN
35:     DEFPUSHBUTTON "&Load...", ID_PB_LOAD, 254, 7, 50, 14
36:     PUSHBUTTON    "&Play", ID_PB_PLAY, 254, 25, 50, 14
37:     PUSHBUTTON    "P&ause", ID_PB_PAUSE, 254, 43, 50, 14
38:     PUSHBUTTON    "&Stop", ID_PB_STOP, 254, 61, 50, 14
39:     PUSHBUTTON    "E&xit", IDCANCEL, 254, 79, 50, 14
40:     CONTROL       "", ID_MP_PLAYER,
41:         "{22D6F312-B0F6-11D0-94AB-0080C74C7E95}", WS_TABSTOP, 6, 7,
42:         242, 172
43: END
44:
45: IDD_PROJECTORBOX DLGINIT
46: BEGIN
47:     ID_MP_PLAYER, 0x376, 344, 0
48:     0x0000, 0x0000, 0x0001, 0x0000, 0x2584, 0x0000, 0x1cf0, 0x0000,
        ↪0x0003,
49:     0xffff, 0xffff, 0x000b, 0x0000, 0x000b, 0xffff, 0x000b, 0xffff,
        ↪0x000b,
50:     0xffff, 0x000b, 0xffff, 0x0000, 0x0002, 0x0000, 0x0000, 0x000b,
        ↪0x0000,
51:     0x0003, 0x0000, 0x0000, 0x0008, 0x0002, 0x0000, 0x0000, 0x0005,
        ↪0x0000,
52:     0x0000, 0x0000, 0x4014, 0x0008, 0x0002, 0x0000, 0x0000, 0x000b,
        ↪0xffff,
53:     0x0003, 0x0000, 0x0000, 0x0005, 0x0000, 0x0000, 0x0000, 0xbff0,
        ↪0x0003,
54:     0x0000, 0x0000, 0x0008, 0x0002, 0x0000, 0x0000, 0x0013, 0x0000,
        ↪0x0000,
55:     0x0013, 0xffff, 0x00ff, 0x0003, 0x0000, 0x0000, 0x0003, 0x0000,
        ↪0x0000,
56:     0x000b, 0xffff, 0x000b, 0xffff, 0x000b, 0xffff, 0x000b, 0x0000,
        ↪0x000b,
57:     0xffff, 0x0008, 0x0002, 0x0000, 0x0000, 0x000b, 0xffff, 0x0003,
        ↪0xffff,
58:     0xffff, 0x000b, 0x0000, 0x0003, 0x0001, 0x0000, 0x000b, 0x0001,
        ↪0x0005,
59:     0x0000, 0x0000, 0x0000, 0x3ff0, 0x0008, 0x0002, 0x0000, 0x0000,
        ↪0x0008,
```

continues

LISTING 21.2 CONTINUED

```
60:     0x0002, 0x0000, 0x0000, 0x0008, 0x0006, 0x0000, 0x002d, 0x0031,
        ➥0x0000,
61:     0x0005, 0x0000, 0x0000, 0x0000, 0xbff0, 0x0005, 0x0000, 0x0000,
        ➥0x0000,
62:     0xbff0, 0x000b, 0xffff, 0x000b, 0xffff, 0x000b, 0x0000, 0x000b,
        ➥0x0000,
63:     0x000b, 0x0000, 0x000b, 0xffff, 0x000b, 0xffff, 0x000b, 0x0000,
        ➥0x000b,
64:     0x0000, 0x000b, 0x0000, 0x000b, 0x0000, 0x000b, 0x0000, 0x000b,
        ➥0x0000,
65:     0x000b, 0x0000, 0x000b, 0x0000, 0x000b, 0x0000, 0x0003, 0x0000,
        ➥0x0000,
66:     0x0013, 0x0000, 0x0000, 0x000b, 0xffff, 0x0003, 0xfda8, 0xffff,
        ➥0x000b,
67:     0x0000,
68:     0
69: END
```

The IDD_PROJECTOR dialog box resource defines the dialog box that will serve as the main application window. This dialog box contains a series of buttons used to manipulate the media player, along with the actual Media Player control. The big number associated with the Media Player control is a class identifier that uniquely identifies the control. A class identifier is required of all ActiveX controls, and is assigned to a control when the control is created. This guarantees that no two ActiveX controls will ever share the same class identifier, which means that all ActiveX controls are easily distinguishable from each other.

You're probably wondering what in the world all that strange code is just below the dialog box resource. This is where things get a little tricky. Unlike other types of controls, ActiveX controls require you to initialize them before they can be used. Because they often have lots of different attributes that need to be initialized, they require the use of a dialog initialization structure. This is the big structure you see toward the end of the Projector.rc resource script.

The good news is that you don't have to worry about what all those numbers mean in the dialog initialization structure. The bad news is that you have to use a visual dialog editor to generate the structure. I used the Visual C++ dialog editor to create the entire IDD_PROJECTOR dialog box. I then copied the dialog resource code to the Projector.rc file and cleaned it up a little. Figure 21.3 shows the IDD_PROJECTOR dialog box in the Visual C++ dialog editor.

Notice in the figure that the Media Player control is selected and the Properties window is displayed. The Properties window shows the different properties of the Media Player control, which are then written to the dialog initialization structure when the resource script is saved. This is one situation where you have to rely on a development tool, the dialog editor, to accomplish the task of constructing the application's frame window.

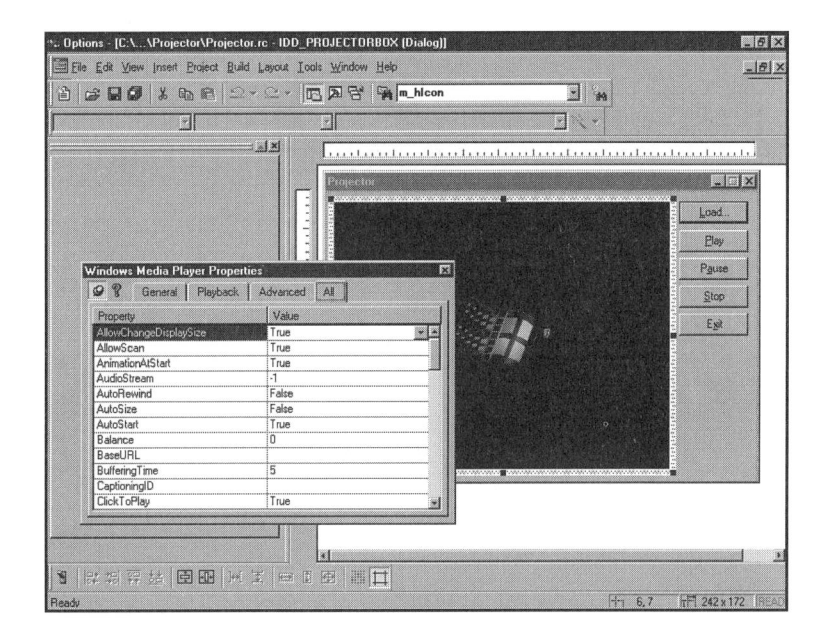

FIGURE 21.3

The `IDD_PROJECTOR` *dialog box in the Visual C++ dialog editor.*

The Application

The Projector application class, `CProjectorApp`, is responsible for creating the application window from the `IDD_PROJECTOR` dialog box resource. Listings 21.3 and 21.4 contain the source code for the `CProjectorApp` application class, which shows how this is accomplished.

LISTING 21.3 THE PROJECTOR.H HEADER FILE FOR PROJECTOR

```
 1: #ifndef __PROJECTOR_H__
 2: #define __PROJECTOR_H__
 3:
 4: //----------------------------------------------------------------
 5: // CProjectorApp Class - Projector Application Object
 6: //----------------------------------------------------------------
 7: class CProjectorApp : public CWinApp {
 8:     // Public Constructor(s)/Destructor
 9: public:
10:              CProjectorApp();
11:
```

continues

LISTING 21.3 CONTINUED

```
12:     // Public Member Functions
13: public:
14:     virtual BOOL   InitInstance();
15:
16:     // Message Map & Runtime Support
17: protected:
18:     DECLARE_MESSAGE_MAP()
19: };
20:
21: #endif
```

LISTING 21.4 THE PROJECTOR.CPP SOURCE CODE FILE FOR PROJECTOR

```
 1: //--------------------------------------------------------------
 2: // Inclusions
 3: //--------------------------------------------------------------
 4: #include "StdAfx.h"
 5: //--------------------------------------------------------------
 6: #include "Projector.h"
 7: #include "ProjectorDlg.h"
 8:
 9: //--------------------------------------------------------------
10: // MFC Debugging Support
11: //--------------------------------------------------------------
12: #ifdef _DEBUG
13: #undef THIS_FILE
14: static char BASED_CODE THIS_FILE[] = __FILE__;
15: #endif
16:
17: //--------------------------------------------------------------
18: // Global Variables
19: //--------------------------------------------------------------
20: CProjectorApp theApp;
21:
22:
23: //--------------------------------------------------------------
24: // Message Map & Runtime Support
25: //--------------------------------------------------------------
26: BEGIN_MESSAGE_MAP(CProjectorApp, CWinApp)
27: END_MESSAGE_MAP()
28:
29: //--------------------------------------------------------------
30: // Public Constructor(s)/Destructor
31: //--------------------------------------------------------------
32: CProjectorApp::CProjectorApp() {
33: }
```

```
34:
35: //-------------------------------------------------------------
36: // Public Member Functions
37: //-------------------------------------------------------------
38: BOOL CProjectorApp::InitInstance() {
39:     // Enable the app to contain ActiveX controls
40:     AfxEnableControlContainer();
41:
42:     // Create the main window as a dialog box
43:     CProjectorDlg dlg;
44:     m_pMainWnd = &dlg;
45:     dlg.DoModal();
46:
47:     return FALSE;
48: }
```

The `InitInstance()` member function of `CProjectorApp` takes on the responsibility of creating the main frame window as a dialog box. It does this by simply creating a `CProjectorDlg` object and calling its `DoModal()` member function. This is no different than the approach you've used to create dialog boxes throughout the book.

You may have noticed that the `InitInstance()` member function calls the `AfxEnableControlContainer()` function just before creating the main frame window. `AfxEnableControlContainer()` must be called in order for an application to support ActiveX controls. This call enables the application as an ActiveX container, which simply means that the application can contain ActiveX controls. The `AfxEnableControlContainer()` function is defined in the standard header file AfxDisp.h, which should be included in the application's StdAfx.h header file.

The Main Window

As you already know, the main frame window of the Projector application is implemented as a dialog box. Listing 21.5 contains the declaration of the `CProjectorDlg` class.

LISTING 21.5 THE PROJECTORDLG.H HEADER FILE FOR PROJECTOR

```
1: #ifndef __PROJECTORDLG_H__
2: #define __PROJECTORDLG_H__
3:
4: //-------------------------------------------------------------
5: // Inclusions
6: //-------------------------------------------------------------
7: #include "Resource.h"
8: #include "MediaPlayer.h"
```

continues

LISTING 21.5 CONTINUED

```
 9:
10: //------------------------------------------------------------
11: // CProjectorDlg Class - Projector Dialog Object
12: //------------------------------------------------------------
13: class CProjectorDlg : public CDialog {
14:     // Member Constants
15:     enum { IDD = IDD_PROJECTORBOX };
16:
17:     // Member Data
18: protected:
19:     HICON           m_hIcon;
20:     CMediaPlayer*   m_pMediaPlayer;
21:
22:     // Public Constructor(s)/Destructor
23: public:
24:                     CProjectorDlg(CWnd* pParent = NULL);
25:
26:     // Public Member Functions
27: public:
28:     virtual BOOL    OnInitDialog();
29:
30:     // Message Handlers
31: public:
32:     afx_msg HCURSOR OnQueryDragIcon();
33:     afx_msg void    OnPaint();
34:     afx_msg void    OnSysCommand(UINT nID, LPARAM lParam);
35:     afx_msg void    OnPBLoad();
36:     afx_msg void    OnPBPlay();
37:     afx_msg void    OnPBPause();
38:     afx_msg void    OnPBStop();
39:
40:     // Message Map & Runtime Support
41: protected:
42:     DECLARE_MESSAGE_MAP()
43: };
44:
45: #endif
```

The CProjectorDlg class defines two member variables, m_hIcon and m_pMediaPlayer. The m_hIcon member stores the application's icon. This is necessary because dialog boxes don't typically have icons associated with them. So, you must manually support an icon in the application using the m_hIcon member variable. The m_pMediaPlayer member stores a pointer to the Media Player control in the dialog box window.

The first three message handlers declared in CProjectorDlg are required because a dialog box has some shortcomings when acting as a main frame window. More specifically, the following aspects of a main frame window must be manually supported when using a dialog box as the main frame window:

- Setting the iconic cursor for the application when it is dragged while minimized
- Drawing the icon for the application window when it is minimized
- Handling custom menu commands via the system menu

The OnQueryDragIcon() message handler takes care of the first task. The OnPaint() message handler is used to draw the icon for the application when it is minimized. And finally, the OnSysCommand() message handler processes system menu commands. Menu items added to the system menu of an application generate system menu commands that are delivered to the OnSysCommand() message handler.

The remaining message handlers in CProjectorDlg are called in response to buttons on the dialog box. These buttons control the Media Player control through their corresponding message handlers.

Listing 21.6 contains the complete source code for the CProjectorDlg class.

LISTING 21.6   THE PROJECTORDLG.CPP SOURCE CODE FILE FOR PROJECTOR

```
 1: //------------------------------------------------------------
 2: // Inclusions
 3: //------------------------------------------------------------
 4: #include "StdAfx.h"
 5: //------------------------------------------------------------
 6: #include <CommDlg.h>
 7: #include "ProjectorDlg.h"
 8: #include "AboutDlg.h"
 9:
10: //------------------------------------------------------------
11: // MFC Debugging Support
12: //------------------------------------------------------------
13: #ifdef _DEBUG
14: #undef THIS_FILE
15: static char BASED_CODE THIS_FILE[] = __FILE__;
16: #endif
17:
18:
19: //------------------------------------------------------------
20: // Message Map & Runtime Support
21: //------------------------------------------------------------
22: BEGIN_MESSAGE_MAP(CProjectorDlg, CDialog)
23:     ON_WM_QUERYDRAGICON()
24:     ON_WM_PAINT()
25:     ON_WM_SYSCOMMAND()
26:     ON_BN_CLICKED(ID_PB_LOAD, OnPBLoad)
```

continues

LISTING 21.6 CONTINUED

```
27:    ON_BN_CLICKED(ID_PB_PLAY, OnPBPlay)
28:    ON_BN_CLICKED(ID_PB_PAUSE, OnPBPause)
29:    ON_BN_CLICKED(ID_PB_STOP, OnPBStop)
30: END_MESSAGE_MAP()
31:
32: //-----------------------------------------------------------------
33: // Public Constructor(s)/Destructor
34: //-----------------------------------------------------------------
35: CProjectorDlg::CProjectorDlg(CWnd* pParent) :
36:    CDialog(CProjectorDlg::IDD, pParent) {
37:    // Load the application icon
38:    m_hIcon = AfxGetApp()->LoadIcon(IDR_PROJECTOR);
39: }
40:
41: //-----------------------------------------------------------------
42: // Public Member Functions
43: //-----------------------------------------------------------------
44: BOOL CProjectorDlg::OnInitDialog() {
45:    CDialog::OnInitDialog();
46:
47:    // Add the About menu item to the system menu
48:    CMenu* pSysMenu = GetSystemMenu(FALSE);
49:    if (pSysMenu != NULL) {
50:      pSysMenu->AppendMenu(MF_SEPARATOR);
51:      pSysMenu->AppendMenu(MF_STRING, ID_ABOUT, "&About Projector...");
52:    }
53:
54:    // Explicitly set the icon since the main window is a dialog
55:    SetIcon(m_hIcon, TRUE);
56:
57:    // Get a pointer to the media player control
58:    m_pMediaPlayer = (CMediaPlayer *)GetDlgItem(ID_MP_PLAYER);
59:
60:    return TRUE;
61: }
62:
63: //-----------------------------------------------------------------
64: // Message Handlers
65: //-----------------------------------------------------------------
66: HCURSOR CProjectorDlg::OnQueryDragIcon() {
67:    // Return the cursor for the minimized application
68:    return (HCURSOR)m_hIcon;
69: }
70:
71: void CProjectorDlg::OnPaint() {
72:    if (IsIconic()) {
73:      // Manually draw the application icon
74:      CPaintDC dc(this);
75:      SendMessage(WM_ICONERASEBKGND, (WPARAM)dc.GetSafeHdc(), 0);
76:
77:      // Draw the icon centered in the client rectangle
78:      CRect rc;
```

```
 79:     GetClientRect(&rc);
 80:     int x = (rc.Width() - ::GetSystemMetrics(SM_CXICON) + 1) / 2;
 81:     int y = (rc.Height() - ::GetSystemMetrics(SM_CYICON) + 1) / 2;
 82:     dc.DrawIcon(x, y, m_hIcon);
 83:   }
 84:   else
 85:     // Perform default painting
 86:     CDialog::OnPaint();
 87: }
 88:
 89: void CProjectorDlg::OnSysCommand(UINT nID, LPARAM lParam) {
 90:   if ((nID & 0xFFF0) == ID_ABOUT) {
 91:     // Display the About dialog box
 92:     CAboutDlg dlgAbout;
 93:     dlgAbout.DoModal();
 94:   }
 95:   else
 96:     // Perform default processing of system menu command
 97:     CDialog::OnSysCommand(nID, lParam);
 98: }
 99:
100: void CProjectorDlg::OnPBLoad() {
101:   // Get the filename of the movie
102:   CFileDialog dlg(TRUE, "asf", "", OFN_FILEMUSTEXIST,
103:     "Active Streaming Format (*.asf)|*.asf|" \
104:     "Active Streaming Redirector (*.asx)|*.asx|" \
105:     "Audio Video Interleave Format (*.avi)|*.avi|" \
106:     "RealAudio/RealVideo (*.rm)|*.rm|" \
107:     "Wave Audio (*.wav)|*.wav|" \
108:     "All Files (*.*)|*.*||");
109:
110:   // Set the movie filename in the media player
111:   if (dlg.DoModal() == IDOK)
112:     m_pMediaPlayer->SetFileName(dlg.GetPathName());
113: }
114:
115: void CProjectorDlg::OnPBPlay() {
116:   // Play the movie
117:   m_pMediaPlayer->Play();
118: }
119:
120: void CProjectorDlg::OnPBPause() {
121:   // Pause the movie
122:   m_pMediaPlayer->Pause();
123: }
124:
125: void CProjectorDlg::OnPBStop() {
126:   // Stop playing the movie and rewind
127:   m_pMediaPlayer->Stop();
128:   m_pMediaPlayer->SetCurrentPosition(0);
129: }
```

The constructor for `CProjectorDlg` loads the application icon, which is drawn in the `OnPaint()` message handler. The `OnInitDialog()` member function adds an About Projector menu item to the system menu. It then sets the icon for the dialog box window and obtains a pointer to the `Media Player` control.

As you learned earlier, the `OnQueryDragIcon()` message handler sets an iconic cursor that is displayed when the minimized application is dragged. The `OnPaint()` message handler checks to see if the window is minimized, in which case it draws the application icon. The `OnSysCommand()` message handler checks for the `ID_ABOUT` menu command and displays the About dialog box in response to it.

The code that deals with the `Media Player` control is isolated in the remaining message handlers in `CProjectorDlg`. The `OnPBLoad()` message handler first obtains a filename from the user by invoking the File Open common dialog box. It then calls the `SetFileName()` member function on the `Media Player` control to set the filename of the media content to be played.

The `OnPBPlay()` message handler simply calls the `Play()` member function on the `Media Player` control to play the media clip. Likewise, the `OnPBPause()` message handler calls the `Pause()` member function on the `Media Player` control to pause the playback of the clip. And finally, the `OnPBStop()` message handler calls the `Stop()` member function to stop the playback of the clip. The `OnPBStop()` message handler also calls `SetCurrentPosition()` and passes in `0` to rewind the Media Player to the beginning of the media clip.

Figures 21.4 and 21.5 show the Projector application playing a couple of different types of media content.

FIGURE 21.4

The Projector application playing the Endorse.asf media file.

FIGURE 21.5
The Projector application playing the Drill.avi media file.

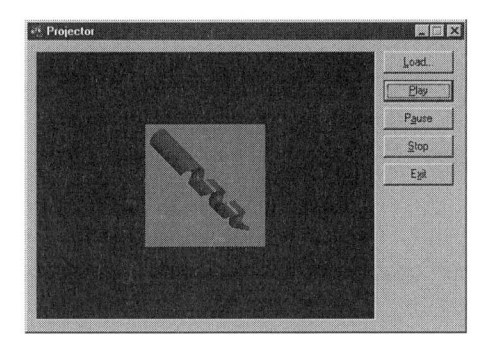

Summary

This hour introduced you to a fascinating area of programming, at least in my mind. Multimedia programming is one of the most challenging, and often one of the most rewarding, areas of software development. This hour explored DirectX, which is Microsoft's expansive multimedia technology that eases the pain typically associated with high-performance multimedia development. You learned about the different parts of DirectX, including the DirectX `Media Player` control. You then focused on how the `Media Player` control is used with MFC. The hour concluded by showing you how to develop an MFC application based on the `Media Player` control.

Q&A

Q How does DirectX allow you to run multimedia applications that require special hardware features such as 3D graphics and sound?

A DirectX provides a Hardware Emulation Layer (HEL) that provides software-based drivers that emulate functionality typically found in hardware. In other words, if DirectX detects that hardware isn't available to accomplish a given task, it will automatically emulate the functionality through the HEL.

Q Why is it necessary to use an MFC wrapper class around the `Media Player` control?

A Strictly speaking, it isn't necessary. However, ActiveX controls aren't used in the same manner as MFC objects, so there is a consistency issue when it comes to mixing the two in an MFC application. It is much more consistent to stick with MFC classes in MFC applications. The `CMediaPlayer` wrapper class provides an MFC wrapper that doesn't harm performance and makes the application code much easier to understand than if you used to ActiveX control directly.

Workshop

The Workshop is designed to help you anticipate possible questions, review what you've learned, and begin thinking ahead to put your knowledge into practice. The answers to the quiz are in Appendix A, "Quiz Answers."

Quiz

1. What is multimedia content?
2. Name at least two multimedia applications that ship with Windows 98.
3. What is the main goal of DirectX?
4. What happens if a DirectX application utilizes 3D graphics features that are typically implemented in graphics hardware, but there is no graphics hardware installed on a user's system?
5. What is DirectX Foundation?
6. What is DirectX Media?
7. What is media streaming?
8. What is the significance of media streaming?
9. What MFC class serves as a C++ wrapper around the Media Player control?
10. What function must you call in order to use ActiveX controls in an application?

Exercises

1. Open the resource script for the Projector application in a visual resource editor and edit the IDD_PROJECTOR dialog box resource. Set the Show Controls, Show Position Controls, and Show Status Bar properties to True and save the resource script. Next recompile the application.
2. Add two new buttons to the IDD_PROJECTOR dialog box named Volume + and Volume -. Create resource identifiers for these buttons named ID_PB_INCVOLUME and ID_PB_DECVOLUME. Now create message handlers for the buttons named OnPBIncVolume() and OnPBDecVolume() that raise and lower the volume of the Media Player control.

Hour 22

Creating DLLs

This hour introduces you to DLLs, which form a very important part of the Windows operating system. You find out in this hour how functional parts of an application can be isolated into separate modules called DLLs. These DLLs can then be linked to dynamically at runtime by multiple applications. DLLs are beneficial in that they promote code sharing and reuse, reduce the memory requirements of applications, and provide developers with a means of updating specific parts of an application.

In this hour, you will learn

- DLL basics
- How DLLs are used with MFC
- How to build an MFC extension DLL and use it within an MFC application

DLL Fundamentals

If you've done much programming with C/C++, you are no doubt familiar with static libraries. Just in case you aren't, they are libraries of compiled code that are made available for inclusion within an application at compile-time; or more specifically, at link-time. Static libraries are combined with compiled application code and linked into an executable .EXE file. As an example, the standard C runtime library is a static library that is linked into every command-line C application.

NEW TERM The *static library* is a library of compiled code that is made available for inclusion within an application at compile-time.

Figure 22.1 illustrates the process of statically linking a static library. Notice that the code in a static library is physically linked into the application's .EXE file at compile-time.

FIGURE 22.1

A static library is statically linked into an application at compile-time.

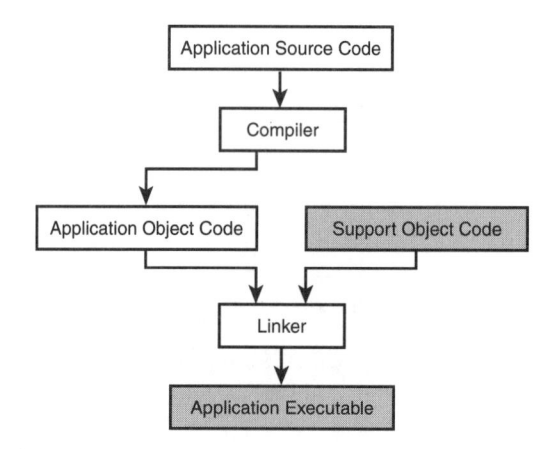

Windows introduced a new twist on the whole linking process with dynamic link libraries, or DLLs. A DLL is like a static library in that it contains compiled code, but DLLs are not statically linked with an application at compile-time. Instead, DLLs are compiled into their own .DLL files and dynamically linked with an application at runtime. The concept of dynamic linking is at the core of the Windows operating system. Dynamic linking gives an application the capability of dynamically calling functions and use resources from outside of the application's .EXE file at runtime.

NEW TERM *Dynamic linking* is the integration of modularized executable support code with an application at runtime.

Figure 22.2 shows how a DLL is dynamically linked to an application at runtime. Notice that the code in a DLL resides in a separate .DLL file and that a special import library is linked in with the application. You learn about import libraries in a moment.

FIGURE 22.2

A dynamic library is stored in a .DLL file and dynamically linked with an application at runtime.

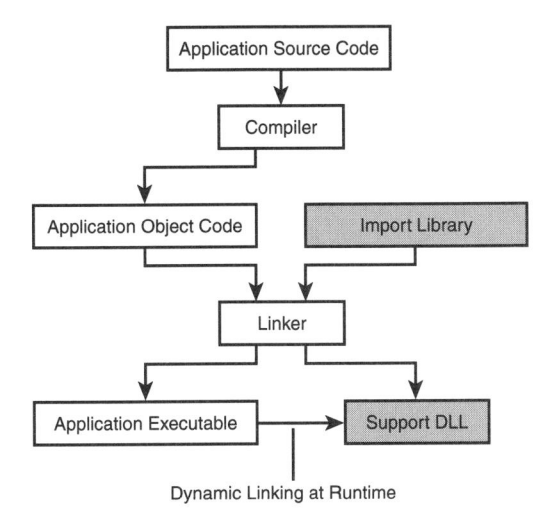

```
          Application Source Code
                    |
                    v
                Compiler
                    |
                    v
        Application Object Code    Import Library
                    |                    |
                    v                    v
                       Linker
                    |                    |
                    v                    v
        Application Executable ----> Support DLL
                    |
          Dynamic Linking at Runtime
```

When using a DLL, an application calls functions in the DLL at runtime. Pushing the link stage to occur at runtime gives developers a lot more flexibility in creating modular applications with plug-in functionality that resides in DLLs. Furthermore, it allows applications to share commonly used code because the code is physically stored in a single .DLL file. Contrast this with copies of the code being statically linked into multiple .EXE files.

> Even though they often contain executable code, DLLs are typically named with the .DLL file extension. By default, Windows 95/98 hides .DLL files in Windows Explorer because they are considered system files. You can change this option using the View, Folder Options command in Windows Explorer, which I suggest doing if you're going to be building your own DLLs.

You might be surprised to learn that Windows itself is just a bunch of DLLs. When you build a Windows application, you don't statically link all the Windows GDI graphics code with your application, for example. Rather, you reference the appropriate header files and link in an import library that contains information about the functions exported in the Windows DLLs. Custom DLLs work in the exact same way. In this sense, you can think of your own custom DLLs as not only extensions to your application, but also as extensions to Windows itself.

New Term: The *import library* is a special library file that contains information about the functions exported by a DLL, but no actual executable code.

> MFC itself is provided as both a static library and a DLL. It is up to you whether you want an MFC application to statically link MFC into the application's .EXE file or dynamically link the application to the MFC DLL at runtime. In general, it is better to use the MFC DLL and dynamically link to it because MFC is relatively large. That's the approach I took in all the examples throughout this book. Just keep in mind that you will need to ship the MFC DLL with your application to end users.

The primary benefit of DLLs is the sharing of code among applications. For example, you could create a spell checker and build it into a DLL. This spell checker DLL could then be dynamically used by any application. Additionally, if you later dreamed up an enhancement to the spell checker, you could update the DLL by itself without having to modify the applications that use it. The applications indirectly gain new functionality through the DLL without having to undergo a rebuild. In fact, from the perspective of the applications, nothing has changed. Users, on the other hand, immediately realize the improved features made available by the DLL. This is a very powerful benefit of DLLs that simply isn't possible through static linking.

To Dynamically Link or Not

One of the most difficult aspects of building DLLs is determining what code is to be placed there. Typically you will be in the midst of developing an application when you run across some piece of functionality that could be separated into a self-contained module. However, is it justifiable to break an application up into DLLs solely for the sake of modularizing the application? In most cases the answer is yes. Generally speaking, it never hurts to move code into a DLL because you are ultimately creating more options for code reuse by doing so.

One drawback to using DLLs involves performance. Because the executable code in a DLL must be loaded and dynamically linked, applications that make heavy use of DLLs may pause from time to time. On the other hand, because the main executable in such an application is so small, the application will start more quickly than a statically linked application. So, the tradeoff involves the speed at which an application initially starts up versus its ongoing performance while in use. If you don't use more than a few DLLs, this is probably not something worth worrying about.

Another potential downside to breaking an application up into DLLs is versioning. The benefits of being able to update a DLL and alter a portion of an application's functionality at runtime come at the cost of potentially creating versioning conflicts. In other words, you have to be very careful that a change in a newer version of a DLL won't break application code that is expecting the older version of the DLL. In any event, planning is the key to making sure applications and DLLs peacefully co-exist.

DLL Mechanics

It is important to understand that DLLs aren't applications and cannot be executed as standalone programs. This makes the structure of DLLs somewhat different from applications. For example, DLLs have a function named `DllMain()` instead of the `WinMain()` function found in Win32 applications. The `DllMain()` function is called by Windows to perform any initialization and cleanup for a DLL:

```
int APIENTRY DllMain(HINSTANCE hInstance, DWORD dwReason, PVOID pReserved);
```

The first argument to `DllMain()`, `hInstance`, is the instance handle for the DLL. The second parameter, `dwReason`, specifies why Windows is calling `DllMain()`, and is used to determine whether initialization or cleanup is to be performed. Finally, the last parameter, `pReserved`, is reserved for use by Windows. If a DLL doesn't have the need for initialization or cleanup code, it can just return `TRUE` from `DllMain()`. DLLs that extend MFC classes do require initialization and cleanup, however, as you learn a little later in the hour.

An application must link in a special import library in order to call functions in a DLL. Import libraries are generated as part of the compilation of DLLs, and contain information about the functions exported by DLLs. Exported functions are functions that DLLs make available for applications to call. DLLs can also have nonexported functions that are used internally by the DLL. You indicate that a function is exported by declaring the function using the `__declspec(dllexport)` modifier. There is also a `__declspec(dllimport)` modifier used to import DLL functions. These modifiers are often defined for reuse in a more readable style:

```
#define EXPORT __declspec(dllexport)
#define IMPORT __declspec(dllimport)
```

For DLLs that extend MFC, there is a special macro called `AFX_EXT_CLASS` that you can use to export and import entire classes. This macro will intelligently export a class during the compilation of the class, and then import the class when the class header file is referenced in application code. You must define the special macro `_AFXEXT` when building a DLL for the `AFX_EXT_CLASS` macro to work properly.

NEW TERM An *exported function* is a function in a DLL that is made available for applications to call.

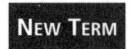

NEW TERM An *exported class* is a class in a DLL that is made available for applications to use.

Managing DLLs with `DLLMain()`

You can create DLLs to contain just about any type of code you want, such as straight C functions, C++ classes, and MFC-derived C++ classes. Because this book obviously is about MFC, I'd like to focus on how to build DLLs containing MFC-derived classes. The type of code included in a DLL impacts the structure and responsibilities of the DLLMain() function. So, let's first analyze the structure of DLLMain().

The second parameter to DLLMain(), dwReason, lets you know whether the DLL is being attached to or detached from an application. This is your cue to perform any DLL initialization or cleanup. You will be on the lookout for a value in dwReason of DLL_PROCESS_ATTACH or DLL_PROCESS_DETACH. Listing 22.1 shows a skeletal DLLMain() function that handles these two DLL states.

LISTING 22.1 A SKELETAL DLLMain() FUNCTION THAT CAN BE USED TO INITIALIZE AND CLEAN UP A DLL

```
 1: extern "C" int APIENTRY
 2: DllMain(HINSTANCE hInstance, DWORD dwReason, LPVOID lpReserved) {
 3:    if (dwReason == DLL_PROCESS_ATTACH) {
 4:       // Perform initialization of DLL
 5:    }
 6:    else if (dwReason == DLL_PROCESS_DETACH) {
 7:       // Perform cleanup of DLL
 8:    }
 9:
10:    return 1;
11: }
```

This code provides a template for initializing and cleaning up a DLL but it doesn't actually do any work. That is where the AFX_EXTENSION_MODULE structure comes into play. The AFX_EXTENSION_MODULE structure is a special data structure used to hold the state of an MFC extension DLL. You must create a static global variable of type AFX_EXTENSION_MODULE to keep track of the state of your MFC extension DLLs:

```
static AFX_EXTENSION_MODULE TipOfTheDayDLL = { NULL, NULL };
```

What is the significance of this global variable? Well, it is used with the MFC functions that take on the responsibility of managing an MFC extension DLL. To understand what

I'm talking about, consider the following three tasks that all MFC extension DLLs must perform in their DllMain() function:

- Call the AfxInitExtensionModule() function to initialize the DLL
- Create a CDynLinkLibrary object if the DLL will be exporting CRuntimeClass objects or has its own resources
- Call the AfxTermExtensionModule() function to clean up the DLL

The AfxInitExtensionModule() function initializes a DLL by making a copy of a DLL's module handle. It is also required as a parameter to the constructor for the CDynLinkLibrary object. This object is responsible for exporting any runtime classes in the DLL, along with any resources defined in the DLL. Finally, the AfxTermExtensionModule() function is called to clean up the extension DLL when each process detaches from the DLL. It's worth noting that these functions are defined in the standard MFC header file AfxDLLX.h, which you should include in the source code file containing the DLLMain() function.

Listing 22.2 shows a completed DLLMain() function that is suitable for use in an MFC extension DLL.

LISTING 22.2 A DLLMain() FUNCTION SUITABLE FOR USE IN AN MFC EXTENSION DLL

```
 1: static AFX_EXTENSION_MODULE TipOfTheDayDLL = { NULL, NULL };
 2:
 3: extern "C" int APIENTRY
 4: DllMain(HINSTANCE hInstance, DWORD dwReason, LPVOID lpReserved) {
 5:    if (dwReason == DLL_PROCESS_ATTACH) {
 6:       // Perform one-time initialization of DLL
 7:       if (!AfxInitExtensionModule(TipOfTheDayDLL, hInstance))
 8:          return 0;
 9:       new CDynLinkLibrary(TipOfTheDayDLL);
10:    }
11:    else if (dwReason == DLL_PROCESS_DETACH) {
12:       // Terminate the DLL before destructors are called
13:       AfxTermExtensionModule(TipOfTheDayDLL);
14:    }
15:
16:    return 1;
17: }
```

Creating an MFC Extension DLL

After you have the necessary ingredients in place for the DLLMain() function, the rest of an MFC extension DLL's code closely resembles normal application code. Let's work through the development of an example DLL to confirm this. The DLL you're going to build is called TipOfTheDay, and implements a Tip of the Day dialog box that displays a random tip about how to use an application. This dialog box is typically displayed when an application first starts. Figure 22.3 shows the completed Tip of the Day dialog box in action.

FIGURE 22.3
The Tip Of The Day dialog box displays a random tip about how to use an application.

> The specifics of compiling and linking a DLL are to a large extent dependent on the development environment you are using. I've provided a Visual C++ project as part of the source code for the book, which is available from the companion Web site. This project includes all the proper compiler switches and linker settings for successfully compiling and linking the TipOfTheDay DLL. If you are using a development environment other than Visual C++, I encourage you to open the TipOfTheDay.dsp file and study the different settings. This file is kind of like a fancy make file for the DLL.

The construction of the CTipOfTheDay dialog box class really isn't much different than if you were developing the class as part of an application. In fact, because the DLL is compiled by itself into a .DLL file, you must provide its own resources just as if it was an application. Listing 22.3 contains the code for the Resource.h header file for the TipOfTheDay DLL.

LISTING 22.3 THE RESOURCE.H HEADER FILE FOR THE TIPOFTHEDAY DLL

```
1: //------------------------------------------------------------
2: // Icons                     Range : 1000 - 1999
3: //------------------------------------------------------------
4: #define IDI_TIPOFTHEDAY       1000
5:
6: //------------------------------------------------------------
```

```
 7: // Dialog Boxes              Range : 2000 - 2999
 8: //---------------------------------------------------------
 9: #define IDD_TIPOFTHEDAYBOX    2000
10:
11: //---------------------------------------------------------
12: // Controls                   Range : 3000 - 3999
13: //---------------------------------------------------------
14: #define IDB_NEXTTIP           3000
15: #define IDS_TIPTEXT           3001
```

These identifiers are used to identify resources in the DLL. Listing 22.4 contains the DLL's resource script, which shows how the identifiers are used by defining the DLL's resources.

LISTING 22.4 THE TIPOFTHEDAY.RC RESOURCE SCRIPT FOR THE TIPOFTHEDAY DLL

```
 1: //---------------------------------------------------------
 2: // Inclusions
 3: //---------------------------------------------------------
 4: #include "AfxRes.h"
 5: #include "Resource.h"
 6:
 7: //---------------------------------------------------------
 8: // Icons
 9: //---------------------------------------------------------
10: IDI_TIPOFTHEDAY ICON "TipOfTheDay.ico"
11:
12: //---------------------------------------------------------
13: // Dialog Boxes
14: //---------------------------------------------------------
15: IDD_TIPOFTHEDAYBOX DIALOG DISCARDABLE  0, 0, 220, 85
16: CAPTION "Tip Of The Day"
17: STYLE DS_MODALFRAME | WS_POPUP | WS_CAPTION | WS_SYSMENU
18: FONT 8, "MS Sans Serif"
19: BEGIN
20:     DEFPUSHBUTTON   "&Close", IDOK, 163, 64, 50, 14
21:     PUSHBUTTON      "&Next Tip", IDB_NEXTTIP, 106, 64, 50, 14
22:     LTEXT           "Did you know...", IDC_STATIC, 39, 7, 79, 8
23:     ICON            IDI_TIPOFTHEDAY, IDC_STATIC, 7, 7, 21, 20
24:     LTEXT           "", IDS_TIPTEXT, 39, 21, 174, 35, SS_SUNKEN
25: END
```

The IDI_TIPOFTHEDAY icon is used in the IDD_TIPOFTHEDAY dialog box resource. This dialog box consists of two buttons, Close and Next Tip. The Close button uses the IDOK identifier to function as an OK button. The Next Tip button, on the other hand, is identified by IDB_NEXTTIP and will require a command message handler in the dialog box class. The other resource with an explicit identifier is the IDS_TIPTEXT static text control. This control is where the actual tip text is displayed for each tip.

The dialog box class for the DLL, `CTipOfTheDay`, is declared in the TipOfTheDay.h header file, which is shown in Listing 22.5.

LISTING 22.5 THE TIPOFTHEDAY.H HEADER FILE FOR THE TIPOFTHEDAY DLL

```
 1: #ifndef __TIPOFTHEDAY_H__
 2: #define __TIPOFTHEDAY_H__
 3:
 4: //----------------------------------------------------------------
 5: // Inclusions
 6: //----------------------------------------------------------------
 7: #include "Resource.h"
 8:
 9: //----------------------------------------------------------------
10: // CTipOfTheDay Class - About Dialog Object
11: //----------------------------------------------------------------
12: class AFX_EXT_CLASS CTipOfTheDay : public CDialog {
13:    // Member Constants
14:    enum { IDD = IDD_TIPOFTHEDAYBOX };
15:
16:    // Public Constructor(s)/Destructor
17: public:
18:                CTipOfTheDay();
19:    virtual    ~CTipOfTheDay();
20:
21:    // Public Member Functions
22: public:
23:    virtual BOOL   OnInitDialog();
24:
25:    // Message Handlers
26: public:
27:    afx_msg void   OnNextTip();
28:
29:    // Message Map & Runtime Support
30: protected:
31:    DECLARE_MESSAGE_MAP()
32: };
33:
34: #endif
```

This header file declares a pretty basic dialog box much like the About dialog box that you've used throughout the book. It declares an `OnInitDialog()` member function to handle dialog initialization. The class also declares an `OnNextTip()` message handler for responding to the Next Tip button. As you no doubt already know, the really interesting stuff takes place in the implementation of the dialog box class, which is shown in Listing 22.6.

LISTING 22.6 THE TIPOFTHEDAY.CPP SOURCE CODE FILE FOR THE TIPOFTHEDAY DLL

```
 1: //-----------------------------------------------------------------
 2: // Inclusions
 3: //-----------------------------------------------------------------
 4: #include "StdAfx.h"
 5: //-----------------------------------------------------------------
 6: #include <AfxDLLX.h>
 7: #include "TipOfTheDay.h"
 8:
 9: //-----------------------------------------------------------------
10: // MFC Debugging Support
11: //-----------------------------------------------------------------
12: #ifdef _DEBUG
13: #undef THIS_FILE
14: static char THIS_FILE[] = __FILE__;
15: #endif
16:
17: //-----------------------------------------------------------------
18: // DLL Support
19: //-----------------------------------------------------------------
20: static AFX_EXTENSION_MODULE TipOfTheDayDLL = { NULL, NULL };
21:
22: extern "C" int APIENTRY
23: DllMain(HINSTANCE hInstance, DWORD dwReason, LPVOID lpReserved) {
24:   if (dwReason == DLL_PROCESS_ATTACH) {
25:     // Perform one-time initialization of DLL
26:     if (!AfxInitExtensionModule(TipOfTheDayDLL, hInstance))
27:       return 0;
28:     new CDynLinkLibrary(TipOfTheDayDLL);
29:   }
30:   else if (dwReason == DLL_PROCESS_DETACH) {
31:     // Terminate the DLL before destructors are called
32:     AfxTermExtensionModule(TipOfTheDayDLL);
33:   }
34:
35:   return 1;
36: }
37:
38: //-----------------------------------------------------------------
39: // Message Map & Runtime Support
40: //-----------------------------------------------------------------
41: BEGIN_MESSAGE_MAP(CTipOfTheDay, CDialog)
42:   ON_COMMAND(IDB_NEXTTIP, OnNextTip)
43: END_MESSAGE_MAP()
44:
45: //-----------------------------------------------------------------
46: // Public Constructor(s)/Destructor
47: //-----------------------------------------------------------------
48: CTipOfTheDay::CTipOfTheDay() : CDialog(CTipOfTheDay::IDD) {
49:   // Seed the random number generator
```

continues

LISTING 22.6 CONTINUED

```
50:     ::srand((unsigned)time(NULL));
51: }
52:
53: CTipOfTheDay::~CTipOfTheDay() {
54: }
55:
56: //-----------------------------------------------------------------
57: // Public Member Functions
58: //-----------------------------------------------------------------
59: BOOL CTipOfTheDay::OnInitDialog() {
60:     CDialog::OnInitDialog();
61:
62:     // Display the first tip
63:     OnNextTip();
64:
65:     return TRUE;
66: }
67:
68: //-----------------------------------------------------------------
69: // Message Handlers
70: //-----------------------------------------------------------------
71: void CTipOfTheDay::OnNextTip() {
72:     static CString sTipList[] = {
73:       "The New command under the File menu is used to create a new " \
74:         "document.",
75:       "The Open command under the File menu is used to open a " \
76:         "document from a file.",
77:       "The Save command under the File menu is used to save the " \
78:         "current document to a file.",
79:       "The Save As command under the File menu is used to save the " \
80:         "current document to a different file.",
81:       "The Print command under the File menu is used to print the " \
82:         "current document.",
83:       "The Exit command under the File menu is used to quit the " \
84:         "application.",
85:       "You can use the buttons on the toolbar to carry out commonly " \
86:         "used menu commands.",
87:       "You can look to the status bar for useful information about an " \
88:         "application such as help messages for menu commands.",
89:       "If you pause with the mouse cursor over a toolbar button, a " \
90:         "tooltip will be displayed.",
91:       "You can click on the toolbar and drag it to transform it into " \
92:         "a floating toolbar window.",
93:       "You can dock a floating toolbar window by dragging it to any " \
94:         "edge of the application window."
95:     };
96:
97:     // Get a random tip
98:     int nTip = ::rand() % (sizeof(sTipList) / sizeof(*sTipList));
```

```
 99:
100:    // Display the new tip
101:    SetDlgItemText(IDS_TIPTEXT, sTipList[nTip]);
102: }
```

Before getting into the code for the CTipOfTheDay dialog box class, the TipOfTheDay.cpp source code file provides an implementation of the DLLMain() function required for MFC extension DLLs. This is the exact same DLLMain() code you learned about earlier in the hour.

Because the dialog box is responsible for displaying a random tip of the day, it is necessary to seed the standard C random number generator in the constructor for CTipOfTheDay. This is accomplished with a call to the srand() function. The companion to srand() is rand(), which actually generates random numbers. You'll get to it in a moment.

The OnInitDialog() member function is used to display the first tip in the dialog box. This is done by directly calling the OnNextTip() message handler. Generally speaking, it isn't a good idea to directly call message handlers because their design dictates that they are called in response to a delivered message. However, it's harmless in this case because the OnNextTip() handler doesn't accept any parameters.

The OnNextTip() message handler begins by defining a static array of strings containing the different tips. The handler then uses the standard C rand() function to generate a random index into the array of tips. This index is used to select a string from the array of tips and set the IDS_TIPTEXT static text control in the dialog box. The SetDlgItemText() member function is used to set the text of this control.

That finishes up the code for the DLL, but you still don't have a means of trying out the DLL. The next section leads you through the development of a simple application to test out the TipOfTheDay DLL. Keep in mind that a successful build of the DLL results in the creation of both a .DLL file and an .LIB import library for the DLL. You'll need both of these files to use the DLL in an application.

Using an MFC Extension DLL

Applications that make use of functionality found in DLLs typically access this functionality by creating objects from exported DLL classes or by making calls to exported DLL functions. Even though the executable code for such classes and functions is located in a .DLL file, application source code still requires knowledge of them. This means that you must include the header file for a DLL in order to use classes and functions in the DLL; this header file must contain declarations for exported DLL classes and functions.

Along with including a DLLs header file in their source code files, applications must also link the DLLs import library in order to be able to access DLL functions. Remember that the import library doesn't contain any code, it just serves as a bridge allowing the application to make calls into the DLL.

Now that you have an idea as to how an application uses a DLL, let's get to work creating such an application. The Tipper application is a minimal application used solely as a test bed for the TipOfTheDay DLL. The application is based on the Skeleton application you've used throughout the book. Listing 22.7 contains the code for the application's `InitInstance()` member function, which creates a `CTipOfTheDay` DLL and invokes it with a call to `DoModal()`.

LISTING 22.7 THE `CTipperApp::InitInstance()` MEMBER FUNCTION FOR TIPPER

```
 1: BOOL CTipperApp::InitInstance() {
 2:   // Create main window
 3:   m_pMainWnd = new CMainFrame;
 4:   ASSERT(m_pMainWnd);
 5:   if (((CMainFrame*)m_pMainWnd)->Create(m_pszAppName)) {
 6:     m_pMainWnd->ShowWindow(m_nCmdShow);
 7:     m_pMainWnd->UpdateWindow();
 8:
 9:     // Display a tip upon startup
10:     CTipOfTheDay totd;
11:     totd.DoModal();
12:
13:     return TRUE;
14:   }
15:
16:   return FALSE;
17: }
```

This code results in the TipOfTheDay dialog box being displayed when the application frame window is first shown. This is the way in which many Windows applications utilize a "tip of the day" feature. For testing purposes, it's also useful to display the dialog box in response to a left mouse button click in the frame window. This requires an entry in the message map for the `CMainFrame` class:

```
BEGIN_MESSAGE_MAP(CMainFrame, CFrameWnd)
  ON_WM_LBUTTONDOWN()
END_MESSAGE_MAP()
```

The associated declaration for the `OnLButtonDown()` message handler follows:

```
afx_msg void  OnLButtonDown(UINT nFlags, CPoint point);
```

Listing 22.8 contains the code for the `OnLButtonDown()` message handler in `CMainFrame`, which displays the Tip Of The Day dialog box.

LISTING 22.8 THE CMainFrame::OnLButtonDown() MESSAGE HANDLER FOR TIPPER

```
1: void CMainFrame::OnLButtonDown(UINT nFlags, CPoint point) {
2:   // Display a tip
3:   CTipOfTheDay totd;
4:   totd.DoModal();
5: }
```

You might be surprised by how straightforward the code is for displaying the Tip Of The Day dialog box. This is a testament to the fact that dynamic linking to a DLL is very simple after you build the DLL and link in the import library to the application. In fact, from a coding perspective, the `CTipOfTheDay` class appears to be a part of the Tipper application.

> In case you're wondering, it is possible to explicitly control the loading and unloading of DLLs from an application. In this case, you wouldn't use an import library but would instead use special functions to perform the dynamic linking. Although there are certainly some situations where this approach is desirable over the implicit approach you've learned about, you will typically be fine using the implicit approach.

Summary

This hour delved into dynamic link libraries (DLLs) and the role they play in Windows. You began the hour by learning the basics of DLLs and their relationship to the Windows operating system and Windows applications. You then learned about the specific support required to create DLLs that act as extensions to MFC. You finished up the hour by creating an MFC extension DLL and then testing it within an MFC application.

Q&A

Q What happens if the .DLL file can't be found for an application that implicitly links to a DLL?

A The application will not be able to execute. When a DLL is implicitly linked to an application via an import library, the .DLL file must be present for the application to successfully initialize. Applications that explicitly link to a DLL are different in this regard and can provide a means of recovering from a missing .DLL file. However, in many situations an application is seriously crippled if a DLL is missing. As an example, MFC applications that dynamically link to the MFC DLL cannot run at all if the DLL isn't present.

Q How does an application use an import library to access code within a DLL?

A When an application is designed to dynamically link to a DLL, it includes references to DLL classes and functions instead of the actual code for them. The import library is responsible for establishing these references when an application is compiled. At runtime, the DLL is dynamically linked to the application and the class and function references are resolved. The neat thing about DLLs is that all this linking takes place behind the scenes, which means the application code looks no different than if the code for the classes and functions had been statically linked with the application.

Workshop

The Workshop is designed to help you anticipate possible questions, review what you've learned, and begin thinking ahead to put your knowledge into practice. The answers to the quiz are in Appendix A, "Quiz Answers."

Quiz

1. What is a static library?
2. What file extension is typically used to identify DLLs?
3. What is the special library file that contains information about the classes, functions, and data exported by a DLL?
4. What is the primary benefit of DLLs?
5. What is the main distinction between DLLs and applications?
6. What function is called by Windows to perform any initialization and cleanup for a DLL?
7. What do you call functions that DLLs make available for applications to call?
8. How are import libraries different from other libraries?
9. What special identifier do you use to export entire MFC classes from a DLL?
10. What standard MFC header file must you include in the source code file containing the `DLLMain()` function for an MFC extension DLL?

Exercises

1. Modify the Doodle application to use the TipOfTheDay DLL. Be sure to link in the import library for the DLL and copy the .DLL file to the directory containing the Doodle.exe application.
2. Add some new tips of your own to the TipOfTheDay DLL. Next rebuild the DLL and copy the .DLL file to the directory containing the Doodle.exe application so that you can test the new tips.

HOUR 23

Creating Custom Controls

In this hour, you learn about custom controls and how to create them. Earlier in the book you learned how controls are used as application building blocks. That's fine, but what if you need special functionality that isn't provided by the standard MFC control classes? You take matters into your own hands and create your own control class that does exactly what you want. This hour covers some fundamentals of control creation and then shows you how to create a couple of custom controls.

In this hour, you will learn

- When to think about creating custom controls
- How to derive a custom control from an existing control class
- How to create a new custom control from scratch

When Standard Controls Aren't Enough

Back in Hour 5, "Making Use of Controls," you learned about the many different controls available for use in MFC applications. You also spent some time creating an application that used some of the controls. You didn't learn, however, what to do in a situation where there isn't a control to accomplish a task required of your application. As useful as standard controls are, situations will arise that require a custom control.

Custom controls are controls that you create to carry out a specific task. Even though this task might initially apply to a specific application, you might end up creating a control that is reusable in other applications. In fact, this should be your goal when creating custom controls. The idea is to package a specific task or piece of application functionality into a single control class that can be easily reused in other applications. Reusability is really the main benefit of moving application functionality into a control. Creating custom controls can lessen your workload in the future and ultimately improve the structure of your applications.

NEW TERM A *custom control* is a user-defined control that is created to carry out a specific task.

There is nothing mystical about custom controls; they are implemented in classes just like standard controls. Custom controls don't even have to use MFC, although I highly suggest it because MFC provides so many useful features. Custom controls can be based on existing controls or they can be created from scratch. Either way, I encourage you to use MFC as the basis for custom controls. Following are the two approaches available to you when it comes to creating a custom control class:

- Derive the class from an existing MFC control class
- Derive the class from `CObject`

Even though the second approach involves deriving from an existing class (`CObject`), from a control perspective it really means that you're creating a control from scratch. In other words, you aren't inheriting any functionality from an existing control class. It's usually smart to derive from an existing control class if the class provides significant functionality that you can take advantage of. Remember that one of the main points of classes and object-oriented programming is to reuse code as often as possible. By inheriting functionality from parent control classes, you're saving yourself unnecessary work.

Although I've only mentioned deriving custom controls from existing control classes, you might also consider deriving some controls directly from the `CWnd` class. The `CWnd` class is the parent of all the standard control classes, so

> if you want to build on basic windowing functionality, CWnd is a good place to start.

There are two types of controls that you can create: visible and invisible. Visible controls are controls that are typically based on the CWnd class and that are visible at runtime. Invisible controls usually aren't based on CWnd and are not visible at runtime. Invisible controls perform tasks that don't require visible output or user interactions, such as timers.

NEW TERM A *visible control* is a control that is visible at runtime.

NEW TERM An *invisible control* is a control that is not visible at runtime.

It is rare that you would want to derive an invisible control from an existing control class. Because they are all visible, the standard controls typically don't provide any features that benefit invisible custom controls. For this reason, you will generally derive invisible control classes from CObject. The audio clip control you develop later in the hour is an example of an invisible control that is derived directly from CObject.

Deriving from an Existing Control

In this section, you develop the CColorBox control class, which implements a color box custom control. The color box control simply draws a colored rectangle based on the value of its color property. The color box control demonstrates how to derive a custom control from an existing MFC control class, in this case CStatic.

Deriving a custom control from an existing control is often as simple as deriving a class from an MFC class and overriding appropriate member functions. In most cases you will also define member data for the control and provide a few public member functions for accessing the data. Listing 23.1 contains the declaration of the CColorBox custom control class.

LISTING 23.1 THE COLORBOX.H HEADER FILE FOR THE CColorBox CONTROL

```
1: #ifndef __COLORBOX_H__
2: #define __COLORBOX_H__
3:
4: //-------------------------------------------------------------
```

continues

LISTING 23.1 CONTINUED

```
 5: // CColorBox Class - ColorBox Control Object
 6: //-----------------------------------------------------------------
 7: class CColorBox : public CStatic {
 8:   // Member Data
 9: protected:
10:   COLORREF   m_crColor;
11:
12:   // Public Constructor(s)/Destructor
13: public:
14:               CColorBox(COLORREF cr = RGB(255, 255, 255));
15:   virtual     ~CColorBox();
16:
17:   // Public Member Functions
18: public:
19:   virtual BOOL  Create(DWORD dwStyle,const RECT& rect,
20:     CWnd* pParentWnd, UINT nID);
21:   COLORREF    GetColor()                    { return m_crColor; }
22:   void        SetColor(COLORREF crColor)    { m_crColor = crColor; }
23:
24:   // Message Handlers
25: public:
26:   afx_msg void   OnPaint();
27:
28:   // Message Map & Runtime Support
29: protected:
30:   DECLARE_MESSAGE_MAP()
31:   DECLARE_DYNCREATE(CColorBox)
32: };
33:
34: #endif
```

The class declaration for CColorBox shows that the class is derived from CStatic. The CColorBox class declares a single member variable, m_crColor, which stores the current color used by the control. The constructor for the class accepts a COLORREF parameter that is used to set the color of the control. Notice that white (RGB(255, 255, 255)) is specified as the default color value of this parameter if no color is provided.

Generally speaking, it is a good idea for all CWnd-derived control classes to override the Create() member function because it plays a vital role in the creation of controls. If you recall, this member function is called to create the underlying window for a control after a control object has been created. The CColorBox class also provides a couple of access member functions for getting and setting the m_crColor member variable. And finally, the OnPaint() message handler is implemented to enable the control to paint itself. Practically all CWnd-derived controls will implement this message handler in order to paint themselves.

Creating Custom Controls

The inner workings of the CColorBox class are revealed in Listing 23.2, which contains the class implementation.

LISTING 23.2 THE COLORBOX.CPP SOURCE CODE FILE FOR THE CColorBox CONTROL

```
 1: //----------------------------------------------------------------
 2: // Inclusions
 3: //----------------------------------------------------------------
 4: #include "StdAfx.h"
 5: //----------------------------------------------------------------
 6: #include "ColorBox.h"
 7:
 8: //----------------------------------------------------------------
 9: // MFC Debugging Support
10: //----------------------------------------------------------------
11: #ifdef _DEBUG
12: #undef THIS_FILE
13: static char BASED_CODE THIS_FILE[] = __FILE__;
14: #endif
15:
16:
17: //----------------------------------------------------------------
18: // Message Map & Runtime Support
19: //----------------------------------------------------------------
20: BEGIN_MESSAGE_MAP(CColorBox, CStatic)
21:    ON_WM_PAINT()
22: END_MESSAGE_MAP()
23:
24: IMPLEMENT_DYNCREATE(CColorBox, CStatic)
25:
26: //----------------------------------------------------------------
27: // Public Constructor(s)/Destructor
28: //----------------------------------------------------------------
29: CColorBox::CColorBox(COLORREF crColor) {
30:    // Initialize the member data
31:    m_crColor = crColor;
32: }
33:
34: CColorBox::~CColorBox() {
35: }
36:
37: //----------------------------------------------------------------
38: // Public Member Functions
39: //----------------------------------------------------------------
40: BOOL CColorBox::Create(DWORD dwStyle, const RECT& rect,
41:    CWnd* pParentWnd, UINT nID) {
42:    return CStatic::Create("", dwStyle, rect, pParentWnd, nID);
43: }
44:
```

continues

LISTING 23.2   CONTINUED

```
45: //-----------------------------------------------------------
46: // Message Handlers
47: //-----------------------------------------------------------
48: void CColorBox::OnPaint() {
49:     CPaintDC dc(this);
50:
51:     // Draw the color box
52:     RECT rc;
53:     GetClientRect(&rc);
54:     CBrush br(m_crColor);
55:     dc.FillRect(&rc, &br);
56: }
```

The constructor for `CColorBox` is very simple in that it just initializes the `m_crColor` member variable. The `Create()` member function is also very straightforward; it calls the parent `CStatic::Create()` member function and passes on its parameters. It does take care of passing an empty string as the caption for the control because the `CColorBox` control doesn't display any text.

The only significant code in `CColorBox` is in the `OnPaint()` message handler, which paints a filled rectangle in the color specified by `m_crColor`. No tricks here!

That finishes up the `CColorBox` control. I know it's a very basic control, but I want to keep things simple and not lose focus on the goal. Besides, you might have the need at some point to display a color in an application, and now you have a control that will do that for you. You test out the `CColorBox` control in an application a little later in the hour.

Creating a Control from Scratch

You learned earlier in the hour that it's possible to create controls that aren't based on an existing control class. In this section you build a control named `CAudioClip` that is derived from the `CObject` class, as opposed to `CWnd`, `CStatic`, or some other control class. The `CAudioClip` control is interesting because it is an invisible control. Instead of performing some kind of visual task, this control plays audio clips. It's not hard to see the reason why a control that plays audio clips is implemented as an invisible control.

Listing 23.3 contains the source code for the AudioClip.h header file.

LISTING 23.3   THE AudioClip.h HEADER FILE FOR THE `CAudioClip` CONTROL

```
1: #ifndef __AUDIOCLIP_H__
2: #define __AUDIOCLIP_H__
3:
```

```
 4: //-----------------------------------------------------------
 5: // CAudioClip Class - AudioClip Control Object
 6: //-----------------------------------------------------------
 7: class CAudioClip : public CObject {
 8:    // Member Data
 9: protected:
10:    CString m_sClip;
11:    BOOL    m_bLoop;
12:    BOOL    m_bAutoStart;
13:
14:    // Public Constructor(s)/Destructor
15: public:
16:            CAudioClip(LPCTSTR psClip = "Chimes.wav",
17:              BOOL bLoop = FALSE, BOOL bAutoStart = TRUE);
18:    virtual ~CAudioClip();
19:
20:    // Public Member Functions
21: public:
22:    void    Play();
23:    void    Stop();
24:    CString& GetClip()                     { return m_sClip; }
25:    void    SetClip(LPCTSTR psClip) { m_sClip = CString(psClip); }
26:    BOOL    GetLoop()                      { return m_bLoop; }
27:    void    SetLoop(BOOL bLoop)     { m_bLoop = bLoop; }
28:
29:    // Runtime Support
30: protected:
31:    DECLARE_DYNCREATE(CAudioClip)
32: };
33:
34: #endif
```

The `CAudioClip` class declares three member variables: `m_sClip`, `m_bLoop`, and `m_bAutoStart`. The `m_sClip` member variable is a string that stores the filename of the audio clip associated with the control. The other two member variables are Boolean values that determine how the audio clip is played. If the `m_bLoop` member is set to TRUE, the audio clip will be looped repeatedly. If `m_bAutoStart` is set to TRUE, the audio clip will begin playing as soon as the control is created.

These three member variables are passed as parameters into the constructor for `CAudioClip`. Each parameter is given a default value that is used if an explicit value isn't provided. The `CAudioClip` class also provides a set of public member functions that are used to play and stop the audio clip, as well as access the audio clip and alter the loop property. The access member functions are all defined inline.

Listing 23.4 contains the implementation of the `CAudioClip` class, which reveals how the control works.

LISTING 23.4 THE AUDIOCLIP.CPP SOURCE CODE FILE FOR THE CAudioClip CONTROL

```
 1: //-----------------------------------------------------------------
 2: // Inclusions
 3: //-----------------------------------------------------------------
 4: #include "StdAfx.h"
 5: //-----------------------------------------------------------------
 6: #include "AudioClip.h"
 7: #include "MMSystem.h"
 8:
 9: //-----------------------------------------------------------------
10: // MFC Debugging Support
11: //-----------------------------------------------------------------
12: #ifdef _DEBUG
13: #undef THIS_FILE
14: static char BASED_CODE THIS_FILE[] = __FILE__;
15: #endif
16:
17:
18: //-----------------------------------------------------------------
19: // Runtime Support
20: //-----------------------------------------------------------------
21: IMPLEMENT_DYNCREATE(CAudioClip, CObject)
22:
23: //-----------------------------------------------------------------
24: // Public Constructor(s)/Destructor
25: //-----------------------------------------------------------------
26: CAudioClip::CAudioClip(LPCTSTR psClip, BOOL bLoop, BOOL bAutoStart) {
27:    // Initialize the member data
28:    m_sClip = CString(psClip);
29:    m_bLoop = bLoop;
30:    m_bAutoStart = bAutoStart;
31:
32:    // Play the clip if AutoStart is set
33:    if (bAutoStart)
34:      Play();
35: }
36:
37: CAudioClip::~CAudioClip() {
38: }
39:
40: //-----------------------------------------------------------------
41: // Public Member Functions
42: //-----------------------------------------------------------------
43: void CAudioClip::Play() {
44:    // Play the audio clip
45:    ::sndPlaySound(m_sClip, SND_ASYNC | SND_FILENAME |
46:      (m_bLoop ? SND_LOOP : 0));
47: }
48:
49: void CAudioClip::Stop() {
```

```
50:     // Stop playing the audio clip
51:     ::sndPlaySound(NULL, SND_ASYNC | SND_FILENAME);
52: }
```

The constructor for `CAudioClip` first initializes the member variables, and then takes on the task of supporting its auto-start functionality. If the `bAutoStart` parameter is `TRUE`, the `Play()` member function is called to play the audio clip.

The `Play()` member function relies on a Win32 function called `sndPlaySound()` to play the audio clip. The `sndPlaySound()` function accepts a string containing the filename of an audio clip, along with a set of properties that dictate how the clip is played. The `SND_ASYNC` property indicates that the audio clip is to be played asynchronously, which results in the `sndPlaySound()` function returning immediately and allowing the application to go about its business while the clip plays. If you didn't specify this property, the application would freeze until the sound finished playing. The `SND_FILENAME` property indicates that the audio clip is stored in a file; you can also use `sndPlaySound()` to play sounds from memory or resources.

The `SND_LOOP` property results in the audio clip being played repeatedly. You stop a looped audio clip by calling `sndPlaySound()` and passing `NULL` as the clip filename. This approach is used in the `Stop()` member function to stop playing the audio clip.

> The `sndPlaySound()` Win32 function expects audio clips to be stored in the Windows WAVE format, which is evident by the file extension .WAV. Windows ships with plenty of sample .WAV audio clips, or you can record your own with the Sound Recorder application that also ships with Windows.

You might have noticed that the AudioClip.cpp file includes a header file called MMSystem.h. This Win32 header file defines all the constants, structures, and functions that comprise the Windows multimedia system. Any application that includes this header file must also statically link the standard WinMM.lib. This also means that any application that uses the `CAudioClip` control class must link in the library. The ControlTest application that you develop in the next section is such an application.

Testing Controls

You've now successfully built two custom controls, but you've yet to see them in action. The remainder of the hour focuses on the development of an application that tests the controls. The application is called ControlTest and is based on the familiar Skeleton application that you've grown so attached to.

All the control-related code in ControlTest is located in the `CMainFrame` frame window class. Listing 23.5 contains the declaration of the `CMainFrame` class.

LISTING 23.5 THE MAINFRAME.H HEADER FILE FOR THE `CMainFrame` FRAME WINDOW CLASS

```
 1: #ifndef __MAINFRAME_H__
 2: #define __MAINFRAME_H__
 3:
 4: //-----------------------------------------------------------
 5: // Inclusions
 6: //-----------------------------------------------------------
 7: #include "ColorBox.h"
 8: #include "AudioClip.h"
 9:
10: //-----------------------------------------------------------
11: // CMainFrame Class - Main Frame Window Object
12: //-----------------------------------------------------------
13: class CMainFrame : public CFrameWnd {
14:     // Member Data
15: protected:
16:     CColorBox   m_ColorBox;
17:     CAudioClip  m_AudioClip;
18:
19:     // Public Constructor(s)/Destructor
20: public:
21:                 CMainFrame();
22:     virtual     ~CMainFrame();
23:
24:     // Public Member Functions
25: public:
26:     BOOL        Create(const CString& sTitle);
27:
28:     // Message Handlers
29: public:
30:     afx_msg int  OnCreate(LPCREATESTRUCT lpCreateStruct);
31:     afx_msg void OnLButtonDown(UINT nFlags, CPoint point);
32:     afx_msg void OnRButtonDown(UINT nFlags, CPoint point);
33:
34:     // Message Map & Runtime Support
35: protected:
36:     DECLARE_MESSAGE_MAP()
37:     DECLARE_DYNCREATE(CMainFrame)
38: };
39:
40: #endif
```

Creating Custom Controls

The first thing to notice about the header file for `CMainFrame` is that it includes the header files for each of the custom controls. This is necessary so that the `CMainFrame` class knows about the control classes. The `CMainFrame` class then declares two member variables to contain one of each of the controls.

The familiar `Create()` function is declared in order to facilitate the creation of the frame window. The `OnCreate()` message handler is used to provide a place to create the color box control. Also, the `OnLButtonDown()` and `OnRButtonDown()` message handlers are used to provide a means of starting and stopping the playing of the audio clip.

Listing 23.6 contains the implementation of the `CMainFrame` class.

LISTING 23.6 THE MAINFRAME.CPP SOURCE CODE FILE FOR THE `CMainFrame` FRAME WINDOW CLASS

```
 1: //----------------------------------------------------------------
 2: // Inclusions
 3: //----------------------------------------------------------------
 4: #include "StdAfx.h"
 5: //----------------------------------------------------------------
 6: #include "MainFrame.h"
 7: #include "Resource.h"
 8:
 9: //----------------------------------------------------------------
10: // MFC Debugging Support
11: //----------------------------------------------------------------
12: #ifdef _DEBUG
13: #undef THIS_FILE
14: static char BASED_CODE THIS_FILE[] = __FILE__;
15: #endif
16:
17:
18: //----------------------------------------------------------------
19: // Message Map & Runtime Support
20: //----------------------------------------------------------------
21: BEGIN_MESSAGE_MAP(CMainFrame, CFrameWnd)
22:   ON_WM_CREATE()
23:   ON_WM_LBUTTONDOWN()
24:   ON_WM_RBUTTONDOWN()
25: END_MESSAGE_MAP()
26:
27: IMPLEMENT_DYNCREATE(CMainFrame, CFrameWnd)
28:
29: //----------------------------------------------------------------
30: // Public Constructor(s)/Destructor
31: //----------------------------------------------------------------
```

continues

LISTING 23.6 CONTINUED

```
32: CMainFrame::CMainFrame() {
33: }
34:
35: CMainFrame::~CMainFrame() {
36: }
37:
38: //-----------------------------------------------------------------
39: // Public Member Functions
40: //-----------------------------------------------------------------
41: BOOL CMainFrame::Create(const CString& sTitle) {
42:     CString sClassName;
43:
44:     sClassName = AfxRegisterWndClass(CS_HREDRAW | CS_VREDRAW,
45:       ::LoadCursor(NULL, IDC_ARROW),
46:       (HBRUSH)(COLOR_WINDOW + 1),
47:       ::LoadIcon(AfxGetInstanceHandle(),
48:       MAKEINTRESOURCE(IDR_CONTROLTEST)));
49:
50:     return CFrameWnd::Create(sClassName, sTitle);
51: }
52:
53: //-----------------------------------------------------------------
54: // Message Handlers
55: //-----------------------------------------------------------------
56: int CMainFrame::OnCreate(LPCREATESTRUCT lpCreateStruct) {
57:     // Create a color box control and set its color to red
58:     RECT rc = { 5, 5, 100, 100 };
59:     m_ColorBox.Create(WS_CHILD | WS_VISIBLE | WS_BORDER, rc, this, 0);
60:     m_ColorBox.SetColor(RGB(255, 0, 0));
61:
62:     return 0;
63: }
64:
65: void CMainFrame::OnLButtonDown(UINT nFlags, CPoint point) {
66:     // Play a music audio clip looped
67:     m_AudioClip.SetClip("Music.wav");
68:     m_AudioClip.SetLoop(TRUE);
69:     m_AudioClip.Play();
70: }
71:
72: void CMainFrame::OnRButtonDown(UINT nFlags, CPoint point) {
73:     // Stop playing the audio clip
74:     m_AudioClip.Stop();
75: }
```

The `OnCreate()` message handler takes on the responsibility of creating the color box control using the `m_ColorBox` member variable. This code closely resembles the control

Creating Custom Controls

creation code you developed back in Hour 5. A rectangle is first created to identify the physical dimensions of the control. This rectangle is passed into the control's `Create()` member function, along with the window styles, parent window pointer (`this`), and identifier for the control. The `SetColor()` member function is then called to set the color of the control to red.

The audio clip control comes into play in the mouse button handlers. The `OnLButtonDown()` message handler uses the `SetClip()` member function to set the audio clip to a music WAVE file, and then sets it to loop with a call to `SetLoop()`. The audio clip is then played with a call to the `Play()` member function. The `OnRButtonDown()` handler stops playing the clip by calling the control's `Stop()` member function.

One thing that you might not have noticed is that an audio clip is played when the control is first created as a member variable of `CMainFrame`. This is due to the fact that the `m_bAutoStart` member variable of `CAudioClip` is set to `TRUE` by default in the class constructor. The result is the default clip Chimes.wav being played. When you run the ControlTest application, you'll notice that a chimes sound is played when the application first starts. Figure 23.1 shows the completed ControlTest application.

FIGURE 23.1

The ControlTest application with a visible color box control and an invisible audio clip control.

> Don't forget that the ControlTest application must link in the standard WinMM.lib library because the `CAudioClip` control uses the `sndPlaySound()` Win32 function. This is necessary because the `sndPlaySound()` function is part of the Windows multimedia system, which isn't a part of the core Win32 library.

Summary

This hour ponders the question of what to do when a standard control doesn't do the trick. Actually, this hour goes far beyond pondering by showing you exactly how to build custom controls. You began the hour by assessing the need for custom controls. You then learned how to build a custom control that is based on an existing control class. From there you moved on to building a custom control that doesn't derive from a control class from scratch. You wrapped up the hour by testing out the controls in an MFC application.

Q&A

Q How do the custom MFC controls covered in this hour relate to ActiveX controls?

A ActiveX controls are special controls based on Microsoft's COM (Component Object Model) specification that are designed for use in a wide range of applications. More specifically, ActiveX controls are required to support a language-independent interface so they can be used in different types of development environments. Unlike ActiveX controls, the custom MFC controls you developed in this hour are limited because they can only be used in MFC applications. You could certainly convert the controls to support ActiveX, however, but it would involve a significant amount of work due to the overhead required of ActiveX.

Q Why doesn't the `CAudioClip` class provide a `Create()` member function for creating the control?

A Because the `Create()` member function is only required for classes that derive from `CWnd`. This is because all MFC window classes have an underlying Win32 window object that must be created via a call to `Create()`. The audio clip control is an invisible control, so it has no need to derive from `CWnd` or to provide a `Create()` member function.

Workshop

The Workshop is designed to help you anticipate possible questions, review what you've learned, and begin thinking ahead to put your knowledge into practice. The answers to the quiz are in Appendix A, "Quiz Answers."

Quiz

1. What is a custom control?
2. What is the main benefit of placing application functionality in a control?

3. When should you derive a custom control class from an existing control class?
4. What MFC class is the parent of all the standard control classes?
5. What is a visible control?
6. What are some differences between visible and invisible controls?
7. From what MFC class is an invisible control usually derived?
8. What member function associated with creation should all `CWnd`-derived control classes typically override?
9. What message handler should all `CWnd`-derived control classes implement in order to paint themselves?
10. What header file and static library are required to use the `sndPlaySound()` Win32 function?

Exercises

1. Try your hand at creating some more color box controls in the ControlTest application and setting them to different colors. You might even experiment with altering the colors based on the user clicking the left and right mouse buttons.
2. Record an audio clip using a microphone and the Sound Recorder application, and then play it using the `CAudioClip` control class in the ControlTest application.

HOUR 24

Creating Wizards

This hour introduces you to wizards, those nifty little user interfaces that guide you through a series of steps to accomplish a given task. Wizards have become very popular in modern Windows applications, and serve a valuable purpose in making the user interface of an application more intuitive. This hour covers the basics of wizards and how they are developed using MFC. Toward the end of the hour you'll create a Wizard using MFC classes and then try it out in an MFC application.

In this hour, you will learn

- How wizards are used to simplify tasks in Windows applications
- About the relationship between property pages and wizards
- How to create wizards using MFC

Simplifying Tasks with Wizards

Wizards represent a relatively new graphical user interface feature in Windows that has caught on and enjoyed widespread use. In case you're new to them, wizards are user interface components that use a multistep questionnaire to gather information from the user. Aside from being used in many Windows applications, wizards are also used throughout the Windows operating system. Have you ever installed a printer in Windows 95/98? If so, then you've already had some experience in using wizards. Figures 24.1 through 24.3 show the Windows 95/98 Add Printer Wizard that is used to install new printers.

NEW TERM A user interface component that uses a multistep questionnaire to gather information from the user is called a *wizard*.

FIGURE 24.1

The first page of the Windows 98 Add Printer Wizard.

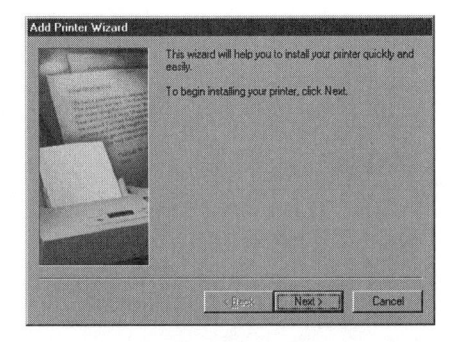

FIGURE 24.2

The second page of the Windows 98 Add Printer Wizard.

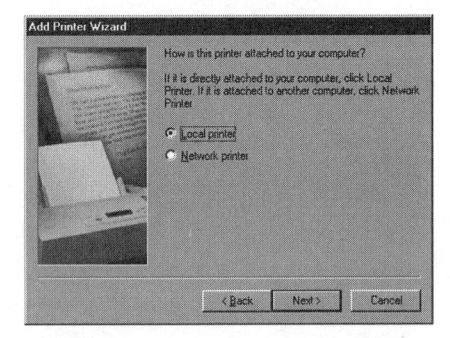

FIGURE 24.3

The third page of the Windows 98 Add Printer Wizard.

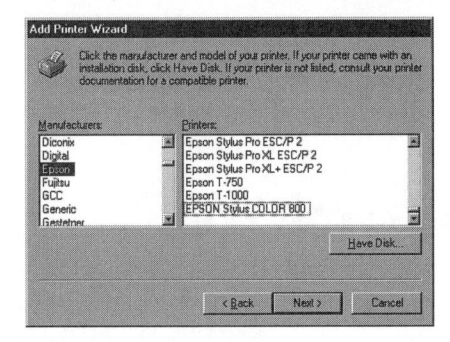

You'll notice from the figures that the Add Printer Wizard involves multiple steps, which are broken down into pages. You can think of a wizard as a type of flip-book questionnaire you proceed through a page at a time. All Wizards support the Back and Next buttons for navigating through the pages. Additionally, the last page of a wizard includes a Finish button, which carries out the task of the wizard. There is also a Cancel button on each page that allows you to cancel out of a wizard.

Although wizards are typically used to automate the process of gathering information for some task such as installing a printer, a wizard can take on the responsibility of performing a task before exiting. For example, you could use a wizard to gather information for a calculation and then display the results in the last page of the wizard. This is the approach you use later in the hour when you build a wizard.

It's important to understand that generally speaking, wizards serve as enhancements to an application's user interface, not as replacements for traditional user interface elements such as menus and dialog boxes. In other words, you should attempt to provide a means of accomplishing a task manually and then build a wizard that helps automate the task. Some power users might prefer to do things manually without the help of a wizard. Understandably, there might be some situations where a wizard is simply the most effective user interface for completing a complex task, in which case you might not be able to provide another option.

Property Sheets, Property Pages, and Wizards

Wizards are very close relatives of property sheets, also known as tab dialog boxes, which represent another user interface feature that has enjoyed widespread use in Windows. A property sheet is a user interface component that presents multiple dialog boxes as pages within a single window; each page is accessed via a tab. The pages in a property sheet are called property pages, and provide a solution to the problem of trying to gather lots of information within a single dialog box. There are physical limitations as to how much information can be gathered from a single dialog box, so property pages effectively enable you to use multiple dialog boxes within the same context, the property sheet. Figures 24.4 and 24.5 show a couple of the pages of the Display Properties dialog box in Windows 98.

> **NEW TERM** A *property sheet* is a user interface component that presents multiple dialog boxes as pages within a single window; each page is accessed via a tab.

> **NEW TERM** A *property page* is a page within a property sheet that is logically equivalent to a single dialog box.

FIGURE 24.4

The Background page of the Windows 98 Display Properties property page.

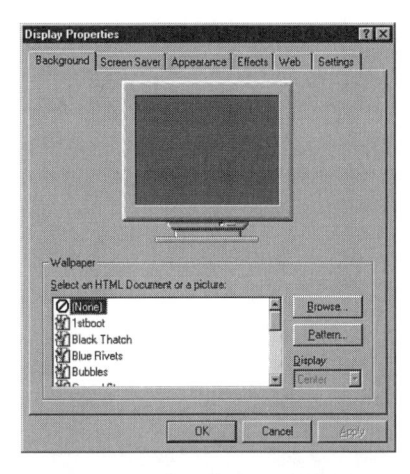

FIGURE 24.5

The Screen Saver page of the Windows 98 Display Properties property page.

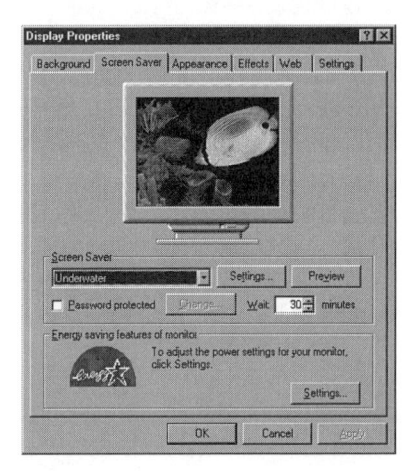

As you can see in the figures, property sheets are similar to wizards in that they are designed to display multiple pages of information. Each property page in a property sheet is logically equivalent to an individual dialog box. In fact, you can think of the property sheet tabs as the names of the different dialog boxes (pages) contained within the property sheet.

> It isn't just a coincidence that property pages appear to be so similar to dialog boxes; property pages are actually implemented as dialog boxes. In fact, you define the layout of individual property pages using dialog box resources. You learn how to do this later in the hour when you build the Investment Wizard.

Property sheets are different from wizards in that property sheets enable the user to click on a tab and go to any page at will. Wizards are more restrictive and enforce an ordered approach to navigating the pages. To enforce this page order, wizards don't provide tabs for page navigation. Also, property sheets don't provide Back or Next buttons to navigate between pages because the user can just use the tabs.

Other than navigational differences, property sheets and wizards are actually very much alike. Following are some of the similarities between them:

- They serve as a container for multiple pages
- Their pages are laid out as dialog box resources
- They provide a means of navigating through the pages
- They automatically provide buttons for performing standard tasks such as OK, Finish, Cancel, and so on.

Although wizards and property sheets differ slightly in their approaches to some of these things, such as navigating through pages, they are still very similar. Consequently, it shouldn't come as too big of a surprise that creating a property page is little different than creating a wizard. In fact, the same MFC class is used as the basis for creating both property pages and wizards. Let's learn how this could possibly work!

MFC's Support for Property Sheets and Wizards

MFC provides wizards with full support based on its support for property pages. You really have to learn about property pages to learn about wizards. There are two MFC classes that encapsulate the functionality of both property pages and wizards:

- CPropertySheet—supports both property sheets and wizards
- CPropertyPage—supports pages within a property sheet or wizard

The CPropertySheet Class

Property sheets and wizards are implemented in the CPropertySheet class, which is derived from CWnd. The CPropertySheet class serves as a container for property pages, which themselves represent dialog boxes. Within an application, a property sheet consists of a CPropertySheet object and multiple CPropertyPage objects. You can communicate with the individual pages in a property sheet by calling member functions of the CPropertySheet class.

Although the `CPropertySheet` class is derived from `CWnd`, interacting with a property sheet or wizard is a lot like interacting with a dialog box via a `CDialog` object. For starters, displaying a property sheet requires the familiar two-step process required of dialog boxes:

1. Create a `CPropertySheet` object.
2. Call the `DoModal()` member function to display the property sheet or wizard as a modal dialog box.

> The `CPropertySheet` class also supports modeless property sheets and wizards, in which case you use the `Create()` member function instead of `DoModal()`. Modeless property sheets and wizards are more complicated to implement than their modal counterparts. Beyond that, it typically doesn't make sense for a wizard to be modeless.

Following is an example of creating a property sheet that is implemented in a `CPropertySheet`-derived class named `CMyPropSheet`:

```
CMyPropSheet propSheet;
propSheet.DoModal();
```

This code looks just like the code for creating and displaying a dialog box. Creating and displaying a wizard requires an additional member function call to indicate that the property sheet is in fact a wizard:

```
CMyWizard wiz;
wiz.SetWizardMode();
wiz.DoModal();
```

The `SetWizardMode()` member function establishes that a property sheet is to operate as a wizard. The result is that the Back and Next buttons are used to navigate the pages instead of tabs. The Finish button is also typically used on the last page to indicate that the user is finished with the wizard. When you call the `DoModal()` member function on a wizard, it will return `ID_WIZFINISH` or `IDCANCEL`, depending on whether the user clicked the Finish button or the Cancel button to exit the wizard.

Getting back to the `CPropertySheet` class, Table 24.1 lists some of the member functions commonly used with wizards.

TABLE 24.1 THE MOST COMMONLY USED CPropertySheet MEMBER FUNCTIONS FOR WIZARDS

Member Function	Description
DoModal()	Displays the wizard as a modal dialog box
SetWizardMode()	Forces the property sheet to operate as a wizard
SetWizardButtons()	Determines which wizard buttons are displayed/enabled
AddPage()	Adds a page to the wizard
RemovePage()	Removes a page from the wizard

You're already familiar with the `DoModal()` and `SetWizardMode()` member functions, so let's focus on the remaining three functions. The `SetWizardButtons()` member function is called to specify which buttons are displayed in the wizard. You will typically call this function within a property page to set the wizard buttons when the page becomes active. `SetWizardButtons()` accepts a flag that can be a combination of the following button identifiers:

- PSWIZB_BACK—Back button
- PSWIZB_NEXT—Next button
- PSWIZB_FINISH—Finish button
- PSWIZB_DISABLEDFINISH—Disabled Finish button

The `AddPage()` and `RemovePage()` member functions of `CProperySheet` are used to add and remove pages in a wizard. Following is an example of how the `AddPage()` function is used:

```
CWizPage1 page1;
page1.Construct(IDD_WIZPAGE1, 0);
AddPage(&page1);
```

This creates a property page and adds it to a property sheet. The property page is based on the dialog box resource identified by `IDD_WIZPAGE1`. This identifier is passed into the `Construct()` member function of the property page.

The CPropertyPage Class

I've mentioned property pages a lot throughout the hour but I haven't said much about the `CPropertyPage` class. This class provides the functionality required of a dialog-based property page. Table 24.2 lists the most commonly used member functions defined in the `CPropertyPage` class.

TABLE 24.2 THE MOST COMMONLY USED CPropertyPage MEMBER FUNCTIONS FOR WIZARDS

`Contruct()`	Constructs the property page
`OnSetActive()`	Called when the page becomes active
`OnKillActive()`	Called when the page is no longer active
`OnWizardBack()`	Called when the user clicks the Back button
`OnWizardNext()`	Called when the user clicks the Next button
`OnWizardFinish()`	Called when the user clicks the Finish button

You saw how to use the `Construct()` member function in the previous section. The rest of the member functions in Table 24.2 are called in response to some event. `OnSetActive()` is probably the most important of these functions because it is a good place to set the wizard buttons and set the values of dialog controls. The remaining member functions are useful within the context of certain wizards.

It's important to understand that the `CPropertyPage` class is derived from `CDialog`, which means that you use it much like you would the `CDialog` class. A property page class derived from `CPropertyPage` can override the `OnInitDialog()` member function to perform any one-time initialization chores. Property page classes also have message maps that enable them to respond to messages just like dialog boxes.

Creating a Simple Wizard

If you recall in Hour 7, "Retrieving Information with Custom Dialog Boxes," you created an application called Finance that used a dialog box to gather information and calculate gains on an investment. Although this dialog box was certainly functional, it could be improved by moving its functionality into a wizard. The remainder of this hour leads through the development of an Investment Wizard that performs a similar function as the dialog box in Finance. You'll also build a Finance2 application that allows you to test the wizard.

The Investment Wizard consists of three pages that gather information about an investment and display the results. Figures 24.6 through 24.8 show the finished Investment Wizard as it appears in the Finance2 application. This should give you a good idea about what you are creating as you work through the code for the wizard.

FIGURE 24.6

The first page of the Investment Wizard.

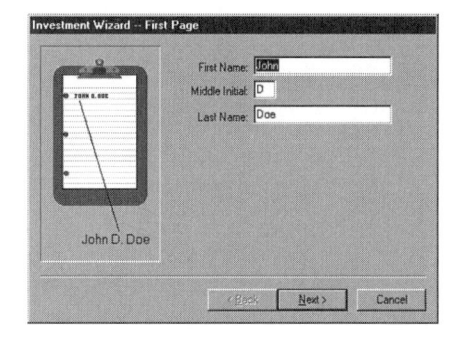

FIGURE 24.7

The second page of the Investment Wizard.

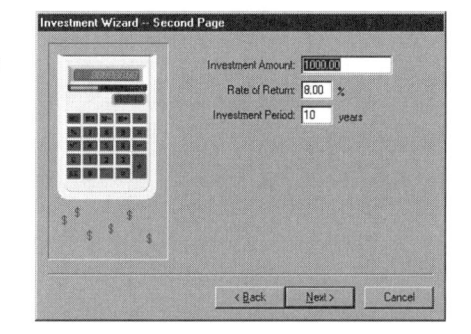

FIGURE 24.8

The third page of the Investment Wizard.

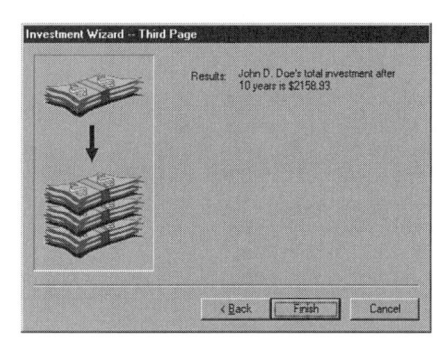

The Resources

The best place to start when building a wizard is to assemble the dialog box resources for each wizard page. Because the Investment Wizard is part of the Finance2 application, its resources must be defined along with the application's resources. Listing 24.1 contains the code for the Finance2 application's Resource.h header file, which includes identifiers for the Investment Wizard's dialog boxes, controls, and bitmaps.

LISTING 24.1 THE RESOURCE.H HEADER FILE FOR FINANCE2

```
 1: //----------------------------------------------------------
 2: // Strings                 Range : 1000 - 1999
 3: //----------------------------------------------------------
 4: #define IDR_FINANCE         1000
 5:
 6: //----------------------------------------------------------
 7: // Commands                 Range : 2000 - 2999
 8: //----------------------------------------------------------
 9: #define ID_FILE_INVESTMENTWIZ 2000
10:
11: //----------------------------------------------------------
12: // Dialog Boxes             Range : 3000 - 3999
13: //----------------------------------------------------------
14: #define IDD_INVESTWIZPAGE1  3000
15: #define IDD_INVESTWIZPAGE2  3001
16: #define IDD_INVESTWIZPAGE3  3002
17: #define IDD_ABOUTBOX        3003
18:
19: //----------------------------------------------------------
20: // Controls                 Range : 4000 - 4999
21: //----------------------------------------------------------
22: #define IDC_FNAME           4000
23: #define IDC_MINITIAL        4001
24: #define IDC_LNAME           4002
25: #define IDC_AMOUNT          4003
26: #define IDC_RETURNRATE      4004
27: #define IDC_PERIOD          4005
28: #define IDC_RESULT          4006
29:
30: //----------------------------------------------------------
31: // Bitmaps                  Range : 5000 - 5999
32: //----------------------------------------------------------
33: #define IDB_INVESTWIZPAGE1  5000
34: #define IDB_INVESTWIZPAGE2  5001
35: #define IDB_INVESTWIZPAGE3  5002
```

The dialog box resources for each page in the Investment Wizard are identified by the constants IDD_INVESTWIZPAGE1, IDD_INVESTWIZPAGE2, and IDD_INVESTWIZPAGE3. The control identifiers are the same ones used in the original Finance application, except for the new IDC_RESULT identifier. You'll learn the importance of this identifier a little later in the hour.

As you might have noticed in the figures showing the completed Investment Wizard, each page of the wizard displays a bitmap. These bitmaps are identified by the constants

IDB_INVESTWIZPAGE1, IDB_INVESTWIZPAGE2, and IDB_INVESTWIZPAGE3. These bitmaps, along with the dialog box resources for the wizard, are defined in Finance.rc, which is shown in Listing 24.2.

LISTING 24.2 THE FINANCE.RC RESOURCE SCRIPT FOR FINANCE2

```
 1: //----------------------------------------------------------------
 2: // Inclusions
 3: //----------------------------------------------------------------
 4: #include "AfxRes.h"
 5: #include "PrSht.h"
 6: #include "Resource.h"
 7:
 8: //----------------------------------------------------------------
 9: // Icons
10: //----------------------------------------------------------------
11: IDR_FINANCE ICON "Finance.ico"
12:
13: //----------------------------------------------------------------
14: // Bitmaps
15: //----------------------------------------------------------------
16: IDB_INVESTWIZPAGE1 BITMAP "IWPage1.bmp"
17: IDB_INVESTWIZPAGE2 BITMAP "IWPage2.bmp"
18: IDB_INVESTWIZPAGE3 BITMAP "IWPage3.bmp"
19:
20: //----------------------------------------------------------------
21: // Menus
22: //----------------------------------------------------------------
23: IDR_FINANCE MENU
24: BEGIN
25:     POPUP "&File"
26:       BEGIN
27:         MENUITEM "&Investment Wizard...",   ID_FILE_INVESTMENTWIZ
28:         MENUITEM SEPARATOR
29:         MENUITEM "E&xit",                   ID_APP_EXIT
30:       END
31:     POPUP "&Help"
32:       BEGIN
33:         MENUITEM "&About Finance...",       ID_APP_ABOUT
34:       END
35: END
36:
37: //----------------------------------------------------------------
38: // Dialog Boxes
39: //----------------------------------------------------------------
40: IDD_INVESTWIZPAGE1 DIALOGEX 0, 0, WIZ_CXDLG, WIZ_CYDLG
41: CAPTION "Investment Wizard -- First Page"
42: STYLE WS_POPUP | WS_CAPTION | WS_SYSMENU | WS_VISIBLE
```

continues

LISTING 24.2 CONTINUED

```
43: FONT 8, "MS Sans Serif"
44: BEGIN
45:     RTEXT           "First Name:", IDC_STATIC, 106, 10, 42, 8, 0
46:     EDITTEXT        IDC_FNAME, 152, 7, 99, 12
47:     RTEXT           "Middle Initial:", IDC_STATIC, 106, 25, 42, 8, 0
48:     EDITTEXT        IDC_MINITIAL, 152, 22, 16, 12
49:     RTEXT           "Last Name:", IDC_STATIC, 106, 42, 42, 8, 0
50:     EDITTEXT        IDC_LNAME, 152, 38, 99, 12
51: END
52:
53: IDD_INVESTWIZPAGE2 DIALOGEX 0, 0, WIZ_CXDLG, WIZ_CYDLG
54: CAPTION "Investment Wizard -- Second Page"
55: STYLE WS_POPUP | WS_CAPTION | WS_SYSMENU | WS_VISIBLE
56: FONT 8, "MS Sans Serif"
57: BEGIN
58:     RTEXT           "Investment Amount:", IDC_STATIC, 112, 10, 64, 8, 0
59:     RTEXT           "Rate of Return:", IDC_STATIC, 112, 26, 64, 8, 0
60:     EDITTEXT        IDC_AMOUNT, 180, 8, 66, 12, ES_NUMBER
61:     EDITTEXT        IDC_RETURNRATE, 180, 24, 23, 12, ES_NUMBER
62:     LTEXT           "%", IDC_STATIC, 206, 27, 8, 8
63:     RTEXT           "Investment Period:", IDC_STATIC, 112, 42, 64, 8, 0
64:     EDITTEXT        IDC_PERIOD, 180, 40, 23, 12, ES_NUMBER
65:     LTEXT           "years", IDC_STATIC, 207, 43, 17, 8
66: END
67:
68: IDD_INVESTWIZPAGE3 DIALOGEX 0, 0, WIZ_CXDLG, WIZ_CYDLG
69: CAPTION "Investment Wizard -- Third Page"
70: STYLE WS_POPUP | WS_CAPTION | WS_SYSMENU | WS_VISIBLE
71: FONT 8, "MS Sans Serif"
72: BEGIN
73:     LTEXT           "Results:", IDC_STATIC, 112, 10, 30, 8, 0
74:     LTEXT           "", IDC_RESULT, 146, 8, 120, 60, 0
75: END
76:
77: IDD_ABOUTBOX DIALOG 0, 0, 217, 55
78: CAPTION "About Finance"
79: STYLE DS_MODALFRAME | WS_POPUP | WS_CAPTION | WS_SYSMENU
80: FONT 8, "MS Sans Serif"
81: BEGIN
82:     ICON            IDR_FINANCE, IDC_STATIC, 11, 17, 20, 20
83:     LTEXT           "Finance Version 2.0", IDC_STATIC, 40, 10,
84:                      119, 8, SS_NOPREFIX
85:     LTEXT           "Copyright (c)1998 Michael Morrison", IDC_STATIC,
86:                      40, 25, 119, 8
87:     DEFPUSHBUTTON   "OK", IDOK, 178, 7, 32, 14, WS_GROUP
88: END
89:
90: //----------------------------------------------------------------
```

```
 91: // Strings
 92: //-------------------------------------------------------------
 93: STRINGTABLE
 94: BEGIN
 95:     AFX_IDS_APP_TITLE    "Finance"
 96: END
```

Perhaps the most important thing to notice about the dialog box resources for the Investment Wizard is their width and height. The dialog boxes are set to the standard wizard page dimensions defined by the WIZ_CXDLG and WIZ_CYDLG constants. These constants are defined in the PrSht.h header file, which is included in Finance.rc.

Although you can't tell it by looking at the resource code, the controls in the wizard page dialog boxes are intentionally placed to the right of the boxes to make room for the bitmaps. The bitmaps are drawn in the source code for the property pages, which you learn about in a moment. Figures 24.9 through 24.11 show the wizard page dialog box resources as defined in Finance.rc.

FIGURE 24.9

The dialog resource for the first page of the Investment Wizard.

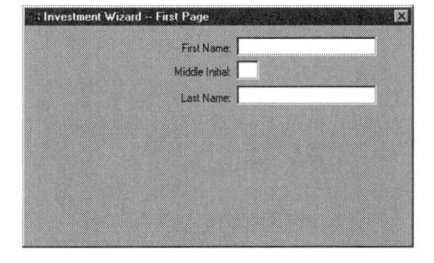

FIGURE 24.10

The dialog resource for the second page of the Investment Wizard.

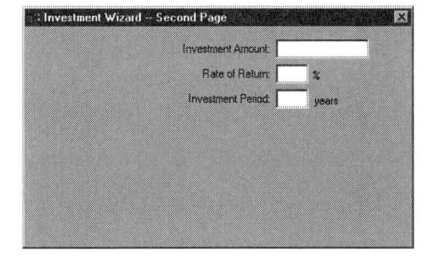

FIGURE 24.11

The dialog resource for the third page of the Investment Wizard.

I wanted to give you a look at the dialog box resources so that you could see how they are impacted when used in the context of a wizard. The wizard class is responsible for displaying the Next, Back, Cancel, and Finish buttons. Each page can tell the wizard which buttons to display or enable, but a page can't directly manipulate the buttons.

The Wizard Data

Before moving on to the page classes and wizard class for the Investment Wizard, it is helpful to define a couple of global variables used by them:

```
CInvestmentWiz* pInvestmentWiz;
CInvestWizData  wizData;
```

These global variables are defined in the InvestmentWiz.cpp source code file along with the page classes and wizard class. The `pInvestmentWiz` pointer keeps track of the wizard object for the sake of the page objects. This is necessary so that the pages can call `SetWizardButtons()` on the wizard to display and enable the appropriate wizard buttons.

The `wizData` global variable is of type `CInvestWizData`, which is a custom data class used to hold the information edited by the user in the wizard. Listing 24.3 contains the declaration of the `CInvestWizData` class.

LISTING 24.3 THE `CInvestWizData` CLASS DECLARATION FOR FINANCE2

```
 1: class CInvestWizData : public CObject {
 2:     // Public Member Data
 3: public:
 4:     CString m_sFName;
 5:     CString m_sMInitial;
 6:     CString m_sLName;
 7:     float   m_fAmount;
 8:     float   m_fReturnRate;
 9:     int     m_nPeriod;
10:
11:     // Public Constructor(s)/Destructor
12: public:
13:     CInvestWizData();
14: };
```

As you can see, the `CInvestWizData` class includes the member variables that appeared in the dialog box in the original Finance application. Sometimes you will want to include member data directly in the property pages but in this case you need to share the information across the entire wizard. So, it makes sense to place the data in a global object. Listing 24.4 contains the code for the `CInvestWizData` constructor, which provides initial values for the member data.

LISTING 24.4 THE CInvestWizData:: CInvestWizData() CONSTRUCTOR FOR FINANCE2

```
 1: //-------------------------------------------------------------
 2: // CInvestWizData Public Constructor(s)/Destructor
 3: //-------------------------------------------------------------
 4: CInvestWizData::CInvestWizData() {
 5:    // Initialize the wizard data
 6:    m_sFName = "John";
 7:    m_sMInitial = "D";
 8:    m_sLName = "Doe";
 9:    m_fAmount = 1000.0;
10:    m_fReturnRate = 8.0;
11:    m_nPeriod = 10;
12: }
```

The Wizard Pages

Finally, it's time to learn how the pages for the wizard are implemented. You'll be glad to learn that the Investment Wizard pages are very simple and closely resemble dialog box classes you've seen throughout the book. Listing 24.5 contains the class declaration for the `CInvestWizPage1` wizard page class.

LISTING 24.5 THE CInvestWizPage1 CLASS DECLARATION FOR FINANCE2

```
 1: class CInvestWizPage1 : public CPropertyPage {
 2:    // Private Member Data
 3: private:
 4:    CBitmap   m_bitmap;
 5:
 6:    // Public Member Functions
 7: public:
 8:    BOOL       OnInitDialog();
 9:    BOOL       OnSetActive();
10:    void       DoDataExchange(CDataExchange* pDX);
11:
12:    // Message Handlers
13: public:
14:    afx_msg void  OnPaint();
15:
16:    // Message Map & Runtime Support
17: protected:
18:    DECLARE_MESSAGE_MAP()
19: };
```

No surprises here, except maybe the fact that the `OnPaint()` message handler is used. Painting on a dialog box isn't all that common, but in the case of wizards it makes perfect sense. Listing 24.6 contains the implementation of the `CInvestWizPage1` wizard page class.

LISTING 24.6 THE `CInvestWizPage1` CLASS IMPLEMENTATION FOR FINANCE2

```
 1: //-----------------------------------------------------------------
 2: // CInvestWizPage1 Message Map & Runtime Support
 3: //-----------------------------------------------------------------
 4: BEGIN_MESSAGE_MAP(CInvestWizPage1, CPropertyPage)
 5:   ON_WM_PAINT()
 6: END_MESSAGE_MAP()
 7:
 8: //-----------------------------------------------------------------
 9: // CInvestWizPage1 Public Member Functions
10: //-----------------------------------------------------------------
11: BOOL CInvestWizPage1::OnInitDialog() {
12:   // Load the bitmap
13:   m_bitmap.LoadBitmap(IDB_INVESTWIZPAGE1);
14:
15:   return TRUE;
16: }
17:
18: BOOL CInvestWizPage1::OnSetActive() {
19:   // Show only the Next button
20:   pInvestmentWiz->SetWizardButtons(PSWIZB_NEXT);
21:
22:   // Set the control values
23:   SetDlgItemText(IDC_FNAME, wizData.m_sFName);
24:   SetDlgItemText(IDC_MINITIAL, wizData.m_sMInitial);
25:   SetDlgItemText(IDC_LNAME, wizData.m_sLName);
26:
27:   return TRUE;
28: }
29:
30: void CInvestWizPage1::DoDataExchange(CDataExchange* pDX) {
31:   CDialog::DoDataExchange(pDX);
32:
33:   // Exchange the dialog data
34:   DDX_Text(pDX, IDC_FNAME, wizData.m_sFName);
35:   DDX_Text(pDX, IDC_MINITIAL, wizData.m_sMInitial);
36:   DDX_Text(pDX, IDC_LNAME, wizData.m_sLName);
37: }
38:
39: //-----------------------------------------------------------------
40: // CInvestWizPage1 Message Handlers
41: //-----------------------------------------------------------------
```

```
42: void CInvestWizPage1::OnPaint() {
43:    CPaintDC dc(this);
44:
45:    // Select the bitmap into a memory DC
46:    CDC dcMem;
47:    dcMem.CreateCompatibleDC(&dc);
48:    dcMem.SelectObject(&m_bitmap);
49:
50:    // Copy the bitmap to the dialog DC
51:    dc.BitBlt(0, 0, 129, 226, &dcMem, 0, 0, SRCCOPY);
52: }
```

The bitmap for the page is loaded in the `OnInitDialog()` member function. The `OnSetActive()` member function is then used to set the wizard buttons for the page, which in this case consists only of the Next button. `OnSetActive()` also takes on the task of initializing the dialog controls with the global wizard data that applies to this page. This global data is updated in the `DoDataExchange()` member function, which wires variables to dialog controls. Finally, the `OnPaint()` message handler handles drawing the page's bitmap on the left side of the page.

The remaining two wizard page classes, `CInvestWizPage2` and `CInvestWizPage3`, are implemented very similarly to `CInvestWizPage1`. Listings 24.7 through 24.10 contain the code for these classes

LISTING 24.7 THE CInvestWizPage2 CLASS DECLARATION FOR FINANCE2

```
1: class CInvestWizPage2 : public CPropertyPage {
2:    // Private Member Data
3: private:
4:    CBitmap m_bitmap;
5:
6:    // Public Member Functions
7: public:
8:    BOOL       OnInitDialog();
9:    BOOL       OnSetActive();
10:   void       DoDataExchange(CDataExchange* pDX);
11:
12:   // Message Handlers
13: public:
14:   afx_msg void  OnPaint();
15:
16:   // Message Map & Runtime Support
17: protected:
18:   DECLARE_MESSAGE_MAP()
19: };
```

LISTING 24.8 THE CInvestWizPage2 CLASS IMPLEMENTATION FOR FINANCE2

```
 1: //--------------------------------------------------------------
 2: // CInvestWizPage2 Message Map & Runtime Support
 3: //--------------------------------------------------------------
 4: BEGIN_MESSAGE_MAP(CInvestWizPage2, CPropertyPage)
 5:   ON_WM_PAINT()
 6: END_MESSAGE_MAP()
 7:
 8: //--------------------------------------------------------------
 9: // CInvestWizPage2 Public Member Functions
10: //--------------------------------------------------------------
11: BOOL CInvestWizPage2::OnInitDialog() {
12:   // Load the bitmap
13:   m_bitmap.LoadBitmap(IDB_INVESTWIZPAGE2);
14:
15:   return TRUE;
16: }
17:
18: BOOL CInvestWizPage2::OnSetActive() {
19:   // Show the Back and Next buttons
20:   pInvestmentWiz->SetWizardButtons(PSWIZB_BACK | PSWIZB_NEXT);
21:
22:   // Set the control values
23:   CString sVal;
24:   sVal.Format("%.2f", wizData.m_fAmount);
25:   SetDlgItemText(IDC_AMOUNT, sVal);
26:   sVal.Format("%.2f", wizData.m_fReturnRate);
27:   SetDlgItemText(IDC_RETURNRATE, sVal);
28:   sVal.Format("%d", wizData.m_nPeriod);
29:   SetDlgItemText(IDC_PERIOD, sVal);
30:
31:   return TRUE;
32: }
33:
34: void CInvestWizPage2::DoDataExchange(CDataExchange* pDX) {
35:   CDialog::DoDataExchange(pDX);
36:
37:   // Exchange the dialog data
38:   DDX_Text(pDX, IDC_AMOUNT, wizData.m_fAmount);
39:   DDX_Text(pDX, IDC_RETURNRATE, wizData.m_fReturnRate);
40:   DDX_Text(pDX, IDC_PERIOD, wizData.m_nPeriod);
41: }
42:
43: //--------------------------------------------------------------
44: // CInvestWizPage2 Message Handlers
45: //--------------------------------------------------------------
46: void CInvestWizPage2::OnPaint() {
47:   CPaintDC dc(this);
48:
49:   // Select the bitmap into a memory DC
```

```
50:     CDC dcMem;
51:     dcMem.CreateCompatibleDC(&dc);
52:     dcMem.SelectObject(&m_bitmap);
53:
54:     // Copy the bitmap to the dialog DC
55:     dc.BitBlt(0, 0, 129, 226, &dcMem, 0, 0, SRCCOPY);
56: }
```

LISTING 24.9 THE CInvestWizPage3 CLASS DECLARATION FOR FINANCE2

```
 1: class CInvestWizPage3 : public CPropertyPage {
 2:     // Private Member Data
 3: private:
 4:     CBitmap       m_bitmap;
 5:
 6:     // Public Member Functions
 7: public:
 8:     BOOL          OnInitDialog();
 9:     BOOL          OnSetActive();
10:
11:     // Message Handlers
12: public:
13:     afx_msg void  OnPaint();
14:
15:     // Message Map & Runtime Support
16: protected:
17:     DECLARE_MESSAGE_MAP()
18: };
```

LISTING 24.10 THE CInvestWizPage3 CLASS IMPLEMENTATION FOR FINANCE2

```
 1: //-----------------------------------------------------------------
 2: // CInvestWizPage3 Message Map & Runtime Support
 3: //-----------------------------------------------------------------
 4: BEGIN_MESSAGE_MAP(CInvestWizPage3, CPropertyPage)
 5:    ON_WM_PAINT()
 6: END_MESSAGE_MAP()
 7:
 8: //-----------------------------------------------------------------
 9: // CInvestWizPage3 Public Member Functions
10: //-----------------------------------------------------------------
11: BOOL CInvestWizPage3::OnInitDialog() {
12:    // Load the bitmap
13:    m_bitmap.LoadBitmap(IDB_INVESTWIZPAGE3);
14:
15:    return TRUE;
```

continues

LISTING 24.10 CONTINUED

```
16: }
17:
18: BOOL CInvestWizPage3::OnSetActive() {
19:    // Show the Back and Finish buttons
20:    pInvestmentWiz->SetWizardButtons(PSWIZB_BACK | PSWIZB_FINISH);
21:
22:    // Calculate the investment
23:    float fTotal = wizData.m_fAmount;
24:    for (int i = 0; i < wizData.m_nPeriod; i++)
25:      fTotal += (fTotal * (wizData.m_fReturnRate / 100));
26:
27:    // Display the result
28:    CString sResult;
29:    sResult.Format("%s %s. %s's total investment after %d years is
       ➥$%.2f.",
30:      wizData.m_sFName, wizData.m_sMInitial, wizData.m_sLName,
31:      wizData.m_nPeriod, fTotal);
32:    SetDlgItemText(IDC_RESULT, sResult);
33:
34:    return TRUE;
35: }
36:
37: //-----------------------------------------------------------------
38: // CInvestWizPage3 Message Handlers
39: //-----------------------------------------------------------------
40: void CInvestWizPage3::OnPaint() {
41:    CPaintDC dc(this);
42:
43:    // Select the bitmap into a memory DC
44:    CDC dcMem;
45:    dcMem.CreateCompatibleDC(&dc);
46:    dcMem.SelectObject(&m_bitmap);
47:
48:    // Copy the bitmap to the dialog DC
49:    dc.BitBlt(0, 0, 129, 226, &dcMem, 0, 0, SRCCOPY);
50: }
```

The most important difference to note between all the wizard page classes is the wizard buttons that each of them displays. Also take note that the third page doesn't provide a `DoDataExchange()` member function because it is an output-only page and doesn't need to store user input.

The Wizard

You might have guessed by now that the majority of the work in a wizard is in creating the wizard pages. This means that an actual wizard class requires relatively little code. Listing 24.11 contains the class declaration for the `CInvestmentWiz` wizard class.

LISTING 24.11 THE `CInvestmentWiz` CLASS DECLARATION FOR FINANCE2

```
 1: class CInvestmentWiz : public CPropertySheet {
 2:    // Private Member Data
 3: private:
 4:    CInvestWizPage1 m_page1;
 5:    CInvestWizPage2 m_page2;
 6:    CInvestWizPage3 m_page3;
 7:
 8:    // Public Constructor(s)/Destructor
 9: public:
10:             CInvestmentWiz();
11:
12:    // Message Map & Runtime Support
13: protected:
14:    DECLARE_MESSAGE_MAP()
15: };
```

The `CInvestmentWiz` wizard class contains the individual wizard pages as member objects. This handles their initial creation but it is still necessary to call the `Construct()` member function on each page to properly construct the pages. This is carried out in the constructor for `CInvestmentWiz`, which is shown in Listing 24.12.

LISTING 24.12 THE `CInvestmentWiz` CLASS IMPLEMENTATION FOR FINANCE2

```
 1: //-----------------------------------------------------------------
 2: // CInvestmentWiz Message Map & Runtime Support
 3: //-----------------------------------------------------------------
 4: BEGIN_MESSAGE_MAP(CInvestmentWiz, CPropertySheet)
 5: END_MESSAGE_MAP()
 6:
 7: //-----------------------------------------------------------------
 8: // CInvestmentWiz Public Constructor(s)/Destructor
 9: //-----------------------------------------------------------------
10: CInvestmentWiz::CInvestmentWiz() : CPropertySheet() {
11:    // Create the investment wizard
12:    Construct("Investment Wizard", this);
13:
14:    // Add the wizard pages
15:    m_page1.Construct(IDD_INVESTWIZPAGE1, 0);
16:    m_page2.Construct(IDD_INVESTWIZPAGE2, 0);
17:    m_page3.Construct(IDD_INVESTWIZPAGE3, 0);
18:    AddPage(&m_page1);
19:    AddPage(&m_page2);
20:    AddPage(&m_page3);
21:
22:    // Set the wizard global variable for page access
23:    pInvestmentWiz = this;
24: }
```

As you can see, the `CInvestmentWiz` class implementation consists solely of a message map and a constructor. The constructor constructs each wizard page and then adds them to the wizard via the `AddPage()` member function. It then sets the global wizard pointer variable, `pInvestmentWiz`. As the code demonstrates, the wizard class intelligently delegates most of its functionality to the wizard pages.

Testing the Investment Wizard

What fun would a wizard be if you didn't have an application in which to test it? The Finance2 application is used to test out the Investment Wizard. The File, Investment Wizard command is the menu command that invokes the wizard. Following is the message map entry for this menu command handler:

```
ON_COMMAND(ID_FILE_INVESTMENTWIZ, OnFileInvestmentWiz)
```

The message handler declaration for `OnFileInvestmentWiz()` follows:

```
afx_msg void  OnFileInvestmentWiz();
```

Listing 24.13 contains the source code for the `CMainFrame::OnFileInvestmentWiz()` message handler, which invokes the Investment Wizard.

LISTING 24.13 THE `CMainFrame::OnFileInvestmentWiz()` MESSAGE HANDLER FOR FINANCE2

```
1: void CMainFrame::OnFileInvestmentWiz() {
2:     // Display the investment wizard
3:     CInvestmentWiz wiz;
4:     wiz.SetWizardMode();
5:     wiz.DoModal();
6: }
```

That's all the code required to invoke the Investment Wizard. At least from an application's perspective, wizards are a piece of cake!

Summary

This hour explored wizards, which are the questionnaire-style user interfaces that are so prevalent for automating tasks in Windows applications. You began the hour by learning the basics of wizards and how they are used in applications. You then learned about the relationship between wizards and property sheets, along with how property pages fit into both of them. From there you moved on to learn about the specific MFC classes used to build wizards and property sheets. You finished up the hour by building a wizard of your own.

Q&A

Q Can I use the `EndDialog()` or `DestroyWindow()` member functions defined in `CDialog` to close a property page?

A No. The wizard or property sheet that contains a property page is responsible for closing the property page. If you manually close a page using the `EndDialog()` or `DestroyWindow()` member functions, the wizard or property sheet will be left displaying a blank page. This doesn't make sense and ultimately gives an application an unprofessional appearance.

Q Can I create a wizard with page sizes other than the standard `WIZ_CXDLG` and `WIZ_CYDLG` sizes?

A Yes. However, Microsoft's Windows style guidelines strongly suggest staying with the standard wizard sizes. If you do decide to use a different page size, it should be consistent across all the pages in the wizard.

Workshop

The Workshop is designed to help you anticipate possible questions, review what you've learned, and begin thinking ahead to put your knowledge into practice. The answers to the quiz are in Appendix A, "Quiz Answers."

Quiz

1. What is a wizard?
2. What two buttons are presented on each page in a wizard?
3. What button is presented on the last page of a wizard to carry out the task of the wizard?
4. What is a property sheet?
5. What dialog box problem do property sheets and property pages solve?
6. How do you define the layout of individual pages in a property sheet or wizard?
7. What MFC class is used to implement a wizard?
8. How do you indicate that a property sheet is to operate as a wizard?
9. How do you know if the user clicked the Finish button to exit a modal wizard?
10. What member function in `CPropertyPage` is useful for placing code that sets wizard buttons and the values of wizard page dialog controls?

Exercises

1. Try out the Investment Wizard in the Finance2 application. Experiment with moving back and forth between the pages and entering different values for the investment parameters. Notice that the third page calculates new results based on the information entered in the first two pages.

2. Modify the code for the Investment Wizard so that it operates as a property sheet. Take note of how it relies on tabs instead of Back and Next navigation buttons; these buttons are automatically hidden in property sheets.

Appendix A

Hour 1, "Welcome to MFC"

Quiz Answers

1. Windows 95, Windows 98, Windows NT
2. The client area
3. A window class
4. Messages
5. The window procedure
6. MFC serves as a wrapper around the Win32 API that packages Win32 functions and data types within C++ constructs.
7. CWnd
8. To speed up compilation
9. A message map
10. Because all resources in an application must have a unique identifier associated with them so that they can be identified and used

Hour 2, "Building MFC Applications"

Quiz Answers

1. It allows an application developer to focus on the information the application manipulates, and logically divide this information from the code that presents the it to the user.
2. The document template
3. The application object
4. The application object's `InitInstance()` member function
5. The application object's `OnIdle()` member function
6. `CDocument`
7. A variable-naming convention where a variable name begins with a lowercase letter or letters that indicate the data type of the variable
8. To distinguish between calling Win32 API functions and MFC member functions of the same name
9. To check the integrity of objects
10. Both macros are used to perform validity tests during the development of an application. However, test code in the ASSERT macro is only compiled in debug mode, whereas test code in the VERIFY macro is compiled in both debug and release modes.

Exercise Answers

1. No answers
2. Following is the completed document string for the `IDR_SKELETON` string resource:

   ```
   IDR_SKELETON "Skeleton\nSkeleton\nSkeleton\nSkeleton Files
   (*.skl)\n.skl\n
     Skeleton.Document\nSkeletoneDocument"
   ```

Hour 3, "Creating and Using Applications Resources"

Quiz Answers

1. A resource script
2. 32×32

3. Because they are defined during the development of an application and are compiled into the executable file of the application
4. To provide keyboard shortcuts for commonly used commands
5. Resource.h
6. An application that creates a binary resource file based on a resource script containing definitions of application resources
7. To store the button graphics for toolbar buttons
8. The specific location in the cursor image that represents the point of the cursor
9. Use the bitwise OR symbol
10. AFX_IDS_APP_TITLE

Hour 4, "Interacting with the User"

Quiz Answers

1. An MFC construct used to associate messages with message handler member functions
2. A message handler
3. Because message maps are much more efficient
4. A virtual key code
5. One
6. WM_CHAR
7. It must have input focus and not be minimized.
8. System keystrokes such as using the Alt key to access menus
9. When a key is held down and the typematic repeat for the keyboard kicks in
10. When the WM_ONMBUTTONDBLCLK() message is sent, which occurs when the user double clicks the middle mouse button, if one exists

Exercise Answers

1. Following is the code for the revised OnKeyDown() message handler:
   ```
   void CMainFrame::OnKeyDown(UINT nChar, UINT nRepCnt, UINT nFlags) {
     CPoint  ptCurPos;

     // Calculate new cursor position based on key press
     if (::GetCursorPos(&ptCurPos)) {
       // Get the client area rect and convert to screen coordinates
   ```

```
        CRect rcClient;
        GetClientRect(&rcClient);
        ClientToScreen(&rcClient);

        switch (nChar) {
          case VK_SPACE:
            ptCurPos.x = ::rand() % ::GetSystemMetrics(SM_CXSCREEN);
            ptCurPos.y = ::rand() % ::GetSystemMetrics(SM_CYSCREEN);
            ::SetCursorPos(ptCurPos.x, ptCurPos.y);
            break;

          case VK_LEFT:
            ptCurPos.x -= 5;
            if (rcClient.PtInRect(ptCurPos))
              ::SetCursorPos(ptCurPos.x, ptCurPos.y);
            break;

          case VK_RIGHT:
            ptCurPos.x += 5;
            if (rcClient.PtInRect(ptCurPos))
              ::SetCursorPos(ptCurPos.x, ptCurPos.y);
            break;

          case VK_UP:
            ptCurPos.y -= 5;
            if (rcClient.PtInRect(ptCurPos))
              ::SetCursorPos(ptCurPos.x, ptCurPos.y);
            break;

          case VK_DOWN:
            ptCurPos.y += 5;
            if (rcClient.PtInRect(ptCurPos))
              ::SetCursorPos(ptCurPos.x, ptCurPos.y);
            break;
        }
      }
    }
```

2. Following is the code for the `OnRButtonDown()` message handler:

```
void CMainFrame::OnRButtonDown(UINT nFlags, CPoint point) {
  // Display a ghostly message
  MessageBox("Boo!");
}
```

Hour 5, "Making Use of Controls"

Quiz Answers

1. A control
2. Traditional Windows controls and common controls
3. Push button, check box, and radio button
4. A special code used to convey information about control events to a control's parent
5. The main difference lies in the motivation for each; the standard dialog box controls were present in the earliest versions of Windows back when the Windows user interface was in its infancy. Common controls are more of an afterthought and are aimed at refreshing the Windows user interface with a more modern look and feel. Also, the standard dialog box controls communicate with applications by sending WM_COMMAND messages, while common controls typically send WM_NOTIFY messages.
6. To distinguish between the different controls in an application
7. The OnCreate() message handler
8. WM_COMMAND and WM_NOTIFY
9. A piece of software isolated into a discrete, easily reusable structure
10. To paint the background of the frame window a different color (light gray)

Exercise Answers

1. The following code must be added to the message map for CMainFrame:

    ON_LBN_DBLCLK(ID_LB_ANIMLISTBOX, OnPBPlayClicked)

2. The following code must be added to the CMainFrame::OnCreate() member function just after the ListBox control is created:

    m_AnimListBox.AddString("Drill.avi");

Hour 6, "Using Common Dialog Boxes"

Quiz Answers

1. A standard dialog box that helps perform a common user interface task
2. Windows 3.1

3. Modal and modeless
4. `CCommonDialog`
5. File Open and File Save As
6. A dialog-specific Win32 data structure
7. By passing parameters to the dialog box object's constructor
8. `DoModal()`
9. By checking the return value of `DoModal()` to see if it is equal to `IDOK`
10. Whether the dialog box is a File Open (`TRUE`) or File Save As (`FALSE`) common dialog box

Exercise Answers

1. Following is the `CMainFrame::OnRButtonUp()` member function with the static color member variable change:

   ```
   void CMainFrame::OnRButtonUp(UINT nFlags, CPoint point) {
     static COLORREF color = RGB(192, 192, 192);

     // Select a background color using the Color dialog box
     CColorDialog dlg(color);
     if (dlg.DoModal() == IDOK) {
       // Set the new background color for the frame window
       color = dlg.GetColor();
       CBrush brBackground(color);
       ::SetClassLong(GetSafeHwnd(), GCL_HBRBACKGROUND,
         (LONG)(HBRUSH)brBackground);
       Invalidate();
     }
   }
   ```

2. Following is the new version of the code that creates a `CFileDialog` object in the `CMainFrame::OnPBPlayClicked()` member function:

   ```
   CFileDialog dlg(TRUE, "avi", "*.avi");
   ```

Hour 7, "Retrieving Information with Custom Dialog Boxes"

Quiz Answers

1. Use a message box.
2. It can be pushed by using the Enter key on the keyboard.
3. `IDOK`

4. `CDialog`
5. A dialog box resource, which specifies the layout of and controls used within a dialog box
6. The `DIALOG` resource statement
7. `DEFPUSHBUTTON` is the dialog box's default pushbutton, whereas `PUSHBUTTON` is just a regular button.
8. The physical positioning of controls is simply too difficult to accurately carry out with straight coding.
9. `DoModal()`
10. Call the `DDX_Text()` function and pass the control identifier and member variable that are to be connected.

Exercise Answers

1. No answer
2. You must override the `OnCancel()` member function defined in the `CDialog` class. Following is the code for the `CPersonalInfoDlg::OnCancel()` member function:

```
void CPersonalInfoDlg::OnCancel() {
  if (MessageBox("Are you sure you want to cancel?", NULL,
    MB_YESNO) == IDNO)
    return;

  CDialog::OnCancel();
}
```

Hour 8, "Manipulating Menus"

Quiz Answers

1. By pressing Alt+Space
2. `GetSystemMenu()`
3. To respond to system menu commands
4. Call the `GetSubMenu()` member function of `CMenu`
5. `MF_SEPARATOR`
6. To indicate that a new menu item is to be inserted at a zero-based integer menu position, as opposed to being inserted at the position identified by a menu command identifier
7. `TrackPopupMenu()`

8. `ON_UPDATE_COMMAND_UI`
9. To provide a consistent means of setting the state of user interface elements in a command update message handler
10. `Enable()`

Exercise Answers

1. No answer
2. The first step in adding a custom floating pop-up menu is to define a menu resource identifier in the Resource.h file:

   ```
   #define IDM_POPUP            5000
   ```

   The second step involves creating a menu resource for the pop-up menu:

   ```
   IDM_POPUP MENU
   BEGIN
     POPUP ""
       BEGIN
         MENUITEM "&Play",      ID_FILE_PLAY
         MENUITEM "&Stop",      ID_FILE_STOP
       END
   END
   ```

   Finally, the `OnRButtonUp()` message handler must be rewritten to load the floating pop-up menu as a resource, and then free it after you're done:

   ```
   void CMainFrame::OnRButtonUp(UINT nFlags, CPoint point) {
     CMenu menu;
     menu.LoadMenu(IDM_POPUP);
     CMenu* pPopupMenu = menu.GetSubMenu(0);
     ClientToScreen(&point);
     pPopupMenu->TrackPopupMenu(TPM_CENTERALIGN | TPM_LEFTBUTTON,
       point.x, point.y, this);
     menu.DestroyMenu();
   }
   ```

Hour 9, "Drawing Graphics"

Quiz Answers

1. A programmatic interface for painting graphics in a generic manner
2. An abstract surface to which graphics are painted
3. It frees applications from the responsibility of supporting specific graphics hardware
4. A palette

5. A graphical image stored as an array of pixels
6. Its X-axis increases to the right, whereas its Y-axis increases down
7. `RGB`
8. When the window needs to be repainted
9. It manages a device context associated with a window's client area
10. Call the `CDC::Ellipse()` function and pass equal values for width and height

Hour 10, "Managing Data with MFC"

Quiz Answers

1. Arrays can't change in size, and you must always access their elements using an integer index
2. A rectangular width and height
3. For efficiency, because structs are more efficient than objects containing virtual functions; however, objects are much more useful if you must alter the data
4. A mechanism for generating classes based on type parameters
5. A map (dictionary)
6. `CDumpContext`
7. To serialize objects, which is the process of reading and writing objects as streams of binary data
8. Because it's possible for the internal memory of the string object to be moved in memory, thus invalidating the pointer
9. An absolute date and time based on coordinated universal time (UTC), which is equivalent to Greenwich mean time (GMT)
10. A `CTimeSpan` object represents the difference between two `CTime` objects

Exercise Answers

1. Following is the answer code:
   ```
   CString fName = "Michael";
   CString lName = "Morrison";
   CString name = fName + " " + lName;
   CString message = "Good afternoon, " + name + "!";
   MessageBox(message);
   ```

2. Following is the answer code:
   ```
   CString fName = "Michael";
   ```

```
CString lName = "Morrison";
CString name = fName + " " + lName;
CTime time = CTime::GetCurrentTime();
CString sTime = t.Format( "%A, %B %d, %Y, %I:%M:%S %p" );
CString message = "Good afternoon, " + name + ", it is " + sTime +
"!";
MessageBox(message);
```

Hour 11, "Organizing Data with MFC's Collection Classes"

Quiz Answers

1. The template-based collections are more modern, more convenient, and provide better type safety than the old collection classes
2. Array
3. List
4. Array
5. A non-indexed data structure containing linked elements that can be navigated in either direction
6. Map
7. Map
8. AfxTempl.h
9. `CArray` is used to store an array of objects, whereas `CTypedPtrArray` is used to store an array of object pointers
10. Because it establishes the size of the array and allocates memory for it, which avoids the frequent reallocation that can result in fragmented memory

Exercise Answers

1. Following is the code for the `messageArray` variable:

   ```
   CArray<CString, CString&> messageArray;
   ```

2. Following is the code for the `propertyMap` variable:

   ```
   CMap<CString, CString&, BOOL, BOOL> propertyMap;
   ```

Hour 12, "Managing Application Data with Documents"

Quiz Answers

1. A special class that stores and provides access to application data
2. As many as it needs
3. Yes
4. It associates a document with its views
5. `CDocument`
6. To store and retrieve document data from a persistent location such as a hard disk
7. It determines if document data has been modified since the last save, and is used as the basis for presenting a prompt allowing the user to save the document before closing it
8. The `UpdateAllViews()` member function
9. By calling the `IsStoring()` member function on the `CArchive` object
10. It is a special number used to distinguish between different versions of a serialized class

Exercise Answers

1. Following is the code for the modified `Serialize()` member function:

    ```
    void CGraphic::Serialize(CArchive& ar) {
      if (ar.IsStoring()) {
        ar << (WORD)m_nType;
        ar << m_rcPosition;
        ar << m_crColor;
        ar << m_sName;
      }
      else {
        WORD w;
        ar >> w;
        m_nType = w;
        ar >> m_rcPosition;
        ar >> m_crColor;
        ar >> m_sName;
      }
    }
    ```

2. No answers

Hour 13, "Viewing Application Data"

Quiz Answers

1. Providing a graphical user interface for interacting with the data contained in a document
2. Views are actually windows and derive from the `CWnd` class, whereas documents derive from `CObject`
3. `CView`
4. `CListView`
5. To render a visual representation of the document data associated with a view
6. When the document data for a view is modified and the view needs to be updated
7. If you are printing a multipage document, or if you want the printed document to somehow look different than it does on the screen
8. To force you to provide an implementation for it in your own view classes
9. Every view is required to implement the `OnDraw()` member function, which is used to draw a document to the screen and to a printer; the `OnPrint()` member function is also sometimes used to prepare a printer device context before calling the `OnDraw()` function to actually perform the printing
10. A *splitter window* is a special window that hosts two or more other windows, called panes, separated by one or more dividers

Exercise Answers

1. No answer
2. Following is the modified `Serialize()` member function:

```
void CDoodleDoc::Serialize(CArchive& ar) {
  // Store/retrieve the current color
  if (IsStoring()) {
    ar << (DWORD)m_crColor;
  }
  else {
    DWORD dw;
    ar >> dw;
    m_crColor = dw;
  }

  // Store/retrieve graphic list
  m_graphicList.Serialize(ar);
}
```

Hour 14, "Enhanced User Interfaces"

Quiz Answers

1. It calls the `Invalidate()` member function to redraw the entire view in response to any change in document data
2. A piece of information used to inform a view of how it is to be updated in response to a document change
3. The `Invalidate()` function invalidates an entire view, whereas `InvalidateRect()` invalidates a rectangular area within a view
4. A rectangle associated with a device context that specifies the area of the device context to which graphics can be drawn; nothing is drawn outside of the clipping rectangle
5. `SetScrollSizes()`
6. Logical coordinates are based on a logical entity such as a document, whereas device coordinates are based on a physical entity such as a window
7. One of a pair of windows that is displayed on either side of a splitter window; moving the splitter window adjusts the sizes of the panes
8. AfxCView.h
9. They determine the number of panes managed by the splitter window, along with their spatial location
10. CListView

Exercise Answers

1. Following is the code for the `CGraphic::GetColor()` member function:

   ```
   COLORREF GetColor() { return m_crColor; }
   ```

2. Following is the new string formatting code for the `CDoodleListView::OnUpdate()` member function that includes the color of each graphic text entry:

   ```
   COLORREF cr = pGraphic->GetColor();
   sItem.Format("%s : %dx%d   Red=%d Green=%d Blue=%d",
     pGraphic->GetTypeAsString(), rc.Width(), rc.Height(),
     GetRValue(cr), GetGValue(cr), GetBValue(cr));
   ```

Hour 15, "Utilizing Control Bars"

Quiz Answers

1. Toolbars can only contain buttons, whereas dialog bars can contain any control
2. `CControlBar`
3. The capability of a floating control bar to be attached to the edge of a frame window
4. You can create a dialog bar from a dialog box resource
5. By tiling each button image from left to right across a single toolbar bitmap
6. By using the `SEPARATOR` identifier in the toolbar resource
7. To establish the status bar panes
8. `ID_VIEW_TOOLBAR` and `ID_VIEW_STATUS_BAR`
9. A shorthand help message that is displayed when you pause the mouse cursor over a toolbar button
10. By inserting a newline (`\n`) character at the end of each help message string resource, followed by the ToolTip text

Exercise Answers

1. I'll trust that you added a new tile to the toolbar bitmap suitable for the About button. Following is the new toolbar resource containing the About button:

   ```
   IDR_DOODLE TOOLBAR  16, 15
   BEGIN
       BUTTON      ID_FILE_NEW
       BUTTON      ID_FILE_OPEN
       BUTTON      ID_FILE_SAVE
       SEPARATOR
       BUTTON      ID_EDIT_CLEAR_ALL
       SEPARATOR
       BUTTON      ID_DRAW_LINE
       BUTTON      ID_DRAW_RECTANGLE
       BUTTON      ID_DRAW_ELLIPSE
       BUTTON      ID_DRAW_CRITTER
       BUTTON      ID_DRAW_CHANGECOLOR
       SEPARATOR
       BUTTON      ID_APP_ABOUT
   END
   ```

2. Following is the status bar message and ToolTip string resource entry:

   ```
   ID_APP_ABOUT "Display program information, version number, and copyright"
   ```

Hour 16, "Managing Multiple Documents"

Quiz Answers

1. The application's main frame window
2. The client window of the main frame window
3. One
4. `CMultiDocTemplate`
5. `CMDIFrameWnd`
6. `CMDIChildWnd`
7. When a child document window of a different type is activated, or when all child document windows are closed
8. Three; one "empty" menu and additional menus for each document type
9. A list of recently used files that appear in the File menu of an application; the user can quickly open any of these files by selecting them from the menu
10. Because the About Doodle menu item would become disabled if all the child document windows (views) are closed, which doesn't make sense

Hour 17, "Inside Printing"

Quiz Answers

1. A visualization of a document on the screen as it will appear on the printed page
2. It uses the `OnDraw()` member function of a view class to print documents
3. `CView`
4. The sequence of steps required to print an entire document
5. `OnPreparePrinting()`
6. Override the `OnPreparePrinting()` member function
7. `OnBeginPrinting()` and `OnEndPrinting()`
8. `CPrintInfo`
9. Shrink the `m_rectDraw` member of the `CPrintInfo` object
10. 300

Hour 18, "Accessing Databases with DAO"

Quiz Answers

1. ODBC and DAO
2. Nothing, they are the same thing
3. A Microsoft Jet database
4. It encapsulates the Microsoft Jet database engine
5. It encapsulates a .MDB Jet database file
6. The `Recordset` object
7. `CDaoRecordView`
8. A `CDaoRecordset`-derived class for each record set that you plan on using in the application
9. It must be overridden in custom record set classes to return the name of the default database
10. It must be overridden in custom view classes to return a pointer to the `recordset` object associated with the view

Exercise Answers

1. No answers.
2. Following is the code for the `CHockeyView::OnFileWorst()` message handler:

   ```
   void CHockeyView::OnFileWorst() {
     // Open the team record set
     CTeamSet teamSet;
     try {
       teamSet.Open();
     }
     catch(CDaoException* e) {
       AfxMessageBox(e->m_pErrorInfo->m_strDescription);
       e->Delete();
       return;
     }

     // Look for the team with the worst points
     int         curPoints, worstPoints = 999;
     COleVariant bookmark;
     if (teamSet.IsOpen())
       while (!teamSet.IsEOF()) {
         // Calculate the current team's points
         curPoints = teamSet.m_Wins * 2 + teamSet.m_Ties;
   ```

```
        // Check to see if the current team has the least points
        if (curPoints < worstPoints) {
          // If so, then bookmark the team
          worstPoints = curPoints;
          bookmark = teamSet.GetBookmark();
        }
        teamSet.MoveNext();
      }
    // Set the current record to the last bookmarked team
    teamSet.SetBookmark(bookmark);

    // Format and display the result
    CString sResult;
    sResult.Format("The %s are the worst team in the NHL with %d wins,
" \
        "%d losses, and %d ties for a total of %d points.",
        teamSet.m_TeamName, teamSet.m_Wins, teamSet.m_Losses,
    teamSet.m_Ties,
        worstPoints);
      MessageBox(sResult);
    }
```

Hour 19, "ADO and the Future of Databases"

Quiz Answers

1. VBSQL, which is a database interface for Visual Basic
2. Relational databases that have an ODBC driver
3. DAO presents an object-based interface for accessing databases, as opposed to a function-based interface (API)
4. Because ADO provides a high-level database interface built on top of OLE DB that is much easier to use than OLE DB
5. Relational databases, non-relational databases, email systems, and file systems
6. The `Command` object
7. It represents a column of data in a record set
8. `MoveNext()`, `MovePrevious()`, `MoveFirst()`, and `MoveLast()`
9. To set connection settings such as the data provider and the database filename
10. The ADO Data control has the advantage of providing graphical navigational support

Hour 20, "Connecting to the Web"

Quiz Answers

1. Internet Explorer 3.0
2. It maintains a history list containing the Web pages that have been opened
3. The `CHtmlView` class contains a `WebBrowser` control that it uses to display Web content
4. AfxHTML.h
5. `Navigate()` only enables you to open Web pages, whereas `Navigate2()` enables you to open both Web pages and other document files
6. Pass the `navOpenInNewWindow` navigation constant as the second parameter to `Navigate()` or `Navigate2()`
7. `GoBack()`
8. Call the `Refresh()` member function
9. Call the `GetBusy()` member function
10. Because the `WebBrowser` control plays an important role in the Internet Explorer application and provides special features solely for Internet Explorer; these features correspond to member functions in the `CHtmlView` class, which only have effect in Internet Explorer

Exercise Answers

1. Following is the new menu resource for the BrowseIt application with the Go, Search menu item added:

```
IDR_BROWSEIT MENU
BEGIN
  POPUP "&File"
    BEGIN
      MENUITEM "E&xit",                ID_APP_EXIT
    END
  POPUP "&View"
    BEGIN
      MENUITEM "&Stop",                ID_VIEW_STOP
      MENUITEM "&Refresh",             ID_VIEW_REFRESH
      MENUITEM SEPARATOR
      MENUITEM "&Toolbar",             ID_VIEW_TOOLBAR
      MENUITEM "&Status Bar",          ID_VIEW_STATUS_BAR
    END
  POPUP "&Go"
    BEGIN
      MENUITEM "&Back",                ID_GO_BACK
```

```
        MENUITEM "&Forward",            ID_GO_FORWARD
        MENUITEM SEPARATOR
        MENUITEM "&Home",               ID_GO_HOME
        MENUITEM SEPARATOR
        MENUITEM "&Search",             ID_GO_SEARCH
    END
    POPUP "&Help"
    BEGIN
        MENUITEM "&About Browse It...", ID_APP_ABOUT
    END
END
```

Also, following is the toolbar resource for BrowseIt with the new Search toolbar button:

```
IDR_BROWSEIT TOOLBAR  20, 20
BEGIN
    BUTTON      ID_GO_BACK
    BUTTON      ID_GO_FORWARD
    BUTTON      ID_GO_HOME
    BUTTON      ID_GO_SEARCH
    SEPARATOR
    BUTTON      ID_VIEW_STOP
    BUTTON      ID_VIEW_REFRESH
END
```

2. Following is the code for the `CBrowseItView::OnGoSearch()` message handler:

```
void CBrowseItView::OnGoHome() {
  // Navigate to the default home Web page
  GoHome();
}
```

Hour 21, "Multimedia and DirectX"

Quiz Answers

1. Audio or video content that is time-based, which means that the content changes over time

2. CD Player, Sound Recorder, and Windows Media Player

3. To eliminate the inconsistencies inherent in low-level multimedia programming

4. DirectX will emulate the 3D functionality

5. It is the low-level layer of DirectX, and supports core multimedia features such as 3D graphics, sound, music, advanced user input, and network support

6. It is the higher-level layer of DirectX that sits on top of DirectX Foundation and provides high-level services such as animation and media streaming

7. The viewing of media content as it is transferred over a network
8. It allows media content to be delivered over a network as a continuous flow of data with minimal wait time before playback begins
9. `CMediaPlayer`
10. `AfxEnableControlContainer()`

Exercise Answers

1. No answers. However, notice that the Media Player control now has its own VCR-style controls that can be used to manipulate the playback of the media clip. Information about the media clip is also displayed in the Media Player control.
2. Following is the code for the `OnPBIncVolume()` and `OnPBDecVolume()` message handlers:

```
void CProjectorDlg::OnPBIncVolume() {
  // Raise the volume
  m_pMediaPlayer->SetVolume(m_pMediaPlayer->GetVolume + 1);
}

void CProjectorDlg::OnPBDecVolume() {
  // Lower the volume
  m_pMediaPlayer->SetVolume(m_pMediaPlayer->GetVolume - 1);
}
```

Hour 22, "Creating DLLs"

Quiz Answers

1. A library of compiled code that is made available for inclusion within an application at compile-time
2. .DLL
3. Import library
4. The sharing of code among applications
5. DLLs cannot execute as standalone programs
6. `DllMain()`
7. Exported functions
8. Import libraries don't contain any executable code
9. `AFX_EXT_CLASS`
10. AfxDLLX.h

Exercise Answers

1. Following is the code for creating a `CTipOfTheDay` dialog box object and displaying the dialog box, which should be placed in the `CDoodleApp::InitInstance()` member function:

   ```
   CTipOfTheDay totd;
   totd.DoModal();
   ```

2. No answers

Hour 23, "Creating Custom Controls"

Quiz Answers

1. A user-defined control that is created to carry out a specific task
2. Reusability
3. If the class provides significant functionality that you can take advantage of
4. `CWnd`
5. A control that is based on the `CWnd` class and that is visible at runtime
6. Visible controls are based on the `CWnd` class and are visible at runtime, whereas invisible controls usually are not based on `CWnd` and are not visible at runtime
7. `CObject`
8. `Create()`
9. `OnPaint()`
10. MMSystem.h and WinMM.lib

Exercise Answers

1. No answers
2. No answers

Hour 24, "Creating Wizards"

Quiz Answers

1. A user interface component that uses a multistep questionnaire to gather information from the user
2. The Back and Next buttons
3. The Finish button

4. A user interface component that presents multiple dialog boxes as pages within a single window; each page is accessed via a tab
5. The problem of trying to gather lots of information within a single dialog box that has physical limitations on how much information can be presented and gathered
6. With dialog box resources
7. `CPropertySheet`
8. Call the `SetWizardMode()` member function on the `CPropertySheet` object
9. The `DoModal()` member function will return `ID_WIZFINISH`
10. `OnSetActive()`

Exercise Answers

1. No answers
2. The only change required to convert the wizard to a property sheet is to remove the call to the `SetWizardMode()` member function in `CMainFrame::OnFileInvestmentWiz()`. Following is the revised `OnFileInvestmentWiz()` message handler:

```
void CMainFrame::OnFileInvestmentWiz() {
  // Display the investment wizard
  CInvestmentWiz wiz;
  wiz.DoModal();
}
```

Appendix B

MFC Information Resources

Like any software development technology, MFC is constantly being enhanced and extended to evolve with the ever-changing computing world. As an MFC developer, you must keep track of the latest MFC trends. This will give you insight into where MFC is headed, along with how it fits into new software technologies.

Aside from keeping up with the future of MFC, you will no doubt encounter situations where you need to find additional information on MFC. This book certainly provides a solid introduction to MFC programming, but there is no way any single book could uncover everything that lurks within MFC. I encourage you to make the most of online MFC resources and printed periodicals. The remainder of this appendix directs you to some very useful MFC resources.

Online Resources

Online MFC resources consist of Web sites, newsgroups, and a mailing list that focuses on developing Win32 applications using MFC. Following are some of the most useful MFC Web sites I've found:

- Microsoft Developer Network—http://msdn.microsoft.com/developer/
- Microsoft Visual C++—http://msdn.microsoft.com/visualc/
- MFC Professional—http://www.visionx.com/mfcpro/
- MFC FAQ—http://www.stingsoft.com/mfc_faq/

In addition to visiting these Web sites, you may want to join a newsgroup because newsgroups typically provide more interactions between MFC developers. Following are the main newsgroups out there focused on MFC discussions:

- comp.os.ms-windows.programmer.tools.mfc
- comp.os.ms-windows.programming.mfc
- microsoft.public.vc.mfc
- microsoft.public.vc.mfc.docview

One final online resource you might want to consider is joining an MFC mailing list. A mailing list is useful because it periodically sends you information and allows you to get into discussions based on MFC programming. The following URL directs you to a Web page that allows you to join an MFC mailing list:

http://www.digiday.com/mfcpro/joinmfcl.htm

Periodicals

If you aren't feeling very interactive, or if you already waste too much time surfing the Web, you might want to consider picking up an MFC magazine. You may even find one you like and decide to subscribe. Following are some useful programming magazines that include articles related to MFC:

- Visual C++ Developer—Pinnacle Publishing
- Visual C++ Developer's Journal—Fusion Interactive (http://www.vcdj.com/)
- Visual C++ Professional—Oakley Publishing
- Inside Microsoft Visual C++—The COBB Group
- Windows Developer's Journal—Miller Freeman Inc. (http://www.wdj.com/)
- Windows Tech Journal—Oakley Publishing

- Microsoft Systems Journal (MSJ)—Miller Freeman Inc. (http://www.microsoft.com/msj/)
- Dr. Dobb's Journal—Miller Freeman Inc. (http://www.ddj.com/)

You may notice that some of the periodicals mentioned also have a Web site. These Web sites typically provide downloadable source code and sometimes even include selected articles from the current issue.

APPENDIX C

MFC and Visual Development Tools

This book focuses on building Win32 applications using MFC without regard to a specific compiler or visual development environment. This approach forces you to dig into the details of MFC without relying on development tool features such as code generation wizards. Granted, wizards can save you lots of time and serve a very useful purpose once you have an MFC knowledge base, but it's important to first learn MFC through straight coding.

Having said all that, this appendix directs you to a few visual development environments that support application construction with MFC. You have the option of using each of these environments simply as a fancy editor/compiler/debugger, or as a full-blown visual development tool. As an example, I used Microsoft Visual C++ to develop all of the sample code in the book, but I didn't rely on any of its helper features such as wizards. I essentially used Visual C++ as a visual editor/compiler/debugger. As you get comfortable with a particular tool, you may decide to use some of the helper features to speed up application development.

Below you'll find a list of MFC visual development tools, along with their respective Web sites:

- Microsoft Visual C++—`http://msdn.microsoft.com/visualc/`
- Symantec C++—`http://www.symantec.com/scpp/index.html`
- Inprise C++ Builder—`http://www.inprise.com/bcppbuilder/`
- Watcom C/C++— `http://www.powersoft.com/products/languages/watccpl.html`

Although I personally use Microsoft Visual C++, it's not my intention to promote it over the others. I encourage you to visit the Web sites for each tool and make an educated decision based on your needs. All four products are published by very respectable vendors in the software development industry, so you should be in good shape regardless of which tool you choose.

INDEX

Symbols

!= (CString overloaded) operator, 186
& (ampersand), 53
> (CString overloaded) operator, 181
>= (CString overloaded) operator, 181
< (CString overloaded) operator, 181
<= (CString overloaded) operator, 181
:: (scope resolution) operator, 31
>> (overridden) operators, 214-215, 226
<< (overridden) operators, 214-215, 226
+= (CString overloaded) operator), 186
. . . (ellipsis), 112
= (CString overloaded) operator, 186
== operator, 112, 186
[ ] (brackets), 180, 326

A

accelerators, 45, 48-49
Access, Jet databases, 318, 328
accessing
  DLLs, 414
  string characters, 186
Active Documents, WebBrowser control, 363
ActiveX. *See also* DirectX; multimedia
  COM basis, 429
  controls
    AfxEnableControl-Container() member function, 398
    COM-based, 93
    custom controls comparison, 429
    data-aware, 357
    initializing, 396-397
    Media Player, 385-388
    MFC-supported, 93
    reusability, 93
    WebBrowser, 363-365
    windows controls comparison, 92
  DirectX Foundation components, 384
  programming language independence, 360
ActiveX Data Objects. *See* ADO
Add Printer Wizard, 433
Add to Custom Colors button, 107

Add() member function, 196
AddGraphic() member function, 226, 244, 250, 315
AddHead() member function, 200
adding
  menu items, 138-140, 273-274
  PreCreateWindow() member function, 40
  splitter windows, 257-258
  string resources, 40
  ToolTips, 274
  views list, 260
AddPage() member function, 440-441
AddTail() member function, 200
ADO (ActiveX Data Objects), 357-360
Advanced Streaming Format (ASF), 382, 386
AFX EXT CLASS macro, 407
AFX EXTENSION MODULE variable, 408
AFX IDS APP TITLE identifier, 19
afx msg keyword, 65
afxDump objects, 182
AfxEnableControlContainer() member function, 398

AFXEXT macro, 407
AfxGetInstanceHandle() function, 19
AfxInitExtensionModule() function, 409
AfxRegisterWndClass() function, 19
AfxTempl.h header files (data collections), 192, 206
AfxTermExtensionModule() function, 409
AIFF (Audio Interchange File Format), 387
ampersand (&), 53
animate controls, 83, 91-92
animation. *See* multimedia
Animator (sample) application. *See* listings
Animator2 (sample) application. *See* listings
Animator3 (sample) application. *See* listings
APIs (programming interface), DirectX, 381
App component (document strings), 221
AppendMenu() member function, 134, 137, 140
application menus, 133, 136-140
application windows, 6, 29, 74
applications
   basic structure, 24-25
   building, 14
   data, 25
      modeling, 28
   dialog-based, 391
   document/view architecture, 22-23
      CDaoRecordView class, 349
      document interaction, 209-210
      document templates, 23-24, 40
   form-based
      CDaoRecordset class, 325-326, 340
      CDaoRecordView class, 324-327, 349
      DDXFieldCBIndex() function example, 349
      dialog boxes comparison, 324
      DoDataExchange() member function example, 349

GetBookmark() member function example, 349
Hockey (sample) application Conferences table example, 330
Hockey (sample) application Divisions table example, 330
Hockey (sample) application Teams table example, 328
Hockey ConferenceSet.cpp source code file example, 341-343
Hockey ConferenceSet.h header file example, 340-341
Hockey DivisionSet.cpp source code file example, 344-346
Hockey DivisionSet.h header file example, 343-344
Hockey Resource.h header file example, 330-331
Hockey TeamSet.cpp source code file example, 337-339
Hockey TeamSet.h header file example, 336-337
Hockey.mdb Jet database example, 328
Hockey.rc resource script example, 332-336
HockeyDoc.cpp source code file example, 348-349
HockeyDoc.h header file example, 346-348
HockeyView.cpp source code file example, 349
HockeyView.h header file example, 349
IsEOF() member function example, 349
IsOpen() member function example, 349
MoveNext() member function example, 349
OnFileBest() message handler example, 349
OnGetRecordSet() member function example, 349

OnInitialUpdate() member function example, 349
Open() member function example, 349
placing recordsets, 327
SetBookmark() member function example, 349
initialization, 19
main frame windows, 25
MDI, 275
   client windows, 282
   CMDIChildWnd class, 283
   CMDIFrameWnd class, 282
   CMultiDocTemplate class, 281, 290-292
   CMultiDocumentTemplate class, 215
   creating, 283-284
   document templates, 281
   document-centric environments, 279-280
   Doodle6 Doodle.cpp source code file example, 290-292
   Doodle6 Doodle.h header file example, 289
   Doodle6 main application string resources example, 288
   Doodle6 MainFrame.cpp source code file example, 292
   Doodle6 MainFrame.h header file example, 292
   Doodle6 menu resource definition example, 286-287
   Doodle6 menu resource definitions example, 286
   frame windows, 281
   icons, 280
   multiple document types, 277
   multiple menus, 283-286
   resources, 284
   SDI comparison, 276-278
   windows hierarchy, 277-279, 292
   Word, 279
multimedia, 378-379
   objects, 16-19, 25-28

resources, 25, 42
    accelerators, 45, 48-49
    bitmaps, 45, 49-50
    compiling, 43-47
    CResourcefulApp::OnApp
        About() message handler example, 58
    cursors, 45, 50
    dialog boxes, 46, 54-55, 58
    editors, 58
    files, 19
    icons, 46, 50
    identifiers, 19, 48
    menus, 46, 51-54
    MFC automatic associating, 58
    Resourceful application class message map example, 58
    standard application data comparison, 42
    string tables, 46, 56-57
    version, 57
    versions, 46
SDI, 276, 279
single document, CSingleDocTemplate class, 215
static libraries, 401-402
StdAfx files, 15-16
user interface elements, 25
Web-enabled
    BrowseIt menu resource definition example, 370-371
    BrowseIt StdAfx.h header file example, 370
    BrowseIt string resources definition example, 372
    BrowseIt toolbar resource definition example, 372
    BrowseItView.cpp source code file example, 375-376
    BrowseItView.h header file example, 373-375
    documents, 376
    Microsoft Money, 363
    Microsoft Office, 362
windows
    main frame, 16, 19
    views, 29
Windows Media Player, 388

arcs, 163
ARG KEY parameter (CMap class), 202-203
ARG TYPE parameter, 195-199
ARG VALUE parameter (CMap class), 202-203
arrays, 175, 179, 188-189, 194-198. *See also* data collections
ASF (Advanced Streaming Format), 382, 386
ASSERT macro, 40
ASSERT VALID macro, 40
AssertValid() member function, 38, 251
assigning CString objects, 185
assigning string literals, 185
AU (UNIX audio), 387
audio. *See* multimedia
Audio Interchange File Format (AIFF), 387
AVI (Audio Video Interleaved) format, 86, 387

B

b prefix, 32
Back buttons, 433, 440
BASE CLASS parameter
    CTypedPtrArray class, 194, 197-198
    CTypedPtrList class, 201
    CTypedPtrMap class, 205
base classes, 194
BEGIN MESSAGE MAP() macro, 64
BitBlt() member function, 168-169
bitmaps, 45, 152-154
    BitBlt() member function, 168-169
    CBitmap class, 168
    defining, 49
    device-dependent, 315
    drawing, 168-169
    LoadBitmap() member function, 168
    loading, 167-168
    OnPaint() message handler bitmap drawing example, 169
    toolbars, 264-267
BITSPIXEL constant, 160
Boolean parameters, CDocument::SetModifiedFlag member function, 221

Boolean value (BOOL) data type, 10
.BMP filename extension, 49
brackets ([ ]) 180, 326
BrowseIt (sample) application. *See* listings
browsers. *See* Explorer; WebBrowser control
brushes, 96, 152-153
building. *See* creating
buttons
    Add to Custom Colors, 107
    Back, 433, 440
    controls, 78-79, 87, 96
    Define Custom Colors, 107, 441
    dialog boxes, defaults, 115
    Finish, 433, 441
    Next, 433, 441
    Printer, 109
    toolbars, 266, 274

C

C
    static libraries, 400
    Watcom C/C++ Web site, 482
C++
    arrays, 175, 189
    Class Wizard, 63
    Inprise C++ Builder Web site, 482
    Inside Microsoft Visual C++, 479
    MFC wrapper classes, 12, 176
    Microsoft Visual C++ Web site, 482
    static libraries, 400
    Symantec C++ Web site, 482
    Visual C++ Developer, 479
    Visual C++ Developer's Journal, 479
    Visual C++ Professional, 479
    Watcom C/C++ Web site, 482
C++ templates
    data collections, 178
        arrays, 179, 188-189, 192-196
        collection-specific coding purposes, 180
        lists, 179, 189-192, 198-202

maps, 179, 189-192, 202-205
  type-safety approaches, 180
  multiple data type class capability, 178-179
  non-template data collection class comparison, 176, 188
CAboutDlg class, 58
CAnimateCtrl, 85
CArchive class, 181
  >> (overridden operators), 214-215, 226
  << (overridden operators), 214-215, 226
  serializing objects, 182-183
CArchive objects, Serialize() member function parameters, 213
CArray class, 195-197
CAudioClip (sample) control. *See* **listings**
CBitmap class, 168, 315
CBRS FLYBY (toolbar style), 274
CBRS SIZE DYNAMIC (toolbar style), 274
CBRS TOOLTIPS (toolbar style), 274
CButton, 84
CClientDC class, 159
CCmdUI class, 147
CColorbox (sample) control, 419-422
CColorDialog class, 102, 106
CCommonDialog class, 101
CControlBar class, 263-264
CCtrlView class, 231
CDaoDatabase class, 322
CDaoQueryDef class, 323
CDaoRecordset class, 323
  document/view architecture, 349
  form-based applications, 324-328, 349
  m_strFilter public member variable, 349
CDaoTableDef class, 323
CDaoWorkspace class, 322
CDC class, 158-160
CDialog class, 119-121
CDialog objects, 120-122, 438
CDialogBar class, 263-265
CDocument class, 28, 33-37, 210-214, 224-226
CDumpContext class, 181

CDynLinkLibrary objects, 409
CEdit class, 84
CEditView class, 231
CFile class, 181-183
CFileDialog class, 102, 105, 110
CFindReplaceDialog class, 102, 108
CFontDialog class, 102, 107
CFormView class, 231
CGraphic class, 205-206, 226
char pointers, strings, 186
CHECKED menu option, 53
child document windows (MDI), 282, 292
CHtmlView class, 232, 365-366
  BrowseItView.cpp source code file example, 375-376
  BrowseItView.h header file example, 373, 375
  documents, 376
  GetAddressBar() member function, 369
  GetBusy() member function, 367, 376
  GetFullName() member function, 369
  GetStatusBar() member function, 369
  GoBack() member function, 366
  GoForward() member function, 366
  GoHome() member function, 366
  GoSearch() member function, 366
  Internet Explorer exclusive member functions, 369-370
  LoadFromResource() member function, 376
  Navigate() member function, 366-368
  Navigate2() member function, 366-368
  OnUpdateViewStop() message handler, 376
  Refresh() member function, 367-368
  SetAddressBar() member function, 369
  SetFullScreen() member function, 370
  SetMenuBar() member function, 370
  SetStatusBar() member function, 369

  SetToolBar() member function, 370
  Stop() member function, 367-368
CImageList, 85
Class Wizard (C++), 63
class wrappers. *See* **classes**
classes. *See also* **data collections**
  base, 194
  CAboutDlg, 58
  CArchive, 181-183
    >> (overridden) operators, 214-215, 226
    << (overridden) operators, 214-215, 226
  CArray, 195-197
  CBitmap, 168, 315
  CCmdUI, 147
  CControlBar, 263-264
  CCtrlView, 231
  CDaoRecordView, 232, 323
    document/view architecture, 349
    form-based applications, 324-327, 349
    OnGetRecordset() member function, 328
  CDC, 158-160
  CDialog, 119-121
  CDialogBar, 263-265
  CDocument, 28, 210
    DeleteContents() member function, 211-212, 226
    Doodle3 DoodleDoc.cpp source code file example, 224-226
    Doodle3 DoodleDoc.h header file example, 222-223
    OnCloseDocument() member function, 211-212
    OnNewDocument() member function, 211-212, 226
    OnOpenDocument() member function, 211-212, 226
    OnSaveDocument() member function, 211-212
    Serialize() member function, 211-214, 226
    SetModifiedFlag() member function, 211-212, 221, 226

CListBox 487

SkeletonDoc.cpp source code file example, 34-37
SkeletonDoc.h header file example, 33-34
UpdateAllViews() member function, 211-212, 226
CDumpContext, 181
CEditView, 231
CFile, 181-183
CFormView, 231
CGraphic, 205-206, 226
CHtmlView, 232
CList, 198-201
CListView, 231, 260
CMainFrame, 19, 206
CMap, 202-204
CMDIChildWnd, 283, 290-292
CMDIFrameWnd, 282, 292
CMenu, 136
CMultiDocTemplate, 281, 290-292
CMultiDocumentTemplate, 215
CObject, 181
   class hierarchy importance, 181
   custom controls derivation, 417, 423
   invisible controls derivation, 418
   serializing objects, 183
control, 83-85
CPoint, 158
CPrintDialog, 109
CPrintInfo, 302
CPropertyPage, 437, 441-442
CPropertySheet, 436-441
CRecordView, 231
CRichEditView, 231
CScrollView, 231, 250-251
CSingleDocTemplate, 215
CSkeletonDoc, 37-39
CSkeletonView, 40
CSplitterWnd, 253, 258
CStatic, CColorbox (sample) control class derivation, 420
CStatusBar, 263-264
CString, 177
   C runtime string functions comparison, 184
   constructors, 185
   creating strings, 185
   MBCS, 179
   overloaded operators, 112, 186
   Unicode, 179
CTime, 177, 186
CTimeSpan, 177, 186
CToolBar, 263-266
CTreeView, 231
CTypedArray, 198
CTypedPtrArray, 194-198
CTypedPtrList, 198-202
CTypedPtrMap, 202, 205
CView, 29, 230
   DoPreparePrinting() member function, 297-298
   GetDocument() member function, 232-233, 237, 240
   OnBeginPrinting() member function, 297-298
   OnDraw() member function, 232-233, 237, 240
   OnEndPrinting() member function, 298, 301
   OnEndPrintPreview() member function, 298, 300
   OnPrepareDC() member function, 297, 299
   OnPreparePrinting() member function, 297-298, 311, 315
   OnPrint() member function, 232-233, 297, 299
   OnUpdate() member function, 232-233
   printing support, 297
   SkeletonView.cpp source code file example, 40
   SkeletonView.h header file example, 39-40
CWinApp, 18
CWnd
   custom controls derivation, 417, 420
   Invalidate member function, 172
   MessageBox() member function, 115
   views, 230
dialog box, 101
   CColorDialog, 102, 106
   CCommonDialog, 101
   CFileDialog, 102, 105, 110
   CFindReplaceDialog, 102, 108
   CFontDialog, 102, 107
   constructing, 130
   CPageSetupDialog, 103, 108
   CPrintDialog, 103
   customizing, 103
   Finance PersonalInfoDlg.cpp source code file, 130
   Finance PersonalInfoDlg.h header file example, 130
   IDD member constant, 130
   member functions, 111-112
existing
   deriving custom controls, 417-418, 420-423
   deriving invisible controls, 418
exported, DLLs, 407
importing DLLs, 407
names, 30
simple collection classes, 193-194, 206
typed pointer collection classes, 193-194
window, 6
wrapper
   ADO, 360
   CDaoDatabase, 322
   CDaoQueryDef, 323
   CDaoRecordset, 323-326, 340, 349
   CDaoTableDef, 323
   CDaoWorkspace, 322
   CHtmlView, 365-369, 373-376
   CMediaPlayer, 389-390, 398
   CPoint, 176
   CRect, 12, 177
   CSize, 177
   CWnd, 12
clicking (mouse), 73
client areas, 6
   mouse messages, 74
   painting, 156
   views, 29
client windows, MDI, 282
clipping rectangles, 247-248
CList class, 198-201
CListBox, 84

CListCtrl, 84
CListView class, 231, 260
close command, 134
closing
   dialog boxes, 130
   property pages, 454
CMainFrame (sample) frame window class, 428-429
CMainFrame class, 19, 206
CMainFrame::PreCreateWindow() member function, 40
CMap class, 202-204
CMDIChildWnd class, 283, 290-292
CMDIFrameWnd class, 282, 292
CMediaPlayer class, 389-390, 398
CMenu class, 136
CMenu objects, obtaining, 134, 137-138
CMultiDocTemplate class, 281, 290-292
CMultiDocumentTemplate class, 215
CObArray base class, 194
CObject class
   class hierarchy importance, 181
   custom controls derivation, 417, 423
   invisible controls derivation, 418
   serializing objects, 183
cocatenating strings, CString overloaded operators, 186
Color Selection dialog box, 100, 106
   Animator2 (sample) application, 112
   selecting colors, 107
COLORREF data type, 158
COLORREF parameter, 420
colors, 155
   Animator2 (sample) application, 112
   Color Selection dialog box, 107
   COLORREF data type, 158
   monitors
      basic colors RGB values, 157-158
      electron guns, 156
   RGB system, 110-112

COM (Component Object Model), ActiveX controls, 93, 429
command identifiers (ID ABOUT), 393
command update message handlers, 147
Command (ADO), 360
commands
   menu, adding, 273-274
   system, 133-134
CommDlgExtendedError() function, 112
comments (TODO), 37
common controls. *See* controls
common dialog boxes. *See* dialog boxes
comp.os.ms-windows.programmer.tools.mfc (newsgroup), 478
comp.os.ms-windows.programming.mfc (newsgroup), 478
Compare() member function, 186
CompareNoCase() member function, 186
comparing
   data collections, 192
   strings, 186
compilers
   MFC compatibility, 19
   resource, 43-44, 47
compiling
   application resources, 43-45, 47
   precompiled headers, 15
Component Object Model (COM), ActiveX controls, 93, 429
components, software, 93
Connection (ADO), 359
ConnectionString (ADO Data Control property), 360
constants
   names, 31
   navigation, 367-368
   resource, defining, 47-48
   WIZ CXDLG, 448, 454
   WIZ CYDLG, 448, 454
Construct() member function, 442
constructing. *See* creating
constructors, 449
   CMainFrame, 206
   CString, 185

control bars, 262. *See also* dialog bars; status bars; toolbars
   CControlBar class, 263-264
   docking, 264
   hiding, 273-274
control notifications, 79
   edit control notification codes, 89
   edit control notifcation message map example, 88-89
   WM COMMAND, 88-92
   WM NOTIFY, 90-91
controls. *See also* specific control types
   ActiveX
      AfxEnableControlContainer() member function, 398
      COM-based, 93
      custom controls comparison, 429
      data-aware, 357
      initializing, 396-397
      Media Player, 385-386, 388
      MFC-supported, 93
      reusability, 93
      WebBrowser, 363-365
      windows controls comparison, 92
   Animator (sample) application, 94
   Animator MainFrame.cpp source code file example, 96
   Animator MainFrame.h header file example, 95-96
   Animator Resource.h header file example, 94-95
   classes, 83-85
   coding, 85-87
   common, 78
      animate, 83, 91-92
      control notifcation, 90-91
      image list, 83
      implementing, 81-82
      list, 82
      messages (WM NOTIFY), 87
      progress bar, 83
      property page, 82
      property sheet, 82
      rich edit, 83
      slider, 83
      spin, 83
      status bar, 82

CToolBarCtrl 489

toolbar, 82
tooltip, 82
tree, 82
Windows 95, 76, 80
Windows Explorer, 83
common/standard dialog box comparison, 81
control notification, 79
   custom controls, 91
   WM COMMAND, 88-89
   WM NOTIFY, 90-91
custom, 415-417
   ActiveX controls comparison, 429
   CAudioClip control AudioClip.cpp source code file example, 425-426
   CAudioClip control AudioClip.h header file example, 423-424
   CColorbox control Colorbox.cpp source code example, 420, 422
   CColorbox control Colorbox.h header file example, 419-420
   CMainFrame frame window class Mainframe.cpp source code file example, 429
   CMainFrame frame window class Mainframe.h header file example, 428-429
   CObject class derivation, 417, 423
   CWnd class derivation, 417
   existing class derivation, 417-418, 420-421, 423
   reusability issues, 416-417
   testing, 428
identifiers, 85
invisible, 418
messages, 87
parent-child relationship, 75-76, 96
positioning, 96
visible, 418
Windows (traditional), 76-77
   button, 78-79, 87, 96
   edit, 78, 88-89
   list box, 78
   scroll bar, 78
   static, 78

converting
   CString objects, 186
   SDI applications, 283
coordinate systems. *See* **mapping modes**
coordinates, 254
CPageSetupDialog class, 103, 108
CPaintDC class, 159
CPoint class, 158, 176
CPoint data type, 10
CPrintDialog class, 103, 109
CPrintInfo class, public data members, 302
CPrintInfo object, 301-302
CProgressCtrl, 85
CPropertyPage class, 84, 437, 441-442
CPropertySheet class, 84, 436-441
CPropertySheet objects/CDialog objects comparison, 438
Create() member function, 19, 96
   CMainFrame (sample) frame window class, 429
   CPropertySheet class, 436
   CSplitterWnd class, 253
   CWnd-class derivation, 429
Create() member functions, 40, 420
CreateStatic() member function, 259
creating. *See also* **defining**
   arrays, 197
   controls
      custom, 415-426
      invisible, 418
      visible, 418
   dialog boxes
      common, 110-112
      classes, 130
      custom, 125-127
      DoModal() member function, 111, 126-127
      resources, 127-130
   DLLs. *See* DLLs
   documents, 216
   form-based applications. *See* applications
   MDI applications. *See* applications
   message boxes, 114, 117

objects
   CDialog, 122
   CTime, 186
pop-up menus, 147
property sheets, 434-437
status bars, 269-274
strings, 185
toolbars, 265-269, 274
views, 234
wizards. *See* wizards
CRecordView class, 231
CRect class, 177
CRect data type, 10-12
CResourceful::OnAppAbout message handler example, 66
CResourcefulApp::OnApp About() message handler example, 58
CRichEditCtrl, 85
CRichEditView class, 231
CScrollBar, 84
CScrollView class, 231, 250-251
CSingleDocTemplate class, 215
CSize class, 177
CSkeletonApp::InitInstance() member function, 40
CSkeletonDoc class, 37-39
CSkeletonView class, 40
CSliderCtrl, 85
CSpinButtonCtrl, 85
CSplitterWnd class, 253, 258
CStatic class, 84, 420
CStatusBar class, 263-264
CStatusBar member variable example, 271
CStatusBarCtrl, 84
CString class, 177
   C runtime string functions comparison, 184
   constructors, 185
   MBCS, 179
   overloaded operators, 112, 181, 186
   strings, creating, 185
   Unicode, 179
CString objects, 185-186
CTime class, 177, 186
CTime objects, 186
CTimeSpan class, 177, 186
CTimeSpan objects, 186
CToolBar class, 263-266
CToolBar member variable example, 268
CToolBar objects, 266
CToolBarCtrl, 84

CToolTipCtrl, 84
CTreeCtrl, 84
CTreeView class, 231
CTypedArray class, 198
CTypedPtrArray class, 195-198
CTypedPtrList class, 198, 201-202
CTypedPtrMap class, 202, 205
.CUR filename extension, 50
cursors, 45, 50, 73
custom controls. *See* controls
custom data collections, 206
custom dialog boxes. *See* dialog boxes
custom resources, 44
customizing. *See also* editing
   CDaoRecordset class, 325
      defining member variables, 326
      DoFieldExchange() member function, 326
      GetDefaultDBName() member function, 325
      GetDefaultSQL() member function, 325
      Hockey (sample) application, 340
      Hockey ConferenceSet.cpp source code file example, 341-343
      Hockey ConferenceSet.h header file example, 340-341
      Hockey DivisionSet.cpp source code file example, 344-346
      Hockey DivisionSet.h header file example, 343-344
      Hockey TeamSet.cpp source code file example, 337-339
      Hockey TeamSet.h header file example, 336-337
      initializing member variables, 326
   CDaoRecordView class
      HockeyView.h header file example, 349
      OnGetRecordset() member function, 328
   colors, 107
   data collections, 206
   dialog boxes, 103-104

CView class, 29, 230-232
   DoPreparePrinting() member function, 297-298
   GetDocument() member function, 232-233, 237, 240
   OnBeginPrinting() member function, 297-298
   OnDraw() member function, 232-233, 237, 240
   OnEndPrinting() member function, 298, 301
   OnEndPrintPreview() member function, 298, 300
   OnPrepareDC() member function, 297-299
   OnPreparePrinting() member function, 297-298, 311, 315
   OnPrint() member function, 232-233, 297-299
   OnUpdate() member function, 232-233
   printing support, 297
   SkeletonView.cpp source code file example, 40
   SkeletonView.h header file example, 39-40
CView::OnFilePrint() message handler, 304
CWinApp, 18
CWinApp::OnFilePrintSetup() message handler, 303, 310
CWindowsDC class, 159
CWnd class
   CDialog class, 121
   custom controls derivation, 417
      OnPaint() message handler, 420
      overriding Create() member function, 420
   Invalidate() member function, 172
   MessageBox() member function, 115
   simplicity, 12
   views, 230
   Win32 API comparison, 12
CWnd objects, 40

D

DAO (Data Access Objects), 317
   advantages, 319
   CDaoRecordView class, 323-327, 349

   Database object, 321
   DBEngine object, 320
   MFC comparison, 322
   Microsoft Jet databases, 318-321, 328
   object model, 320
   ODBC comparison, 318
   QueryDefs object, 322
   Recordset object, 322
   simplicity, 355
   TableDefs object, 321
   Workspace object, 321
   wrapper classes
      CDaoDatabase, 322
      CDaoQueryDef, 323
      CDaoRecordset, 323-326, 340, 349
      CDaoTableDef, 323
      CDaoWorkspace, 322
      exceptions, 323
      hidden database engine, 323
Data Access Objects. *See* DAO
data collections, 187. *See also* arrays; lists; maps
   AfxTempl.h header file, 206
   AfxTempl.h header files, 192, 206
   C++ templates, 188
      collection-specific coding purposes, 180
      multiple data type class capability, 178-179
      type safety approaches, 180
   comparing, 192
   custom, 206
   importance, 174
   non-template, 176, 188
   programming, 194-195
   simple collection classes, 193-194, 206
   typed pointer collection classes, 193-194
   Win32, minimizing overhead, 177
data modeling (CDocument class), 28
data objects. *See* resources
data structures. *See* data collections
data types
   COLORREF, 158
   CPpoint, 10

CRect, 10, 12
    with overridden operators,
        226
    prefixes, 31-32
    Win32
        BOOL, 10
        handles, 8-9
        names, 31
        POINT, 10
        RECT, 10-12
**data-aware controls, ActiveX,
    357**
database interfaces. *See* **specific
    database interfaces**
Database object (DAO), 321
databases
    interfaces. *See* specific data-
        base interfaces
    Microsoft Jet, 318-321, 328
DBEngine object (DAO), 320
**DDV (dialog data validation),
    121**
**DDX (dialog data exchange),
    120-121, 349**
**DDX Check() member function,
    126**
**DDX Radio() member function,
    126**
**DDX Scroll() member function,
    126**
**DDX Text() member function,
    126, 130**
**DDXFieldCBIndex() function,
    349**
DEBUG macro, 38
**DECLARE DYNCREATE
    macro, 19**
**DECLARE MESSAGE MAP
    macro, 19**
**DECLARE MESSAGE MAP()
    macro, 63**
declaring. *See* setting
    declspec(dllexport) modifier
        (DLLs), 407
    declspec(dllimport) modifier
        (DLLs), 407
**default buttons, dialog boxes,
    115**
**Define Custom Colors button,
    107**
defining
    accelerators, 48-49
    bitmaps, 49
    cursors, 50

dialog boxes, 55
    controls, 124-125,
        129-130
    DIALOG resource state-
        ments, 123
    DIALOGEX resource
        statements, 119, 129
    resource definition exam-
        ple, 55
    resources, 122
    styles, 124
handles, 9
menus
    menu item names, 53
    templates, 51-53
resource constants, 47-48
resources, 130
string tables, 56-57
**DEFPUSHBUTTON controls,
    130**
**DeleteContents() member func-
    tion, 211-212, 226**
**DeleteMenu() member function,
    137**
deriving. *See* **creating**
**DestroyWindow() member
    function, 454**
destructors, 206
**detecting errors, common dia-
    log boxes, 112**
**development-environments,
    DLLs, 406**
device contexts, 154
    clipping rectangles, 247-248
    device-independence,
        151-152
    printing, 294
device coordinates, 254
**device independence (graphics),
    151-152**
device-dependent bitmaps, 315
dialog bars, 262-265. *See also*
    **control bars; status bars;
    toolbars**
dialog box controls, 81
**dialog box resource definition
    example, 55**
dialog box templates, 117
dialog boxes, 46. *See also* **prop-
    erty sheets; wizards**
    Animator2 (sample) applica-
        tion, 112
    buttons, default, 115

classes
    CColorDialog, 102, 106
    CCommonDialog, 101
    CFileDialog, 102, 105,
        110
    CFindReplaceDialog, 102,
        108
    CFontDialog, 102, 107
    constructing, 130
    CPageSetupDialog, 103
    CPrintDialog, 103
    customizing, 103
    Finance
        PersonalInfoDlg.h head-
            er file example, 130
    IDD member constant,
        130
    member functions,
        111-112
    Win32 programming com-
        parison, 105
closing, 130
common, 97
    Animator2 (sample) appli-
        cation example, 112
    Color selection, 100,
        106-107, 112
    consistency issues, 104
    constructing, 110-112
    defined, 99
    detecting errors, 112
    File Open, 100, 106
    File Open dialog box file-
        name retrieving exam-
        ple, 111
    File Save As, 100, 106
    Find text, 100, 108
    Font selection, 100,
        107-108
    history, 98-99
    Page setup, 100, 104,
        108-109
    Print Setup, 104
    Replace text, 100, 108
    resource files, 112
controls, 124-125, 129-130
custom, 113, 125-129
defining, 55, 124-125
DS MODALFRAME style,
    124
ellipsis (. . .), 112
GUI elements, 54, 58
as main frame windows, 398
modal, 99, 105, 117-119

dialog boxes

modeless, 99, 105, 118-119
Printer Properties, 109
property pages comparison, 434
resource definition example, 55
resources, 117, 122
   constructing, 127-130
   DIALOG resource statement, 123
   DIALOGEX resource statement, 119, 129
   Finance menu resource definition example, 130
   IDD PROJECTOR, 396
   visual dialog box editors, 120
TipOfTheDay (sample) DLL, 410
variables, 120-121
WS CAPTION style, 124
WS POPUP style, 124
WS SYSMENU style, 124
dialog data exchange (DDX), 120, 349
dialog data validation (DDV), 121
DIALOG resource statements, 123-125
dialog-based applications, 391
DIALOGEX resource statements, 119, 129
dictionaries. *See* **maps**
Direct3D, 383
DirectAnimation, 385
DirectDraw, 383
DirectInput, 383
DirectMusic, 383
DirectPlay, 384
DirectShow, 385-386
DirectSound, 383
DirectX, 378-379. *See also*
   ActiveX; multimedia
   APIs, 381
   automated programming, 381
   combining multimedia content, 381
   Foundation, 382-384
   goals, 380
   Media, 382
      DirectAnimation, 385
      DirectShow, 385-386
      DirectX Transform, 385
      Explorer supported, 384
      SDK (Software Development Kit), 389

Media Player control, 385
   building applications, 391-394, 396-398
   CMediaPlayer class, 389-390
   m pMediaPlayer member variable, 398
   programming, 387
   Projector (sample) application, 391-395, 397-398
   supportable nonstreaming media formats, 386
   supportable streaming media formats, 386
   Windows Media Player, 388
Microsoft's DirectX Web site, 382
DirectX Transform, 385, 441
disabling default menu items, 147
displaying. *See* **viewing**
DllMain() function. *See* **DLLs**
DLLs (dynamic link libraries), 399. *See also* **dynamic linking**
   AFX EXT CLASS macro, 407
   AFX EXTENSION MODULE variable, 408
   AFXEXT macro, 407
   AfxInitExtensionModule() function, 409
   AfxTermExtensionModule() function, 409
   CDynLinkLibrary objects, 409
   compiling resources, 42-43
   declspec(dllexport) modifier, 407
   declspec(dllimport) modifier, 407
   development-environment specific, 406
   DllMain() function, 405-409
   exported classes, 407
   exported functions, 407
   files, 401-402, 414
   import libraries, 403, 406, 414
   MFC, 402
   sharing code benefit, 403-404
   static libraries comparison, 402

TipOfTheDay (sample) DLL, 410-414
versioning issues, 405
Windows, 403
docking
   control bars, 264
   toolbars, 274
DocName component (document strings), 221
DocType component (document strings), 221
document strings, format, 40
document templates, 23-24, 40
document-centric applications
   document templates, 23-24, 40
   document/view architecture, 22-23
document/view architecture, 13, 19-23. *See also* **documents; views**
   automatic nature, 211
   CDaoRecordView class, 349
   InitInstance() member function, 40
   Skeleton (sample) application, 33
documents, 207. *See also* **document/view architecture; views**
   Active, WebBrowser control, 363
   application-specific nature, 210
   CDocument class, 28, 33-37, 210-214, 224-226
   creating, 216
   CSkeletonDoc class, 37-39
   defined, 22
   document/view architecture, application interaction, 208-210
   main purposes, 209
   MDI applications, 275-278
   SDI applications, 276
   serialization, 213-215, 226
   size, 248-250, 260
   strings, 221-222
   templates, 215, 281
   Web-enabled applications, 376
DoDataExchange() member function, 130
   Finance2 (sample) application, 453
   Hockey (sample) application, 349

DoFieldExchange() member function, 326
DoModal() member function
  CPropertySheet class, 438-440
  dialog boxes, constructing, 111, 126-127
Doodle (sample) application. *See* **listings**
Doodle2 (sample) application. *See* **listings**
Doodle3 (sample) application. *See* **listings**
Doodle4 (sample) application. *See* **listings**
Doodle5 (sample) application. *See* **listings**
Doodle6 (sample) application. *See* **listings**
Doodle7 (sample) application. *See* **listings**
DoPreparePrinting() member function, 297-298
double-clicking (mouse), 74
Dr. Dobb's Journal, 479
dragging (mouse), 74
Draw() member function, 315
drawing. *See also* **painting windows**
  bitmaps, 168-169
  ellipses, 165-166
  graphics, 170-172
  lines, 163-164
  primitives, 162
  rectangles, 165
  text, 166
DS MODALFRAME style (dialog boxes), 124
dump contexts, 182
Dump() member functions, 38, 251
dwReason parameter (DLLs), 406-408
DYNAMIC DOWNCAST macro, 244
dynamic link libraries. *See* **DLLs**
dynamic linking, 404. *See also* **DLLs; static linking**
  application speed issues, 404
  explicit control, 413
  exported classes, 407
  exported functions, 407
  import libraries, 406, 414

  missing .DLL files, 414
  versioning issues, 405
dynamic splitter windows, 253, 260

E

edit controls, 78, 88-89
editing. *See also* **customizing**
  fonts, 108
  menus
    application, 136-140
    system, 134-136
  page setup information, 109
  printer configuration, 109
  text, 108
editors
  resource, 58
  visual dialog box, 120
EDITTEXT controls, 129
electron guns (monitors), 156
ElementAt() member function, 197
Ellipse() member function, 165
ellipses (. . .), 112, 166
Enable() member function, 147
END MESSAGE MAP() macro, 64
EndDialog() member function, 130, 454
Error (ADO), 360
errors, detecting (common dialog boxes), 112
Errors (ADO), 360
event-driven programming, 8, 11
.EXE files, 44, 401-402
executable files, compiling resources, 44-45
ExitInstance() member function, 28
Explorer. *See also* **WebBrowser control**
  ADO, 359
  DirectX Media, 384
  exclusive member functions, 369-370
exported classes, 407
exported functions, 407
.Ext component (document strings), 222
extensions (filenames)
  .BMP, 49
  .CUR, 50
  .DLL, 401-402, 414

  .EXE, 44, 401
  .ICO, 51
  .LIB, 414
  .MDB, 318
  .OBJ, 44
  .RC, 46
  .RES, 44

F

Field (ADO), 360
Fields (ADO), 360
file extensions. *See* **extensions**
File Open dialog box, 100, 106, 111
File Save As dialog box, 100, 106
filenames. *See* **names**
files
  .BMP, 49
  CFile class, 182
  .CUR, 50
  .DLL, 401-402, 414
  .EXE (executable), 44-45, 401-402
  header
    AfxTempl.h, 192, 206
    BrowseIt StdAfx.h header file example, 370
    BrowseItView.h header file example, 373-375
    CAudioClip control AudioClip.h header file example, 423-424
    CColorbox control Colorbox.h header file example, 419-420
    CMainFrame frame window class Mainframe.h header file example, 428-429
    DLLs, 414
    Doodle Resource.h header file example, 170-171
    Doodle2 Graphic.h header file example, 205-206
    Doodle2 StdAfx.h header file example, 206
    Doodle3 DoodleDoc.h header file example, 222-223
    Doodle3 DoodleView.h header file example, 234-236

494 files

Doodle3 Graphic.cpp source code file example, 226
Doodle3 Graphic.h header file example, 226
Doodle3 Mainframe.h header file example, 217
Doodle4 DoodleListView.h header file example, 260
Doodle6 Doodle.h header file example, 289
Doodle6 MainFrame.h header file example, 292
Finance2 Resource.h header file example, 444-445
Hockey DivisionSet.h header file example, 343-344
Hockey Resource.h header file example, 330-331
Hockey TeamSet.h header file example, 336-337
HockeyDoc.h header file example, 346
HockeyView.h header file example, 349
MMSystem.h (Win32), 428
Projector Resource.h header file example, 392
Projector.h header file example, 397
ProjectorDlg.h header file example, 398
Resourceful AboutDlg.h header file example, 58
SkeletonDoc.h header example, 34
SkeletonView.h header file example, 39-40
StdAfx.h header file example, 258
TipOfTheDay DLL Resource.h header file example, 410
TipOfTheDay.h header file example, 412-413
.ICO, 51
.LIB, 414
.MDB, 318
MRU, 288, 292
.OBJ, 44
.RC, 46
.RES, 44

resource
  common dialog boxes, 112
  Doodle.rc resource file example, 171-172
  Resourceful Resource.h header file example, 57-58
  Skeleton.rc resource file example, 19
source code
  BrowseItView.cpp source code file example, 375-376
  CAudioClip control AudioClip.cpp source code file example, 425-426
  CColorbox control Colorbox.cpp source code example, 420-422
  CMainFrame frame window class Mainframe.cpp source code file example, 429
  Doodle3 DoodleDoc.cpp source code file example, 224-226
  Doodle3 Mainframe.cpp source code file example, 217-218
  Doodle4 DoodleListView.cpp source code file example, 260
  Doodle6 Doodle.cpp source code file example, 290-292
  Doodle6 MainFrame.cpp source code file example, 292
  Hockey ConferenceSet.cpp source code file example, 341-343
  Hockey DivisionSet.cpp source code file example, 344-346
  Hockey TeamSet.cpp source code file example, 337-339
  HockeyDoc.cpp source code file example, 348-349
  HockeyView.cpp source code file example, 349

  MainFrame.cpp source code example, 19
  Projector.cpp source code file example, 398
  ProjectorDlg.cpp source code file example, 398
  Resourceful AboutDlg.cpp source code file example, 58
  Skeleton.cpp source code file example, 17-18
  SkeletonDoc.cpp source code file example, 34-37
  SkeletonView.cpp source code file example, 40
  TipOfTheDay.cpp source code example, 413-414
StdAfx, 15-16
.WAV, 427
FileType component (document strings), 221
FillRect() member function, 165
Finance (sample) application. See listings
Finance2 (sample) application. See listings
Find text dialog box, 100, 108
Find() member function, 201
FindIndex() member function, 201
Finish buttons, 433, 441
flags
  InsertMenu() member function, 139-140
  TrackPopupMenu() member function, 146
floating pop-up menus, 145-147
focus, 68-69
Font Selection dialog box, 100, 107
Font selection dialog box, 108
fonts, 108, 152-154
form-based applications. See applications
Format() member function, 186
frame windows (MDI), 281
functions
  AfxGetInstanceHandle(), 19
  AfxInitExtensionModule(), 409
  AfxRegisterWndClass(), 19
  AfxTermExtensionModule(), 409
  bitmaps, 152-154, 167-169
  brushes, 152-153
  CDC class, 158-159

functions 495

DDXFieldCBIndex(), 349
DllMain(), 405-409, 414
device independence, 151-152
EndDialog(), 130
exported, 407
fonts, 152-154
Get StockObject(), 96
graphics, 315
graphics device context, 151, 154, 247-248
importing, 407
member
   Add(), 196
   AddGraphic(), 226, 244, 250, 315
   AddHead(), 200
   AddPage(), 440-441
   ADO, 360
   AfxEnableControlContainer(), 398
   AppendMenu(), 134, 137, 140
   AssertValid(), 38, 251
   BitBlt(), 168-169
   CMainFrame::Create() member function example, 141-142
   Compare(), 186
   CompareNoCase(), 186
   Construct(), 442
   Create(), 19, 40, 96, 253, 420, 429, 436
   CreateStatic(), 259
   DDX Check(), 126
   DDX Radio(), 126
   DDX Scroll(), 126
   DDX Text(), 126, 130
   DeleteContents(), 211-212, 226
   DeleteMenu(), 137
   DestroyWindow(), 454
   dialog box classes, 111
   DoDataExchange(), 130, 349, 453
   DoFieldExchange(), 326
   DoModal(), 111, 126-127, 438-440
   DoPreparePrinting(), 297-298
   Draw(), 315
   Dump(), 38, 251
   ElementAt(), 197
   Ellipse(), 165
   Enable(), 147
   EndDialog(), 454
   ExitInstance(), 28

FillRect(), 165
Find(), 201
FindIndex(), 201
Format(), 186
GetAddressBar(), 369
GetAt(), 186, 196, 200
GetBookmark(), 349
GetBuffer(), 186
GetBusy(), 367, 376
GetCount(), 199, 203
GetCurrentPosition(), 390
GetCurrentTime(), 186
GetDay(), 186
GetDayOfWeek(), 186
GetDefaultDBName(), 325
GetDefaultSQL(), 325
GetDeviceCaps(), 159-160, 315
GetDocument(), 40, 232-233, 237, 240
GetFullName(), 369
GetHead(), 199
GetHeadPosition(), 200
GetHour(), 186
GetMenu(), 137
GetMenuItemCount(), 137
GetMinute(), 186
GetMonth(), 186
GetNext(), 200
GetNextAssoc(), 204
GetPrev(), 200
GetSecond(), 186
GetSize(), 196
GetStartPosition(), 203
GetStatusBar(), 369
GetSubMenu(), 136-138
GetSystemMenu(), 134
GetTail(), 199
GetTailPosition(), 200
GetTypeAsString(), 260
GetVolume(), 389
GetYear(), 186
Ghost
   CMainFrame::Draw-Boo() support member function example, 74
GoBack(), 366
GoForward(), 366
GoHome(), 366
GoSearch(), 366
InitInstance(), 19, 27, 218-219, 290-292, 414
document/view architecture, 40

InsertAfter(), 200
InsertAt(), 196
InsertBefore(), 200
InsertMenu(), 137-138
Internet Explorer exclusive, 369-370
Invalidate(), 172
IsEmpty(), 201, 204
IsEOF(), 349
IsOpen(), 349
LineTo(), 163
LoadBitmap(), 168
LoadFrame(), 292
LoadFromResource(), 376
LoadMenu(), 147
LoadStdProfileSetting(), 292
Lookup(), 204
LPCRECT(), 159
message handlers, 61, 65-66, 69-70, 74
MessageBox(), 115
ModifyMenu(), 137
MoveNext(), 349
MoveTo(), 163
Navigate(), 366-368
OnBeginPrinting(), 297-298
OnCloseDocument(), 211-212
OnCreate(), 96, 112
OnCreateClient(), 258
OnDraw(), 40, 232-233, 237, 240, 246-247, 296, 299, 313-314
OnEndPrinting(), 298, 301
OnEndPrintPreview(), 298-300
OnFilePersonalInfo(), 130
OnGetRecordset(), 328, 349
OnIdle(), 28
OnInitDialog(), 130, 414, 442, 453
OnInitialUpdate(), 252, 349
OnKillActive(), 442
OnLButtonDown(), 254-256
OnNewDocument(), 37, 211-212, 226, 260
OnOpenDocument(), 211-212, 226, 260
OnPBPlayClicked(), 112

OnPrepareDC(), 297-299
OnPreparePrinting(),
  297-298, 311, 315
OnPrint(), 232-233,
  297-299, 315
OnSaveDocument(),
  211-212
OnSetActive(), 442, 453
OnUpdate(), 232-233,
  243-246, 253, 312-313
OnWizardBack(), 442
OnWizardFinish(), 442
OnWizardNext(), 442
Open(), 349
operators [ ] (brackets),
  197, 204
Pause(), 390
Play(), 390, 426, 429
PreCreateWindow(), 40,
  96
PrintPageHeader(), 315
Rectangle(), 165
Refresh(), 367-368
ReleaseBuffer(), 186
RemoveAll(), 197, 201,
  204
RemoveAt(), 196, 200
RemoveHead(), 200
RemoveKey(), 204
RemovePage(), 440-441
RemoveTail(), 200
Run(), 27
Serialize(), 37, 211-214,
  226, 249
SetAddressBar(), 369
SetAt(), 186, 196, 200,
  204
SetAtGrow(), 196
SetBarStyle(), 274
SetBookmark(), 349
SetCheck(), 147
SetClip(), 429
SetCurrentPosition(), 390
SetDlgItemText(), 414
SetFileName(), 389
SetFullScreen(), 370
SetLoop(), 429
SetMenuBar(), 370
SetModifiedFlag(),
  211-212, 221, 226
SetRadio(), 147
SetSize(), 194-196
SetStatusBar(), 369
SetText(), 147
SetToolBar(), 370
SetVolume(), 389

SetWizardButtons(), 440
SetWizardMode(),
  439-440
Stop(), 367-368, 390, 429
TextOut(), 166
TrackPopupMenu(),
  145-146
UpdateAllViews(),
  211-212, 226
names, 30
palettes, 152-154
pens, 152
pixels, 172
rand(), 414
sndPlaySound() (Win32), 426
  static linking WinMM.lib,
    429
  .WAV files, 427
srand(), 414
virtual, message maps comparison, 62-63
Win32
  CommDlgExtended
    Error(), 112
  Win32 API, names, 31
  WinMain(), 10-11, 26

G

GetAddressBar() member function, 369
GetAt() member function, 186, 196, 200
GetBookmark() member function, 349
GetBuffer() member function, 186
GetBusy() member function, 367, 376
GetCount() member function, 199, 203
GetCurrentPosition() member function, 390
GetCurrentTime() member function, 186
GetDay() member function, 186
GetDayOfWeek() member function, 186
GetDefaultDBName() member function, 325
GetDefaultSQL() member function, 325
GetDeviceCaps() member function, 159-160, 315

GetDocument() member function, 40, 232-233, 237, 240
GetFullName() member function, 369
GetHead() member function, 199
GetHeadPosition() member function, 200
GetHour() member function, 186
GetMenu() member function, 137
GetMenuItemCount() member function, 137
GetMinute() member function, 186
GetMonth() member function, 186
GetNext() member function, 200
GetNextAssoc() member function, 204
GetPrev() member function, 200
GetSecond() member function, 186
GetSize() member function, 196
GetStartPosition() member function, 203
GetStatusBar() member function, 369
GetStockObject() function, 96
GetSubMenu() member function, 136, 138
GetSystem Menu() member function, editing system menus, 134
GetTail() member function, 199
GetTailPosition() member function, 200
GetTypeAsString() member function, 260
GetVolume() member function, 389
GetYear() member function, 186
Ghost (sample) application. *See* listings
global variables, wizards, 448
GMT (Greenwich Mean Time), 186
GoBack() member function, 366
GoForward() member function, 366

GoHome() member function, 366
GoSearch() member function, 366
graphic cards, optimizing views, 242
Graphical User Interfaces (GUIs), 54, 58
graphics, 149-150, 170-172
   color, 155
      COLORREF data type, 158
      RGB, 156-158
   GDI (Graphics Device Interface), 151, 315
      bitmaps, 152-154, 167-169
      brushes, 152-153
      CDC, 160
      CDC class, 158
      device-dependent bitmaps, 315
      device-independence, 151-152
      fonts, 152-154
      graphics device context, 151-154, 247-248
      palettes, 152-154
      pens, 152
      pixels, 172
   mapping modes, 154-155
   primitives, 162-165
   variables, 172
graphics device contexts, 154
   clipping rectangles, 247-248
   device-independence, 151-152
   printing, 294
Graphics Device Interface. *See* GDI
GRAYED menu option, 53
Greenwich Mean Time (GMT), 186
GROUPBOX controls, 129
GUIs (Graphical User Interfaces), 54, 58

H

h prefix, 31
handles, 8-9
Hardware Emulation Layer (HEL), 398
header files. *See* files
headers, precompiled, 15

help
   MFC FAQ Web site, 478
   MFC mailing list, 478
   MFC Professional Web site, 478
   Microsoft Developer Network Web site, 478
   Microsoft Visual C++ Web site, 478
   newsgroups, 478
   periodicals, 479
   ToolTips, 274
HELP menu option, 54
hiding control bars, 273-274
hInstance parameter (DLLs), 405
hints (views), 243
Hockey (sample) application. *See* listings
HRZRES constant, 160
HORZSIZE constant, 160
hot keys, 45, 48-49
hotspots, 73-74
Hungarian notation, 32-33

I

.ICO filename extension, 51
ICON statements, 19
icons, 46, 50
   defining, 19, 51
   MDI applications, 280
   size, 51
IDD member constants, 130
IDD PROJECTOR dialog box resource, 396
identifiers, 303-304
   AFX IDS APP TITLE, 19
   command control, 85
   handles, 8-99
   ID ABOUT command identifier, 393
   ID APP EXIT, 40
   ID FILE MRU FILE1, 288
   ID FILE PRINT, 304
   ID FILE PRINT DIRECT, 304, 309
   ID FILE PRINT PREVIEW, 304
   ID FILE PRINT SETUP, 303, 310
   IDD PROJECTORBOX, 393
   IDR SKELETON, 40
   PSWIZB BACK, 440

   PSWIZB DISABLEDFINISH, 441
   PSWIZB FINISH, 441
   PSWIZB NEXT, 441
   resource, 19
   SEPARATOR, 268
   standard MFC, 48
   UINT pane identifiers, 272
   virtual key codes, 68
image list controls, 83
IMPLEMENT DYNCREATE macro, 19
IMPLEMENT SERIAL macro, 226, 315
implementing common controls, 81-82
import libraries, 403, 406, 414
importing, 407
INACTIVE menu option, 54
Indeo 5, 387
initializing, 19
   ActiveX controls, 396-397
   applications, 19
   CMainFrame class, Create() member function, 19
InitInstance() member function, 19, 27, 40
   Doodle3
      CDoodleApp::InitInstance member function example, 218-219
   Doodle6 (sample) application, 290-292
Inprise C++ Builder Web site, 482
input focus, 68
InsertAfter() member function, 200
InsertAt() member function, 196
InsertBefore() member function, 200
InsertMenu() member function, 137-140
Inside Microsoft Visual C++, 479
instance initialization, 19
Internet applications. *See* applications
Internet Explorer. *See also* WebBrowser control
   ADO, 359
   DirectX Media, 384
   exclusive member functions, 369-370

Internet Information Server
4.0, 358
Invalidate() member function,
172
Investment wizard (sample)
application, 439, 443-447
building pages, 450-454
CInvestmentWiz class, 454
global variables, 448
invisible controls, 418
IsEmpty() member function,
201, 204
IsEOF() member function, 349
IsOpen() member function, 349

J-K

Jet databases
.MDB extension, 318
DAO, 318, 320
Hockey.mdb Jet database
example, 324

KEY parameter, 197-199
keyboard shortcuts, 45
keyboards
Doodle7 keyboard accelerator
resource definitions example, 304
focus, 64
keyboard/mouse balance, 60
messages, 64-65
virtual key codes, 64
keys (maps), 189
keywords, 62

L

l prefix, 27
.LIB files, 411
libraries. *See also* DLLs
import, 402-403, 414
static, 399, 402
WinMM.lib, 423, 427
lines, 157-158
linked lists, 189
linking. *See* dynamic linking;
static linking
list box controls, 77
list controls, 79
listings
accelerator resource definition, 45-46
animate control notification
message map example,
85

Animator MainFrame.cpp
source code file, 89-93
Animator MainFrame.h header file, 87-88
Animator Resource.h header
file, 87
Animator2
CMainFrame::OnCreate()
member function, 107-108
Animator2 CMainFrame::
OnPBPlayClicked()
member function, 108-109
Animator2 CMainFrame::
OnRButtonUp() message
handler, 110
Animator3 animation control
message handlers, 144
Animator3
CMainFrame::Create()
member function, 137
Animator3
CMainFrame::OnCreate()
message handler, 137-138
Animator3 CMainFrame::On
RButtonUp() message handler, 141
Animator3 CMainFrame::On
SysCommand() message
handler,
134
Animator3 command update
message handlers, 145
Animator3 menu resource,
136
bitmap drawing OnPaint()
message handler, 162-163
BrowseIt menu resource definition, 367-368
BrowseIt StdAfx.h header
file, 367
BrowseIt string resource definitions, 369
BrowseIt toolbar resource
definition, 368-369
BrowseItView.cpp source
code file, 370-373
BrowseItView.h header file,
369-370
CAudioClip control
AudioClip.cpp source code
file, 421-423
CAudioClip control
AudioClip.h header file,
420-421

CColorbox control
Colorbox.cpp source code
file, 419-420
CColorbox control
Colorbox.h header file,
417-418
CMainFrame frame window
class Mainframe.cpp source
code file, 425-426
CMainFrame frame window
class Mainframe.h header
file, 424-425
CMainFrame::PreCreateWind
ow() member function, 36
CResourceful::OnAppAbout
message handler, 62
CResourcefulApp::
OnAppAbout() message
handler, 54
CSkeletonApp::InitInstance()
member function, 35-36
dialog box resource definition, 50
DIALOG resource statement
example, 118
Doodle CMainFrame menu
command message handlers, 167
Doodle CMainFrame menu
command update message
handlers, 168-169
Doodle CMainFrame message
handlers, 168
Doodle CMainFrame message
map, 166
Doodle CMainFrame::
OnLButtonDown message
handler, 169-171
Doodle Resource.h header
file, 163-164
Doodle.rc resource file,
165-166
Doodle2 CMainFrame::
OnLButtonDown()
message handler, 203-204
Doodle2
CMainFrame::OnPaint()
message handler, 204-205
Doodle2 Graphic.cpp source
code file, 200-202
Doodle2 Graphic.h header
file, 199-200
Doodle2 StdAfx.h header file,
203

listings

Doodle3 CDoodleApp::InitInstance() member function, 214-215
Doodle3 DoodleDoc.cpp source code file, 218-220
Doodle3 DoodleDoc.h header file, 217-218
Doodle3 DoodleView.cpp source code file, 234-238
Doodle3 DoodleView.h header file, 232-233
Doodle3 Graphic.cpp source code file, 222-224
Doodle3 Graphic.h header file, 221-222
Doodle3 Mainframe.cpp source code file, 213-214
Doodle3 Mainframe.h header file, 212-213
Doodle3 menu resource definition, 215-216
Doodle4 CDoodleDoc::AddGraphic() member function, 243, 246-247
Doodle4 CDoodleDoc::OnNewDocument() member function, 258
Doodle4 CDoodleDoc::OnOpenDocument() member function, 258-259
Doodle4 CDoodleDoc::Serialize() member function, 246
Doodle4 CDoodleView::AssertValid() member function, 247
Doodle4 CDoodleView::Dump() member function, 248
Doodle4 CDoodleView::OnDraw() member function, 244-245
Doodle4 CDoodleView::OnInitialUpdate() member function, 248
Doodle4 CDoodleView::OnLButtonDown() member function, 249-251
Doodle4 CDoodleView::OnUpdate() member function, 243-244, 248-249
Doodle4 CGraphic::GetTypeAsString() member function, 257
Doodle4 CMainFrame::OnCreateClient() member function, 253
Doodle4 DoodleListView.cpp source code file, 255-257
Doodle4 DoodleListView.h header file, 254
Doodle4 StdAfx.h header file, 252
Doodle5 CMainFrame::OnCreate() message handler, 265-266
Doodle5 final CMainFrame::OnCreate() message handler, 271
Doodle5 menu resource definition, 269-270
Doodle5 revised CMainFrame::OnCreate() message handler, 268
Doodle5 status bar help message string resource definitions, 267
Doodle5 status bar keyboard status indicator string resource definitions, 267
Doodle5 status bar revised help message string resource definitions, 272
Doodle5 toolbar resource definition, 264-265
Doodle6 Doodle.cpp source code file, 285-287
Doodle6 Doodle.h header file, 284-285
Doodle6 main application string resources, 283
Doodle6 MainFrame.cpp source code file, 288-290
Doodle6 MainFrame.h header file, 287-288
Doodle6 menu resource definition, 283
Doodle6 menu resource definitions, 282
Doodle7 CDoodleDoc::AddGraphic() member function, 310-311
Doodle7 CDoodleView message map, 304
Doodle7 CDoodleView::OnDraw() member function, 306-307
Doodle7 CDoodleView::OnLButtonDown() message handler, 309-310
Doodle7 CDoodleView::OnPrint() member function, 307-308
Doodle7 CDoodleView::OnUpdate() member function, 306
Doodle7 CDoodleView::PrintPageHeader() member function, 308-309
Doodle7 CGraphic::Draw() member function, 312-313
Doodle7 keyboard accelerator resource definitions, 304
Doodle7 revised menu resource definitions, 301-303
Doodle7 revised toolbar resource definitions, 303-304
edit control notification message map, 82-83
ellipse drawing OnPaint() message handler, 159
File Open dialog box filename retrieving, 106
Finance CMainFrame::OnFilePersonalInfo() member function source code, 127-128
Finance menu resource definition, 126-127
Finance PersonalInfoDlg.cpp source code file, 125-126
Finance PersonalInfoDlg.h header file, 123-124
Finance2 CInvestmentWiz class declaration, 450
Finance2 CInvestmentWiz class implementation, 451-452
Finance2 CInvestWizData class declaration, 444
Finance2 CInvestWizData::CInvestWizData() constructor, 444
Finance2 CInvestWizPage1 class declaration, 445

Finance2 CInvestWizPage1 class implementation, 446-447
Finance2 CInvestWizPage2 class declaration, 447
Finance2 CInvestWizPage2 class implementation, 448-449
Finance2 CInvestWizPage3 class declaration, 449
Finance2 CInvestWizPage3 class implementation, 449-450
Finance2 CMainFrame::OnFileInvestmentWiz() message handler, 452
Finance2 Finance.rc resource script, 441-443
Finance2 Resource.h header file, 439-440
Ghost CMainFrame::DrawBoo() support member function, 70-71
Ghost CMainFrame::OnKeyDown() message handler, 66-67
Ghost CMainFrame::OnLButton() message handler, 70
Hockey ConferenceSet.cpp source code file, 333-335
Hockey ConferenceSet.h header file, 332-333
Hockey DivisionSet.cpp source code file, 336-337
Hockey DivisionSet.h header file, 335-336
Hockey Resource.h header file, 325-326
Hockey TeamSet.cpp source code file, 330-332
Hockey TeamSet.h header file, 329-330
Hockey.rc resource script, 326-329
HockeyDoc.cpp source code file, 338-340
HockeyDoc.h header file, 337-338
HockeyView.cpp source code file, 341-346
HockeyView.h header file, 340-341
line drawing OnPaint() message handler, 158

MainFrame.cpp Skeleton source code, 14-15
MainFrame.h Skeleton header file, 13-14
menu resource definition, 48
MFC Extension DLL DLLMain() function example, 405
Personal Information dialog box resource definition, 122-123
Personal Information dialog box resource definition example, 122-123
Projector Resource.h header file, 385
Projector.cpp source code file, 390-391
Projector.h header file, 389
Projector.rc resource script, 386-388
ProjectorDlg.cpp source code file, 393-396
ProjectorDlg.h header file, 391-392
rectangle drawing OnPaint() message handler, 159
required implementation file message map macros, 61
Resource.h header file resource identifiers, 122
Resourceful AboutDlg.cpp source code file, 55-56
Resourceful AboutDlg.h header file, 54-55
Resourceful application class message map, 54
Resourceful message map, 61
Resourceful Resource.h header file, 51
Resourceful.rc resource script, 52-53
skeletal initialization DLLMain() function, 404
Skeleton Resource.h header file, 16, 45
Skeleton.cpp source code file, 11-12
Skeleton.h header file, 11
Skeleton.rc resource file, 16-17
SkeletonDoc.cpp source code file, 29-30
SkeletonDoc.h header file, 28-29
SkeletonDV menu resources, 38

SkeletonDV string resources, 37
SkeletonView.cpp source code file, 33-34
SkeletonView.h header file, 32
slider control notification message map, 84
StdAfx files source code, 10-11
string table resource definition, 50-51
text drawing OnPaint() message handler, 160
TipOfTheDay DLL Resource.h header file, 406
TipOfTheDay.cpp source code file, 408-411
TipOfTheDay.h header file, 408
TipOfTheDay.rc resource script, 407
Tipper CMainFrame::OnLButtonDown() message handler, 412
Tipper CTipperApp::InitInstance() member function, 412
lists, 176, 188-190, 194-197. *See also* **data collections**
LoadBitmap() member function, 162
LoadFromResource() member function, 375
loading
  bitmaps, 162
  Web pages, 375
LoadMenu() member function, 142
LoadStdProfileSettings() member function, 287
logical coordinates, 249
Lookup() member function, 198
lp prefix, 27
LPCRECT() member function, 159
lpsz prefix, 27
LTEXT controls, 123

M

m bAutoStart member variable, 421, 427
m bLoop member variable, 421
m bPreview (public data member), 298

menus

m ColorBox member variable, 427
m hIcon member variable, 392
m nCurPage (public data member), 297
m nDrawMode variable, 167
m nNumPreviewPages (public data member), 297
m pen variable, 167
m pMediaPlayermember variable, 392
m rcColor member variable, 418
m rectDraw (public data member), 298
m sClip member variable, 421
m strFilter public member variable, 348
macros
   AFX EXT CLASS, 403
   AFXEXT, 403
   ASSERT, 35
   ASSERT VALID, 35
   DEBUG, 31
   DECLARE DYNCREATE, 15
   DECLARE MESSAGE MAP, 15
   DYNAMIC DOWNCAST, 244
   IMPLEMENT DYNCREATE, 15
   IMPLEMENT SERIAL, 224, 311
   message map
      BEGIN MESSAGE MAP(), 61
      DECLARE MESSAGE MAP(), 61
      END MESSAGE MAP(), 61
      ON COMMAND, 62
      ON MESSAGE, 62
      ON NOTIFY, 84
      ON UPDATE COMMAND UI, 62
      ON WM XXXX, 62
      required implementation file message map macros example, 61
   ON COMMAND, 132
   ON UPDATE COMMAND UI, 142
   T, 179
   Win32 API, 110
magazines, 478-479

mailing lists, 478
main frame windows, 11-15, 23
   dialog boxes, 392
   views, 26
main() function, 7
MainFrame.cpp Skeleton source code example, 14-15
MainFrame.h Skeleton header file example, 13-14
mapping modes, 152
   device coordinates, 249
   logical coordinates, 249
   MM LOENGLISH, 300
      Doodle7 (sample) application, 305
      MM TEXT comparison, 301
   MM TEXT, 152-153, 299
   pixels, 171
maps, 176, 188-190, 197-198. *See also* data collections
maximize command, 132
MB ABORTRETRYIGNORE style (message box), 114
MB APPLMODAL style (message box), 114
MB DEFBUTTON1 style (message box), 115
MB DEFBUTTON2 style (message box), 115
MB DEFBUTTON3 style (message box), 115
MB ICONEXCLAMATION style (message box), 115
MB ICONINFORMATION style (message box), 115
MB ICONQUESTION style (message box), 115
MB ICONSTOP style (message box), 115
MB OK style (message box), 114
MB OKCANCEL style (message box), 114
MB RETRYCANCEL style (message box), 114
MB SYSTEMMODAL style (message box), 115
MB YESNO style (message box), 114
MB YESNOCANCEL style (message box), 114
MBCS (Multibyte Character Sets), 179
.MDB extension, 318

MDI (Multiple Document Interface), 215, 275-276
MDI applications. *See* applications
MDICLIENT class, 279
Media Player control (ActiveX), 385
   applications, building, 384-396
   CMediaPlayer class, 383-384
   DirectShow (DirectX media), 381
   m pMediaPlayer member variable, 392
   programming, 387
   Projector (sample) application
      Projector Resource.h header file example, 385
      Projector.cpp source code file example, 390-391
      Projector.h header file example, 389
      Projector.rc resource script example, 386-388
      ProjectorDlg.cpp source code file example, 393-396
      ProjectorDlg.h header file example, 391-392
   supportable nonstreaming media formats, 382
   supportable streaming media formats, 381
   Windows Media Player, 382
media streaming, 381
member functions. *See* functions
member variables. *See* variables
memory device contexts, 312
MENUBARBREAK menu option, 49
MENUBREAK menu option, 49
menus
   application
      editing, 134-136
      system menu comparison, 132
   BrowseIt menu resource definition example, 367-368
   CMenu objects, 135
   commands, adding, 269-270
   Doodle3 menu resource definition example, 215-216

Doodle6 menu resource definition example, 282-283
Doodle7 revised menu resource definitions example, 301-303
items
    adding, 135-136
    default disabling, 143, 146
    names, 49
    state, 142
multiple, MDI applications, 280-282
ON COMMAND macro, 132
options, 49
pop-up, 135-136, 140-142, 146
Recent File menu item (Windows), 283
resource definition example, 48
as supplemental user interfaces, 138
system, 132-134
templates, 47-48
WM COMMAND message, 132
WM SYSCOMMAND message, 133

message boxes, 114-115
message handlers, 60
    afx msg keyword, 62
    Animator3 animation control message handlers example, 144
    Animator3 CMainFrame::OnCreate() message handler example, 137-138
    Animator3 CMainFrame::OnRButtonUp() message handler example, 141
    Animator3 CMainFrame::OnSysCommand() message handler example, 134
    Animator3 command update message handlers example, 145
    Animator3 new menu command message handlers example, 139
    command update, 142-143, 146

CResourceful::OnAppAbout message handler example, 62
CView::OnFilePrint(), 298
CView::OnFilePrintPreview(), 299
CWinApp::OnFilePrintSetup(), 298, 304
Doodle CMainFrame menu command message handlers example, 167
Doodle CMainFrame menu command update message handlers example, 168-169
Doodle CMainFrame message handlers example, 168
Doodle CMainFrame::OnLButtonDown message handler example, 169-171
Doodle2 CMainFrame::OnLButtonDown() message handler example, 203-204
Doodle2 CMainFrame::OnPaint() message handler example, 204-205
Doodle7 CDoodleView::OnLButtonDown() message handler example, 309-310
Finance2 CMainFrame::OnFileInvestmentWiz() message handler example, 452
Ghost CMainFrame::OnKeyDown() message handler example, 66-67
Ghost CMainFrame::OnLButton() message handler example, 70
Ghost OnKeyDown() message handler declaration example, 66-67
Ghost OnLButton() message handler declaration example, 69
OnANStart(), 93
OnANStop(), 93
OnChar(), 65
OnCKTransparency(), 93
OnCreate()
    CMainFrame (sample) frame window class, 425-426
    creating toolbars, 265

Doodle5 CMainFrame::OnCreate() message handler example, 265-266
Doodle5 final CMainFrame::OnCreate() message handler example, 271
Doodle5 revised CMainFrame::OnCreate() message handler example, 268
toolbars, docking, 271
OnEditClearAll(), 221
OnFileBest(), 346
OnKeyDown(), 65
OnKeyUp(), 65
OnLButtonDblClk(), 69
OnLButtonDown(), 68, 412, 425-427
OnLButtonUp(), 68
OnMButtonDblClk(), 69
OnMButtonDown(), 68
OnMButtonUp(), 69
OnMouseMove(), 68
OnMouseMove() message handler declaration example, 69
OnNextTip(), 411
OnPaint(), 156-157, 170
    CWnd class-derived controls, 418
    Finance2 (sample) application, 447
OnPBPlayClicked(), 93
OnRButtonDblClk(), 69
OnRButtonDown(), 68, 425-427
OnRButtonUp(), 69, 110
OnSysCommand(), 133-134
OnSysKeyDown(), 65
OnSysKeyUp(), 65
OnUpdateEditClearAll(), 221
OnUpdateViewStop(), 373
parameters, 63-65
Projector (sample) application, 392-393
Resourceful message handler declaration example, 62
WM COMMAND, 83
WM NOTIFY, 84
message maps, 15, 60
    animate control notification example, 85
    Doodle CMainFrame message map example, 166

newsgroup 503

Doodle7 CDoodleView message map example, 304
edit control notification example, 82-83
macros, 61-62, 84
Resourceful application class message map example, 54
Resourceful message map example, 61
slider control notification example, 84
virtual member functions comparison, 60-61
MessageBox() member function, 114-115
messages, 59
control notification, 82-84
keyboard, 64-65
MFC/Win32 comparison, 60
mouse, 67-69
virtual member functions, 61
windows, 5-8
WM COMMAND, 132
WM PAINT, 156
WM SYSCOMMAND, 133
MF BYCOMMAND flag, 136
MF BYPOSITION flag, 136
MF CHECKED flag, 136
MF DISABLED flag, 136
MF ENABLED flag, 136
MF GRAYED flag, 136
MF HILITE flag, 136
MF POPUP flag, 136
MF STRING flag, 136
MF UNCHECKED flag, 136
MF UNHILITE flag, 136
MFC FAQ Web site, 478
MFC mailing list, 478
MFC Professional Web site, 478
Microsoft
Access, 318, 324
ADO products, 355
database interfaces, 352
Jet databases, 320, 324
Microsoft Developer Network Web site, 478
Microsoft Internet Explorer. *See* Explorer
Microsoft Systems Journal, 479
Microsoft Visual C++. *See* C++
Microsoft Visual C++ Web site, 478, 482
Microsoft Visual Studio, 63, 355

Microsoft's DirectX Web site, 379
Microsoft's Windows Media Web site, 383
Money, 362
MSN Web site, 373
newsgroups, 478
Office, Web enabled, 362
Word, as MDI application, 277
MIDI (Musical Instrument Digital Interface), 382
minimize command, 132
MM LOENGLISH mapping mode, 300-301, 305
MM TEXT, 152-153, 299
MMSystem.h header file, 423
modal dialog boxes, 99, 105, 115-117
modeless dialog boxes, 99, 105, 116-117
modeless property sheets, 436
modeless wizards, 436
modeling data, CDocument class, 25
modifiers, DLLs, 403
modifying. *See* editing
ModifyMenu() member function, 134
monitors, electron guns, 153
most recently used (MRU) file, 283, 287
mouse, 67-69
MOV (QuickTime), 382
move command, 132
MoveNext() member function, 346
MoveTo() member function, 157
moving (mouse), 68
Moving Picture Experts Group (MPEG), 382
MPEG-1 (Moving Picture Experts Group standard 1), 382
MPEG-2 (Moving Picture Experts Group standard 2), 382
MPEG-3 (Moving Picture Experts Group standard 3), 382
MRU (most recently used) file, 283, 287
Multibyte Character Sets (MBCS), 179

multimedia, 377. *See also* **ActiveX; DirectX**
applications, 378
ASF (Advanced Streaming Format), 381-382
AU (UNIX audio), 382
Audio Interchange File Format (AIFF), 382
AVI (Audio-Video Interleaved), 382
content, time-based, 378
Indeo 5, 382
media streaming, 381
Microsoft's Windows Media Web site, 383
MIDI (Musical Instrument Digital Interface), 382
Moving Picture Experts Group (MPEG), 382
QuickTime (MOV), 382
RA (RealAudio), 382
RV (Real Video), 382
Sound File (SND), 382
VOD (Video on Demand), 381
WAV (Waveform Audio), 382
Multiple Document Interface (MDI), 275
Multiple Document Interface applications. *See* MDI applications
Musical Instrument Digital Interface (MIDI), 382

N

\n (newline) characters, 37
names, 26
classes, 27
constants, 27
filename extensions, 42, 45-47
functions, 27
menu items, 49
variables, 27-28
Win32, 27
Navigate() member function, 364-365
Navigate2() member function, 364-365
navigating
property sheets, 435
wizards, 433-435
navigation constants, 365
nChar parameter, 65
newline (\n) characters, 37
newsgroups, 478

Next buttons, 433, 437
nFlags parameter, 65, 69
nonclient areas (application windows), 4, 68
notification codes, 83
notifications. *See* control notifications
nRepCnt parameter, 65
NUMCOLORS constant, 156

O

.OBJ filename extension, 42
objects
    ADO, 351-359
    afxDump, 177
    application, 11-13, 23-25
    CArchive, 210
    CDialog, 117-118, 436
    CDynLinkLibrary, 405
    CMenu, 133-135
    CPrintInfo, 297-298
    CPropertySheet, 436
    CRect, 8
    CString, 179-182
    CTime, 182
    CTimeSpan, 183-184
    CToolBar, 264
    CWnd, 8, 34
    DAO. *See* DAO
    dialog boxes, 106
    recordsets, form-based applications, 323
    serializing, 177-178
obtaining objects, CMenu, 133-135
ODBC (Open Database Connectivity), 318, 353. *See also* DAO
Office, Web-enabled, 362
OLE DB (OLE Database), 354
ON COMMAND macro, 62, 132
ON MESSAGE macro, 62
ON UPDATE COMMAND UI macro, 62, 142
ON WM XXXX macro, 62
OnANStart() message handler, 93
OnANStop() message handler, 93
OnBeginPrinting() member function, 295-296
OnChar(), 65
OnCKTransparency() message handler, 93

OnCloseDocument() member function, 209
OnCreate() member function, 93, 107-108
OnCreate() message handler, 265-268, 271, 425-426
OnCreateClient() member functions, 253
OnDraw() member function, 35, 230-231, 234, 296
    device independence, 238
    Doodle4
        CDoodleView::OnDraw() member function example, 244-245
    Doodle7
        CDoodleView::OnDraw() member function example, 306-307
    printing, 294
one-time initialization, 13
OnEditClearAll() message handler, 221
OnEndPrinting() member function, 295-297
OnEndPrintPreview() member function, 295-297
OnFileBest() message handler, 346
OnFilePersonalInfo() member function, 127-128
OnGetRecordset() member function, 324, 346
OnInitDialog() member function, 128
    Finance2 (sample) application, 447
    overriding, 438
    TipOfTheDay (sample) DLL, 411
OnInitialUpdate() member function, 248, 346
OnKeyDown(), 65
OnKeyUp(), 65
OnKillActive() member function, 438
OnLButtonDblClk(), 69
OnLButtonDown(), 68, 249-251
OnLButtonDown() message handler, 425-427
OnLButtonUp(), 68
OnMButtonDblClk(), 69
OnMButtonDown(), 68
OnMButtonUp(), 68
OnMouseMove(), 68

OnNewDocument() member function, 31
    automatic calling, 209
    Doodle3 (sample) application, 220
    Doodle4
        CDoodleDoc::OnNewDocument() member function example, 258
OnNextTip() message handler, 411
OnOpenDocument() member function, 209, 220, 258-259
OnPaint() message handler, 158-163, 170
    CWnd class-derived controls, 418
    Finance2 (sample) application, 447
OnPaint() message handler bitmap drawing example, 162-163
OnPaint() message handler ellipse drawing example, 159
OnPaint() message handler line drawing example, 158
OnPaint() message handler rectangle drawing example, 159
OnPaint() message handler text drawing example, 160
OnPBPlayClicked() member function, 108-109
OnPBPlayClicked() message handler, 93
OnPrepareDC() member function, 295-296
OnPreparePrinting() member function, 295, 305, 314
OnPrint() member function, 230-231, 295-296, 307-309
OnRButtonDblClk(), 69
OnRButtonDown(), 68
OnRButtonDown() message handler, 425-427
OnRButtonUp(), 69
OnRButtonUp() message handler, 110
OnSaveDocument() member function, 209
OnSetActive() member function, 438, 447
OnSysCommand() message handler, 133-134
OnSysKeyDown(), 65
OnSysKeyUp(), 65
OnUpdate() member function, 230-231, 306

programming

Doodle4
    CDoodleView::OnUpdate() member function example, 243-244, 248-249
    DYNAMIC DOWNCAST macro, 244
    optimizing views, 242-243
OnUpdateEditClearAll() message handler, 221
OnUpdateViewStop() message handler, 373
OnWizardBack() member function, 438
OnWizardFinish() member function, 438
OnWizardNext() member function, 438
Open Database Connectivity (ODBC), 318, 353. *See also* DAO
Open() member function, 346
operators
    >> (overridden), 211-212, 225
    << (overridden), 211-212, 225
    [ ], 180, 193, 198
    overloaded
        == operator, 109
        CString, 181-182
        LPCRECT() member function, 159
    scope resolution (::), 27
optimizing views, 241-245. *See also* editing
options (menu), 49
overriding
    Create() member function, 418
    OnInitDialog() member function, 438

P

p prefix, 27
Page Setup dialog box, 99, 104
painting windows. *See also* drawing
    client areas, 156
    OnPaint() message handler, 156-157
    WM_PAINT message, 156
palettes, 151-152
panes, 252
Parameter (ADO), 356
parameters
    Boolean, 221
    CArray, 192-193

CList, 195
CMap, 197
COLORREF, 418
CTypedPtrArray, 194
CTypedPtrList, 196
CTypedPtrMap, 199
dwReason, DLLs, 403-404
hInstance, DLLs, 403
message handlers, 63-65
mouse, 69
Navigate() member function, 365
Navigate2() member function, 365
pReserved, DLLs, 403
Parameters (ADO), 356
Password (ADO Data Control property), 358
Pause() member function, 384
pens, 151
periodicals, 478-479
Personal Information dialog box resource definition example, 122-123
physical coordinates, 249
pies, 157
pixels, 171
placing record sets (form-based applications), 323
Play() member function, 384
    CMainFrame (sample) frame window class, 427
    sndPlaySound() Win 32 function, 423
POINT data type, 7
point parameter, 69
POINT structure, 158
pointers
    char, 182
    typed pointer collection classes, 191
polygons, 157
pop-up menus
    AppendMenu() member function, 136
    floating, 140
        command update message handlers, 146
        constructing as resources, 142
    GetSubMenu() function, 135
    InsertMenu() member function, 135
positioning controls, 94
precompiled headers, 10
PreCreateWindow() member

    function, 34-36, 39, 92
prefixes (variables), 27
pReserved parameter, DLLs, 403
primitives (graphics), 157-159
print commands, identifiers, 298-299, 304
Print dialog box, 99, 105
print jobs, 295
Print Preview, 294
Printer buttons, 104
Printer Properties dialog box, 104
printers, 104-105, 314
printing, 293
    CPrintInfo class, 297-298
    CPrintInfo object, 297-298
    CView class, 295
    default support, 294
    device contexts, 294
    device-dependent bitmaps, 311-312
    device-independent architecture, 293
    mapping modes, 299-301, 305
    Page Setup dialog box, 104
    print commands, identifiers, 298-299
    Print dialog box, 105
    print jobs, 295
    Print Preview, 294
    Printer Properties dialog box, 104
    views, 228
    Win32 comparison, 294
PrintPageHeader() member function, 308
procedural programming, 7
procedures, windows, 5
programming
    controls, 81
    data collections
        AfxTempl.h header files, 192, 202
        example, 191-192
        simple collection classes, 191, 205
        type pointer collection classes, 191
    event-driven, 6-7
    Media Player control, 382
    minimizing overhead, Win32 data structures, 175
    procedural, 7
    Win32 API, 4

programs. *See* applications
progress bar controls, 79
Projector (sample) application. *See* listings
Properties (ADO), 356
properties (SND), 423
Property (ADO), 356
property page controls, 79
property pages, 434-438, 454
property sheet controls, 79
property sheets 433-437. *See also* dialog boxes; wizards
PSWIZB BACK identifier, 437
PSWIZB DISABLEDFINISH identifier, 437
PSWIZB NEXTidentifier, 437
pt prefix, 27
public data members, CPrintInfo class, 297-298
PUSHBUTTON controls, 123

Q-R

QueryDefs object (DAO), 320
QuickTime (MOV), 382

RA (RealAudio), 382
rand() function, 411
.RC filename extension, 45
rc prefix, 27
RDO (Remote Data Objects), 353
RealVideo (RV), 382
Recent File menu item (Windows), 283
records, [ ] (brackets) character, 322
Recordset (ADO Data Control property), 356-358
Recordset objects (DAO), 320
RecordSource (ADO Data Control property), 358
RECT data type, 7-8
rectangles
 clipping rectangles, 245
 FillRect() member function, 159
 OnPaint() message handler rectangle drawing example, 159
 Rectangle() member function, 158
Red Green Blue color system (RGB), 110, 154

Refresh() member function, 364-366
RegName component (document strings), 216
RegType component (document strings), 216
ReleaseBuffer() member function, 182-184
Remote Data Objects (RDO), 353
RemoveAll() member function, 193, 196-198
RemoveAt() member function, 193, 196
RemoveHead() member function, 196
RemoveKey() member function, 198
RemovePage() member function, 437
RemoveTail() member function, 196
removing Create() member functions, 36
Replace text dialog box, 99, 103
.RES filename extension, 42
resource compilers, 42
resource editors, 57
resource files, common dialog boxes, 111
resource scripts. *See* resources
Resource.h header file resource identifiers example, 122
Resourceful (sample) application. *See* listings
resources, 25
 accelerators, 44-46
 bitmaps, 44-46
 BrowseIt menu resource definition example, 367-368
 BrowseIt toolbar resource definition example, 368-369
 compiling
  DLLs, 42-43
  executable files, 43
  resource compilers, 42, 45
 constants, 45
 CResourcefulApp::OnAppAbout() message handler example, 54
 cursors, 44-47
 custom, 44
 dialog box, 117-118
  constructing, 121-123, 126-128
  controls, 119-120, 123
  defining, 49

DIALOG resource statement, 118-119
DIALOGEX resource statement, 119-123
Finance menu resource definition example, 126-127
GUI elements, 49, 56
IDD PROJECTOR, 396
Personal Information dialog box resource definition example, 122-123
Resource.h header file resource identifiers example, 122
visual dialog box editors, 120
Doodle7 keyboard accelerator resource definitions example, 304
Doodle7 revised menu resource definitions example, 301-303
Doodle7 revised toolbar resource definitions example, 303-304
editors, 57
filename extensions, 42, 45-47
Finance2 Finance.rc resource script example, 441-444
floating pop-up menus, 142
Hockey.rc resource script example, 326-329
icons, 44, 47
identifiers, 16, 48
MDI applications, 281-283
menus, 44
 Doodle5 menu resource definition example, 269-270
 menu item names, 49
 menu resource definition example, 48
 options, 49
 templates, 47-48
MFC automatic associating, 53
Projector Resource.h header file example, 385
Projector.rc resource script example, 386-388
Resourceful application class message map example, 54
Resourceful Resource.h header file example, 51

scripts, 45, 52-53
Skeleton.rc resource file
    example, 16-17
standard application data
    comparison, 42
string, 37-38
    BrowseIt string resource
        definitions example, 369
    status bars, 267-268
string tables, 44, 50
    defining, 50
    definition example, 50-51
    TipOfTheDay.rc resource
        script example, 407
    versions, 44, 51
    Win32, MFC comparison, 44
restore command, 132
retrieving records, [ ] (brackets), 322
RGB (Red Green Blue) color system, 110, 154-155
rich edit controls, 79
RTEXT controls, 123
Run() member function, 25
RV (RealVideo), 382

S

schemas, 224-225
scope resolution operator (::), 27
scripts, resource
    .RC filename extension, 45
    compiling, 45
    Resourceful.rc resource script
        example, 52-53
scroll bar controls, 77
scrolling views, 245
    CScrollView class, 247
    Doodle4
        CDoodleView::Assert
            Valid() member function
            example, 247
    Doodle4
        CDoodleView::Dump()
            member function example,
            248
    Doodle4 CDoodleView::On
        LButtonDown() member
        function example, 249-251
    setting views scroll size,
        248-249
SDI (Single Document Interface), 276
SDI applications

MDI comparison, 276
WordPad, 277
SDK (Software Development Kit), DirectX Media, 383
searching text, 103
selecting colors
    Animator2 (sample) application, 109
    Color Selection dialog box, 102
SEPARATOR identifiers, 265
Serialize() member function, 31
    automatic calling, 209
    CArchive object parameter, 210
    CGraphic class, 225
    Doodle4
        DoodleDoc::Serialize()
            member function example, 246
serializing
    CGraphic class, 221-225
    documents, 210-212, 225
    objects, 178
    schemas, 224-225
SetAddressBar() member function, 366
SetAt() member function, 180, 193, 196-198
SetAtGrow() member function, 193
SetBarStyle() member function, 270
SetBookmark() member function, 346
SetCheck() member function, 143
SetClip() member function, 427
SetCurrentPosition() member function, 384
SetDlgItemText() member function, 411
SetFileName() member function, 384
SetFullScreen() member function, 366
SetLoop() member function, 427
SetMenuBar() member function, 366
SetModifiedFlag() member function, 209-210, 221
SetRadio() member function, 143
SetSize() member function, 193-194

SetStatusBar() member function, 366
SetText() member function, 143
setting
    constants, 443, 453
    default buttons (dialog boxes), 115
    document size, 245-246, 259
    views scroll size, 248-249
SetToolBar() member function, 366
SetVolume() member function, 384
SetWizardButtons() member function, 437
SetWizardMode() member function, 436-437
sharing code, DLLs, 402
shortcuts (keyboard), 45
simple collection classes, 191, 205
Sin City Web site, 373
Single Document Interface (SDI), 276
sites (Web)
    Dr. Dobb's Journal, 479
    Inprise C++ Builder, 482
    MFC FAQ, 478
    MFC Professional, 478
    Microsoft Developer
        Network, 478
    Microsoft MSN, 373
    Microsoft Systems Journal, 479
    Microsoft Visual C++, 478, 482
    Microsoft's DirectX, 379
    Microsoft's Windows Media, 383
    Sin City, 373
    Symantec C++, 482
    Visual C++ Developer's
        Journal, 478
    Watcom C/C++, 482
    Windows Developer's
        Journal, 478
size (documents), declaring, 245-247, 259
size command, 132
sizing icons, 47
Skeleton (sample) application.
    See **listings**
SkeletonDV (sample) application. *See* **listings**
slider controls, 79, 84
SND ASYNC property, 423

SND FILENAME property, 423
SND LOOP property, 423
sndPlaySound() function (Win32), 423
   .WAV files, 423
   static linking WinMM.lib, 427
software components, 86
Software Development Kit (SDK), DirectX Media, 383
Sound File (SND), 382
source code. *See* files
spin controls, 79
splitter windows, 229, 251
   adding, 252-253
   CSplitterWnd class, 252
   dynamic, 253, 259
   panes, 252
   static, 253, 259
SQL (Structured Query Language), 319, 322
srand() function, 411
state, menu items, 142
statements, ICON, 17
static controls, 76
static libraries, 399-402
static linking, 400, 423, 427. *See also* DLLs; dynamic linking
static splitter windows, 259
status bars. *See also* control bars; dialog bars; toolbars
   application-specific, 273
   controls, 79
   creating, 266-268
   CStatusBar class, 262-263
   string resources, 267-268
StdAfx files, 10-11
Stop() member function, 364-366, 384, 427
string literals, 179
string resources
   adding, 37-38
   BrowseIt string resource definitions example, 369
   document strings, 37-38
   status bars, 267-268
string tables, 44, 50-51
strings
   characters, accessing, 180
   comparing, 181
   concatenating, 181
   converting to char pointers, 182
   creating, 179-180
   CString class, 179

document, 216-217
   Format() member function, 183
Structured Query Language (SQL), 319, 322
subscript operators ([ ]), 180
switch statements, 60
Symantec C++ Web site, 482
system menus, 132-134
sz prefix, 27

T

T macro, 179
tab (\t) characters, 49
tab dialog boxes. *See* property sheets
TableDefs object (DAO), 320
tables, 324-325
templates
   C++, 176-177, 188
   document, 23, 36, 215, 279
   menu, defining, 47-48
   window classes, 4
testing
   controls, 423-427
   wizards, 454
text
   drawing, 160
   Find dialog box, 103
   Replace text dialog box, 103
TextOut() member function, 160
TipOfTheDay (sample) DLL. *See* listings
Tipper (sample) application, 412
TODO comments, 31
toolbars, 261-263. *See also* control bars; dialog bars; status bars
   bitmaps, 263-264
   button images, 264, 273
   CBRS SIZE DYNAMIC style, 271
   controls, 79
   creating, 264
      BrowseIt toolbar resource definition example, 368-369
      CToolBar member variable example, 265
      Doodle5 CMainFrame:: OnCreate() message handler example, 265-266

      Doodle5 toolbar resource definition example, 264-265
      Doodle7 revised menu resource definitions example, 303-304
      OnCreate() message handler, 265
      SEPARATOR identifiers, 265
   CToolBar class, 262-264
   docking, 271
   ToolTips, 270-272
tools, visual development, 482
tooltip controls, 79
ToolTips, 270-272
TPM CENTERALIGN flag, 140
TPM LEFTALIGN flag, 140
TPM LEFTBUTTON flag, 140
TPM RIGHTALIGN flag, 140
TPM RIGHTBUTTON flag, 140
tracking accessed Web pages, WebBrowser control, 364
TrackPopupMenu() member function, 140
traditional Windows controls. *See* controls.
tree controls, 79
TYPE parameter, 192-196
typed pointer collection classes, 191

U-V

UINT pane identifiers, 268
Unicode, T macro, 179
Unicode character set, 179
UNIX audio (AU), 382
UpdateAllViews() member function, 209-210, 221
user input. *See* messages
user interface elements, 23, 26, 241, 431. *See also* views
user-defined resources, 44
UserName (ADO Data Control property), 358

validating dialog box member variables, DDV, 117
VALUE parameter
   CMap class, 197
   CTypedPtrMap class, 199

values (map), 189
variables
  AFX EXTENSION MODULE, 404
  CStatusBar member variable example, 268
  CToolBar member variable example, 265
  dialog box, 117-118
  global, wizards, 444
  m nDrawMode, 167
  m pen, 167
  member
    defining, 323
    initializing, 323
    m bAutoStart, 421, 427
    m bLoop, 421
    m ColorBox, 427
    m hIcon, 392
    m pMediaPlayer, 392
    m rcColor, 418
    m sClip, 421
  names, 27-28
  prefixes, 27
  public member, 348
VBSQL (Visual Basic SQL), 352
version resources, 44, 51
VERTRES constant, 156
VERTSIZE constant, 156
video. *See* multimedia
Video On Demand (VOD), 381
viewing
  files, .DLL, 401
  fonts, 103
  printer configuration, 105
  WebBrowser control, 363
views, 227. *See also* document/view architecture; documents; windows
  CCtrlView class, 230
  CDaoRecordView class, 230
  CEditView class, 230
  CFormView class, 230
  CHtmlView class, 230
  CListView class, 230, 253-257
  creating, 232
  CRecordView class, 230
  CRichEditView class, 230
  CScrollView class, 230
  CSkeletonView, 34-35
  CTreeView class, 230
  CView class
    DoPreparePrinting() member function, 295

GetDocument() member function, 230-231, 234, 238
OnBeginPrinting() member function, 295-296
OnDraw() member function, 230-231, 234, 238
OnEndPrinting() member function, 295-297
OnEndPrintPreview() member function, 295-297
OnPrepareDC() member function, 295-296
OnPreparePrinting() member function, 295, 305, 314
OnPrint() member function, 230-231, 295-296
OnUpdate() member function, 230-231
CWnd class, 229
defined, 22
document/view architecture, 227-228
form-based applications, 323
hints, 242
multiple views, 228, 251
optimizing, 241-245
printing, 228
scrolling, 245-249
setting scroll size, 248-249
user interface elements comparison, 26
user interface responsibilities, 239
virtual member functions, 60-61
visible controls, 417
Visual Basic SQL (VBSQL), 352
Visual C++. *See* **C++**
Visual C++ Developer, 478
Visual C++ Developer's Journal, 478
Visual C++ Professional, 478
visual development tools, 482
visual dialog box editors, 120
Visual InterDev, ADO, 355
Visual Studio
  ADO, 355
  Class Wizard, 63
VOD (Video on Demand), 381

W-Z

w prefix, 27
Watcom C/C++ Web site, 482
WAV (Waveform Audio), 382
.WAV files, 423
Web browsers. *See* Explorer; WebBrowser control
Web pages, 363-364, 375
Web sites. *See* sites (Web)
Web-enabled applications. *See* applications
WebBrowser control. *See also* Explorer
  CHtmlView class, 364-366
  non-HTML documents, 363
  Web pages
    accessed pages list, 364
    viewing, 363
What You See Is What You Get (WYSIWYG), 300
Win32, 3
  data structures, minimizing overhead, 175
  data types
    BOOL, 7
    handles, 6
    names, 27
    POINT, 7
    RECT, 7-8
  event-driven programming, 6-7
  functions, 111, 423, 427
  header files, 423
  resources, 44
    accelerator, 44-46
    bitmap, 44-46
    cursor, 44-46
    dialog box, 44, 49-50, 56
    icon, 44, 47
    menu, 44, 47-49
    MFC comparison, 44
    string table, 44, 50-51
    version, 44, 51
  switch statements, 60
  Win32 API
    basis for MFC, 4, 7
    common dialog boxes, 98-100
    dialog boxes, 97
    function names, 27
    GetStockObject(), 92
    MDI, 276
    MDICLIENT class, 279
    MFC C++ wrapper classes, 7, 175
    POINT structure, 158

programming, 4
RGB macro, 110
virtual key codes, 64
WinMain(), 7, 24
windows. *See also* **views**
  application, 4, 26, 68
  classes, 4
  controls
    ActiveX controls comparison, 85
    coding, 81-82
    common, 76-79
    common/standard dialog box comparison, 78
    control notification, 77-78, 82-84
    identifiers, 81
    messages, 82
    parent-child relationship, 75-76, 94
    positioning, 94
    traditional Windows, 76-77, 87, 93
  defined, 4
  focus, 64
  main frame, 11-15, 23, 392-393
  MDI, 276, 279-280, 291
  messages, 5-8
  painting, 156-157
  panes, 252
  procedures, 5
  splitter, 229, 251-253, 259
  views, 26
  WS CAPTION style, 119
  WS POPUP style, 119
  WS SYSMENU style, 119
Windows
  brushes, 92
  colors, 110
  DLLs, 400-401
  MDI/SDI applications comparison, 278
  MM TEXT, 152-153
  Print Preview, 294
  Recent File menu item, 283
  RGB, 154-155
  WinMM.lib, 423, 427
Windows 95, 3, 76-78
Windows 98, 3
Windows Developer's Journal, 478
Windows Explorer, common controls, 79
Windows Media Player, 382
Windows multimedia system,

WinMM.lib, 423, 427
Windows NT, 3
Windows Tech Journal, 478
Windows WAVE format (.WAV) files, 423
WinMain() function, 7, 24
WIZ CXDLG constant, 443, 453
WIZ CYDLG constant, 443, 453
wizards. *See also* **dialog boxes; property sheets**
  Add Printer Wizard, 432-433
  Back buttons, 433
  Class Wizard (C++), 63
  constants, 443, 453
  CPropertyPage class, 435-438, 443, 453
  CPropertySheet class, 435-437, 443, 453
  CPropertySheet objects, 436
  Finish buttons, 433
  Investment wizard (sample) application, 438-444, 450-452
  modeless, 436
  Next buttons, 433
  pages, building, 445-450
  properties sheets comparison, 433-435
  PSWIZB BACK identifier, 437
  PSWIZB DISABLEDFINISH identifier, 437
  PSWIZB FINISH identifier, 437
  PSWIZB NEXT identifier, 437
  uses, 433
WM CHAR, 65
WM CLOSE message, 6
WM COMMAND, 82-83
WM CREATE message, 6
WM KEYDOWN, 65
WM KEYUP, 65
WM LBUTTONDOWN, 6, 68
WM LBUTTONUP, 68
WM MBUTTONDBLCLK, 69
WM MBUTTONDOWN, 68
WM MBUTTONUP, 69
WM MOUSEMOVE, 6, 68
WM NOTIFY, 82-84
WM PAINT message, 6, 156-157
WM RBUTTONDBLCLK, 69
WM RBUTTONDOWN, 68

WM RBUTTONUP, 69
WM SYSCOMMAND message, 133
WM SYSKEYDOWN, 65
WM SYSKEYUP, 65
Word, as MDI application, 277
WordPad, as SDI application, 277
Workspace object (DAO), 320
wrapper classes. *See* **classes**
WS CAPTION style (windows), 119
WS POPUP style (windows), 119
WS SYSMENU style (windows), 119
WYSIWYG (What You See Is What You Get), 300

Other Related Titles

Sams Teach Yourself Database Programming with Visual C++ 6 in 21 Days
0-672-31350-2
Lyn Robison
$34.99 USA /
$49.95 CAN

Sams Teach Yourself Visual C++ 6 in 24 Hours
0-672-31303-0
Mickey Williams
$24.99 USA /
$35.95 CAN

Sams Teach Yourself Visual C++ 6 in 21 Days
0-672-31240-9
Davis Chapman
$34.99 USA /
$49.95 CAN

Sams Teach Yourself C++ in 24 Hours
0-672-31067-8
Jesse Liberty
$24.99 USA /
$35.95 CAN

Sams Teach Yourself Visual Basic 6 in 24 Hours
0-672-31306-5
Greg Perry; Sanjaya Hettihewa
$19.99 USA /
$28.95 CAN

Sams Teach Yourself Database Programming with Visual Basic 6 in 21 Days
0-672-31308-1
Michael Amundsen
$45.00 USA /
$64.95 CAN

Sams Teach Yourself OLE DB and ADO in 21 Days
0-672-31083-X
John Fronckowiak
$39.99 USA /
$57.95 CAN

Sams Teach Yourself Database Programming with Visual Basic 6 in 24 Hours
0-672-31409-6
Dan Rahmel
$19.99 USA /
$28.95 CAN

Sams Teach Yourself Visual InterDev 6 in 21 Days
0-672-31251-4
L. Michael Van Hoozer, Jr.
$34.99 USA /
$49.95 CAN

Programming Windows 98/NT Unleashed
0-672-31353-7
Viktor Toth
$49.99 USA /
$71.95 CAN

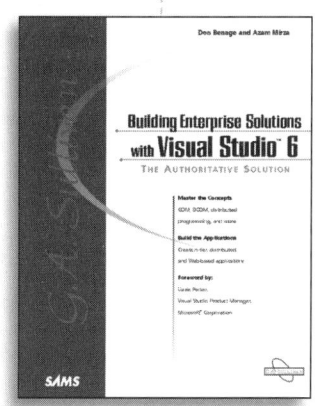

Building Enterprise Solutions with Visual Studio 6
0-672-31489-4
G.A. Sullivan
$49.99 USA /
$71.95 CAN

SAMS
www.samspublishing.com

All prices are subject to change.

mcp.com
The Authoritative Encyclopedia of Computing

- Resource Centers
- Books & Software
- Personal Bookshelf
- WWW Yellow Pages
- Online Learning
- Special Offers
- Site Search
- Industry News

▶ Choose the online ebooks that you can view from your personal workspace on our site.

About MCP · Site Map · Product Support

Turn to the *Authoritative* Encyclopedia of Computing

You'll find over 150 full text books online, hundreds of shareware/freeware applications, online computing classes and 10 computing resource centers full of expert advice from the editors and publishers of:

- Adobe Press
- BradyGAMES
- Cisco Press
- Hayden Books
- Lycos Press
- New Riders
- Que
- Que Education & Training
- Sams Publishing
- Waite Group Press
- Ziff-Davis Press

mcp.com
The Authoritative Encyclopedia of Computing

When you're looking for computing information, consult the authority. The Authoritative Encyclopedia of Computing at mcp.com.

Get the best information and learn about latest developments in:

- Design
- Graphics and Multimedia
- Enterprise Computing and DBMS
- General Internet Information
- Operating Systems
- Networking and Hardware
- PC and Video Gaming
- Productivity Applications
- Programming
- Web Programming and Administration
- Web Publishing